THE COUNSELOR
AND THE GROUP

THE COUNSELOR AND THE GROUP

Integrating Theory, Training, and Practice

Third Edition

James P. Trotzer, Ph.D.

USA	Publishing Office:	ACCELERATED DEVELOPMENT *A member of the Taylor & Francis Group* 325 Chestnut Street Philadelphia, PA 19106 Tel: (215) 625-8900 Fax: (215) 625-2940
	Distribution Center:	ACCELERATED DEVELOPMENT *A member of the Taylor & Francis Group* 47 Runway Road, Suite G Levittown, PA 19057-4700 Tel: (215) 269-0400 Fax: (215) 269-0363
UK		ACCELERATED DEVELOPMENT *A member of the Taylor & Francis Group* 1 Gunpowder Square London EC4A 3DE Tel: 171 583 0490 Fax: 171 583 0581

THE COUNSELOR AND THE GROUP: Integrating Theory, Training, and Practice

1 2 3 4 5 6 7 8 9 0

Printed by Edwards Brothers, Ann Arbor, MI, 1999.
Cover design by Joe Dieter.

A CIP catalog record for this book is available from the British Library.
∞ The paper in this publication meets the requirements of the ANSI Standard Z39.48-1984 (Permanence of Paper)

Library of Congress Cataloging-in-Publication Data

Trotzer, James P., 1943–
 The counselor and the group: Integrating theory, training, and
practice / James P. Trotzer. —3rd ed.
  p. cm.
 Includes bibliographical references and index.
 ISBN 1-56032-699-9 (case: alk. paper)

  1. Group counseling. I. Title.
BF637.C6T68 1999
158'.35—dc21

99-20506
CIP

ISBN 1-56032-699-9 (case)

To Toni, my intimate partner, friend, confidante,
and coleader in life.

CONTENTS

5   **Process to Practice** 116

9   Multicultural Group Work

Rod J. Merta

10   Differentiating Groups

14 Family Theory as a Group Resource   416

15 The Case for Group Research   448
Rex Stockton, Paul L. Toth

LIST OF FIGURES

PREFACE

My understanding of the role and purpose of a Preface in a textbook is that it is 1) the least likely part of the book to be read or referred to, 2) essentially a place for the author to elaborate on the background dynamics and formulation forces that prompted the work as a sort of ritualistic, cathartic exercise before the book is published, and 3) the place where acknowledgments and appreciation are expressed to persons, places, events, and experiences that have contributed to the book's material and conceptual essence. I suspect that all three factors are accurate and in spite of the delimitation of the first factor, I make the following request of the reader (if noticed): *Please read the preface before reading any other portion of the book. It will provide the necessary perspective that will enhance the usefulness and your understanding of the group process as it is detailed in the text.*

I ask your indulgence regarding the boldness of the following statement, but it is my confirmed belief that the model of group process presented in this text is a model whose time has come. Despite the fact that the model has been on the professional scene for over thirty years, it is in the context of contemporary pressures for efficiency and fiscal mandates for economy that the relevance and utility of the model as presented is realized in the therapeutic domain. Secondly, since the character and nature of group process is now recognized as an essential component of all groups, whether therapeutic or task, the utility presented is even more apparent. With that said, let me elaborate on the developmental dynamics of the current edition of *The Counselor and the Group: Integrating Theory, Training, and Practice.*

In writing this third edition I have made a concerted effort to maintain the integrity of the text as developed in the first two editions. The theme of integration, the purpose of practicality and the format combining explication and application have been sustained. As noted in the Preface of the first edition, group counseling is a helping process that is used increasingly in agencies, schools, inpatient settings, and private practice. As the viability of this means of helping people resolve their problems grew, so did the need for trained group leaders. This book parallels that growth by providing information about group process, dynamics, skills, techniques, and experience that knowledgeable leaders require to be effective.

There are four prerequisites for an effective group leader: 1) cognitive knowledge about group process, 2) involvement as a participant in group interaction, 3) skills and techniques for use in the leadership capacity, and 4) supervised experience in the leadership role. This text provides the means and direction for acquiring all four because it contains a wealth of information about *applying* knowledge to process.

This book is for persons in the helping professions who wish to develop or improve not only their understanding of the group process but also their leadership skills and the application of that process across a broad spectrum of groups including counseling/therapy groups, task groups, and other free standing or temporary groups in which counselors lead or become members. The book specifically lends itself to use by counselor educators who teach group courses, students in training to become group counselors, counselors in mental health agencies, private practices and schools that use groups, and consultants in group process in community organizations, business, and industry. Professionals who by the very nature of their professions may wish to enhance their group leadership capacities will find this book useful.

The format of this book is directed toward immediate integration of knowledge, experience, and application. Suggested activities are designed to demonstrate the concepts and provide first-hand involvement with the dynamics of the group counseling process. In addition, most of the activities serve a dual purpose—demonstrating cognitive components of the group counseling process and providing prospective leaders with techniques to use in groups of their own. As such, this book is most appropriate for an initial group course or as a text to accompany a supervised group internship or practicum. It is also designed as a handbook for clinicians to use in developing and enhancing their group knowledge and skills and as a resource for understanding group dynamics and implementing group leadership methods and techniques.

In May 1985 a special issue of the *Journal for Specialists in Group Work* (Vol. 10, No. 2) entitled "Critical Issues in Group Work: Now and 2001" addressed the nature and prospects of group work in the 1980s and 1990s. A diverse group of contributors confirmed the presence and essence of group work and pronounced the group modality as a fundamentally sound professional tool in response to the therapeutic needs of our human environment. While endorsing the relevance of group work as a humanizing counter force in a society characterized by the dehumanizing forces of technology (information overload and interpersonal isolation), the inherent vulnerabilities of the group approach were also identified. In spite of an evolving history that had substantiated group work as effective across a wide range of helping disciplines, inherent weaknesses were noted that, if allowed to persist without remedy, would not only jeopardize the effectiveness of group work, but threaten its very existence. The weaknesses noted were encapsulated in three main categories: 1) inconsistent and insufficient training of group leaders, 2) need for a more substantial link between theory, research, and clinical practice, and 3) the necessity of integration in terms of theory, training, and practice across all therapeutic modalities (individual, group, marriage, and family) and across disciplines. As this edition is published, I am happy to report that this text along with the group work profession and professionals who enact group work have responded to that mandate. Those weaknesses have been and continue to be addressed as a means of enhancing and solidifying the place and relevance of group work now and in the future.

Modifications, additions, and revisions of the current edition reflect the progress that has been realized in group work, the contemporary status of group work, and the future prowess of the field. A substantive literature review of group articles published in the last decade served the purpose of updating both references and content to reflect the contemporary state of the field. Additional chapters were solicited and developed to emphasize and complement contemporary issues and cutting edge trends integrated into the text. Specifically chapters on best practices in group counseling, the multicultural and diversity dynamics of group work, and research in group work were added to the text. Each of these chapters not only brought greater relevance, depth, and breadth to the text but also incorporated cutting edge perspectives from the respective authors who are leaders in the group field and experts on their respective topics.

Lynn Rapin and Bob Conyne collaborated in translating the ethics of group work into a chapter entitled *Best Practices in Group Counseling* (Chapter 8). Lynn served as cochair of the Association for Specialists in Group Work (ASGW) Ethics Committee that developed the Best Practices Guidelines adopted by ASGW in March, 1998. She is now in private practice as a licensed psychologist and a counselor educator at the University of Cincinnati. Bob is widely published and has served in multiple leadership capacities in ASGW including President and Editor of the *Journal for Specialists in Group Work*. He is Professor of Counseling and Program Coordinator at Teachers College, University of Cincinnati.

Rod Merta has written and presented extensively in the group work field and is recognized as a leader with respect to multicultural and diversity aspects of group work. He contributed Chapter 9, *Multicultural Group Work*, which takes a pragmatic and realistic view of multicultural and diversity dynamics with respect to group process. Rod is a licensed psychologist and Associate Professor at New Mexico State University at Las Cruces.

Rex Stockton and Paul Toth combined their many faceted talents in research, writing, teaching, and practice in the group field to present a unique and necessary chapter on research in group work. Addressing a topic often underemphasized or excluded in group texts, their chapter, *The Case for Group Research: A Practitioner Friendly Proposition*, presents an informative, practical, and viable perspective for group practitioners relative to the vital link between research and practice. Rex is a recognized authority in group research, has served ASGW as President and in many other leadership roles and has an extensive record of publications in the group work field. He is Professor of Counselor Education at Indiana University. Paul, also a noted author and practitioner, is currently staff psychologist at the Indiana University Student Counseling Center.

Acknowledgments for this third edition span more than three decades of people, places, experiences, and events. Without them the cumulative result and continuing evolution of this text and my own experience and expertise would diminish. My interest and training in group work was initiated and nurtured into existence by Al Roark and Bill Sease, my mentors at the University of Colorado who gave me my first opportunities to study, research, and practice group work.

The extended group leadership experience that really taught me about group process, group dynamics, and therapeutic factors in groups occurred in the Intensive Treatment Unit of the Minnesota State Prison. I consider that first experience as my experiential doctorate in group work. I am sure I learned more than the inmates benefitted, but I am deeply grateful to them. Combined with the many graduate student training group experiences and the groups I have been privileged to run in agencies, schools, and private practice, the debt to group members is only partially repaid by passing on what I have learned and taught. I have been fortunate to have had many perceptive and dedicated graduate students who have encouraged—and many times forced—me to grow and learn.

To Dr. C. S. Peng, Chair of the Guidance Department at Taiwan Provincial College of Education (now National Changhua University of Education) I owe a special debt of gratitude for his role in motivating and encouraging me to write the first edition of this text during my tenure there as a visiting professor.

Professional colleagues during both my first and second "tour of duty" as a counselor educator have been and are stimulating contributors to the content and perspectives of the text. Wayne Kassera, Jim Lipsky, Dan Ficek, John Hamann among others at the University of Wisconsin-River Falls and Murray Finley at Rhode Island College are particular persons who merit acknowledgment. During the interim period of private practice and agency work, I am indebted to Ralph Fessler and Fred Bemak (formerly) of The Johns Hopkins University who made it possible for me to maintain my teaching orientation and formulate my conceptual framework while engaged in clinical practice by giving me the opportunity to teach group and family courses during summer sessions.

To Joe Hollis (now retired) and his staff at Accelerated Development who assisted me in the renovation project that became the second edition of this text I owe a great deal of thanks. The input of their work and insight continues to reverberate in this edition. To the current Taylor & Francis staff, especially acquisitions editor Tim Julet, editorial assistant Jill Osowa, and production editor Stephanie Weidel, I owe special thanks for the rigorous and stimulating process of refining this current edition into reality.

Finally, I wish to acknowledge my long term association with the group of dedicated and talented group work professionals who are the Association for Specialists in Group Work. Past, current, and ongoing relationships have immensely affected me personally and professionally, and activities engaged in under the auspices of the organization and its leaders have contributed significantly to the content of this book. Special recognition goes to the following:

- Ben Cohn who initially provided me with a forum for developing and presenting my ideas about group work by including me in his team conducting group counseling workshops across the country.
- Marguerite "Peg" Carroll who as ASGW President recruited me to head up the ASGW Family Counseling Commission whose activities, presentations, and articles prompted much of the material for Chapter 14 (*Family Theory as a Group Resource*) and who later as Director of the ASGW Training Institute Program enlisted my services as an Instructor.
- Bob Conyne who as editor of the *Journal for Specialists in Group Work* during my 3 year stint on the editorial board challenged and motivated me to think more seriously about writing and who as President continued to encourage and solicit my professional input.
- Diana Hulse-Killacky who as President literally propelled me into the group work spotlight and has subsequently been a supportive and stimulating colleague.
- Beverly Brown who offered me the opportunity to serve as Process Observer for the Executive Council during her term of office. That experience served to solidify and promote my interest and expertise in the process application of group dynamics to task and organizational groups and resulted in a series of articles included in the Appendices of this text.
- Michael Hutchins and Jeremiah Donigian who enlisted my services as co-coordinator of the Education and Training Cluster which gave me access to personnel and resources tapped for various aspects of this edition.

My current professional status relative to group work is directed once again to training masters level practitioners in group and family counseling. Specifically, I am emphasizing the adaptation of my model of group counseling to problem solving that is solution-focused and brief and can be adapted and applied in therapeutic, school, community, organizational, and work settings. As a process consultant I am active in serving work and organizational groups as a process observer, trainer, and workshop leader. My role as Director of the Multicultural/Bilingual Counseling program at Rivier College prompted my involvement in the New Hampshire Multicultural and Diversity Task Force and the Nashua Hispanic Network where my group expertise is continually being expanded and challenged. I have realized more than ever that, like the "Force" in the Star Wars trilogy, group process is always with you.

My experience in writing this third edition has been both a humbling and a growth experience. The humbling part emanates from the change in perspective that has evolved over the three editions. When I wrote the first edition I was in my 30s and the finished product represented everything I knew about groups. When in my 40s I completed the second edition—which had expanded from 200 to 500 pages of text—I had the illusionary or delusionary feeling that it represented everything there was to know about groups. Now in my 50s, as I complete this third edition, I am astounded and amazed by how much I don't know about groups and how much there is to know. That is the humbling part. The growth part is that because of those same realizations there is always the excitement of learning more about group work.

My hope is that this third edition of *The Counselor and the Group* will continue to be a functional tool in the training process and practice of group work. Someone once compared teaching with doing and noted that doing is the humbler work. This book is thus dedicated to the doers, the group practitioners, in hopes that it will serve as a resource in the often difficult and thankless occupation of helping people. However, like growth, group work is dynamic not static and as such is energizing in itself. Just as growth never stops so the process of helping people grow must never stop—otherwise, we become impediments to growth and healing rather than facilitators or stimuli to them. Therefore I present this edition to you with the sincere desire that it will spur your professional development in group work in a constructive and fulfilling manner just as preparing it has done for me.

And finally, (and this is really just for me) I want to express my appreciation and gratitude to my ever expanding primary group, my family, who daily teach me about the joys and challenges of intimate group interaction, and who continue to encourage, demand, and invite me to grow as a person and a group member.

Jim Trotzer

PROLOGUE

The emergence of the metaphor as a pragmatic and creative tool in the conduct of counseling and psychotherapy has provided clinicians with a resource that can be adapted to any client, context, and modality. A metaphor is a word, picture, or analogy that conveys information and meaning that has therapeutic impact cognitively, behaviorally, and affectively. Clinically, metaphors "represent words, analogies, non-verbal expressions and stories in which thoughts and feelings about an emotionally charged situation have been transferred to an analogical situation that preserves the original dynamics" (McClure, 1989, p. 239). As such, metaphors create analogies that substitute "a non-threatening external subject for a threatening internal one" enabling clients to experience affectively charged "worlds of meaning from a safe distance"(Rossel, 1981, p. 120). Gladding (1984, 1992a, & 1992b) explicated the metaphor as a particularly relevant tool in group work (Campbell, 1996).

Metaphors serve to enhance learning and therapeutic impact in many ways. They inform (establish meaning), amplify (expand meaning), illuminate (supply meaning), and provide material for interpretation (suggest meaning) (McClure, 1989). As such the metaphor has impressed me with its usefulness in both clinical practice and teaching. For the past few years I have started each group class I have taught by developing and sharing a metaphor for group work. I have also incorporated these metaphors into the initial sessions of my counseling and therapy groups. The result has typically been constructive. So as we begin our journey together into this third edition of *The Counselor and the Group*, I would like to share a metaphor for group work:

Every group is a puzzle:
The members are the pieces and the leader is the puzzlemaker.

☐ The Picture

Every group puzzle produces a different picture. Although the frame or form of the puzzle may be depicted by the type of group (counseling, therapy, psychoeducational, or task), each picture will be unique and different. The picture itself is dynamic and emerges as the process of putting the pieces together occurs. In a sense every group is a living puzzle. The picture is framed by the ground rules, parameters, and purposes of the group. But just as puzzles have different shapes and contents so will groups, and the finished product will always have its own identity.

☐ The Puzzle Pieces

The members as the pieces of the puzzle contribute to the nature of the picture. The pieces, like the picture, are dynamic. In becoming part of the puzzle, they both affect the puzzle and are affected by it. Each piece has a place in the puzzle that must be found in the course of the puzzle's development. In that process the pieces may change in shape and fit over time. They may look one way at the beginning of the group and differently at the end. Some pieces look alike and others look very different. Some pieces find their place in the context of similarity and sameness and others in the context of difference and diversity. Yet each piece is worthwhile, valuable, and necessary. In addition, each piece of the puzzle will see the picture from a different perspective both while the puzzle is emerging and after it is completed. Each piece will take away an impression in the form of experience and memory that is at the same time similar to other pieces and unique.

☐ The Puzzlemaking

Just as puzzles vary in size and complexity, so do groups. As membership increases there are more pieces to the puzzle, and as complexity increases, the pieces become more puzzling. The process of the group is also reflected in puzzlemaking. At the beginning the pieces appear disconnected and disarrayed. Often groups begin a lot like puzzles: You dump out the box and some pieces land face up and others face down. The first task in puzzlemaking is to turn all the pieces face up so the process can begin. At times the process of putting the puzzle together will get stuck or bogged down generating frustration, anger, and discouragement. At other times the pieces will fall into place and fit together generating a sense of connectedness and progress. Over the course of putting the puzzle together learning and experience occur, and when the puzzle is completed, i.e., the group is concluded, the process as much as the product will define the result. Each piece will disassemble and go its own way, but will carry with it the imprint of the process and the impact of the product.

☐ The Puzzlemaker

The leader is the puzzlemaker. Different leaders use different styles and approaches to putting the puzzle together—some direct, others facilitate; some work from the outside in and others from the inside out. Some go with the flow and others make things happen. Some use structured methods and activities and others rely on member initiatives. There are common tools and skills all puzzlemakers use as well as unique techniques related to the school of puzzlemaking in which the leader was trained and holds allegiance.

My task as the author of this manual on puzzlemaking is to help you make sense of and master the art of puzzlemaking. I hope to pique your curiosity, elicit your interest, stimulate your desire to become puzzlemakers, and encourage you to take up the challenge of solving the puzzles that are group work.

Putting together a puzzle is a lot like life. Sometimes the going is easy and things fall into place without effort. Other times nothing seems to fit and you just get frustrated and want to quit. Sometimes you get angry and try to force the pieces into place. Other times you pull back, detach, relax, turn away, and take a respite. Then, when you return to the puzzle, you see things differently and the pieces begin to make sense again. There is a sense of satisfaction and frustration that attends to the process of puzzlemaking as you go along. However, when it is finished, you see the whole picture for a moment, put it in your memory and experience and then go on to the next puzzle. Hopefully you will enjoy and be challenged by the process and will continue to seek out more puzzles to put together. After all, life itself is one big puzzle, and as a professional counselor and group worker, you have a lot to offer your clients and group members as they each seek out the pieces and form the picture that is their life.

As you begin this book, I wish you the very best in your learning and effort to become a master puzzlemaker.

☐ Learning Activity

As you read this book develop a metaphor that captures the essence of group work for you. Keep a log or journal with ideas and applications gleaned from your reading and experiences. As you read each chapter, develop the metaphor to incorporate key concepts that are presented. When you have finished the book, write a comprehensive explanation of your metaphor representing your understanding and perspective of group work. If you are in a class or group setting share the metaphor with your colleagues in an interactive forum. If you are leading a group, share the metaphor with the group as a means of generating group process. To assist you in your initial thinking about a metaphor read the following example as a resource to stimulate your creative thinking (Breier, 1997, p.12).

☐ Group Counseling is Like . . .
by Christine A. Breier

. . . a track event because everyone can't go forward if there is a false start.

. . . a beard because it can get a little hairy at times.

. . . photography because you give it your best shot and see what develops.

. . . carbon monoxide because an unacknowledged presence in the room can be fatal if not caught in time.

. . . the deep south because sometimes you've got to take the heat.

. . . a ball point pen because sometimes it rolls and sometimes it doesn't.

. . . a side-view mirror because sometimes things are bigger than they appear.

. . . ironing because sometimes a little steam is necessary to work the wrinkles out.

. . . fishing because sometimes the fish are biting most when the surface is calm.

. . . a geode because there are many sparklies waiting to be found inside.

. . . e-mail because there's no communicating if the system crashes.

. . . a microwave because there's warmth created when lives touch and bounce off one another.

. . . a turtleneck because some people can feel warm while others feel choked.

. . . a smoke detector because it intermittently chirps loud when it needs more energy to do its work.

. . . an abacus because it can be counted on.

. . . a postage stamp because oftentimes the parts that are the most gluey stick best over the long haul.

. . . a washing machine because you might have to go around and around before you come clean.

. . . a computer keyboard because you have to enter and then return.

CHAPTER 1

Introduction and Context

☐ Our Changing World

The evidence is overwhelming that the world around us is changing at an ever increasing rate and that we as individuals are faced with an ever more complex environment. We are constantly forced to adapt if we want to achieve our potential, individually and collectively. Over a quarter century ago Gazda (1971a) pointed out that "the world each of us personally inhabits grows steadily and rapidly larger. No (person) today has any choice but to be part of a greater and more diverse community" (p. 6). That observation has not only been realized, but accelerated by the technological advancements of the computer age.

The primary indicator of our expanding world is that we are inundated with the exponential development of new information often referred to as the knowledge explosion. Access to that new knowledge is promulgated by the perpetual evolution of the information superhighway that gives us rapid retrieval through computer technology, the internet, email, fax machines, and cellular phones. So sophisticated is consumer access to information that Waitley's (1978) observation that we are bombarded with eight times the amount of information that our grandparents were exposed to in a lifetime is archaic. Futurists drumming the perspective of space age technology indicate there is no possibility of human beings keeping up with the development of new knowledge in any discipline without the assistance or rather the necessity of computers. No wonder people who have not grown up with computers as their mode of communication feel completely overwhelmed. Even those with computer competence and allegiance have difficulty keeping pace with the rapid changes in the information industry.

Information overload that encourages and demands dependence on technology not only overwhelms individuals but produces a by-product of isolation (Klein, 1985). As individuals, our sense of identity is eroded as it becomes modified by and melded with the mechanics of knowledge rather than forged in the cauldron of human interaction. As this experience escalates, the seeds of dehumanization are planted and nurtured.

The problems of adjusting to such a world, however, are not the result of the essence or speed of change itself nor the nature or plethora of knowledge, but rather are the result of the conflict that is produced because individual adjustment to change is a slow process. C. Gilbert Wrenn (1962 & 1971) one of the forefathers of the counseling movement and a great humanitarian noted that the critical conflict of the human experience is associated with the discrepancy between what he called outer reality and inner reality. Outer reality—the world outside the boundaries of the individual person—changes very quickly. Inner reality—each person's personality, identity, values, attitudes, and perceptions—changes very slowly. Consequently, all human problems are adjustment problems. The clash between these two realities sums up the basic stress we all experience and provides a context for the problems that confront us.

Since the pace of scientific and technological change far exceeds that of social change, each of us is confronted with the task of not only getting ourselves together but also developing the interpersonal skills necessary to meet our needs in a global, mobile, and changing society. This requires each individual to be strong, flexible, and able to act interdependently. Each of us must increase what Toffler (1970) called our "cope-ability" capacity defined as the speed and economy with which we adapt to change.

The personal consequences of change in our environment are readily evident. The individual is bombarded with the inconceivable nature of change, the futility of understanding or impeding it, and the inability to change quickly enough to adapt to it. "We have more knowledge than we know what to do with, more people than we know how to live with, more physical energy than we know how to cope with, and in all things a faster rate of change than we know how to keep up with" (Dyer, 1967, p. 4). The implications of these realizations on our existence has effected a massive shift in our patterns of life and our sense of security.

Life styles have paradoxically taken on characteristics of a global expansiveness communicationally while generating relational reclusiveness personally. A person can do business by fax, email, phone, or the internet all over the world but remain isolated relying on technology to stay in contact rather than making a connection personally. In addition, physical mobility has produced life styles of a nomadic nature as opposed to a stationery one associated with a community. Career experts Tiedeman and Tiedeman's (1973) observation that "Today we move more, change jobs more and ourselves more and rely on faster and more elaborate technology and communication" (p. 336) is both prophetic and understated. Technology has affected the very nature of occupation by causing many jobs to become archaic, creating jobs requiring different skills and functions and making other jobs obsolete if not upgraded with computer capabilities and competencies. Without word processing skills and computer proficiency neither professors nor secretaries can function effectively in their respective capacities. Katz's (1973) projection that the concept of "job" would be phased out in favor of a view of "occupation" as more of an attitude toward learning was short sighted. Now you do not necessarily have to know how to do things as long as you know how to outsource or access information and resources.

Expanded communication capabilities expose us to problems and social concerns that intrude upon our lives and demand our attention. Wars, racism, sexism, terrorism, ageism, poverty, inflation, overpopulation, ecology, global warming, corruption, crime, and disasters of human and natural causality, local or global, confront us each day. As a result, we can be assured that we will face the prospect of changing old relationships and beginning new relationships throughout our lives. We must learn the efficacy of saying goodbye to the old and hello to the new as part and parcel of daily life. But at the same time we must learn how to retain the positive and critical aspects of our past experience to assure our present and future growth. Change and retention are facets of life adjustment that must be balanced so that stability and progress are possible.

☐ The Domain of Choice

What then are the implications for the child, the adolescent, and the adult whose personality and identity are constantly developing and emerging through the process of interaction between the self and the rapidly changing world they live in? Individuals must be prepared to engage in a continual process of decision making to maintain purposeful and responsible control over their own lives because of the ever increasing variety of attitudes, values and life styles that are becoming part of the domain of choice.

Children are more aware of the diverse elements of their environments than ever before. Mass media, computers, family mobility, and educational systems that stress exposure and experience all contribute to this awareness of an ever increasing range of possible behaviors and life styles. Preteenagers and adolescents are faced with choices earlier and in a more intense manner than ever before. Drugs, sex, morals, values, occupational choices, relationships, identity, and sexual orientation all must be grappled with. Neither is the adult freed from the necessity of choosing. Social awareness developed through education and the media impede acting in ignorance or irresponsibly. The economy, occupational evolution, increased leisure time and value changes continually force adults to reassess themselves and their life style. Even the aging process is complicated by issues of quality of life, health choices, living wills, and the prospect of living but being unable to care for oneself. Thus the domain of choice is not only larger but extends over a longer period of time as life span and life expectancy increases.

The common element needed for successful resolution in all these cases is the ability to make good decisions based on accurate self-knowledge and relevant knowledge of the environment. Victor Frankl once observed that "man ultimately decides for himself." As such, education, counseling, therapy, or any learning experience must move human beings toward having the "ability to decide."

The development of decision making skills including the processes of introspection, communication, and relationship formation are necessary because only through the process of self-exploration and feedback from others can a person become fully aware of those options and consequences that must be considered in making the best decisions possible. Through the process of effective decision making we as individuals, whatever our age or circumstance, can retain control over our lives and destinies in spite of pressures brought to bear on us by our changing world.

☐ The Need for Group Counseling

Groups and group work are peculiarly and uniquely designed to address the problems of living in our contemporary society. Hulse (1985) stated that "against the backdrop of a complex and highly technological world and our own needs for connections and support, the group emerges as a potentially humanizing force" (p. 93). Dies (1985) elaborated noting that the

> heightened individualization of learning and sense of isolation . . . threatens to undermine the sense of personal relatedness that provides the foundation of human interaction. The feeling of universality and cohesiveness and the quality of interpersonal learning . . . of group experiences promise to be effective antidotes to counteract these depersonalizing forces (p. 70).

He continued to state that groups "will be used to rehumanize the educational process for children . . . and revitalize adults who feel alienated in a technological society" (p. 71). Conyne, Dye, Gill, Leddick, Moran, and Ward (1985) concurred with this view and predicted that groups "will become major forces in combatting the increasing depersonalization and anomie that are likely to accompany the computer and `high tech' revolution" (p. 114).

Dye (DeLucia, 1991) pointedly states that "counseling groups are places where people exchange ideas and teach each other and learn from each other" (p. 68). In a practical sense, the counseling group is also a valuable tool in helping people improve their ability to make decisions and act in a manner that is personally meaningful, constructive, and socially relevant. The positive aspects of the helping process are incorporated into the group setting and facilitate the transfer of learning more readily to the ongoing life of the participant. The group counseling process if properly constituted and led meets the demands of an effective learning environment because it is safe, understanding, participating, and approving (Ohlsen, 1977). In addition, the process is directed toward self exploration, encouraging introspection and feedback so that communication can occur and relationships can develop. Therefore, it establishes the fundamental basis needed to make good decisions. Consequently, "it is the content and process of group involvement that impacts the very essence of our lives and leads us to new possibilities" (Gladding, 1990, p. 130).

The group process is also a most appropriate means of meeting the personal needs of individuals who often feel isolated, alienated, confused, frustrated, or lost in a world characterized by change, bureaucracy, and bigness. The group supplies a personal touch to the individual's life, serving as an oasis in the wasteland of an impersonal existence that is often a byproduct of scientific and technological advancement. It is a means whereby we as individuals can reconstitute and revitalize the type of personal experience that gives meaning to human existence and generates the impetus to incorporate those experiences into our daily lives.

Group counseling has broad applicability, encompassing the needs of persons from a wide variety of backgrounds and age groups. For individuals who have identifiable problems that interfere with their lives, group counseling can help them resolve their concerns in a personally responsible and realistic manner. For individuals who do not have specified concerns, the group process can help them improve themselves developmentally and serve as a preventative measure to ensure continued adjustment and personal satisfaction in their lives.

The flexibility of group counseling facilitates adaptability to a broad range of helping environments and programs. It is a relevant means of helping clientele in schools, mental health centers, correctional institutions, halfway houses, drug treatment programs, employment agencies, welfare programs, homeless shelters, and many other organizations whose purpose is to help people with their personal development and concerns. It is also an appropriate and effective modality in an organizational sense where the goals are improved productivity and more effective utilization of human resources. (See Association for Specialists in Group Work, 1982).

However, the need for group counseling extends beyond the persons and organizations served. A professional need exists to develop group counseling as a vehicle for providing helping services to the counselor's clientele thereby expanding the counselor's effectiveness. In this age of accountability the counselor must become a visible professional and be willing to demystify the nature of the helping process (Ivey & Alschuler, 1973). Groups can be used to increase client-counselor contact and to extend the role of the counselor by providing services to larger numbers of persons in the schools and in the community (Cottingham, 1973). The group process can be the key to providing the helping process in a manner that will best serve the interests of the clients, the educational or therapeutic staff and setting, the community, business and industry, and the counseling profession.

☐ The Need for Training

The success and impact of group work is primarily dependent on the ability of a competent leader. Most counselor training programs recognize the need to train future counselors in group procedures and incorporate at least one course in group process into their requirements. Professional standards developed by relevant professional organizations and their derivatives (e.g., American Counseling Association and their credentialling counterparts, Council for Accreditation of Counseling and Related Educational Programs [CACREP] and National Board of Certified Counselors [NBCC]) have all promoted the requirement of competency in group work. The Association for Specialists in Group Work (ASGW) specifically emphasizes group work as a fundamental competency for all counselors (Conyne, 1996). State licensing boards and certification agencies have followed suit by incorporating professional credentialling requirements or specifying their own stipulations relative to group work. However, most counselors complete their training at the master's degree level with only one or two group courses and possibly some supervised group experience during their practicum or internship (Huhn, Zimpfer, Waltman, & Williamson, 1985). This factor prompted Stockton (Morran, 1992) to state, "I am often impressed with the large number of counselors who have graduated from training programs with solid individual counseling skills and minimal group counseling skills" (p. 7). Thus they venture forth to their jobs with a minimum of training and a maximum of timidity with respect to implementing group work.

Counselors who were trained prior to the 70s and have not subsequently pursued specific additional training in group work also may lack the skill and possibly even the philosophical basis for group counseling. Group counseling demonstrations, continuing education presentations, and professional conference programs serve to promote the group modality as a viable procedure. At best the training value of these programs is questionable and the impact sporadic. Counselors often come away from these programs with enthusiasm and some new techniques but without the depth necessary to develop functional and comprehensive group programs.

Katz (1973) pointed out that an abundance of persons want to participate in experiential groups, but few persons are qualified to organize and lead them. Aubrey (1973), in discussing models to expand the effectiveness and role of the counselor, identified the group as the primary means of doing so. Carroll (1973) in her discussion of the "supracounselor" (a counselor who is expert as a helper and in training others to be helpers) also affirmed that need. Conyne et al. (1985) flatly stated that in spite of the growing need for groups in our society there is "a disappointingly insufficient supply of well trained group workers." They also cited poor leadership training as the "single weakest area in the group work field today" (p. 113).

As a result, a great need exists for the development of training programs at graduate, postgraduate, continuing education, and inservice levels to prepare competent group leaders. Lifton (Christensen, 1990) opined, "We need trained group counselors to be counselor trainers, because counselors will find themselves in many settings where group skills will be needed, and the people won't know how to apply them or how to use them" (p. 138). Conyne, Harvill, Morganette, Moran, and Hulse-Killacky (1990) have observed,

> In general, counseling graduates are moving into work sites with some knowledge of group counseling, a lesser amount of competency training in group membership and leadership and with severely limited supervised experience in actually leading groups. Group leadership effectiveness cannot be accomplished under these training conditions (p. 31).

Recently, professional development workshops sponsored by the American Counseling Association and the Association for Specialists in Group Work have begun to make inroads into upgrading professional competence in group work. However, much more emphasis is needed. Therefore the task before us and the purpose of this book is to train counselors 1) to work effectively with their clients in group settings, 2) to share their expertise by training others to be effective group leaders, and 3) to share their group process expertise in all types of groups thereby enhancing their consultative and resource roles in a wide variety of settings.

☐ Basic Training Components

As stated in the Preface, the four basic training prerequisites for becoming an effective group leader are

1. acquisition of cognitive knowledge and information about group process,
2. experiential involvement as a participant in group process,
3. development of strategies, skills, and techniques to use in the leadership capacity, and
4. supervised experience in the leadership role.

Cognitive knowledge is necessary to provide the counselor with a philosophical, theoretical, and technical understanding of the group process. This information—encompassing group theory, dynamics, and process—serves the counselor well in terms of understanding and directing the group process and in describing its nature to others. Often cognitive awareness of the goals and dynamics of group counseling is required by prospective group members and other significant persons before they will agree to participate in or support group counseling as a helping procedure. Similarly, cognitive understanding of the group process and leadership role lays the foundation for self-confidence as a group leader. Reading, listening (class lectures, audio and video tapes, etc.) research projects, and class discussions can provide much of the needed intellectual basis for leading groups. Observation of professional leaders as role models complements the cognitive learning and was considered by Shapiro and Shapiro (1985) as an essential part of training. Tape series such as Carroll's (1986) *Group Work: Leading in the Here and Now* and Stockton's (1992) *Developmental Aspects of Group Counseling: Process, Leadership and Supervision* available from the American Counseling Association are excellent learning tools. However, a cognitive understanding of the dynamics and process of group work in and of itself is insufficient.

Prospective leaders must complement cognitive learning with *experiential involvement* in the group process. This involvement must occur on two levels. First is the personal involvement level where prospective leaders become members of an ongoing group process. The process of becoming an effective group leader begins within the realm of one's own experience. Personally participating in the group process enables the prospective leader to fully understand the impact of group pressures and dynamics and facilitates firsthand learning about the process intended for helping others. Without this kind of experience group counselors will lack the depth necessary to give their approach to leadership personal integrity.

Two types of personal group experience are advisable. The first type is as a member of a counseling group composed of members drawn from a common context. This experience is typically obtained in graduate school as part of group process courses where groups are formed that consist of graduate students who are peers. The second type of personal group experience is being in a group composed of members drawn from populations that are not relationally connected other than in the group. Shapiro and Shapiro (1985) identified personal group therapy as one of their core training components, and therapy groups are usually composed of members who have no other common relational context. The reason these two types of experiences are recommended is to acquaint potential group leaders with the dynamic differences that ensue when working with related versus nonrelated group members.

The second level of experiential involvement is experimental involvement. This is necessary to help prospective leaders learn and understand the *concepts, skills,* and *techniques* associated with the group process. A laboratory milieu involving experiential learning centering on specific techniques is useful in complementing didactic learning about group process. These experiences help bridge gaps between the cognitive process and personal experience as a group member. They are important in initial training to help leaders enhance their ability and develop a repertoire of methods, techniques, and activities for use in groups. They provide the foundational competencies for effective practice. Once the foundation has been laid, attending group workshops and group presentations at professional meetings and conventions is invaluable to the continued development of leadership competence.

Finally, the old adage "there's no substitute for experience" applies to the group leader. Until the counselor has the opportunity to function in a leadership capacity and try out methods, skills, and techniques in actual situations, learning is incomplete. The process of obtaining leadership experience should begin in training under competent supervision in a group practicum or internship or as part of a general practicum or internship. All too often, however, counselors are left on their own to take care of this aspect of their development. This book will describe some possibilities for initial leadership experiences and will make additional suggestions for getting the necessary experience to become a competent group leader.

☐ Book Format

The objective of this book is to provide the group leader with the first three prerequisites mentioned above and to initiate the process for realizing the fourth. Each chapter is composed of didactic discussion and experiential activities to complement the discussion. The information included was selected on the basis of its particular relevance to agency, private practice, and educational settings, although the appropriateness for other helping and group oriented environments is not excluded.

The second criterion in selecting information was practicality because my intent is that this book will have merit on the basis of its usefulness rather than its erudite scholarship or theoretical prowess. Techniques and exercises were chosen or developed on the basis of their applicability to learning and using the group process. Special attention was given to include activities that can be used in training *and* practice. The hallmark of any good technique is that it substantially aids the group process and at the same time teaches the group members about the group process. Therefore many of the techniques or adaptations of them will be useful to group leaders in conducting their own groups.

Finally, the information and activities can be used in total or in part since much of the emphasis in this book is directed toward utilization. The book is written so that selective usage or adaptation will not interfere with the fluidity of the presentation. Therefore readers are encouraged to complement, supplement, revise, delete, or adjust the concepts and activities of this book to meet their own needs.

☐ Strategies for Obtaining Group Experience

Strategies for obtaining group experience (the second prerequisite) are included in this first chapter because cognitive learning and experiential learning need to proceed hand in hand. In this way prospective leaders are allowed the opportunity to approach their group experience with their own expectations rather than expectations gleaned from reading or lectures. They also begin the process of testing knowledge against experience immediately. Strategies are broken down into two groups, the first directed toward counselor trainees and the second toward practicing counselors who wish to develop their group skills.

Strategies for Counselor Trainees

Most training in group counseling begins with a formal course in group process. For example, Hetzel, Stockton, and McDonnell (1994) found that an introductory group course was part of the curriculum in 98% of the counseling departments that responded to their survey. Merta, Wolfgang, and McNeil (1993) found that 88% of the counselor education programs they surveyed included experiential groups as a component of training in group practice. Corey and Corey (1992) have stipulated that group experience should be a requirement of an initial, or any, group counseling course. Therefore the first strategies discussed are intended for incorporation into a class format. While the specific proportion of experiential vs. didactic training varies, a reasonable balance is one-third to one-half experiential and the remainder didactic. Some programs have implemented experiential group process courses extending the requirements to a sequence of two courses, one focusing on cognitive learning and the other on experiential learning. The following strategies suggested will still apply but with the added adaptation and advantage that the group process course can be administratively recognized as part and parcel of an instructor's teaching load. The first step is to divide the class into counseling size groups (preferably eight members per group) and organize a schedule of meetings for the entire quarter or semester. A general rule of thumb is to have at least one group meeting for each week of the term.

Since the publication of the second edition of this book, extensive discussions of the nature of the experiential group requirement have occurred both in the literature (Donigian, 1993; Forester-Miller & Duncan, 1990; Lloyd, 1990; Merta & Sisson, 1991; Williams, 1990) and in the annals of professional organizations and credentialing agencies responsible for setting training standards and licensing/certification requirements (ASGW, 1991; CACREP, 1994). Primary concern has been to ensure both quality training *and* ethical practice relative to trainees in group work. (Ethics in the form of Best Practices in group counseling will be discussed extensively by Rapin and Conyne in Chapter 8.) The general consensus of that debate is that group experience should be a required dimension of group courses, but the experiential aspect itself should not be evaluated as a portion of the student's academic grade in the course. Pierce and Baldwin (1990) summarized the issue effectively as follows:

> In the context of teaching students to become group counselors, students become clients whose welfare must be protected. This means that group leadership in a counselor education program must be fair, do no harm, respect the individual's right as a free agent and yet at the same time, do them some good in being able to participate constructively and to use and control self disclosure effectively (p. 149).

Therefore the standard parameters for implementing any and all of the following strategies are:

1. Required participation in experiential groups as part of graduate training in group work is not to be evaluated as part of the student's grade.*
2. The requirement of participation in experiential groups (however framed) is mandatory, *but* the depth of involvement and self disclosure is the option of the student.

   Note: Most training programs reserve the right to review a student's appropriateness for the program at any time which is different from the limitation with respect to group participation and grades (Sklare, Thomas, Williams, & Powers, 1996).

Group Strategy 1: Instructor as Group Leader

This approach requires the leader to wear two hats, instructor and group leader. The advantage of this approach is that an immediate integration of the instructor's cognitive expertise and leadership style is realized. He or she becomes both expert and model, which provides the class members with an example of how the two fit together. The disadvantage is that one or the other of the roles or the dual role itself may be an inhibiting factor to class members' participation. Similarly the leader may have difficulty switching hats and may experience added pressure if a discrepancy occurs between what he or she says and does.

Group Strategy 2: Outside Professional as Group Leader

This strategy involves the instructor enlisting the cooperation of trained leaders from among the counseling staff or faculty to lead the facilitated group experience part of the class. Sometimes instructors can trade services or responsibilities to facilitate this strategy. If the training program has a doctoral component, advanced degree students can also be utilized as group leaders. The advantage of this approach is that group members do not have to encounter the dilemma of the instructor being the leader and can experience the group in a more natural, autonomous manner. As such the experience tends to approximate the manner in which most groups are conducted in field settings—where the counselor has no role in the lives of group members other than group leader. The disadvantages of this approach are that instructors lose the opportunity for more personal contact with students that takes place in the group and have more difficulty assessing student needs and thus planning their instruction accordingly. In addition, the mentoring dimension of instruction is limited.

Group Strategy 3: Outside Professional, – observe Instructor-Observer

This strategy requires the cooperation of a trained leader and a facility that will allow for unobtrusive observation by the instructor (preferably a group room with a one way mirror, audio system and video taping capability). The distinct feature of this strategy is the incorporation of a feedback session in which the instructor-observer shares perceptions of the group interaction for purposes of educating members and elucidating group process. The feedback sessions are critical to this approach but can cause difficulties if comments are not made tentatively and time is not allowed for discussion and processing of the process observation.

With the advent of the process observer emphasis and orientation in group work (Bieschke, Matthews, & Wade, 1996; Hulse-Killacky, 1996), this particular strategy has almost unlimited potential. Using a microlab format the instructor can divide the class into two groups and lead a process observation group with one group while the other group is participating in an experiential group process. The process group can learn from the experiential group and contribute feedback thereby multiplying the learning potential of both group experiences. The student gains experience as a group member and a process observer as each group alternately observes while the other experiences. Professional growth is also stimulated in the leader and instructor who can try out new ideas and get immediate feedback as to their relevance and meaning.

Group Strategy 4: Leaderless Group, Instructor-Observer

The basic advantages of this method are that the instructor does not have to depend on outside help and that less time is involved since more than one group can be going at a time. The same types of facilities are necessary as for Strategy 3 but the group functions without a designated leader. Structuring or nonstructuring is the prerogative of the instructor. Feedback sessions at the end of each session or in separate sessions are also important. The instructor can keep pace with the group members' experiences, provide important insights, intervene when necessary, and structure teaching around group process. The disadvantage is that the group does not have a designated leader to provide a model or supply expertise to help develop the flow of group interaction. In addition, less similarity occurs to the nature of the groups used in professional settings that tend to follow a leader-member group model. The process observation group variation mentioned in Strategy 3 can also be incorporated into this option.

Group Strategy 5: Required Participation in an Outside Group

Basically this strategy requires class members to participate in a group counseling experience outside of class as a supplement to their learning in the course. If this strategy is used the instructor should screen and approve class members' choices to ensure greater relevance to the course. The instructor also may locate groups and then encourage or require class members to choose from an approved list. The advantage of this approach is that the range of class members' group experiences are broader which leads to— if the instructor can facilitate discussion of these experiences within limits of confidentiality—a very positive result.

If this option is pursued two guidelines are helpful and necessary for ethical purposes. First, members are required to inform their group that they are in a group class, are participating as a requirement of that class, will be processing their experience with their instructor as part of the learning experience, and need to obtain the group's permission to do so. Second, a ground rule is established that discussion will only pertain to the member's own experience and observations of the group process. In addition, it is usually beneficial to have members keep journals of their experiences and than discuss them with the instructor in light of the course content. (Regardless of the strategy chosen, the journal idea is a good one because it helps group members consolidate their experiences and integrate them with their cognitive learning.) The disadvantage of this strategy is the complete lack of contact with the actual experience of the group members and that even when the preceding guidelines are followed, the experiences chosen or obtained may not be relevant. Opportunity to mentor and model is again limited.

Group Strategy 6: Designated Leader, Instructor-Observer

The format of this strategy entails designating leaders from among the group trainees as an added dimension to their experiential learning. As designated leaders for one or more sessions (coleaders can also be used), trainees obtain firsthand experience in the leadership role whetting their appetites for further experience and initiating the process of deciphering differences between member and leader roles in the group. The instructor observes incorporating feedback to the designated leader(s) and the group as part of a follow-up session. Leaders can be video taped and review their work with the instructor and other students to enhance the learning experience.

Whitman, Morgan, and Alfred (1996) describe a coleading training experience that pairs a student with a senior therapist. Their model could be adapted to an introductory course. However, since coleadership adds another process variable to the group dynamics, their model may be more appropriate for more advanced courses where students have more experience and training before they move into a coleader position.

The disadvantages of this strategy are that the group process may become disjointed as leadership is rotated and members do not get an experienced leader as a role model. These disadvantages tend to outweigh the advantage of a brief leadership experience for trainees. *Note*: A variation combining aspects of strategies 3, 4, and 6 using fishbowl methodology is described by Kane (1995).

Group Strategy 7: Structured vs. Nonstructured Group Leadership

This strategy is more of a modification of Strategy 1 (Instructor as Group Leader) than an alternative. The group process is divided into two parts, the first in which the leader takes a facilitative, nondirective role and the second in which the leader structures group interaction using communication exercises and directed focus activities to generate group interaction. This strategy gives members a sense of where they function best relative to the structure/nonstructure continuum both as individuals and as potential group leaders. The disadvantages are those of administration and orchestration rather than experience. Some instructors, including the author, resolve this dilemma by incorporating structured activities into the cognitive portion of the course using experiential activities to demonstrate group concepts, process, and dynamics.

Additional Considerations. Whenever the group experience is organized around subgroups of an entire class, the very nature of group experience can cause factionalism, coalitions, and polarization. The instructor when approaching the class must take this into account and organize class experiences that tend to offset the tendency toward group cliques. Changing the environment also may be a useful intervention in organizing group experiences. Sometimes changing rooms for class and group experiences helps ease the transition from one experience to the other.

Strategies for Practicing Counselors

Practicing counselors who wish to develop their expertise in leading groups sometimes have a difficult time arranging learning experiences due to lack of time in their own schedules and lack of opportunities in their immediate environment. The first possibility is to take a graduate level group course, either by audit or on a credit basis. Prior to enrolling the counselor should check with the instructor to determine the amount and types of experiences expected.

Group courses can be selected from a variety of professional fields including counselor education, psychology, social work, human relations, or communications programs. When group process courses are selected from fields outside of counselor education, counselors may have to rely on their experiences and previous training for adapting and applying the course information and experience to their own settings and use. The advantage of selecting courses from counseling related fields is that counselors may be able to apply credits earned toward an advanced degree, meet professional continuing education requirements, or realize increments on a salary schedule while at the same time improving their professional skills. The advantage of a counselor education group course is the direct relationship the course has to the counselor's role in the agency, school, or private practice setting in which he or she works. It provides the opportunity for the immediate integration of training and practice.

Many counselors choose to pursue group training in noneducation settings such as private, profit and nonprofit organizations, professional associations, or training institutes that provide courses and programs on a per person cost basis. Examples of these programs are National Training Laboratories (NTL), Esalen Institute and Western Behavioral Science Institute. In addition, a host of organizations have emerged in the wake of licensure/certification continuing education requirements that advertise and provide training in group work. Professional organizations such as the American Group Psychotherapy Association (AGPA) and the American Counseling Association (ACA) of which the Association for Specialists in Group Work (ASGW) is a division sponsor regional and national training programs as part of their continuing education thrust. Some of these programs may lead to a credential in group leadership. Whenever one of these programs is selected, counselors should again determine the nature of the experience and assess its relevance to their own settings prior to becoming involved. This requires professional judgment as well as a cognitive grasp of the group process prior to investigating the various group programs.

Local continuing education or inservice training in group process may be the most viable and relevant means of obtaining group expertise. The counselor can organize a group of professionals interested in learning the group counseling process and then bring in an outside consultant who has the most appropriate credentials and experience to serve as group leader. The advantages of this approach are numerous. There is greater assurance that the desired experience and the resulting experience will be similar because the counselor has input into the organization of the experience and the selection of the leader. Cooperation between the educational setting and the group leader's university or professional organization is facilitated, increasing the amount of input from outside experts and stimulating the professional life of the counselors and staff. Since the program is organized in the field setting, the time involved is reduced and attendance is more convenient. Administrators look favorably on programs such as this and may provide financial support for the group leaders and salary reinforcement to the participants. Inservice programs have some inherent disadvantages including lack of interest and motivation due to fatigue of the participants and difficulty in locating an expert who will be stimulating and relevant at an affordable price. Careful planning directed toward meeting the need for effective group counseling programs and wise selection of the consultant can overcome these difficulties.

The Mythical, Ideal, Ultimate, Basic Group Course

In spite of all the discussion and research in training group workers and the development of training and certification standards and requirements, the fact remains that the vast majority of masters level counselors and clinicians will complete their training with only one group class and possibly some supervised group work experience in their practicum or internship. Consequently I would like to conclude this chapter with a brief sketch of an ideal group course that identifies the components, experiences, and requirements necessary to provide an adequate foundation for group work competence.

Class Format: The class format should incorporate lecture/presentation, structured group activities for demonstration, and facilitated group process for personal experience.

Academic Requirements: Reading requirements should include an appropriate group text, supplemental reading and familiarization with the group work literature (professional journals). Writing projects should include a minimum of three projects identified as follows:

1. A research paper on the ethics of group work.
2. A research paper on a selected group topic using current professional group literature.
3. A group proposal or plan for a specific population, situation or setting.

Experiential Requirements: The class framework should provide the following experiences as an integral dimension of the course:

1. A facilitated group experience (required but nongraded) of at least 10 sessions. This experience should be facilitated by a trained and experienced leader. A journal should be required but not read or evaluated by the instructor.

Note: A follow up activity to the experiential group could involve the student writing a 2–5 page summation of their group experience to be discussed with the group instructor after the academic work is completed (grades are in) as part of an overall assessment of the student's learning, progress, and appropriateness for group work.

2. Each student should have the opportunity to serve as a process observer for at least one class session and have their process observation incorporated in the class process.

Note: Preparation for the process observer experience can involve required reading of the *Gleanings of a Process Observer* in Appendix E (pp. 565–571).

3. Each student should have one group leadership experience consisting of a minimum of 20–30 minutes in the leadership role (preferably video taped). Group composition is the class or subgroups of the class. The focus of the group can be getting a group started, demonstrating a structured group activity, or an evolving focus reflecting the development of the group process (stage related and class related). Feedback by the instructor and class members can be incorporated into the experience and the tape (if available) can be reviewed by the student individually, with peers, and by the instructor as a leadership learning experience.

Definitions and Distinctions

☐ A Group is a Group (or Is It?)

Each one of us spends a significant portion of our lives in groups: family groups, work groups, neighborhood groups, church groups, social groups—the list could go on ad infinitum. Periodically, in the course of our interaction in these groups, we find ourselves sharing or disclosing personal information about our hopes or disappointments, joys or pain, problems or achievements. These disclosures may emanate from the turmoil or excitement within ourselves, from the perceived amenability to sharing observed or experienced in the nature of the group itself, or some combination of the two. What triggers these disclosures are the rudiments upon which the group process as a helping modality is built.

Vignettes of naturally occurring therapeutic group interactions abound:

Jane, a 31 year old mother of two, discloses to three neighborhood women friends that she has discovered a lump in her breast and is scared to death to tell her husband or go to a doctor.

Bill, a 43 year old middle manager gets into his office car pool angry on Monday morning and proceeds to tell the passengers about an argument he and his wife had over the weekend which continued unresolved right up to the point he got into the car.

Diane, an executive secretary, gathers each day for a coffee break with other women in similar positions in the corporation. A main topic of conversation is female issues so they name this group "OVA" and make efforts to get together outside office hours.

Dierdre at age 16 talks enthusiastically and intensely about her new boyfriend with a group of three or four close friends.

Billy, age 4, tells his playmates at his preschool that his parents are getting a divorce.

Jim, 22 and in his first year of teaching, receives an offer for a three year doctoral fellowship and talks it over with fellow teachers in the teachers' lounge asking, "What should I do?"

Ben talks excitedly with a group of coworkers about the birth of his new daughter.

All these examples reflect the personal nature and helping capacity of groups, but what distinguishes a counseling or therapy group from these or any other personally meaningful group interactions? Answering that question is the focus of this chapter.

☐ General Nature of Groups

The purpose of this chapter is to define group counseling and discuss the characteristics that distinguish it and give it an identity of its own in the broad spectrum of group processes and group work. To accomplish this we first must look at the general nature of groups so we can develop some guidelines for delimiting the context in which we will consider group counseling.

Slavson (1952) stated that a group consists of "at least three persons because it is the third and succeeding persons who introduce problems and stresses that do not ordinarily exist in two person relationships" (p. 223). This definition denotes the minimum number of persons required for the group process to occur and distinguishes a group from a dyadic relationship (for example, individual counseling) based on the inclusion of group dynamics. With three or more persons new forces and pressures are introduced into the group as members attempt to relate, communicate, and achieve objectives. The interaction becomes more complex, communication is more difficult to follow, and control is less easily obtained.

Coalitions can now form that precipitate the creation of subgroups. Additionally the emergence of multiple member roles can occur (e.g., in a three person interaction there can be a message-sender, a message-receiver, and an observer of the transaction). These dynamics escalate with expanding group size and necessitate the establishment of an optimal group size. This is a difficult task because no clear basis exists for determining a specific number above which a group becomes impersonal or nontherapeutic—a point beyond which an individual's identity is submerged or lost in the group.

Some guidelines are available to help us determine a general perspective on the optimal group size necessary to maintain personal and therapeutic group interaction. Homans (1950) defined a therapeutic group as a "number of persons who communicate with one another over a span of time and who are few enough so that each person is able to communicate with others, not at second hand through other people, but face to face" (p. 1).

This definition stresses the importance of groups maintaining a size where members can communicate directly and personally with one another. A therapeutic group must be small enough so that the identity of the individual is preserved and each member has some degree of reciprocal influence on each other (Schmuck & Schmuck, 1971). When a group becomes so large or develops a style of communication that prohibits personal and direct contact between members, its therapeutic nature is severely restricted.

A maximum size limit depends, to some extent, on the purposes and type of group involved, the nature and maturity of the group members, and/or the experience and expertise of the group leader. However, once a group exceeds a range of 8 to 12 members, the therapeutic atmosphere and impact become proportionally less evident. A general rule of thumb relative to an effective group size is 5 to 12 members (Roark & Roark, 1979). Specifically by age group, recommended group size is

1) elementary school age, 4 to 6 members;
2) middle school to junior high age, 6 to 8 members;
3) high school age, 8 to 10 members; and
4) young adult to adult age, 8 to 12 members.

Groups with the elderly vary in size depending on the interactive capabilities of the participants ranging from adult group size (8 to 12 members) to smaller groups of 3 to 6 members. Group size will be addressed more specifically in Chapter 10, but in general we will be considering a group size of 3 to 12 members as the range within which the group counseling process operates.

☐ Group Counseling Definition

A comprehensive and operational definition of group counseling must include comments on the following components: process, atmosphere (climate) of the group, purpose (focus), membership, and leadership. With these components in mind let's turn our attention to the definition of group counseling as it will be used throughout this book. This definition is designed to answer three basic questions—What?, Who?, and Why?—with respect to group counseling.

What

Group counseling is the development of an interpersonal network.

This network is what creates the atmosphere and milieu necessary for the helping process to work. The ingredients that are essential to a therapeutic relationship must therefore be present in the interaction between the leader and group members. These characteristics include trust, acceptance, respect, warmth, communication, and understanding.

Trust is basically the experience of feeling safe and secure in sharing one's self with others without fear of rejection or reprisal. It involves both trusting others and being trustworthy. The development of trust is the cement that secures confidentiality into place as the cornerstone of the group process.

Acceptance is the quality of being allowed to be freely yourself regardless of problems you have in your life. Victor Hugo captured the essence of this characteristic when he stated that "the supreme happiness of life is the conviction that we are loved, loved for ourselves or rather, loved in spite of ourselves."

Respect is the willingness to relate to one another based on the uniqueness, inherent worth, and dignity of each person and the commonality of humanness we all share. Yalom (1995) referred to the connectedness of human experience as the principle of "universality." The quotation "every person is in certain respects like all other persons, like some other persons, like no other person" expresses the thought very clearly. John Ruskin, the English literary critic, accentuated the importance of respect for the worth of each person when he noted, "the weakest among us has a gift, however seemingly trivial, which is peculiar to him (her) and which worthily used will be a gift to his (her) race forever."

Warmth is the human capability that is best described as unconditional positive regard. It combines the elements of caring, nonpossessive love, prizing, and liking and is difficult to measure except in terms of one's own experience and feelings. Its presence is completely dependent on the sensitivity of each person to recognize and receive it and the ability of each person to feel and express it.

Communication is also a necessary relational factor in that it provides the means whereby meaningful interaction between persons is facilitated. The type of communication referred to here is two-way communication in which all persons involved have the desire and ability to initiate, respond to, and receive the communication process (Johnson, 1972; Johnson & Johnson, 1997; Schmuck & Schmuck, 1971).

The final ingredient is _understanding,_ referred to by Rogers (1961) as empathy and Truax and Carkhuff (1967) as accurate empathy. Understanding is the ability to see things from the other person's frame of reference, to be able to step into another person's shoes but at the same time maintain your own identity and reality. It is the capacity to perceive another person's perspective or experience _as if_ you were that person but without losing the "as if" quality. Rogers (1952) felt that the ability to "listen with understanding" removes barriers in communication that often develop from our tendency to evaluate communications we receive.

If we are successful in creating relationships within the group characterized by these qualities, a therapeutic or helping atmosphere will be the end product.

Who

(through which) A counselor and several clients come into contact.

This aspect of our definition gives the principals involved in the process. The counselor is a person with professional training in guidance, counseling, or psychotherapy and who has specific competence as a group leader (Cohn, 1967). In this sense he or she is the "more knowing" person in the group who combines professional expertise and personal commitment to help the clients. The clients are considered "less knowing" individuals because they are experiencing problems and concerns that, for reasons known or unknown to them, they have not been able to resolve on their own. Feelings of being unable to cope or at least the discomfort of having problems they can't resolve supply the impetus for convening the group (Trotzer, 1975).

Ultimate responsibility for leadership is on the shoulders of the counselor although each counselor's personality will determine the nature or style of leadership and the amount of responsibility shared by group members. Counselors have responsibility *to* their clients in that they use their expertise, knowledge, and personality to facilitate the group process, help the clients whenever possible, and protect or defend their clients' well being if that becomes necessary. However, the counselor is not responsible *for* the clients since the members are individually responsible for decisions, actions, and changes in their own lives. (*Note*: The exception to this perspective otherwise known as the free agency of the client involves clear and present danger situations and duty to warn provisions of ethical and legal codes that govern the practice of professional counselors.)

Why

In order to help each other confront unsatisfactory or problem areas in the clients' lives and discover, understand, and implement ways of resolving those problems and/or dissatisfactions.

The focus of group counseling is on problems. It is oriented toward helping members express and explore their difficulties and concerns in an effort to use the group's resources to find ways of overcoming these difficulties and living more fulfilled and satisfying lives. This integration of process and purpose is a prominent element in our definition. Process involves two basic phases. The first is characterized by relationship development that leads to self-disclosure and understanding of one's problems, the second is associated with action directed toward resolving the problems. During the action phase the client uses the group to help him or her discover alternatives, evaluate their implications and probabilities of success, and then practice and implement them to solve the problem. Thus the purpose of group counseling is to deal directly with a client's difficulties, stresses, frustrations, problems,

concerns, and dissatisfactions in an effort to remove them as factors impeding the client's growth, development, and personal fulfillment. The unique
aspect of group counseling is the "helping each other" process, which will
be discussed in greater depth a little later in this chapter.

The group counseling definition in total is:

> Group counseling is the development of an interpersonal network character-
> ized by trust, acceptance, respect, warmth, communication and understand-
> ing through which a counselor and several clients come in contact in order to
> help each other confront unsatisfactory or problem areas in the clients' lives
> and discover, understand and implement ways of resolving those problems
> and dissatisfactions (Trotzer, 1972).

This definition differentiates counseling or therapy groups from other group
experiences or interactions based on the mobilization of interpersonal human resource potential in relation to a helping objective. Several key points
are emphasized. As an interpersonal network the counseling group represents a human process reflective of the domain of human relationships in
which members are experiencing their problems.

Second, the traits of that therapeutic network only have meaning in a
relational context. Trust, acceptance, respect, warmth, communication, and
understanding can only be experienced if interpersonal relationships are
present. Third, there is a built-in interpersonal growth dynamic in that the
process depends on members helping each other. And finally, the focus and
purpose of the group are explicit. Counseling groups are initiated for the
purpose of problem solving. As such the counseling group represents a
temporary interventive modality in each group member's life, the therapeutic impact and duration of which is governed by the intention on the
part of both leaders and members to dissolve the group by resolving the
problems (Trotzer, 1985).

☐ Advantages of Group Counseling

Advantages of the group counseling modality can be considered from several perspectives. The first is in contrast to individual counseling, noting
those helping characteristics the group can provide that are not readily
available to the counselor in one-to-one relationships. Second is the perspective that views group counseling as an entity in and of itself with its
own merit and advantageous characteristics. Third is the viewpoint that
presents advantages but takes particular care to define the qualifications
and conditions under which they operate and limits that must be observed
to prevent an asset from becoming a liability. A fourth perspective projects
constructive assets and qualities of group dynamics beyond the therapeutic
setting. These dynamics are called process dynamics and reflect generic
qualities endemic to all group work. All four of these vantage points will be
incorporated into our succeeding discussion.

The reader should keep in mind that different group approaches may emphasize different positive qualities of the group process. It is possible for all advantages to be evident at some time during the group process. However what is more likely is that only a few will be consistently prominent. The following list of advantages/assets is comprehensive in nature encompassing a broad spectrum of approaches rather than a definitive list of advantages characterizing every group approach.

Safety Factors in Groups

Group counseling provides group members with an automatic camouflage if they desire to use it. Due to the fact that each member of the group is a client, an initial feeling of safety exists because the probability of being the center of attention decreases in direct proportion to the size of the group. In addition, the feeling that there is strength in numbers also is present. These assumptions may be enough to encourage group members to embark on the journey toward working on their problems in the group. Members often are more willing to discuss feelings, concerns, attitudes, and beliefs in groups of peers than in individual counseling (Dinkmeyer & Muro, 1971). In fact, Ohlsen (1970) pointed out that "some clients find it easier to discuss difficult subjects in group counseling" than in one-to-one counseling (p. 5).

The climate of the group generated by the relationships formed is also a factor in members feeling safe. In the first place, relationships are developed in an atmosphere of controlled intimacy, which reduces the risk in forming relationships and the contingent obligations that usually result from them (Mahler, 1969). Secondly, members have a natural feeling that fellow clients will accept them and empathize with them which makes facing up to problems and weaknesses safer (Ohlsen, 1977).

Problems can result from these safety factors. Individual members can successfully lose themselves in the group and never have to confront their problems. When this occurs the safety in numbers influence undermines the helping process. Another problem results when the group becomes so safe nothing is risked and therefore no action toward resolving problems is taken (Vorrath, n.d.). When either of these two situations arises the group leader must take steps to create tension in the group or confront the group to activate the helping process once again.

Sense of Belonging

William James (1890) once wrote:

We are not only gregarious animals liking to be in sight of our fellows, but we have an innate propensity to get ourselves noticed, and noticed favorably, by our kind. No more fiendish punishment could be devised were such a thing physically possible, than one should be turned loose in society and remain absolutely unnoticed by all the members thereof (p. 293).

The enticement of group counseling is that it spawns the conditions that enable both the *noticing* to occur and the *ignoring* to be avoided.

Lakin (n.d.) pointed out that one of the key distinctions between individual and group psychotherapy is that the group has the capacity to provide members with an experience of belongingness. Thus the group member has the opportunity to feel a part of a social group, one of our essential needs as human beings. While deep intimacy and closeness are still the bailiwick of the dyadic relationship, the group can provide social support in the form of group membership, which can never be an element of the one-to-one relationship. When members experience acceptance, understanding, and cohesiveness in the group, they begin to realize they are important and worthwhile. They feel they need the group and are wanted by the group, which is the essence of belonging. The key dynamic operating here is that 1) groups help individuals create their personal identity, and 2) individuals influence the traits that groups exemplify. The interaction of these two processes helps members find belongingness, which provides them with the support they need to work on improving themselves.

The problem presented by the group's belongingness factor is that members may lose sight of the fact that the counseling group is intended to be transitional in nature rather than permanent. In other words, group counseling is not a process designed to give group members a permanent social group within which to operate and meet their needs. Rather the group is a temporary stopping-off place where members can reconstrue themselves for the purpose of living more effective lives in their regular environments. The element of belonging is only useful as it aids the member in achieving a better life outside the group. A derivative of this same problem is that the sense of belonging may also be a manipulative tool in the hands of the members or leader. Careful attention must be given to whether its impact is constructive or simply a power play used by the group to dominate, control, or manipulate individual members.

Social Value of Group Counseling

In the literature there is clear consensus that group counseling has definite social qualities that make it particularly relevant for helping people solve their problems. Groups by their very nature tend to take on social characteristics representing the environment in which they are formed. Individual members through their input into the group represent the broader society in which their learnings and experiences have occurred (Trotzer, 1975). Gazda (1968) referred to this phenomenon when he stated that the group is "a microcosm of social reality" (p. 1). Dinkmeyer and Muro (1971) called the group a "reflection of society as a whole" (p. 60). Hinckley and Herman (1951) commented that the group resembles "true-life situations" where dependence and independence are constantly interchanging, and Vorrath (n.d.) stressed the role of the group as an "ongoing community." Matthews (1992) has noted that people in society dance to the oscillating dynamic described as a conflict between responsibility to self versus responsibility to the group. Counseling and "therapy conducted in groups has the advantage of treating the members in the context of this fundamental dance of life" (p. 162). In all cases the affirmation is that groups are mini-societies, that reflect to some degree the reality of the outside world.

Very early in my work as an individual therapist I realized a major discrepancy existed between what happened in the counselor's office and the client's life. The best laid plans tended to go awry once the client encountered the expectational pressures of the real world. Consequently, the necessity of upgrading the transferability potential in counseling became paramount. The social environment of the counseling group does just that. In group counseling an inherent transitional value bolsters the probability of successful implementation of change outside the group. This transferability dynamic is a major therapeutic asset.

The group then is a valuable tool in the hands of a trained counselor because it is a social laboratory where results obtained have transitional properties to implement in real life. The group has the advantage of being a laboratory where individuals are able to understand the social meaning of thoughts, feelings, and behaviors because they are being reviewed and experienced in a social context (Dinkmeyer & Muro, 1971). Since we as human beings are social by nature, to fully understand our actions is difficult if we divorce them completely from the social milieu and the systems in which we function. The group can retain this dimension, while individual counseling must depend almost entirely on verbal description to account for it. The group atmosphere provides the opportunity for members to learn more about themselves because it gives them a broader social mirror in which to view themselves than does individual counseling. In fact, individual change may actually be an easier process in groups. Kurt Lewin once observed that "it is easier to change individuals formed into a group than to change any of them separately" (Maples, 1992, p. 145).

The group is an arena where social comparisons can be made and evaluated. Members have the advantage of practicing behavioral and attitudinal changes prior to attempting them in real life situations. This process, called reality testing, is a major ingredient in the successful resolution of problems. Members can assess the probability of success by using the group as a sounding board in formulating, developing, and evaluating alternatives. By using the group in this way members also can develop the self-confidence needed to implement the changes outside the group.

The extent to which groups are representative of society is difficult to determine and for this reason must be carefully considered in the inter-action of any group. Lakin (n.d.) warns that groups are not only capable of defining social reality but are capable of defining it in such a way that it is distorted. When this occurs the resulting perceptions and changes may in fact be detrimental to problem resolution rather than therapeutic.

An example of reality distortion occurred in an adolescent girls' counsel-ing group where group members, in response to one girl's disclosure of her loneliness and desire to have a boyfriend, coerced a boy to invite her to a dance. This was done outside the group without the knowledge of the group leader. The girl was noticeably overweight and when the two appeared at the dance, the boy became subject to cat calls and snide remarks with negative innuendos. He became embarrassed and incensed and made an impulsive decision to leave the girl standing alone in the middle of the dance floor thus devastating her already fragile sense of self-esteem. The group had failed to consider the reality factors in attempting to respond helpfully to the girl's problem as they perceived it. Leaders are responsible for preventing reality distortion and must be willing to bear the negative reactions of members when they intervene to maintain a realistic focus in the group.

Group as Power

The aspect of group process that triggers the most varied and intense reac-tion is its power. Agreement is plentiful that the group process is powerful, however, no end is in sight regarding the controversy as to if and how that power should be used to change persons' lives. To review this subject is beyond the scope of this book, therefore, we will turn our attention to the issue of power in the context of group counseling. Suffice it to say that the influence of groups and group dynamics is inevitable in each of our lives, and our task is to define those elements that make the group counseling process a beneficial tool in the hands of the counselor.

The power of the group centers around peer group pressure and influ-ence. One of the most important aspects in the development of every person is the reaction of those persons in his or her peer group. This is particularly true during adolescence but is no small matter in the lives of children and adults—from young adults to the elderly. Group counseling harnesses this power of the peer group in an effort to make it a construc-tive influence in helping group members resolve their problems. One of the most surprising revelations that occurs again and again as one works with groups is that individuals in many cases know what they want to do or should do to better themselves but will not act on that knowledge until they feel it is acceptable and valued by their peer group.

The power of the peer group is revealed in the natural tendencies of the group to influence individuals in terms of conformity, identity, reward and punishment, and social controls. In each of these cases the counseling group uses peer group dynamics to help individual members live more satisfying lives and act constructively in resolving problems. As a result, the counselor has available vastly expanded resources that can be used in counseling. Individual counseling does not have these resources directly available since the counselor is usually not a member of the client's peer group and is not in a position to engage significant peers in the counseling process. Peer influence therefore becomes the vehicle of change in the group counseling process. Vorrath (n.d.) felt this was such an important aspect of the group process that he built his entire approach to working with adolescent delinquents around it.

In addition to the forces already mentioned, the use of peer group dynamics provides a buffer zone between the adult world and the child or adolescent. Ohlsen (1974) gave a brief description of how it works:

> When some members of the group fail to act, other members can put pressure on reluctant actors without arousing the defensiveness that results when parents and teachers pressure adolescents to behave differently (p. 144).

This process helps bridge the generation gap by improving communication. Group members can say the same things and require the same things that adults would but without the contingent emotional resistance. Among adults this same phenomenon can be observed based on the distinction of emotional involvement. The same input that would be resisted or rejected out of hand when given by spouses, bosses, close friends, or parents of adult children is received as revelation, insight, or helpful when obtained from a noninvolved third party of the same age or role category.

As with any source of power the group's power also can be abusive and destructive. If peer pressure is directed toward achieving unrealistic goals or used to force individuals into actions detrimental to themselves or others, the group leader must take steps to intervene. Group pressure is only beneficial if it facilitates the process of self-development on the part of individual group members. Its influence should not become the all consuming power in the client's life. As in the case of belongingness, the group must exert its power to get members out of the group via successful resolution of problems and not attempt to totally immerse them in a process that is an end in and of itself.

Helping and Being Helped

Group counseling provides members with the opportunity to both help and be helped. Lakin (n.d.) credited the availability of this option in the group to the group's capacity to redistribute power. The counselor is not the only one who can aid members and indeed should not be since the members are invaluable resources in the helping process. That is why Conyne (Ward, 1993) called members "the most important resource in the whole group" (p. 103). More than any other this characteristic of mutual help contributes to the appeal of group counseling. In individual counseling, clients seldom if ever have the opportunity to help the counselor. They are always in the position of being the ones with the problems who are being helped. In the group they can still get the help they need but in addition they can maintain and build their self-respect and self-worth by assisting others with their problems. Vorrath (n.d.) stressed this concept of "doing things to help one another" as the key therapeutic element in the group process. The impact of this dynamic creates a spiral effect in the group. As members see help being given or give help, they become more willing to ask for and accept help for themselves. As more members ask for help a greater opportunity exists to be helpful, and so on. Ohlsen (1970) observed that when members discover others struggling with similar problems, their own problems become more acceptable. Seeing others learn to cope with their problems is encouraging and helps them increase their sense of self-respect. "Thus group counseling . . . enables them (the members) to satisfy some of their strongest needs, especially in providing real assistance to peers while obtaining assistance from them" (Ohlsen, 1970, p. 206).

The only problems with this group counseling dynamic are associated with the manner and content of the help that is given. In most cases members provide assistance in the form of feedback and alternatives that are realistic and relevant to the concerns of the members being helped. In giving assistance, however, the one being helped must retain the right to weigh and select the alternatives and perceptions that he or she views as most helpful. In that way ultimate responsibility for change is on the shoulders of the member not the group. Also, the leader is responsible for making sure the help given is realistic and that all members have equal access to the group's assistance, intervening when individual members become dominant or isolated with respect to obtaining help in the group.

Self-Correcting Group Dynamics

Counseling and therapy groups have certain inherent self-monitoring and self-correcting tendencies. These tendencies are resources which are naturally available and are mobilized as the flow of the group interaction evolves. However, these dynamics are not absolute and can be obliterated or negated by circumstances, events, and conditions that occur in the group. The most prominent of these tendencies is the dual dynamic of countering ostracism and enmeshment in the group. The best illustration of this dynamic is your hand. Attempt to disassociate one finger from the rest of your fingers. As you do so you will feel a natural resistance and a pressure to pull that finger back in thereby reducing the tension. The same phenomenon occurs in groups when one member or several members become peripheral or ostracized. The group finds ways of pulling the detaching or isolated members back in by shifting focus or attention or by siding with and defending extruded members.

Now, clench your hand into a fist asserting all the pressure you can to hold it closed. Note that tension once again is evident precipitating an impulse to relax the hand thereby separating its members (the fingers) from such close proximity. The same dynamic occurs in groups when intensity becomes overwhelming. A natural tendency exists on the part of individuals and the group to lighten up. This may be done through humor, a shift in focus, or a direct confrontation of the fact that things are too tight. Members may even suggest physical activities to relieve the stress of becoming so embroiled in the group.

Another self-correcting group trait is *centering* where group members act to draw the group back from tangents or distractions to a theme or focus of personal relevance. Frustration or the desire to get something out of the group are motivators for members to get the group to center. These self-correcting traits are unique to group counseling, not being available at all in individual counseling, and being superseded by homeostatic forces in family counseling. However, they are not sufficient to insure that groups will function therapeutically. Group leaders may rely upon them as the first line of defense against excesses or distortions, but must be ready to intervene if the group does not mobilize them. Donigian and Malnati (1997) make the further point that these same self-regulating processes function to maintain the status quo or homeostasis and as such may represent resistance. Consequently, the leader may have to intervene to generate tension so that the group and its members can move ahead with the change process. Also, one of the reasons leaderless groups are vulnerable to nontherapeutic interactions is that the group process can generate dynamics that exhaust or mitigate against these natural helping and healing properties of the group substituting negative dynamic processes that proceed unchecked.

Curative Factors in Groups

Yalom (1975) coined the term *curative factors* to describe components of the group process that account for the therapeutic impact of group. He considers these factors to have a common manifestation across the "entire spectrum of therapeutic groups among a wide variety of populations" (MacDevitt, 1987, p. 76). Based on a foundation of research, clinical practice and theoretical conceptualization, Yalom (1995) identifies the components that characterize therapeutic groups. Summarized by MacDevitt (1987) they are as follows:

1. Altruism: the process of helping others
2. Cohesion: feeling that one truly belongs to the group

3. Catharsis: being able to express feeling and concerns to others
4. Insight: Acquiring self-knowledge or self-understanding
5. Interpersonal learning-input: receiving feedback from other members
6. Interpersonal learning-output: acquiring interpersonal skills
7. Guidance: receiving advice and suggestions
8. Family reenactment: experiencing and learning from the group as if it were one's family
9. Instillation of hope: being encouraged by seeing that others have solved or are solving their problems
10. Universality: realizing that one is not so different from others
11. Identification: modeling oneself after another member or the therapist
12. Existential factors: realizing important, painful truths about life (pp. 76–77)

Together these factors interrelate in such a way to both create conditions for change and generate change. They are interdependent but have properties that allow them to be identified and isolated for conceptualization purposes. As such they account for the distinctive nature of group counseling and are the assets that advocate the use of groups as practical and effective in helping clients.

Donigian and Malnati (1997) contribute four additional factors to the above list. In their system the group processes of contagion, conflict, anxiety, and consensual validation are therapeutic factors that make change possible in groups. *Contagion* is when one member's actions or expressions create ramifications that impact the group. *Conflict* is the dynamic that provides focus and focal direction in the group and raises issues that become the work of the group. *Anxiety* is the tension or fuel that drives the group. It reflects both past conflicts (e.g., unresolved family of origin issues) and present manifestations of conflict from past and/or current (ingroup) sources. *Consensual Validation* is the opportunity for group members to check out their behavior with other members and receive feedback.

Bemak and Epp (1996) have proposed *love* as another curative factor in groups. They describe nonsexual love as a unique characteristic of therapeutic groups that is not accessible in such a potent form in any other counseling modality. Due to the fact that American pop culture has distorted love by entangling it with eroticism, sensuality, and sexuality, counseling theorists have had to "intellectually disguise love's positive non-erotic role in the therapeutic process" (p. 119). Consequently terms such as "unconditional positive regard," "positive reinforcement," "transference," "countertransference," and "positive strokes" have been devised as "love's euphemistic disguises" (p. 120). The fact that groups can provide these powerful nurturing dynamics definitely has curative implications. Even Freud noted the propensity for group members desperate for nurturing "to find someone to hate so they could band together in love" (Bemak & Epp, 1996, p. 123). As such love qualifies as a potent asset in groups, a fact echoed by Gawrys and Brown's (1963) observation that being accepted and understood by a counselor is a satisfying experience but being accepted, understood, and cared for by a group is profound.

Spectator Therapy

A derivative of the social laboratory characteristic of group counseling is what Dinkmeyer and Muro (1971) called "spectator therapy." Each group member has the opportunity to see someone else talk about a problem similar to her or his own and watch the other member work through it in the group. Thus the members can experience the benefits of the group without revealing their own problems. This is certainly not a characteristic of individual counseling and therefore is unique to the group process. The inherent weakness of this trait is an obvious one—if everyone observes, no one will work on problems and nothing will be learned by being a spectator.

Feedback for Growth

The nature of communication in group counseling is special because of the opportunity for members to receive multiple feedback. While individual counseling enables the client to receive feedback from an understanding and helpful expert, the group incorporates both that feedback and feedback from peers. Paraphrasing Cohn (1967) the impact of this process is as follows:

> When persons are placed within the context of a group they cannot continue to rely only upon their own perceptions for a view of themselves. Through the process of group interaction each person comes in contact with the group's perception of what he or she is or what he or she purports to be. Thus it is within the context of the group that each person gains greater self-awareness (p. 1).

Group counseling effectiveness is related to the quantity and quality of the feedback. As members receive feedback about their actions, feelings, thoughts, and problems, they become more clearly aware of the impact of their behavior on others and others' problems and concerns. In addition they find out more about themselves, which gives them a stronger basis on which to make decisions beneficial to their lives.

Groups must guard against using feedback in a destructive, pejorative, or personally damaging manner. When used for the purpose of ostracizing, scapegoating, or criticizing with no positive purpose in mind, the person and the group process are damaged. Groups must establish guidelines for feedback (see Figure 2.1), and the leader must act to facilitate positive use of feedback while safeguarding individuals and the group from using it negatively.

Feedback is a way of helping others to consider changing their behaviors. It is communication to a person (or a group) that gives that person information about how he or she affects others. Like a guided-missile system, feedback helps individuals keep behavior on target and thus achieve their goals. It is a shared corrective mechanism for the individual who wants to learn how well behavior matches intentions. The following guidelines were listed by David W. Johnson (1972) in his book entitled *Reaching Out: Interpersonal Effectiveness and Self-Actualization* on pages 16–17.

1. Focus feedback on behavior rather than on the person.
2. Focus feedback on observations rather than inferences.
3. Focus feedback on description rather than judgment.
4. Focus feedback on descriptions of behavior that are in terms of "more or less" rather than in terms of "either-or."
5. Focus feedback on behavior related to a specific situation, preferably to the "here and now," rather than on behavior in the abstract, or in the "there and then."
6. Focus feedback on the sharing of ideas and information rather than on giving advice.
7. Focus feedback on exploring alternatives rather than on giving advice.
8. Focus feedback on the value it may have to the receiver, not on the value of release that it provides the person giving the feedback.
9. Focus feedback on the amount of information that the person receiving it can use rather than on the amount that you have and would like to give.
10. Focus feedback on time and place so that personal data can be shared at appropriate times.
11. Focus feedback on what is said rather than on why it is said.

FIGURE 2.1. Guidelines for feedback.

Personalizing the Learning Process

The group process by its very nature enhances the learning process (Hulse-Killacky, 1986). Therefore, group counseling is especially helpful in educational settings because it contributes to the personalization of the learning process by providing an environment in which members can discuss their unique and common problems. It has all the properties of an ideal learning environment in the sense that it has a trained leader, involves peer group dynamics, and takes into account individual differences of the group members. The focus is personal and problem oriented, and members are given the opportunity to deal responsibly with themselves and their concerns (Trotzer, 1972). Immediate integration occurs with the education process because members are encouraged to discover more effective methods of living their lives.

Group counseling presents a helpful alternative to students who have difficulty functioning in the less personal environment of the classroom or who shy away from the intensity of individual counseling or psychotherapy. By working on problems in a group setting, individuals realize the school or the community has resources for helping them and has a personal interest in them. This creates a greater personal commitment to the school and the educational process in general. Thus group counseling is a means of maximizing the educational process by making contact with the personal lives of students in a manner that is meaningful to both parties in the learning relationship—the student and the school.

Hulse-Killacky (1996) has posited even broader relevance to this personalization of the educational process. "As group work is recognized more and more as a broad methodology, there will be new and rich opportunities to link group work with teacher education, special education and educational leadership programs." (p. 166). Thus the reality of group work in educational settings personalizing the learning process is validated and the potential is unlimited. However, the personalization of learning in groups extends beyond the educational domain. Groups conducted in agencies and private practice settings provide participants with a host of opportunities for personalized learning about themselves and their problems. A growing trend in business and industry is to use groups called *quality circles* to enhance productivity, improve efficiency, and boost morale. Essentially quality circles use the group as an environment to facilitate workers learning from each other—all in the best interests of the company or corporation. In a sense there is no limit to the applicability of group process to enhance personal and interpersonal learning regardless of purpose or setting.

Increasing Counselor Contact

Since its inception, group counseling has always been promoted as a means of increasing the amount of counselor-client contact time and thereby expanding the impact of the counselor's professional role. The only logical conclusion is that if a counselor effectively spends one hour per week with eight clients in a group as opposed to one hour per week with each of those clients individually, he or she will choose the group approach. That decision makes for the most efficient use of counselor time.

Strangely enough, though, group counseling still does not have the unequivocal support from counselors, administrators, counselor educators, and consumers that individual counseling does. Part of the reason for this is the lack of training and training programs (Carroll, 1985; Conyne et. al., 1985; Shapiro & Shapiro, 1985). But the more important reason seems to be a complex problem of hesitancy regarding the group process and lack of motivation to try it on the part of counselors. As Dansby (1996) indicated "there is evidence that the belief in the importance of group far exceeds the actual practice" (p. 232). Inevitably, actual priorities in guidance, counseling, and psychotherapy programs place group work low on the list regardless of its position idealistically. However, the recent emergence of cost consciousness promulgated by insurance companies and managed care has raised the cost effectiveness benefit of group work. Consequently, counselors are being encouraged to use the group modality for mental health treatment and are doing so effectively. The fact that this trend is pragmatic from a business or profit standpoint as opposed to a concern for people is moot. The benefits of group work are relevant regardless of motive. If this trend continues advantages of greater counselor-client contact and expanded counselor role will be realized.

☐ The Group Work Umbrella

Since the publication of the second edition of this text, the field of group work has expanded and developed to a point where an umbrella construct encompassing a veritable rainbow* of group modalities and processes has emerged. The Association for Specialists in Group Work has developed Professional Standards for the Training of Group Workers (ASGW, 1991) that delineate four specific arenas of group practice (see Appendix A). Figure 2.2 presents a brief summary of the four specializations. The discussion that follows has been subsumed by the umbrella, but has also served as its inception and impetus when the first edition of this text was published (Trotzer, 1977). Appropriate adaptations have been made, but the wheel has not been reinvented or relabeled since the ASGW standards and the material that follows are quite compatible.

The definition of group counseling would not be complete without a discussion of its relationship to guidance/psychoeducation groups and psychotherapy groups. Figure 2.3 presents a graphic illustration of the relationship among these three group processes and details the essential characteristics of each one. You will notice overlap between group guidance/psychoeducation groups and group counseling and between group counseling and group psychotherapy. These processes are not mutually exclusive entities but are on a continuum. Although we can identify specific characteristics that generally apply to each process, in practice some degree of commonality does exist. The group leader, therefore, must maintain a flexible attitude in working with these processes and recognize that their characteristics are fluid rather than rigid.

Group guidance/psychoeducation groups involve the process of providing personally relevant information of a developmental nature to group members. This information may be in terms of facts and figures, procedures,

---

*The "Group Work Rainbow" was conceptualized by Dr. Robert K. Conyne and promulgated during his tenure as President of ASGW, 1995–96.

(Compiled from: Association for Specialists in Group Work: Professional standards for the training of group workers (Association for Specialists in Group Work, 1992, p. 13; Conyne, 1996, pp. 157–158).

I. Task/Work Groups

The task/work group specialization refers to the utilization of group dynamics, organizational development, and team building to enhance group members' skills in task accomplishment and group maintenance. The focus is on the application of group process skills, principles, and dynamics to improve, practice, and achieve realization of identified work goals. The scope of practice for task/work group specialists includes normally functioning individuals who are members of naturally occurring task or work groups typically operating in organizational settings such as businesses, industries, schools, health care environments, institutions of higher learning or religious organizations.

II. Guidance/Psychoeducation Groups

The guidance/psychoeducation group specialization refers to the utilization of the group modality for educative and preventive purposes. The guidance/psychoeducation specialist uses the group medium to educate and assist group participants who are at risk for, but presently unaffected by, environmental threats (e.g., AIDS), who are approaching a developmental transition point (e.g., preparing for college), or who are embroiled in the turmoil of coping with a life crisis (e.g., suicide of a loved one). The overarching goals of guidance/psychoeducation groups are to assist members in present adjustment and prevent future development of debilitating dysfunction while strengthening coping skills and self-esteem. The scope of guidance/psychoeducation group practice is essentially normally functioning individuals who are in need of information, skills, and guidance in a wide range of settings.

III. Counseling/Interpersonal Problem Solving Groups

The counseling\interpersonal problem solving group specialization addresses the task of helping group participants resolve the usual, yet often difficult, problems of living through interpersonal support and group problem solving. Group counselors help participants develop their existing interpersonal problem solving competencies so that they can resolve current problems and be better able to handle future problems of a similar nature. The scope of group counseling practice includes individuals who are experiencing nonsevere career, educational, personal, social and developmental concerns.

IV. Psychotherapy/Personality Reconstruction Groups

The group psychotherapy specialization addresses the concerns of individuals who are in need of reconstructive or remedial psychological treatment. Group psychotherapy is focused on helping individuals with acute or chronic mental or emotional disorders evidenced by marked distress or impairment in functioning for the purpose of generating major personality change.

FIGURE 2.2. ASGW group work specializations.

Information ⋯⋯⋯⋯

Leader ――――
Structure

Leader Training ‐‐‐‐‐

Emotional
Involvement ‐○‐

Group Guidance/   *Group Counseling*   *Group Psychotherapy*

**Group Guidance/
Psychoed Groups**

1. Preventative
2. Developmental
3. Personally relevant information
4. Cognitive
5. Environmental emphasis
6. Presentation and discussion
7. Leader directed
8. Topic-oriented
9. Planned activities
10. Skills
11. Common goals

Group Counseling

1. Remedial
2. Normal individuals
3. Thoughts, feelings, and behaviors evaluated
4. Problem-oriented
5. Focus determined by individuals
6. Situational (organized as needed)
7. Relationship important
8. Empathy and support stressed
9. Tendency toward homogeneity (common problems)
10. Verbal techniques
11. Feelings and needs emphasized
12. Conscious awareness
13. Leader facilitates
14. Present-oriented
15. Nonmedical setting
16. Relatively short longevity

Group Psychotherapy

1. Reconstructive, reeducative or rehabilitative
2. Personality change
3. Focused support
4. Past history included
5. Conscious and unconscious awareness
6. Deep neurotic conflicts, deviant behavior, or severe emotional problems
7. Individuals considered sick or mentally ill
8. Long duration
9. Homogeneous or heterogeneous
10. High emotional involvement
11. Depth analysis and involvement
12. Primarily verbal techniques
13. Individual development primary
14. Leader facilitates and directs as needed

FIGURE 2.3. Group guidance, group counseling, and group psychotherapy. (Material for this diagram was collected from these sources: Dinkmeyer & Muro, 1971; Gazda, Duncan, & Meadows, 1967; Goldman, 1962; Mahler, 1969; Ohlsen, 1970, 1974; Schmidt, n.d.; Trotzer, 1975. Partially adapted from L. M. Brammer & E. L. Shostrom, 1976, *Therapeutic Psychology: Fundamentals of Counseling and Psychotherapy* (3rd ed.). Reprinted by permission.)

requirements, or skills necessary to help them in their lives. The focus of the process is decidedly cognitive in nature with emphasis on environmental factors, content, and topics. Methods are usually centered on presentation and discussion with the leader taking the primary responsibility for organizing and directing the group. Although members should collaborate in selecting topics that are in line with their interests and needs, Mahler (1969) pointed our that "in schools group guidance is usually oriented toward telling students what adults think the youngsters should know about themselves" (p. 11). The most common themes involve teaching coping skills and supplying information that facilitates understanding of self, others, and the environment to enhance the prospect of effective adjustment in group members and help individuals more fully realize and apply their human potential (Robinson, 1980).

The main emphasis in guidance/psychoeducation groups is dealing with people on the basis of their developmental status in life. As such the process takes on dimensions of being preventative and facilitative in nature. Group members often know what they want to do but don't know how to do it. Efforts are directed toward supplying members with essential skills and information that will enable them to address current developmental tasks and prevent or circumvent problems in the future. The primary by-product of such groups is effective decision making based on relevant knowledge of one's self and one's environment. The different types of guidance/psychoeducation groups are discussed in detail in Chapter 10 (Differentiating Groups), and more specific examples are included there.

In contrast to guidance/psychoeducation groups, *group counseling* is primarily remedial in nature. It deals with normal individuals who are experiencing problems that are interfering in some respect with their lives. As a result, the development of a group relationship characterized by empathy and support is stressed where members can evaluate their thoughts, feelings, and behavior in a safe yet social environment. Counseling groups are formed in light of certain personal and interpersonal problems and therefore tend to be homogeneous in nature. Members are organized into groups that discuss problems with which they can identify, at least to some extent. Groups meet until the problems are solved for the most part and tend to be of relatively short duration. Counseling groups tend to mirror quarter or semester time frames in schools and extend three to nine months in other settings depending on their purposes and organizational formats. Members are encouraged to work toward dissolving the group by resolving their problems.

Because of the emphasis on personal problems the focus of the group is determined by the members, and a contingent emphasis on feeling is due to the emotional involvement required to engage in self-disclosure and feedback. The leader is primarily a facilitator who uses verbal techniques, stresses conscious awareness, and keeps the group oriented to the here and now problems of group interaction and member concerns (Carroll, 1986; Carroll

& Wiggins, 1997). These groups are usually conducted in nonmedical settings, such as schools, agencies, private practices and other helping institutions catering to normal clients.

The distinction between group counseling and group psychotherapy is associated more with the type of clients than the process itself. *Group psychotherapy* is utilized to work with clients who are nonnormal, dysfunctional, or psychiatrically impaired in some respect. They may be considered sick, mentally, ill, or emotionally disturbed, or have psychotic traits, tendencies, or deep neurotic conflicts, or engage in deviant behavior. In any event, the causes of the problems are related to personality dynamics and development. Therefore, the purpose is to effect personality change with group effort directed toward reconstructing, reeducating, or rehabilitating individual members relative to personality characteristics that are creating problems in their lives. In addition, psychotherapy groups may be utilized to help members maintain functional lifestyles in spite of psychiatric maladies and support independent living of members who might otherwise require institutional care. Since the focus is on personality, the process tends to be quite long in duration because personality patterns develop over a long period of time and are therefore resistant to change. Support is necessary to the process in the sense of 1) providing it when clients are working on their issues and patterns and 2) when they need therapeutic intervention to circumvent relapses or to maintain functionality. Often clients in group therapy try to avoid working on their problems because of the effort required to change. If the group supports members actions that are not associated with the task of changing or maintaining functionality, the whole process is undermined. Therefore support is used as a reinforcement that focuses on encouraging and promoting individual efforts toward resolving personality problems and maintaining accountable functionality.

Group psychotherapy may be composed of either homogeneous or heterogeneous members and is characterized by a high degree of emotional involvement. The leader facilitates or directs as is necessary and uses primarily verbal techniques. Conscious and unconscious awareness, a concern for the past history of the client, and depth analysis and exploration may be involved in the process with the expertise of the leader being essential to the constructive use of these procedures. Groups are organized in medical or institutional settings on an inpatient basis or in private practices, mental health clinics, counseling centers, or agencies where referred clients (including self-referred ones) are treated as outpatients.

General trends evident on a continuum from group guidance/psychoeducation groups to group psychotherapy are that the role of cognitive information and the amount of leader structure decreases while the degree of emotional involvement (affect) and required leadership training and expertise increase. In addition, elements of guidance and counseling groups may be integrated into psychotherapy groups, and counseling groups often include guidance or psychoeducational dimensions. However, when individuals present issues or problems in guidance or counseling groups that significantly derail or distract the intended process, referral to the appropriate therapeutic entity is in order.

☐ Relating Focus and Process

Figure 2.4 illustrates the relationship among group guidance/psychoeducation groups, group counseling, and group psychotherapy with the basic focus of each process. The essence of every person's identity is the result of continual interaction between personality, thoughts, feelings, behaviors, and environment. Personality is the aspect of a person that develops over time and is characterized by a consistency that gives each person a uniqueness unparalleled by any other human being. Personality is composed of the patterns and characteristics that are generally stable and that change at an increasingly slower rate as one matures and grows older. These patterns and traits dictate each person's adjustment to life and the concomitant satisfaction or dissatisfaction that he or she experiences. When a person develops characteristics that consistently and continually create frustration, anxiety, problems, and dissatisfactions, efforts must be made toward changing those traits and developing different or revised characteristics to facilitate satisfactory adjustment. The process of group psychotherapy is directed to that end.

Thoughts, feelings, and behaviors are the three components of one's experience that have the dual role of expressing personality and affecting personality. The characteristic that distinguishes these components from personality is their tendency to fluctuate according to situations and experiences one is exposed to or solicits. A person often shows markedly different behavior at a party than on the job. Similarly, a person's feelings sometimes change very rapidly with the advent of an unexpected gift or visit from an important person in one's life.

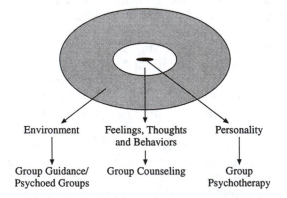

FIGURE 2.4. Relating process and focus in groups.

The whole process of education is such that a person often has learning experiences that change their thinking in a very short period of time. In any case, the changes occur quickly and can be accounted for by any number of reasons including role demands, expectations, events, circumstances, or inner turmoil. Attesting to the importance of these components as the moderators between one's personality and one's environment is the fact that theories of counseling and psychotherapy focus on them as channels for instituting change in a person's life. For example, Carl Rogers' (1951) Person-Centered Therapy focuses on feelings, William Glasser's (1965) Reality Therapy and Albert Ellis' (1971) Rational-Emotive Therapy emphasize thinking and cognitions while behaviorists such as John Krumboltz and Carl Thoreson (1976) zero in on behavior.

Problems occur in people's lives when they cannot adjust to changes in any or all of the three areas. The problems may be the result of a change that occurs too quickly (traumatic events), or is too intense (crisis situations), or is so divergent and varied as to become unsettling to the person. When individuals cannot understand, cope, or deal adequately with their thoughts, feelings, or behavior and feel something must be done to rectify the situation, they may look outside themselves for a source of help. Group counseling is one process that can effectively provide the help in a meaningful and constructive manner. Its focus is on evaluating thoughts, feelings, and actions of normal human beings for the purpose of helping them adjust adequately, cope effectively, grow developmentally, and live more satisfying and productive lives.

Each person lives in an environment or life space that provides experiences, opportunities, and pressures or stresses that must be dealt with to achieve personal fulfillment. To do that individuals must implement decisions based on their knowledge of that environment and the interaction of their own selves within it. Decisions that are based on accurate information about one's self and one's world and include steps to develop the personal skill necessary to carry out those decisions are by far the most rewarding. They accelerate one's progress and achievement and create a more satisfying lifestyle. The process of group guidance and psychoeducation groups is directed at providing the information and skills that are personally relevant and that facilitate the decision making process in the manner just described.

☐ Learning Activities

The Nature of Group

The following activities can be used in classes or groups to help members assess the characteristics of groups and the group process. Since their purpose is to integrate experience and cognition, these activities require both involvement and observation on the part of each participant.

Building Blocks Dyads (Option 1)

This technique is particularly useful in the beginning stages of group development since it encourages getting to know one another and at the same
time demonstrates some of the peculiar properties that differentiate group
and dyadic (one-to-one) relationships.

Have class members pair off with a person they do not know or know
least well in the group. Give them 5 to 10 minutes to get to know each
other as best they can. About half way through the time allotted, stop the
discussion and have each partner write down an initial impression of their
partner. Then allow the conversation to continue to the end of the stated
time period. At the end of the time period form the dyads into groups of
four (two dyads to a group) and have the dyad members introduce their
partners and give their initial impressions. After each member has been
introduced, each group can proceed to get better acquainted. At the end of
about 10 minutes form the groups of four into groups of eight and instruct
them to get to know each other without any specific directions. After 15
minutes of discussion form the groups of eight into groups of 16 (or some
number larger than eight depending on class size), and once again give
them about 15 minutes to get to know each other. The total time involved
should be about 45 to 60 minutes.

Discuss the experience in terms of the purpose (getting to know one
another) and the characteristics revealed about groups and group process.
What differences were noted between one-to-one and group relationships?
What impact did the size of the group have on the nature of the discussion?
Did dyads and subgroups retain their identity when merged into a larger
group? What happened to communication and to the influence of the individual as groups changed in size?

Building Blocks Dyads (Option 2)

A variation of the technique just described is to divide the class in half. In
one group, follow the procedures described above starting with dyads and
them proceeding to four and eight and so on up to the total size of the
subgroup. With the other half of the group, reverse the procedure moving
from the large group by one-halves down to two persons (dyads). For example, if there are 16 people in the subgroup, your groups would start with
16. Then they would divide into eight, four, and two, in that order. At each
level, give the members a personal sharing task to perform. Examples that
could be used follow:

1. Share a meaningful experience you have had recently.
2. Share one thing about your personality that you feel is a positive
   attribute.
3. Share one thing about yourself that you would like to change.

4. Share a problem in your life right now that you have not been able to deal with satisfactorily.
5. Share one negative and one positive thing about your (job, family, school, and so on) that you are aware of right now.

(These types of personal sharing tasks also are useful in group counseling as initiating procedures that help group members interact and get material to be worked with out on the table.)

Allot an appropriate amount of time at each level of interaction so that members have sufficient time to discuss the personal sharing tasks in some depth. After all steps have been completed, conduct a follow-up discussion based on the processes and reactions of members in the various sized groups. Contrast the experience of moving from the large group to dyads and from dyads to the large group.

Dyads versus Groups (Option 1)

To compare the process of individual counseling with group counseling more directly, try the following exercise. Using the personal sharing tasks previously listed or similar ones, have members of the class pair off and discuss the chosen task in detail. Then divide the class into small groups (six to eight members) and repeat the process using a different personal sharing task. It is not necessary that persons who were partners in the one-to-one sharing be in the same group. In fact, it is usually a good idea to split them up. Allot plenty of time for discussion in each exercise and then process it in terms of similarities and differences between the two experiences.

Dyads versus Groups (Option 2)

Using the same format as that just described, we can add the dimension of process observation. In the first phase use triads (groups of three) instead of dyads. Two persons interact using one of the personal sharing tasks and the third person observes. After an appropriate length of time (10 to 15 minutes) the observers give feedback to the two persons who participated in the sharing. This procedure is repeated three times with three different personal sharing tasks until each person has had the opportunity to be the observer.

For the group phase, use the fish bowl approach. Divide the class into subgroups large enough for each one to be subdivided into two smaller groups of three to five members each. One small group sits in an inner circle and proceeds to discuss one of the personal sharing tasks. The other small group sits in an outer circle observing the interaction of the inner group. Each member in the outer circle should be assigned one person in the inner circle to observe in addition to the group process. At the end of the discussion each observer sits down with the person he or she was observing and gives feedback on his or her participation and reactions in the group. During the feedback session the person receiving the feedback initially is not allowed to comment until the observer finishes. After the feedback is completed discussion can ensue. After individual feedback has been given and discussed, the outer circle members convene and discuss together their observations of the inner group process while the inner group listens. Repeat the whole process reversing the inner and outer circles and making sure each person in the observer circle is assigned a different person to observe than the one who observed her or him in the first round. On completion of both phases hold a general discussion comparing and contrasting the dyadic and group processes.

Consensus

The consensus exercise entitled "Agree-Disagree," described in Figure 2.5 is another useful method of learning about group process. This exercise has a great deal of flexibility and can be utilized effectively in a variety of group situations that require group decision making. The statements used

---

Directions
1. Read each statement individually and decide whether you agree or disagree with it.
2. Select another person, and the two of you come to agreement on each of the statements. Words may be changed or added in order to come to an agreement. If you don't agree with the statement as it stands, you must come up with a revision that each person agrees with at each level.
3. After each statement has been discussed and agreement reached, select two other people who have reached agreement. The four of you now go through the process of reaching agreement on each of the statements.
4. After the four of you have reached agreement, select another foursome and the eight of you try to come to an agreement.

Sample Statements
1. Sex education is the responsibility of the family; the schools should not become involved.
2. Learning disabled children are basically mean kids who don't listen and are lazy.
3. Students should not be allowed to have a voice in school administration or curriculum matters.
4. Black people have less ability that Whites and should be treated accordingly.
5. No prison inmate or ex-convict should ever be trusted.
6. Law and order is the cure for our social problems today.
7. Radical students are really knowingly or unknowingly the spokespersons for anarchy.
8. Individual freedom should be guaranteed at all costs.

FIGURE 2.5. Agree-disagree activity.

for generating discussion can be varied to fit the situation, the nature of the group members, and the purpose for which the group was formed. After completing the exercise discuss the factors involved in reaching consensus as the group became larger.

Starting a Group From Scratch

This activity is particularly effective if utilized at the very inception of a class or group experience since it reduces social stimuli to a minimum and accentuates the dynamics that individuals experience as they encounter the task of becoming part of a group process. The following sequence of steps is suggested:

1. Blindfold each group member as they arrive and lead them to a seat in a circle of chairs that have been set up beforehand. (An alternative method is to let members sit in the circle upon arrival, give them a blindfold and instruct them to blindfold themselves.)

2. When all members are blindfolded and seated, explain that the group has begun and that the first part of the experience will be nonverbal. Have group members stand and begin to mill around within the perimeter of the chairs (as the leader you can direct people back into the group if they wander out.) While milling, they are to make physical contact with other members making an effort to greet each person with whom they come in contact. (This is to be done completely without talking).

3. Each group member is to make contact with at least five different people during the milling. When a member makes contact with the sixth person, they are to nonverbally signal that person that they want to be their partner. If that person has made contact with five other people already they signal agreement. If they have not connected with five other people, they must refuse the invitation (nonverbally) and both continue to mill in search of a partner.

4. When all group members have found a partner based on the five contacts criteria, the leader assists each dyad to find seats for the next phase which is getting acquainted (both remain blindfolded). Have partners get to know each other in two ways. First by using the question "Who are you?" and second by sculpting. Partners alternate asking "Who are you?" repeatedly with the requirements that *each answer be different* and neither party give his or her name. Allow three to four minutes for the "Who are you?" repetitions, and then instruct the partners to sculpt each other's head to get a sense of their partner's physical features. *Note*: Obtain prior consent for the sculpting activity in order to adapt the activity in consideration of individual members cultural or religious beliefs which may mitigate against physical contact.

5. When the sculpting is completed, the leader separates the partners and forms two lines of chairs which are back to back so that partners will have restricted visual access to each other when the blindfolds are removed.

6. Give each member an 8½ × 11 (or larger) sheet of paper and a magic marker. Remove the blindfolds and instruct each person to create a "Wanted" poster by drawing a picture or caricature of their partner's head or face on the top half of the sheet and describing them with identifying data on the bottom half.

7. When the "Wanted" posters are complete, use masking tape to post them on a wall for all to see. Give each member another sheet of paper and have them number the sheet from 1 through X (number of people in the group). Number the posters 1 through X and have group members independently match posters and people, writing down the correct name next to the appropriate number on their sheets.

8. When most or all have been identified, review the posters as a group and place the members's names on each poster.

9. Process the activity in light of individual member's feelings and experiences and in terms of group process dynamics.

An alternative to the poster procedure (steps six to eight) is to separate partners in step five and place them in separated places in the circle. Remove the blindfolds and complete the identification phase verbally by having each person describe their partner and try to identify them in the group.

Group Counseling Definition and Advantages

A Cognitive Exercise

Have each class member write his or her own definition of counseling or psychotherapy. Encourage members to use their own words and to focus on aspects particularly meaningful to them. The definition need not be comprehensive, but it should reflect the unique perception of each class member. Discuss the definitions in class, noting on the board the different characteristics pointed out by class members. Then have the class members write out their own definitions of *group* counseling or *group* psychotherapy following the same guidelines of using their own words and focusing on aspects each person deems important. Discuss these definitions in the same manner as before, and then compare the two in an effort to identify similarities between them and differences that can be attributed to the special qualities of the group process.

"Ask the Expert" Activity

(Adapted from Crowley, 1989, pp. 173–75). Follow the sequence of steps below.

1. Divide the class into subgroups of three to four members and instruct them to come up with three questions they want to ask the expert about group counseling or group work.

2. Each subgroup presents their questions to the class.
3. The subgroups are then redirected to come up with an answer to one of their own questions.
4. Each subgroup presents their answer to the class.
5. Process follow-up: The instructor can a) facilitate a follow-up discussion bringing out the group's expertise, and/or adding/sharing her or his expertise or b) use the material presented by the subgroups as a springboard into appropriate lecture or presentation material.

Curative Factors Activity (Option 1)

(Adapted from Sklare, Thomas, Williams, and Powers, 1996, p. 268.) This activity is based on Yalom's 12 curative factors listed on pp. 30–31 of this chapter. It has most relevance after the class or group has had a number of class/group sessions to generate experiences for the class members to draw upon.

1. Divide the class in into triads. Each member of the triad is asked to share a personal group experience related to one of the therapeutic factors in groups. (A total of three different experiences will be shared by the end of the activity.)
2. Rotate triad group membership and repeat the sharing two more times.
3. The instructor then introduces the 12 (or more) curative factors in group counseling and facilitates a discussion of the class members' group experiences relative to the factors.

Curative Factors Activity (Option 2)

(Adapted from Hetzel, Barton, & Davenport, 1994, pp. 58–59.) Devise a set of Q Sort cards for each class member composed of the curative factors or advantageous characteristics described on pp. 23–35 in this chapter. Following a group process experience in class, have members sort the cards based on their experience in the group. Process the group experience 1) identifying the top ranked curative factors and noting common and divergent member perceptions of the group process, and 2) noting present and absent therapeutic factors as indicated by the rankings. This activity can be used periodically or routinely as a process activity to accentuate learning of the curative factors in group process.

Group Dynamics

The following activities can be used to illustrate some of the various characteristics unique to the group process described in this chapter. Many similar activities can be found in the books listed in the references (Bates, Johnson,

& Blake, 1982; Corey, Corey, Callanan, & Russell, 1992; Hamachek, 1971; Johnson, 1972; Johnson & Johnson, 1997; Katz, 1973; Moustakas, 1972; Pfeiffer & Jones, 1969–85; Rosenthal, 1998; Schutz, 1967; Stevens, 1971). The examples included here were selected because they involve a physical dimension and demonstrate a psychological concept. Using techniques of this nature may be particularly effective with certain populations (e.g., adolescents or young adults) in certain settings (e.g., adventure learning or outward bound programs) and can help facilitate clearer understanding of group dynamics while at the same time adding diversity and variety to the group process experience. However, as with any activity involving physical contact, appropriate precautions must be followed and informed consent obtained before engaging group members in them.

Breaking Out

Place one member in the center of the group and have other members form a tight ring around him or her. The person in the center is instructed to try to get out of the group in any way possible without resorting to physical violence and the group is instructed to prevent such an escape. The leader should keep close control over the action to prevent excesses that might cause physical harm, and members should be cautioned not to exert themselves if they have some physical problem that might be aggravated. This exercise should seek its own level of time and participation.

Follow-up discussion should center around the member's experience and the implications of the exercise relative to group process characteristics and the power of the group. Emotions elicited and strategies used to escape from or conform to group pressure in the exercise tend to reflect the actual feelings and reactions of members regarding group pressure toward conformity, identity, and loss of individual uniqueness. (This exercise may also be useful in group counseling when individual members are dealing with problems of dependency or lack of individual initiative.)

Breaking In

This exercise is the converse of the previous one. One member is placed outside the group, and the other group members form a tight unit that the outsider is instructed to try to get into. The same precautions relative to control of excesses and limiting participation in case of physical disabilities should be followed. This exercise has relevance for demonstrating the group's capacity for cohesiveness and members' needs for belongingness that the group can meet. It also demonstrates the power of the group in preventing members from joining. The appeal of group membership must be grappled with by the outsider and involves making decisions as to the amount of personal effort that will be exerted to get into the group. Time involved and participation again are dependent on the situation.

Discussion should relate to members' experiences and eventually move into the domain of relating the exercise to the power of the group and its dynamics. In group counseling this exercise is sometimes used to help members who feel isolated or lack commitment to the group understand their feelings and behavior more clearly.

Behind-the-Back Technique

This technique developed by Corsini (1968) demonstrates the intense power of the group process when used in the manner described by its creator. Corsini developed the method in his work with prison inmates and used the negative feedback of the group to break down the personality attributes of individual members that were creating problems for them. A greatly modified version can be useful in group counseling.

One member of the group is asked to sit with his or her back to the group. He or she is instructed to listen and at no point is allowed to respond or react until the feedback is completed. The rest of the group proceeds to discuss their perceptions and feelings about the person relating both negative and positive reactions. It is necessary to let this proceed for an extended period of time for its full impact to be realized.

On completion of the feedback, the member turns into the group and shares the feelings experienced during the feedback session. She or he should be encouraged to comment on the accuracy of the group's response from a personal point of view, and group discussion should attempt to clarify misunderstandings and mediate possible differences of perception. The feelings experienced by members usually reflect the helplessness people often feel in the face of group pressure and the fear that the group will respond negatively. Follow-up discussion should make members aware of using feedback and the group's power in a therapeutic manner. Efforts should be made to help the member receiving the feedback make constructive use of relevant material and discard the rest. In psychotherapy groups more intense focus may be placed on the feedback itself since personality traits and change are at stake.

CHAPTER

Rationale for Group Counseling

☐ The Development of a Psychological Framework

Group counseling has relevance and meaning only if it is understood and applied in the psychological context of human growth and development. A psychological framework is needed to guide the process, evaluate its impact, and provide a rationale for its use. However, while such a framework is a necessity, Jourard (1968) pointed out that to simply imitate someone else's theory or rationale is not sufficient. Each helping person must develop his or her own theoretical viewpoint to be truly effective in helping others. The development of a personal approach is necessary for a counselor to make the best use of the resources available in providing therapeutic help to other people. Major resources include the counselor's personality, knowledge, and training. These resources combined with each helping experience enable the counselor's theoretical approach to come to fruition.

The general impact of training and practice on the development of one's own approach to group counseling is illustrated in Figure 3.1. In training, the counselor is given an overview of the group process, which is implemented from a variety of theoretical perspectives. Each of the theories utilizes certain techniques that can be learned and applied in the group setting. Once a counselor has an understanding of the process, an initial commitment to a theoretical model that is congruent with her or his personality, and has acquired techniques relevant to that theory, then she or he is ready to apply that learning in a supervised setting.

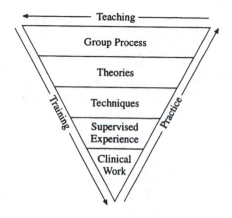

FIGURE 3.1. A model relating training and practice.

Practice operates in the opposite direction of training, helping counselors develop their own rationales and approaches to group counseling. From their very first experience as group leaders, counselors begin to evaluate their knowledge and skills relative to the group process. They develop, adapt, revise, and delete methods and techniques to improve effectiveness. They weigh the theoretical concepts they've learned, affirming some and refuting others, reorganizing, refining, or rejuvenating still others, and discovering new ones that fit the reality of their experiences in group counseling. It is at this point that each counselor develops a personal conceptualization of the total group process. Thus individual personality, training, and experience have become intertwined in a dynamic relationship that will continue to develop throughout a professional career.

Keep this conception of the relationship between training and practice in mind while I present the psychological rationale for group counseling that will be used in this book. Remember that my perspective and subsequent framework is the result of the interacting forces of my training, group membership, leadership experience, and teaching. All of these have provided input for my understanding of the group process and influence how I teach that process to prospective group leaders.

☐ The Psychological Rationale for Group Work

The psychological rationale for group work entails the dynamic interaction of three generic psychological components (Trotzer, 1997d). The nature and substance of every group construed under the group work umbrella described in the last chapter results from the interaction of *persons, process, and purpose.* First of all, every group is composed of individuals, each of whom brings with him or her needs, abilities, expectations, and experiences. These persons provide the resources and raw materials out of which the group emerges. As individuals interact, process is conceived. Process refers to the relationship that eventuates between members over the course of the group's life. This relationship is critical to the impact and results of the group experience. As Gladding (Campbell, 1996) observed, "process truly drives content, . . . relationships between members . . . either (make) or (unmake) the productivity in groups" (p. 74).

The impetus for process that brings individuals (persons) together in groups is the reason for which the group is formed. Consequently, purpose is the final component that supplies the nature and character of the group. It contributes the overall identity of the group. For example, guidance/psychoeducation groups are formed to educate or inform, counseling groups to solve problems, therapy groups to change personality, and work groups to accomplish the task or mission for which it was convened.

In this chapter the person component will be presented in terms of Maslow's (1970) hierarchy of human needs. The process component will be addressed utilizing an adaptation of Luft and Ingham's (Luft, 1984) Johari Window, and the purpose component will incorporate a generic problem solving model. Subsequently, the psychological rationale for group counseling presented in this book can be summarized by the following formula:

Individual Needs + Relationship Development + Problem Solving = Group Counseling
(Person Component)   (Process Component)   (Purpose Component)

In other words individual members motivated by their respective needs interact in a group milieu to develop a relationship in which they work to address and resolve their personal problems.

☐ The Person Component

The basic supposition of the person component of my rationale is that each person has certain human needs that are met primarily through social interaction with other human beings. The extent to which our needs are met is dependent on the type and quality of interpersonal relationships we have with others. The manner in which we meet our needs supplies the foundation of our life styles, and the relationships we develop form the bulwark of our identity. Our needs are the motivators of our behavior and are hierarchical in nature. Our environment and heredity provide us with opportunities we can utilize in meeting our needs (Jourard, 1968), but we basically depend on our interpersonal relationships to determine how. The ordering of our needs reflects the developmental process of the group within which the relationships formed provide the means to resolve problems that are curtailing effective adjustment, growth, and self-fulfillment.

☐ **Basic Human Needs**

Maslow (1943, 1954, and 1962) developed the hierarchical conceptualization of human needs that is used as the basis for our discussion of the person component. Figure 3.2 presents an adapted and embellished version of Maslow's original hierarchy. Maslow contended that people have certain basic needs that motivate them to behave in a manner to satisfy those needs. Our needs are differentiated and have prepotent qualities that influence which need is going to be called into play as predominant and which need will emerge upon satisfaction of a prior need. Maslow postulated five basic needs including (in order of priority): physical needs, safety, love and belonging, esteem, and self-actualization. He stressed, however, that the individual should be viewed as a total person and that any motivated behavior can satisfy many needs at the same time. His main thrust was that human beings are dominated by wants and not by satisfactions because once a

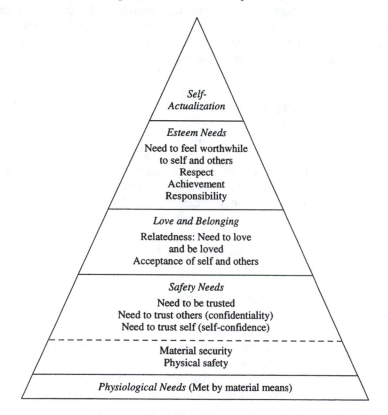

FIGURE 3.2. Hierarchy of human needs. (Data for diagram based on Hierarchy of Needs in "A Theory of Human motivation" in *Motivation and Personality,* 2nd edition. Abraham H. Maslow (1970). Used by permission.)

need is satisfied or even partially satisfied, other needs emerge that must be dealt with. Carroll (1969) noted that this situation usually results in people being "partially unsatisfied in all (their) needs," which he called "a normal state of affairs to which a person learns to adjust" (p. 27). In addition, Laird and Laird (1967) in discussing the relationship among our different needs observed that under stress the higher order needs (called "wants" in their terminology) tend to peel off. This creates a situation where individuals are forced to operate on a less sophisticated level until they can once again proceed up the hierarchy.

Besides the priority aspect of our needs, Maslow noted an important distinction between our lowest order physiological needs (food, clothing, and so on) and the progressively higher order needs of safety, love and belonging, esteem, and self-actualization. Physiological needs are meant to be gratified and not deprived so that the higher order needs and their goal directed behaviors can emerge. These higher order needs are social needs, and an individual's drive to satisfy them is much more critical in human motivation than is physical need gratification. This is particularly true in our society, where for all practical purposes most people have access to the means of satisfying their physiological needs.

The needs hierarchy and the physical-social need distinction have direct application to counseling. If our clients are experiencing deprivation in any of these areas, that area most likely will be the focus of or at least an impediment to the counseling process. An overall goal of group counseling is to help clients meet their lower order needs in a consistent manner, which will enable them to progress toward self-actualization. In addition, the social nature of the higher order needs suggests that the group counseling process is a plausible means of helping clients meet these needs. Let's turn our attention then to a specific discussion of each of these needs and consider their implications for group counseling.

Physiological Needs

All of us have experienced being too tired, too cold, or too thirsty to think about anything other than alleviating that sensation. Deprivation of our physical needs alters our perceptions drastically and effectively distorts our view of human nature and life (Maslow, 1943). Tolerance levels naturally vary and can be substantially altered in some cases, but ultimately failure to meet these needs is self-destructive. Our most basic drive, self-preservation, usually takes the form of making sure we have sufficient food, clothing, and shelter to sustain life. However, even in a society with an adequate level of material wealth, often cases of deprivation interfere with learning and the process of self-development. Students in a classroom who have not had sufficient rest the night before are difficult to motivate. People who have missed breakfast or lunch often find it difficult to concentrate on their jobs. Teachers who must participate in inservice meetings at the end of a teaching day may lack alertness due to fatigue. Group members who should be interacting may be distracted by such physical discomforts as a chilly room or uncomfortable seating. Group leaders who have physical ailments such as a cold or headache may be inattentive or distracted. In any case physiological needs can create havoc with our concentration and make it difficult to utilize our abilities to their fullest potential.

Physiological need fulfillment is a prerequisite for everything, including group counseling. The group process specifically—and human relationships generally—can't directly reduce that need. An effective group process depends on having members at a point where they are ready to work on meeting their higher order needs. Physiological deprivation of members may pose insurmountable barriers to the group process. A group leader should be aware of this possibility, both in the obvious sense (members dozing or inattentive) and in the subtle sense (pride may prevent acknowledgement of hunger caused by poverty or parental neglect). This second case is sometimes manifested in hostile or antagonistic behavior on the part of the member who for fear of losing esteem in the group's eyes will not admit to the lack of physiological requirements. For example, a 12 year old inner city youth from an economically deprived family consistently acted out during mid-morning group sessions at a child guidance center. When the group leader, in consultation with a social worker, discovered that the boy seldom ate breakfast she instituted a snack at the beginning of each group session, which substantially reduced the boy's disruptive behavior. Leaders therefore must try to identify physiological needs when they account for unusual member actions and suggest activities and make arrangements that will alleviate those needs if members can't do so on their own.

In contrast, however, group leaders also must be alert to group members using physiological need ploys to resist involvement in or obstruct the group process. In my work with inmates in a prison setting one of their biggest complaints was that the physical environment was not conducive to group therapy and the therapeutic process. Another group of educators at a weekend inservice program conducted in a hotel setting raised such a fuss about the physical conditions that we spent the first day in search of an appropriate setting moving from auditorium to secluded lobby to a hotel room to a member's home who lived nearby and finally in frustration disbanded to a lounge. The second day we reconvened in the original location with the group rule of "no moves" and the group finally formed and started to work.

Safety Needs

The desire for safety is basic to every human being. Our greatest frustrations are most often associated with our fear of the unknown, in social as well as physical situations. When we lack knowledge or commitments on which we can depend, we lose touch with our sense of confidence. That in turn gives rise to anxiety and the urge to protect ourselves.

The need for safety is related to the essential nature of trust, which is the ability to and experience of depending on something or someone as the stabilizing force in our lives. Franz Kafka acknowledged the importance of this need when he wrote that "man cannot live without a lasting trust in something indestructible within him, but both his trust and its indestructible object can remain forever concealed from him." Maslow (1943) has indicated that the safety need is the driving force behind our preference for routine, our withdrawal from the unfamiliar, and our mobilization of resources in times of emergency. Adler (Carroll, 1969) was even more emphatic, calling security man's basic drive and adding that "it is the feeling of inferiority, inadequacy, insecurity, which determines the goal of an individual's existence" (p. 25). The emphasis on this need for security places it near the very core of human existence and demands our active attention to satisfy it.

In Figure 3.2 are indications that safety needs are manifested in five specific ways. The desire for physical safety is foremost, although individuals often risk endangering their bodies to achieve certain valued objectives. Individuals may choose to endanger their physical well being in exchange for thrills or a sense of accomplishment when they engage in certain forms of recreation or sports such as rock climbing or stock car racing. Or, they may choose occupations that have high physical risk integrated into the performance of their job. Generally, however, people are cautious and concerned about protecting themselves from physical harm.

The guarantee of physical safety to group members while in group counseling is a standard requirement. Ethical principles of group practice dictate that groups be conducted in a manner such that clients never feel physically endangered or intimidated; members should not be forced to risk physical harm doing group activities (Corey, Corey, & Callahan, 1993). The group has no control over outside dangers other than to help members develop precautionary guidelines if they are concerned about situations in which they may experience physical harm. However, the group leader has an ethical responsibility and a legal obligation to invoke interventive action if a clear and present danger situation in a group member's life surfaces in the course of group interaction. This duty to warn mandate applies to both ingroup and out of group situations the leader becomes aware of.

The need for material security is also a concern of most people, especially where value systems and life styles are based on material acquisition and monetary self-sufficiency. The terminology of economics and the banking industry clearly reflect this need, with words such as "trust fund," "securities," and "low risk investments." This need becomes increasingly important as one grows older. Retirement benefits are always a key concern in labor negotiations and in occupational choices. Some people spend their entire work lives preparing for a retirement in which they will be financially solvent.

The material aspect of the safety need can be met by the process of attaining financial security in the form of secure employment, well paying jobs, insurance policies, retirement programs, bank accounts, debt free possessions, investments, and the like. But group counseling has little direct relationship to meeting this need. The group can help individuals develop and understand their values with respect to material acquisitions. It can also help members develop self-knowledge relative to educational and vocational planning, that contribute to meeting the need for material security. Some groups for the elderly are formed for the specific purpose of helping members deal with problems of physical and material security that often face them in their older years. Counseling groups for workers who are within a few years of retirement are becoming more prevalent in business and industry. However, groups of this nature often move from a materialistic emphasis to a consideration of the higher order needs, which must be dealt with to develop a personally meaningful existence in retirement and old age.

The other three aspects of safety needs are person oriented and relational in nature and are set apart from physical and material security by a broken line in Figure 3.2. We all have the need to trust ourselves, to trust others, and to be trusted by others. The need to trust ourselves, to have self-confidence, is perhaps the most elusive personal characteristic we attempt to establish. We strive to build a sense of personal security in an ever increasing number of situations as we mature. We tend to become involved when we feel sure of ourselves, and we tend to avoid or resist becoming involved in situations in which we lack confidence. Even as experience positively affects our self-confidence, we need to continually reaffirm it. Most people experience frustration with regard to self-confidence, feeling they never have enough. Although some people may be accused of being overly self-confident, in most cases their behavior is an overreaction to their lack of self-confidence. Even people who appear to have a healthy self-assurance report they experience doubts and anxieties about their ability to trust themselves. Only as we meet this need can we experience any satisfaction in our growth and accomplishments, and only on the basis of self-confidence can we build a predictable stability to pave the way for personal fulfillment in social situations.

The need for self-confidence is typically associated with the problems of most members in a counseling group. Either lack of self-confidence or ostentatious self-assurance used to defend against one's fears is common. The group therefore must provide an atmosphere where threat to one's personal security is minimal and where members can develop the ability to trust themselves. This ability is particularly important at the point of implementing change. The group is only the testing ground, and it depends on the individual to determine whether change will materialize. Thus the amount of confidence individuals feel in themselves is directly related to the probability of successful change.

The needs to trust others and to be trusted by others are the foundation of our social relationships and are essential therapeutic elements in the group process. We can only meet these two needs through our personal contacts with others, and in most cases they have a reciprocal effect. The need to trust others is our desire to place ourselves or some aspect of ourselves in the confidence of another person. This need is the foundation dynamic of confidentiality in groups. May (1953) had the idea that each person has a natural thrust beyond himself or herself toward others, and this is partly manifested in the need to trust others. Johnson (1981) has indicated that human beings have a relationship imperative which motivates them to reach out in confidence to others. However, a subtle but critical relational counterpart to that thrust in each of us is needed. An ancient Chinese proverb states that "a sure way to help someone is to let them help you." When we confide in (trust) another person we invoke self-confidence in that person and invite reciprocity. This precipitates bonding in the relationship while enhancing the security of the individual. Our need to trust propels us to overcome our aloneness and sets the stage for deeper emotional attachment to others. Our need to trust generates opportunities to rely on other people as resources in our growth and development and in problem solving. That need to trust is a motivating force in the group counseling process that enables self-disclosure to occur and gives psychological credence to sharing.

The need to be trusted by others promotes the group process of identity formation and opens the door for constructive feedback in our relationships. Our need to be trustworthy is evident in our desire for relationships that result in increased self-respect and self-confidence. As others share themselves with us, we perceive ourselves as important and capable of caring and respect. The need to be trusted enables our social interaction to become a dynamic growth process, giving us both the capacity to depend on others and to be depended on by others. In the group process the need to be trusted encourages members to supply therapeutic help to their fellow members. It motivates them to demonstrate their trustworthiness by their care, concern, and resourcefulness, which is reflected in their feedback. This trustworthiness is a vital personality trait that forms the basis for positive interpersonal relationships. It acts as a lubricant reducing the social friction created by group dynamics and pressures and ameliorates the defensive posture of individuals that produces resistance to both the group process and individual change.

Love and Belonging

Several years ago I came across a quotation by John E. Largients, which expresses emphatically the nature of the need for love and belonging. He wrote, "Not many men may be willing to die for love these days. But you can't escape the fact that millions are dying daily for lack of it." Maslow (1943) pointed out that we all have a desire for affectionate relations with people and for a place in a group. The absence of these relationships with family, friends, or people in general results in loneliness and social isolation. Glasser (1965) affirmed that the need for relatedness or the need to love and be loved is basic to human beings. Dinkmeyer and Muro (1971) stated that people have affection needs that are expressed in their desire to belong, help, and be helped. Common agreement is that every human being experiences an essential necessity for love and that our need for love is not one-sided. To give love to others is equally important as to receive it from others. Stendhal summarized this quality of love when he said that "love is a well from which we can drink only as much as we put in."

Many levels of this need for love and belonging exist, ranging from simple acceptance to the complex intimacy of a love relationship in a marriage or family. Our need for love is initially exhibited in social situations by our desire for acceptance by individuals or groups that are attractive to us. When we experience acceptance by others, we experience fulfillment and a sense of belonging. This leads to an association with the person or group who accepted us, thus contributing to our identity. This experience of acceptance by others is a reflection of their own acceptance of themselves. We not only have a need to be accepted by others, but we also have a need to accept ourselves. The relationship between acceptance of self and the ability to accept others is pointed out in the Judeo-Christian commandment "love your neighbor as yourself." If we have little love for ourselves, then only little love can be shown to those around us. Wrenn (1971) related this idea to counselors when he wrote that the amount of caring counselors can show their clients can be measured by the amount of caring they show for themselves.

In group counseling the members usually are struggling with this need for acceptance in some way. They may be experiencing problems in their social relationships that make them feel isolated from and unaccepted by others. They may have negative feelings about their own selves, not liking who they are and therefore being unable to accept themselves. Their behavior may be such that they experience rejection from others, including their families. The group process therefore must take the need for love and belonging into account. An atmosphere must be created in the group where the members feel accepted and free to share their true selves with others, thus resulting in greater self-acceptance. If the need for acceptance is not met in the group, members will use their energies to defend themselves and resist the process. Whereas trust is the foundation of the group process, acceptance is the framework around which it is built. If members can feel accepted even though they have unresolved problems and difficulties, facing up to the task of change is less threatening.

Esteem

The need for esteem is unique because it possesses a quality that can drive people to make extreme sacrifices in its pursuit. We can find many examples of people who have severely taxed their minds and bodies, sacrificed values, and renounced friends and family to attain the fame, fortune, or status they feel will give them esteem. However, in such efforts the meaning of esteem is frequently lost or confused. Maslow's (1943) idea of esteem centers around seeking recognition from others and from oneself as a worthwhile person. This need is satisfied when one experiences feelings of worth, strength, usefulness, and confidence. Unfortunately the need for esteem has too often been associated with financial success, social position, role attainment, material acquisition, and accomplishments. This has caused confusion leading to the simplistic notion that achievement equals esteem, which is inaccurate.

The need for esteem is very complex and involves an integration of the elements of worth, respect, achievement, and responsibility. Glasser (1965) stated that the second basic human need is the need for respect or the need to feel worthwhile to self and others. In his description we have the essence of esteem. It is a human feeling that can only be transmitted on an interpersonal basis. The meaning of esteem comes from within oneself and from others. It does not come with achievements, position, or money, although these things can be used to command the attention that relates to esteem. Without the psychological reaction of self-respect or self-esteem generated by one's accomplishments, the accomplishment is personally meaningless. Without the respect communicated by other people, position or wealth fails to give us feelings of worth. In other words, the esteem need can only be met through a reciprocal interaction with other human beings who value us in conjunction with our own inner perception of our self as worthwhile.

Another characteristic of the esteem need that is overlooked at times is its relationship to responsibility. We can only experience feelings of worth to ourselves and others if we act in a responsible manner. The relationship between responsibility, achievement, and respect is circular. To achieve something we must take responsibility. Once we have taken responsibility and realized an accomplishment, respect is generated both from ourselves and from others. To maintain this respect, we must continue to be responsible, and so on. The amount of responsibility we assume is directly related to what we accomplish and the amount of respect we experience. The reverse of this relationship is equally valid.

Low self-esteem and feelings of worthlessness are common in group members. As individuals experience problems they can't resolve themselves, the natural tendency is to think less of themselves and to feel that others think less of them. This downward spiral must be broken by the group process. Within the group the client should realize feelings of worth. The climate should be characterized by a positive attitude that takes into account the strengths of individual members as well as their weaknesses. The group can meet client needs for esteem initially by focusing on individual assets. By allowing members to experience responsibility for themselves and by encouraging them to help one another, the group can facilitate the process of solving individual member problems while at the same time meeting the need for respect.

Self-Actualization

To begin with we must distinguish between self-actualization and the need for self-actualization. The former is a state of being, and the latter is a motivating force that influences our actions. Although the tendency is to relate self-actualization to an utopian life style devoid of problems and full of peace, fulfillment, and satisfaction, a more realistic perspective is to view it as a state in which all of one's energy can be mobilized to achieve one's potential. This definition has potent import, because one goal of the group process is to help individuals utilize all their resources in resolving their problems.

Many descriptions of a self-actualized person can be given, all of which reveal the positive quality of the state. Gilmer (1970) described self-actualized people as fully functioning; they think well of themselves and others and view relationships with others as important investments and as opportunities for developing their own selves. The self-actualized person according to Johnson (1972) is "time competent, that is (one) having the ability to tie the past and the future to the present in a meaningful continuity while fully living in the present" (p. 2). Hesse (1971) captures this conception of self-actualization in his discourse on the river. The following excerpts are examples.

> Today he saw one of the river's secrets, one that gripped his soul. He saw that the water continually flowed and flowed and yet it was always there; it was always the same and yet every moment it was new (p. 102).

> The river is everywhere at the same time, at the source and at the mouth, at the waterfall, at the ferry. In the ocean and in the mountains, everywhere and. . . . The present only exists for it, not the shadow of the past, nor the shadow of the future (p. 107).

Finally, Carroll (1969) summarized the characteristics of self-actualized persons in practical and specific terms. They are spontaneous and feel free to be themselves because they have confidence in and acceptance of themselves. They are self-sufficient but have feelings for mankind. They have a strong desire to help others, have a good social conscience, are creative, natural, and flexible. They are problem-centered rather than self-centered and are able to tolerate ambiguity.

Although describing a self-actualized person is relatively easy, being one is much more difficult. The experience of being self-actualized is difficult to identify because when one is in that state it is not necessary to think about being self-actualized. In fact, one of the cues that a person is no longer self-actualized or has not yet become so is when he or she is concerned about being self-actualized. Self-actualization is therefore a transient state for most people that is moved into and out of with the flow of life experiences and relationships with others. One is aware of it as a goal to be strived for or an identifiable condition that has passed. The more relevant consideration then is the drive to become self-actualized, which has implications for the group counseling process.

Maslow (1954) ascribed the need for self-actualization to "man's desire for self-fulfillment; namely to the tendency for him to become actualized in what he is potentially" (pp. 91–92). Combs and Snygg (1959) called self-actualization humanity's basic need and describe it as "that great, driving, striving force in each of us by which we are continually seeking to make ourselves more adequate to cope with life" (p. 46). The desire to realize our potential is the motivating force that drives all of us to attempt to remove obstacles from our lives and is the therapeutic generator of efforts made by group counseling members to resolve their problems. Even though we can never completely fulfill our potential the striving to do so is the self-actualization process. The concept of self-actualization is not a static state that, once attained, can be maintained indefinitely. Rather it embodies a continual growth process, which is characterized by momentary peak experiences and plateaus of satisfactory fulfillment but which pushes us toward continual self-development throughout our lives.

Bach (1970) presented this perspective of the continuous self-actualizing process in his book *Jonathan Livingston Seagull: A Story*. The excerpt that follows points out the unceasing nature of the drive toward fulfillment of one's potential (Jonathan Livingston Seagull is speaking to his protege' Fletcher Seagull as he is about to send him out into the world on his own):

> You don't need me any longer. You need to keep finding yourself, a little more each day, that real unlimited Fletcher Seagull. He's your instructor. You need to understand him and to practice him (p. 92).

The impact of the need for self-actualization in group counseling has several dimensions. As group members' needs for safety, love, and esteem are met, they have access to those resources of energy that had previously been used to meet those needs. The need to actualize oneself emerges as the important motivator in clients' lives through which they not only gain a greater awareness of their potential but also find ways of using it to improve their lives. *Growth groups* are formed for the express purpose of helping members expand their awareness and utilize their potential more fully. These groups use encounter or T-group methods and are designed to help adequately functioning people become even more effective. In counseling groups, however, as lower order needs are met in the group, clients can focus attention more intensively on their problems and a work oriented atmosphere develops. Group members can attack their difficulties in a pragmatic manner without the emotional overtones usually associated with confronting personal problems. In accord with the idea that self-actualized people are not devoid of problems, the group members not only learn how to solve specific problems but learn general problem solving skills that will be useful to them in the future.

☐ Needs and Relationships: Formation of the Self/Viewing Man in a Social Context

The question "What is Man?" always leads to an answer that construes human beings in some social context. Whether given extensive or minimal credit, the interpersonal environment must always be accounted. William James' (1890) observation that "no more fiendish punishment could be devised, were such a thing physically possible, than that one should be turned loose in society and remain absolutely unnoticed by all the members thereof" (p. 293) underscores the crucial relevance of our interpersonal network—without it we simply would not be. Johnson (1981) pointed out that human beings "desire and seek out relationships with others" and "have personal needs that can be satisfied only through interacting with other humans" (p. 1).

Interpersonal relationships are extremely important in meeting our basic human needs. Relationships with others are required to adequately satisfy our needs for safety, love and belonging, and esteem. Having positive relationships with others is a key quality of a self-actualized person. Because of this basic dependence on human relationships, people are primarily social in nature. Interpersonal contacts not only meet our needs but also develop the qualities that make us uniquely human. Therefore we need to look intensely at interpersonal relationships to determine their impact on the human growth process and their relevance to group counseling.

☐ The Process Component

Schmuck and Schmuck (1971) stated that "human beings develop in a sequential and systematic manner, not because of the gradual unfolding of instinctual tendencies, but because they experience a regular sequence of interpersonal interactions in their lives" (pp. 11–12). Gazda (1971b) added that "it is primarily through people that we grow into what we are today, and it is primarily through our relationships that we grow into what we will be tomorrow" (p. 1). The importance of the group process stems from the fact that we are social beings who develop through adequate and meaningful exposure to social situations and relationships. Clearly we can neither meet our needs nor develop our humanness in isolation. We must have contact with others, and these contacts must qualify as relationships for their influence to be realized.

Our relationships have a socializing effect on our lives, not only shaping our behavior to conform to the standards of society, but also having a differentiating impact that enables each person to develop a unique personality, self-concept, and identity. Johnson (1981) stated that "our identity is built out of our relationships with other people. As we interact with others we note their responses to us, and we learn to view ourselves as they view us" (p. 2). In fact he went so far as to state that our "psychological health depends almost entirely on our relationships with other people. The ability to build and maintain cooperative, interdependent relationships with other people is often cited as a primary manifestation of psychological health" (p. 3).

Combs and Snygg (1959) stipulated that our self is basically a social product that arises out of our experience with other human beings. Self-image and the self-system acquired through social contact are built on experiences of approval or disapproval and are called *reflected appraisals* by Sullivan (1953a). In other words, the essence of a person's identity depends on social interactions, that help the person differentiate himself or herself from the environment, others, and to be a person in his or her own right (Allport, 1960).

Our interpersonal relationships form the learning environment in which we acquire self-knowledge. "We learn about ourselves not only by experiencing our own actions, but also by experiencing the action of others, who serve as both mirrors and models for imitation" (Carroll, 1969, p. 270). Sullivan (1953b) contended that personality is almost entirely the product of interaction with other significant human beings. Who we are is forged in the cauldron of our human relationships. Even Carl Rogers' (1951) self-theory acknowledges the impact of interpersonal relationships. One of his 19 propositions states: "As a result of interaction with the environment and *particularly, as a result of interactions with others,* one's picture of oneself is formed" (Italics added) (p. 483). The importance of this self-knowledge was underscored by Kubie (1958) as the key to effective maturation and development: "Without self-knowledge in depth . . . we can have no adults, but only aging children who are armed with words and paint and clay and atomic weapons, none of which they understand" (p. 133).

The group is one of the primary vehicles that provides us with self-knowledge. Family, peer group, school group, occupational group, religious affiliation or church fellowship, and social set supply us with the interaction whereby we learn about ourselves. Mahler (1969) effectively tied this influence of groups to the group counseling process when he stated,

> A major goal of group counseling is to develop a relationship which will enable the counselor to meet the important developmental needs of (clients) and to help them with the identity-seeking process. Group counseling provides an

opportunity for (clients) to examine in a friendly and permissive atmosphere their feelings and attitudes and the ideas they have about themselves and the world (p. 141).

Group counseling has process merit for another reason. Although our relationships are the key to meeting our needs and developing our personality, they also are the core of most of the problems we experience. Dinkmeyer and Muro (1971) said that "all human problems are primarily social" (p. 9). Gazda (1971b) said that "Many of our real problems in living are interpersonal in nature. Therefore it seems reasonable to help (clients) develop skills necessary for establishing and maintaining effective interpersonal relationships . . . we must help (clients) become socially competent" (pp. 6–7). Mahler (1969) added that "the major concerns people bring to group counseling focus around the basic socialization process" (p. 11). The social milieu of the counseling group is conducive to helping members deal effectively with their concerns, because it stresses effective relationship development as a means of learning about oneself and finding socially relevant solutions to personal problems.

☐ The Johari Window

Since relationships are the key to meeting many basic needs and are also the means by which we develop identity and self-concept, the nature of our relationships takes on strategic value in our growth and development. To understand how relationships develop and how positive ones differ from negative ones is imperative. This understanding is necessary from a psychological standpoint and a group counseling frame of reference. In this regard Luft and Ingham (Luft, 1984) designed a relationship development model called the Johari Window to explain the process of relationship development. Figure 3.3 presents an adapted form of their basic model.

Relationships develop as a result of interaction between people in which information is exchanged. The extent to which a relationship develops depends on the intensity of the interaction involved and the nature and depth of the information shared.

In any relationship, two person components—self and others—and two information components—known and unknown—exist. Juxtaposed to one another a grid of four quadrants is created which can be used to graphically illustrate the nature of all relationships from initial contacts or acquaintances to our most deeply intimate associations. By modifying the size of the various quadrants we can graphically illustrate the nature of all relationships from superficial (small open area) to deeply intimate (large open area). No intrinsic value orientation is implied in the model to infer that all our relationships should be characterized by a certain degree of openness. Rather the model is a descriptive tool for studying relationships, and it provides a

FIGURE 3.3. Johari window. From *Group Processes: An Introduction to Group Dynamics,* Joseph Luft. Reprinted by permission.

basis for assessing their nature and growth. Typically our relationships run the full gamut of the openness continuum from small open area to extensive open area. However, no human relationship can be characterized as being completely open. Construing any relationship as totally open would extinguish individuality by default and eliminate the growth dynamic in relationships.

Quadrant I is called the *open* area and represents all information that is mutually accessible to all participants in the relationship. This information may range from the mere exchange of names with a first time acquaintance to a deep sharing of our innermost thoughts and feelings with an intimate partner. As relationships develop and grow, the open area expands. Note that we have relationships of all degrees of openness, and that the open quadrant increases in size as a result of interactions where information drawn from the other quadrants of the grid is exchanged in the relationship.

Quadrant II is called the *hidden* area and represents information known to the self but not shared with others. This quadrant encompasses all our self-knowledge accrued through personal experience and learning. This area is the domain which houses the real you. Only when you want others to know does information pass into the open quadrant through a process known as self-disclosure. The important characteristic of this area is that you control the nature and amount of information which is disclosed. You usually make the decision as to what and when based on the level of trust and acceptance sensed in the relationship. Any time you choose to self-disclose you take a risk because now others have access to the information and as such you lose control of it. John Powell (1969) in his book *Why Am*

I Afraid to Tell You Who I Am?, discussed many of the barriers that hinder us in telling others about ourselves. However, the more we do disclose, the greater the likelihood that others will know us as we really are.

Quadrant III is called the *blind* area. This area contains information, i.e., knowledge and perceptions, others know about us but have not shared with us. Each of us develops impressions of those to whom we relate. However, until we tell them what our perceptions are, that information remains part of the blind area in the relationship. The only way to remove this barrier in a relationship is through the communication mechanism of giving feedback. However, feedback involves risk just as self-disclosure does. Therefore, we usually hold back giving feedback until 1) we are sure that the relationship will not be jeopardized, 2) we feel the relationship will improve because of it or 3) the need to express it exceeds the concern for its impact on the relationship.

Quadrant IV is called the *unknown* area and represents the potential for growth that is a part of all relationships. Information from this quadrant materializes as a relationship progresses through its various stages of development. For example, we all have the capacity to love. However, until we become involved in a relationship where we experience loving and being loved, that information is an unknown entity. Similarly, as we relate to others over time, aspects of ourselves emerge that neither we nor our partners knew existed. Information seldom moves directly from the unknown to the open; it usually follows a route through either the hidden or blind quadrants into the open area.

The factor governing the amount of self-disclosure and feedback that occurs in relationships is *risk.* As human beings, we are endowed with self-protective defense mechanisms which intercede whenever we sense we are vulnerable to reprisal or rejection. Consequently, we do not unleash overly personal, positive, or negative information unless we are somewhat assured that we will not be punished or hurt or that the relationship will be able to stand it.

Very little risk occurs in disclosing something about yourself that is already obvious or in giving feedback that a person is familiar with already. However, as the material shared becomes more personal in nature, the element of risk increases. Risk is taking the chance that others will reject us or that we will experience some form of reprisal as a result of what we share. For this reason we tend to guard against letting others know us or sharing our perceptions of others until we are reasonably sure that such action will be received in a nonthreatening manner or will accomplish a desired result. However, a certain degree of risk taking must occur for any relationship to grow. Benjamin Franklin's old adage, "nothing ventured, nothing gained," is applicable to the arena of relationships. Generally speaking, when we risk self-disclosure or feedback and experience positive results, we become more willing to do so again. Thus a positive growth cycle is initiated in the relationship. On the other hand, if we experience negative consequences, we are less likely to risk again which inevitably results in relational stagnation, deterioration, or termination.

In everyday relationships and in group counseling, risk is reduced when trust, acceptance, respect, communication, and understanding characterize our interpersonal contacts. Self-disclosure and feedback can then operate freely, generating more opportunities for personal learning and growth. In addition, a reciprocal effect occurs: as conditions suitable for personal sharing improve the quantity and quality of self-disclosure and feedback increase, and as more self-disclosing and feedback occur, the conditions for doing so improve. In group counseling then, the leader must help develop a climate where members can take risks, thereby enabling the mechanisms of self-disclosure and feedback to function in a constructive manner.

☐ Putting it All Together

Figure 3.4 illustrates the development of personality, identity, and self-concept based on the interaction between basic human needs and relationships with others. Personality is the behavioral dimension of our self which develops over time and is manifested in the manner in which we relate to the world around us. It includes our traits, habits, and basic tendencies that characterize us over time and across circumstances. Identity is the cognitive component of our self and encompasses all information that we perceive to pertain directly and indirectly to answering the question "Who am I?" for ourselves. Self-concept is the affective element of the self that contains our subjective valuative conclusions of how we feel about our self at any point in time. Our self-esteem may be positive or negative, high or low depending on circumstances and situations. But the composite of all evaluations in both a contemporary and longitudinal sense forms our self-concept.

Glasser (1965) pointed out that our needs can only be met through involvement with other human beings. Relationships with others help us develop our individual uniqueness and adapt to societal standards. White (1966) indicated that one primary growth trend is that of developing better interpersonal relationships to improve our lives. In this case our needs motivate us to form relationships that will help us achieve our potential and in that manner improve our lives. The overall result of this interactive process is the personhood of each human being. It must be noted that this illustration is an oversimplification of a very complex process, the dynamics of which affect the development of each person throughout life.

☐ The Purpose Component

The representation in Figure 3.5 depicts the overall relationship between the psychological framework discussed in this chapter and the group

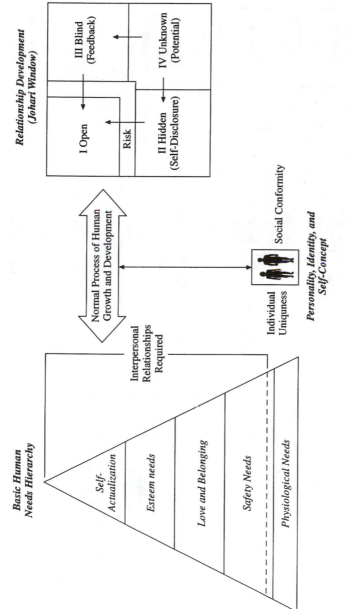

FIGURE 3.4. Needs, relationships, and personal development.

69

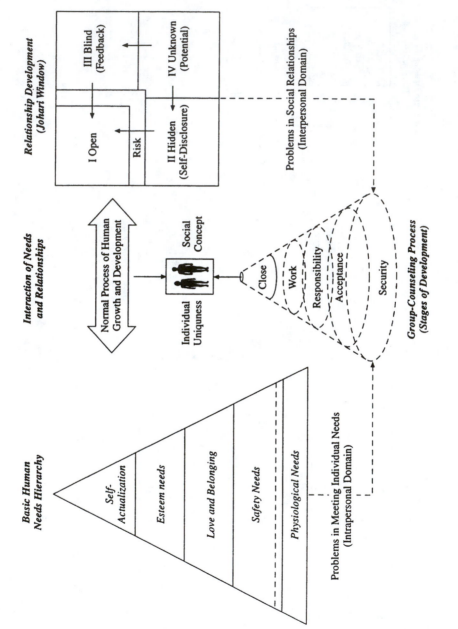

FIGURE 3.5. The psychological rationale and the group counseling process.

counseling process. The normal process of growth and development entails the interaction between our needs and our relationships and results in the nature of our personal identity. However, within that process obstacles in the form of problems occur that impede our growth. These problems generally fall into two generic categories: problems in meeting our individual needs and problems in social relationships. These categories are certainly not mutually exclusive but each has one basic distinguishing characteristic. Needs problems tend to be *intrapersonal* in nature, while social problems are *interpersonal*. In any case the problems have a symbiotic relationship to each other in the sense that problem resolution is contingent on the interaction of needs with relationships.

In some ways these two problem categories are reciprocal, i.e., unmet individual needs will contribute to relationship problems, and relationship problems present obstacles to getting personal needs met. In most instances an interpersonal component to all human problems must be addressed when presented in counseling (Trotzer, 1985). Yalom (1995) confirmed this view noting that in therapy goals often shift from relief of suffering (intrapersonal) to goals that have relational implications (interpersonal). Patients who come into therapy desiring release from anxiety or depression move to wanting to improve communications, develop relationships, learn to trust others, love, or be honest in their relating. This interpersonal factor in and of itself commends group counseling/therapy as a more comprehensive therapeutic modality. Consequently, the group counseling process must account for the needs of the individuals and the social relationships required to meet those needs. This creates a climate conducive to helping clients resolve problems in their lives and thus validates the purpose for forming groups as a helping modality.

The problem solving process itself contributes merit to the purpose dynamic in group counseling. When faced with issues or problems one cannot resolve on her or his own, turning to others for assistance is a common option. For that option to be effective a set of typical steps is usually involved. These basic elements of problem-solving are:

1. Identifying a safe context (relationship) in which to talk about, share and address the problem.
2. Accepting the problem as part of one's self, i.e., perceiving the problem as ego syntonic rather than ego dystonic.
3. Owning responsibility for the problem, i.e., acknowledging an internal locus of control rather than an external locus of control.
4. Devising a means to resolve the problem that involves the following:
   a. Identifying alternative ways of viewing the problem and/or alternative solutions to resolving it, i.e., using the brainstorming capacity of divergent thinking to assess the problem and identify possible means of resolving it.

b. Evaluating alternatives to establish the most relevant perspective of the problem and most plausible solution, i.e., using the mental capacity of convergent thinking to specify a focus and direction.

c. Making a decision, i.e., choosing an alternative to apply to the problem.

d. Planning a course of action.

e. Practicing the alternative if possible (as in a group setting).

f. Implementing the plan.

g. Evaluating whether the problem is solved.

Group counseling provides a context where these steps can be experienced and implemented.

☐ Relating the Rationale to the Group Process

The developmental sequence of the group counseling process falls into a series of stages that reflect the *person* component (basic human needs), the *process* component (relationship development generating qualities amenable to self-disclosure and feedback) and the *purpose* component (resolving intrapersonal and interpersonal problems). As indicated in Figure 3.5, the sequence includes the following stages in order of occurrence: *Security, Acceptance, Responsibility, Work,* and *Closing.* The characteristics and dynamics of each of these stages and their corresponding developmental tasks will be discussed in the following chapters.

☐ Learning Activities

The learning activities selected for this chapter relate to the basic needs hierarchy and relationship development pertaining to self-disclosure and feedback. In most cases the exercises are very flexible in terms of purpose; therefore, follow-up discussion may result in widely varied reactions. Each exercise has relevance to the group counseling process from both a teaching and a practicing perspective.

Needs and Groups: A Self Assessment Exercise

The purpose of this exercise is to demonstrate the relationship between our needs and relationships with respect to identity development. It is useful as an assessment tool for the purpose of setting interpersonal and personal growth goals in group counseling. Each person completes the exercise individually as a prerequisite to group interaction.

Instructions:

1. Make an exhaustive list of all the groups of which you are a member.
2. Identify those groups which meet the needs listed below and place them in the appropriate column.

SECURITY	LOVE AND BELONGING	ESTEEM

3. Using only your group memberships as material write a one paragraph description of your identity.
4. Identity Self-assessment
   a. List those groups that you value highly and which contribute positively to your identity.
   b. List those groups you think contribute negatively to your identity.
   c. List those groups with whom you would like to disassociate yourself.
   d. List groups with whom you would like to join or increase your participation.
   e. Based on your entries in b, c, and d, set goals for yourself to work toward.

Coming to Life Activities

Physiological needs, particularly those associated with fatigue, boredom, and tension can be effectively dealt with through the use of physical activities that stimulate physical and mental alertness and relieve tension and anxiety. The following are examples of activities that can be done individually, in dyads, or in groups. An excellent sequence to follow in a group situation is to select one activity from each category and build from individuals to dyads to groups. These activities are most useful as icebreakers at the start of the group sessions or energizers when group members indicate a need for a physical break from the psychological strain of group interaction (Kassera & Kassera, 1979).

Individual Activities

Deep Breathing

Disperse group members around the room. Have each group member take three deep breaths, increasing the volume of air intake with each successive breath. Have members follow your example so that everyone is doing the same thing. Then have members inhale and hold their breath for 15 seconds. At the end of 15 seconds, have them exhale forcefully making their own personal sound in unison with the group. Take several easy breaths to relax. Have them repeat the breath holding sequence, this time for 20 seconds. Once again breathe easily to relax. Repeat a third time for 25 seconds. (*Note*: You may vary the amount of time your clients spend holding their breath up to as much as 45–60 seconds.) At the end of this exercise members should experience rapid heartbeats. Relax with easy breathing and move on to the next activity.

Isometrics

Isometrics utilize mental imagery as the means of simulating physical exertion thereby stimulating physical alertness. Have group members stand with hands extended slightly above their heads. Tell them to imagine that a 2-ton elevator is descending on them and at your signal they must hold the elevator up to prevent being crushed. Signal the members to start, allowing them to exert themselves for 15 seconds. Repeat this process three times, allowing time for members to relax and breathe easily between each effort. Encourage members to put their whole bodies into the effort. Repeat this same sequence using the concept of two walls closing in a la a *Star Wars* trash compactor. The members must hold the walls off by extending their hands out from their sides. On the third trial of each isometric sequence have group members succeed, i.e., tell them to push the elevator up or the walls out as far as they can.

Dyad Activities

Mirroring

Pair group members off and have them face each other. Appoint one as the actor and one as the mirror. The objective is for the mirror to imitate all motions and actions of the actor. Have the actor begin slowly and gradually, quicken the pace to a point where it is impossible for the mirror to follow, and then gradually slow down again. Reverse roles and repeat the exercise. You also may want to have your clients switch partners several times or form an inner and outer circle of partners and then rotate one of the circles.

Hand Dancing

Have partners face each other and place their hands, palms extended, approximately 1 inch from each other. Have one partner begin to move his or her hands slowly. The other partner is to follow the actions of the first pair of hands maintaining the 1-inch distance and not touching. Tell your clients to speed up the process to the point where following is impossible and then slow down. Reverse roles, and repeat the same process.

An alternative form of hand dancing that can be used to help group members focus on the nature of relationships and communication is a three step sequence that uses three different versions of hand dancing. First, have members do the hand dancing activity as previously described but with hands about six inches apart. Second, have members clasp hands. Use the same leader-follower instructions, but at some point add an instruction for the follower to resist following. Third, have partners touch hands (palms and fingers). Repeat leader-follower and resister instructions. Upon completion of the sequence, process the activity in light of members' experiences and relate these experiences to the nature and effectiveness of communication in relationships.

Back Breakers

Have partners stand back to back locking their arms at the elbow. Instruct them to cooperate in turning side to side and stretching each other's arm and shoulder muscles. Then have one partner bend over slowly pulling the other on to his or her back, holding the person there for a short time. Have partners reverse the process and repeat the exercise three or four times. This exercise should be done slowly and carefully so the participants can feel the stretching; they shouldn't overdo either the lifting or the strain of being stretched.

An added task can be to have partners work together to sit down on the floor and get back to their feet while retaining their back to back, arms locked position.

Trust Walk

The concept of trust in our lives is sometimes easier to come to grips with if we can experience it physically. The trust walk is one example of a concrete experience that can be used to understand the abstract concept of trust. Pair group members off and designate one or the other of the partners as blind. You may wish to use blindfolds to prevent peeking but simply having the partner close his or her eyes is sufficient. In fact, not using artificial means of blinding puts added pressure on the blind partner. The seeing partners are then directed to take their blind partners on a walk, giving them as many experiences as possible but always maintaining responsibility for their safety. The entire exercise should be conducted without words. Partners must work out their own strategies for nonverbal communication. After a designated period of time (10 minutes or more), reverse the roles and re-peat the exercise. Follow-up discussion should relate the members' experi-ences to trusting oneself, trusting others, and being trustworthy. The dis-cussion can easily be directed to a consideration of the security factor in group dynamics.

Note: It is often appropriate to demonstrate several versions of leading and following as part of the introduction to the activity. This tends to alleviate some of the anxiety associated with touch and introduces modeling as a legitimate learning tool in the group.

Trust Fall

Another way of demonstrating the concept of trust physically is using the trust fall, which is usually more threatening than the trust walk. Have each dyad move to an area free of objects and with sufficient room to conduct the exercise. Have one partner stand facing away from the other partner with feet together, eyes closed, and body rigid. Simply instruct the person to fall backward when ready. The other partner is instructed beforehand to catch the person. It is usually a good idea to demonstrate this exercise first, especially in terms of showing group members how to catch their partners and modeling how to engage in the falling-catching sequence by degrees. Persons with physical problems, such as bad backs, should be cautioned before becoming involved. After several falls reverse positions and repeat the exercise. Discussion can be much the same as with the preceding exercise, but you may wish to add the dimension of relating the trust-falling experience to sharing personal problems with other people you do not know or trust.

Group Activities

Human Machine

Have one member of the group begin a motion of some kind. A second member attaches physically to the first, adding another motion but keeping in tune with the first. The rest of the members attach themselves one at a time until the whole group is functioning as a machine. Once the whole group is involved moderate the motion by directive, speeding up and slowing down. At least once accelerate to the point of disintegration to demonstrate the importance of group coordination and teamwork.

Circle Massage

Have group members stand in a circle shoulder to shoulder. Have them take a right face, form cupped hands, and begin to beat on the back of the person in front of them in a rapid staccato manner moving all around the person's back. Have them switch to a neck and shoulder massage after about 30 seconds. The circle will often begin to move around of its own volition. After a suitable time period have the group do an about face and repeat the same process.

Group Hop

Form the group into a circle standing shoulder to shoulder. Have the group make a right face placing their left hand on the left shoulder of the person in front of them and reaching down with the right hand to pick up that person's right ankle. When the group is steady, instruct them to hop forward and then backward. Next, instruct the group to make an about face and repeat the activity using right hands on shoulders and left hands holding ankles.

Dr. Untangle

Have group members (at least six) stand in a circle. Number off the group 1-X (number in the group). Have them raise their arms over their heads and clasp hands as follows:

1. In even numbered groups, have the odd numbered persons grasp the left hand of the next highest even numbered person with their right hand. (Each person in the circle should have one free hand remaining.)
2. Instruct group members to grasp the free hand of another person in the group who is NOT standing immediately to their right or left.
   Note: In odd numbered groups the last odd numbered person must grasp the respective hands of the last highest even numbered person and the number one person, i.e., the last odd numbered person must take the hand of the person on each side of him or her.
3. Once all members are appropriately clasped, instruct them to untangle themselves without letting go of their hands. (Properly completed the result will be a full circle with members holding hands.)

The Knot

Another version of the untangling task is to have members stand in a line holding hands. As leader, grasp the hand of the person at one end of the line and proceed to weave, snakelike in and out of the line with members following your lead as best they can. When you have the group sufficiently tangled up, connect the person's hand you are holding to the free hand of the last person in the line. Instruct the group to untangle the knot without letting go of hands. The successful result will be a connected circle.

Coin on the Forehead

With group members standing in a circle, place a coin (quarter or nickel) on the forehead of one member. Instruct the group to pass the coin forehead to forehead without using their hands to touch the coin. Group members may assist each dyad making the pass as long as they do not touch the coin with their hands.

Trust Ring

A group version of the trust fall is to have group members form a ring around one person who stands erect, feet together, arms folded across their chest, and eyes closed. Upon a signal (verbal or a slight push from the leader) the center person falls toward the ring which is then responsible for catching and moving the person around while maintaining responsibility for his or her safety.

In this activity an important procedure is for the leader to demonstrate appropriate ways of catching and touching especially for female members. Females can fold their arms over their breasts and catchers from the front can be directed to arms and shoulders rather than the chest area. This activity demonstrates the dynamic of group trust especially in regard to the individual-group interaction. In fact, this activity can be helpful in assisting individual members who are hesitant to place their confidence in the group. Once they experience the group's capability relative to their physical safety, they may be more confident that the group also can be trusted with their psychological safety.

Three Secrets

This exercise gets at the importance of safety and security on a more personal and psychological level. Have each group member write three secrets that they would not tell the group under any circumstances at this point in time. Assure them that they will not have to share their secrets and that no tricks are involved. On completion of the writing have members put the secrets away for safe keeping, and conduct a discussion centered around why they would not want to share their secrets in the group. Focus attention on the need for developing trusting relationships and confidentiality in the group. Help members come to grips with the threat involved in sharing their private world with others. The information written in this exercise often surfaces later voluntarily when members feel the group can be trusted. Members who decide to share their secrets will usually preface or follow their self-disclosure by telling the group that they would not have been able to do so before. This tends to bolster the morale of the group and serves as an indication that a trusting climate is developing. This activity also serves to demonstrate that boundaries will be respected in the group relative to a member's privacy.

Note: This activity was developed by Dr. Dan Ficek of the University of Wisconsin-River Falls Student Counseling Center.

Self-Collage

Self-knowledge, self-disclosure, and self-acceptance are intricately interwoven in the fabric of our identity. This exercise ties these threads together in a manner that is useful in the group counseling process. Have each person develop a collage using magazines, newspapers, photos, and so on, centered around the question "Who am I?" Have each person share his or her collage with the group and describe the connection between the items included and his or her personality and life style. On completion of the descriptions, have group members comment on aspects of the collage that stand out for them and that they identify with or admire. The focus of this feedback should be on appreciation and affirmation (rather than analysis or criticism) and as a means of identifying and valuing similarities and differences among group members. In the follow-up discussion relate the experiences in this exercise to the process of self-disclosure and self-acceptance.

A Symbol of You   brinj to class

This exercise has merit because it encourages self-disclosure in initial group sessions. Have each person bring to the group a material object that represents something meaningful in his or her life. Each person in turn presents the object to the group and describes what it is, what it symbolizes, and why it was chosen. A variation of this activity is to have group members go outside and find some object of nature that represents who they are or how they feel. When they return ask each person to show the object and describe its meaning.

One Thing You Value

The concept of acceptance is sometimes difficult to comprehend. This activity can serve the purpose of more clearly differentiating between acceptance and judgment. Have the members think of something they value deeply as a part of themselves. It can be an attitude, belief, characteristic, or possession, but it must be something they hold dearly. Form dyads and have the partners in turn describe their valued entity. Instruct the listener to help the speaker explain what they value by reflecting or asking questions, but under no circumstances must the listener make an evaluation of any kind. Stress this last point emphatically. After both parties have had the opportunity to be speaker and listener, discuss the experience. Ask if the members followed the rules or if some made evaluations in their minds like that's "like me" or "not like me" or, "I believe that, too." Most likely all group members broke the rule because it is impossible to keep if you become at all involved in the other person's sharing. Point out that acceptance does not mean no evaluation occurs, but it does mean that judgments are not passed. Acceptance is also distinct from condoning, because the latter implies a choice not to act on a judgment that has already been made.

What's Your Bag? (or Pushing the Envelop)

The following activity is an excellent advance organizer for discussion of the Johari Window and relationship development. Pass out crayons or magic markers and brown paper lunch bags (You can use grocery bags if you want this to be a big production, or envelops and pens or pencils can be substituted.). Have members decorate the outside of the bag with their name and words, symbols, and pictures that portray things about themselves that they would share easily with other people. Once the bag is completed, pass out three blank slips of paper and ask them to write three things about themselves they do not easily share with others. Have them fold each slip and place it inside the bag. Assure group members that they will not be required to share what is on the slips of paper inside the bag. Finally, pass out a fourth slip and ask them to write one thing they absolutely would not share with the group. Place that slip inside the bag also. (You may want to color code the final slip.) Have members close their bags or seal their envelops. Process the activity:

1. Have group members share the outside of their bags with the group one at a time.
2. When all have shared the outside of their bag *invite* them to share one item from inside the bag. Indicate that each person may choose to decline the invitation.
3. When all have either shared or declined, process the activity in light of self-disclosure relating it to the hidden and open quadrants of the Johari Window model of relationship development.

Circles of Relationships

Have each group member create a relationship map using the diagram in Figure 3.6. In each circle have members identify by first name or initials, persons in their life who fit in each of the circles. In addition, have them use arrows to represent persons who are moving away or toward them. Solid arrows can be used to designate movement they actually perceive is occurring and dash line arrows can be used to designate persons they would like to move toward or away from. As in indicator of group development have members place group members in their relationship maps. Use the maps as a springboard to discuss characteristics of relationships, identify relationship problems, and assess the current status of relationship development in the group. This activity is an excellent means of helping group members discuss the ethical issues of contact between members outside the group and maintaining boundaries that differentiate membership in the counseling therapy group from other relationships.

Road of Life

A person's life story is sometimes more readily told as a series of critical incidents that stand out in memory. This exercise can be used to effect self-disclosure through the process of describing key experiences in the life of

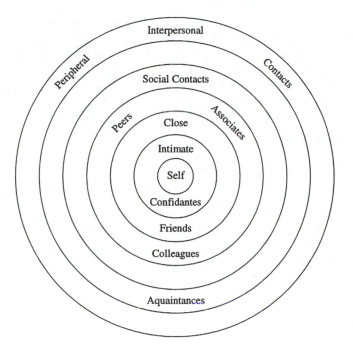

FIGURE 3.6. Relationship map. (Trotzer & Trotzer, 1986)

each group member. On a blank sheet of paper, have each person place a dot on the left hand side of the sheet representing birth and a dot on the right hand side representing death. Have them draw a curvy road representing life's ups and downs between the two dots. Designate a point on the road as the present. Using symbols such as balloons or clouds attached to the road, have each person indicate past, present and anticipated future experiences (critical or important incidents or events) that are meaningful to them. Then have each person share their road with the group. Group discussion can revolve around similarities and differences between members and stress the uniqueness of each person as well as the mutuality of human experience.

Impression-Go-Round

This simple activity is effective in demonstrating the feedback mechanism in group counseling. Have each person in the group give their impression of every other person in the group. This can be handled in one of two ways. The first is to have one person at a time give their impression of every other member. When that person has completed the impression-go-round, the next person does the same and so on. The second method is to have one member be the focal point and the other members in turn give their impressions.

When all members have given their impression of the spotlighted member another member gets the limelight, and the process is repeated until each person has received feedback from all the others. Variations of this impression-go-round include using animals or colors that represent each member's impression of each of the other members of the group. The members in turn share their choices and explain why they chose them.

Self-Actualization (Cognitive Exercise)

Because the nature of self-actualization is very complex and frequently confusing, this exercise can serve to help clarify its meaning. Have each class member write down a personal definition of self-actualization. The definition need not be comprehensive but should reflect the most important aspects of the term in each member's mind. Discuss the definitions, listing on the board the various characteristics. Then divide the class into small groups of four to eight, and have them develop a comprehensive definition of self-actualization.

CHAPTER

Process of Group Counseling

☐ Background

Group theory, research, and practice have all provided evidence to substantiate the premise that therapeutic groups evolve through a developmental process characterized by identifiable phases that are recognizable, verifiable, and consistent within and across groups (Trotzer, 1985, p. 94). These phases may vary in number and nomenclature according to author but have a generic commonality that gives them concurrent relevance across perspectives and theoretical models.

Cohn (Osborn, 1990) pointed out that "in group counseling there is a testing period, then a working through period followed by an analyzing period and finally a follow-up period" (p. 5). These process components are often consolidated into stages and labeled. For example, Tuckman (Tuckman, 1965; Tuckman & Jensen, 1977) identified five stages using the dynamic descriptors of forming, storming, norming, performing, and adjourning to depict the group process. Corey (1995) describes the stages more generally as initial, transition, working, and termination. Clark (1992) used broader strokes to delineate group development as three stages: relationship, integration, and accomplishment. And Anderson (1984) coined the rubric TACIT to emphasize the group process: *T*rust, *A*cceptance, *C*loseness, *I*nterdependence and *T*ermination. A simple perusal of these varied process descriptions reveals the correlational affinity of the distinctive labels to the generic process.

The process of group counseling presented in this chapter has emerged from experience in a variety of settings and with a wide range of clients and age groups. Contributing to this model have been my involvement and leadership experience in schools with middle, junior high, and senior high students; at the Minnesota State Prison doing group therapy with inmates and group training with staff; at the university level working with undergraduate and graduate students; in numerous human relations workshops with a variety of educators; in church related youth retreat groups; in interracial and multicultural groups; and in other diverse settings as a consultant. Recently, leading and supervising counseling and therapy groups in both private practice and a mental health agency has further helped me develop and refine this model.

Contrary to what might be expected from reading the previous chapter, the basic framework of this process model was developed first (Trotzer, 1972), and the rationale supplied later. In this sense the model is experience based rather than theory based and is rooted in observation of actual group interaction rather than in empirical assessment of hypothetical constructs. However, the theoretical, training, and research literature of the group field has consensually validated its process components as relevant and applicable in the practice of group work (Conyne, 1985; Corey, 1995; Gazda, 1984a; Johnson & Johnson, 1997; Rogers, 1970; Yalom, 1995).

☐ Nature of the Process

The model described presents a developmental perspective of group counseling that is intended for use as an aid in understanding and directing the group process and as a framework for many different theoretical approaches and techniques. The group process itself is divided into five stages. However, the stages are not autonomous or independent of each other. Each stage has certain characteristics that distinguish it, but their meaning and impact are obtained only within the context of the total group process. The duration of each stage is dependent on the nature of the leader and group members and the interaction between them (Donigian & Malnati, 1997). In some cases, the stages turn over very rapidly; in some, the stages are almost concurrent; and in others, a particular stage may continue for a long period of time and can lead to stagnation in the group process, especially if this occurs early.

Rogers' (1967) description of the group process correlates well with this idea of stages emerging and submerging in group interaction: "The interaction is best thought of, I believe, as a varied tapestry, differing from group to group, yet with certain kinds of trends evident in most of these intensive encounters and certain patterns tending to precede and others to follow" (p. 263). Each stage of the group is like a wave in the sea that has a momentary identity as it crests but whose beginning and demise are swallowed up in the constant movement of the water.

☐ Group Process and Problem Solving

The stage cycle of the group process reflects characteristics of our basic human needs and depicts the essential qualities of good interpersonal relationships. In group counseling the model also mirrors a basic pattern for successful problem solving. The integration of the stages (see Figure 3.5) into a conceptualization of a method for resolving problems is readily evident. The stages of security, acceptance, responsibility, work, and closing (Termination) are easily translated into a step-by-step procedure for resolving personal concerns (see Figure 4.1). First of all, as we experience

Process (Group Dynamics)	Content (Problem Solving)
I. Security Stage: Develop a psychologically safe environment in which each member can feel secure and free to talk about themselves and their problems.	1. Find a person or place where it is safe to admit to and talk about problems.

Individual Need: Security;
Relationship Trait: Trust

II. Acceptance Stage: Form a milieu in which members experience a sense of belongingness and acceptance as a person and as a member with and in spite of problems or issues they are dealing with.	2. Accept problems as part of one's self.

Individual Need: Love and Belonging;
Relationship Trait: Acceptance

III. Responsibility Stage: Develop an atmosphere that emphasizes individuality in a group context and develop a norm of owning responsibility for one's self and one's problems.	3. Take responsibility for one's own problems and commit to resolving them.

Individual Need: Esteem;
Relationship Trait: Differentiation and Accountability

IV. Work Stage: Develop a working together culture where group members work together to help each other deal with their issues and solve their problems.	4. Identify, clarify, understand the problem and work to resolve it (planning, practice, implementation, and evaluation).

Individual Need: Self-Actualization;
Relationship Trait: Cooperation

V. Closing Stage: Formulate closure with an emphasis on transfer of learning, internalization of change, affirmation, and confirmation.	5. Problem is solved and problem-solving process is learned.

FIGURE 4.1. Group process and problem solving.

problems we can't solve, a natural tendency is to hide or deny them because we don't want negative repercussions in our self-image or in reactions of others around us. Problems threaten our security as persons and
our relationships with others. Therefore problems are only shared with
others if an atmosphere of safety is part of our relationship with them. The
first step is *security*. Feelings of trust and confidence reduce resistance and
risk and facilitate our sharing of personal concerns with others. The amount
of trust necessary for disclosing our problems is a product of the combined
emotional seriousness of the problem and the quality of our relationships.
Some problems we experience force us to use disclosure as a means of
developing a trusting climate. For example, a client who has recently under-
gone a traumatic experience—say a close friend was injured while riding in
a car the client was driving—may be motivated by intense emotional feelings to share the problem without first determining if the atmosphere is
safe. Such risks are sometimes taken without a foreknowledge of trust in
the relationship. However, other problems may have emotional or social
overtones or undercurrents that demand an atmosphere of confidentiality
before any self-disclosure follows. Examples of these kinds of problems include sex problems, drug problems, and difficulties in relationships with
significant others such as bosses, coworkers, parents, teachers, or an intimate partner. In any event, step one in resolving our problems is to find a
safe place physically, psychologically, and relationally where we can talk
about them.

The second step is associated with *acceptance*. Although the term acceptance encompasses a broad range of concepts, such as acceptance of self,
acceptance of others, and acceptance by others, a key point in solving a
problem is to accept that problem as a part of ourselves. Until we recognize
that the problems we experience are part of us, we cannot act constructively to resolve them. Denial and unwillingness to face our problems are
the biggest deterrents to their resolution. The old adage "a problem faced is
a problem half solved" expresses the importance of this step. In order to
accept our problems, we need to know that recognition of them as our own
will not be devastating to ourselves or to our relationships with others. In
other words, our own acceptance of our problems is contingent to a large
degree on the reactions or the perceived reactions of others. If we sense we
are accepted by others as persons with and in spite of our problems; if we
feel we can let them see who we are including our problems and be received with empathy, we are more willing to identify, share, and acknowledge our problems.

Taking *responsibility* is the third step in the problem solving process. After
we acknowledge our problems, we also must admit to our part in their
cause and shoulder the responsibility to act positively to resolve them. Responsibility brings into focus the action phase of problem solving. The realization that problem solving is an active process and that the individual
with the problem is primarily responsible for that action is a difficult but

necessary step toward resolution. Clients often hope that once they have admitted to, identified, or accepted their problems something almost magical will occur and the problem will be resolved. They sometimes feel that because they have made the courageous effort to reveal themselves, their reward should be instant resolution, or at least that the counselor should take over. Therefore the process of getting clients to take responsibility for themselves is another key step in successful resolution.

The fourth step is to *work* out the means whereby the problem can be solved. This involves understanding the problem, identifying alternative solutions, evaluating them, planning and practicing new attitudes or behaviors, and trying them out in the real world. The helping relationship at this point is a working relationship in which all parties exert energy and intelligence toward helping the individual find and implement a successful solution.

The final step is to *terminate* the relationship when clients begin to experience success more than failure in their attempts to implement and integrate changes into their lives. In terminating, clients should not only realize problem resolution but should also have learned the problem solving process and increased their confidence in using it.

The following discussion will describe the life cycle of a group in which the problem solving characteristics just detailed will be related to the group counseling process. Each stage will be discussed separately, considering factors such as major identifying characteristics, focus, leader role, and resulting impact. The ABCs of group dynamics will be incorporated into the description of each stage from both the member and leader perspective. *A* stands for the *A*ffective component and represents emotions experienced in the group. *B* is the *B*ehavioral dimension that indicates how participants act or behave, and *C* is the *C*ognitive aspect of group experience that identifies how participants think and perceive.

☐ The Security Stage

The initial stage of the counseling group is characterized by tentativeness, ambiguity, anxiety, suspicion, resistance, discomfort, and other such emotional reactions on the part of both the members and the leader. Members experience these reactions because they are entering a new social situation in which they cannot predict what will occur and they are not confident of their ability to be in control of themselves or relate well to the group. Even though orientation procedures may be used, once the group comes together and interaction begins, the cognitive preparation gives way to the normal emotional reactions experienced in new social situations. Uncomfortable feelings also arise because each member is aware that he or she is in counseling and has personal concerns that are not easily shared under any circumstances.

An example of the inner turmoil a group member experiences was demonstrated by a young woman who requested admittance to a therapy group at a university counseling center. During the first session she paced and stood outside the room, struggling with the decision of whether to enter or not. The group leader, aware of her fears and misgivings about the group, left the door open and indicated to her that she could come in when she was ready. Toward the end of the session she entered the room and stood against the wall but did not join the group until the second session. So extensive was her discomfort that she did not participate until the fourth session and did not risk disclosing anything about herself until much later. Although most group members do not experience reactions to that extent, feelings of discomfort in the early sessions are always prevalent.

The security stage is a period of testing for group members. Much of this testing can be categorized as resistance and is displayed in the form of passivity, withdrawal, distractibility, uncooperativeness, or hostility. Bonney (1969) pointed out that "resistance and hostility toward the leader and conflict among group members are . . . expected outgrowths of the basic insecurity of procedural direction and uncertainty concerning the capacity of the group to achieve its proposed aims" (p. 165). The testing takes many forms and is aimed in many directions but the most common challenges are leveled at leader competency, ground rules, and other members' actions. Rogers (1967) felt that negative expressions are a way of testing the trust-worthiness and freedom of the group. All persons in the group experience some form of nervousness that generates defending types of behaviors rather than the authentic sharing of feelings and thoughts.

The focus during this initial period must take into account these insecure feelings of members. Underlying concerns that brought the members to the group should be set aside for the moment, and the here and now discomfort facing the group should be worked with. Some leaders like to use group warm-ups to help members express and work through these initial feelings and to establish a comfortable rapport within the group. The individual problems of members, though they may be categorically similar, are most likely quite dissimilar in the perception of each member at this point. Thus an important procedure in the forming stage of a group is to establish a common ground so that members can make contact with each other, get acquainted, and open lines of communication.

Since each member is preoccupied with dissatisfactions in his or her own life, an immediate focus on any one problem can lead to a rather disjointed process or generate a high risk of losing the involvement and cooperation of all the members. This type of emphasis might also allow some members to go too deep too quickly and scare off others. Cohn (1973) warned leaders to avoid this possibility and stressed that one essential feature of the group process is that members must be moved to deeper levels of interaction together. In a sense the first and most important task of a group leader is to get all the members on the same page. By initially focusing on the discom-fort that all are experiencing, a common ground is established that moves the group toward more cohesiveness. This identification with one another helps members overcome feelings of isolation and lays the foundation for the development of trust (Trotzer, 1972).

A significant aspect of the security stage is the leader's part in sharing the discomfort. Seldom will a leader enter a group without some feelings of uneasiness and hesitancy. These feelings do not necessarily reflect the skill, experience, and expertise of the counselor but rather are indicative of the effort involved in working toward closeness between people and helping people with problems. If leaders do not enter groups with some of these feelings, they are probably not prepared to become involved in the very personal worlds of the members.

The leader's role in the security stage is to perform what Lifton (1966) called *security-giving operations*. Leaders must be able to gain the confidence of the members, display warmth and understanding, provide for the various needs of members, and create and maintain a friendly and safe atmosphere in the group. Sensitivity, awareness, and an ability to communicate feelings and observations to the group without dominating it are important qualities of group leadership at this stage of the group's development.

As the group resolves the discomfort of the artificial social situation, members can begin delving into the problems in their lives. As members share their common feelings and perceptions, trust develops. Cohn (1964) emphasized this concept of trust, suggesting that once group members trust and are trusted the groundwork is laid for making the effort needed to improve their real life situations. Rogers (1967) stated that the "individual will gradually feel safe enough to drop some of his(her) defenses and facades" (p. 8). The members will become more willing to show their inner selves rather than just their outer selves. They will begin to direct energy toward *expression*—communication that allows oneself to be known to others authentically and transparently—rather than *impression*—communication that involves putting on a face in order to attract others (Schmuck & Schmuck, 1971).

Ohlsen (1970) also described the impact of the security stage: "When clients come to feel reasonably secure within their counseling group, they can be themselves, discuss the problems that bother them, accept others' frank reactions to them and express their own genuine feelings toward others" (p. 91). In other words, the development of trust provides the basis for getting down to the business of working on one's problems. Vorrath and Brendtro (1974) added that the most dynamic experience members gain from the group is that they learn to trust people. Therefore, "group leaders need to work on not taking the lack of trust personally while at the same time, helping members experience being able to trust in the group" (McBride & Emerson, 1989, p. 29). As such, trust has a process dimension and an outcome dimension that give it a two-fold impact in the group process. During the security stage the development of a trusting, nonthreatening atmosphere is the primary objective. This objective is in accord with each member's basic human need for security. As trust increases, the willingness for personal involvement and commitment increases. Members are more likely to risk letting themselves and their problems, frustrations, joys, and successes be known. Because of the atmosphere created by the movement toward trust, the individual members feel freer to be themselves. When this occurs the transition into the second stage of the group counseling process takes place.

From the leader perspective, the affective dynamics tend to be a modified, mirror image of members' feelings. Whereas, members may be uneasy, resistent, anxious, and filled with self-doubt, leaders typically experience similar feelings in the form of performance anxiety, anticipatory nervousness, and doubts relative to self-confidence and leadership competence. In the cognitive realm, leader and member expectations may be slightly or greatly incongruent. Member expectations (cognitions relative to how they perceive the group) are influenced by past group experiences, pregroup orientation (if used) or how the group is introduced, and what they have heard or read about group counseling. Leader expectations tend to be based on their conception of what the group is for and where he or she would like it to go in a general sense. This variation in perception contributes to the ambiguity and lack of clarity as to group purpose and focus. Leader-member cognitive disparity combined with emotional uneasiness produces behavioral activity in the group that validates the underlying discomfort. Nervous gestures and person specific, social idiosyncracies occur. Overtalking or undertalking coupled with nonverbal cues and messages that are noted but not acknowledged verbally, pursued interactionally, or clarified communicationally typify early group interaction.

Leader preparation for the security stage involves pregroup consideration of the following questions:

1. Why is the group being called into existence and what implications does that have relative to process dynamics?
2. What do you want the group to accomplish (goals/objectives)?
3. How will you help the group accomplish the goals for which it was formed?
4. How will you set parameters and ground rules and clarify expectations?
5. How will you proceed in your first session?

Mental imaging is a useful tool in the consideration of all these questions. Basic involvement for group leaders at the security stage is to be willing to participate in the affective discomfort of the group, have cognitive clarity about a direction for the group, and have a behavioral repertoire of responses to model, generate, and facilitate effective adjustment in the group. The interaction of these three elements creates a sense of security in the group that leads to a basic trust level that will enable the group to make the transition to the acceptance stage.

☐ The Acceptance Stage

The acceptance stage is directly related to our need for love and belonging and therefore has many derivatives that influence the direction of the group process. Generally this stage is characterized by a movement away from resistance and toward cooperation on the part of group members. As members begin to overcome the discomfort and threat of the group, grounds for their fears dissipate and they become more accepting of the group situation. As they become more familiar with the group's atmosphere, procedures, leader, and members, they become more comfortable and secure in the group setting. They accept the group structure and the leader's role. This acceptance does not mean the purpose of the group is clear to members, but it does mean they are accepting the method. The meaning and purpose of the counseling group must be derived from the group members not from the group structure.

Inherent in the group members' acceptance of the group as a vehicle for their interaction is their need to belong and the need for relatedness. The members' desires to be a part of the group emerges as an important motivating factor. This desire is inwardly evident to the individual from the outset of the group. But at first it is stifled for fear of acting in a manner that might ultimately jeopardize that belonging. However, with the foundation of trust established, the members are more willing to be their real selves and risk being known for the sake of being accepted. A journal entry of a 34-year-old Vietnam veteran who chose an alcohol treatment center rather than jail effectively depicts the acceptance stage of the group process:

> At first there was no way I was going to admit to being an alcoholic or even that I had a drinking problem. But as I listened to the other guys talk about booze in their lives, I began to realize they were all talking about many of the same experiences I had. The first thought that came to me was "Hey, you can't fool these cats because they've been there." I felt lots of pressure to 'fess up' but still held back because I wasn't sure how they (the group) would take me nor was I sure I could stomach myself if I did. I finally decided to share my drinking problems when I saw the group treat another Nam vet in the group in a sensitive way, giving him support and help with a problem I thought was even worse than mine. When I did admit I had a drinking problem, the group seemed to open up to me and let me in, and I also liked myself better.

As acceptance is experienced, relationships grow and cohesiveness develops. Cohesiveness is important to the group process because it makes group members more susceptible to the influence of each other and the group. It also provides the impetus for group productivity. It is a key factor in the helping process in groups because "those who are to be changed and those who influence change must sense a strong feeling of belonging in the same group" (Ohlsen, 1970, p. 88). Thus group cohesiveness meets the members' needs to belong, provides them with a temporary protective shield from the outside world, and is a potent therapeutic factor in the change process.

The therapeutic influence of cohesiveness makes use of peer group dynamics as its key resource in the group. As members experience genuine acceptance by fellow members, self-esteem is enhanced, ego is strengthened, self-confidence is bolstered, and they develop more courage in facing up to their problems. The impact of feeling accepted by a group of one's peers was stated succinctly by Gawrys and Brown (1963): "To be accepted and understood by the counselor is a satisfying experience; to be accepted and understood by a number of individuals is profound" (p. 106). Within this context, then, the potential of peer group influence can be used in a positive manner by the counselor. The group leader's role in this stage is no small factor in generating an accepting atmosphere in the group and contributing directly to the individual members' experiences of feeling accepted. Leaders must be models of acceptance from the onset of the total group process. They must demonstrate a genuine caring for each of the group members. Their leadership must be characterized by acceptance of each person regardless of the differences or characteristics each person presents or the behaviors he or she has exhibited outside the group. The process of acceptance is initiated by leaders who practice Rogers' (1962) concept of unconditional positive regard and who value diversity whether of a volitional (individual beliefs, values, or choices) or predetermined (race, culture, or ethnicity) variety. Two basic leadership skills are essential at this stage of the group. The first is "active listening" (see pages 245–246) where leaders communicate empathic understanding to each group member. The second is "multi-directed partiality" (Boszormenyi-Nagy & Krasner, 1986) where leaders communicate partiality, i.e., side with or demonstrate empathy for each member in the presence of the other members in spite of acknowledged differences. This skill creates a context in which members experience acceptance while at the same time establishing the basis for dialogue as a resource for acknowledging, valuing, and resolving differences. As members experience acceptance from the leader, they feel more accepting of themselves and follow the leader's model in their actions toward one another. As members feel more accepting of themselves and other members, an atmosphere of acceptance as a norm is created.

This brings us to the primary objective of the acceptance stage from a problem solving perspective—developing acceptance of self. For members' problems to surface in the group they must feel free to truly be themselves without fear of rejection or reprisal. As already stated, members cannot deal effectively with their problems without recognition that the problems are a part of them. Further, they must know that even though they have problems they are still persons of worth and importance. All people have the desire to like and accept themselves and to be liked and accepted by others. This desire is what the group utilizes in helping members deal with their problems. When each member can accept feelings, thoughts, and behaviors, whether positive or negative, as part of self and still feel accepted as a person, a big step has been taken in the helping process of the group.

The focus during the acceptance stage should be on the whole person and not just on isolated problem areas. In order to attain self-acceptance and acceptance of others, members must work with the total picture of themselves and others. Getting to know oneself and each other, and engaging in "Who am I?" and "Who are you?" activities, serve to promote self-disclosure. As individuals share themselves and describe their problems, accepting problems as part of themselves occurs more naturally and is less threatening. Many leaders like to integrate the first two stages of security and acceptance, using structured, personal sharing activities and techniques. In this way sharing promotes trust, and trust encourages sharing. Members find that many of their concerns are similar to those of other members if not in content at least on an affective level. This similarity among members leads to identification with each other and facilitates openness. As members can speak more freely about their problems, they find they can embrace these problems without losing self-esteem or position in the group; this experience paves the way for the more individualistic stage of responsibility.

The acceptance agenda of the second stage represents a big order to fill in a relational, practical, and conceptual sense. However, results, when attained, unleash acceptance as a powerful force in facilitating the problem solving process. When established, acceptance removes many of the roadblocks in the counseling process. It enables the group to begin constructive individual help. The development of acceptance accomplishes three main objectives (Trotzer, 1972).

1. It aids the group in becoming cohesive and connected thus meeting Gendlin and Beebe's (1968) guideline that *closeness must precede unmasking*.
2. It helps each individual feel accepted as a person of worth even though life is not satisfactory at the moment. This meets Gendlin and Beebe's (1968) guide-line of putting *people before purpose*.
3. It releases the potential of peer-group influence to be used in a positive rather than negative manner.

The affective dynamics of the acceptance stage place leaders in somewhat of an emotional quandary as they grapple with their role in the group. As members feel more comfortable and experience a growing sense of camaraderie and belonging, leaders feel a sense of being in between. Issues such as, "Am I part of this group or not part of this group?" and "How much should I be a leader, and how much should I be a person?" emerge to create mixed emotions that pull them into the group and push them out at the same time. Feelings of wanting to be more personal contrast with the desire to maintain an emotional objectivity or detachment.

In the cognitive domain the leader is aware of the need for personally relevant topics and information to be shared and that a total person emphasis needs to be maintained to give the group balance and stability as the relational bonding occurs. Norms are forming which give the group security and predictability, but the leader is responsible for seeing that these norms are dynamic and therapeutic and not forged at the expense of differences.

Behaviorally, the leader notices that self-disclosure increases and that feedback is given on an experimental basis. He or she sees members exhibit the rudiments of helping behaviors and realizes more dramatically the importance of leadership in generating, modeling, and facilitating appropriate group actions. Content of the group interaction addresses the purposes and problems that called the group into existence, and the leader must act to meld the relational and helping dynamics to key the transition to responsibility.

The following are questions leaders must ask and answer at the acceptance stage:

1. What is my relationship as a person and a professional in the group?
2. How can I best assist the bonding process of the group?
3. What norms are forming in the group, and are these norms conducive to therapeutic impact?
4. How does the content being shared relate to the purposes of the group?
5. What can I do to merge the relationship development process and the problem solving process?

As the leader addresses these questions in a framework of developing a group identity and building cohesiveness, the groundwork is laid for movement into the responsibility stage of the group process.

☐ The Responsibility Stage

The third stage of the group counseling process is characterized by a movement on the part of group members from acceptance of self and others to responsibility for self and to others. A subtle but distinct difference exists between acceptance of and responsibility for self. Acceptance helps members realize and admit that problems are a part of their selves. However, acceptance alone leaves members with an avenue of retreat away from working on their problems. Members can say "Yes, that's the way I am" or "All right, that's my problem" but can disclaim any part in its cause or rectification. Acceptance alone allows members to claim no fault and negates any responsibility for doing anything about changing. The inclusion of responsibility, however, moves members toward resolution. The combination of acceptance and responsibility encourages members to state "Yes, that's my problem, and I have to do something about it." The ground is thus made fertile for constructive change to take place.

A divorced mother with two children shared her problems and frustrations in a women's counseling group at a mental health center. Her story exemplifies the difference between acceptance and responsibility. During the fourth group meeting she talked extensively about the pain of her divorce and the subsequent difficulties of trying to raise her children alone. She became very emotional at times, and the group facilitated catharsis in a very sensitive manner. At the end of the session the group leader helped the woman put herself back together emotionally and solicited feedback from the group couched in terms of support. During the following session she was again the focus of attention, but this time members began to suggest alternatives that could possibly help her improve her life. To each alternative she responded by saying, "I already tried that" or "I don't think that would work." After several attempts to get her to consider alternatives failed, one member observed that maybe she really didn't want to do anything different in her life to overcome the problems. The woman denied that but soon afterward asked that the focus of the group attention be directed elsewhere. During the following sessions this woman's situation was brought up several times by herself, other group members, or the leader, but the discussion always stalemated at the point of her taking any responsibility for the problems or for initiating changes. Eventually she told the group that she felt her problems were the result of others being unfair and insensitive to her and that she was a victim and not a cause in her situation. Soon afterward she left the group. She was willing to share her problems in the group but was not able to see herself as a contributor or take the initiative to work toward resolving them.

The issue of responsibility in the group emanates from both our needs as human beings and the nature of the problem solving process. Members can only meet their need for esteem and respect through actions and achievements that require the person to take responsibility. If members feel causes are external they will also feel the cures must come from sources external to themselves and not from their own efforts, resources, and initiatives. Both differentiation and empowerment are critical to the responsibility stage. Members need to differentiate as individuals within the group and experience the sense of empowerment necessary to take ownership and responsibility for themselves and their issues.

Our needs are reflected in the pressure of the counseling group to move on. The social aspect of cohesiveness developed in the acceptance stage wears thin after a while, and a natural tendency is toward getting down to the business of problems. This tendency, according to Bonney (1969), is a mark of group maturity in that group members begin to accept responsibility for the management of the group and exert their energies to the task of problem solving. As members take increased responsibility for themselves and the therapeutic process, their chances for growth within the counseling group improve. In fact, Lindt (1958) found that only those who accepted responsibility in the helping process of the group benefited from their experience.

During the early stages of the group process the task is to develop trust and acceptance by focusing on similarities among members. This process universalizes. It helps members recognize that their problems are experienced by others (universality), even though individual differences are apparent (Dinkmeyer & Muro, 1979; Yalom, 1995). During the responsibility stage the focus changes to individualization and differentiation based on each person's uniqueness and responsibility. The atmosphere of the group provides for considerable personal freedom with the implication that members have permission to 1) explore their weaknesses, strengths, and potentialities; 2) determine a way of working on problems; and 3) express feelings. The here and now emphasis is a key component in the responsibility stage, but it takes on a broader, problem oriented perspective. During the early stages of the group the here and now is directed to present feelings about the group and one's part in it. At this point, however, the focus expands to the individual lives of the members and helps them to focus on their here and now problems outside the group as well. This can be done in a step by step process in which expression of feelings is the starting point. The expression of personal feelings and perceptions about one's self and others is one basis for learning responsibility in the group. To emphasize taking responsibility for what one thinks and feels, leaders can ask members to state their own perceptions or feelings and to tack on the statement "and I take responsibility for that." In this manner members learn to take responsibility for expressing anger and caring and can offer constructive criticism without the threat and risk usually associated with the expression of such feelings or observations.

As the members learn to accept responsibility for their personal feelings and perceptions, accepting responsibility for their actions, and eventually their problems, becomes easier. These steps must be taken if the counselor and the group are to have any significant impact on the individual member's life. Mahler (1969) emphasized the importance of responsibility for oneself: "Counselees must realize the importance of being responsible for their own lives, behavior, and actions, making their own decisions and learning to stand on their own perceptions" (p. 140). He added that, "People need opportunities to learn that only by taking actions, making decisions, and accepting responsibility for their own lives can they become adults in the full sense of the word" (p. 141). Group counseling gives them that opportunity.

The leader's role during this stage centers around helping members realize self-responsibility. Lakin (1969) and Glasser (1965) stressed the modeling nature of the leader role in which the counselor's actions must depict the proper attitude toward responsibility. Glasser felt that responsibility can only be learned through involvement with responsible people. Therefore the member's primary example to follow in the group is the leader. At this point the leader must help members maintain a focus on themselves and their problems rather than on events, people, or situations external to the group and beyond its influence. The counseling group can only affect people and situations through its effect on the person in the immediate presence of the group. The counselor must stress an internal frame of reference rather than an external one. The question that ultimately must be faced is not "What can others do?" but "What can I do?"

The leader faces a crucial issue during the responsibility stage, and a word of caution is apropos. In our concern for our clients to make it on their own, we often see opportunities in the group process that could be used to *make* members be responsible. This situation must be handled carefully. For group members to become responsible they must experience responsibility, not be told about it or forced into it. At times the issue of responsibility can be appropriately brought up and addressed as a topic in a teachable moment. At other times confrontation may need to be used with members who have not recognized their responsibilities. Regardless of other actions, the choice to be responsible is best left to members. Mahler (1969) went so far as to state that "counselors who teach in group counseling violate the concept that basic responsibility for management of one's own life is up to the individual" (p. 103). Therefore leadership should be directed toward helping members feel accepted and responsible without domination. When successful, members will feel a more personal, individual responsibility, experience empowerment, and exhibit less dependency.

The responsibility stage sets the tone for the remainder of the group counseling process. Once members realize their responsibility for themselves and understand that while the leader and the group will hold them accountable neither will infringe upon this responsibility, members can direct their entire attention to problem solving. The responsibility stage affirms the inherent worth of members, assures them of respect as human beings, and points out qualities necessary to enhance self-worth and resolve problems. Those qualities are self-assessment, congruence, honesty, responsibility, and commitment. When the members willingly engage in the introspective process, self-disclose, demonstrate their acceptance of others and willingness to help others, and—with very little or no help from the leader—take responsibility, the work stage of the counseling process is imminent.

The affective dimension of leadership experience is a useful gauge reflecting the process dynamics in the responsibility stage. As members struggle emotionally with responsibility and commitment the leader experiences a greater sense of clarity as to his or her role in the group. A sense of confidence evolves that facilitates ease of movement as a leader and enables him or her to be resourceful and maneuver effectively using a variety of appropriate roles. Leaders begin to trust their intuitions and impulses in this particular group and feel more capable in the leadership position.

In the cognitive domain, the leader consciously shifts focus from a "forest-trees" point of view to a "trees-forest" perspective. Whereas, in the earlier stages leader emphasis is given to context (forming the group out of individual components), the focus now changes to components (differentiating individuals in the group context). The uniqueness of each person and each person's role becomes important and the goal evolves from giving members an "I belong" experience to giving them an "I contribute" experience as they transition from being part of to taking part in the group.

Leaders also notice significant behavior changes in the group. Members begin to use more "I" language increasing their reliance on and utilization of first and second person pronouns rather than third person referents in their interaction with each other. Concreteness increases in member disclosures. Members are more prone to describe their actions in specific terms rather than using general descriptions, jargon, or colloquial aphorisms. Finally, more confrontations begin to arise drawing the leader into a mediating role.

While the responsibility stage is the most difficult to delineate as a stage, it is of crucial importance to the group process because of its impact on the group's ability to engage in critical thinking which is so essential to problem solving. Janis (1971; 1972) identified and researched the phenomenon of *groupthink,* a process that cohesive and bonded groups substitute for critical thinking. He stated: "the more amiability and esprit de corps there is among members of a policy-making ingroup, the greater the danger that independent critical thinking will be replaced by groupthink, which is likely to result in irrational and dehumanizing actions directed against outgroups" (p. 44). Applied to the group counseling process, this means that groups that develop through the security and acceptance stages but do not move into responsibility will introduce interactive mechanisms and behaviors that will undermine and subvert critical thinking, distort reality, suppress individuality, and generally detract from therapeutic problem solving. Consequently, leaders must be especially sensitive to danger signals that come not only from individuals (members who resist being responsible for their own lives) but from the group as well.

McClure (1990) characterized groups that stagnate prior to the responsibility stage as *regressive*. These groups put forth a demeanor that creates a harmony illusion. "The group creates a public myth that there are no conflicts or intellectual differences among group members" (p. 161). Furthermore these groups consciously and unconsciously avoid conflict, abdicate responsibility, and experience psychic numbing. These dynamics in turn lead to scapegoating, group narcissism, suppression of divergent thinking, inability to resolve internal group conflict, and self-interest. Subsequently one of the critical channels through which individuation and productive group development occurs—the emergence and resolution of conflict—is stymied.

McRoy and Brown (1996) have stipulated that "conflict in small groups is inevitable, and . . . without conflict development into a productive group may be impaired" (p. 12). They point out that theorists and researchers concur that "groups develop in stages and conflict occurs naturally as the group strives to reach a productive or problem-solving stage" (p. 12). Therefore, one of the traits that may signal the emergence of the responsibility stage is conflict. To respond effectively the leader must be cognizant of the contest between the dynamics of suppression that may emanate from the cohesiveness of the acceptance stage and the growth oriented dynamics of expressiveness that propel the group into the productivity of the work stage.

The following are key leadership questions for the responsibility stage:

1. What can I do to enhance the emergence of each member's individual identity in the group?
2. How can I facilitate individual responsibility for self and problem ownership as a group norm?
3. Is the dual commitment of taking from the group (group as a resource for individual problem solving) and giving to the group (being a resource to other members) emerging?
4. Are the interactions and perspectives emerging in the group in touch with reality in spite of the supportive bonding in the group?
5. What obstacles (resistances) stand in the way of the problem solving process, and how can they be addressed?

As noted, the responsibility stage is the least definitive process-wise, but the most critical progress-wise, so answering these questions will prepare the way for therapeutic work.

☐ The Work Stage

The character of the work stage organizes itself around the individual problems and concerns of group members. As trust, acceptance, and responsibility are experienced and learned, what becomes increasingly evident is that some areas in each member's life are not satisfactory and could benefit from change. When these areas are pinpointed and discussed specifically, the work stage goes into full operation. Vorrath and Brendtro (1974) felt that the core of the group process is reached at this point because the goal of any counseling or therapy group is to work on problems and get them solved.

The work stage of group counseling is exemplified by the interaction of a human relations group designed to improve communication and relationships between racial groups in a large urban high school. The members decided that the basic problem was not knowing how to approach students who were racially different from themselves. They tended to be hesitant, fearing overtones of prejudice or racism might be communicated. To work on this problem, the leader first had racially similar members discuss their perceptions of themselves and racially different groups and then make suggestions that they felt would facilitate better relationships. After each subgroup had discussed their perceptions and made their suggestions, a comprehensive list of suggestions was developed in terms of skills. The leader then formed racially mixed dyads to try out the suggestions. During the work stage, partners were rotated periodically to give members the experience of trying out alternatives and building their skills and confidence with all racial groups represented.

The basic purposes of the work stage are to give group members the opportunity to 1) examine personal problems and issues closely in an environment free of threat, 2) explore alternatives and suggestions for resolving the problems, and 3) try out new behaviors or attitudes in a safe setting prior to risking changes outside the group (Trotzer, 1972). The energy of the group is concentrated on accomplishing these three purposes through the use of clarification, feedback, support, encouragement, information giving, skills training (Gazda and Brooks, 1985), strategic planning, and in vivo practice. Once in motion the productivity of the group is quite amazing and at times needs to be held in check because of the tendency to begin to solve problems before they are fully understood.

The leader role in the work stage is extremely vital from two perspectives. Leaders must be both facilitator and expert. They must be able to facilitate the discussion of problems, bringing out as many facets as possible, and create an atmosphere where alternatives can be suggested. These two processes entail mustering the total perceptual and experiential resources of the group. After a particular problem has been discussed and alternative solutions suggested, leaders must use their expertise to provide vehicles for examining the consequences of the suggestions as a means of aiding the decision making process. These activities can take the form of role playing, sociodramas, communication exercises, or discussion. In this way alternatives can be assessed and evaluated, thus avoiding shot-in-the-dark failures. This type of reality testing in the group provides the group member with an idea of both the feasibility of a specific alternative and the effort involved in using it to resolve the problem. It also provides the member with an opportunity to develop self-confidence before attempting to make any specific changes in the more threatening world outside the group.

Another important facet of the group process that surfaces during the work stage is the dual role of the group member as both the helper and the helped. When any one member of the group is working on a particular problem, the other members provide help through their feedback, sharing, suggestions, discussion, and participation in group activities. The experience of being in the helper role increases members' feelings of self-worth because now they are in the position of giving rather than receiving. The ancient oriental proverb that says "The best way to help a person is to let him or her help you" captures the impact of the helper role in groups. The giving of assistance to others raises ones self-esteem and also produces a more congenial attitude toward receiving assistance from others. The two way process of helping and being helped is thus established. This process makes good use of members' altruistic tendencies and allows them to engage in *spectator therapy* where they benefit from watching others work out their problems.

During this stage the group also represents *society in microcosm* (Gazda, 1968); that is, group members represent, as best they can, the forces, attitudes, reactions, and ideas of the world outside the group. Through the process of feedback the group helps each member develop realistic alternatives to problems that can reasonably be applied in their lives outside the group. This mini-society, laboratory function is important because of its transitional value in preparing members for the task of implementing changes. The greater the approximation of societal or community reality, the greater the probability of effective change or resolution.

In the work stage the *healing capacity* (Rogers, 1967) of the group emerges, and the specific goals and objectives of the counseling group are dealt with. Each group has different objectives based on the diversity of the group membership and the setting in which the group is formed. However, since most counseling groups are usually organized to deal with specific problems, this point in the group process is where efforts are focused on resolving them. The work stage prepares members for reentry into the world where they are experiencing their problems. They are armed with a well-conceived and evaluated plan, and self-confidence has been shored up through practice and personal encouragement. However, individuals do not have to make the changes and implement their plans without some support which the group provides until such time as termination is appropriate.

The approach-avoidance dynamics of initiating change and resisting change that emerge in the work stage can be emotionally draining. Leaders often experience this stage as a combination of excitement and frustration. As members mobilize around the motivation provided by their need to actualize their potential, they run smack into resistances that hinder their growth and development. Their resulting frustration may be shared by the leader who has become personally attached in some degree to each group member and the process of problem solving each person is experiencing. When added to the leader's professional commitment to being personally effective, a sense of challenge may emerge that entices leaders to overstep boundaries of responsibility and try to do too much for their clients. This emotional bonding is indicative of effective process dynamics, but must be kept in balance by parallel dynamics in the cognitive domain.

Leaders are cognitively aware that the norm of problem solving is operationalized and must keep in mind the parameters that will most effectively ensure that both the process and product are personally relevant to each group member. So, while being emotionally supportive, leaders must actively remind themselves of their role in being a reality check to the group process and its members. In addition, maintaining a clear conceptual perspective of the fundamentals of effective problem solving is essential. This awareness produces leader behavior that facilitates helper-helpee role reciprocity in group members and enables the leader to act as a resource in problem solving. Behaviors that present the process expertise of the leader emerge as he or she provides tools and vehicles (e.g., initiates activities such as role playing) to help group members address their problems.

The more capable leaders are of monitoring their own affect, cognition, and behavior, and the more successful they are in maintaining a balance between support for and perception of group members, the more effective their actions will be in the work stage. Following are questions that help leaders apprize their role at this stage:

1. What is my relationship to each group member? (How do I see each person and the problem(s) each is addressing?)
2. What resources do I have that can be mobilized to guide, direct and assist the problem solving process?
3. How can I most effectively carry out my role with respect to the relationship between group process and social reality?
4. How can I most effectively mobilize group resources in doing therapeutic work?

As each of these questions are answered, the resulting success in problem solving will naturally raise the issue of termination for individual members and/or the group as a whole.

☐ The Closing Stage

The final stage of the group counseling process is mainly supportive in nature and is characterized by feedback, encouragement, perseverance, accountability, and acknowledgement. Although group members may successfully work through their problems within the group, they still face the difficult task of modifying their behavior and attitudes outside the group. The expectations of significant others outside the group are still based on past experience with the group member, thus making it difficult to give encouragement or reinforcement to the member for acting in new or different ways. The group is a place where members can share their frustrations, successes, and failures and also reassess their actions for possible changes that will increase their effectiveness. Without a source of support, the potential for regression to old ways is greater.

The group also serves as a motivator. Part of this function entails rejecting excuses and confronting members with their own lack of commitment and effort if need be. Sometimes members need to be pushed out into the real world when they cannot venture forth on their own. The group has uncanny competence in assessing whether members are authentic in their efforts and whether they have performed up to their capability. During this stage the group can provide both a sounding board function and an accountability function.

Group support facilitates the integration of change into the client's life. Efforts to change and the change process itself are supported until internalization of change takes place individually and reinforcement occurs in members' lives outside the group. As changes become a more natural part of their lifestyles, the difficulty of adapting new behaviors, feelings, and attitudes decreases. The support of the group is only necessary until the balance between ease and difficulty in implementing change swings to the ease side of the scale.

The focus of the group thus turns to members' behaviors and experiences outside the group and deals with the progress they are making. The leader helps members discuss their experiences and feelings and offers support, understanding, and encouragement. The leader also helps members begin to take credit for their own changes instead of giving credit to the group or the counselor. In this way the individual members can integrate their new behaviors and attitudes into their everyday lives and can feel reinforcement from within themselves rather than from the group.

The closing stage for individuals may take many different forms. For example, a student who had been a member of a therapy group at a college counseling center for three years began to miss group meetings, showing up periodically but with longer time lapses between attendance. As he entered the final semester of his senior year, he relied less and less on the group for feedback and support and took more and more responsibility for himself. His need for the group and his involvement in the group lessened, with termination coinciding with graduation.

Another example of the closing stage is the standard procedure used at an alcohol treatment center when individual patients are preparing to leave treatment. The patient's group holds a graduation ceremony for the departing member during which that person makes a commencement address reviewing and summarizing their treatment and describing goals and objectives for the future. The group then engages in a serenity prayer during which group members give support, feedback, and encouragement to the graduating member. The person is then presented with a coin that has a missing piece symbolizing the unending process involved in rehabilitation and growth. The ceremony thus serves to summarize and reinforce changes that have occurred but also prepares the person for the rigors of adjusting to life outside the treatment center.

The point at which a group or individual member should terminate is sometimes difficult to determine. For this reason groups are often terminated on the basis of a preset time schedule, for example, after 10 sessions or at the end of a semester. However, ending a group is also appropriate when group members experience more success than frustration in solving their problems and feel intrinsic rather than extrinsic reinforcement for their actions in doing so. As members become more autonomous, they lose their dependence on the group. As they resolve their problems and learn how to solve problems, they no longer need the group. When any of these situations occur the group has run its course and should be disbanded.

The leader's affective experience of the closing stage typically includes ambivalence. Personally, a certain amount of over-involvement may have occurred that mitigates against members terminating. Professionally, the realization that the effort expended to make this group work will have to be repeated with another group may produce feelings of resistance relative to closure. The natural inclination to desire affirmation as a person and professional may produce feelings of incompleteness or even insecurity if such feedback is not forthcoming. Consequently, for leaders to have emotional approach-avoidance tussles with respect to closing is not unusual.

Cognitively, the purposes of termination are quite clear:

1. to translate closing into commencement;
2. to continue the impetus of the change process beyond the life of the group;
3. to ensure that closure does not disrupt or undermine growth or generate regression;
4. to provide a therapeutic exodus from the group for each participant, including the leader; and
5. to enable group members to assume credit and responsibility for their own changes.

These purposes can be addressed through behaviors that incorporate a process and product review regarding the history of the group and each of its members. Using self-disclosure and feedback tools, specific marker events, successes, failures, and the nature of the experience can be shared. Looking ahead to future goals and anticipating potential predicaments is also common in the closing stage. Sometimes members, out of a sense of nostalgia or simply to hang on, will manufacture problems or recycle old problems to keep the group going. This tends to be rather short lived, however, since the momentum to get on with life already has set the disbanding process in motion. Celebratory and symbolic termination gestures reflecting individual personalities and the group milieu emerge enabling members and leader(s) to say goodbye.

The following are questions leaders need to address in the closing stage of the group process:

1. How can I assist members in detaching and/or the group in disbanding in a therapeutic manner?
2. What is the degree of my investment in the group and what do I need to do to detach effectively?
3. How can I facilitate closing so that it preserves progress and serves as a commencement to continued growth?
4. What resistances to closing are evident, and how can they be reframed into initiatives for ending?

With termination, the history of the group as an entity is complete. However, the impact of the group may carry beyond the life of the group itself involving the leader in individual member's lives either by choice (follow-up) or circumstance. Either way, the closing stage may include some spillover dynamics that will persist even though for all intents and purposes, the group officially ends with the last meeting.

☐ A Precautionary Note

Viewing group counseling as a developmental sequence of a set number of stages raises the possibility of unnecessary and undesirable rigidity in conceptualizing the group process. To circumvent this and maintain flexibility in this group model, it is necessary to remember that within each stage there can be many levels. Different degrees of trust, acceptance, and responsibility are reached by the group and its members at different times. Some problems discussed in the group require less trust than others. At other times recycling the process may be necessary to develop deeper levels of trust, acceptance, or responsibility in order to deal with a particular problem. Bonney (1969) labeled this phenomena *retransition* referring to the tendency of groups to go back through the early phases of group development before proceeding to a deeper level. At any one time and with any one problem or person the group may have to retreat to a previous stage before it can move to the next one. In fact, all stages may recur several times before the group has run its course.

The recycling of stages is particularly evident in open ended groups where individual members terminate and other members join, all in the course of the ongoing group life. Each exit and entrance sets off dynamics that are the impetus for recycling elements of earlier group stages so as to reform the group into a therapeutic entity consisting of the current participants.

Another consideration is that components of two or more stages may be prominent in the group at the same time. The group may be learning trust, acceptance, and responsibility while working on a particular problem. The group does not develop in a lock-step manner even though general trends can be noted and specific characteristics consistently appear at certain points in the group's development. Neither can the group process be forced to conform to an external standard or model. Rather, it is a responsive and flexible process that is influenced by the leader's personality, differences between people and their problems, and variations in the rate at which different people develop relationships and work out individual change.

☐ Concluding Comments

Group counseling brings into perspective the relationship between psychological needs and the socialization process, whereby human learning and problem solving occur through interpersonal interaction. It accentuates the social learning process by focusing on the dynamics of the group itself rather than on some environmental context. Group members are given the opportunity to learn how they function individually and socially. They can do this because the leader and other members have created a climate or atmosphere characterized by psychological safety and acceptance where they can take responsibility for their own lives. In such a situation members can experience the healthy attributes of individuality or uniqueness and re-latedness or conformity. They learn both autonomy and interdependence.

Members can express themselves freely and engage in open and honest interaction with other members without the fear of rejection or reprisal that so often tempers interaction in one's environment. Within the group, members can experience and learn responsibility. They can confront prob-lems openly, knowing they will obtain support and assistance as needed. Members experience the interchanging role of being the helper and the helped as they work on their own problems and assist others with theirs. The member can discover and evaluate alternative solutions to personal concerns while at the same time building self-confidence and personal se-curity, that serve as enabling factors in implementing change outside the group. Thus group counseling provides both a setting and a process whereby the basic objectives of counseling and therapy can be attained.

☐ Learning Activities

Activities presented here are organized in sequence to relate to the stages of group development discussed in this chapter. Although the primary characteristic and use of each activity is stage related, each can be used for many other purposes. These activities are versatile and adaptable, depending on the leader's approach and the nature of the group.

Trust Ring

Option 1

This activity is useful in demonstrating the characteristics of trust and con-fidentiality that are necessary for a group to work effectively. Have all group members stand in a circle in an area that is free of material objects such as chairs or tables. Have group members join hands strongly gripping the hand or wrist of the persons standing beside them. Members should have a strong grip on each of their partners' hands or wrists. Then have the group extend out as far as possible forming a taut circle. Instruct all members to lean back exerting pressure on the circle and slowly move their feet toward the center of the circle creating a centrifugal pressure on the group. Have the group move in a clockwise direction maintaining this centrifugal pressure. After a few moments reverse the direction. Follow the activity with a discussion of each person's reaction in terms of the amount of pressure he or she was personally willing to place on the group and feelings regarding his or her partners and the total group. Stress the importance of the whole group going to the aid of individuals who were slipping in order to protect them and maintain solidarity in the group. Discussion also can focus on the amount of pressure the group as a whole exerted relating it to risk taking in self-disclosure and feedback.

Option 2

A variation of this exercise is to have members stand in a circle shoulder to shoulder. Instruct members to interlock their arms around the back or waist of the persons beside them. Then have group members lean inward and slowly move their feet away from the center of the group creating a centripetal force on the group. Have the group move alternately in a clockwise and counter clockwise manner. At the conclusion of the exercise have the group members retain their interlocking positions in the circle and discuss the reactions in the same manner as described in Option 1. An added feature of this discussion can be the impact of closeness created by the "arms around each other" dimension, relating it to the effect of warmth and closeness in developing cohesiveness and trust in the group.

The Trust Ring exercises of Options 1 and 2 were developed by Jim Ross and demonstrated in my group counseling class at the University of Wisconsin-River Falls.

Closed Fist

This activity lends itself to a consideration of strategies used by people in negotiating trust in human relationships. It is particularly applicable to group counseling because of the risk intrinsic to the process of sharing. Break the group down into dyads. Ask partners to exchange some material object that they value (such as a ring, a picture, or a wallet). Have each partner put the object away out of sight for the time being. Then instruct members to think of something that is extremely valuable to them, something they would not wish to give up under any circumstances. This may be a material object or a conceptual object. Give the group a few moments to choose something. Then ask one of the partners to figuratively place the visualized item of value in a closed fist without telling their partner what it is. Instruct the other partner to try to get it. Allow this process to proceed for a time without any intervention. Then ask for an account of what happened, noting the different strategies that were used to obtain the object and pointing out their relevance to the group process. After this discussion ask members to negotiate retrieval of the actual objects they exchanged initially.

Important factors to consider in this activity are the type of exchange strategies that produce competitiveness, cooperation, ill will, intimidation, and positive interpersonal feelings. Strategies that are conducive to positive relationships should be used in the group. Also, note that the value of the objects exchanged reflects the amount of commitment and trust in the relationship. Members will share more willingly and at a deeper level if other members share reciprocally.

This exercise was demonstrated by Dr. Dan Ficek in a Human Relations Workshop he and I led in Red Wing, Minnesota.

Life Story

Vorrath & Brendtro (1974) used this technique to introduce new members into the group. It is especially appropriate for ongoing counseling groups that experience member turnover. New members after a brief period of time in the group are asked to tell their life stories as completely and as accurately as they possibly can. The life stories should include a description of problems that brought the new people into the group. The other group members have the responsibility of facilitating the new member's efforts. Under no circumstances should views of the person be challenged at this point. After the story is completed the group can begin to work with discrepancies or other factors that might relate to examining and resolving the member's problems. The main impact of this technique is that members realize their side of the story is going to be heard first. They receive guarantees that their frame of reference is important and will be considered by the group. They experience acceptance and find the group is a safe place to air their problems.

Poem of Self

This activity helps establish a minimum level of self-acceptance for each group member and helps the group become involved in introspection and self-disclosure essential to the group process. Use the following directions in carrying out the exercise.

1. List four adjectives that describe what you look like.
2. List four adjectives that describe what you act like (personality).
3. List five words ending in "ing" that describe things you like to do (if you like to read, put reading). Words may be created by adding -ing to any word that represents an activity, e.g., tennis-ing.
4. List six things (nouns) that would remind people of you (possessions, such as a guitar, or roles you play, such as a student, for example).
5. List four places you would like to be.
6. On a sheet of paper draw the following diagram or hand out a copy of the diagram.

7. On the first line of the diagram write your full given name.
8. Choose one word from list 1 (what you look like) and one word from list 2 (what you act like) and place them in the blanks on line 2.
9. Choose three words from list 3 (things you like to do) and insert them in the blanks on line 3.
10. Choose four words from list 4 (things that remind people of you) and write them in the blanks on line 4.
11. Choose two words from list 5 (places) and write them in the blanks on line 5.
12. On the bottom line write a nickname or any name by which you are called other than your given name. (This may be a derivative of your given name, such as "Toni" for Antoinette.)

On completion of the poem have each member read his or her poem to the group twice, the first time quickly with rhythm and poetic expression and the second time slowly so that they can catch all the words. After everyone has read and explained the meaning of the words in their poems discuss how the activity contributed to getting to know one another.

Coat of Arms

The coat of arms has more depth to it than the poem of self and can be used in conjunction with it. This activity gets at more varied aspects of each person's life and provides a good beginning for the actual counseling process. It also combines the medium of illustration with verbal description, which makes sharing an easier process. Give each person a sheet of paper with the following diagram on it or have the people draw it. Then have them fill in the numbered sections of the shield according to the following instructions.

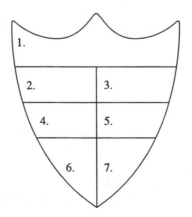

FIGURE 4.2. Personal coat of arms diagram.

1. In the section numbered 1, write a motto or phrase that describes how you feel about life or that is a guide to your life style. (Some people create their own; others use slogans, proverbs, quotations, poems, or Bible verses.)
2. In section 2, draw a picture that represents your greatest achievement or accomplishment (no words).
3. In section 3, draw a picture that represents something other people could do to make you happy (no words).
4. In section 4, draw a picture that represents a past failure or disappointment in your life (no words).
5. In section 5, draw a picture that represents the most significant goal in your life right now (no words).
6. In section 6, draw a picture that represents a problem you would like to work on in this group (no words).
7. In section 7, write three things you would like people to say about you if you died today (or write your epitaph).

After all the members have completed the shield, have each member share it with the group and explain the meaning of each section. This exercise has the positive impact of acceptance since it deals with each person's strengths, weaknesses, goals, relationships with others, and problems. The instructions for the various parts can be changed to meet the demands of the situation and the needs of the members, thus making this activity a flexible and effective tool in the hands of the group leader.

Alternative instructions:

Draw a picture that represents:
- a talent, ability, or gift you have.
- an important person in your life.
- an important decision you have made.
- a special interest, hobby, or recreational pursuit.
- write your pet peeve.

Gestalt Interventions

One of the ways we avoid being responsible for ourselves and in control of our own lives is through the words we use in communication (Stevens, 1971). The following intervention techniques drawn from the Gestalt approach to group therapy can be used to help group members take responsibility for their own thoughts, feelings, and behaviors and ultimately for their problems.

Questions or Statements

Many questions that group members ask are really camouflaged statements. Before responding with an answer, ask the questioner to change the question into a statement that expresses personal perceptions, observations, or feelings.

I Can't/I Won't Statements.

Members often use the words "I can't" in discussing problem situations, that give the impression that control is really outside of themselves. When you hear an "I can't" statement ask the member to repeat the statement using "I won't," to convey the message that the person has a choice in the matter. "I just can't talk to my father" changes to "I just won't talk to my father."

I Have to/I Choose to Statements

Have group members make a list of "I have to" statements describing all the things in their lives they feel they have to do. Have them share their lists in the group. Then have them change "have" to "choose" and discuss the difference such a change makes in their perception of their list. Discussion usually pinpoints quite clearly the issue of personal responsibility and choice. As a group leader you also can ask members to substitute "I choose to" for "I have to" during group discussions. In doing this the members realize that they are responsible, and that they do have a choice.

I Need/I Want Statements

Group members often express desires as needs, creating the impression that severe personal consequences will result if needs are not met. They say "I need" which depicts whatever it is as essential to their well being. To define more accurately what really is and isn't needed, have members change "I need" statements to "I want" statements and discuss which is more appropriate. Incorporate feedback from other members as to the accuracy of the statement.

Strength Bombardment

Otto (1967) first posited the idea that problems could be solved by starting with people's strengths and then focusing on their weaknesses. That premise is particularly relevant to the responsibility stage of group development. One means of helping group members accept responsibility for themselves is to approach it from a perspective of strengths, assets, and accomplishments of which the member is already aware. This activity uses the processes of self-disclosure and feedback to help members take responsibility for their behavior.

First, have each group member develop a list of accomplishments or achievements. Encourage the members to feel completely free about the list and not to think about the reactions of others or about the ego related emotional connotations such a request usually conjures up. Upon completion of the list, have the members write a paragraph, starting with "I am," that describes only their positive qualities. Assure them that no one else will see the paragraph, but indicate that they should include only positive qualities and not put in any negative ones. When the paragraph is completed have members put it away, stating that they can do what they want with it, possibly keeping it tucked away to pull out for a rainy day ego boost. Now have the members share their initial list of accomplishments with the group. Then place two chairs facing each other in the center of the circle. Ask one member to volunteer to take one of the chairs in order to receive positive feedback from the other members. When one person has taken a chair, each other person in turn gets up, sits in the opposite chair and gives the first person only positive feedback. There should be no "I would like you if . . ." or "I like you but . . ." comments, and the person receiving the feedback can only respond with expressions of appreciation, not with denials or counter remarks. This process continues until each person has received positive feedback from every other person in the group. On completion of the activity, relate the experience to the issue of responsibility and discuss how one's positive qualities can be used as resources to help overcome one's negative qualities and problems. This activity is useful as a springboard to the work stage of the group process.

Awareness and Responsibility

This technique was developed out of the Gestalt approach to group therapy and combines the concepts of personal awareness and individual responsibility. It has relevance to group counseling because it clarifies where members are personally and helps them take responsibility for their own thoughts, feelings, and behaviors in the group. Each group member is asked to share with the group thoughts, feelings, and perceptions or observations using the format: "Right now I am aware... (members complete the statement describing what they are aware of), and I take responsibility for that awareness." The last part of the statement is added to get individuals to affirm their own part in feeling, acting, or thinking the way they do and to prevent them from putting responsibility on others. A leader can effectively use the last part of the statement by simply asking members to add it to any statement involving a personal emotion, accusation, interpretation, or perception. In this way, the impact of the statement becomes just one person's frame of reference and allows other members the freedom to respond as they see fit without feeling threatened by the imposition of another person's point of view on them.

Problem Identification and Rating

The work stage is the point in the group process at which problems should be dealt with directly. This activity pinpoints problems that are pertinent to individual members and are relevant to other members' lives as well. Give each member a card to anonymously write a description of a problem he or she would be willing to discuss with the group. Stress the willing to discuss aspect. When the descriptions are finished, read them one by one to the group. After each problem is read, ask members to individually rate it on a 1 to 5 scale (5 is high and 1 is low), showing their interest in discussing the problem, their perception of its seriousness, and their identification with it. Record each individual rating on each card (remember, this is a rating not a ranking). After reading and rating all the problems, add up the total ratings on each card. A hierarchy of problems develops based on the scores. Reread the highest rated problem and ask the person who wrote it to own and describe it in detail. The group can then work with that specific person and problem.

This procedure results in a hierarchical agenda, but if the group is particularly effective in helping the first person, other members may decide to reveal deeper problems with which they want help. The problem agenda and hierarchy should be adhered to only if it is in the best interests of the group. Rigid structuring of the group focus based on the ratings could deter progress if flexibility is not incorporated into the processing.

Behavioral Problem Solving

Many times group members have difficulty resolving their problems because they lack specificity. Have members write down and then briefly describe to the group three personal concerns with which they are struggling. Then have each member select one of his or her concerns and describe it in detail following the four basic behavioral steps:

1. Describe in behavioral terms what you do not like or what is wrong (*problem*).
2. Describe in behavioral terms what you would like to change or how you would like to be (*goal*).
3. Discuss with the group how you might be able to accomplish your goal and develop a strategy for doing so (*plan*).

4. Try out the plan and report back to the group on your progress (*evaluation*).

For the last two steps a contract system (Dustin & George, 1973) is helpful where the group member writes the plan in the form of a contract. He or she signs it in the presence of witnesses which increases the individual's commitment and gives the group a solid basis for follow-up, reinforcement, accountability, encouragement, and evaluation of progress. Some groups use *Goal-Boards* to keep the group cognizant of each person's goal and progress. A check-in system is then used each session to chart the change process.

Go-Round

Good way to begin — tie up loose ends

One of the simplest and yet most versatile and effective exercises that can be used in group counseling is the go-round. As the name implies this technique involves going around the group person by person, giving each a specific opportunity to respond. This technique has many variations and purposes and fits at any stage of group development. For instance, a go-round is a good way to begin a group to find out what everyone is thinking or feeling and to get some cues about how to proceed. A go-round when a group ends gives members the opportunity to say what they have not had a chance to say and is a good way to tie up loose ends. During the group sessions, go-rounds immediately following critical incidents are useful to air feelings and release tension, as well as to move the group on to the next phase of the process.

Feelings Face

This activity is a useful tool for ending an individual group session or an overall group experience. Have group members draw a caricature of a face that represents their feelings about the group experience on an 8 × 11 sheet of paper. On each corner of the paper have members write a different word or phrase describing their experience in the group. When completed, have them fold the corners of the page back so only the face is showing. Instruct the group to mill around the room showing their faces to other members on a one to one basis. Members are to guess what the other person's face is portraying. After guessing, each shares one of the words or phrases written on a corner explaining the reasons for their feelings. When each group member has shared all their corners (four in all), they turn their faces in to the group leader.

  An alternative mode for processing the feelings face is to share the faces and the feelings in the group. The leader also can have each member share the face and feelings with him or her as an exit visa from the group.

Feelings Doodles

A modification of the previous activity is to have members create an eyes closed doodle attempting to portray their feelings. The same format can be used to process the doodle as is described in the Feeling Face activity. Or, the created doodles can be used as a kind of group Rorschach activity. Have members pass their doodles to you as leader without any identification. Show the doodles to the group one at a time and ask for projective feedback responses. Questions like, "What do you see in this doodle?" can be used to elicit input. Once the group has responded to the doodle, the person who drew it can be asked to identify himself or herself and respond to the group's perceptions. Projected feelings as perceived by the group and acknowledged feelings of the person can be discussed as a processing activity.

Appleton and Dykeman (1996) have noted that this activity has cultural relevance when working in groups with Native Americans. The shapes, symbolism, and images facilitate expressiveness and communication from a cultural heritage that has long used and valued symbols.

Process to Practice

☐ Turning Group Dynamics into Form and Function

Developmental psychology's most significant contribution to our knowledge of human beings emanates from the basic premise that by understanding normal functionality, we are able to facilitate and enhance normality as well as accommodate to and correct abnormality. Its methodology entails studing organism change phenomena and identifying sequences of events that constitute normal growth and development over the organism's life cycle. Once clarified these sequences or stages serve as the reference base when any individual unit of the organism is encountered. Consequently, development principles are relevant to any organism or organization that evolves through developmental phases that have sequential and life cycle dimensions. Individuals, relationships, systems, and groups all qualify as being developmental in nature. As we have seen in the previous chapter, the group process is a specific example of the developmental psychology perspective.

☐ Developmental Perspective

Simply understanding the development of a counseling or therapy group is insufficient since the utility of that process only has meaning if transformed into a pragmatic application that helps people change. In other words, process dynamics must be translated into form and function as well as serve as our evaluative criteria for determining if the process is evolving appropriately. This chapter is designed to bridge the gap between process and practice. The developmental concept most relevant to this chapter is that given typical conditions, growth or change in any organism unfolds predictably in a sequence of stages each of which involves certain developmental tasks (Havighurst & Neugarten, 1968). These tasks must be addressed for successful completion of a particular stage to occur and serve as the basis for proceeding to the next stage. These stages are the building blocks of the organism's growth and development. How they are addressed determines how a particular organism will adjust and function. Over time, how these tasks are handled will indicate where the organism will fall on the continuum of normality and whether it will be typical or atypical. The stages of the group process contain such developmental tasks. They are embedded in the interactional dynamics of the ongoing process. The purpose of this chapter is to identify those tasks and demonstrate their relevance to the structure and utility of the group as a therapeutic change agent. Each group stage will be deconstructed in terms of specific developmental tasks. Implications for using the tasks as a basis for structuring the group process will be discussed. The phases of an individual group session which generally reflect process dynamics and developmental tasks in prototypical form will also be described. The chapter will conclude with a set of task related group activities.

Developmental Tasks: Seeds of Form and Function

Every group has a structure that develops and evolves during the course of the group forming and interacting through its life cycle. Landreth (1973) has pointed out that the question is not whether structure exists in groups but rather what kind of structure exists and how it is generated. Impetus for structure emanates from any number of sources alone or in combination.

> Leader personality, training and theoretical orientation, the focus and purpose of the group and the individual and collective nature of the group members all affect group structure. In addition, contemporary group process has been influenced by the evolution of group techniques and activities that are being used as structuring tools to implement and facilitate the group process (Trotzer, 1979, p. 177).

These structural agents, however, require material to respond to for their impact to be realized in the group. That material is supplied by group dynamics of which developmental tasks are an integral part. Each stage of the group process has inherent tasks that depict the sequential nature of the group's development.

A developmental task is an objective, need or responsibility which must be addressed in the group in order to insure therapeutic and constructive progress. As these tasks are dealt with effectively, the result is a stronger foundation for group interaction and an achieved readiness to continue the group process through closure. If inappropriately handled or ignored, these tasks can present obstacles that disrupt the group or become the basis for resistance which is detrimental to group development. Thus effective group interaction is contingent upon a structure which considers the developmental tasks as the group moves through its life cycle. (Trotzer, 1979, pp. 179–80)

The interface between the structuring agents and the developmental tasks creates the actual form of the group and produces the function that the group serves in the lives of its members. The tasks are guideposts to which structural factors can relate in guiding, stimulating, and facilitating the group.

The developmental tasks corresponding to each group stage will now be described. Figure 5.1 graphically depicts the relationship among stages and tasks. A brief summary of each stage will precede explication of its developmental tasks

As described in Chapters 3 and 4 the process of group counseling/therapy is composed of five stages that reflect characteristics of our basic human needs, qualities of therapeutic, interpersonal relationships, and dynamics

Group Process Stages					
	Security	**Acceptance**	**Responsibility**	**Work**	**Closing**
D E V E L O P M E N T A L **T A S K S**	S1. Getting Acquainted S2. Interpersonal Warm-up S3. Setting Boundaries S4. Building Trust A1. Personal Sharing A2. Giving Feedback A3. Building Group Cohesiveness A4. Accepting Self A5. Accepting Others R1. Self-Assessment R2. Recognizing Ownership R3. Building Responsibility R4. Giving Respect R5. Doing a Fair Share W1. Problem Solving W2. Mobilizing Group Resources W3. Reality Testing C1. Giving Support C2. Addressing Unfinished Business C3. Affirming and Confirming Growth C4. Saying Goodbye C5. Follow-Up				

FIGURE 5.1. Group process: Stages and development tasks.

of problem solving. Each stage has certain traits which distinguish it, but its meaning and impact are evident only in terms of the total group process. Although leadership style, techniques, group purpose, and membership vary, these stages tend to emerge and evolve as part and parcel of most group interactions (Trotzer, 1985).

☐ Security Stage

The initial stage of the group process is characterized by feelings of discomfort common to forming interpersonal relationships in a new social environment. Group members are reluctant to interact because their presence in the group is contingent on some recognized purpose that requires personal vulnerability. The purpose of this stage is to develop an atmosphere in which members can relate without hesitancy and where discomfort is alleviated as trust develops. This stage is referred to as the security stage because it must account for each group member's needs for psychological safety and initiate trust which is essential to therapeutic interaction and necessary for members to disclose personal problems.

The developmental tasks of the security stage collectively combine to accomplish the objectives of getting the group started, generating forming dynamics, and laying a foundation of trust which can be broadened and deepened as the group interacts. Four developmental tasks are identified for the security stage.

Task S1: Getting Acquainted

The goal of this task is to help group members make initial contact with one another and exchange basic information about each other. This task is particularly important when convening groups composed of members who do not know each other. Getting acquainted breaks the social ice of new relationships and provides a means by which members can begin to move toward one another in their relationships. It also enables members to begin to find their place in the group and alleviates some of the ambiguity associated with possessing little knowledge of the people with whom the individual member is interacting. As members become acquainted with each other, an important security plank is laid for relationship development between members.

Task S2: Interpersonal Warm-Up

This task relates to the period of time at the beginning of each group session that group members need to warm-up to one another and addresses the interpersonal stiffness that commonly pervades the reconnecting experience in groups. As such, its goal is similar to getting acquainted with more far reaching implications. Group members have social muscles which need to be warmed-up each time the group reconvenes. Group members need to have the time to focus—to move from their lives outside the group to their experience in the group. Interpersonal warm-up enables them to do that. Group participants must be helped to get totally into the group in a way that does not precipitate undue stress and that alleviates the problems of jumping in too fast. Effective interpersonal warm-up allows members to get in touch with themselves, the group, and their confidence in the group and is essential to developing a sense of security.

Task S3: Setting Boundaries

Boundaries or ground rules serve an important security-giving function for members. By establishing guidelines under which the group will operate, members sense limits which remove much ambiguity. Boundaries also help the group members get a grasp on where they are, how they are expected to fit in, and what they can expect. The group environment becomes more predictable and thus more within the member's control. Boundaries also provide a focus for testing—sometimes producing storming dynamics and resistance—which in turn further clarifies the arena of interaction for members. Boundary formation may be addressed in several ways. Leaders may determine the ground rules and inform group members of them during pregroup screening and orientation or during the first group session. Or, leaders may give the group the task of developing the boundaries and ground rules for the group in the first group session. Some leaders use a combination of these two approaches identifying one or two critical boundaries and then relying on the group to flesh out the rest. A final method used most typically in growth, sensitivity, or encounter groups is to convene group interaction and address the task of boundary setting as the need arises. Whether group rules are established by the leader, developed by the group, or invoked as the need arises, they facilitate trust by providing members with concrete guidelines to govern their interaction. They are a form of protection and insurance against personal harm in the group, and they are the seeds from which group norms develop. (See Figure 5.2 for examples of group groundrules.)

Task S4: Building Trust

The goal of this task is to help group members deal with the dynamic of trust in the group. It involves both experiencing and understanding trust as it pertains to interpersonal relationships in the group. Members must confront what is meant by trusting themselves and others and come to

I. Guidelines for Group Members

1. Let others know what your ideas are. What every member has to say is important. Sharing your thoughts and reactions with the group will stimulate other members and will help them to share what they are thinking about.
2. Ask questions. If you have a question or there is something you want to know more about, ask. There is no such thing as a stupid question in this group. Several other members probably want to know the same thing.
3. Don't do all the talking. Others want to participate also and they can't if you take too long to express your ideas.
4. Help other members participate. If someone looks as though he wants to say something but hasn't, encourage him or her to do so. You could say "Joe, you look as though you'd like to say something." Silent members may especially need your support and encouragement to participate verbally. Don't overdo it though. A member doesn't have to talk to be involved in what is going on.
5. Listen carefully to other members. Try to listen so intently that you could repeat what the other member has said to his or her satisfaction. You aren't listening effectively if you are thinking about what you are going to say when you get the chance. Give the other person's ideas a chance and try to understand what he or she is saying. Listen to him or her the way you would want him or her to listen to you.
6. Group members are here to help. Problems can be solved by working cooperatively together. In the process of helping others, you can help yourself. The information you have can be helpful to others. Suggesting alternatives or causes can help other members to make better decisions.
7. Be willing to accept another point of view. Don't insist that you are right and everyone else is wrong. The other person just might be thinking the same thing. Try to help other members understand you rather than trying to make them understand.
8. Keep up with the discussion. If the discussion is confusing to you, say so.
9. In this group it is okay to talk about your feelings and reactions.

From "Group Counseling: To Structure or Not to Structure," G. L. Landreth, *The School Counselor* (1973). Reprinted by permission.

II. Ground Rules for Group Sessions

1. Everyone who is here belongs here because he or she is here, and for no other reason. (This is our top rule. It depends on nothing else. Nothing changes it.)
2. For each person what is true is determined by what is in him or her, what he or she directly feels and finds making sense in him or herself and the way he or she lives inside him or herself.
3. Our first purpose is to make contact with each other; everything else we might want or need comes second.

Figure 5.2. Guidelines and ground rules.

4. We try to be as honest as possible and to express ourselves as we really are and really feel just as much as we can.
5. We listen for the person living and feeling inside.
6. We listen to everyone.
7. The group leader is responsible for two things only: he or she protects the belonging of every member, and he or she protects their being heard if that is getting lost.
8. Realism: if we know things are a certain way, we do not pretend they are not that way.
9. What we say here is confidential; no one will repeat anything said here outside the group, unless it concerns only him or herself. This applies not just to obviously private things but to everything. After all, if the individual wants others to know something, he or she can always tell them him or herself.
10. Decisions made by the group need everyone taking part in some way.
11. New members become members because they walk in and remain. Whoever is here belongs.

From "An Experiential Approach to Group Therapy," E. T. Gendlin and J. Beebe, III. *Journal of Research and Development In Education* (1968). Reprinted by permission.

III. How to Get the Most Out of Group

1. No matter how hard it may be for you, participate. You cannot make progress unless you get involved and allow yourself to experience your true feelings and reactions to others in the group. Question, challenge, say what you feel. Try to be as open and honest with yourself and others as you possibly can.
2. Make the group part of your life. In other words, don't think of group as something that happens one day and then forget about it until the next day. After the group session, think over what happened. What feelings did you feel when you talked about yourself? You may feel depressed or happy after group. Try to figure out why you are feeling this way. Take a few minutes to write these things down. Discuss it next group.
3. You are not in group to be tactful or popular. Be yourself whatever that takes. Show the group all sides of your personality.
4. Don't wait for a golden opportunity before you start talking or getting into your feelings. Make your own openings. Likewise, if you feel bored and think that the person who holds the floor is going nowhere, tell him or her so!
5. This is your group. If it is not moving in the direction you would like it to move, say so!
6. Try to move into areas that are emotionally uncomfortable to you, both inside and outside the group. You grow in your treatment only by going beyond the limits you have set for yourself in the past.
7. Experiment in and outside the group with new forms of behavior. Unless you start to act differently and take some risks, you will not change!

Figure 5.2. Guidelines and ground rules (*Continued*).

IV. Therapy Group Ground Rules

1. *Confidentiality*: Everything shared and discussed in group remains in the group. Do not discuss content, observation, or reactions outside the group. Any discussion outside the group should pertain only to yourself. All other discussions outside the group are breaches of confidentiality.

2. *Contact Between Group Members*: There is to be no contact in person or by telephone (or other electronic communication device, e.g., e-mail, voice mail or FAX) between members outside the group. Any inadvertent or informal or formal contact must be reported to the group.

3. *Purpose of the Group*: Each person has been selected and invited to be a member of this group because he or she has both assets and issues. The intent of the group is to work on your issues and use your assets to help yourself and each other.

4. *Content of the Group*: Issues and content that brought you into this group may derive from the past, present, or future of your life, but will be addressed in a here and now context for the purpose of resolution, personal empowerment, and growth.

5. *Group Attendance*: Members must commit to a minimum of 10 sessions and must make every effort to attend each session. In the event of an emergency that interferes with attendance, please call to inform the leader of your absence.

6. *Charge for the Group*: The charge for each group session is $____. You may pay in advance or at each group session. Place your check or cash (clipped with your name) into the envelop that will be passed at the beginning of each session. No group time will be used to collect fees.

7. *Group Time Frame*: Each group session will be one and one-half hour (90 minutes) in length beginning at _____ and ending at _____ on _____ evenings. Please plan to arrive a few minutes early so the group can begin promptly.

8. *Responsibility of Group Members*: It is the responsibility of each group member to participate in the group on the basis of awareness in the following areas:
   a. Awareness of what you bring with you to the group.
   b. Awareness of what is going on in you while in the group.
   c. Awareness of what is going on with each group member as they share in the group; and
   d. Awareness of what is going on in the group.
   Participation is primarily through the vehicles of self-disclosure (personal sharing) and giving feedback.

9. *Commitment of the Group Members*: Each member is committed to interact as openly and honestly as possible in a context where each person's dignity, worth, and personal boundaries are respected.

I have read the above ground rules and agree to them as the basis for my participation in this therapy group conducted by (*leader's name*).
Signature_____

Figure 5.2. Guidelines and ground rules (*Continued*).

grips with where they are as both trusting and trustworthy individuals within the group. Members need to realize and be open to the developmental nature of trust as the foundation upon which risk taking in the group is based. Trust building, once initiated, is an ongoing task that, by necessity, must be continually responded to if the group is to develop an indepth personal quality to its interaction.

☐ Acceptance Stage

The acceptance stage of the group process focuses on the development of group cohesiveness which is an outgrowth of our psychological need to belong. Caring and being cared about are essential therapeutic qualities in this stage because members need to experience acceptance as a total person before they are willing to disclose those parts of themselves that require change. As group cohesiveness develops, a supportive milieu is formed in which the norm of personal sharing is reinforced and where disclosing problems is an integral part of a total person perspective. The tasks associated with the acceptance stage are directed toward pulling the group together as a unit in which communication channels are opened and where members are experiencing belongingness, warmth and acceptance.

Task A1: Personal Sharing

The goal of this task is to establish self-disclosure as one of the primary means of interacting in the group. Personal sharing involves learning the skill of self-disclosing and the presentation of self as a total person including problem areas. Individuals make choices that begin the process of letting the group know who they are. The information shared is that which they are in control of and generally involves some risk taking. Luft (1970) refers to this information as the *hidden* area of the person that in a relational context is subject only to that person's recall and choice relative to disclosure. This task is essential because it provides the main communication channel by which the group can come to know and understand its members. It is also the major means available to members to let others know who they are. Personal sharing is progressive in nature because the degree of self-disclosure increases within the context of group interaction—provided conditions are supportive. Personal sharing opens the door for potential connectedness and closeness in the group, and paves the way for personal vulnerabilities and resources to emerge.

Task A2: Giving Feedback

The task of giving feedback is essential to the group process because it provides the communication channel whereby members can disclose their perceptions and observations about each other. It is also crucial to problem solving in the group context. Members need to learn the skill and precautions of giving feedback (see Figure 2.1). Feedback is a means of increasing members' awareness and self-knowledge in that it taps into what Luft (1970) referred to as the *blind* area—things others know about us that we do not know. Like personal sharing, giving feedback involves risk taking and is progressive in nature as facilitated by conditions in the group. Giving feedback provides another major channel of communication in the group that is necessary for an atmosphere of a therapeutic nature to be realized and the group's resources to be mobilized in a helping manner.

Task A3: Building Cohesiveness and Closeness

This task develops a positive relationship between group members by harnessing the power of peer influence to generate group cohesiveness. The goal is to achieve togetherness and identification with the group thus providing members with a sense of belongingness. It is based on helping members recognize similarities and common characteristics and falls in line with Gendlin and Beebe's (1968) concept that closeness must precede unmasking. It is intended to help the group realize their connectedness and experience working together under the common bond of their group experience.

Task A4: Learning to Accept Self

The main point of this task is to help group members learn to accept themselves more readily through expression of their identity and characteristics in an atmosphere of support. As group members experience the acceptance of the group, they become more cognizant of their own selves and their own needs to accept themselves. This results in a greater feeling of self-confidence and self-worth and provides a stimulus to treat others in a like manner. It also makes members more open to looking at those aspects of self that are not as desirable with the intention of initiating a serious effort toward change.

Task A5: Learning to Accept Others

This task is important to the development of sensitivity among group members. Through the process of supportive listening, observing leader and member acceptance models, and risking one's own self through self-disclosure, members find their own feelings of worth are enhanced because others treasure and desire their acceptance. As members risk being open to and accepting other members who are different from themselves, they realize the value of difference and diversity and the merit of differentiation.

In reality, these last two tasks are reciprocal in nature. Either can be the initial thrust but once in motion, the two become self-perpetuating. Therefore, groups often move quickly to a cohesive state once these two tasks have been addressed.

☐ Responsibility Stage

The responsibility stage of the group process emerges from our psychological need for esteem (respect) which is acquired through responsible individual action and experiences in therapeutic relationships where individuals are perceived as worthwhile. Members move from an emphasis on acceptance of self and others to evaluating self and others in terms of ownership of behaviors, feelings, and thoughts and taking responsibility for one's own part in them. The problem solving process is contingent on individuals recognizing responsibility for their problems and group members making a commitment to help each other work on them. As this occurs, the group moves into the working phase of the group process.

The responsibility stage tasks seek to generate individual commitment to the group in terms of willingness to be accountable for one's own behavior and to contribute responsibly to the group process.

Task R1: Self-Assessment

The focus of this task is to give members an opportunity to engage in self-evaluation as a means of identifying their own uniqueness. The thrust of self-assessment is to focus on individualization and differentiation between members to get members to view responsibility from an internal perspective. Members must realize that looking at oneself realistically is essential and that engaging in constructive self-criticism is healthy. In doing so, the foundation for responsible action is laid.

Task R2: Recognizing Ownership

Part of being responsible for self includes taking ownership of thoughts, feelings, and behaviors. The goal of this task is to help members adopt an internal frame of reference with respect to claiming their own actions. This is especially important in group problem solving because if members do not perceive themselves as contributors to their concerns and problems, they will not view themselves as responsible for changing to resolve them. If causes are viewed as external (someone else's fault), then cures will be perceived in the same manner.

Task R3: Experiencing and Building Responsibility

The main purpose of this task is to help members engage in actions that make them take the initiative in being responsible as opposed to just telling them to be responsible. Since responsibility is so closely tied to self-worth, this task purports to enhance self-worth by helping members put them-selves directly on the line relative to their interaction in and out of the group.

Task R4: Giving Respect

This task presents a balance to the self-oriented thrust of the responsibility stage. It is important as a means of checking the tendency of the group to encourage individuals to do their own thing even to the detriment of others. Giving respect entails recognizing other people's needs and rights in the process of attempting to meet one's own needs and claim one's own rights. This task asserts that mutual respect is an essential entity if different individuals are to grow in different directions with each other's help. Glasser (1965) has noted that the mark of a responsible person is being able to meet one's needs without depriving others of meeting their needs. This task assists members in their growth toward being responsible people.

Task R5: Doing a Fair Share

The goal of this task is to attain and actualize a commitment from indi-vidual members to help one another by serving as a constructive resource when another member is working on a problem or concern. This task also provides a balancing effect that enables group members to continue to contribute their fair share to the therapeutic endeavors of others regardless of their own status at the time. This task has special impact because it teaches interdependency and helps members realize a necessary balance between self-interest and social responsibility.

☐ Work Stage

The purposes for which the group was formed and the relevance of the group to individual members emerge as focal points in the work stage of the group process. The atmosphere and relationships in the group are such that individuals can examine personal concerns without fear of reprisal or rejection, explore alternatives for resolving problems, and experiment with new behaviors in a safe environment prior to risking changes in the outside world. Members participate in the interaction as both helpers and helpees and have the opportunity to engage in spectator therapy as they observe other members working on concerns that may be similar to their own. The leader, as both expert and facilitator, contributes to the process by encouraging members to be resources to persons working on their problems and by keeping the group in touch with reality. The work stage prepares group members for reentry into the world outside the group by arming them with well thought through plans, plausible skills or behaviors, and bolstered self-confidence. Emphasis is on implementation and integration of change, but not without the continued support of the group.

The primary purpose of the tasks in the work stage is to put the group to work on the collective and individual issues that brought the group into being.

Task W1: Problem Solving

The major goal of this task is to help members learn and experience the problem solving process. This process includes:

1. identifying, clarifying, and understanding the problem;
2. generating alternatives to resolving the problem (divergent thought processes, creative thinking, and brainstorming);
3. evaluating alternatives (convergent thought processes, critical thinking, and reality testing);
4. decision making (choosing a viable alternative);
5. planning (developing a strategy for implementation);
6. practice (trying out new behaviors in the social laboratory of the group);
7. implementing (introducing changes into the world outside the group and reporting results and experiences to the group); and
8. evaluating (determining if changes have resolved the presenting problem).

Task W2: Mobilizing Group Resources

The ultimate effectiveness of a group is determined by the extent to which resources of that group are utilized to achieve the best possible solution relative to individual needs and problems. The purpose of this task is to facilitate the helper role of group members and make good use of their resources that encompass a broad range of life experiences, diversity, knowledge, and skills. Mobilizing group resources extends the helping potential of the group and is a means of enhancing the self-esteem of group members who realize their own value through giving assistance to others.

Task W3: Reality Testing

The goal of this task is to make sure that the group engages in interaction that results in a realistic understanding of problems and their solutions. The importance of this task is tied to the fact that members must function effectively outside the group. Therefore, to promote the mental health of members and to increase the probability of constructive change occurring in their lives, the group must act responsibly in terms of providing realistic feedback, alternatives, and information. If group members do not embrace this responsibility, they are acting in a manner detrimental to the therapeutic process.

☐ Closing Stage

Since the overriding objective of any therapeutic group experience is ultimately to dissolve the group by resolving the presenting concerns for which the group was organized, the closing stage serves a valuable transitional function. It is characterized by members actively pursuing change in their lives outside the group while still experiencing the support, encouragement, and accountability of the group. The members use the group as a sounding board and the group acts as a reinforcing and motivating agent. Once the individual has begun to experience success, either through external or internal means, and has begun to take credit for the change, termination is appropriate. Closure brings the group experience to an end by enabling members to be responsible for themselves, reinforcing changes that have occurred, and giving members help in moving smoothly back into the mainstream of their own lives. The basic objective of the closing stage tasks is to help members effectively conclude their group experience.

Task C1: Giving Support

The goal of this task is to give members psychological and emotional support during the period of time when they are implementing changes in their lives outside the group. This support may take the form of encouragement, reinforcement, or confrontation designed to foster positive action by members in their own environments. The intent is to provide support without creating dependency so that members can learn to function effectively on their own. Part of this task may include revising, substituting, or refining action plans to facilitate effective change in the member's life. The provision of support is necessary only until members have integrated the changes into their lives to the point of experiencing internal reinforcement and positive recognition from their environment.

Task C2: Addressing Unfinished Business

As groups move toward termination, unfinished business may emerge as a critical component of the ending process. Unfinished business issues may stem from a variety of sources and how they are addressed carries significant weight in the overall effectiveness of the group. Notice that the unfinished business task is process oriented (*addressing*) rather than product oriented (*finishing*). It is generally improbable and unfeasible that all issues can be resolved before a group terminates but a valid and serious effort needs to be made to address them.

The source of unfinished business may be individual group members or the group process. Individuals may feel they still have unidentified issues on which to work or that their concerns have not been completely resolved. Interpersonal interactions within the group may produce unresolved relational issues and unsettling or uncomfortable events in the group's history may still need processing before the group can effectively end.

The goal of this task is to allot time and energy to address unfinished business—whatever its source—as a means of clearing the way for termination.

Task C3: Affirming and Confirming Growth

The goal of this task is to review, summarize, and reinforce what has been learned through the process of group interaction. It builds self-confidence in members and generates a dependence on self rather than the group. Affirming growth relates to each member's self-disclosures of learning and change that have occurred as a result of group involvement. Confirming growth relates to group feedback acknowledging change in individual members thus giving credence and value to the process of change and the result.

Task C4: Saying Goodbye

The goal of this task is to provide an opportunity for members to terminate their group experience. Saying goodbye provides a stepping off point at a time when ending may be difficult due to relational bonds forged in the group, time restrictions, or the particular focus of interactions in the group. It precipitates closure to the group experience when an individual leaves, a group session ends, or a group disperses and eases the transition of members back into their ongoing life experiences.

Task C5: Follow-Up

This particular task is sometimes difficult to address effectively but is important if the impact of the group is to be minimally sustained. The goal is to make a provision for postgroup contact with group members for purposes of assessing whether changes that have been realized and continue to be an integral part of group members' lives. Another feature of follow-up is as a stimulus to rekindle motivation to change and growth that may have receded since the group disbanded.

☐ Structural Dynamics

The relationship between group process and group structure becomes clearer in the context of developmental tasks which elucidate the life cycle of a group. These tasks both substantiate and facilitate the group process and provide a focal point for the various factors that constitute structure. As counseling and therapy groups proceed through the tasks of various stages, structural dynamics are revealed in different ways.

One or all of the structural dynamics noted may be operational in a group at any particular time. However, whether their impetus is purposes, leader, activities, members, or any combinations thereof, stage related developmental tasks provide a concrete conceptual basis for construing group process.

Natural Progression

Groups which have clearly defined and consensually agreed upon purposes move naturally through the various developmental tasks and stages enroute to achieving their objectives. The impetus for this progression is the group's *purpose* but since groups have an inherent life cycle, the group interaction accounts for the tasks thus making both the process and the outcome therapeutic. In other words, purposes impose a structure that process carries out in order for those purposes to be effectively realized.

Noting Obstacles

Barriers evident in a group at any one time are usually indicative of the stage the group is in and pinpoint tasks that need to be addressed to move the group forward. Identification of impasses and resistances and initiating appropriate action to overcome them are the bailiwick of the group *leader*. For example, if the group is characterized by suspicion and distrust, the leader might initiate or facilitate a focus on the developmental tasks of the security stage. Thus the leader's impact on structure materializes.

Structuring the Group Process

Group leaders can control the sequence and flow of group interaction by using the developmental tasks as the basis for selecting group *activities*. These activities are incorporated directly into the group process and create a structure that has conceptual validity.

Member Initiatives

Within each individual group member a drive is toward self-enhancement which often surfaces as the motivating force to move the group along in the developmental process. Boredom or frustration among members stuck in one place in the group process, pain of individual problems that need attention, and individual enthusiasm to grow and learn will stimulate *members* to press the issue of structure in order to deal with appropriate developmental tasks that will help the group progress.

☐ Individual Group Sessions

Each individual group session represents in prototypical fashion the overall group process and elements of developmental tasks that pertain to the stage of development the group is in as well as certain tasks that pervade the entire group process. As such, each session is a picture in miniature of the total process as well as a step in the evolution of that process. Just as the life cycle of a group has stages, a group session has sequential phases that are distinguishable. These phases evolve and merge as the group interacts, but in most cases they are evident to some degree in each session. Acknowledging, understanding, and accounting for these phases will enhance the group process and facilitate the most effective interactive pathway for the group to follow. The basic phases of each session are

1. the energizing phase;
2. the advance organizing phase;
3. the working phase;
4. the processing phase; and
5. the closing phase.

Each will be elaborated upon identifying key characteristics and developmental tasks that pertain to each phase and its role, purpose, and focus relative to the group process (Trotzer, 1980).

The phases of a group session as described in this section can be used as a cognitive overlay for groups at any point in the group process. Doing so enables the group leader to maintain a balanced perspective of both the overall group process and the specific events of a particular session. This produces a flexibility and dynamism that avoids the errors of not seeing the forest for the trees (getting myopic with regard to a specific group session) and not seeing the trees for the forest (missing the specificity and importance of individual group sessions in the overall process).

Energizing Phase

The energizing phase is the period of time at the beginning of each group session that is used to get members connected or reconnected to each other and the group. It is the timeframe during which group members shift focus from their lives outside the group to their experience in the group. During the early stages of the group process, this phase is closely related to the Getting Acquainted task but throughout the group process it is related to the Interpersonal Warm-Up task and serves the purpose of mobilizing group member energy.

The transition from outside the group to inside the group is always an important issue each time a group assembles. Kassera and Kassera (1979) pointed out that leaders can facilitate more effective beginnings if they make an effort to recognize and respond to the dynamics involved in initiating a group interaction. For example, activities called *energizers* can be used to facilitate contact between group members and prepare them for interacting with one another and tuning in to the focus of the group session.

The key goals of the energizing phase are to stimulate a here and now perspective and generate a present oriented readiness to concentrate on the tasks and experiences of the group session. This phase is primarily one in which members clear their minds of distractions and attain an ingroup focus laying the groundwork for the advance organizing phase. Initially, and at certain resistance points in the group process, the energizing phase may be extended to as long as 15 to 30 minutes but once the group is formed beyond the security stage, the time needed for members to clear their minds and connect with each other is generally reduced to 5 to 10 minutes.

Advance Organizing Phase

The initial struggle of any learning effort is to connect the attention of the learner to the material to be learned. This is particularly crucial to the personal learning involved in counseling or therapy. If something can be done to trigger curiosity, invoke relevance, stimulate interest, or enhance motivation, the whole process of learning is accelerated and becomes more exciting and engaging. The advance organizing phase of a group session is the period of time during which the group moves from being in the group to being involved in the group. While the energizing phase serves to energize individual members and connect them with the group and each other, the advance organizing phase serves to direct that energy and connect the group to the focus for which the group was convened.

The advance organizing phase is an ingroup transition phase in which members' interests are aroused and connected to the theme, purposes, and business of the group. Advance organizers designed to prepare members for involvement or set a group agenda are helpful in this phase. For example, many groups use go-rounds to identify topics, problems, or issues that members wish to discuss during the session as a means of planning the agenda for the session and allocating time.

Developmental tasks of the various stages often surface as content areas during the advance organizing phase. Issues such as trust, cohesiveness, or accountability/responsibility may be raised as the group works on making itself a more therapeutic environment. Once the group is fully operational, however, the tasks of the work stage tend to predominate as members focus on problem solving.

Except for periods when the group is at an impasse or when resistance emerges either in the form of process obstacles or member's obstructing their own process, the advance organizing phase of a group session tends to be brief and concrete, signaling the group to get down to business.

Working Phase

The working phase is the heart of a group session. Whether the work is process work (dealing with the forming process of the group) or content work (dealing with the purposes for which the group was formed and problems of individual members), this phase carries the most weight both in terms of time and effort. Here again, the developmental tasks of the stage the group is in are reflected in the work being done. The group addresses the agenda items created in the advance organizing phase and uses its energy to do the therapeutic work it was formed to do. Members work on problems, try out solutions, practice skills, and generally use the group as a social laboratory for problem solving. Or, they may focus on themselves as persons or the group as an entity. Either way, the group is activated in the working phase.

Processing Phase

The processing phase of a group session is complementary to but distinct from the working phase. It has meaning because of what occurs in the working phase, but adds an invaluable dimension to the work because it consolidates, validates, and integrates the learning that has taken place. The processing phase is the time period near the end of each session in which the group reviews or reflects back on what occurred in the session. It recycles the energy of the group by shifting emphasis from the hands on, experiential work of the session with its affective nature to the integrative work with its cognitive bearing. Processing may be directed at either the group's functioning or the individual members' efforts or both. The closing stage tasks of giving support, unfinished business, and affirming and confirming growth are reflected in the processing phase.

The processing phase is a first step in detaching from the group experience as the group and its members step back to look at themselves and their efforts. As they do so a shift occurs from being experientially engaged to being cognitively engaged. Processing is essential because it helps members summarize, personalize, and generalize what they have learned about the group, each other, and themselves. During this phase members synthesize and apply their group experience making it a more integral part of their lives.

A typical tool of the processing phase is the *go-round* in which members share their reactions, insights, and perspectives on the group experience. The timeframe tends to be relatively brief, normally 5 to 15 minutes, but under certain circumstances this can be extended. Certain events in the group or particularly crucial incidents may require extensive processing for the group or certain individuals. Under such circumstances processing may dominate a significant portion of the session. In more structured groups where agenda items direct the work phase, processing may be interspersed during the course of the session after each item on the agenda has been addressed. However, the typical case is for processing to be relatively brief and serve as a springboard for the closing phase of a session.

Closing Phase

The closing phase deals with the dynamics of leaving a group session. Just as starting is an issue at the beginning of a session, closing is an issue at the end. The closing phase should provide a meaningful transition from the world inside the group to the world outside the group by winding down the group energy and redirecting individual member enery to their life beyond the group. It should aid and facilitate leaving, opening the door for members to reconnect with their world outside the group, but should also project their thoughts toward the next session. As such, closing is a delicate process because it is done under time constraints (most groups have a scheduled ending time), but it must account for the past, present, and future in some way. Helping members reconnect with their lives without carrying disturbing unfinished business from the group and positively anticipating the next session is no small assignment. Yet, the closing phase is designed to do just that.

The developmental tasks of the closing stage (such as saying goodbye) are activated in this phase. Although closing tends to be brief, it is significant. Left unattended or mishandled, it can seriously jeopardize the therapeutic progress. Structured activities and closing rituals are helpful in handling this phase. In addition, some leaders add a feedback or evaluation component to closing to assist them in thinking about and planning future group sessions.

☐ Learning Activities

In this section learning activities are organized sequentially with regard to developmental tasks of the group process described in this chapter. Activities have been related to each task or to a group of tasks to exemplify how structured activities can be used to address specific group tasks. However, remember that activities themselves may be utilized flexibly and related to other tasks as well. In addition, keep in mind that other structuring agents (leaders, purposes, members, etc.) may address the tasks without using structured activities.

☐ Learning Activities for Security Stage

Task S1: Getting Acquainted

Personality Profile

Pass out a 3 × 5 card and pencil to each group member informing them that this is their personality profile. Ask members to congregate in the center of the room with their cards and pencils. Explain that they will have to make a series of choices that will reflect the characteristics of their personality. They are to first make their choice by physically moving to one side of the room or the other as traits are identified and then record their choice on the card. Present the following (or other) polarity choices to the group using the directive: "If you are more like _____ move to the right side of the room, and if you are more like _____ move to the left side of the room.

Ground rules:

1. a choice must be made (no middle ground)
2. all choices are final

Polarity samples:

flower - rock	heart - brain
night - day	work - play
steak - hamburger	mountain - valley
think - feel	push - pull
anger - hurt	thunder - lightning
lake - river	together - alone
talk - listen	early - late
lead - follow	spontaneous - deliberate
hug - handshake	mall - mail order catalog

(Use at least 10 varied polarity choices to create a profile of traits)

After the choices have been made have members circle the five choices most descriptive of their personality. Have them study their own profiles for a minute or two and then write a narrative personality description on the back of the 3 × 5 card.

Sharing: Have group members share the five choices and their reasons for selecting them as a way of getting acquainted with each other. (If the group is large, this can be done in subgroups of three to four members). Close the sharing by having each person read their personality statement.

Name Saying

Split the group in half forming two concentric circles facing each other. Using the statement, "My name is _____," have the outer circle members rotate around inner circle members introducing themselves to each other. Repeat this rotation four times alternating, having the outer circle move and the inner circle move. Each time, create a different demeanor for presenting the introduction.

Examples: Introduce yourself by expressing the introductory statement:

1. Casually (laid back)
2. Very formally (formal occasion like meeting the President of the United States)
3. Lovingly (like you want to sweep the person off his or her feet)
4. Angrily (like you are irritated or angry at the person)

This activity is useful for groups who have never met before and tends to be a tension breaker as well as starts the process of getting to know each other's names.

Task S2: Interpersonal Warm-up

Balloon Game

Assemble the group in a circle holding hands. Present them with the task of keeping a balloon aloft without letting go of each other's hands and without letting the balloon hit the floor or get away from the group. Once they seem to be mastering the task, add a second, third, and fourth balloon until the group is in chaos. Process the activity in light of group dynamics. This activity not only warms people up, but accentuates the working together dimension of the group and serves as a metaphor for the complications of dealing with the varied concerns of the group members.

Place and Space Activity

As an initiating activity, have group members mill around the room without talking, trying to find a comfortable place in the room in relation to the other members. Allow enough time for members to experiment with different places and spaces. Once the group has formed up in a solidified manner, have members explain how they arrived at their place and space. Reassemble the group and process the activity in light of group dynamics.

Task S3: Setting Boundaries

List of Group Rules Activity

Have each group member create a list of rules they think are important/ necessary for the group to be effective. Have them place a star by those rules that they believe are a necessity for them to feel at ease in the group. Have members share their lists and personal requirements as a means of addressing the formation of ground rules for the group.

Create Your Own Ground Rules

Present the group with the task of devising a set of ground rules for the group. This activity is best conducted over two sessions where the first produces the basic rules and the second refines, redefines, adds, or deletes rules so that the group has a set of workable guidelines. The rules generated also may be periodically reviewed as a means of evaluating the group atmosphere and keeping the group on target therapeutically.

Task S4: Building Trust

Anonymity Bag

One of the reasons people keep things inside is because they don't know how people will respond to what they think or feel. Therefore, they choose not to say anything because they would be personally accountable and possibly vulnerable. This activity is designed to provide an anonymity cushion so members can get a sense of how the group will respond to their input without having to directly risk putting themselves on the line.

Have group members write down anonymous statements about what they think, feel, and believe about themselves, the group, or someone else in the group. These statements are placed in a bag. The statements can be processed in one of two ways.

> *Leader Processing:* The leader selects a statement from the bag, reads it to the group and facilitates a discussion regarding the statement.

> *Member Processing:* The bag is passed around and each member draws out a statement making sure it is not his or her own. In turn, each member reads the statement to the group and gives his or her reaction or opinion as to its

meaning and relevance. This process continues until all statements have been discussed.

I Can Hardly Believe It

Using the stimulus statement, "Something I find hard to believe about my-self is _____," invite group members to disclose elements of them-selves that 1) they are not really sure are a part of their person, and 2) they would not usually risk saying are a part of who they are. Create a risk inviting atmosphere by making the activity light, experimental, and fun. Encourage the sharing idea of ideals, fantasies, and exaggerations about themselves that members often toy with in their minds, but tend not to disclose. After sharing, process the information in relation to each person's goals, problems, or desires for change.

☐ Learning Activities for Acceptance Stage

Task A1: Personal Sharing

Who Am I Hierarchy

Pass out five 3 × 5 cards to each group member. On each card members are to write different responses to complete the statement, "I am a person who _____." Once they have the five cards completed, have them rank the cards based on the importance of each statement to them as persons (one = most important, 5 = least important). Process the activity in the group by having each member share their statements starting with number five and working up to number one. They are to share the statement and then comment on, "What life would be like if that statement was not part of who I am." This activity serves as a means of identifying and appreciat-ing qualities in a person and pinpointing areas that may benefit from work in the group.

5 × 8 Sharing

Pass out 5 × 8 cards to each member. Have them draw a diamond in the center of the card and write their name in it. Have them complete the following statements in each of the areas of the card designated by the instructions:

> Upper left corner: I am . . .
> Upper right corner: I worry about . . .
> Lower left corner: I am here because . . .
> Lower right corner: By the end of the group I will . . .

When the task is completed have group members share their statements either sequentially using one stem at a time or by having each member share their entire card. Process relative to the dynamics and purpose of the group.

Task A2: Giving Feedback

OTINAY and MIOYI

Introduce this activity by writing one of the above combinations of letters on the board and explaining that it stands for an ancient oriental ritual that is eminently growth producing. The letters actually stand for one of the following phrases:

> "*O*ne *T*hing *I* *N*oticed *A*bout *Y*ou . . ." and
> "*M*y *I*mpression *O*f *Y*ou *I*s . . ."

Using one of these statements, have group members engage in a feedback activity either by designating one person at a time to be the focal point or doing it spontaneously until all members have given and received feedback. These terms sometimes become symbolic and members may ask for feedback or for permission to give feedback by referring to OTINAY or MIOYI at any point in the group process.

Making The Shoe Fit

Have group members remove one of their shoes and place it in a pile in the center of the group. Each member selects a shoe other than their own and puts it on (actually or symbolically). Their task is to explain what they perceive it is like to be the person whose shoe they have on.

A variation of this activity is to have members remove both shoes and exchange them with another group member. This activity called *Walk a mile in my shoes* requires that each person become the person whose shoes they are wearing for a significant amount of time. This activity is very useful as a feedback exercise after the group members have gotten to know each other fairly well and can carry out the other person's role in the group in a realistic manner for a reasonable period of time.

Task A3: Building Cohesiveness and Closeness

2-Foot Square

This energizer draws attention to the importance of cohesiveness and closeness with respect to working together effectively as a group. Using masking tape or chalk, mark out a square on the floor that is smaller than a group can easily fit into (a 2-foot square is an approximate size for a six to eight person group). Inform the group that their task is to get everyone inside the square with no physical part touching the floor outside the designated area. If the group is outdoors, a stump or stone can be used for the same purpose. Tell the group you will not help them in any way, but you will determine if and when they have succeeded. Give the group sufficient time to accomplish the task and then process it in light of the group dynamics involved in completing the task and generalizing to the developmental dynamics of the group.

Group Recipe

Have each group member write two ingredients (on separate slips) that they believe they contribute to the group. Place these ingredients in a bag. Process this activity in two steps:

1. Draw out the slips ingredient by ingredient writing them on a chalk board or newsprint. As each ingredient is drawn, the group gives feedback on why that ingredient is important to a group. Optional: The group may also guess who supplied the ingredient as a means of affirming the person who contributed it.
2. When all the ingredients are listed, have the group discuss what the result of their group recipe is. Members can be asked to write a summary description of the group as a means of initiating discussion, or a group summary can be facilitated through discussion.

Task A4 and A5: Learning to Accept Self and Others

Attitudes Toward Self and Others Activity

The following activity combines the acceptance of self and others tasks and uses self-disclosure as the interactive mechanism. Pass out an 8½ × 11 sheet of paper and pencil to each group member. Divide the sheet into two columns labeling them *self* and *others*. Further divide each column in half to create four quadrants. Finally, divide the upper quadrant of each column into two columns so the sheet of paper looks like this. . . .

In the two columns under *self* place the stems "I like these things about me . . ." and "I dislike these things about me. . . ." Have group members list those things they like and dislike about themselves in the respective columns.

In the two columns under *others* write the stems "I am attracted to people when . . ." and "I am turned off to people when. . . ." Have group members list those things that attract them to people and turn them off to people in their respective columns.

In the bottom quadrant of each column have the group members write two paragraphs. Under the *self* column they are to start the paragraph with "I am a person who . . ." and use all the information from the like and dislike lists. Under the *others* column they are to start their paragraphs with "My attitude toward others is . . ." and use all the information from the attracted to and turned off lists.

This activity is facilitated timewise if a prepared sheet with the above described design and information is passed out to the group.

When the members have completed their lists and paragraphs, have them share their observations about themselves and others by reading their paragraphs. Start with the *self* paragraphs and then move on to the *others* paragraphs. Facilitate interaction using their self-disclosures to further address the acceptance tasks in the group process.

☐ Learning Activities for Responsibility Stage

Task R1: Self-Assessment

*Creating Your Own Birthday Celebration**

One of the ways to teach and experience the task of self-assessment is to provide group members with choices they have to prioritize according to their own interests, values, and inclinations. Pass out two sheets of 8½ × 11 paper to each person. Have them fold the two sheets so that each sheet has 12 sections. (Sequence: fold in half then in half again to produce quarters. Fold quarter size sections into thirds so that when you open the sheets you will have 12 sections). Direct members to number the sections consecutively 1–12 on one sheet and then tear or use a scissors to cut the second sheet into 12 separate sections. Introduce the activity with the following instructions:

> You are going to have a birthday and you must decide what you want to do to celebrate it. I will give you your choices one at a time. Write a key word or phrase on one of your 12 slips and place it on your numbered sheet starting with number one. As each choice is given you may rearrange your choices.

Present the following presents or activities the person could choose for their birthday (key word or phase is in italics)

---

*This activity was demonstrated by Sydney Simon in a values clarification workshop attended by the author.

1. Have someone write a *poem* in honor of your birthday.
2. Receive an *expensive necessity* as a present.
3. Have a number of people give you *precious validations* confirming your importance and worth as an individual.
4. Slips of paper with *personal messages* hidden around the house (one for every year of your life).
5. Gifts of *socks* and *underwear* or *panties* and *pantyhose*.
6. Receive *homemade gifts*.
7. Have your *birthday ignored*.
8. *Cake, ice cream* and *candles* to celebrate.
9. *Surprise party*.
10. *Coupons of Time*: someone gives you coupons that you can redeem for extra time when you need it.
11. Have a *week-long celebration*.
12. *Write your own*: have each person write their own idea for how they would celebrate.

When members have completed their prioritizing, have them share and explain their top three or four choices.

This activity can be adapted to any group situation where priorities are involved. Simply construct 11 items that fit the situation and present them one at a time and add a "write your own" item. It can be helpful in assessing motivational factors, (why people want to be in a group, part of a program, or picked for a position), identifying problems and planning agendas (what should be addressed first), and identifying key functions or roles that are part of a job description.

Tasks R2 Through R5: Responsibility Stage Tasks

One activity can often be designed to address more than one developmental task. In fact, structured activities by their very nature tend to incorporate more than one task. The following example is an activity that addresses all the developmental tasks of the responsibility stage in the context of one structured experience.

Diamond and 4 Activity

Instructions for members:

1. Draw a large diamond in the center of an 8½ × 11 sheet of paper.
2. In the diamond, write a brief description of a problem you have been unable to resolve or something you have always wanted to do, but haven't been able to.
3. On each side of the diamond write a brief description of an obstacle or

barrier that has stood in the way of solving your problem or doing what you want to do (identify four barriers or obstacles).

4. Divide the group into subgroups of at least four members. (If the group is small enough and time allows, the following steps can be completed using the entire group).

5. Processing the material (this is a timed activity).

   a. Member 1: spend 60 seconds describing to the group the problem and the obstacles. (1 minute)

   b. Group members: member 1 turns his or her back to the group and listens as the remaining group members discuss the problem or situation and seek to identify ways of overcoming the obstacles or barriers. (2 minutes)

   c. Member/group interaction: the member and the group discuss the ideas that have been generated relative to the problem. (3 minutes)

   d. Repeat the sequence with each member in the group.

Evidence of the responsibility stage developmental tasks are as follows:

Instructions 1 through 3: Self-Assessment (R1)
Instruction 5: Recognizing Ownership (R2), Giving Respect (R4) and Doing a Fair Share (R5)
Instructions 1 through 5: Experiencing and Building Responsibility (R3)

The *strength bombardment activity* described on pp. 111–112 is another activity that lends itself well to integrating the tasks of the responsibility stage.

☐ Learning Activities for Work Stage

Tasks W1 through W3

Reality Therapy Problem Solving

Glasser's (1965; Glasser & Wubbolding, 1995; Wubbolding, 1991) reality therapy approach translates into six basic steps that adapt nicely to the developmental tasks of the work stage. The following steps can be taught to the group and used as an agenda for personal problem solving.

1. *Wants*: What do you want? The group member describes generally and specifically what he or she wants in life immediately and long term.

2. *Direction and Doing*: What are you doing? The group member describes what he or she is doing in a particular circumstance or relationship and how he or she acts.

3. *Evaluation*: Is what you are doing helping or hurting you? The group member evaluates whether or not what they are doing is resulting in the kind of experience desired. (If yes, stop or start over; if no, go on to Step 4.)

4. *Planning*: Can we work out a plan to make your life more successful? Focus group resources on helping the group member develop a plan which will successfully resolve his or her problem.
5. *Commitment*: Will you commit to the plan? Obtain a personal commitment from the group member to carry out the plan.
6. *Persistence*: No excuses; no punishment; no withdrawal. Hold the person to their commitment, revising the plan if necessary to ensure success. Respect the person's efforts but accept no excuses for not following through on the commitment.

All work stage developmental tasks are addressed in the context of this activity format. A method of problem solving is taught and used by group members. The *we* in the planning step directly mobilizes group resources and reality testing is built into Step 3. (evaluation) and Step 4. (planning) via the criteria of improving one's life and making it more successful.

☐ Learning Activities for Closing Stage

Task C1: Giving Support

Gift Giving

As a closing activity inform group members they will be exchanging gifts as part of the last group session. Have them think of a gift they would like to give each group member as that person leaves the group and goes on with their life. Gifts may take any shape or form and may be concrete or abstract, but each gift should in some way be related to the work that person had done in the group.

Gifts may be exchanged either spontaneously with members picking individual gifts off their gift list until all gifts have been exchanged or one person at a time may be designated as the receiver or giver depending on the inclination of the group. Create a festive atmosphere for this activity.

Task C2: Addressing Unfinished Business

The Unfinished Business Card

A tool to assist group members in addressing unfinished business that stems from interaction between individual members in the group is the unfinished business card. Distribute the card (as depicted in Figure 5.3) to group members several sessions (two or three) prior to the group's designated termination session. Have them place the name of each member in the Group Member column and a brief description of any unfinished business they believe they have with any member. The Contact column refers to

| Group Member | Unfinished Business | Contact | Status | |
			Complete	Incomplete
1.				
2.				
3.				
4.				
5.				
6.				
7.				
8.				
9.				
10.				
11.				
12.				

FIGURE 5.3. Unfinished business card.

whether time and attention were devoted to the unfinished business, and the Status column indicates whether the unfinished business was completed or left incomplete as the group ends.

The card may be used solely to stimulate group members to think about unfinished business with the initiative to address the unfinished business left up to the members, or specific time can be allocated in the final sessions to deal with the input from the cards. Either way, do not expect that all unfinished business between members will be addressed before the group ends.

Task C3: Affirming and Confirming Growth

Rock, Scissors, Paper (adapted)

The old game of rock, scissors, paper involves two people who, on the count of three, flash a hand signal: fist for rock, flat hand for paper, and two fingers separated in a V for scissors. The sequence of ascendence is:

1) paper covers rock,
2) rock crushes scissors, and
3) scissors cuts paper.

The winner gets rewarded. Using this game, have group members pair off for the purpose of disclosing what they have gained from the group (affirming personal growth) and giving their partner feedback as to how he or she was perceived to grow in the group (confirming growth). The person who wins the game gets to go first disclosing their own growth or change and receiving feedback. Their partner goes second. Rotate partners until each group member has been paired with every other group member. Process the activity as a group focusing on how the group has impacted upon group members' lives.

Task C4: Saying Goodbye

Annual Signing Party

As a closing activity, fashion booklets out of four sheets of 8½ × 11 paper cut in half lengthwise, folded, and stapled in the center. Each member is given a booklet and asked to design their own cover representing the group. Have each member place their name on the front of the booklet accompanying their designs. Booklets can then be exchanged for group members to write in, reflecting on their view of the person and the group experience. This activity works well if the group is inclined to close with a commencement atmosphere or celebration. Allot time for the members to write in each others books as a lead in to closing.

Circle For Closure

This activity is specifically designed as a final group experience. Have group members form a circle with arms locked around each other. Ask members to share brief thoughts about the group in either a go-round or spontaneous manner. When completed, have members silently make eye contact with each group member signaling acknowledgment and goodbye nonverbally. When eye contact has been made with each person, have members close their eyes. Using guided imagery, verbally instruct the group to visualize the group's history and their own part in it. Have them visualize each group member and think a specific thought about that person. Finally, have them think about themselves and their experience in the group.

At this point have the group drop their locked arms position (eyes still closed) and clasp hands. Introduce the idea of closure by informing the group the time has come for the group to end. Have members drop hands to their sides and take an about face. Instruct them to say goodbye to the group in their minds. Ask them to think about what is coming up for them in their lives in the next few days or weeks. Have them think specifically about what they will be doing next (after the group). Instruct them to take one step forward (away from the group circle), open their eyes and go about their business.

Task C5: Follow-Up

A Letter To Myself

This terminating activity can be used to extend the impact of the group and serves to remind group members about changes they have made or plans they intend to carry out. During the last session of the group have members write letters to themselves in which they state where they would like to be with regard to their goals or problems at some future date (one month hence or six months, and so on). Then have group members address and seal envelops with their letters in them and turn them over to the group leader who serves as the sender. As a group agree on a sending date. Variations of this activity could involve phone calls, individual interviews, or a reconvening of the group by the group leader.

6

Group Leader

The objective of this chapter is to describe and delineate the qualities, skills, and functions of effective group leaders. The inherent difficulty in this task is related to the wide variety of characteristics that can be attributed to effective leadership. This variability is the result of differences in leader personalities as well as divergent training programs, philosophies, and theories. The diversity in member personalities and the varied purposes for which groups are formed also must be considered in discussing successful leadership. Therefore any effort to describe the perfect leader would be a useless academic exercise and have little relevance because of its nearsightedness. Describing basic tendencies that seem to have commonality among effective leaders and discussing a broad range of leadership traits, skills, functions, and issues seems to be a more plausible manner of accomplishing the stated objective of this chapter. In this way the prospective leader can assess the information in light of her or his own personality and theoretical convictions.

This chapter includes such topics as the personality of the group counselor, training for group leadership, leader skills and functions, basic issues in group leadership, and special considerations for the group leader. It includes suggested activities for obtaining supervised leadership experience that is so imperative in developing expertise in group counseling and concludes with learning activities that focus on leadership dynamics and characteristics.

☐ Personality of the Group Leader

In any treatise on effective therapeutic intervention, whether in the form of psychiatry, psychotherapy, or counseling, with individuals or in groups, the one overriding characteristic that is discussed repeatedly is the personality of the individual who is cast in the helping role. This is only logical since the service performed is basically a human service and therefore remains just out of reach of empirical and laboratory controls that could mechanize the process. Although this is true, it raises some difficult problems in distinguishing who the most effective helpers are and what qualities describe them (Stockton & Morran, 1982; Stockton, Morran, & Velkoff, 1987). This same problem confronts leaders and trainers in group counseling/therapy.

The professional literature is replete with articles and books that stress personal characteristics as the most important aspect of a counselor's ability to counsel (Corey, 1995; Corey & Corey, 1992; Mahler, 1969; Yalom, 1995). Since each individual is unique, he or she brings to the helping role his or her own particular capacities and incapacities that enhance or deter the helping process. To know which traits are assets and which are liabilities the counselor must engage in an introspective process to attain the knowledge that will help him or her decide which qualities to use, which to modify or develop, and which to circumvent. Therefore the first characteristic of an effective leader is *self-awareness*. Self-awareness or self-knowledge is the very personal education that enables us as persons and leaders "to listen to almost anything without losing our temper or our self-confidence" (Robert Frost).

Self-awareness is important because the group leader influences the nature of the group. How the leader acts determines to a great extent how the group will respond. Leaders must know what qualities about themselves make them attractive to the group. They must know how they influence others and how others affect them. Mahler (1969) pointed out that awareness of one's self and one's personality must involve "knowing strengths, weaknesses, conflict areas, motivations and needs" (p. 170). Without this knowledge leaders not only open themselves up for potential problems in the group but also jeopardize their effectiveness in utilizing their own personal resources in directing the group.

Dustin and George (1973) stated that leaders' self-awareness must include a thorough knowledge of their own rewards in relating to others. Without knowing what personal attributes reinforce other people, the leader cannot be effective in helping members modify and change their behavior. Lakin (1969) went a step farther and stressed that group leaders must be clear about their own intentions and goals. Lack of such understanding can result in damaging indecisiveness on the leader's part. It can also subject the group to unnecessary pressure and lead to the use of unethical practices under the guise of leadership expertise.

Without self-awareness leaders may become subject to emotional responses emanating from their own issues without knowledge of their origins. As such, self-knowledge becomes a fundamental component of leadership relative to facilitation and intervention in groups. Kline (1990) stressed self-monitoring and conducting self-inventories as a routine practice for group leaders. He noted that "when leaders encounter their limitations or identify their own personal issues in others they are likely to respond emotionally" (p. 196). Such awareness behooves the leader to proceed carefully and take steps to clarify their interventions before responding. Yalom (Forrester-Miller, 1989) validated this point of view stating that "no one can effectively lead a group who is unwilling or unable to look at his or her own feelings and neurotic conflicts" (p. 199).

The counselor's *attitudes* also are important components of self-awareness. They will eventually become apparent to group members in any event; therefore, counselors need to have a firm grasp on their value structure and attitudes so that they can be as transparent to the group as possible. This enables them to interact with members more freely. One value of special import to the leader is that of valuing self-awareness since the whole group counseling process centers around self-disclosure and feedback, which is designed to promote the members' self-knowledge and to help them use this knowledge to solve their problems. Leaders who do not value self-knowledge for themselves can hardly expect group members to see it as important in their lives.

Leader *personality* is the core of leadership style, and if leaders do not know of what that core consists, they have nothing on which to build their approach nor can they authenticate their style. During the beginning stages of the group process, personality characteristics of the leader determine how quickly rapport is established. As the group develops the counselor's personality is the factor that defines the ultimate limits of the group experience because anything considered is contingent on the value system of the leader. In fact, when problems or impasses arise in the group a good rule of thumb is for leaders to first look at themselves before trying to determine if the causes come from sources in the group. Substantial self-knowledge is thus mandatory as a leader personality trait in successful group leadership.

Openness and *flexibility* are two personality characteristics that lend themselves well to effective group leadership. There is a direct positive correlation between the possession of these two qualities and the range of people with whom the counselor can effectively work. This is not to imply that counselors who set no limits or boundaries and make no demands are the most effective. Rather, these qualities help the leader develop parameters appropriate to the nature of clients and their problems. *Openness* is that quality that stems from a secure knowledge of one's self so that the ideas of others can be received without feeling personal threat. Leaders, because of their own self-knowledge, can open themselves to the exposés of their clients without using judgment as a protective device. Instead they communicate an appreciation of diversity which Hulse (1985) considered an essential attribute of effective group leaders. Clients experience this openness in the form of acceptance, which paves the way for further self-disclosure on their part.

Flexibility is an outgrowth of the leader's confidence and sensitivity to the needs of the clients. The less confidence leaders have in themselves the more rigid they tend to become. Dogmatic nonstructuring by a leader is an example of high rigidity rather than the ultimate in flexibility. Flexible people know their own boundaries but are willing to vary within those boundaries and are continually testing their limits to reaffirm their where-abouts. One error that group leaders often make is that they go through the limit-testing process once, define for themselves what the extremities of their effectiveness are, and then never test them again. This is a sure way to stifle growth because, as one's experience increases, *self-confidence* increases, and with added self-confidence, flexibility increases. However, if counselors lapse into rigid patterns of operation they will curtail their creativity and never realize the gain in flexibility.

Allied closely with openness and flexibility is *tolerance of ambiguity*. This term is often narrowly construed as the ability to keep quiet in silent periods. Although at times this is indeed an example of being tolerant of ambiguous circumstances, it is a shallow test in most cases because silence can be more a matter of resistance than constructive or therapeutic action. A more viable definition for the group counselor is *the ability to act constructively in the interest of the group in the absence of knowledge about what is in the minds of group members*. This may take the form of being silent and allowing the pressure of silence to produce meaningful disclosures by sharing or of breaking the silence to alleviate tension that is inhibiting interaction. In any event the most effective leaders have personalities that can carry them through new and ambiguous situations without imposing their will on others simply to resolve their own discomfort. Or as Lao-Tse has noted, sometimes "a leader is best when people barely know he(she) exists."

Effective group counselors are essentially *positive individuals*. People who think positively about life tend to have a constructive influence on those around them. The positive person is also in a good position to see strengths in others. This is an important asset in group counseling because clients steeped in their own problems sometimes fail to see the positive aspects of their lives. There must be a diplomatic aspect to the leader's positivity, however, in order to make the best use of it as a resource. Members can be turned off by a "look at the good side" routine, and therefore the positive perspective must be tempered with a sensitivity to the negative side of things so the clients are assured that their perspectives are valued also.

A number of leader personality traits can be grouped under the general heading of *human qualities*. These characteristics tend to encourage others to have good feelings about themselves and help in developing therapeutic relationships. They can be described as social interest traits and they give the counselor a good rapport with people. *A genuine and sincere interest in others* is one of these qualities. People who find other people interesting, intriguing, and exciting and can convey that enthusiasm in a nonthreatening manner make good group counselors. This is especially true if that interest can be attached to the specific individual in the group as well as to the group as a whole. This interest, coupled with a _sensitivity to others_ that allows the counselor to put members and their interests and problems first, is a potent force in a group setting. Some people have a natural _empathic ear_ and others have to develop it, but the counselor who can tune in to the lives of others without disturbing or possessing them has the capability of being especially effective in group counseling.

Warmth and _caring_ are also human qualities that effective group leaders tend to have. The impressive thing about these qualities is that they can be conveyed in innumerable ways. Some people do it by their effervescence and enthusiasm, others by their smiles or attention, and others use their seriousness or quietness to show their depth of concern. The means of expression are not limited to one style, and if warmth and caring are present, usually no confusion exists on the part of the message receiver. Being a caring person is a must for group counselors. It provides them with the necessary fortitude to deal with people who have problems. It gives them leverage in the group interaction because of its importance to group members. It provides a model for others to follow, and it lays the groundwork for strong mutual liking and respect in the group which is essential to success.

Birnbaum (1969) cited _human objectivity_ as a necessary quality for persons engaged in the helping professions. This characteristic allows the counselor to be involved with others but at the same time be apart from them in order to assess things more rationally and objectively. It might be equated with the as _if_ quality in Rogers' (1962) definition of empathy: the counselor becomes involved in another's life _as if_ actually being that person but without losing personal identity and perspective in the process. People who are able to think clearly when emotionally involved and under pressure tend to function well as group leaders. People who can be receptive to others, who can function in accord with their own values, and who have their own opinions make good group leaders.

Finally, effective group counselors are _mature_ and _integrated_ persons who identify with the struggles involved in the process of life and can appreciate the efforts of members who are working on personal problems. They are able and willing to share themselves if necessary and in the best interest of the group. They are not devoid of problems and concerns in their own lives but are able to put them into proper perspective while working with group members. They have _integrity,_ which carries them through their own personal struggles and facilitates their handling of problems in the group process. They are strong enough not to wield their power to direct and badger members and strong enough to admit their own weaknesses. They are true to themselves, their clients, and their professional responsibility. Effective group leaders are people who can deal successfully with life's tasks and who are able to function interdependently with others. They are active and growing human beings who are continually striving for self-actualization without depriving others of opportunities to do the same.

The personality characteristics described here may not be definitive, but they do provide a strong basis for effective leadership when combined with the unique therapeutic qualities of individuals and the philosophical, theoretical, and technical factors provided by training. Hogan, Curphy and Hogan (1994) have identified the essential nature of effective leadership as a form of persuasion. Adapted to therapeutic group leadership the implication is that leaders are effective when members "willingly adopt, for a period of time, the goals of a group as their own" (p. 493). Leadership is not domination. "Persons who can require others to do their bidding because of their power are not leaders" (p. 493). Rather leadership involves persuading group members to work toward a common goal that is important to the welfare of the group while benefitting its individual members. Leaders who manifest the characteristics described above tend to be persuasive in a therapeutic manner.

Many individuals display the aforementioned qualities naturally but still may not know how to use them effectively in group counseling. Training, which is the topic of the next section, is the means whereby personality characteristics are translated into leadership skills that enhance the group counseling process.

☐ Training Group Counselors

In 1985 Carroll (1985), Shapiro and Shapiro (1985) and Conyne et al. (1985) all specified insufficient and inadequate training of group leaders as a major critical issue for group work. Even Yalom (1985) noted that without constant and continual attention to training, group counseling and group therapy naturally declines toward a second rate status as a helping modality. The view of these experts was that even with the maturation of group work as a full fledged professional entity, we are continuing to turn out professional counselors who have some knowledge and interest in group work but who are lacking in the technical skills and experience needed to implement a group program on the job or in clinical practice. Thus, the process that for years has been acclaimed as a potential means of solidifying and promoting the counselor role still receives but scant emphasis in comparison to its supposed impact. In addition, the underlying assumption that if counselors are competent in individual counseling they will also be proficient in groups is still embedded in the core of most training programs implicitly or explicitly.

Long ago Mahler (1969) pointed out the fallacy of this assumption, arguing that the reverse is much more likely to be the case—a person who is effective in group probably also would do well in individual counseling. In addition, Pearson (1981) noted that group skills tend to be viewed as extensions of one-to-one skills. The focus tends to be on similarities rather than on the differences between group skills and basic individual counseling skills. Harvill (Conyne, Harvill, Morganette, Morran, & Hulse-Killacky, 1990) further stressed that due to the emphasis in group process training in most programs, teaching leadership facilitation via specific skills—the "how to" of group leadership—has been missing. The need then is for delimited programs, i.e., master's programs with highly structured degree and licensure/certification requirements, to emphasize a group focus that is separate from and in concert with the individual orientation that predominates if competent group leaders are to be prepared.

Dinkmeyer and Muro (1971) were forward looking in affirming that the skill of utilizing group process must become the primary emphasis of training counselors. This is important according to their purview because counselors place their skills at the disposal of a vast range of clientele and significant others in their clients' lives. Without adequate group skills, counselors' direct and indirect service functions are severely curtailed because they have neither the time nor the tools to meet the needs of these people individually.

Lakin (1969) proffered a more somber perspective and warning. If proper attention is not given to training effective group leaders while promoting the group process as a viable means of helping people, we risk having "vast numbers of inadequate [leaders] who practice their newly discovered insights on others in the naive conviction that they have all but mastered the skills involved" (p. 927). Thus we may have to face charges of incompetence leveled at group leaders who were inadequately trained and lack the skills to function effectively in group settings. As was pointed out in Chapter 2, the group has unique characteristics that require knowledge and experience to handle appropriately, so the need for training is clearly obvious. But what should that training entail?

Training Standards and Competencies

In response to the aforementioned concerns and issues, the Association for Specialists in Group Work (ASGW, 1991) developed the Professional Standards for the Training of Group Workers that appears in Appendix A. Their purpose is to assist training programs in preparing group leaders while holding them accountable for quality preparation and competent performance (Conyne et al., 1992). These standards define group work and delineate its knowledge, skills and experiences into *core competencies* and *group work specializations*. The expectation is that training programs in group work will provide the core group competencies as the minimum level of proficiency for entry into the field and advanced training to generate group work specialists in one or more of the four group work specialties. For example, masters level graduate programs—the programs that produce the majority of group practitioners in professional settings—are expected to provide the core group competencies with access to the specialization level in at least one type of group work. Currently this expectation is still relegated to one, or at most two, required courses in group dynamics and process and sporadic attention in practicums or internships.

In reality, the application and implementation of the training standards is a work in progress (Conyne, Wilson, Kliner, Morran, & Ward, 1993). For specific examples of training models in each of the group specializations and for curricula in compliance with ASGW Professional Training Standards the reader is referred to Conyne, Wilson and Ward (1997) *Comprehensive Group Work: What it Means and How to Teach It.*

Group textbooks, professional literature, and professional standards all emphasize three specific areas in the training and development of competent group leaders. The first is the vast body of knowledge associated with the group modality as an entity in and of itself. The second is concentrated involvement in groups—as members and leaders—to integrate knowledge and practice and to develop a conceptualized framework for working with groups. And the third is professional commitment to continually update group work knowledge and skills concomitant with the practical experience of conducting groups on the job. In line with these three areas of concentration the following components are described as generic resources for the effective preparation of counselors to work in groups.

General Coursework

These courses should form a broad foundation for group counselor training, as well as providing supplemental knowledge about the group process. The basic requirements of most counselor education programs can supply this foundational aspect, and courses drawn from psychology, sociology, and human relations can provide the supplemental. Preference should be given to courses that use group process methods as part of their format (Hulse-Killacky, 1996).

Group Coursework

Every group counselor should have the equivalent of two courses in group work, one that emphasizes group dynamics and process and one that involves theories, techniques, skills, and procedures—including training in a least one of the group work specializations. These courses should be taken in the department that is most closely allied to the setting in which the counselor wishes to work. Although it might be advantageous to have more group course work, most programs do not have the resources or flexibility to provide them. Besides, once the basic coursework is taken, preference should be given to the experiential domain rather than the academic.

Membership Experience

Every group counselor should be required to participate in at least one intensive, ongoing group counseling experience. (See Chapter 1 for examples and details.) The ongoing nature of the experience is stressed to ensure that synthesis of the cognitive and experiential learning processes takes place over time and has more opportunity to develop. One shot marathons or short term group experiences can certainly provide supplementary data but can't substitute for the extended process of the typical therapeutic group.

Practicum/Internship Group Experience

Specific requirements to engage in a variety of groups should be a part of the general field work for counselor trainees. Minimally the practicum student/intern should conduct an ongoing counseling/therapy group, a series of psychoeducational/guidance groups and/or classroom meetings (in schools) or a series of structured preventive mental health groups (in agencies), in addition to the usual one-to-one counseling and other requirements. These experiences give potential group leaders the opportunity to develop expertise in groups on an equal footing with individual counseling.

Formal Group Practicum/Internship

This requirement needs to be added in most training programs. A specific field experience concentrating entirely on the development of the counselor's group leadership ability in a preferred setting is a necessity. Supervision should concentrate on the development of personal qualities and competence of the leader and provide technical skills for organizing and conducting group programs and developing one or more of the group work specializations.

On-the-Job Leadership Experience

No substitute exists for experience and once counselors have completed their training and are out on the job, they should proceed immediately in getting groups started. Many counselors never use their training in group counseling because they never get started—a reason not to always exists and plenty of other things can be found to do. Carroll (1985) has observed that the systemic expectations of the counselor role in schools often undermine implementation of group programs by school counselors. Yalom (1985) cited the old nemeses of groups being "second rate," "superficial or dangerous," and "only useful if individual counseling is not available as factors that impede group work" (p. 515). Nevertheless, group counselors must take the initiative, set and stick with priorities, and place groups at the head of the list.

Personal Reading

The professional journals are continually adding to the information in the field of group work, and group leaders should make every effort to keep themselves current. Three recommended journals that have stood the tests of time and relevance as to group work are the *Journal for Specialists in Group Work, the International Journal of Group Psychotherapy,* and *Small Group Research: An International Journal of Theory, Investigation,* and *Application.* New books and materials are also reviewed in these journals periodically, so there is no excuse for not keeping abreast of new ideas, research, and practices in the group domain. The very fact that the last 30 years have witnessed vast and penetrating changes in the area of group counseling should be reason enough to stay well read.

Professional Organizations, Workshops, and Meetings

Membership in professional organizations such as the Association for Specialists in Group Work (a division of the American Counseling Association), Group Psychology and Group Psychotherapy (Division 49 of the American Psychological Association) and/or the American Group Psychotherapy Association is imperative. Such membership provides plenty of opportunities to participate in or observe group programs at professional meetings or conventions, in workshops, and in inservice situations. Counselors who lead groups should make a concentrated effort to attend these sessions and to contribute to them as well. Sharing experiences is an excellent way to develop new ideas and get feedback on your own.

If prospective group leaders can acquire training and experience in each of these categories, they will have a substantial basis on which to build an effective group leadership style that will be professionally competent, personally satisfying, and meaningfully therapeutic in the lives of the group members with whom they work.

Specialized Training

Specialized training in the following areas will accentuate effectiveness and provide invaluable resources in leading counseling and therapy groups.

Assertiveness Training

Many client problems revolve around the issue of assertiveness. Realizing the need for and learning appropriate assertive behavior skills is one way of assisting group members in their relational dilemmas. Most assertiveness training programs utilize group process. For example, Lange and Jakubowski (1976) presented extensive structured exercises and illustrations depicting cognitive, affective, and behavioral procedures for increasing group members' responsible assertiveness. Alberti (1977) and Alberti and Emmons (1995a; 1995b) also are helpful resources with respect to assertiveness training.

Interpersonal Skills Training

Training in this area includes a wide range of skills encompassing communication, relationship development, self-awareness, social skills, and interpersonal problem solving. Interpersonal skills are the links that connect the individual and other people and determine the quality and satisfaction of our relationships. A major portion of those links involve communication. Satir (1972) wrote that once a human being has arrived on this earth, communication is the single largest factor determining what kinds of relationships he (she) makes with others and what happens to him (her) in the world about him (her)" (p. 30). Miller, Nunnally, and Wackman (1975) added that "communication is both a vehicle for creating relationships and an index of relationships" (p. 279). Consequently knowing how to assist group members in acquiring interpersonal skills is vital. In fact, Yalom (1985) pointed out that socializing techniques are a curative factor that operate in all helping groups.

Several sources for content and techniques in this area are Johnson (1981), Hamachek (1978), Miller, Nunnally, and Wackman (1975), Satir (1972), Tubbs and Moss (1978), and Platt and Spivak (1976).

Social Learning Techniques and Behavior Modification

A wide range of methods and techniques based on social learning theory and behavioral principles are applicable to personal problem solving. Techniques that stress imitative, cognitive, cognitive-behavioral, emotional, or operant learning all provide helpful tools to the group leader. Helpful resources in this area are Agras (1978), Bandura (1969), Krumboltz and Thoreson (1976), Kanfer and Goldstein (1975), Wolpe (1990), Beck and Weishaar (1995), and Meichanbaum (1977; 1985).

Marital and Family Processes and Dynamics

Many of the interpersonal concerns members bring to group emanate from their family relationships. Yalom (1970) even went so far as to say that "without exception patients enter group therapy with a history of highly unsatisfactory experience in their first and most important group—their primary family" (p. 12). Satir (1972) stated simply that "troubled families make troubled people" (p. 18). Seigelman (1983) said that the greatest interpersonal risks are related to marriage, separation, divorce, confronting family members, and raising children. Finally, Yalom (Forrester-Miller, 1989) noted emphatically "when you work with any patients who are having problems in living, everybody comes from a dysfunctional family" (p. 199). It stands to reason then that extensive knowledge and understanding of the dynamics of marital and family relations is vital in group counseling (Matthews, 1992). A background in family systems theory related to nuclear and extended family interaction, understanding family constellation and ordinal position, and a myriad of other concepts drawn from marriage and family therapy are vital (Trotzer & Trotzer, 1986). More attention will be given to this area in Chapter 14 in which we will focus on family theory as a group resource.

Conflict Resolution and Mediation

Conflict in relationships is inevitable and often surfaces as the focus of attention in counseling groups. Johnson (1981) pointed out that "an interpersonal conflict exists whenever an action by one person prevents, obstructs, or interferes with the actions of another person" (p. 195). Given the fact that conflict typically arises in groups (McClure, 1990) effective conflict resolution is a necessity. Conflict resolution is often the key to not only solving the presenting problem for members, but future problems as well. (Chapter 9 in Johnson, 1981 is an excellent chapter on resolving interpersonal conflicts.) Developing expertise in teaching conflict resolution strategies is thus another valuable asset to the group leader.

Mediation training is also a valuable adjunctive resource for group leaders providing principles, formats, tools, and procedures that can be adapted for use in the group and taught to group members relative to conflict situations outside the group. Resources for mediation training include:

1. Academy of Family Mediators
   355 Tyrol West
   1500 S. Highway 100
   Golden Valley, MN 55416
2. American Arbitration Association
   E. 140 West 51st St.
   New York, NY 10020-1203
3. Society of Professionals in Dispute Resolution
   815 15th St. NW, Suite 530
   Washington D.C. 20005

Values Clarification

Many interpersonal difficulties stem from a lack of understanding of one's values or from values conflicts. Knowing values clarification strategies and techniques will prove valuable in group counseling. Helpful sources include Kirschenbaum (1977); Raths, Harmin, and Simon (1966); Harmin, Kirschenbaum, and Simon (1973); and Simon, Howe, and Kirschenbaum (1972).

Violence and Abuse

Specific training for assessment, intervention, and treatment across the broad spectrum of violence and abuse is critical for group leaders. Training in the recognition and treatment of the following and other similar areas will enhance leader effectiveness:

1. substance abuse
2. violence in its many aspects—family and intimate (domestic) relationships; community, workplace, and school locations; victim and perpetrator assistance; and prevention, intervention and treatment (Koss et al., 1994; Brown, 1991)
3. sexual abuse in its various forms including assault, rape, sexual harassment, and incest (Rencken, 1989; Courtois, 1988)
4. emotional abuse
5. the whole range of posttraumatic stress disorders

Training and expertise in these areas provide a necessary background for the group leader who works extensively in schools, community agencies, or private practice and will help the leader anticipate the types of problems that will arise in counseling groups.

Group Leadership Skills

The function of training should be to help group practitioners develop the interpersonal skills that translate personality, academic, and theoretical factors into practical tools for use in group counseling. These designated leadership skills certainly are not an exhaustive list but they are representative of the wide range of skills recognized as valuable to group leaders. Pearson (1981) has divided leadership skills into the two basic categories of *teaching skills* and *group management skills*. Teaching skills include explicit teaching (e.g., information giving, skills training, mini-lecturing), implicit teaching (e.g., modeling, in vivo experiences), and process observation (see Appendix E). Group management skills include convening, eliciting, channeling, limit-setting, and protection. Jacobs, Harvill, and Masson (1988) have identified 12 basic skills for group leaders, and Corey and Corey (1977) described 15. For our purposes group leadership skills will be discussed under the three major categories of reaction skills, interaction skills, and action skills.

Reaction skills are responsive in nature and aid the leader in being receptive to individuals and the group as a whole. *Interaction skills* serve a mediating/moderating function in the group. They provide the leader the wherewithal to control and guide the group interaction and they facilitate therapeutic impact. *Action skills*, as their title implies, are vehicles that the leader can use to be proactive in promoting and directing the group process. They serve to increase the depth of group interaction and provide the means whereby leaders can assert their expertise for the good of certain individuals or the group.

The overarching nature of these skills is that they qualify as here and now intervention skills (Carroll and Wiggins, 1997) which experts in the field assert are essential for conducting the group process (Toth & Stockton, 1996). The specific skills in each of these categories are listed and briefly described in this section.

Reaction Skills

Active Listening

The skill of active listening is the most important skill a group leader can develop. Listening is all too frequently taken for granted as a natural part of the communication process that occurs automatically. That assumption is exactly where the problem lies. Because of the emphasis on and need for verbal expression in most areas of our lives, we work very hard at developing our expressive abilities but do very little to improve our receptive abilities. Group leaders must develop their potential as listeners to ensure understanding of the members, their problems, and their communications in the group. The listening skill must be active and not passive in nature; its influence is only useful if counselors can put into words what they are hearing and sensing so that all can benefit from their understanding. In other words, what is received in the private domain of the counselor's person must be returned to the public domain of the group for best results.

Group leaders who listen actively communicate four very important therapeutic qualities to the members of the group. They communicate *acceptance*, because they are willing to hear what clients have to say in a responsive manner rather than in a judgmental or pejorative manner. They communicate *respect* by giving members the opportunity to express how they see things without demeaning them or their perceptions. They communicate empathic *understanding* through the process of returning to the client what they understand the client's words to mean. And they communicate *caring* because of their interest in the member's point of view. All the other skills discussed in this category are really subskills of active listening. When combined they communicate all four of these qualities in a manner that accentuates the helping process.

In addition, active listening skills provide the means by which leaders determine what Makuch, Robison and Stockton (1998) call the *focus of leader interventions* in their recently developed Leadership Characteristics Inventory. As such these skills provide a basis for assessing leadership style from a process perspective. Categories of style include

1. *Individual-directed* intervention style
2. *Group-directed* intervention style
3. Focus on *thinking*
4. Focus on *feelings*

5. Group *process* focus
6. Group *topic* focus

Consequently the content of a leader's active listening responses are critical to his or her influence in the group.

Restatement

Restatement is the skill of repeating the basic content of a member's communication using much the same language and syntax. Its main purpose is to convey to the speakers that they are being heard and that the leader is with them at the moment and following attentively in their discussion. This skill is relatively easy to develop but can become sterile if overused. It is mainly effective in the beginning stages of communication and loses some of its utility as the depth of conversation increases.

> *Member*: I have to make a decision about college right away because my parents are getting impatient.
>
> *Leader*: You must decide about college soon because your parents are losing their patience with you.

Reflection

Reflection is the skill of expressing the meaning of the members' communications, indicating that they are not only heard but understood. Reflections can focus on the content of the communication or on the feelings that constitute the member's affective stance in regard to the communication. Reflection is useful because it helps the leader tune in to the internal frame of reference of the group member and because it helps members express what they might not have been able to express under other circumstances or when left to their own resources. It also assists other members in developing empathy for the speaker and models effective receptive responses for them.

   Reflection is a very complex skill because it encompasses both verbal and nonverbal communication and in its most sensitive form can penetrate to the very core of the client's being. As such it is also a potentially threatening mechanism that can frighten members if it is not adjusted to the level at which they are operating. Moving too quickly or too deeply in a reflective manner can create the impression that the leader is seeing right through the person. This can interfere with the group's progress and create a barrier between the members and the leader.

> *Member*: I have to make a decision about college right away because my parents are getting impatient.
>
> *Leader*: It sounds like you are feeling a lot of pressure from your parents about college but that you are still not sure what you want to do.

Clarifying

Clarifying is the skill of improving communication by responding to confusing and unclear aspects of a message in order to better understand it. Sometimes simply asking the member to say it again removes difficulties and clarifies the communication. At other times the leader may have to help members find the words necessary to relate their meaning. Clarification is used to consolidate and accentuate the key components of the speaker's statement so that the whole group is mutually cognizant of them. It is also useful in addressing process dynamics of the group that may be obscure but inhibiting or detrimental to group progress.

> *Member*: I'm experiencing so much failure lately that I'm beginning to think there is no hope at all for me to be happy. My grades are all Ds, I flunked my driver's test, and my parents are breaking up. I guess I'll just have to roll with the punches.
>
> *Leader*: Could you explain that to the group again. At the beginning it sounded like you were so discouraged that you were on the brink of giving up, but at the end you sounded more resilient.

Summarizing

Summarizing is the skill of pulling together the important elements of a particular conversation or a group session and presenting them in capsule form. Often summaries are offered in a concluding manner, but they also are useful for transitional purposes to stimulate further reactions on the part of the group members. However used, the tying together aspect of a summary is a very useful learning experience for members.

> *Leader*: Our discussion so far seems to have centered on our difficulties in relating to teachers who have old fashioned ideas. It seems some of you like these teachers because you always know what's expected, but that the rest of you feel they're "out of it" and that they're poor teachers. It also seems like the problems you mentioned are those teachers' responsibilities. So I'm wondering what part, if any, you think you play in the problems.

Tracking

Tracking is the nonverbal prerequisite to verbal expression. The leader utilizes eye contact and attending behavior to demonstrate interest and attention in the member who is speaking and follows the verbal flow of the group as it moves from member to member. Tracking supplemented with preverbal acknowledgements (head nodding) and limited verbal notations (e.g., "uh-huh," "I see") demonstrates the leader's involvement in the group interaction and in each participant as their participation evolves. It provides the basis or stimulus for verbal expression using the skills previously mentioned.

Scanning

Scanning is the nonverbal counterpart to tracking that incorporates the nonspeaking group members into the leader's purview. As one member is talking, sharing, or disclosing, the leader visually scans the rest of the group to observe their actions and reactions and notes their attentiveness. This skill provides valuable input to the leader relative to the interactive dynamics occurring in the group and helps the leader keep in touch with the other members while one member holds the focus. It serves as the means by which reaction skills can be extended to the group generally and, more often than not, provides the springboard for shifting into the use of the interaction and/or action skills described below.

Effective leaders maintain an equitable balance between tracking and scanning as the baseline for insuring their involvement with both the individual members and the group interaction.

Interaction Skills

Moderating

Moderating is a regulatory skill used by a leader to govern the group interaction, ensuring that all opinions, perceptions, thoughts, and feelings are aired. Moderating is also used to maintain a mode of discussion that's fair to all members. It requires a certain objectivity on the part of the leader to perform so as not to be viewed as biased by members.

> *Leader*: There seem to be two sides of this issue in our group. We just heard from those who are against any curfew. Now what about those of you who see a curfew as a positive thing.

Interpreting

Interpreting is the skill of relating material and feelings being discussed to an external criterion as a frame of reference to help members gain insight and understanding (Clark, 1993). In most cases the frame of reference is not cognizant to members and requires the leader's expertise to relate it to the situation being discussed. Group interpretations—interpretations that focus on the functioning of the group rather than on an individual in the group—help the group readjust communication patterns in a manner beneficial to therapeutic growth.

> *Leader*: The group is jumping from topic to topic and person to person so quickly today that it's difficult to follow. We might be using this scatter gun approach to avoid getting personal because we really don't trust each other.

Linking

Linking is the skill of tying together common elements in the communication of individual members to help them identify more closely with one another. It is a very useful tool in developing cohesiveness in the group. Linking also is used to pinpoint subgroups who have different perceptions on the same issue. At times it is useful in bringing to the surface underlying dynamics occurring in the group among members, and is a means of making the implicit explicit by verbalizing the nonverbal signals that are evident in the group.

> *Leader*:   Bill and Cheryl seem to think alike on the idea that dating should be done in groups, while Mary and Frank seem to favor the individual couples approach.

Blocking

Blocking is the skill of stepping in to prevent the execution of an undesirable, unethical, or inappropriate action by the group or some of its members. This skill requires leaders to use their knowledge of the group process as well as their sensitivity to individual member's rights, needs, or values to intercept, divert, or stop group actions that are detrimental to the members or the group. It is imperative that the leader using this skill be warm but firm and not influenced by the emotional climate that may prevail in the group at the moment that may be prompting detrimental dynamics.

> *Member*:   Betty has missed one group session, has been late to the other two, and isn't here today. I don't think she cares about our group at all, and that we should just boot her out
>
> *Members*: (Chorus of "I agree")
>
> *Leader*:   I'm not sure why Betty has acted the way she has, but I think you should bring this up to her in the group. You can't just eliminate her without hearing her side of it.

Supporting

Supporting is the skill of providing reinforcement, encouragement, and backing to group members in their efforts to interact in the group. It is most useful when members are disclosing difficult personal information or giving emotionally tinted feedback. It also is useful for drawing out quiet members and aiding shy individuals to express themselves. The giving of support also implies that it can be withdrawn and therefore it can be used as a means of modifying members' behavior in both a positive and negative sense.

> *Member*:   I guess what I have really been wanting to say but couldn't is that I would like the group's help in overcoming my shyness in relating to people.

Leader: John, you showed a lot of courage in sharing that, and maybe you have just taken an important first step in overcoming your fear of relating to other people.

Limiting

Limiting is the skill of defining boundaries to give structure or direction to the group. It provides the framework within which the group can interact and prevents excesses and deviations that will infringe on the rights of members or result in irresponsible actions in the group. It cuts two ways at once because it curtails harmful interaction from occurring while at the same time denoting guidelines for therapeutic interaction.

Leader: It's in the best interest of the group and of each of the members if we don't discuss with others what we talk about in here. That way we won't run into problems like gossiping or breaking confidences.

Protecting

Protecting is the skill of preventing individual members from being unduly criticized, scapegoated, or hurt in a nontherapeutic manner. This skill is essential in combating the overwhelming force of group pressure, which can become a problem at times. In most cases it's necessary to defend single members from the onslaught of the group, but sometimes it's also necessary to protect subgroups of members who are being treated unfairly or inappropriately. This skill demands the ultimate in sensitivity because the leader must be aware of the individual member's limits and ploys, the group's intentions, the possibility of protection coming from within the group, and personal responsibility for making the decision to protect. It is particularly relevant in regard to recognizing and respecting cultural characteristics and diversity factors represented in group members.

Leader: It seems like everyone in the group has had something to say about Joanna, but no one has mentioned anything positive. I feel she has held up very well under all that pressure, but now I think maybe we should look at the group's behavior for a while to find out what is happening to make us so caustic.

Consensus Taking

Consensus taking is the skill of finding out where members stand in their perceptions of the various topics and problems that are being considered in the group. Of particular importance is to tap all divergences of opinion in the group so that members clearly understand where they are in relation to each other. This skill is useful when topics of intense personal or emotional content are discussed and the conversation becomes heated and difficult to follow. It settles the group down and clears the air, making it possible to proceed with both better understanding and less affective interference. It is useful in processing group experiences and events facilitating integration and closure.

> *Leader*:   We have been hard at it for the last 15 minutes about how much commitment we really have to this group, and it has been heavy and a little difficult to come to grips with. Maybe we could do a go-around where each one of you speaks only for yourself, giving your own feeling of commitment. Bill, would you start it off?

Action Skills

Questioning

Questioning, according to Benjamin (1987), is another of those natural tendencies that needs to be refined and developed before it has a positive impact on the helping process. Our automatic reliance on the question is a dependency that must be overcome if we are to be effective in groups. If we don't develop alternatives and vary the nature of our questioning we not only limit the effectiveness of the helping process but also model less effective questioning styles for group members to use in their interaction with each other. The negative effect is cumulative. With these reservations, the skill of questioning is still an important and highly relied on tool in the group process. Clark (1989) delineated the qualities of effective questioning into the following categories. Effective questions are:

1. *Supportive*: allow the respondent independence and latitude to reflect and respond;
2. *Relevant*: relate to the "immediate experience of the group member and lead to productive discussion."
3. *Regulated*: frequency and timing are critical and in the control of the group leader;
4. *Expansive*: enable or facilitate member expressiveness as opposed to closed questions which curtail response; and
5. *Open ended*: prompt members to generate material and expand expressiveness (pp. 121–122)

He also advocates the use of questions as processing tools in the group for purposes of assessing, convening, confronting, expanding, universalizing, linking, and controlling.

Questions can be used to help group members consider aspects of themselves and their concerns they haven't thought of before. Questions also can serve to transfer ambiguous silences into productive discussion. The types of questions used should typically open the door for further discussion. Closed ended or yes/no questions create unbalanced conversation patterns and seldom result in spontaneous discussion.

Member: I'm afraid my parents no longer trust me and that there's nothing I can do that will change their minds.

Leader: It sounds like you feel you might have violated their trust to a point where it's irreparable. But you seem to know what they do expect. Could you tell us what you think their standards of trust are for you?

Probing

Probing is the skill of helping group members go more deeply into themselves and their problems under the direction of an outside source such as the leader. Members often will not take responsibility upon themselves to go more deeply into their problems but will consent to do so if the leader takes a more active role in the process. Effective probing requires the leader to be aware of the sensitive points in the client's frame of reference and the limits to which the client can be asked to go. Awareness of cultural and diversity factors is particularly relevant when probing is considered. Probing should be tentative, always leaving an avenue open for the client to back off if the procedure gets too threatening. Probing is useful in helping members learn the process of introspection and can be an effective means of gradually moving the group to deeper levels of interaction and problem or issue examination.

Member: I know I have some real feelings of anger inside me, but I don't really know where they come from.

Leader: So you know you feel angry but don't know why. I wonder, could you identify any situations where you feel more angry than in other situations?

Tone Setting

Tone setting is subtle but crucial to the atmosphere and attitude of the group. It is the process of establishing a qualitative standard the group can observe and to which it can respond. Leaders can establish the tone of the session in many ways, including the arrangement of the physical setting, the personal mood that they express to the group, the character of their actions in the leadership role, and the activities or suggestions they propose in the group. Tone setting is important in the initial moments of the group session but also can be extremely useful when the group could benefit from a change in mood. For example, comic relief often serves the purpose of pulling the group out of extended discussions that have become emotionally draining. Tone setting gives members a base rate to use in gauging their own behaviors, feelings, and thoughts and provides them with a means of determining how to respond appropriately.

> *Leader*: We've been struggling along here talking about all the things we have to change about ourselves, so as a point of contrast lets have each person share a couple of things about themselves or their life that don't need changing.

Confronting

Confronting is the skill of getting members to face things about themselves that they are blatantly or subtly attempting to avoid. The use of this skill can have potentially explosive repercussions, which may be detrimental to the group and its members if not handled appropriately and sensitively. In group counseling confrontation should generally be tentative and should never force a member into a corner with no escape. This skill is most useful in helping the group deal with discrepancies and inconsistencies in individual and group behavior. It also is helpful in getting members to face responsibility in regard to their problems and behavior.

Confrontation should only be used after a foundation of trust and acceptance has been laid and when the dynamics in the group are cohesive in nature. With these safeguards the members realize that confrontation is directed at their actions, not their persons, and is motivated by intentions that are constructive rather than destructive.

> *Member*: I am doing everything I possible can to fulfill my contract of studying one hour a day at home, but I just can't make it.

> *Leader*: As you came in today, Jack, I heard you telling Sally you watched TV for three hours last night and never cracked a book. How do you explain that in connection with what you just said?

Personal Sharing

Personal sharing is the means by which leaders disclose themselves to the group. It is an important skill because any time leaders do give of themselves by sharing personal concerns or perceptions it usually has a significant effect on the group. Seldom is the impact neutral. For this reason the leader's personal self-disclosure can facilitate the group process as well as help him or her deal with what is going on inside. Of course, leaders must be sensitive to the amount and depth of personal revelation that is appropriate and that the group can handle. Personal sharing is useful in setting an example for group members and helps them see the leader as a fellow human being. It also serves the function of demonstrating that the leader is willing to engage in the same process in which the members are expected to become involved. The overriding purpose of personal sharing, however, should be for the benefit of the group and its members. If personal issues emanating from the group or the leader's life outside the group emerge and need attention, the more appropriate forum is consultation, supervision, or personal counseling.

Leader: I guess I'm really not with it today. My mind keeps wandering ahead to vacation next week when I'll be having surgery.

Member: I thought you were kind of daydreaming today, but I guess you're just a little uptight about your operation.

Modeling

Modeling is the skill of demonstrating by exemplary action the qualities, characteristics, and skills that members may need to learn to function effectively in the group and in their personal lives. Leaders are models whether they choose to be or not because of their position in the group. Therefore leaders must make the best use of the situation rather than leaving their modeling impact to chance. Modeling is helpful in teaching members important interpersonal skills that will make communication and interaction in the group more effective. It also is useful in alleviating the problems of orientation in the group process. Members can take their cues from the leader and model their own behavior and involvement accordingly.

Leader: Today I would like to begin the session by having each of you describe yourself as if you were your own best friend. Use your first name and the third person at all times in describing yourself. I'll start with myself and you can see how it works. Jim is. . . .

☐ Group Leadership Functions

Skills are only the building blocks that leaders use to perform their functions. The manner in which the leader uses his or her skills is determined by the leader's personality, theoretical orientation, and the nature of the group process. Which skills are used at what time and for what purpose depict *the functions of group leadership*. The generic functions of leaders in counseling and therapy groups include initiating and maintaining effective group process, helping members establish goals, protecting members from harm, and effecting appropriate termination (Kaplan & Saddock, 1993). The content of those functions outlined by Polcin (1991) include:

1. *emotional stimulation*: fostering expressions of feelings, values, beliefs, and emotional concerns;
2. *caring*: expressions of warmth, acceptance, concern and genuineness;
3. *meaning attribution*: providing cognitive understanding to members, and
4. *executive leadership*: setting limits, suggesting norms, pacing, managing time, blocking, and interceding (p. 10).

Functions are also the means by which leaders help the group process develop in accord with the needs of the group members and the goals of the group.

Leader functions embody the essential components of a leader's group theory and approach. Although the manner of carrying out the various functions is influenced by training, theoretical orientation, and leader personality, their basic impact on the group remains much the same. The specific functions explicated below are not mutually exclusive, but they do tend to be relatively comprehensive and particularly relevant to the group counseling process.

Promoting Interaction

One of the primary functions of the group leader is to promote interaction in the group. An atmosphere of interaction accelerates group integration, and so leaders must do their utmost to promote its development. This function is as much a contingency of what leaders do not do as it is of what they do. Leaders who dominate, sermonize, evaluate, teach, and moralize in group counseling tend to deter interaction rather than promote it. In fact, leaders who manifest aggressive leader attributes, are charismatic, or use the power of their personality or position to control are associated with negative outcomes in groups (Korda & Pancrazio, 1989). In contrast, leaders who are able to share leadership responsibility, relinquish the role of expert by encouraging members to help each other, and include all the group members in the discussion create conditions that are highly conducive to therapeutic group interaction and member involvement. Dye (De-Lucia, 1991) emphasized that "leaders should be as active as they need to be to get those vital (group) processes going. Once they do get them going, it's time to get out of the way and let the people work things out on their own" (p. 68). In support of this view Conyne et al. (1990) stipulated, "If group leaders can consistently exhibit high levels of facilitative responses, serve as a model to the group, function as a director of communication and be a catalyst to move the process, the consequences would be demonstrated by changes in member behavior, attitudes and/or affect" (p. 33).

Leaders also can promote interaction by the physical arrangements they set up in the group. Groups that meet in comfortable rooms and sit in a circle as opposed to a square or ellipse find it much easier to relate and communicate with one another. The use of a skill such as linking to promote member-to-member communication is very useful in carrying out this function. Another effective technique is personal sharing. If leaders share their feelings and perceptions—especially early in the group's development—they will encourage members to interact with each other in much the same way. The overall purpose of this function is to create an atmosphere that encourages honest, spontaneous give-and-take discussion among members.

Facilitating Interaction

The facilitating function, though similar to the promoting function, has several unique qualities that merit its separate consideration. Lakin (n.d.) stated that one essential function of any group leader is to facilitate social interaction. Facilitation implies that action is taken to enhance interaction that is already occurring. In other words, facilitating is a responsive function. It depends on the group to provide the stimulus that propels it into action. The leader responds to the action by suggesting methods that make communication patterns more meaningful and effective. Facilitation is directly related to increasing understanding in the group. Its effective use is dependent on the group leader's sensitivity and awareness and hinges on the ability to express one's self clearly to the group members. Stockton (Morran, 1992; Stockton & Toth, 1996) has broken down the facilitating function into component parts of perceiving what is occurring in the group, mentally devising or developing an appropriate leadership response, and expressing that response as an intervening activity. He noted that "the three components of perceiving, developing strategies, and intervention are inextricably intertwined" (Morran, 1992, p. 8). Chapter 13 includes a discussion of the use of communication exercises in performing the facilitating function.

Initiating Interaction

The initiating function refers to the leader's active role in structuring the interaction of the group. It can be utilized to generate interaction and determine what the focus of that interaction will be or how it will proceed. The action skills are very important in performing this function, as are activities designed to make things happen in the group. The effective use of this function depends on the leader's knowledge of the group process and his or her expertise in determining the needs of the group members. In most cases initiating is done to direct the group to considerations the leader deems beneficial to the members or the group process. The initiating function also is useful in alleviating anxieties caused by unstructured situations. Chapter 13 describes the use of communication exercises in carrying out the initiating function and gives more details as to its nature.

Guiding Interaction

The guiding function of the group leader has been alluded to in Hulse's (1950) description of the dynamics of group therapy. "Tension is the motor which keeps the therapeutic group going. Anxiety is the fuel that makes the motor run. The group therapist becomes the responsible conductor of this vehicle" (p. 834). The group, because of its complex and potentially destructive nature, needs someone to keep it goal oriented and to steer interaction into the most beneficial channels. Dinkmeyer and Muro (1971) stated that this guiding function helps the group move toward its accepted goals and is the "sum total of the counselor's efforts to utilize effectively the unique benefits of the group situation for personal growth" (p. 118). Lakin (n.d.) refers to this function as the leader's role in "intermanaging interaction." The skills of most consequence in performing this function are the interaction skills, although other skills such as tone setting and questioning are also useful.

Some theorists stress the guiding function as primary and cast the leader in the role of a participant-observer who refrains from personal involvement, stepping in only to guide the group when it deviates from its set purpose and then stepping out again. Vorrath and Brentro's (1974) Positive Peer Culture Groups operate on this model. An important aspect of this function is the leader's ability to control the speed and depth of involvement and interaction. Leaders must be able to encourage members to recognize feelings and proceed to deeper levels and yet maintain a modulated pace that does not leave members behind or hanging. In either case, however, effective leadership requires "spontaneous and creative responses to complex, unrehearsed situations" (Conyne, et al., 1990, p. 33).

Intervening

The intervening function is used to protect group members and contain excesses in the group process. It is used to ensure that each member can exercise the right to be heard and retain the right to privacy. Intervening is necessary to counter the dangers of the group process. Groups may not give support when it is needed, may distort reality, or create pressures that lead to loss of control (Lakin, n.d.). If any of these situations becomes imminent, the leader must intervene to prevent them from damaging individuals or disrupting the group process. Dinkmeyer and Muro (1971) listed several instances in which leader intervention may be appropriate:

1. When individuals are victimized by group forces.
2. When groups create excessive anxieties or pressures for conformity.
3. When hostility is misdirected.
4. When the majority (consensus of opinion) may be incorrect.
5. When individuals are forced to accept group solutions.
6. When groups become too comfortable and no action toward resolving problems occurs.

Intervening may also entail keeping time limits and bringing the group discussion back to its proper focus. Most of the interaction skills are useful in performing this function and the leader must be willing to take responsibility to preserve the psychological well being of members and the therapeutic intent of the group process. Hansen, Warner, and Smith (1980) referred to actions involved in intervening and the rules-keeping function described next as *executive functions*.

Rules-Keeping

Rules-keeping is one of the more technical but necessary functions the leader performs in the group. Its basic intent is to see that the group interaction stays within the framework of the guidelines established to govern that interaction. These guidelines or rules may be imposed by the leader at the outset of the group (see Figure 5.2), can be developed cooperatively between the leader and members, or can be allowed to evolve during the course of group interaction. In any event the leader's function is to see that they are maintained and use the authority of the leader role to prevent any infractions that might develop. The performance of this function should not be arbitrary but should be solidly based on the leader's knowledge of what constitutes therapeutic group interaction and a sensitivity to member needs (Polcin, 1991).

Consolidating

The consolidating function of the leader is the action he or she takes to draw things together in a meaningful way so that group members can relate to them. It also may involve tying together numerous thoughts and feelings in a brief and coherent way. Leaders must be aware of the consensus in the group in order to perform this function effectively. They also must realize that differences of opinion will exist and use this function to help members communicate and understand their differences and similarities. Skills that facilitate this function are clarifying, summarizing, and linking. The main purposes of the consolidating function are to keep the group members at the same level of understanding as the group process unfolds and develops and to help them differentiate, acknowledge, and value diversity in the group.

Enhancing Communication

The function of enhancing communication serves to help group members express themselves more precisely and understand each other more accurately. The leader is able to perform this function by focusing attention on each client's needs and exhibiting genuine caring but at the same time maintaining a healthy separateness to allow for objectivity. Ohlsen (1970) described the nature of this function as follows: "When he (she) is at his (her) best, a counselor can feel deeply with a client without experiencing emotional reactions which are deleterious to the counseling relationship" (p. 2).

The leader who operates in this manner builds relationships in the group by being empathic. The skills of greatest use for enhancing communication are the reaction skills, all of which depend on the counselor's ability to listen actively and to understand members sensitively (Egan, 1986). Leaders must be aware of multiple levels in the member's verbalizations. They must be able to take words and actions at face value while at the same time realize that an underlying ambivalence may be in the message. The leader who can work to merge external expression with internal motivation in the member's communication will be making significant progress in securing a foundation of understanding in the group. The effectiveness of this function depends on the leader's ability to observe and deal with the impact of each member's communication on the rest of the group. Ohlsen (1974) stated that "While trying to detect the speaker's feelings, encouraging him (her) to act and reinforcing his (her) desired behaviors, the counselor also must note how the speaker's behavior is influencing others and how the behavior of others is influencing the speaker" (p. 144). In this way the leader can work with the total process—encompassing expression, reception, and response—and thus increase the influence of communication in the helping process.

The group leader can accelerate and enhance communication by encouraging members to speak directly to each other rather than to the leader (Yalom, 1985). Getting members to send "I messages," using first and second person pronouns (I, me, you), has a significant effect in drawing members together. This personalization of communication clarifies meaning and makes speakers more cognizant of their own motivations, thus improving the quality of their messages.

Resolving Conflicts

If one adage about the group process consistently holds true, it is that the course of group counseling never runs smooth. Inevitably in the process of intense interpersonal interaction, conflicts will arise (McClure, 1990). Not only is conflict inevitable but how it is addressed is a crucial factor in the movement of the group toward productive results (Rybak & Brown, 1997). In a sense, conflict serves a functional purpose in groups since it represents both an enhanced level of relationship development and requires cooperation and continued communication to resolve. If not resolved groups can get stuck or side tracked. The group leader's task is to see that conflicts are addressed and resolved beneficially if not harmoniously for all parties involved. This function requires all the skill and sensitivity the counselor can muster to effect it constructively. It requires that the leader be aware of sources of conflict such as frustrated individual needs, conflicting goals, hidden agendas, disappointment with leader functioning, groping for structure, and anxiety over a new and novel situation. This function requires that leaders know how to implement strategies for conflict resolution. Rybak and Brown (1997) describe two perspectives for dealing with conflict: *conflict management* and *conflict resolution*. They note that "conflict can be destructive to a group, but as members experience satisfactory resolution of conflict, they learn to trust the constructive dialogue that led to resolution" (p. 31). Conflict management takes into account the norms of the group in accordance with cultural and personal values regarding conflict (Merta, 1995). Conflict resolution relates to the manner in which conflict is addressed. When conflict emerges, leaders must know how to respond, when to step in, and when to allow the group or the particular members to work it out. Most of all they must be willing to acknowledge conflict and deal with it therapeutically, attempting to identify its roots and use it constructively in helping group members grow (McRoy & Brown, 1996).

Mobilizing Group Resources

This function more than any other determines the optimum level of a group's helping effectiveness. Unique to group counseling is that it offers the individual many potential sources of help as opposed to just one. The effective group leader therefore is able to assess what the group resources are and mobilizes them for the benefit of the individual and the group. The more successful leaders are in performing this function the less pressure and responsibility they will feel in being the expert in the group. The more adept they are at drawing upon group resources, the more self-esteem members will experience which in turn will improve the morale of the group. The purpose of this function is to get group members to help themselves by helping each other. Group leaders who function well in this way find that many of the other functions are no longer necessary because the group will take responsibility for performing them.

Most of the skills described earlier assist the group counselor in performing this function but the key to its effectiveness is the leader's willingness to operate behind the scenes through group members rather than in a direct helping capacity. Leaders who actively share, redistribute, and defer power and use *contingent statements* rather than *direct approach statements* in responding to members (Rybak & Brown, 1997) are more successful in carrying out this function. Counselors who prefer to do the counseling themselves often do not utilize the group's helping potential to the fullest possible extent.

☐ Issues in Group Leadership

Leaders must grapple with several basic issues in developing their own approaches to group counseling. The manner in which they resolve these issues determines their leadership style. Although theories and training influence and guide the leader's development, the responsibility still remains for each person to decide how to function in the group. The purpose of this section is to elucidate those basic issues confronting all group leaders, the resolution of which affects the group process and molds the unique style of the leader's approach.

Responsibility

The issue of responsibility is always difficult to clarify. It can be discussed on a philosophical level, looking at the helping process and making corresponding assumptions about the basic nature of personhood. On the one hand, if people are viewed as incapable of helping themselves, then the helping process must take responsibility to direct and influence them to help them resolve their problems and live more satisfying and fulfilling lives. On the other hand, if people are viewed as capable and having sufficient resources to help themselves, the helping process need only entail providing a set of conditions or an environment where those resources can emerge and be used by the individual to resolve problems and enhance life adjustment. In between these two extremes are a multitude of positions that different theories expound as the proper perspective on the responsibility issue in the helping process. However, the transition from theory to practice is difficult, especially in group counseling where the leader must cope with a wide variety of expectations and pressures from group members in addition to handling the responsibility issue in a professional manner.

Leader responsibility is an issue on a continuum, with one extreme stressing the leader as totally responsible for all the interaction and impact of the group and the other extreme placing the responsibility totally on the group. Somewhere in between is Mahler's (1969) position, which states that "the main responsibility for growth of the group rests with members but the leader does all he (she) can to facilitate that process" (p. 194). Although these positions describe the relationship of leader responsibility to the group, they do not elaborate on how responsibility is actually manifested.

Leaders who assume total responsibility actually take charge of the entire experience of the group and its members and operate in much the same manner as the director of a movie. They direct, maneuver, push, confront, structure, and demonstrate to bring out the best possible picture or result. This result should be in accord with individual needs and group goals but the extent to which the group experience coincides with those needs and goals is entirely the responsibility of the leader. The weaknesses of this type of leadership are much the same as those of autocratic leadership styles. Members do not learn to take responsibility for themselves, they learn dependence rather than autonomy, and their needs are met only to the extent that leaders personally can extend themselves and their expertise to encompass them. Since most group approaches aspire to increase individual responsibility rather than decrease it, this particular approach to leadership is seldom seen in total. Some leaders, however, begin by taking more comprehensive responsibility and gradually shift responsibility to the members as they see them develop the competence to handle it. This process of responsibility transfer is usually concurrent with the developmental process of problem solving, which gradually moves the members from dependence on outside help at the beginning to independence or autonomy at the end of the group process.

Leaders who invest total responsibility in the group tend to operate from a frame of reference that is based on confidence and trust in the members and the group to do what is best for their own growth. They depend on the group to monitor its excesses and negative reactions. The group's ability to function in a responsible manner is often demonstrated by members stepping in to give support and diverting overly emotional or unjust feedback into more positive channels. Members in this type of group certainly learn responsibility but may at times mistake freedom for license. Because of the extensive pressure groups can exert, at times members become so embroiled in the interaction of the moment that they miss the cues that indicate potential psychological or personal damage is imminent. In these instances this style of leadership breaks down and could have adverse effects on the total group process.

The key considerations in handling the responsibility issue relate to the general group goal of helping members learn individual responsibility and guaranteeing their personal well being in the group process. However the leader decides to operate, responsibility must always be evaluated in terms of its impact on the members' ability to function adequately on their own. If the leader's actions do not increase member independence and autonomy in resolving their personal concerns and problems, those actions are antitherapeutic. If, however, the leader's stand on responsibility accentuates member self-sufficiency in a constructive and growth producing way, then those actions are congruent with the intent of the helping process.

In my opinion the leader is always ultimately responsible for the well being of group members and for ensuring that the group interaction is constructive in nature. In other words, leaders, because of their training and professional commitment, are remiss if they do not exercise their responsibility to prevent negative consequences in the group. Leaders can share responsibility to a very large degree, but they can never abdicate their responsibility. Doing so completely undermines the nature of the helping profession and is detrimental to positive therapeutic intervention. Leaders must be willing to divert topic and conversational trends that seem to be shaping into negative and damaging content (Blaker & Samo, 1973). They must be willing to intervene to protect members and to serve as a reality check if the group does not do so. As Lakin (1969) noted, responsibility must be consciously exercised and modeled by the leader if the group is to qualify as a professional therapeutic venture.

Many, if not most, of the following issues are contingent upon the stand the group leader takes regarding responsibility. Leader decisions about structure and role are particularly tied in with responsibility.

Role of the Group Leader

The role of the group leader is not only a composite of functions performed but a manifestation of the philosophical biases held. The role issue primarily concentrates on how leaders interact in the group in terms of behavior. In actuality the leader role is a conglomeration of subroles that emerge on the basis of interaction among the group leader's personality, philosophical orientation, and the needs of the group. Those subroles that are most frequently used tend to form the character of the leader's style and influence the nature of the group process.

The most common subroles are those of director, facilitator, participator, observer, and expert. The *director* takes an active role in determining the nature and focus of group interaction; the *facilitator* is responsive to what is already occurring in the group; the *participator* operates on an equal level with other group members in the discussion; the *observer* stands apart from the interaction interjecting comments as they appear necessary or appropriate; and the *expert* is the source of knowledge, information, and wisdom that can be utilized to help members or improve the group process. These roles are not always separate entities, but they do involve significant identifiable characteristics that perpetuate the group process. Each will be discussed in turn.

The *director* role helps the group process by giving it structure and direction. It is closely aligned with the philosophy that places responsibility in the hands of the leader. It enables group leaders to assert themselves in the group process and gives members respite from struggling with ambiguous circumstances. The use of the director role should be to either meet individual needs in the group or initiate useful group interaction. Too heavy a dependence on this role reduces opportunities for group members to assert themselves and reduces flexibility in the group.

The *facilitator* role depends on the group for an impetus to action. It helps the group process develop by responding to the direction and goals initiated by the group. This role is related to the position where responsibility is placed in the hands of group members. Members feel more freedom to direct their own interactions but are also confident the leader will step in to make suggestions or help when appropriate. Total reliance on this role may create undue pressure and frustration in the group and may even lead to disenchantment with the group process as a whole. Mahler (1969) pointed out that some counselors confuse the facilitation role by combining it with a misconceived notion of permissiveness. "Some counselors appear to be comparable to indecisive and insecure parents; they hope that their `per-missiveness' will enable (clients) to find themselves. However, counselors must have a sense of purpose and direction or they will be able to accomplish very little" (p. 17). In other words, the facilitator role is enacted according to a specific purpose and is not just a matter of rolling with the tide of group interaction.

The *participator* role probably gives group leaders the most difficulty. Knowing when and how to participate with members is hard to determine. Sometimes members really do not want to know about the leader and prefer to have him or her help out only in times of crisis. Other times leaders may think they are participating on an equal level only to find they are being perceived by members as dominating. Of particular importance in this role is the amount and type of sharing the counselor does. The decision about how deeply counselors can or should go into their own lives and feelings is a difficult one. Mahler (1969) indicated that the participatory leader has the most positive impact on group morale and feelings. Through leader participation members come to see the leader as real human being and do not feel that they are being forced to engage in things the leader is not willing to do. Dinkmeyer and Muro (1971) also pointed out that the effective group counselor is one who is viewed by group members as being with them, and for them, as individuals. Participating can contribute to that perception. An effective participator can usually be active in the group without creating the undesirable side effects usually associated with subroles that cast the leader in a more separated position from members. Participating is a good alternative to passive group leadership for those leaders who want to be active but do not want to dominate the group process.

The *observer* role is one of the most flexible roles the leader can play because it can usually be combined with other roles (participant-observer, director-observer). In its more pure form leaders attempt to maintain an objective yet sensitive awareness of what is transpiring in the group. At times it can rankle members because they feel they are being analyzed and watched. This reaction can cause rifts between the members and the leader. If, however, leaders can parlay their observations into meaningful comments that are beneficial to individuals or the group process, the leader's role as observer can be vindicated and negative reactions curtailed.

The *expert* role of the counselor is potentially both the most detrimental and most useful role the counselor can play in the group. The temptation to be the expert is one of the major pitfalls of many group leaders. Because of it leaders sometimes get themselves into an advice giving bind from which they have difficulty extricating themselves. Mahler (1969) stated the basic problem with leaders who are too quick to use their expertise: "A counselor is lacking in knowledge and understanding of how behavior is changed if he (she) is too eager to give answers, solutions to problems or advice instead of helping individuals discover answers and solutions for themselves"

(p. 17). The counselor as expert is also a necessary and useful aspect of the group leadership role. Leader training, experience, and knowledge are invaluable assets in helping individuals with their problems and in developing a therapeutic group atmosphere. Striking a balance between using expertise and refusing to do so is a complex task for the group leader. One general guideline in determining whether the leader should opt for the role of expert or not is to assess the motivation for that action. If it is in the best interests of an individual or the group process, most likely the effect will be positive. If, however, it is motivated by self-gratification or ego reinforcement on the counselor's part, it should be used hesitantly. Since expertise inherently carries some residual of personal gratification, enhancing the group process and assisting individuals should predominate as the impetus for its use.

The interplay between these roles is of significant import to the group process. The leader must carefully assess their utility and influence in order to function in the most positive manner as a leader and develop professional competence as a group counselor.

The Structure Controversy

The controversy of structured groups versus unstructured groups has been with us almost as long as the group movement itself (Journal for Specialists in Group Work, 1979). Although some would argue that lack of structure by the group leader is in itself a form of structure, a semantic battle does little to help the group leader resolve this issue. Landreth (1973) zeroed in on this issue definitively when he wrote that "the basic question is not whether or not to structure but rather what kind of structuring is needed and how much to structure" (p. 371). Bednar and Langenbaum (1979) added that a linear polarity of structure to nonstructure does not exist because the nonimposition of expectations (ambiguity) is in and of itself a structure. From these premises then our discussion will derive.

Nonstructured groups basically mean that the leader does little to initiate group interaction and functions in the more responsive capacity of a facilitator a la Carl Rogers. *Structured groups* usually refer to groups that the leader directs and runs in an initiating manner, often with the help of structured activities and with ostensible control over the interaction. In the former case the leader's image is submerged in the group process to a point where his or her eminence as the titular head of the group is diffused. In the latter case the leader is always an obviously significant person who seldom loses either position or influence as the leader of the group. Between these two are many positions that reflect more or less the basic positions.

A perusal of the pros and cons of these basic positions on structuring reveals the surprisingly complementary nature of the two positions. What is an advantage to one side is a disadvantage to the other and vice versa. Thus when viewed through a flexible perspective, movement one way or the other on the structure continuum becomes less a liability and more an asset in making the group counseling process effective. Thus we come full circle to Landreth's (1973) position.

The arguments for nonstructured groups revolve around the learning by experience philosophy. Group members, in struggling with the lack of structure, come to realize the need for and nature of positive structure and work to develop it. In this way they learn personal responsibility and identify more closely with their work. Less structure gives more opportunity for individual differences to be accounted for and provides members with more freedom to act constructively on their own behalf and in helping others. The leader in nonstructured groups needs to tolerate ambiguity and risk member dissatisfaction and negative feedback during the initial phases when members are grappling with a nonstructuring leader situation. When successful the nonstructured approach creates strong group cohesiveness, high morale, and a positive therapeutic milieu in which members can help and be helped without the prior sanction of the group leader to do so.

Arguments for the *structured group* more than compensate for the weakness of the nonstructured approach, just as the strengths of the nonstructured approach counter the deficiencies of structured groups. Dinkmeyer and Muro (1971) referred to structuring as programming. "To program a group means that the group counselor, the official group leader, chooses to initiate specific group behaviors of his (her) own choosing at some time in the group's life. Spontaneous interaction, of course, refers to behaviors that originate within the context of the group life itself" (p. 122). Bach (1954) enumerated several advantages to structuring. It enhances cooperation in early group life, decreases leader and member anxiety, enlarges weak minority participation, contrasts individual performance against group performance, differentiates group life from the outside world culture, and reduces emotional anxiety over free expression without altering the leader's role. Landreth (1973) added that structuring may help leaders approach the group with more self-confidence, a prerequisite to the development of a cohesive group. By structuring, group members know what is expected and can therefore concentrate their energies toward accomplishing the goals of the group and resolving their own problems.

Caple and Cox (1989) investigated the relationship between structure and the variables of cohesion and attraction in groups. They found that initial group sessions that were too ambiguous produced anxiety that was detrimental to self-disclosure and deterred both cohesion and attraction. On the other hand, "groups on which structure was imposed reported higher levels of attraction" (p. 22). In contrast, too much structure resulted in lower group cohesion. Over time, however, both structured and unstructured groups evened out relative to self-disclosure and subsequent levels of attraction and cohesion. These findings led them to recommend the use of structure initially to facilitate self-disclosure and thereby enhance the development of attraction and cohesion. Hetzel, Barton and Davenport (1994) supported this finding and stipulated that structured activities are particularly relevant for initiating men's groups. Initial structuring reduces anxiety and improves communication which opens the way for group dynamics to develop.

The point of the matter is that the need for structure varies from group to group and leader to leader. Some groups do not need any help in structuring, while others need help because they will not, or do not, know how to assume responsibility for doing so. In addition, the purpose for which groups are formed greatly affects the need for structure. Thus the resolution of this issue is contingent on a variety of factors. The most important variable seems to be the leader's propensity to determine how much structure is needed and to act in accordance with that awareness.

Group Leadership: Art or Science?

Max DePree (1989) in his classic leadership primer entitled *Leadership is an Art* states the following:

> The first responsibility of a leader is to define reality. The last is to say thank you. In between the two, the leader must become a servant and a debtor, That sums up the progress of an artful leader (p. 11).

Although emanating from the world of business and Fortune 500 companies, there is a lot of wisdom to be gleaned from DePree's perspective in the field of human services—specifically group leadership. He emphasizes that the signs of outstanding leadership appear primarily among the followers, in this case members of the group. Are they "reaching their potential? Are they learning? Do they achieve required results? Do they change with grace? Manage conflict?" (De Pree, 1989, p. 12). What better criteria to determine the merit of leadership in counseling and therapy groups.

The art versus science dilemma often is raised in the helping professions, particularly those which are concerned with helping people resolve psychological and personal-social problems. However, this issue need not force a group leader into a decision one way or the other since in all probability leading a group is a combination of both. Mahler (1969) described leadership as a science because its methods and procedures are exposed to objective assessment for validation. Leadership is also an art because it depends on the "counselor's intuitive sensitivity in knowing when to make a suggestion or provide information, when and how to challenge clients to action, and when to support client efforts to face disturbing feelings" (p. 12). Dinkmeyer and Muro (1971) stated that successful group counselors are an integrated blend of specialist and artist. Ohlsen, Horne, and Lawe (1988) referred to the leader as both a scientist and a practitioner.

Leaders must be scholars who keep themselves continually abreast of new knowledge pertaining to the field of group work. They must be scientists who use empirical methods to assess the impact of the group process and evaluate results. And they must be artists who can use their knowledge and the results of scientific inquiry to meet the needs of group members, help them resolve their problems, and guide the group process. Any time leaders lose sight of the personal element by attempting to conduct groups according to standardized scientific principles, they will become rigid and inflexible, jeopardizing the effectiveness of the group in helping individuals. Any time leaders rely only on their own personality and artistic prowess in leading a group, they lose the perspective of objective evaluation that is necessary to elicit the benefit and consistency of the group process in helping people resolve their problems. So the resolution of this whole issue is to develop a balance between leadership as an art—accounting for the subjective nature of human beings, their needs, differences and uniqueness—and leadership as a science—supplying structure and direction to the therapeutic process and objectivity to its impact. In this way the best qualities of both can be used to make the group counseling process a dynamic and viable method of helping people.

Rules for Group Interaction

One of the most important issues that demand the attention of the group leader is the development of agreed upon rules to govern the group's interaction. This issue has been referred to as a developmental task in groups (setting boundaries) and as a function of the group leader (rules-keeping) but needs to be reiterated here for emphasis.

Many strategies are available for handling the rules issue in groups. Some leaders prefer to establish a comprehensive set of ground rules, discussing them thoroughly with group members either in a screening interview or during the first session of the group. Others present a skeleton list of basic rules and then rely on the group to develop additional rules relevant to that particular group. Other leaders make the development of guidelines to govern interaction a group task. Together with the leader the group works out the rules by which they will relate. Leaders who prefer this method praise it as an excellent means of developing cohesiveness and commitment to the rules and the group. A final strategy is to develop ground rules as the need arises. In this approach the guidelines take on a developmental perspective, since needed rules are invoked as the group moves from stage to stage in its life cycle. In all approaches are two main similarities; 1) the group needs to arrive at consensus regarding the rules and be willing to act in accord with them, and 2) the leader is responsible to see that they are sufficiently comprehensive, reasonable, and adhered to.

Ethical Practice

Certainly group leaders have a professional commitment to function in accordance with the ethical codes developed by the American Counseling Association (see Appendix B), the American Psychological Association and other professional organizations which devise ethical standards to govern professional conduct. In addition, acting in accordance with *Best Practices in Group Counseling* (Chapter 8) and ASGW's Best Practice Guidelines (see Appendix C) is imperative. Beyond that the implications of many of the leader skills and functions already discussed that relate to protection of the individual, maintaining rules, and containing excesses are geared to helping group counselors operate in an ethical manner. Leaders have a professional obligation to function in the best interests of group members, the setting in which they function, and the community to the maximum degree possible. Of course there will always be conflicts of interests, ambiguous situations, and crises in which counselors will have to make decisions based on their own professional judgment and their commitment to their clients. These decisions are never easy, require careful consideration before acting, and are best made under the auspices of ethical guidelines. Ultimately, group leaders are always responsible for ethical practice in their leadership role. Dye (1981) defined ethical practice as the "consensus of judgment on the part of competent, experienced practitioners" (p. 234). As such, familiarity with ethical parameters along with ongoing consultation, supervision, and keeping abreast of current developments in the profession provides the leader with the necessary background for making judgments in any particular group situation.

One pitfall that needs to be specifically mentioned about ethical practice relates to depending on group approval as a means of deciding whether a particular experience, method or technique is ethical or not. Leaders must always be aware of their own professional responsibility and the variety of personality and cultural differences among group members. The simple fact that professional people advocate an experience, or that members involved agree to an experience, does not necessarily justify those experiences as ethically defensible, culturally appropriate, or psychologically sound. Any experiences, interactions, or activities of a questionable nature in the group require the maximum use of counselor competence and resources to support their inclusion. Sensitivity to and resolution of ethical dilemmas is a necessary element of effective leadership.

Group Leader Orientation: Individual, Group, or Theory

Group leaders are often faced with decisions about whether they should act in the interests of an individual, in support of the group, or in accord with a theoretical framework. Sometimes counselors feel caught between the "devil and the deep blue sea" when individuals lock horns with the group or when the group makes demands that are out of step with the counselor's theoretical rationale. Although no easy solution exists to this issue, Dinkmeyer and Muro (1971) cast some light on the subject: "No individual is sacrificed for a theory, no participant is required to respond to a given group technique, and no group member is in any way made to respond to queries that the counselor himself (herself) would not care to have asked of him (her)" (p. 95). The implication seems to be that the interests of the individual come first, the group next, and the theory last. And the key criterion should be whether counselors are willing to put themselves in a similar spot.

These ideas help, but they also are a bit naive in light of pressures placed on leaders in training and the leader's more extensive personal experience and maturity. (Leaders may be willing to do some things that are beyond the capability of the members.) Training programs consciously and unconsciously mold leaders according to certain theoretical and philosophical biases that are difficult to lay aside in the interests of groups or individuals. Similarly, certain individuals in the group who disrupt, resist, and abuse the group process may be difficult to support even when support is professionally appropriate. The solution to this situation therefore requires that leaders develop their own approach under the auspices of acceptable professional practice standards and ethical guidelines and then face individual instances of conflict with openness and flexibility to be sure the best possible route is followed.

As indicated at the beginning of this section, the manner in which group leaders resolve these issues determines leadership style and effectiveness. Leadership style is influenced by leader personality and training, the needs of group members, the nature of their problems, and the goals of the group. An effective leadership approach accounts for all these factors in resolving the issues of group leadership. In addition, it operates within the context of group development. Effective leaders are able to guide their individual behavior so that what they say and do and how they handle the various issues of leadership are not antithetical to therapeutic group functioning.

Special Considerations

What might be termed special considerations for the group leader may have many dimensions. Every group member potentially qualifies as a special consideration on the basis of his or her individual uniqueness. The different purposes associated with different types of groups call upon leaders to make special efforts. But the intent of this discussion is to denote several areas that subsume individual cases and diverse groups and that when realized give the leader a sense of appreciation for the struggle, turmoil, and pressure group members experience in garnering benefit from the group process.

The first area is the realization that *personal growth and change is a difficult and often painful process,* especially when associated with the psychological and personal-social components of one's life. Maslow (Katz, 1973) perhaps stated it best:

> We must appreciate that many people choose the worse rather than the better, that growth is often a painful process and may for this reason be shunned, that we are afraid of our own best possibilities in addition to loving them, and that we are all of us profoundly ambivalent about truth, beauty, virtue, loving them and fearing them too (p. 80).

When we group leaders begin to feel frustrated with members' inabilities to act in ways to improve their lives, we must try to stop and sense the real effort, almost superhuman at times, required to do so. What may seem to all outward appearances the best and most sure fire solution to a client's problems may for that person be a nemesis. What to the leader and the group is an obviously good, appropriate, and possible action may be totally threatening to the person who must carry it out. Thus when encountering resistance we must bear in mind the possibility that the inner fear of change is a stifling factor in members' desires for and thrusts toward growth. Seigelman (1983) noted that, "Major life change is not made easily. It usually takes some external deadline . . . some outrage, or burnout . . . or some outside pressure . . . to get us moving. We don't divert the course of our lives lightly or easily—at least not if we are prudent" (p. 77).

Resistance to change by members in the group *may be the result of an internal conflict* associated with the needs to be adequate in coping with life. Combs and Snygg (1959) have proposed that two major forces that motivate us to be more adequate in our lives also are the cause of resistance. Every person experiences a desire to maintain the self as it is known (self-preservation) and a desire to improve the self (self-enhancement). These desires create a major conflict because in order for the latter to succeed some part of that which is dear to the former must be given up. This struggle is one of the major barriers facing group members in their effort to change. The risk of giving up that which is known about oneself, even though it causes problems, in exchange for something promising but unknown and untested is not easy. The group leader's ability to acknowledge and relate to this perpetual human dilemma in members can do much to turn a confounding barrier into a facilitating resource.

While these first two areas deal with the special consideration of common psychological factors within individual members, the third area concerns the relationship of individual members in the group. The reaction of individual members in the group generally epitomizes humanity's lifelong struggle to "differentiate (a self) while retaining a feeling of unity with others" (Mahler, 1969, p.33). The whole maturation process is a journey from dependence to independence to interdependence. Every human being wishes to be his or her own person while at the same time feeling part of a group. Finding the right balance is an extremely difficult task and maintaining it in all situations once found is nearly impossible. In interpersonal relationships the quest for autonomy and for intimacy and connection often creates our greatest frustrations. No wonder then that group members at times flounder desperately in striking a suitable equilibrium between independence and conformity in the group process. Not surprisingly this equilibrium is easily upset, throwing both the individual and the group into a dither of defensive maneuvers and assertive challenges. Rybak and Brown (1997) frame the struggle as follows:

> Once members have developed some cohesion and a beginning level of integration, the next developmental task is for members to differentiate enough from each other so that each finds a unique place and role in the group (p. 40).

These dynamics pose a critical question for group leaders at any given moment in the group. Is integration that draws members together or differentiation that individuates members most important? Leaders "must decide whether to pull members together as a group or let them differentiate as individuals. The orchestration of such decisions is the way they guide the group through its developmental stages" (Matthews, 1992, p. 163). The group leader who is sensitive to the existence of these connecting-differentiating dynamics and cognizant of the fragile nature of individual-group relationships negotiated in the group will be able to act more constructively, less critically, and more patiently in helping the group prosper.

The importance of these *special considerations* has primary relevance to the leader and subsequent relevance to group members. Leaders who understand the pain of growing, sense the fear of change, feel the inner conflict in the struggle to improve one's self, and appreciate the battle waged between individual dynamics and group pressures will have a more caring attitude in working with the group. This attitude will relieve many of the pressures and anxieties leaders experience, especially when groups do not go well. They will spend less time worrying, expend less energy in group- or self-flagellation, and concentrate more intensely on helping the members and promoting a therapeutic atmosphere in the group. It will also help the leader create a "loving therapeutic atmosphere" and be a "loving figure" thereby defusing the transferential issues that can emerge if members become defensive, frustrated, or disappointed (Bemak & Epp, 1996, pp. 122–123). This attitude of patience, encouragement, understanding, peace, and confidence will be transferred to group members, and give them reassurance that their struggles are worthwhile and that they are understood and appreciated.

☐ **Learning Activities**

The activities described in the following section fall into two categories. The first is methods or strategies for obtaining leadership experience that are

grounded on a solid base of professional training and supervision principles. The first eight learning activities are within this category. The second
category contains exercises designed to assess leader characteristics or abilities and develop leader competencies. The last eight activities are in this
second category.

Leadership Training and Supervision Experiences

Leading Groups in Undergraduate Classes

Many undergraduate classes in education, psychology, social work, human
relations, and other disciplines incorporate small group experiences into
their requirements. These groups tend to have specific course related goals
and are required so that attendance is mandatory. Even when provided as
an adjunct option for extra credit or broadening the learning endeavor, the
groups are well received. Instructors are often amenable to graduate students in group classes leading these groups. The work load for professors is
reduced, the learning potential for their students is extended, and graduate
students receive an excellent opportunity to acquire valuable group leadership experience. A formal program of cooperation between the graduate
and undergraduate instructors is preferable. However, if such an agreement
does not exist, personally contacting undergraduate instructors and working out an individual independent study or field work experience is suitable. An advisable procedure is to be under some type of formal supervision
(for credit) for liability purposes rather than volunteering your services.

Rotating Group Leadership

One method of obtaining an initial exposure to group leadership is to rotate leadership responsibility among members of groups formed as part of a
group counseling course. A schedule can be organized beforehand designating the sequence of leaders and subgroup membership. This type of experience serves the purpose of introducing prospective leaders to the role and
function of group leadership and exposes them to a number of leadership
styles, since each member's approach will reflect his or her own personality. A more important purpose is to give members an opportunity to assess
the skills and characteristics of effective leadership. These sessions can be
video taped for purposes of feedback and discussion of the individual's approach and issues of group leadership. The psychological pressure of this
experience should be low key because members will not get an indepth
leadership experience, probably leading the group only once or twice during the course of a quarter or semester. The focus on general group leadership dynamics should be retained as the main emphasis, and the evaluation
of individual performance should be secondary.

Rotating Co-Leadership

A variation of the method just mentioned, which gives added depth to the leadership experience, is to rotate coleadership responsibility in the group. In this way two members can be in charge for longer time periods—say three to five sessions—and get a more definitive picture of the leader's role. Sessions can be video taped and feedback from the instructor and the group can be given to the coleaders after each session. An overall evaluation can be conducted at the conclusion of their sessions. This strategy also lends itself to variations such as alternating partners, matching coleaders on the basis of personality similarities or differences, and having coleaders model specific philosophies or theories of group leadership to expose members to a broader range of leadership possibilities. It also places members who assume the leadership roles under less pressure since they have a mutually available source of help and reinforcement in the form of the coleader.

Coleadership with an Experienced Leader

One of the very best ways to develop group leadership skills is the mentoring or apprenticeship process where a prospective leader coleads with an experienced professional. According to McCue-Herlihy (1996) "mentoring is an intentional, insightful, supportive process in which a more skilled or experienced person serving as a role model, nurtures, befriends, teaches, sponsors, encourages and counsels a less skilled or less-experienced person for the purpose of promoting the latter's professional and/or personal development" (p. 171). The advantages of this approach are numerous. The experience is an intense and complete immersion in the leader's role. It supplies the prospective leader with a role model to follow and a source of support in crisis situations. It helps the new leader understand the responsibility involved by placing that responsibility directly on his or her shoulders, and it provides a safe place to experiment with the development of a personal style and approach. The difficulty in implementing this approach is finding enough experienced leaders to serve as mentors. Even then problems may occur in arranging schedules and getting the necessary approval to participate. However, these problems should not deter the counselor trainee or counselor educator from trying to develop such a program. If conscientious efforts are made to locate groups and experienced leaders, professional leaders are usually more than willing to take on novices as coleaders and teach them the ropes.

Coleadership with Supervision

Another good way to develop valuable leadership experience is to have two potential leaders colead groups under the supervision of an experienced group leader. When experienced leaders can't be found to take on a coleader, this alternative serves equally as well. It has many of the same mentoring advantages as the previous strategy and may be less threatening to the potential leaders. Sometimes new leaders tend to be withdrawn and passive in the presence of an experienced leader. In this case, both leaders are on an equal footing, feel more responsibility, and have less opportunity to be passive. This type of experience tends to be more action oriented and less observation oriented. An added dimension that serves as a control factor and a learning impetus is the inclusion of a supervisor. This method requires less time on the counselor educator's part than coleading but still gives new leaders the benefit of experience and knowledge through feedback and evaluation sessions. Supervision of this nature introduces additional variables into the group process like video taping or observation, but these tend to be accommodated easily by both the leaders and the group.

One problem with coleadership (this pertains to all the strategies that involve coleading) is that success depends on the ability of the coleaders to work out an effective team approach to the group. Sometimes personality conflicts and differences of group leadership style become obstacles that interfere with the development of a therapeutic group atmosphere. Coleadership thus adds an important variable to the process. Coleadership is recommended generally as a viable leadership form by many group experts (Corey, 1995; Donigian & Malnati, 1997; Gladding, 1991) and advocated for certain types of groups (e.g., groups which focus on gender issues, relational problems, or intimacy difficulties). Carroll and Wiggins (1997) discuss in detail the advantages and disadvantages of coleadership (pp. 83–85) and note that in practice coleadership is for "experienced counselors, not for two neophytes who feel insecure in their role and lack confidence in their leadership" (p. 83). As a training format, however, prospective leaders can examine the utility and relevance of coleadership knowing that when coleadership is appropriate and coleaders develop a positive relationship in their group approach, they have a greater capacity for helping individuals and the group than a single leader.

Supervised Leadership in Practicum, Internship or Field Work

As has already been indicated, group leadership experience should be the focus of a separate field work experience. Once the counselor has developed a solid cognitive and experiential background in group work, the only way left to develop group leadership ability is by leading groups. The advantages of a practicum/internship setting should be utilized to facilitate that process. The supervision provided by the trainee's field supervisor and the practicum/internship director are invaluable sources of learning. In addition, the sharing of experiences with other practicum students or interns adds significantly to the learning and experience of the group leader. More effort is required, however, in establishing specific group counseling field placements to complement the general field work requirements. In this way counselors in training will have access to a more formal means of developing their group abilities on an experiential level.

Groups for Group Leaders

One specific type of leadership training format is the group for group leaders. The general nature of this procedure is to draw together a small group (six to eight members) of counselors who are interested in further developing their expertise in groups. Under the direction of one or more qualified group experts, the group functions as both an intensive group experience and a leadership training process. In other words, the group leaders themselves form the group in which they gain their leadership experience. There are three basic components to this approach. The first, of course, is the personal experience of each person as a member of the group. The second is related to those activities in the group that are designed to give the members experience in the leadership role, and the third is a cognitive component involving feedback and discussion of various leadership skills, functions, and issues.

This format allows much room for flexibility. One variation is for the group to be handled by two experienced group experts using a format of one experiential session and one cognitive session each week. One expert serves as the facilitator of the experiential session, while the other observes the experiential session, using observations as the basis for discussion and feedback in the cognitive session. During the experiential session members can rotate leadership responsibility or simply work with leaders as they emerge. The facilitator is there not to lead the group but to lend expertise, become personally involved, and assume ultimate responsibility in case negative circumstances arise in the group. The follow-up session is an analysis of the experiential session concentrating on group dynamics and essentials of group leadership.

Peer Consultation

One of the often untapped resources among professional counselors is the knowledge and experience of colleagues. The unfounded myth that seeking assistance from fellow professionals is tantamount to an admission of incompetence has long been an inhibitor to sharing expertise. The group counseling field has been no exception. However, due to the increased concern for promoting and assuring ethical practice and with a substantial push from credentialling and licensing/certification requirements where peer consultation is more typically being mandated, this resource can and should be used to acquire group leadership expertise.

Several suggestions for making effective use of peer consultation as a professional resource in regard to developing group counseling expertise follow:

1. Obtain a total department/agency commitment to the use of group methods in counseling and therapy so that all members have a vested interest.
2. Develop a group program so that the need for expertise becomes apparent to all concerned.
3. Set aside specific time slots for consultation to occur rather than depending on catch-as-catch-can meeting arrangements.
4. Arrange schedules that allow for observation and don't create added pressures on either the group leader or peer consultant.
5. Develop settings where observation can take place without causing embarrassment to the group, the leader, or the observer and without interfering in the group process.
6. Exchange roles so that equal opportunity is afforded to be the consultant and the consultee. Nothing is more irksome than to always be asking for consultation and never being asked for feedback in return.
7. Develop guidelines for consultation that specify criteria for evaluation and establish a format for giving feedback. These guidelines should be the product of discussion and input involving all parties in the consulting relationship and should be agreed upon prior to any consultation occurring.

If these general guidelines are used, the threat involved in exposing one's methods to one's colleagues is alleviated. As such, peer consultation is a professionally enhancing method of improving one's group skills while insuring ethical and competent practice. It can also be a morale building experience for the total department, agency, or group practice.

Leadership Training Activities

Group Leaders in My Life

Divide an 8½ × 11 sheet of paper into three columns both lengthwise and widthwise (nine sections total). In each section of column 1 identify one group in which you have been a member and from which you have personally benefited. In each section of column 2 identify the names of the leader(s) of each of those groups. In each section of column 3 describe the characteristics or traits of each group leader. Circle or underline the traits you believe you have. In small groups (three to four persons) share the characteristics identified in the third column, including your own. Use data from the activity to discuss traits of effective group leaders.

Classified Ad

Write a classified ad for a group leader. Include information such as personality traits, training, qualifications and credentials, expectations of the leadership role, setting, and clientele of the group. This activity may be used to initiate a discussion of the essential nature and qualifications of a group leader. Instructions may be varied so that members write a classified ads for themselves as group leaders. Have group members read their classified ads to the group and facilitate a discussion around content. An effective follow-up activity is to have the group write a composite classified ad using the data and discussion from the individual ads.

Consensus Leadership Traits

Have each person in the group write down two or three traits that represent effective group leadership. Form dyads and have the two members develop a composite list. Continue to merge subgroups (dyads to foursomes and foursomes to groups of eight, etc.) until a total group consensus or composite is attained. Use the consensus traits to initiate a discussion of effective group leaders.

Dimensions of Group Leadership

Using the Dimensions of Group Leadership scale in Figure 6.1, have each group member place an asterisk at the point on each continuum that reflects his or her self-perception on that polarity. When completed, have members connect the marks to create a profile. Have each person present his or her profile to the group. Discuss results in terms of similarities and differences. Use the continuum constructs to derive goals for individuals to work on as group leaders. Continuum items may be added or deleted to create a scale that is appropriate to the group.

As a group leader I am:		
Talkative	_/_/_/_/_/_/_/_/_/	Quiet
Directive	_/_/_/_/_/_/_/_/_/	Nondirective
Humorous	_/_/_/_/_/_/_/_/_/	Serious
Confident	_/_/_/_/_/_/_/_/_/	Hesitant
Prepared	_/_/_/_/_/_/_/_/_/	Unprepared
Structured	_/_/_/_/_/_/_/_/_/	Nonstructured
Confrontive	_/_/_/_/_/_/_/_/_/	Supportive
Comfortable	_/_/_/_/_/_/_/_/_/	Ill at Ease
Personable	_/_/_/_/_/_/_/_/_/	Aloof
Authoritative	_/_/_/_/_/_/_/_/_/	Facilitative

FIGURE 6.1. Dimensions of group leadership.

A modification of this activity is to use the line-up format described on page 412 and have group members physically place themselves on each continuum so that both self-assessment and comparative personality data are available for discussion. This version allows access to feedback from others in the process as group members jostle to find their place and space in relation to others on each of the variables.

Personality Inventory Analysis

Since personality is a crucial factor in group leadership, the personality characteristics in Figure 6.2 enable prospective leaders to assess for them-selves—and obtain feedback as to—their primary personality traits. Using the Personality Inventory Analysis or a modification thereof, have each member place a check mark in column one (self) identifying three charac-teristics that describe the general type of personality they portray to others most of the time. Then have members write in the names of the other group members (one in each column) and place check marks by three traits that they believe best describe each person's personality. Share these data by having each person first share his or her own perception and then get feedback as to what other members perceive. Process the information in light of similarities and differences in perceptions. Seek to build self-knowl-edge, self-awareness, and self-esteem since each of the descriptions can be construed as constructive. Also, help members create composite personality sketches by combining traits and integrating self and other perceptions.

Nature of Leadership
(adapted from Johnson and Johnson, 1982, pp. 36–39)

The nature of group leadership can be summarized in two key polarity perspectives. The first is *leaders make the group versus the group makes the leader.* In this perspective the leader is either the one who controls the fortunes of the group or is a pawn in the hands of the group that controls its own fortune. The second is *leaders are born, not made versus leaders are made, not born.* This perspective contrasts innate ability of the leader with learned ability as the key to effective leadership.

Divide the group in half; in one half, the leader makes the group perspec-tive and in the other half, the group makes the leader perspective. Have each group discuss its position and make a case for its accuracy (10–15 minutes). Then create dyads by pairing partners from each group and giv-ing them 10 minutes to convince each other of the correctness of their position. Repeat the same process, using the leaders-are-born and leaders-are-made perspectives. First, have the group discuss their position and then form dyads. After each polarity has been addressed, conduct a brief follow-up discussion to cull the group's reaction and position on each perspective. A final activity is to have each person present their position on the two

1. Put a check mark in column one after the three characteristics you feel describe the general type of personality you portray most of the time as a group leader.
2. After doing the above place the first name of each of the other members of your group in one of the other columns. Then check the three characteristics you think best describe each of them as group leaders.

	ONE (Self)	(Other Member Names)				
gentle						
gracious						
agreeable						
understanding						
considerate						
calm						
soft spoken						
reserved						
quiet						
sincere						
warm						
sweet						
cheerful						
carefree						
confident						
witty						
decisive						
dominant						
intellectual						
serious						
dignified						
mature						
animated						
enthusiastic						
outgoing						
radiant						
vivacious						

3. Share perceptions in the group giving an explanation for each rating.

FIGURE 6.2. Personality inventory analysis.

This form is to help you think about your leadership attitudes and behavior in groups.

Directions:

1. For each item, circle a number along the 5-point scale that fits you best.
2. When you have completed all the items, go back and star three or four scales you would like most to change.
3. Draw an arrow (← or →) to show in which direction you want to change.
4. Select one group skill (from the three or four starred scales) that you would be most willing to work on during this class or supervision period.
5. Write a contract with yourself to improve this behavior or skill. In the contract, identify specific behaviors that you would like to develop. This contract will be renegotiated periodically.

   a. Ability to listen to others in an alert and understanding way

   Very poor   1   2   3   4   5   Very high

   b. Ability to express ideas and thoughts clearly

   Very poor   1   2   3   4   5   Very high

   c. Willingness to tell others what I feel

   Conceal everything   1   2   3   4   5   Reveal everything

   d. Willingness to accept direction from others

   Usually unwilling   1   2   3   4   5   Very willing

   e. Tendency to take over and dominate a group

   Don't ever try   1   2   3   4   5   Try very hard

   f. Reactions to comments about my behavior

   Ignore them   1   2   3   4   5   Incorporate them

   g. Understanding why I do what I do in groups (insight)

   Don't usually know   1   2   3   4   5   Understand very well

   h. Reaction to conflict and expressions of anger in a group

   Become immobilized   1   2   3   4   5   Become stimulated and
   and ineffective   more effective

   i. Reaction to expressions of affection and warmth in a group

   Become immobilized   1   2   3   4   5   Become stimulated and
   and ineffective   more effective

   j. Tolerance for opinions and viewpoints different from my own.

   Very low   1   2   3   4   5   Very high

   k. Ability to lead in a group

   Very low   1   2   3   4   5   Very high

FIGURE 6.3. Analysis of group skills.

polarities. When all individuals have presented, facilitate a group discussion on the merits of the various perspectives and come up with a general group view. This activity tends to elicit many tangential issues relative to group leadership, which may be valuable to pursue.

Analysis of Group Skills

The form in Figure 6.3 is useful in helping prospective group leaders assess their attitudes and behaviors in the group and determine goals for themselves with respect to improving skills. Items may be added or changed to depict any of the skill areas described earlier in the chapter.

Problems Leading Groups

This activity is useful in eliciting discussion of leadership problems in supervision. Pass out 3 × 5 cards and have each member describe a problem he or she is having as a group leader. The cards are placed in the center of the table and each person draws a problem making sure it is not his or her own. Each person reads the problem to the group, discusses it, and makes suggestions as to how he or she might deal with it. The group then discusses the problem sharing ideas and perceptions. Repeat the process until all problems have been addressed.

CHAPTER

Group Member

☐ Nature, Roles, and Behaviors

The most valuable resources a counseling group has at its disposal are its members. The members are crucial to the success of the group and it is imperative that group leaders understand them and their behaviors. Of primary importance is the relationship of each member to the group. The individual decisions of members regarding their own involvement determines the impact of the group as a therapeutic tool for solving problems. Each member has to decide whether he or she is in the group to relate to others with mutual respect and personal self-reference or for exploitation. "The group is completely dependent upon the decision and capacity of each person to share his (her) self-perceptions and to encourage others to do the same" (Dinkmeyer & Muro, 1971, p. 74). Even when a positive commitment is made to become involved, however, problems created by group membership are many.

The fact that counselors must work with a group of clients at one time creates a number of problems for both the leader and members. Lakin (n.d.) enumerates several of these problems: 1) A basic problem of control occurs because the leader is not always able to stay on top of the process and members are not always sure of the authority structure. 2) The issue of responsibility is clouded. Throughout the group process members and the leader engage in a jousting contest over the nature and allocation of responsibility. 3) Although closeness and cohesiveness are continually developing as a group matures, the extent of that closeness is difficult to define for group members. Intimacy is still primarily a dyadic quality, and therefore group relationships have more social attributes than affectional qualities. The problem, however, is knowing where to draw the line. 4) Even though direct communication in counseling groups perpetuates the helping process, that communication is sometimes difficult to follow. The multiplicity of member actions and reactions gives members and the leader a vast amount of input to comprehend. 5) The numerical superiority of members creates a competitive possibility that challenges the expertise and leadership of the counselor directly and indirectly.

The leader must be able to cope with each of these situations and adequately deal with them for the good of the group and its members. Understanding the dynamics of member behavior can provide a solid foundation for doing so. The purpose of this chapter is to consider the various aspects of group membership of which a group leader needs to be aware. Topics covered will include the nature, roles, and behaviors of group members.

☐ Nature of the Group Member

The group member is really a unique form of client. This is because each one brings to counseling all the individuality that personality differences allow for (Krause & Hulse-Killacky, 1996), and each one must learn to cope with and make use of both the counselor and the group process. This combination of personal diversity and the task of functioning adequately as a client in a group gives the group member a quality that is not characteristic of clients in individual counseling, consulting relationships, or even in marital/family counseling where each client's place is circumscribed by a preexisting relational unit.

Just as in leadership, the key factor in membership is personality. Groups are composed of individuals who "overtly and covertly present their unique needs, likes and dislikes, strengths and weaknesses" in the group (Krause & Hulse-Killacky, 1996, p. 91). Those various and sundry characteristics clients manifest in their personal lives are part and parcel of the group process, weaving an intricate pattern in each group that can never be replicated or even simulated in another group. This attribute makes group counseling the dynamic process it is and makes every group a new and challenging experience to the sensitive and aware group leader.

To enumerate all the personality traits that are conducive to good group membership would be an impossible task. However, one general characteristic appears to be mandatory. *The effective group member must be able to relate fairly well in a small group situation.* This rather simple social criterion is essential for both the person to benefit and the process to work. Clients who are antisocial, severely shy, or withdrawn don't have the social ability to function in groups. Other extremes in personality dynamics such as hostility, narcissism, depression, psychosis, total noncompliance, conduct disorders, oppositional defiance, and borderline features may also mitigate against group participation (Jacobs, Harvill, & Masson, 1994; Ohlsen, Horne,

& Lawe, 1988; Yalom, 1995). Such clients are best worked with individually or referred to professional resources for intensive treatment including therapy groups designed specifically for severely dysfunctional clients. However, if the client can function at a minimal level of effectiveness in a small group, all other personality traits that may disrupt or impede the group process and the individual's growth can be worked with to some degree, as the remainder of this chapter will show.

The basic criteria for determining minimal group effectiveness is the client's responsiveness to the leader and other members as noted in the screening interview and the first few group sessions. If evidence exists of interactive qualities in the person that 1) enable a process of give and take to occur, 2) demonstrate a degree of interpersonal initiative, and 3) indicate awareness of the interpersonal influence of others, the probability of adjusting to the group is increased.

Beyond the individual differences and the group adaptability requirement, group members have several other factors in common. These factors define the general nature of the group member. As we've already discussed, all human beings have the same essential needs that motivate their behaviors and direct their courses of action. In most cases typical group members are experiencing deprivation in meeting some of these needs. Therefore they tend to be wary of any procedure that purports to meet their needs when they have not been able to do so themselves. Although naturally wary of the group, most members also experience a hope (usually unexpressed and secret in the initial stages of the group) that the group will be a place where they can find fulfillment and learn the means of satisfying their needs.

Since most of our human needs are met through the process of social interaction and relationship formation, the typical group member is usually experiencing difficulties in relating to others. This difficulty may be with one or two specific relationships or relationships in general, encompassing peer, family, work, community, and school associations. Due to the existence of these inherent relational difficulties in the individual member's lives, each person tends to be hesitant to interact unreservedly in initial group sessions for fear that relational difficulties will also emerge there. Most group members would like to interact amiably, freely, and personally in the group, but this desire is normally camouflaged by caution. Pistole (1997) notes that "as the group develops into a social microcosm, members begin to exhibit their typical patterns of relating and thereby present their interpersonal problems in group interaction" (p. 13).

The character of group members' relational problems are described categorically by the Interpersonal Problem Matrix depicted in Figure 7.1. While this schemata is useful in delineating the nature of the group relative to focus, content, membership, and level of therapeutic intervention, it is included here to explicate the interpersonal difficulties group members bring into the group. Levels I and II are most relevant for our purposes in discussing member behaviors and Level III indicates the prospective interventive

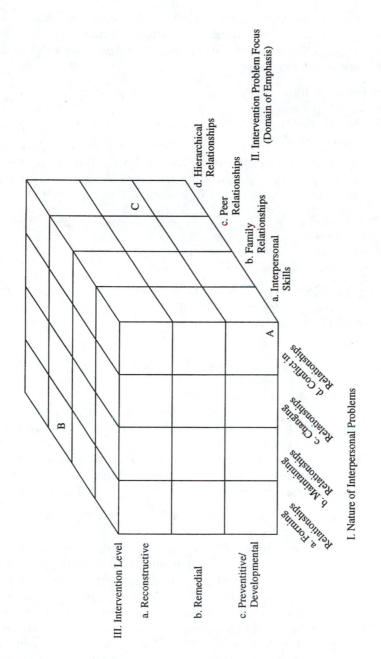

FIGURE 7.1. Trotzer's interpersonal problem matrix.

III. Intervention Level

a. Reconstructive

b. Remedial

c. Preventitive/
Developmental

B

C

A

d. Hierarchical
Relationships

c. Peer
Relationships

b. Family
Relationships

a. Interpersonal
Skills

II. Intervention Problem Focus
(Domain of Emphasis)

d. Conflict in
Relationships

c. Changing
Relationships

b. Maintaining
Relationships

a. Forming
Relationships

I. Nature of Interpersonal Problems

mode that relates to the type of group process that is most relevant (Trotzer, 1985).

The matrix is generated by intersecting three dynamic dimensions of interpersonal problems. Level I (horizontal axis), Nature of Interpersonal Problems, depicts four categories of interpersonal problems emphasizing the dynamics involved. These problems are:

a. Forming Relationships
b. Maintaining Relationships
c. Changing Relationships
d. Conflict in Relationships

Level II (diagonal axis), Interpersonal Problem Focus, is divided into four broadly construed categories representing the basic relational domains in which we experience our interpersonal problems. These categories are:

a. Interpersonal Skills
b. Family Relationships
c. Peer Relationships
d. Hierarchical Relationships.

Level III (vertical axis), Intervention Level, depicts the purpose of group counseling relative to the degree of difficulty or seriousness of the interpersonal problems and the intensity and timing of the intervention itself. The three categories are:

a. Reconstructive, referring to a focus that is personality-specific and designed to help clients make extensive personal changes in order to improve their interpersonal effectiveness.
b. Remedial, referring to an interventive focus that is problem-specific and designed to resolve interpersonal concerns that are impeding growth and development of the individual.
c. Preventive/Developmental, referring to the process of providing personally relevant information and skills in order to help clients prepare for, work through, and/or circumvent typical interpersonal problems.

Each of these levels translates into a type or form of group work delineated elsewhere in this text (Chapters 2 and 10).

The interaction of these three vectors generates descriptive cubicles that suggest the general nature of relational problems, the domain in which problems occur, and the basic character of the group process needed to rectify them. For example, the cube labeled *A* in Figure 7.1 represents a *conflict/interpersonal skills/preventive* interaction. Since we know that conflict in relationships is inevitable and actually a means by which relationships grow and develop (Rybek & Brown, 1997), we can propose a counseling group that teaches conflict resolution skills as a preventive measure. Such a group would be relevant to any number of target populations. Cube *B* (Figure 7.1) is *forming relationships/peers/reconstructive*. An example of this cube would be a therapy group for individuals who are social isolates that is designed to help them form friendships. The group process would be extensive and intensive to enable the group members to make personal changes and acquire the interpersonal skills necessary to form friendships in their social network (peers). Cube *C* (Figure 7.1) is *changing relationships/ hierarchical/remedial.* An example is group counseling for supervisors who had been promoted to positions of authority over former peers and who are struggling personally with this new relational pattern.

While the matrix does not produce mutually exclusive categories, or cover all possible permutations of interpersonal problems, it is very useful in conceptualizing and planning group counseling with respect to relationship issues. Combined with a particular group model for structuring group counseling (e.g., Trotzer, 1979, 1980), it has considerable utility for addressing members' interpersonal concerns.

Beyond relationship difficulties specific problems also exist that bring each individual to group counseling in the first place. This then is another common characteristic of group members. All are in group counseling because they are experiencing a problem or problems that they have not been able to resolve satisfactorily on their own. The fact that they have problems and have indicated an inability to solve them is a duality that generates frustration and creates a natural defensiveness in a social milieu like the group. A basic assumption and expectation from both the clients and others' perspectives is that one should be able to handle one's own problems and that failure to do so suggests inadequacy, weakness, and lack of determination and drive. In addition cultural, ethnic, or family values and mores that mitigate against displaying vulnerability may be at work. As a result, members generally experience a great deal of ambivalence when they enter group counseling. No matter how well prepared they are, when the group begins to interact most members experience an internal conflict between sharing themselves and their problems and retaining an aura of privacy and self-concealment. Matthews (1992) reframed this typical member experience as follows: "One motive (of member behavior) is the desire to escape from group experience with their old way intact. Another is the contradictory desire to use the experience to actualize new potential. Maslow (1967) calls these two motives the omnipresent defensive and growth impulses" (p. 165).

Members experience this approach-avoidance conflict in groups for a variety of reasons. They are not sure what others in the group will think if they reveal their problems. They are not sure of the nature of the group counseling process itself, and they are not sure of themselves and their own role in the group. This being the case, the group is doomed to fail unless a trump card can be played that will tip the balance in favor of proceeding. That something extra can either be the personality of the leader, the internal emotional pressure created by the members' personal concerns, the attraction of the group, or the generic value of the therapeutic group process.

The counselor who can obtain member confidence and is viewed as a caring, supportive, friendly, and helpful person is a vital force in securing commitment to group counseling on the part of members. On the basis of leader explanations beforehand and conduct during initial sessions, many members decide whether they will risk involvement.

Psychological turmoil is another factor that often influences members to commit themselves to group counseling. When the pain, frustration, or anxiety caused by personal problems becomes great, the risk involved in sharing one's issues in the group becomes a lesser and often secondary consideration. The need to ventilate issues and obtain the group's help overcomes the fear of self-disclosure and the need to protect oneself. This motivation, however, often places individual members at risk because they sacrifice their defenses for the sake of psychological relief thus becoming vulnerable. Therefore, the group atmosphere in general—and actions of the group leader in particular—must be such that the relief of pain incentive does not devastate the individual or undermine the group's development as an effective therapeutic process.

The attraction of the group is probably the most influential in convincing members to involve themselves in the group as a means of working on their problems. Cartwright (1951) stated that "the more attractive the group is to its members, the greater is the influence the group can exert on its members" (p. 388). Ohlsen (1970) affirmed this notion, calling the attraction of the group one of the key dynamic forces in its effectiveness. When the member is attracted to the group, the group becomes a setting where individual behavior can be affected (Fullmer, 1971). The group's attractiveness derives from many sources: the social nature of the process, the promise of personal need fulfillment, and the anticipation of help for one's problems (Caple & Cox, 1989). Whatever the reason, members react to the group's appeal by immersing themselves in the process.

Finally, Corey, Corey, and Callahan (1990) have noted that the therapeutic process in groups purports to offer and invoke certain values and incentives. These include: "Self disclosure, risk taking behavior, learning to be direct, questioning of one's life, choosing for oneself, increasing awareness, and autonomy" (p. 69). These factors separately or combined may be the impetus for member involvement.

The final common factor among most group counseling members is a deep and sincere desire for success. This desire also tends to be covered by the defensive mechanisms of members as they enter into the nebulous domain of the group, but it is usually clearly revealed when an atmosphere of trust and safety is created. Even when obstacles to change seem insurmountable, members tend to retain a glimmer of hope that things will work out. Usually when this flickering flame of optimism is extinguished, group counseling loses its impact and more intensive psychotherapeutic treatment is required. At times, however, group counseling may have to rekindle that flame in some clients, which accounts for the overlap between counseling and psychotherapy mentioned in Chapter 2.

☐ Roles of the Group Member

The role of the group member is crucial to the nature and effectiveness of the group. Systemically, roles in groups always imply relationships and interpersonal functions (Rugel, 1991). That fact is certainly relevant in group counseling. The role of each group member is a composite of subroles and role functions. MacKenzie (Rugel, 1991) has delineated four functional roles that emerge in the course of counseling and psychotherapy groups. They are the "structural, social, divergent and cautionary roles" (p. 75). For purposes of our discussion these functional dynamics will be addressed in the context of four subroles: the client, the helper, the model, and the reality check.

The *client role* is self-explanatory. It is that aspect of a member's involvement when the group is focusing on that individual's concerns. All members who are in group counseling have problems. Therefore at some point they must assume the position of being helped in order to make effective use of the counseling process. When the client role is mobilized in group counseling the member is functionally task or goal oriented and as such lends a structural impetus to the group in line with the group's purpose (Rugel, 1991). Members who continually refuse to explore their concerns in the group deny the most vital component of their group membership and thus obstruct any efforts made to help them. Ohlsen, Horne and Lawe (1988) referred to these members as *nonclients* and Corey and Corey (1977) cited eight reasons that may explain such *nonparticipating behavior*. They are:

1. The feeling that one doesn't have anything worthwhile to say.
2. The feeling that one shouldn't talk about oneself or that one should be seen and not heard.
3. Fear of looking foolish; not knowing the appropriate thing to say or do.
4. Fear of certain members in the group or of the authority of the group leader.
5. Resistance, particularly if the person doesn't really want to be a member of the group.
6. Uncertainty about how the group process works.
7. Fear of being rejected or of being accepted.
8. Lack of trust in the group; fear of leaks of confidentiality (p. 40).

These reasons should be explored in the group. Functionally, members who avoid the client role may be manifesting what MacKenzie (Rugel, 1991) called the *cautionary role* where their wariness of overdependence on the group motivates them to maintain a psychological distance. Members who relentlessly function in this manner may not be appropriate for group counseling and should be offered individual counseling where the role of being a client is clearly defined.

The *helper role* has already been alluded to. One of the advantages of group counseling is that the member has the opportunity to be both the helper and the helped. In the helper role members seek to give assistance in whatever way possible to the member who happens to be working on a problem or in need of support, understanding, encouragement, or even confrontation. The functional dynamic involved in the helper role is focused on the needs of other group members for emotional support and acceptance (Rugel, 1991). This *sociable role* assistance may take the form of listening, sharing, giving feedback, suggesting alternatives, confronting, or participating in group activities such as role playing. The helper role has a real therapeutic impact on the client being helped and on the helper. The client values the help received because it originates from peers. For helpers the opportunity to be of assistance builds self-confidence and self-esteem. It provides them with another perspective that takes their minds off their own concerns temporarily and restores a psychological balance. Each helper adds a dimension to the counselor and the group and increases the group's resources in a geometric progression because of the subsequent interaction between unique member personalities. The more willing, creative, and effective the helper is, the more efficient the group process will be. Members who refuse to show concern for others in the group and fail to function in a helping capacity risk not getting the group's help when they need it. In addition, some members resist giving up the client role, continually demanding the group's help and attention in a self-centered manner. They are inconsiderate of other members' needs in this regard and must be helped to realize that their function as helpers in the group is equally important as their client role.

The group member is in a *model role* as well as observing others. Dustin and George (1973) pointed out that group members offer a great number of models and sources of reinforcement. This behavioral learning dynamic functions in the group to help members learn socially adaptive behaviors and skills by emulating fellow members who already exhibit them. The variety of personal attributes among group members accounts for many modeling opportunities during counseling. Some members may be models because of their verbal skills, others because of their personal attractiveness, social skills, emotional sensitivity, common sense, or intellectual abilities. Sometimes leaders include members in the group to serve as models. For example, sociometric stars and isolates are placed together in the same group with the intent being that the isolates will identify with and pattern their behavior after the socially effective stars. Always a good idea is to know the particular area in which each group member can serve as a model so that modeling may be utilized appropriately. Being a model also gives members feelings of worth and helps them learn responsibility.

Besides demonstrating relevant adaptive behavior as models, group members also represent the society outside the group. As such they function as a *reality check*, helping other members assess their concerns in light of realistic criteria and select alternatives that have a reasonable chance of working.

This role is part of the group's society in microcosm characteristic and functions effectively only when members do not deny reality, distort their perceptions, or hesitate to express honest opinions out of fear of or sympathy for the member whose problem is being discussed. This aspect of the member role has tremendous vitality because no matter what the circumstances or setting the group is in, members usually know what is necessary to adapt themselves constructively. The problem is that they are not always willing to admit it. Thus the leader must see that members handle this role responsibly and to the benefit of the group and its members.

The model role and reality check role provide the context in which the divergent nature of member functionality emerges (Rugel, 1991). Models can be detrimental or negative and reality can be denied or distorted. Consequently oppositional dynamics can emerge in the group and generate conflict and problems. The path toward constructive, realistic solutions and resolutions is often strewn with obstacles emanating from perspectives of difference. This process, however, is helpful to the group because it helps the group develop norms for dealing with conflict (Rybek & Brown, 1997).

All the members will demonstrate strengths in certain of these aforementioned roles and weaknesses in others. But at some time during the group process all members must portray each of these four roles to some degree if the group is to maintain mutual responsibility, commitment, and therapeutic influence.

☐ Behaviors of the Group Member

Group members exhibit many kinds of behavior in the group. These behaviors are the material with which the group and the leader must work in accomplishing the purposes of the group and in helping individual members resolve their problems. Five generic categories of member behavior will be discussed here: resisting behaviors, manipulating behaviors, helping behaviors, emotional behaviors, and subgrouping behaviors. Effectively understanding these behaviors will make dealing with them an easier task.

Resisting Behaviors

Resistance is perhaps the biggest nemesis the group counselor faces in the effort to develop a therapeutic milieu. The source of this resistance is within members themselves. Resistance is usually more blatant during early stages of the group and tends to become more subtle and potentially destructive during the later stages. Ohlsen, Horne, and Lawe (1988) describe resistance as the failure to cooperate in the therapeutic process or the blocking of another client's treatment in the group. Members resist the group process for many reasons. They fear that other members will not accept them if they disclose their problems. They worry that if they share one problem it will lead to others, creating a snowballing effect that they cannot control. Some members resist because they are not willing to suffer the pain involved in solving their problems, and others resist simply because they feel incapable of making changes or achieving their goals. For these reasons Rybek and Brown (1997) refer to resistance in group members as *avoidance behaviors* because they are characterized by actions that inhibit the flow of information and disclosure from within and between members.

Dinkmeyer and Muro (1971) pointed out that resistance to personal explorations is particularly evident during early sessions when trust and cohesiveness are minimal. This social resistance is common in most new social environments. Social resistance is the most easily overcome because once common ground is established, rapport develops quickly and the foundational elements of a sharing relationship are formed. Resistance later on in the group when members are confronting their problems becomes a more individualized form of resistance to taking the steps necessary to work out problems. This type of resistance is sometimes very difficult to detect and must be watched for closely by both members and the leader.

Ohlsen (1970) gave four reasons for discouraging resistance in any form. 1) Resistance increases the possibility that confidentiality will be broken. Members who do not commit themselves personally to the group are much more apt to divulge proceedings to outsiders. 2) Resistance increases the amount of acting out behavior. Members who have no ties to the group have less to risk and therefore are more willing to engage in overt disruptive behavior in order to escape from group pressure or protect themselves against involvement. 3) Resistance encourages members to be dependent on each other for meaningful relationships rather than working on improving their lives. Members may resist making changes in order to turn the group into a permanent social gang rather than the temporary therapeutic milieu it is supposed to be. 4) Resistance helps members escape responsibility for coping with their unwillingness to cooperate in the group process. If members never have to face up to their resistant behavior, they will not have to confront the painful areas of their lives or have to expend the energy necessary to change.

Overcoming resistance is a ticklish issue but one that must be faced. Social resistance during the early stages of the group is best handled with methods characterized by warmth and acceptance. Establishing a common ground of experience through group activities or sharing here and now feelings about the group tend to be very effective. For the more complex and serious forms of individual resistance, the possibilities are not so well defined nor is effectiveness assured. Ohlsen (1970) noted that two common techniques used to cope with resistance are interpretation and confrontation. He added, however, that both are questionable because "interpretation tends to encourage intellectualization and to make clients dependent" and confrontation places members on the hot seat where "the full therapeutic impact of the group is no longer felt continuously by the client" (p. 138). Both of these techniques, however, do have utility once a solid relationship of trust and acceptance is established between members. If interpretation is used prior to a good relationship being formed, members may resent the intrusion into their privacy and become even more resistant. However, interpretation at the proper time and stated in a tentative manner can be very helpful. The same is true of confrontation. Often at the point where individual members are resisting, a well timed confrontation can have a meaningful result. This is especially true if the confrontation is generated by group members who have already clearly demonstrated their acceptance and caring for the individual being confronted.

Ohlsen (1970) pointed out another appropriate method of coping with resistance. He suggests utilizing the screening interview as a means of preventing resistance by turning responsibility for convincing the counselor of readiness for group counseling over to the prospective client. Giving clients responsibility for convincing the counselor that they are ready for group counseling, committed to its purposes, prepared to work toward achieving their own individual goals, and willing to develop and maintain a therapeutic climate enables them to accept considerable responsibility for their own growth. Within such a climate, clients tend to perceive resistance as deviant behavior (p. 120).

Resistance is portrayed in many different ways, but whatever its behavioral manifestation, the objectives of protecting oneself and preventing contact remains the same. Some of the more common resisting behaviors are discussed in the paragraphs that follow.

Monopolizing

There are many descriptions of monopolizing group members (Carroll & Wiggins, 1997; Donigian & Malnati, 1997; Higgs, 1992). Dinkmeyer and Muro (1971) described them as persons who must hold the group's attention and who become anxious when the focal point shifts to another member. This type of behavior may be a defensive overreaction to fear of attack or isolation from the group. Ohlsen (1970) said the monopolist "does seem to be a self-centered recognition-seeker who tries to maintain a place for himself (herself) in the center of the stage" (p. 188). Kranzow (1973) stated simply that a monopolist dominates group discussion. A monopolizing member stymies group interaction because other members do not get the opportunity to react or to present their own concerns and points of view. This form of resistance also can create many negative, unexpressed feelings in group members. They dislike having one person monopolize the discussion but do not have the courage or opportunity to take the floor themselves. They therefore internalize their feelings and express them through nonverbal reactions, may become passive-aggressive or make debilitating, behind-the-back comments outside the group. The leader should tune in to these reactions drawing the members out and helping them express their feelings. This will curtail out of group comments and also may help monopolists see that they are generating negative attitudes toward themselves.

The group members may unwittingly reinforce monopolizing behavior by expecting the monopolist to take over in periods of ambiguity and tension. Members can develop a subconscious dependence on this type of group member to take over, so even though they do not particularly relish the idea of a one person show, they do nothing to prevent it. Monopolists also provide a handy excuse for other group members not to reveal themselves. Thus even when a monopolizing person desires to change, expectations are such that he or she will receive little support for not monopolizing. This situation may have to be pointed out to the group from time to time in order to help the group understand and cope with all the dynamics of monopolizing.

Monopolists are often not aware of their behavior and may actually feel that they are behaving correctly. Dinkmeyer and Muro (1971) stated,

> Even when an individual is revealing what appears to be significant aspects of self, he (she) may be either consciously or unconsciously trying to control the group's potential impact on him (her). As long as an individual is speaking he (she) holds the group's attention, prevents interaction, and minimizes the probability of being confronted by another group member (p. 20).

Monopolists tend to be very verbal and therefore initially can put everyone at ease, including the leader. Once monopolists are established the only way to unseat them is through some form of confrontation, which may reverberate in negative repercussions throughout the group process. Therefore it is necessary to identify this behavior early and to act to create a more balanced pattern of communication characterized by total member participation. Yalom (1985) noted that the key to dealing with monopolizing members is not to silence them. "You do not want to hear less from (them); instead, you want to hear more" (p. 378). The message to be conveyed to monopolizers is that you want to hear more meaningful disclosures. If, however, monopolists persist, they may need to be offered individual counseling as a substitute until they can function more effectively in the group.

Excessive Talking

A mild form of resistance that is often mistaken for monopolizing is excessive talking (Higgs, 1992). This phenomenon is typically evident in early stages of the group process and during periods of heightened anxiety. Verbal members of the group may respond to anxiety or tension by increasing their verbal output as a protective or stress reduction mechanism. The characteristic that distinguishes excessive talking from monopolizing is that it tends to be "catching," i.e., other members' verbalizations are elicited and the group begins to babble. In these situations interventions to slow down the pace and giving process feedback to the group noting the phenomena help the group and individual members reduce or restrain their talking. In addition, as the anxiety in the group is alleviated by rapport and acceptance and the contingent issue generating the tension is addressed, the pace of verbalizing also recedes to a more serious and constructive level.

Hostility

Hostile members exhibit a form of resistance that is difficult to work with because very few avenues of approach are open to the group for making personal contact and gaining trust and confidence. Hostility is usually the result of being hurt, let down, or abandoned by someone whose love and acceptance were needed. On the basis of this experience the hostile person no longer expects to be accepted or loved and therefore tends to be demanding, brutal, sullen, and defiant. Detection of hostility is as much an emotional process as it is a behavioral one. Hostile clients tend to generate visceral reactions of fear, edginess, tension, and even anxiety in those around them. Thus other members attempt to either avoid or placate them, both reactions that interfere with constructive group interaction.

Hostile clients require infinite patience tempered with firmness and caring. They must be given an open invitation to let down defenses and join the group on a personal level and must be made aware that the group understands how difficult that may be. On the other hand hostile members must not be allowed to control the group by attitudes and behavior. In fact, if the group can become involved in personal, warm, trusting, accepting interaction in spite of the hostility, it may convince hostile members of the group's sincerity. Reflection and empathic understanding are the best methods of approach (Ohlsen, Horne, & Lawe, 1988), and confrontation is the most dangerous because it only gives the hostile member a good reason to fight back under the pretense of being attacked. If members can convince hostile clients that they really care and make good on their commitments, these clients can be worked with.

Silence

Silent periods and silent members usually cause feelings of uneasiness, tension, or consternation in the group (Carroll & Wiggins, 1997; Donigian & Malnati, 1997; Higgs, 1992). But a distinction must be made between silence that is constructive and silence that is resistant and destructive. A warm and accepting silence that gives individuals time to think and reflect is useful in the group. This type of silence can be a motivating factor when the ambiguity it creates results in tension that influences members to share themselves or their feelings in a personally relevant way. Similarly, some group members can become deeply involved in the group interaction even though they do a minimum of talking. These members may in fact use silence as a means of removing defenses and with time the effect becomes evident. Other members usually are quite adept at recognizing this type of silent member.

A destructive silence generally results in tension and anxiety in the group that interferes with effective action. It is motivated by fear of self-disclosure and elements of confusion and insecurity. It is an effective resisting behavior because it places the responsibility and pressure on other members or the leader to carry on the group process while at the same time protecting the individual from self-revelation. Hinckley and Herman (1951) indicated that silence may mean 1) members are holding back as a punitive measure against the leader or certain members, 2) members are avoiding reality and/or escaping conflict, 3) a particular client is hiding, or 4) certain members have difficulty in communicating with others. In some cases individual members are silent because they do not get the opportunity to talk, are not assertive in speaking out, or simply do not want to interrupt. In other cases, cultural factors may account for silence (Ho, 1984; Ipaye, 1982; Kaneshige, 1973; Merta, 1995). For example, Native Americans and Asian clients may view silence as a mark of respect rather than as resistance. Lifton (1966) added that silence may be a reaction of shock or support. Personality traits that tend toward quietness in social situations and verbal patterns that are deliberate and slow paced also contribute to silence in individual members.

In dealing with group silence the leader must develop an ability to determine the tolerance level of members and the point at which the ambiguity is no longer producing therapeutic results. At this point intervention is appropriate either in the form of initiating a group activity, reflecting the leader's own feelings, reflecting the leader's perception of the group atmosphere, or asking a leading question. Often this type of intervention is greeted with spontaneous relief by the members who then assert themselves verbally in an effort to purge their anxious feelings and prevent the recurrence of that type of silence.

Individual silent members must be encouraged to talk but not necessarily put on the spot to do so. Opportunities can be provided to them in the form of go-rounds or questions directed to the group so that the silent member's participation is in the context of just another perspective. Responding to nonverbal cues that indicate the silent member is thinking, feeling, reacting, or about to say something also can facilitate participation. Use simple statements like "Cheryl, you seemed to be thinking about something just now, and I wonder if you would share it with us?" or "Daniel, you seemed to react to what Jack just said; would you explain what you felt?" Note the tentative nature of these statements. Too forceful or too direct statements may increase resistance. Always give the silent client an option rather than forcing the issue. Response to nonverbal cues is an important skill to develop in working with silences or silent members. This skill is not only important for the leader to develop but for members to master as well.

Withdrawal

Withdrawal and silence tend to go hand in hand, but silence is not necessarily indicative of withdrawal. Withdrawal is usually associated with a negative self-concept in members and may be reflected in the positional dynamics that emerge between members and the leader. Referred to as *proxemics* by Donigian and Malnati (1997), withdrawal is the emotional and physical distance that emerges between a member and the group or between the group and the leader. Group members may resist involvement by maintaining or encouraging social distance between themselves and the group. This may be communicated by a member actually placing his or her chair apart from the group or sitting in a manner which creates physical barriers or distance between themselves and the group. The member may take on the role of an isolate in the group, maintain an observer posture, or resist involvement by criticizing what is going on, either verbally or nonverbally (Kranzow, 1973). Withdrawal tends to be an obvious challenge to group members to demonstrate their care and concern by making a supreme effort to bring the person into the group, or it enables members to resist having to reveal and work on their problems in the group. The withdrawn member, however, usually does not cut off all communication with the group. In fact, often while seeming withdrawn, the person is actually listening intensely. I recall an incident in my therapy group at the Minnesota State Prison where an inmate refused to participate in the group and would go into his cell when the group would convene. His cell was just off the area where the group met. During one of the sessions he yelled out a comment as the group was interacting indicating that despite his withdrawal he was avidly aware of what was going on. To work effectively with withdrawal, an avenue must be located and used to expand the withdrawn member's participation in the group. Many of the same techniques used in silence are relevant for withdrawal, and in certain cases confrontation is also useful, especially if the member does not know how to ask for the group's help.

   Leaders may inadvertently reinforce withdrawal dynamics in the group by not recognizing it as a group phenomenon where the group maintains a distance from the leader as a protective device. This makes it easier for individual members to further withdraw without notice because it occurs in the context of a group norm or tendency. "The greater the distance between group members, the less likely they are to reveal their personal thoughts and feelings and the more likely they are to engage in restrictive solutions such as denial and intellectualization" (Donigian & Malnati, 1997, p. 19). Thus leaders need to maintain active involvement with both members and the group in order to circumvent such systemic dynamics.

Absences

One of the easiest ways to avoid involvement in the group and resist its therapeutic impact is to simply not show up for the group meeting. Absences early in the group process may indicate members' lack of interest, lack of commitment, or fear of the unknown. If the group process is not clearly explained, and if a commitment to participate is not obtained beforehand or at initial contact, absences can be expected. Later in the process absences take on a different meaning. Hinckley and Herman (1951) stated that members may use absence as a means of testing the limits of acceptance in the group and to determine their status. Johnson (1963) added that as a group develops and members sense that subsequent interaction may penetrate into areas that are frightening, potentially harmful, or embarrassing, they may use absence as a means of resistance and escape.

The peculiar aspect about absence is that being out of sight does not mean being out of mind as far as other group members are concerned. A natural tendency is for the group to discuss absent members, especially if other members have feelings they will not express when the absent person is there. This may itself be a form of resistance, and the leader must see to it that the group does not use it to avoid confronting their own concerns. On the other hand, this can be an opportunity for members to work with their feelings in preparation for constructively dealing with the absentee. Often when members find out about the tendency to discuss the absentee, they will make more concerted efforts to attend the group sessions rather than risk being talked about.

Absence can be handled by simply contacting the absentee in a nonconfrontative manner to demonstrate concern. At the same time, the responsibility issue can be stressed. Once clients have indicated they will be in the group, they have an obligation to themselves and other members to be there. Of course, a positive group relationship and climate reduces absences. In cases where absence is obviously an effort to avoid responsibility for one's problems, confrontation may be called for.

Cross Talking

A group form of resistance behavior is cross talking where group members engage in parallel conversations simultaneously disrupting both the flow and the focus of the group. Cross talking is a natural phenomenon in most groups but usually dissipates as the group gets down to business either on its own or at the behest of the leader. However, it becomes problematic when a pattern emerges where it erupts spontaneously and continues in spite of or in direct disregard to leader intervention or member discomfort. This behavior must be dealt with directly on a here and now process level because of its disruptive influence and propensity to undermine cohesiveness and generate chaos in the group.

This phenomenon occurs frequently in groups that lack clear purpose and commitment, where members are required to participate, or where the general purpose of the group is growth or learning rather than therapy or counseling. A specific example of this latter case is required group experience in graduate classes in group work. Cross talking as a pattern is also a signal that the group may be of excessive size for the purposes involved to the point where effective group cohesiveness and atmosphere is delimited. If that is the case, the appropriate intervention is to subdivide the group into smaller units and/or design smaller groups in future planning.

Intellectualizing

Probably the most uncomplimentary label that has developed in the annals of group work is *intellectualizing*; in some ways no more negative charge can be leveled at a group member. Intellectualizing as such basically implies that members are not personally involved and are using the cognitive domain as a shield (Higgs, 1992). Because of the exaggerated overtones of this term, its real meaning has been distorted. Its connotations are more feared though much less distinct and less understood than the denotative qualities of the term. As a result, members and leaders hesitate to point it out when it occurs because of the strong reaction that might be stimulated.

Intellectualizing is nevertheless a very common resistance mechanism in the group. Most members realize that discussing a topic is easier than talking about themselves. They also know that interacting in discussions is easier when devoid of emotional qualities and personal implications. They prefer to discuss how they got to be like they are (there and then), or what they would like to be (if and when), rather than become involved in a discussion of their present thoughts, feelings, behaviors, and problems (here and now). Whenever verbalizations take on qualities that move the focus away from the person to a topic, event, situation, or issue that has little relevance to the group or its members' problems, intellectualizing is occurring. This does not mean these discussions are uninteresting or unemotional. In fact, the contrary is quite often the case. But the point is that the work of the group is not being attended to.

The best safeguard against intellectualizing is to encourage members always to relate their discussions directly to themselves and to keep the focus within the group rather than outside the group. Intellectualizing is often a means of keeping the group going to avoid silence or keeping the leader happy, especially when members are not sure of the group's purposes. Clear and specific goals can help circumvent this problem so that members can address themselves to communication that is personally meaningful and facilitative of group progress. In addition, helping members personalize their comments through reflection, restatement, clarification, modeling, tone setting, and probing can prevent intellectualizing from impeding group progress. Poppen and Thompson (1974) described the nature of nonintellectualizing communication: "Talking about something one of the group members likes becomes more meaningful when he (she) describes his (her) complete feelings about it, indicates how important its value is to him (her), or states how he (she) acts in accordance with this value" (p. 96). The purpose of working with intellectualizing is not to eliminate thinking from the group process. It is to make the cognitive process a resource to the person in working out problems rather than a wall to hide behind. The therapeutic counterpart of intellectualizing is cognitive restructuring which is a legitimate group focus and process

The Old Pro

As more and more individuals have experienced involvement in small group interaction of a therapeutic nature, another resistance phenomenon has emerged—the old pro syndrome. Increasingly likely is that membership in any particular counseling group will include one or several members who have had previous small group experience. Accordingly, an experiential differential exists such that members can be used by the more experienced member to avoid personal involvement. The old pros manifest themselves in a variety of ways. They may exude a sophistication that is read as "I know what this is all about and it doesn't threaten me a bit." They may make numerous references to their previous group experience to solidify their position, impress other members or the leader, justify their actions in the group, or indicate they have less need for help than the others. A common reaction of the old pro is to become "Mr. or Ms. Cocounselor," to minimize personal involvement by assuming a quasi-leadership role (Dinkmeyer & Muro, 1971). This type of member also may begin to share seemingly personal information early in the group, which turns out to be a rehash of what they have already said or dealt with in previous group experiences.

Old pros have the potential of being helpful or detrimental influences in the group. If the leader can help them model effective membership behaviors to help other members overcome fear and distrust of the group, they can be tremendous assets. In fact, this type of person may be able to accommodate very well to functioning as a leader in the peer facilitated groups described in Chapter 10. However, remember that this member's first purpose is to work on personal concerns. If past experience is being used to avoid that purpose, it must be dealt with immediately.

Experienced members can generate negative feelings in other members who resent their superiority. Old pros also may engage in advice giving, which can be disturbing to other members and is in itself a form of resistance. Powdermaker and Frank (1953) explained that giving advice diverts attention away from one's own problems, exhibits superiority to others in the group, and may conceal contempt and hostility for the one seeking assistance. Finally, the old pro may attempt to become the group's superego, the one who keeps telling the group what it should or should not do (Kranzow, 1973). This type of member may represent a direct challenge to the leader and a divisive threat to the group process. For all these reasons old pros must be dealt with as quickly as possible to prevent problems.

But oddly enough the group leader often fails to spot the old pro before some damage has already occurred. Leaders wanting to facilitate a positive group experience may be extremely appreciative and condoning of the behavior of the old pro initially. As a result this person becomes firmly entrenched in that role before the group leader realizes it. Therefore several precautions should be taken. Placing experienced members together in a group counters using their experience as a resistant tool because they can keep a check on each other. An individual interview with the experienced member before or during the group to point out the member's position, enlist cooperation, and reaffirm the basic purpose for being in the group may be all that is needed. During group sessions, probing and questioning the old pro may be effective and drawing out other members' feelings in the form of feedback to the experienced member is invaluable. Remember though that the old pro image may be no more than a facade with very little solid basis. If confronted too strongly such a person may become confused, hurt, and even devastated. Feedback therefore should help them realize what they are doing and amply encourage them to continue to function in a helping capacity with other members. The difference between advice and support or assistance can be pointed out, along with reinforcement for suggesting alternatives and not for telling members which alternative to choose.

The Joker

Humor is probably the least offensive form of resistance in the group. The member who can get the group laughing helps relieve strain and tension and removes some of the pain of considering problems. The humor also calls attention to the person but often at the cost of serious consideration of certain necessary and personal factors. The joker has a lot of group support because group members tend to associate laughter with happiness, and certainly no one should be criticized for making others happy. Therefore the joker has a natural defense alliance that is difficult to penetrate, especially early in the group. Unfortunately, the joker's problems are usually so well camouflaged in joviality that other members seldom take them seriously. The group may depend on the joker to lighten things up when interaction gets too heavy making it difficult for that member to give serious input or get help from the group when needed. This locks the joker into a circumscribed role that conveys an expectation obligating the member to serve as the group's court jester.

The most effective way of coping with humorists is through reflection of the underlying serious aspects of their communication. To be able to laugh with them and yet respond to them seriously and personally will not only help them overcome the use of humor for resistance but also will help other members see them in a different perspective.

The Housekeeper

Dinkmeyer and Muro (1971) described this resistant member as the person who is doing everything for the group except participating in it. Housekeepers set up the room, get extra chairs, pass out materials, and generally take care of any possible technical details of the group. They are especially adept at running errands. They associate with the group but don't involve themselves in the interaction. Reinforcement of their participation and control of the amount of chores they do will help this type of member make therapeutic use of the group more likely. Encourage housekeepers to engage in self-disclosure and giving feedback. In this way housekeepers feel useful to the group and become more involved in it as they engage in give and take discussion with the members on a personal level.

The Help-Rejecting Complainer

Yalom (1985) has identified the help-rejecting complainer (HRC) as one of the most frustrating resistive group members. A subcategory of the monopolizer, the HRC is a discloser, but not a closer. This type of member holds the focus of the group with an unending litany of complaints or problems which by definition are insolvable. No matter how understanding the group is, catharsis does not generate a shift in emphasis and no matter what the group suggests, an obstacle always is present. HRC's are master "yes-butters" and their standard response is often "I tried that and it didn't work."

The HRC is almost completely self-centered and has difficulty tolerating anyone else being in the limelight. They solidify their position in the group early because of their seeming willingness to discuss their problems, but that's as far as they go. As the group continues they generate an underlying tension in the group that manifests itself as irritability, frustration, and anger either stifled or expressed impulsively as group members struggle with the discomfort of dealing with the HRC.

One of the more common interactions that emerge in the group is when an HRC and an advice giver lock horns. Since both members are engaging in nonproductive group behavior, the tension level in the group escalates. This tension can be used constructively if the leader or other group members can shift the focus from content (the topic of the interaction) to process (what's happening in the group). This detaches the group from the grip of the HRC and gives an opportunity to look directly at the behavior and impact of the person in the group.

The key to coping with an HRC is not buying in emotionally to the plight of that member's life. Instead, focus on process, zero in on how the person is coming across, and solicit feedback about the behavior manifested in the group rather than trying to solve the problems being described in the HRC's discourse. Additional measures are *limit setting* where specific boundaries are established around how much group time the HRC can use for themselves and *paradox* where the leader goes with the flow overstating the insolubility of the HRC's problems. Both of these methods make use of boundaries to generate change in behavior. In the first case, boundaries are set and adhered to placing the responsibility for staying within them on the HRC, while in the second case the HRC'S own boundaries are breached creating the reactive initiative to change behavior to regain a sense of being in control.

Since a common dynamic of HRC behavior is "to frustrate and defeat the group and the therapist" (Yalom, 1985, p. 391), mobilizing group resources to address the problem is vitally important. If the group is not stimulated to respond constructively, neither the group nor the individual will realize the therapeutic potential of the group process.

The Self-Righteous Moralist

Another resistant group behavior pattern identified by Yalom (1985) is the self-righteous moralist (SRM). "The most outstanding characteristic of the self-righteous moralist is the need to be right and to demonstrate that the other person is wrong" (Yalom, 1985, pp. 392–393). The critical distinction here is not that the member is secure in his or her own values and lives up to them irrespective of circumstances or negative repercussions—a quality that generally garners respect even from those whose values differ. Rather, the SRM's mission is to be right and superior to others to the point where what others think or feel about him or her is unimportant and/or disparaged. A SRM's security is based totally on personal ascendence which has the tendency to generate intense resentment in other group members. This reaction develops quickly and locks the SRM into a role that is difficult to escape. Members no longer see the SRM as a person because every comment he or she makes generates a negative emotional reaction even among members who may generally espouse the same values.

Yalom (1985) identified the dynamic of shame as the force that undergirds the SRM's behavior. Due to feelings of inferiority stemming from lack of success or recognition, the SRM seeks superiority on the basis of "mobility of character rather than achievements" (Yalom, 1985, p. 393). Another dynamic of the SRM's behavior is projection. Often the SRM takes an uncompromising stand on things that internally stem from a distinct sense of vulnerability. SRMs believe and feel that if they don't take an absolute position and hold it, the next step is to be totally consumed by the very thing they are so against. This facet becomes especially evident when issues related to sex, drug and alcohol use/abuse, authority, beliefs and values, or character traits such as honesty, trustworthiness, and fidelity arise in group discussions.

Given the fragility of their shame based defensive mechanisms, their intrinsic fear of vulnerability, and the group's emotional reactivity, dealing with the SRM is an extremely delicate and often unsuccessful process. Once again separating content from process is recommended because it takes the focus off of the topic upon which the SRM solidifies his or her position and places it on the person. However, because the importance of others is often disregarded by the SRM, very little leverage can be generated from group dynamics. Confrontation places the SRM at risk due to the brittle nature of their defenses. More often than not the SRM is ostracized rather than worked with. However, if group members' feelings can be processed sufficiently to the point where the group can endure or even benevolently tolerate the SRM's participation, over time he or she may be able to risk (experiment with) softening his or her stance and learn a more flexible mode of interpersonal relating that begins to reconstruct the basis of achieving a sense of self-esteem.

The Rescuer

One of the more subtle resisting behavior patterns is the rescuer (Jacobs, Harvill, & Masson, 1994). The rescuer is mobilized into action whenever negative intensity arises in the group. Rather than face and work through negative affect, the rescuer rushes to the aid of the upset member via smoothing, reassurance, and sympathy. They engage in what Corey and Corey (1977) call "band-aiding" behavior by which they try to turn the focus from pain to feeling better without addressing the basis or cause of the distress. They patronize rather than support and try to change the level of interaction from personal to social and the emphasis from personal pain to pain avoidance.

Rescuers can be helped to understand and change their behavior by processing their actions after an incident of rescuing occurs. They also can be tutored via modeling and direct instruction to respond empathetically rather than sympathetically. At critical times their rescuing attempts can be blocked or diverted so that therapeutic business can be attended to. Most important is to work on facilitating self-disclosure by rescuers so that they can experience first hand the helping process and then translate it into use with others. In most cases a rescuer can be transformed into a vital helping resource in the group.

Kottler (1992) has identified 14 characteristics of difficult clients (see Figure 7.2) which in turn have been translated into four categories of difficult group members (Kottler, 1994b). These categories effectively summarize the nature of resisting behaviors. The categories are:

1. The "characterologically difficult" or members "who exhibit rigid personality traits such as character disordered clients (who) may not do well in group settings" (p. 4);

2. Acting out group members who behave "provocatively, seductively or aggressively" (p. 5);
3. The entitled member who seeks control by dominance in time and focus (p. 5); and
4. The manipulative member (pp. 6–7 and discussed in detail later in this chapter).

Kottler (1994) noted that difficult members (and resistant behaviors) "are as much a matter of the leader's perception as are their actual behavior" (p. 7). For this reason leaders must have the ability to deal with difficult members while protecting the rights and well being of other members in the process.

Responding to Resisting Behaviors

Several basic strategies that pertain specifically to resisting behaviors are presented in the following discussion. They are identified in a general hierarchical order of preference from the perspective of 1) relevance and potential for effectiveness, 2) degree of seriousness with respect to the behavior, and 3) appropriateness with respect to timing (earlier versus later in the group process). The general rule of thumb to responding to any potentially detrimental group member behavior is based on a "for the good of the group" criteria. When any behavior persists to the extent that the therapeutic effectiveness of the group is jeopardized, action to deal with the behavior first as an ingroup task and second via referral or removal of the member from the group must be initiated.

---

1. Have chronic, uncontrollable diseases that impair interpersonal functioning.
2. Have hidden agendas that they are unwilling to reveal.
3. Ignore appropriate boundaries.
4. Refuse to accept responsibility for their plight and tend to blame others.
5. Are argumentative.
6. Fear intimacy.
7. Are impatient and unrealistic about what group work can do for them.
8. Are inarticulate or lack verbal skills.
9. Are unduly literal or concrete, or have an intolerance for ambiguity.
10. Are significantly divorced from reality.
11. Are "empty" inside and unable to access internal states.
12. Are despondent and express abject hopelessness.
13. Have little impulse control and are prone to explosive tantrums or outbursts.
14. Feel entitled to special privileges. (Kottler, 1994b, p. 4)

FIGURE 7.2. Kottler's characteristics of difficult clients

Empathy

First and foremost is the use of empathy as a means of dealing with resisting behaviors. Since most resistances are essentially defense strategies the impact of an empathic ear goes a long way in establishing a trust base that enables the group member to risk vulnerability. In fact, the more aggressive the resistance, the more potent accurate empathy becomes.

Limit Setting

This tool is especially appropriate for resisting behaviors that manifest themselves via garnering an inordinate amount of the group's time and attention (Kottler, 1994 b). Placing limits on the amount of time a person can retain the group's attention and holding vigorously to those limits places the initiative for responsible group participation on the shoulders of the resistant member.

Using Paradox

Based on the premise that resistance is a matter of gaining control, going with rather than blocking resisting behaviors creates a paradox where the group member gets more control, attention, and affirmation than he or she is comfortable with. This produces a reactive change in the direction of more appropriate boundaries both as a person and as a group participant.

Contingency Contracting

This strategy is particularly relevant to resisters who are big on problem sharing but come up short on problem solving. Contract with the group member for time in the group based on action outside the group or behaviors/conditions inside the group. Such contracts may be in the simple form of a ratio of responding to others statements versus self statements. For example, five responsive statements must be made before one self statement can occur. Contingency contracting raises the issue of accountability both in and out of the group.

Giving Responsibility

In some cases resisting behaviors can be translated into effective group behaviors by assigning a resister responsibility to assist another person in the group. This technique is useful for resisters whose patterns of behavior are based on inferiority, low self-esteem, or lack of self-confidence. It is also helpful with members who have difficulty when the focus is not on themselves. It is guardedly appropriate for persons who resist involvement via patterns such as the old pro.

Confrontation

Confrontation whereby the behavior of the group member is addressed on a here and now process level is the ultimate ingroup format for dealing with resistant behaviors. Confrontation is often necessary when the other methods have not worked and the resisting behavior is jeopardizing the group process. However, several basic guidelines are necessary for effective confrontation to occur. Johnson and Johnson (1982) note that confrontation is not hit and run. Make sure time is sufficient to work through the confrontation. Take time to hear and understand all points of view (both the group members' and the resister's) and define the problem as a mutual problem (a problem for the group) and not just the confronted member's problem. Keep feedback directed at the behavior rather than the person and make sure each person owns rather than projects their feelings. Allow the confrontee to sift through and cull out relevant data and express positive potential for redirection rather than threaten whenever possible.

Removal From the Group

Ultimately some group members will not be able to accommodate to the group and will place the whole group at risk if they maintain their involvement. In such cases removal from the group is appropriate. If at all possible, this process should be implemented with options for continued therapeutic help such as individual counseling or referral to another more appropriate group. The task of ending should be addressed with the leaving member if possible, but whether or not the departing group member participates, those that remain should be given an opportunity to process their thoughts and feelings.

Manipulating Behaviors

The primary difference between resisting behaviors and manipulating behaviors is that the former are used as a direct protection of self, and the latter are used to control others. In either case the resulting interference with therapeutic growth is the same. Manipulating behavior is directed at getting others to act in a way that is not threatening to self and enables the person to feel in control. It is steering the group and its members to meet one's own needs without their knowledge. Shostrom (1967) pointed out that manipulation is actually one end of a continuum; the other end is actualization. All manipulating behaviors have counterparts that are potentially beneficial to the effector and the recipient of the action. This is also true within the group process. The idea is not to eliminate these behaviors but rather to translate them into their actualizing forms so that the group and its members can benefit and progress.

Manipulation is another of those terms that raise the hackles of purported targets. It can be used to mount an attack against those who are seemingly restricting one's psychological, physical, social, or intellectual freedom. Manipulation—or the suspicion of it—motivates members to watch out for their own hides in order to prevent becoming helpless pawns in the hands of a ruthless controller. It generates distance, blocks communication, prevents cohesion, and generally creates a group atmosphere characterized by restraint and distrust.

Interestingly enough the group leader is usually the first to be suspected of manipulating and only later does the suspicion transfer to members. This is mainly because the group is not clear about the leader's role or intentions. But group members are likely to be manipulative in their actions toward the leader and fellow members. The interplay of multiple personality variables and ambiguous nature of the group situation makes this an inevitable and natural consequence. The purpose of this section is to point out some of the more common types of manipulating behaviors and to discuss their relevance to group counseling. As Shostrom (1967) so aptly observed, manipulation need not be directed from a position of strength and power but can also be done effectively from a position of weakness. Figure 7.3 clearly demonstrates this possibility and shows the positive quality of each type of manipulating behavior. Note the counterparts of each

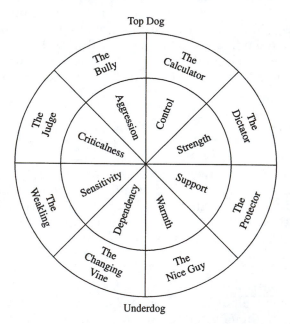

FIGURE 7.3. The manipulative types. (Adapted from *Interpersonal Diagnosis of Personality: A Functional Theory and Methodology for Personality Evaluation*, Timothy Leary (1957) and from *Man, the Manipulator*, E. L. Shostrom (1967). Reprinted by permission.)

behavior and that each can exert a great amount of influence on others regardless of position.

Socializing

Socializers interact extremely well in the group, but their purpose is to extend the counseling relationship into a social relationship rather than to work toward the goals of the group. Ohlsen (1970) described a socializer as "a person who so thoroughly enjoys the quality of his (her) relationships with the members of his (her) counseling group that he (she) may wish to substitute these relationships for those with his (her) important others" (p. 180). Socializers correspond to Shostrom's (1967) nice guys, who can control the actions of others because they are pleasant, friendly, and well liked. They are people no one wants to harm. Nice guys, also can influence members to not upset things by getting into nitty gritty problems. They may misuse the capacity for exuding warmth to reinforce nontherapeutic behaviors in the group members.

Socializers need to be reminded of the purposes and intent of the group. Sometimes it is necessary to block suggestions and input of this type of member so that the group does not become distracted and lose sight of its goals. Socializers can be helped to use their abilities as models, especially for those members who lack social skills. However, they also must be encouraged to utilize their social competence outside the group as appropriate. Once they realize they can function authentically in their relations with significant others they will have no more need to manipulate group members into social alliances and will be able to approach them openly in the context of doing therapeutic group work.

Scapegoating

This behavior directs attention toward another individual or group of individuals in order to divert attention from oneself and avert responsibility, fault, or blame. An individual member is consciously or unconsciously identified as the personification of all that is wrong in and/or out of the group. Through the use of projection or displacement, members can attribute their own problems to others and thus avoid any personal responsibility. The subject, willingly at times and unwillingly at others, is made to feel responsible and required to do penance for the entire group.

Scapegoating is obvious when the entire group gangs up on one particular individual in a barrage of negative feedback. It also can be more subtle, as when the group consistently turns its attention to a key person only when the interaction gets to be particularly disturbing or threatening. In either case the skills usually needed to deal with it are blocking, protecting, and confronting. Leaders must intervene to protect the well being of the persecuted member and to get members to face up to their actions and take responsibility for themselves. Of special importance for the leader is to see that the group does not use scapegoats that are outside the group so all can concur and thus avoid responsible action.

Clark (1997) identified the dynamic of scapegoating as projective identification. When a member who experiences marked self-contempt or low self esteem projects those feelings on to another member in the group, and that person absorbs, internalizes, and enacts the projection, the dynamic of scape-goating is generated. When this occurs other group members are enticed to join in the projection or an antithetical response in the form of subgroup counter attacks is produced. Both responses are harmful to the group process and require leader intervention. The intervention must have a dual focus that acts to protect the target member and at the same time acknowledges the instigator's underlying feelings. Consequently combining skills like blocking, reframing, empathy, cognitive restructuring, and confrontation may be required.

Dependency

Dependent clients operate from a position of weakness. They need someone else to show them the what, how, and why of everything they need to do in order to solve their problems. They treat others as experts and as the only means of help available. In this way they force others to take control and thus do not have to face the anxiety of being independent or autonomous. Ohlsen (1970) stated that "dependent clients have had their dependent behaviors reinforced by persons who needed to have someone dependent upon them or by important others such as parents and teachers who did not bother to teach them, during the normal process of growing up, how to behave independently" (p. 167). Shostrom's (1967) representation of this type of person is the clinging vine. These people completely entwine themselves around others, allowing the others to guide and direct them and shield them from autonomy or independence.

Leaders and members both fall subject to the dependent client because of the appeal to one's pride, sympathy, and expertise. The lesson, of course, that dependent clients must learn is responsibility for self. They must learn to engage in independent behavior, make their own decisions, and avoid dependency reinforcing relationships. Leaders and members alike must refuse to make decisions for the dependent client and must firmly resist taking control. Reinforcement of independent actions within the group is a good place to start and placing the member in choice making situations is very helpful. Affirmation, empowerment, encouragement, and accountability are all critical elements in addressing dependency.

Submissiveness

Submission differs from dependence in that not only do the clients want someone else to tell them what to do but they also want someone else to do it for them. Submissive clients are completely other-controlled persons who will do almost anything to get the approval of people that they treasure (Ohlsen, Horne, & Lawe, 1988). They correspond in some ways to Shostrom's (1967) weaklings because they have no authority or will power to act on their own and they lack even a minimum of courage to assert themselves in any way. They present such a pitiful countenance that others automatically come to their aid. In group situations they are difficult to deal with because any direct contact with them must be made through a wall of defenders who completely blunt any hurtful intrusions. The weakling also tends to be the dominant focal point because no one else seems to need as much help. Such a person may control the group action and emphasis and effectively disable the helping process from having an impact on anyone else.

The all or nothing feature of the submissive client is its source of power. I recall an inmate in my Intensive Treatment Unit therapy group at the Minnesota State Prison who was so thoroughly submissive that fellow inmates, guards, and even administrative officials took over responsibility for his well being and care. So "weak" was this person that normal responsibilities such as obtaining meals, exchanging linens, and performing required routines were carried out for him by others in a joint care taking effort by inmates and prison officials.

Two things submissive clients must learn are to be assertive and to take a positive social interest in the welfare of other group members. The use of modeling and role playing can be very helpful in accomplishing the first and structuring interaction through the use of interpersonal activities will facilitate the second. In addition, empathy expressed through reflection can be beneficial. However, if a tendency toward sympathy and overprotectiveness on the part of members does occur, the leader should step in to redirect and limit the interaction.

Aggression

The aggressive group member has been labeled variously as a pusher (Kranzow, 1973) and a bully (Shostrom, 1967). Both labels represent key identifying traits since the first emphasizes a desire to move ahead as quickly as possible and the second refers to methods used. Aggressive members are very active, influencing the pace and direction of the group by sheer willfulness and a desire to have others see and do things their way. They instill fear and timidity in other members and can single handedly create a stalemate in the group progress. Aggression is often combined with hostility, which results in a formidable challenge for even the most experienced and competent group leader. The Achilles' heel of aggressive clients, however, is that they are usually overreacting to a basic feeling of insecurity that they feel will make them susceptible to being hurt, embarrassed, or disliked. Their aggression, therefore, is an attempt to act first in what they are sure is a situation designed to reveal their weaknesses and make them vulnerable to attack.

Aggressive members must learn that the group is a safe place to let down defenses and that other people are not out to harm them. They need to experience support and acceptance from the leader, who as an expert represents a special threat, and the members. The leader can encourage other members to stand their ground to the threatening forays of the aggressive member and at the same time help the aggressive member realize that other members' independence does not constitute a personal attack or diminish their own importance in the group.

Criticism

Being critical is an effective way to put people on the defensive and control their actions. The key features of this manipulative behavior are evaluation and judgment. Evaluation is based on one's own frame of reference and criteria, while judgment attributes a negative or positive quality to the results of that evaluation. Critical group members may operate under the guise of objectivity so that their assessments seem to be nonpersonal observations of behavior. In reality, however, they may simply be using the role of judge to invoke their own rules and thereby direct the interaction of the group. Criticism also tends to make others avoid contact with the critic and hide true feelings. It communicates the opposite of acceptance, which is disruptive to the group.

Constructive feedback is definitely a valuable part of the group process when it is given in the interests of the receiver and out of a sincere concern for his or her welfare. When used as a tool of control, however, it is unwarranted. The leader must be careful not to model critical behaviors that can be misconstrued by members and emulated to accomplish their own selfish motives. Ground rules are helpful in keeping critical feedback in check; asking members to speak only for themselves and their own perceptions is also important. Poppen and Thompson (1974) stated that criticism should be directed only at those things a person can change and should be concerned with the here and now and questions of "what" and "how" not "why." Since much criticizing is done to avoid being criticized, members must learn both how to receive and how to give feedback. Especially important is for critical members to experience being constructively criticized. In this way they realize the impact of their behavior and can make alterations accordingly.

Domination

Domination is distinct from aggression and monopolizing because it pertains to every aspect of group life, from members to goals to topics of discussion. Dominators through force of strength control the action of the group. They may do it verbally and actively or passively and nonverbally. Shostrom (1967) referred to this type of person as the dictator or someone whose will must be done. Dominating group members can determine the entire character and personality of the group if allowed to act unopposed and unquestioned in the group. Thus channels of interaction and diversity of communication patterns are restricted, and in turn the flexibility and freedom of the group are limited in meeting individual needs. Dominating members usually pose the most serious threat to the leader because they like to call the shots. The most difficult form of dominating member is the one who acknowledges the group leader on the surface but works behind the scenes to subvert the leadership role.

Dominators must learn to use personal power constructively to facilitate rather than restrict freedom and openness. They should be given ample opportunity to lead but must not be given any more authority or control in the group than other members. Leaders should welcome the challenge to their leadership role as an opportunity to find out more about their own attitudes toward domination and authority. By supporting the independent actions of other members and respecting the input of the dominating member, without giving it more credence than that of other members, the leader can effect a constructive balance of power that will help the dominator learn interdependence in relationships inside and outside the group.

Mothering

The mothering group member creates dependency by being the shield and buttress for other members in the face of adversity, attack, or crisis. By supplying this support the mother garners a position of power in the group, which can be wielded to stifle interaction or direct it in a more personally desirable vein. This control can be maintained simply by threatening to remove the support and thus is a potent force in the group's development. Shostrom (1967) referred to this type of person as the protector, who becomes the chief defender of the rights and welfare of others. This type of person is usually above reproach in the eyes of the group members and successfully avoids dealing with any personal problems by continually supporting others as they work on their own.

The mother role (Kranzow, 1973) is a positive addition to the group in that it sees that the needs of members are met. However, this type of member must learn to expose personal needs so that others can respond in kind, thereby creating a symbiotic relationship that leads to mutual growth. As in real life, where mothers must learn to give up their nurturing role as their offspring mature, so the mothering group member must realize members must be granted independence, autonomy, responsibility for their own lives, and freedom from emotional badgering.

Calculating

The calculator (Shostrom, 1967) is a very special type of group member who can steer the group by gauging input for effect and then interjecting it at the precise moment when it will have the most impact. Calculating members are hard to pin down because they are usually very intelligent in the use of their involvement and have the patience to withstand attacks while waiting for the proper moment to counterattack. The calculator often makes highly sensitive and penetrating remarks that contain an element of surprise. Calculators are capable of submarining unsuspecting group members and devastating them at will. As a result, other group members keep a wary eye on them.

Calculators must be handled carefully in the group and, in fact, may not be good group member material. The reason is the difficulty encountered in engaging them in the continuous interaction of the group since they have enough self-control to decide when and if they will participate. They must learn to be sensitive to the feelings of others since their remarks smack of intellect rather than emotion. They may have to be taught through modeling how to both self-disclose and give constructive feedback. If they are willing or can become willing to receive the group's help, they can be valuable assets because they can estimate accurately the impact of certain behaviors. But if they can't be brought around to full time, personal participation, probably the better procedure is to work with them on an individual basis.

In responding to manipulating behaviors leaders must walk a careful path between compassion and confrontation. They must avoid the "compassion trap" of reacting "too sympathetically or treating group members as more fragile than they really are" (McBride & Emerson, 1989, p. 28). And they must act firmly and directly to intercept detrimental actions. "Because manipulative clients thrive in an atmosphere of tension, conflict, hostility and chaos where they feel more powerful, it is especially important to rely on confrontation rather than interpretation as the preferred intervention" (Kottler, 1994b, p. 7). Combining caring, directness, and firmness in responding to manipulative behavior produces best results.

Helping Behaviors

Helping behaviors are those behaviors members engage in that stimulate and promote the therapeutic group process to the mutual benefit of members. They constitute what Rybek and Brown (1997) call approach behaviors and incorporate many skills and functions described in Chapter 6. The leader therefore has a responsibility to model and teach them to members so they can help one another. In addition, many members have a lot of natural ability in helping others that combined with altruistic motives contribute meaningfully to the helping process. The major helping behaviors are discussed in the following paragraphs. A direct correlation exists between the presence of these behaviors and the effectiveness of the group.

Listening

Active, nonjudgmental listening is a necessity in effective groups. Members who conscientiously listen to one another communicate the essential ingredients in therapeutic helping relationships. This type of listening conveys empathy, acceptance, caring, and respect to the speaker. It is a means of valuing the other person and indicates openness. One of the basic ground rules in any group should be that members are to listen to everyone for the purpose of understanding who they really are and what they really think and feel. Reaction skills described in Chapter 6 are the core of effective listening. Group members can learn them through the use of such exercises as Active Listening, described at the end of this chapter. Listening facilitates the group process by establishing the kind of communication base upon which trust and helping relationships can be constructed.

Facilitating

This behavior is important because its purpose is to engage all group members in the interaction of the group. Kranzow (1973) described the facilitator as a person who sees that everyone's needs are met and that all cards are out on the table. Facilitators make efforts to draw group members together, help them talk about themselves, and share their concerns. They tune in to nonverbal cues to draw out less verbal members, ask leading questions, and solicit feedback. Facilitating behaviors assist the problem-solving process because they bring out material for consideration that is crucial to constructive action. They are other-directed and therefore are an integral part of the helper role. As more facilitating is done by members, less responsibility is felt by the group leader, and the members grow in self-confidence, self-esteem, and responsibility in the group.

Leading

At different times during the group process different members may emerge in a leadership capacity. This fluctuation is a common feature of all groups, and group counseling is no exception. Leadership may be assumed or given for a specific purpose or period of time or may be a more permanent role function throughout the group process.

Leading in the therapeutic sense means that the member functions to help group members resolve their problems and accomplish group purposes or tasks. Leading behaviors are important because they serve to disperse responsibility among group members, lifting the burden of responsibility from the leader and giving members the opportunity to take responsibility for the direction of their own lives and the group. They provide an important learning experience that helps members be more assertive and responsible in their lives outside the group. Leading may manifest itself in relation to content or process and incorporate a variety of methods ranging from reflecting feelings, making suggestions, and directing organized activities to leading by example. Leading helps provide structure to the group interaction, decreasing ambiguity and making the group a comfortable and predictable social environment in which to discuss problems.

Self-Disclosing

Johnson (1972) defined self-disclosure as revealing how a person is responding to a present situation, "giving any information about the past that is relevant to understanding how he (she) is reacting to the present" (p. 10). It is the ability to share oneself with others on a personal level. Pierce and Baldwin (1990) describe appropriate self-disclosure as

> sharing ones persistent reactions to what is happening in the group, and it is revealing current struggles, unresolved personal issues, goals and aspirations; pain, joy; strengths and weaknesses; and the meaning of certain personal experiences. Appropriate self-disclosure is *not* revealing one's innermost secrets or digging into one's past; it is not expressing every fleeting reaction to others; it is not telling stories about oneself, and it is not letting the group pressure dictate the limits of one's privacy (p. 152).

Self-disclosing is at the center of the client role. If clients cannot learn to reveal themselves, especially in regard to their problems, they have little chance of benefiting from the group. Self-disclosure depends on an atmosphere of trust, warmth, and acceptance but is a very specific behavior that can only be performed by the particular individual. To self-disclose for someone else is impossible; the material shared is from the hidden or private sector of one's own life. Self-disclosure initiates the problem solving process in the group and paves the way to understanding, on which action and change are based.

Giving Feedback

Johnson (1972) referred to feedback as self-disclosing how one person is reacting to the way in which another person is behaving. Feedback is the mechanism through which the group can give assistance to individual members. It is the means by which reality testing is incorporated into the group and is the process involved in helping members arrive at specific decision points regarding change. Feedback is basically the ability to share one's perceptions without stating that they are absolutely correct and without forcing the recipient to accept them. As part of the helper role it is designed to provide as accurate and as comprehensive a picture as possible to the client but always allows the client to make the final decision about what to accept or reject. In giving feedback maintaining a tentative posture and expressing it in a personalized manner is of particular importance. Feedback is only one person's perception of reality and must be expressed as such.

Leveling

This helping behavior is really the combined action of self-disclosing and giving feedback. Leveling is the open expression of members as they really are and really feel (Satir, 1972). It involves awareness of one's bodily reactions, thoughts, and feelings and utilizing this knowledge in one's communication with others. Perhaps Rogers' (1962) description of congruence— where internal awareness and external expression are one—is an appropriate definition of leveling. Leveling is the basis of open and honest communication and is the principal means of assuring authenticity and genuineness in group relationships. This behavior is especially important when feelings, reactions, and perceptions are being withheld from the group for some reason, causing a stoppage of therapeutic action and communication in the group. Many times the group needs to engage in leveling so as to clear the air of old feelings that are interfering with an individual's freedom to interact or curtailing free expression in the group. Leveling is both a remediating group behavior and a developmental one.

Keeping Confidence

Confidentiality in the group is the responsibility of all group members, and keeping confidence is the specific behavior that carries out that responsibility. Poppen and Thompson (1974) contrasted keeping confidence with gossiping, pointing out that the latter is destructive to the group process, implies lack of commitment to the group, and is a violation of group trust. The trust issue is certainly at the root of this behavior. If members do not feel their disclosures will remain only within the group, they will not risk exposure. Keeping confidence is therefore one important means of establishing trust. It is also a very individual behavior. Vorrath and Brendtro, (1985) pointed out that each member must realize that the development of trust in all its dimensions is completely dependent on him or her. If members cannot keep each other's disclosures and the group's interactions confidential, the meaning and importance of both will either deteriorate or never materialize. A basic ground rule therefore must be the establishment of confidentiality, and group members must be made aware of their obligation to respect the confidence of each other.

Personalizing Communication

This behavior basically refers to communication within the group that utilizes first and second person pronouns (I and you) rather than third person (he/she, him/her and they/them). Poppen and Thompson (1974) referred to this as the use of I-language. Third person references are an attempt to dissociate oneself from one's own behavior or from direct contact and communication with others. A simple comparison of the difficulty in using the various personal pronouns in conversation makes this fact clear. The third person is the easiest form of pronoun to use because it implies objectivity and personal distance in one's communication. Thus, referring to a member in the group as "he" or "she" avoids making the comment directly to the person and means you are talking *about* the person rather than *to* the person. The second person pronoun is more difficult to use because it makes the communication relate directly and specifically to another person. Feedback should always be stated in terms of "you" rather than "he" or "she" so that the message is personal rather than impersonal. The only exception to this guideline is when a particular communication exercise is being used that incorporates a third person approach into its format. Examples of this would be the behind the back technique or describing yourself as your own best friend.

The first person pronoun is the most difficult to use because it places the speaker on the firing line. It is the principal means of exposing one's perceptions, feelings, and opinions. This being the case, members often resort to third person references to avoid personal involvement or to defuse emotional communications. However, the group leader should model personalized communication and request members to use it as well. In this way they learn to take responsibility for their own actions in the group. They also become more careful about what they say and how they speak to each other, which effectively improves the nature and usefulness of communication in the group. Group members can learn to use this type of communication very quickly if the leader simply asks them to repeat their third person statements using appropriate first or second person pronouns. In this way group communication becomes either a personal expression of one's own frame of reference or a personal message to another member.

Emotional Behaviors

The next category of member behaviors is composed of actions characterized by emotional qualities that are difficult for the behaver and the group to cope with effectively. These behaviors are generally associated with the extremes of normal feelings and usually involve overt physical or verbal expressions that tend to stymie even the most experienced and sophisticated leaders and members. Emotions, especially in extreme form, are always difficult to comprehend and tend to either stimulate a natural reaction of avoidance or withdrawal or generate escalation as members catch the emotions and spread them throughout the group. For this reason ambivalence is the order of the day whenever someone begins to express strong feelings negatively or positively. Yet a well known fact is that group dynamics often generate strong feelings. If these reactions are not handled appropriately and responsibly, they can do untold damage to individuals or the group itself. Rather than approaching these behaviors in the blind hope that all will turn out well in the end, a better procedure is for the leader to be prepared in the advent of their occurrence and have some strategies and ideas as to how to respond in a therapeutic manner. This section will only discuss a few of the most common emotional behaviors that occur in the group, but the concepts and principles noted can form a basis for dealing with many group behaviors related to the affective domain.

Venting Negative Feelings

In an atmosphere of safety members frequently verbalize strong negative feelings such as anger, hatred, hostility, and frustration toward people and situations both in and out of the group. This type of ventilation can scare members but is usually therapeutic if members do not overreact by withdrawing from or attacking the member and if follow-up action is taken to help the person work through the feelings. Because social mores generally restrain the expression of strong negative feelings, these feelings sometimes have a tendency to accumulate within the individual rather than dissipate. This is especially true if the individual is continually exposed to the situation or the person that stimulates those feelings. The group's first task is to hear the person out and in the process try to determine if the feelings are temporary or the result of a chronic situation or relationship. If the former, simple catharsis may be sufficient with follow-up to develop preventative measures that will reduce the possibility of recurrence. In the latter case a more problem oriented approach must be taken in which plenty of opportunity is provided to express feelings but with an emphasis on understanding the problem, developing alternatives, forming a plausible plan, and acting to implement it.

When members are experiencing strong negative feelings, they are more likely to take risks that they would not normally take. Thus after feelings are expressed and calm restored, the member may feel sheepish and embarrassed especially if the atmosphere in the group is ominously neutral or quiet. This may cause the person to draw back and develop hostile feelings toward the group. Therefore, the objective is to get the feelings and reactions of group members out in the open as quickly as possible after ventilation has occurred. In this way the focus is directed to others and the member can calm down.

Members who ventilate can't always remember what they said afterwards. Therefore an important procedure is to get back to that member after a short respite to work through the feelings and situation again. The member can determine the role emotion played in the situation by obtaining feedback from other members and can be helped to think more rationally about alternatives and options available.

When negative feelings are directed toward another member in the group the handling of the interaction is a much more serious matter because the welfare of the group is at stake. This type of behavior is often a derivative of confrontations that take place in the group. Also, strong feelings built up over time in the group make the ground fertile for a verbal attack in which these feelings come pouring out in rapid order. A preventative measure is to encourage members to express their feelings as they occur, emphasizing immediacy rather than holding them back in hopes they will disappear. During the exchange keep in touch with reactions of the one being attacked/addressed and restrict ventilation to one person at a time so that a ganging up effect doesn't materialize. At this point deal with the feelings of the expressor/attacker rather than allowing the focus to turn to the receiver. The ventilator must first come to grips with personal awareness before benefiting from anything the recipient of the barrage might say. The follow-up then can then shift to the receiving member and the group's reactions. Other members' perceptions can be used as a means of dealing with allegations made. The total group should be involved so that a precedent of one member attacking and another defending is not set. Maintaining the perspective that venting negative feelings is primarily therapeutic to the person doing it is a necessity. Otherwise much damage can be done if too much stock is placed in the emotional charges leveled at another member. Once emotional equilibrium has been restored the charges can be reevaluated but without the contingent threat introduced by the emotional component of the communication.

Physical Aggression

Physical aggression directed toward persons has no place in group counseling. To assuage that possibility, a very clear and firm ground rule against it must be laid down, with violation resulting in immediate consequences including expulsion from the group. However, the possibility is real that some members may attempt to vent their feelings through physical means because they are not capable of verbal expression or because verbalization alone is not a sufficient outlet. In these cases to use physically expressive activities to release the feelings without a personal attack is appropriate. For example, arm wrestling or attempting to push one another to the floor by pressing on shoulders are useful exercises. Punching bags, batakas, cushions, and pillows also can be used. Another exercise is to have a physically aggressive person lie on the floor and have all other members take a firm hold on the person's arms and legs. The person then tries to get up while the members do all they can to restrain him or her. The strenuous nature of this exercise tires the member quickly and by doing so greatly lessens tension and the emotional impulse to be physically aggressive. Verbal follow-up after this activity helps the member deal constructively with the situation that caused the feelings. Note that these physical activities are relevant in very limited situations where clear boundaries and expectations exist and appropriateness is predetermined.

With members who have a tendency toward being violent, a prearranged agreement can be worked out so that the member is isolated when aggressive feelings begin to emerge. The use of timeout partners, described at the end of this chapter, is also effective in dealing with this type of member behavior. Purposes are to calm the person down, temporarily interrupt the situation that is generating the feelings, and allow for time to think.

The physically aggressive or violent member must be helped to find better ways of reacting. This may involve several steps such as 1) physical expression in a nonthreatening and nonharmful manner, 2) substitution of verbal expression for physical expression, and 3) development of self-monitoring cues that can help prevent impulsive physical outbursts. The member can then become a more productive and adjusted individual who can seek self-expression and fulfillment in socially appropriate ways.

Crying

Probably the most uncomfortable emotional behavior experienced in the group is crying. Even though crying is a natural reaction to sharing a very painful experience or situation, the psychological pressure involved in breaking down is tremendous. Social attitudes about crying, especially for male members, insinuate weakness and lack of self-control. A great resistance often exists to crying because of the fear of what others' reactions will be. As one young woman blurted in reaction to breaking down during her discussion of a particularly hurtful relationship, "I'm afraid you all think I'm just a slobbering idiot." The fear of embarrassment and being seen as a weak person forces many members to contain their tears. This frequently results in mounting pressure, especially if the member continues to work with the painful material. The end product of this buildup then is, in the mind of the crier, far worse because no control over feelings exists. For this reason members often withdraw from the arena of action when they suspect tears are imminent in an effort to avoid a gusher.

Seeing a person cry also has significant impact on other members. They want to help the person but may not really know how. They also may develop the attitude of "boy, that's not going to happen to me," and then withdraw or pursue an entirely cognitive course in the discussion of their problems. This hesitance and inaction often makes the person who cries feel isolated. If the group does not react spontaneously to support and affirm the member, the leader must take steps to do so. Verbalization on the part of others especially in the form of reflection is necessary. And some form of physical gesture such as touching the person's arm or putting an arm around his or her shoulder may be appropriate depending on the person, cultural mores, and situation. Supportive touch when initiated by group members is usually quite impactful, but may need to be modeled by the leader to assure appropriateness. More than anything the group must communicate that they are aware of the various implications that make crying difficult and at the same time convey the message that crying is a normal expression of one's feelings in many situations.

The characteristics of trust and acceptance—if intricate parts of the group atmosphere—alleviate much of the resistance to crying. However, the group must take care not to seduce a member into crying just to demonstrate its ability to handle it or to prove vulnerability. Some leaders function under the misguided notion that crying is synonymous with deeply meaningful group interaction or personal disclosure and direct their efforts to see that members reach that point. Group members need to view crying as a natural part of certain self-disclosures requiring the support and attention of the group. However, it isn't necessarily a symbol of group progress. Nor should efforts be made to belabor distraught members. They should be helped to regain their composure after a reasonable period of time. This is particularly important if the member must leave the group to attend classes, go home, go to work or relate in other social situations. Nothing is more embarrassing than to have to face outsiders knowing your eyes are red and swollen from crying. If not in appropriate control at the end of the group session, the member should be retained or worked with until he or she is able to function in their typical demeanor outside the group.

Crying is another form of ventilation that can be therapeutic. In some cases really no other way exists to express one's pain so effectively. Once these feelings are out the task of working on problems that generate them is easier. Group members understand the seriousness and have a deeper sense of the person. The overreaction that must be guarded against is when the member begins to wallow in self-pity or to use crying to demand the group's attention. When this happens the leader should intervene to bring the member up to a more cognitive level, with emotions placed in proper perspective, and turn attention to coping, managing or making necessary changes.

Affection

Extremes in negative or painful emotions are not the only emotional behaviors difficult to cope with in groups. Extremes in positive feelings, especially related to affection, also cause problems. Normally much more social restraint is related to the expression of affection than to the expression of negative feelings. The reasons for this are that erotic or sexual implications may be associated with showing warm feelings (Bemak & Epp, 1996) and that rejection is a much more threatening force than punishment. If someone expresses warmth, caring, affection, or love in an overt manner, it may raise questions about the real motivation behind the actions. Similarly if a person reveals a positive feeling to another person, who rejects it, little recourse is available for the rejected person other than to withdraw with hurt feelings. If someone addresses us negatively, however, the possibility is always open to respond in kind. Strong positive feelings therefore remain quite disguised in many social situations.

In a cohesive and close group the possibilities of overt physical and verbal expression of affection increase. As Bach (1954) stated:

> in giving of love and sympathy the group as a rule naturally goes much further in overt expressions than any other professional therapist (or counselor) would, could, or should ever do. At such moments the group demonstrates a truly remarkable intensity in its expression of support (p. 96).

In most cases the physical expression of affection is what causes the most concern. Authorities, family members, and other significant persons with a vested interest in the group members or the group process may perceive any expression of physical affection with suspicion. They may even exert pressures on the leader and/or group members that produce inhibitions, create feelings of guilt, and cast a negative reflection on the entire group process. Ethical practice guidelines restrict the extent of physical touch to appropriate supportive contact and touch. Thus the spontaneous expression of physical affection is judiciously limited. In addition, structured activities that involve physical touch should have clear guidelines and precise purposes. Generally speaking with respect to affection members should be encouraged to utilize verbal means of expression.

In the verbal domain expressions of warmth should be tempered by an awareness of how the receiver may respond. They should never be used to embarrass or make another person feel uncomfortable for the sake of gratifying one's own ego. Neither should verbal expressions incorporate a demand to which the other person must respond. They must simply be a reflection of one's own feelings. Following these guidelines can alleviate much of the discomfort and difficulty associated with affectionate behaviors and can make them a viable therapeutic influence in the group process.

Acting Out

Acting out behaviors may incorporate any number of previously mentioned resistant, manipulative, or emotional behaviors but constitute a very special category (Kottler, 1994b) because of their intent to flaunt the authority of the group leader or the freedom and acceptance of the group. Johnson (1963) felt that a frequent cause of acting out behavior is the negative feelings individuals have toward the group leader that cannot be expressed. As a result the member engages in overt acts which are designed to threaten, frustrate, irritate, and intimidate the leader. Ohlsen, Horne, and Lawe, (1988) presented a varying perspective indicating that acting out may simply be a matter of members using treatment as an excuse to do things they ordinarily would not do. Acting out behavior may take the form of tardiness, absences, use of drugs or alcohol, or overt, ingroup, aggressive actions. In all cases they immediately bring attention to the member and usually are disruptive to the group process.

Acting out also may be a group test administered by the member to determine boundaries of group interaction and to find out exactly where he or she stands with the leader and members. Whatever the motive, efforts should be made to involve all members in the discussion rather than letting the acting out behavior degenerate group interaction into a one-to-one confrontation. This is difficult to do especially if the overt behavior is directed at the leader. Other members are naturally curious about how the leader will handle it. Nevertheless the leader should attempt to get members to express their feelings and perceptions so that the instigator is given feedback from a variety of viewpoints. In this way the entire group takes responsibility for coping with the acting out member. Another effective approach is to use Glasser's (1965) question "What are you doing?" (avoid asking "why," which would lead to rationalizations). This request makes the member assess his or her own behavior rather than forcing others to react. If these ingroup strategies do not work, then an alternative is to ask the acting out person to take a break and return to the group when functioning in an acceptable manner. If acting out continues unabated in a disruptive fashion, individual counseling may be more appropriate because the member will not have an audience. In more extreme cases the need may be to make a referral to inpatient psychotherapy.

Subgrouping Behaviors

The generic definition of a group is *three or more persons* because with the introduction of the third and succeeding members the phenomenon of group dynamics emerges. Part of those dynamics is the potential for coalitions to form. Consequently, the formation of subgroups is a naturally occurring aspect of all groups including counseling and therapy groups. As a group develops, coalitions become an integral part of group life. As such, subgrouping is one of the major group member behaviors of which leaders must be aware and must learn to utilize effectively.

In one sense subgrouping behavior serves as a barometer of group health. If subgroups emerge, dissolve, and reemerge in the course of group interaction, and the membership of coalitions varies from topic to topic and issue to issue, the group has fluidity which enables it to maintain resiliency and flexibility. On the other hand, if subgroups solidify with the same members coalescing all the time regardless of the topic or issue, the group develops a rigidity that interferes with and undermines the therapeutic nature of the group. Therefore, as long as subgroups retain variable membership, reorganize in response to different focal points, and function generally within the overall norm structure of the group, no particular concern need be raised. However, if persistent patterns of polarization combined with consistent subgroup membership continually emerge across all group interactions, action to dissolve or de-rigidify the subgrouping process is necessary.

Yalom (1985) noted that subgrouping or fractionalization is an inevitable part of the group process and if not attended to can be a destructive force. Subgrouping may occur in one of two general ways: 1) within the context of the group itself, and 2) as a result of external group contact and interaction. Within the group, subgrouping is by far the easiest to deal with because the dynamics are present in a first hand, here and now form that can be processed as they are occurring. In heterogeneous groups, coalitions between members with more similar concerns, problems, values, or perspectives tend to occur. Such coalitions provide excellent material and opportunities for learning acceptance, generating dialogue, and appreciating diversity. These are commodities that have unlimited value in relating to and coping with the world outside the group. The primary facilitative factor in dealing with ingroup subgrouping is raising what is happening to the awareness of the group members rather than letting such dynamics hover beneath the surface where assumptions and suppressed emotions can begin to ferment into misunderstandings that will jeopardize healthy group functioning.

Out of group subgrouping dynamics are much more complicated to cope with. Subgroups with an out of group derivation may arise in several different ways: 1) members may seek out contact with other members based on what they have observed or heard in group; 2) social contact outside the group such as getting together for a beer or cup of coffee may serve as impetus for a subgroup emerging, and 3) on occasion, intimacy between two group members may generate a dyadic coalition. Note that while social incentives motivate members to connect outside the group, equally strong privacy incentives inhibit group members from becoming intimately involved with each other so as not to become group material. Members often view socializing as nonproblematic but tend to draw the line on close relationships at least until the group is over.

Yalom (1985) depicted the problem of subgrouping as stemming "from the belief of two or more members that they can derive more gratification from a relationship with each other than one from the entire group" (p. 334). With respect to dyadic intimacy he stated, "members who become involved in a love-sexual relationship will almost inevitably award their dyadic relationship higher priority than their relationship to (the) group" (p. 335). He added that members who "violate group norms by secret liaisons are opting for need gratification rather than pursuit of personal change" (p. 337). Thus, the evidence is that subgrouping in any of its derivatives is potentially destructive to the group.

Out of group connections that lead to subgrouping are not all negative. In fact, outside contact negotiated in the group for purposes of accountability and support may be an effective means of extending the group's therapeutic influence. Women's groups at times use the *in-relation* propensities of women to therapeutic advantage by incorporating out of group contact. (Juntunen, Cohen, & Wolszon, 1997; McManus, Redford, & Hughes, 1997). If such contacts occur in the context of overall group goals and norms and do not lead to collusion and the emergence of a no talk subterfuge, they can be very helpful and therapeutic. The obvious key is that any significant out of group contacts or experiences are open and above board and that material from such contacts is accessible to the group. Yalom (1985) observed that "it is not the subgrouping per se that is destructive, but the conspiracy of silence that surrounds it" (p. 339). His research has indicated that such suppression of expression not only leads to a deterioration in therapeutic group process, but also is a contributing factor to attrition and drop outs as individuals fail to cope with being included or excluded in a subgroup.

The general guidelines for dealing with subgrouping behavior are as follows:

1. Make expectations relative to subgrouping behavior clear both in screening interviews and in the context of group interaction. Some group leaders make specific groundrules that delimit or specify out of group contact. While subgrouping can not likely be absolutely forbidden, actions that would encourage or exploit it are to be avoided.
2. Bring all coalescing, colluding, and subgrouping behavior that occurs in the group to the group's attention.
3. Establish a guideline and expectation that the group be informed about extra group activity among members.
4. As a group leader, do not collude with subgroups overtly or covertly by not disclosing what you perceive and/or know about the subgroup.

☐ Concluding Remarks

Most group member behaviors, as diverse as they are, can be predicted according to the climate of the group, the leader's knowledge of human reactions, and the dynamics involved in bringing the individual to the group. Most of the detrimental effects of the negative behaviors described in this chapter can be prevented or at least curtailed if precautionary measures are taken to ensure a healthy group atmosphere and if the leader is willing to act to work with and redirect the behaviors. The positive behaviors, whether actualized counterparts of negative behaviors or helping behaviors, can also be incorporated into the group process by laying clear ground rules and by modeling, teaching, and intervening when necessary.

☐ Learning Activities

The following activities can be used to teach members effective group behaviors and skills, help them understand their own and other members' actions in the group, and help them cope with the more difficult emotional behaviors that may occur. Generally, the activities included in this section pertain to enhancing appropriate and therapeutic member behaviors and to understanding the nature of member actions and experiences in the group.

Active Listening

This activity can be used to teach members the helping behavior of listening by developing the specific skills of restatement, reflection, summary, and clarification. The exercise has four parts and requires at least an hour to do. Even more time is preferable, and the exercise can be done in two sessions, concentrating on Parts 1 and 2 in the first session and 3 and 4 in the second.

1. Making Contact

Have members pair up with another group member, usually a person they know least well. This can be done nonverbally through the use of milling, or it can be accomplished simply by numbering off. Once partners are together have them disperse around the room so that there will be as little noise interference as possible during the exercise.

2. Hearing and Being Heard: The Skill of Restatement

1. Verbal Communication. Have one partner make a personal statement about himself or herself. The other partner must repeat that statement word for word exactly as it was said. If the statement is repeated with even the slightest variation, the first partner must reply with an emphatic "No, you're not listening," and then reiterate the statement until it is repeated exactly right. Each partner does this with three different statements. When repeated accurately, confirm the listener with positive feedback: "That's right, good listening!"

2. Inflection or Tone of Voice. Repeat the procedure as described in 2.1. except this time incorporate an emotional quality in the statement expressed through fluctuation in the speaker's tone of voice. This time the partner must repeat the statement exactly, word for word and in the same tone of voice. Do this three times each.

3. Nonverbal Communication or Body Language. Repeat the procedure as described, but this time include gestures for emphasis in the statement. The partner must repeat the statement exactly, word for word, in the same tone of voice, and using the same gestures.

This part of the activity teaches the skill of *restatement* and focuses on the various levels of communication: the verbal level (word for word), the inflection level (same tone of voice), and the nonverbal level (same gestures).

3. Transition: Restating in Your Own Words

Have the partners carry on a conversation on any topic they choose for a period of 10 minutes. However, before adding to the conversation each person must summarize in their own words what their partner just said. The following ground rule must be followed:

> Once the first statement has been made the other person can make a statement only after summarizing the ideas and feelings of the first speaker accurately and to that speaker's satisfaction. All individual comments must be restated satisfactorily before continuing. See to it that this rule is followed for the entire 10 minutes.

The purpose of this segment of the exercise is to help members realize how often their own thoughts interfere with hearing other people out. By repeating their partner's statement before making one's own comment, chances are greater that complete communication will take place. The object is to concentrate on what the other person is saying rather than on organizing what is about to be said. The skill of *summarization* is also learned.

4. Understanding and Being Understood.

1. Declarative Statements: The Skill of *Reflection*. Have one partner make a personal declarative statement about himself or herself, or his or her life, thoughts, or feelings. The other partner then responds by saying "do you mean. . .?" and adding what she or he perceives the meaning of the statement to be. If the statement is accurate the first partner says "yes" and if inaccurate "no." The responding partner must get three "yes" answers to the same statement before she or he proceeds to make her or his own statement. Repeat this process three times for each partner using a different statement each time. This part of the activity teaches the skill of reflection.

2. Personal Questions: The Skill of *Clarification*. Have one partner ask the other partner a personal question. Instruct them to make the questions as personal and honest as possible because the questions will not have to be answered. The questioned partner responds by saying, "Are you asking . . . ?" and then adds what is perceived to be the meaning and intent of the questioner. She or he must get three "yes" answers from the questioner before asking his or her own personal question. Repeat this process three times for each partner using a different question each time. The basic premise behind this exercise is that most questions are essentially camouflaged declarative statements representing a directive or reflecting the questioner's point of view or expected answer. The skill taught in this part of the exercise is clarification.

The complex nature of communication is pointed out using the two basic forms of expression: the declarative statement and the question. The activity reveals how one person really has difficulty in understanding another's personal communication and stresses the fact that one statement or question can have a multitude of meanings.

Nonverbal Communication Exercise

The purpose of this exercise is to help members develop their skills in nonverbal communication of feelings and utilizing them to improve the communication process in the group. It is also an effective device for leading members in a step by step manner into dealing with feelings that are a part of their personal lives.

1. Recognizing Feelings

Divide the group into dyads and have them sit facing each other with one partner facing the chalkboard and the other facing away from it. The leader writes a feelings word from the following list on the board and the person facing the board tries to communicate that feeling nonverbally and as naturally as possible to the partner. After five seconds, call time and have the observer try to identify the feeling using reflective leads like "You seem to be feeling. . . ." Repeat this activity about four times and then reverse positions and do it again with different words. Then ask partners to think of a feeling they have experienced often or recently and try to communicate it nonverbally to each other. Discuss the difficulties involved in communicating and identifying feelings using only nonverbal cues. Also discuss the differences in communicating positive and negative feelings noting similarities and contrasts. Here are some feelings words that can be used.

Hostility	Anger	Love
Joy	Happiness	Anxiety
Frustration	Confusion	Suspicion
Satisfaction	Pride	Fear

2. Feelings and Situations

Since most feelings are hard to separate from the situations they are associated with, it is often easier to communicate the feelings given a context in which they occurred. Divide the group into subgroups of four. Ask one member of each group to come to you and give that member a description of one of the following situations. The member then returns to the group and attempts to naturally and nonverbally communicate the emotions associated with the situation. Other situations can be substituted or added at the leader's discretion. The other group members try to determine the feelings and make educated guesses about what the situation might be. Repeat this procedure until all four members have had the opportunity to communicate a situational feeling.

1. You are bored and tired during a class discussion. How do you portray that feeling nonverbally?
2. Another person does something or says something that hurts your feelings deeply. How do you portray those feelings nonverbally?
3. You feel affection for another person but at the same time you are not sure the other person feels the same way you do. How do you show your feelings nonverbally?
4. Your closest friend is leaving town for long time and you will have no chance to see her/him while she/he is gone. How do you show your feelings nonverbally?

3. Personal Situations

Reconvene the entire group if it is a counseling size group or stay with groups of four if larger. Have the members think of a recent past experience that was quite emotional for them. Have individual members in turn demonstrate those feelings nonverbally while the group observes. Observers then discuss what they perceived without comment from the person who expressed the feelings. After the discussion is concluded the presenter indicates how accurate the group's perceptions were and shares the situation and feelings with them. Repeat this process until all have participated in conveying a personal feeling.

This particular segment of the exercise was suggested by Dr. Wayne J. Kassera, College of Education, University of Wisconsin-River Falls.

Barriers to Communication

Sometimes members can understand communication barriers more clearly if they are depicted in a physical manner. The purpose of this exercise is to help group members realize the importance of communication in the group and think about strategies for overcoming obstacles.

Form dyads and have members begin a personal sharing type of discussion. Instruct them to sit back to back as they talk and not to turn around. After several minutes have them change their position to side by side but without looking at each other. Then have them face each other but avoid eye contact. During these changes they should continue to share. Finally have them carry on a normal face-to-face conversation. Stop the conversation after a few minutes and ask for reactions and feedback. Point out the importance of eye contact and careful listening in communication.

Then have the partners reengage in their discussion. Number members in each dyad as a one or a two. Start with both partners *sitting*. After a few minutes ask the *ones* to stand up while continuing the conversation. A few minutes later ask the *ones* to stand on their chairs while talking. Again after a few minutes instruct the *ones* to sit down. Repeat the entire procedure giving the same instructions to the twos. When both are at an equal level sitting again, ask for feedback and reactions, paying special attention to the impact of position and role on the communication process.

Cartoon of Member Reactions

The caricatures depicted in the cartoon in Figure 7.4 can be duplicated and passed out to members to help them discuss and understand the various defensive reactions or postures members display in groups. The handout can be used in several ways:

1. It can be used simply as an open ended stimulus for discussion;
2. Members can write and discuss captions for each figure, attempting to identify the message that is being conveyed;
3. Members can label each figure with an appropriate name that represents the behavior displayed (for example, Hostile Harry); or
4. Members can use the cartoon as a means of identifying their own and others' reactions, placing names of the members beneath the caricatures and then getting feedback from others as to what they think.

Since the caricatures are exaggerations they should be used in a light-hearted vein and not as a means of castigating any one member for unusual behavior or for giving negative feedback. Follow-up discussion might center on how to help each of these types of persons be more comfortable, involved, and open in the group.

Time Out Partners

The time out partner activity (Poppen & Thompson, 1974) lends itself well to working with the more negative or counter productive member behaviors. At any point in the action the leader can call "timeout" and members pair off for a short time to counsel or coach each other. Partners can be selected at random, the same partners can meet together for a period of time, or some criterion (such as using stars with isolates) can be used to match partners. The idea is to stop the group interaction temporarily to give individuals a respite from the pressures of group interaction and to provide them with time to relax and reassess their involvement and behaviors. Members usually respond well to this activity and occasionally initiate the request for a time out period themselves. The time out concept can also be applied on

FIGURE 7.4. Caricature of group member reactions.

an individual basis where certain members or the entire group go off by themselves for a short time and then return to the group. This technique can easily be adapted to a variety of different group settings, such as the classroom, psychoeducation or guidance groups, and psychotherapy groups.

Dollar Game

An excellent activity for helping group members understand manipulative behavior is to have each member bring a dollar to the group meeting (fifty cents or a quarter can be used for children). Instruct the members to place their dollars in the center of the group. Then tell them that their task is to decide as a group which individual is to receive all the money. No deals to share the money can be made and the individual chosen will in fact get all the money for personal use. Allow the group to interact until they reach consensus on the group member who is to receive the money. Give the money to that individual. Conduct a follow-up discussion directed at sharing feelings and reactions to the task particularly emphasizing values and strategies used in the negotiation process. After some discussion pass out a copy of Shostrom's (1967) Top Dog/Underdog diagram (Figure 7.3) and have members assess the types of manipulative strategies that were used in the group interaction. Have members identify their own strategies and also give their perceptions of other members' strategies.

A variation of this activity for children is to use a free trip to a special place like Disney World as the thing group members must decide to give to one member. Also, the Closed Fist exercise described at the end of Chapter 4 can be used for the same purpose as this activity.

Sharing Fears Activity

As a stimulus to introduce the helping behavior of self-disclosure, Childers and Couch (1989) suggest an anonymous fear sharing activity. Members are asked to write their fears, anxieties, or concerns about the group on 3 × 5 cards which are then passed to the leader. The leader randomly selects and reads the cards anonymously, solicits group discussion, and processes member's responses. As the cards are read and processed, self-disclosing by members begins to occur.

Name and Sign Activity

The following activity is designed to dissolve the barriers to connecting and communicating that exist in first or early group sessions. It helps members feel at ease, participate effectively in the group, and as a group and helps members get to know one another in a nonthreatening manner.

Instructions:

1. Members stand in a circle with the leader(s).
2. The leader begins the activity by giving his/her name and making a physical sign: "My name is Jim and my sign is (enacts a gesture, e.g., wave, hand signal, dance).
3. The group responds in unison by saying: "You are Jim and your sign is (the group makes the gesture).

The process then moves clockwise or counter clockwise with each member giving his/her name and sign. After each new person's disclosure, the group responds in unison starting with that person and then repeating the name and sign of each previous person. Continue until the entire circle of members has been introduced and the group has responded in unison to the entire circle. This activity can be replicated as an interpersonal warm-up at the beginning of succeeding group sessions as a means of helping members remember names and connect socially with each other.

Lynn S. Rapin
Robert K. Conyne

Best Practices in Group Counseling

☐ Introduction by James P. Trotzer

Professional ethics and standards of professional practice have catapulted to the forefront as predominant concerns in the helping professions. Encompassed in the tumultuous maze of legal, ethical, and professional dynamics are the providers, consumers, and overseers (professional organizations and governmental agencies) of mental health services. Codes of ethics and statutory parameters to govern and guide professional practice have been established and are in a perpetual state of being devised and defined, revised and refined, tested and applied. The field of group work is no exception to this emphasis and process. Consequently, the inclusion of a specific chapter on best practices in group counseling is designed to provide you with the most current perspectives on professional and ethical practice in group work.

Pedersen (1998) has noted that "ethical guidelines are a necessary but not sufficient condition for promoting ethical behavior"(p. 23). Herlihy and Corey (1996) have explicated the functions of ethical codes as educational tools relative to professional conduct, sources of accountability relative to professional responsibility, and catalysts relative to improvement of the profession. The purpose of this chapter by Lynn Rapin and Bob Conyne is to incorporate those elements into the training dimension of this text with regard to group counseling.

The emphasis of the chapter is to develop a pragmatic connection between codes of ethics, standards of practice, and literal performance. The relationship of the chapter to professional ethics is to provide concrete group counseling guidelines and practices that will implement the moral principles which undergird codes of ethics (Kitchener, 1984; Welfel & Kitchener, 1992). These principles include:

1. *Autonomy*: Preserving the free agency and self-determination of the client.
2. *Beneficence*: Promoting that which is good (therapeutic) for the client and facilitating the client's growth and development.
3. *Nonmalfeasance*: Applying the first directive of the Hippocratic Oath which stipulates "above all else—do not harm." Refraining from engaging in any actions that are hurtful to the client.
4. *Justice and fairness*: Treating all clients equally and with equity.
5. *Fidelity*: Being honest, reliable, faithful in conduct and not engaging in deceptive manipulative or exploitative behaviors.

Referring to the Best Practices Guidelines as explicated, and learning and engaging in Best Practices behaviors will assist you in understanding and implementing both the spirit and the letter of ethical codes of professional conduct.

In relationship to a specific code of ethics (American Counseling Association [ACA] Code of Ethics and Standards of Practice, 1995: See Appendix B), the following statement will suffice:

> Best Practices in Group Work Guidelines
> "are intended to clarify the application of the ACA Code of Ethics and Standards of Practice to the field of group work by defining a group worker's responsibility and scope of practice involving those activities, strategies and interventions that are consistent and current with effective and appropriate professional, ethical and community standards" (p. 1) (Excerpted from ASGW Best Practices Guidelines by Lynn Rapin and Linda Keel, adopted by ASGW Executive Board March 29, 1998.)

In relationship to the helping modalities, this chapter delineates group work as an entity that presents certain unique issues compared to the other helping modalities (e.g., individual counseling, couple, or family counseling). Group counseling—while in some respects ameliorating some of the ethical dilemmas attendant to individual counseling and family counseling—raises its own challenges to ethical practice due to the nature of the process and its reliance on group dynamics and peer pressure. Consequently the best practices as elucidated will be of utmost utility.

Finally, this chapter in some respects is the core of the text as all the other chapters are reflected in it and reflect on it. You will note as you read, the direct relationship the guidelines have to the other sections of the text. Therefore, it is with a great deal of enthusiasm and confidence that I introduce you to Lynn Rapin and Bob Conynes' chapter *Best Practices in Group Counseling*. I believe that its merit will be self-evident and that you will benefit conceptually and practically from its content and activities.

☐ Overview

Group counseling practice can be enhanced and barriers to its implementation can be reduced or eliminated through the proper application of best practices. Our purpose in writing this chapter is to provide a basic primer on best practices in group work, with special emphasis on group counseling.

Definition of Best Practices in Group Work

Best practices in group work refer to those activities, strategies, and interventions that are consistent and current with effective and appropriate professional, ethical, and community standards. In group counseling, these practices should address not only what occurs within group sessions but, also, necessary activities and involvement occurring before and after group sessions. That is, best practice guidelines for group work, and specifically group counseling, need to be comprehensive in scope.

Evolution of Best Practices in Group Counseling

ASGW Ethical Guidelines for Group Counselors

The most recent edition of the ASGW's Ethical Guidelines for Group Counselors (1989) has been supplanted by the ACA Code of Ethics and Standards of Practice (1995). This action by the ASGW Executive Board was taken at the request of the ACA to reduce the legal liability of any ACA division, including ASGW, that had developed a set of ethical standards, and to promote the unification of the counseling profession.

ACA Code of Ethics and Standards of Practice

Now, any ethical complaints submitted are processed in accordance with the ACA Code of Ethics and Standards of Practice (ACA, 1995, see Appendix B). However, much of the contents of the ASGW 1989 guidelines remain germane to guide best practices in group work.

ASGW Ethics Committee Project on Best Practices

The Ethics Committee of ASGW was given the charge of producing a best practices in group work document that would include relevant features from the previous guidelines document as well as other necessary elements. The work of that committee produced the Best Practices in Group Work Guidelines adopted by the ASGW Executive Board March 29, 1998.(Keel & Rapin, 1997; Rapin & Keel, 1996a, 1996b, 1997, 1998).

Group Counseling Focus

In this chapter, we draw upon the formulating work and development that resulted in ASGW's Group Work Best Practices Guidelines (see Appendix C). In keeping with the focus of this book the contents of this chapter are centered on group counseling, rather than the broader range of group work. In addition, chapter contents represent our own thinking and should not be construed as being in any way an official statement of ASGW.

Planning, Performing, and Processing

We organize the best practice guidelines into categories representing the three Ps of group work leadership practice: *Planning*, *Performing*, and *Processing* (Conyne, 1997, as reported in Conyne, Smith & Wathen, 1997; Conyne, in press).

Planning

In planning, group counseling leaders must be concerned with all steps that are preliminary to conducting the first group session. This includes but is not limited to designing the group, choosing appropriate meeting space, publicizing the group, and recruiting and selecting group members.

Performing

In performing, group leaders apply the group counseling plan effectively and appropriately to positively affect group members. Some important components of performing include the delivery of core competencies in group work, attending to confidentiality throughout the sessions, and developing therapeutic conditions.

Processing

In processing, leaders meet in supervision or with peers or coleaders between sessions to reflect on and evaluate what occurred in the preceding session, derive meaning from events and experiences, and consider any impact on the next and upcoming sessions. In addition, in the case of coleaders, processing involves examining the nature and quality of their interaction during group sessions.

Ethical choice points and dilemmas can occur at every planning, performing, and processing step. As this text is organized, you will find that many of the guidelines in the current chapter match content headings of other chapters. This is understandable because the group leader has ethical responsibilities in every aspect and stage of group work, from participation as a student leader in training through direct experience with group members to professional instruction, evaluation, and consultation about groups.

We propose that orienting yourself to the best practice elements of planning, performing, and processing will assist you in identifying and limiting potential ethical dilemmas. At the same time, we appreciate that guidelines can only serve as a road map to decision making. The unique personal attributes of the group leader, leader skills, member needs, group goals, leader and member roles, and behaviors in interaction with the particular group and theoretical orientation combine for a wide range of decision points.

As you read through the guidelines, consider potential choice points and options you have for responding. The reader can also increase understanding of ethical issues by consulting other ethics sources including two special issues of the *Journal for Specialists in Group Work* (1982, 1990), and texts devoted entirely to ethical practice (Burke & Miranti, 1992; Corey, Corey & Callahan, 1993; Herlihy & Corey, 1996).

The guidelines that follow are organized in the sequence of the ASGW Best Practices Guidelines but are presented in the form of a directive or action statement relative to group counseling. Within each statement the topic heading derived from the ASGW document is accentuated with italics.

☐ Section A: Best Practices in *Planning* Group Counseling: Guidelines

A1: Be Aware of *Professional Context and Regulatory Requirements*

Codes of Ethics

Counselors have both professional and regulatory obligations that guide their practices. Codes of ethics define the ethical responsibilities required of members of professions toward the persons they serve. Further, accompanying standards of practice provide minimum expected behaviors required of practicing professionals. Specific procedures must be followed when there is a complaint about the ethical practice of a professional association member. There are a number of ethical decision making models (Forester-Miller & Davis, 1995; Forester-Miller & Rubenstein, 1992; Kitchener, 1984) that can assist you at ethical decision points.

Current published codes of ethics, standards of practice, and complaint procedures are available to present and future members of professional organizations and their clients. Ethical codes are not static but are revised periodically to reflect contemporary practice. Changes in professional training, delivery, and reimbursement systems, for example, may influence specific ethical principles or standards of practice.

Counselors look to their primary national, professional organization, the

American Counseling Association, and its divisions to guide their group practice (ACA, 1995). Counselors or their colleagues may have membership in other professional associations which also have codes of ethics and practice standards germane to group work. Some of these include the American Psychological Association (1992), the National Association of Social Workers (1993), and the American Group Psychotherapy Association (1991).

Licensure, Certification, and Accreditation

Counselors are regulated by state licensing bodies and they can be certified as being properly trained and educated, for example through the National Board for Certified Counselors (NBCC) (1989) and National Certified Group Psychotherapists (NCGP). As of this writing, 43 states and the District of Columbia have counselor licenses and one has state certification (NBCC, 1997b). A growing number of counselor education training programs are accredited by the Council for the Accreditation of Counseling and Related Educational Programs (CACREP)(1993) as meeting at least the minimal standards for counselor training, including the area of group work.

Absorbing all the professional practice context components we have briefly summarized above may seem overwhelming to the counselor in training or new graduate. However, the professional context that emerges strongly influences group counseling training and practice, requiring practitioners to be cognizant and responsive as they engage in group counseling best practice.

A2: Develop a *Scope of Practice and Conceptual Framework* for Group Counseling

Value of Groupwork

Many counselors do not feel confident or competent to lead groups. Others do not set group work as a priority (Dansby, 1996), and some do not believe that group counseling is effective. However, evidence to the contrary is building that group counseling is equally as effective as individual counseling and sometimes more so (Seligman, 1995; Sleek, 1995). Therefore, group counseling needs to be valued as an essentially important helping approach. According to Corey and Corey (1997), ". . . groups are the treatment of choice, not a second rate approach to helping people change" (p. 5).

Scope of Practice

Defining scope of practice is of essential importance for all group workers (Conyne, Wilson, & Ward, 1997). The ASGW (1990) Training Standards require group workers to be able to define group work in general, the core competencies that all counselors should be able to deliver, and each of the four group work specializations (task, psychoeducation, counseling, and psychotherapy groups). Advantages and disadvantages of each specialization and the conditions under which each can properly be used also need to be understood. Counselors need to be aware of their own strengths and limitations in relation to performing group work leadership. Awareness and knowledge of all these areas allow counselors to select a scope of group work practice that suits their assets and which fits presenting situations. Those selecting group counseling as a focal area will be aimed at helping ". . . group participants to resolve the usual, yet often difficult, problems of living through interpersonal support and problem solving . . . (so) that they may be better able to handle future problems of a similar nature. . ." (ASGW, 1990, p. 14).

Conceptual Framework

Group counselors cannot be driven solely or predominantly by techniques, presenting issues, or intuition (Corey, Corey, Callahan, & Russell, 1992). It is necessary for them to develop a general conceptual framework that will provide practical guidance that includes a basis for predictability, interpretation, evaluation, and reality testing. For some group counselors, development of a conceptual framework may involve drawing from the individually oriented counseling and personality based theories such as the psychodynamic, behavioral, cognitive-behavioral, humanistic, or transpersonal orientations (Corey, 1995; Peterson & Nisenholz, 1995), and applying them to group counseling. Corey and Corey (1997), for instance, prefer a combination model drawn from selected theories, that they describe as "thinking, feeling, and behaving." For others, it may involve focusing on interpersonal, interactional, social- psychological, or systemic models of change (e.g., see Forsyth, 1990; Napier & Gershenfeld, 1993; Shaw, 1981), and applying them to group counseling. Chapters 3–5 of this text present a psychological rationale and process model for group counseling. In all cases, conceptual underpinnings need to be integrated with personal values, strengths, and limitations, as well as account for cultural and situational demands. These considerations are typically reflected as Practice Guidelines on Professional Disclosure Statements and in Professional Development.

A3: Conduct an Ecological *Assessment*

An ecological assessment provides the group counselor with an understanding of the cultural, demographic, economic, political, social, health, and psychological needs of community members. In addition, community members' attitudes toward group counseling as influenced by factors of culture and diversity are of primary importance and must be addressed in any ecological assessment.

Multiple Assessment Issues

The group counselor must become focused on understanding the local community with regard to issues that need to be addressed. Critical questions include:

1. What needs exist in this community that group counseling might be able to address?
2. What resources could be mobilized in order to provide groups?
3. How would group counseling fit within the organizational mission?
4. How could group counseling services be developed and delivered using strategies that are culturally appropriate and which include adequate opportunities for community participation? (See Chapter 11, Organizing for Group Counseling, for specific strategies.)

Likewise, the counselor needs to research the professional literature to discover what counseling approaches have worked elsewhere. In doing so, leads can be found to suggest how successful group counseling might be adapted to local use.

Formation of a small, representative, planning group is usually advantageous for conducting an effective ecological assessment for two reasons: 1) the process is too complex for one person to accomplish well alone; and 2) involvement of significant others at the assessment stage can facilitate their later approval, assistance, and support.

Match Group Work Type

Counselors can choose from a variety of group work types (task, psychoeducation, counseling, and psychotherapy groups) to serve the needs of their clients. In many cases more that one type of group could be used with clients. For example, at risk populations could be served by both psychoeducational and counseling groups.

A4: Implement *Program Development and Evaluation* Principles

Group Goals, Themes, and Activities

Once an ecological assessment has produced information allowing for identification of the type of group(s) to be offered for specified client populations, the group leader needs to define the purpose of the group(s) and set specific group goals for both leader and members. The leader should further use program development skills to formulate the activities or themes of the group and to identify potential techniques which might be most appropriate for the group type, theoretical orientation, and population (McKay & Paleg, 1992).

Evaluation Plan

An evaluation plan should be developed to look at both process (formative evaluation) and outcome (summative evaluation) dimensions (Fitz-Gibb on & Morris, 1987). Evaluation questions, measures, and tools should be identified prior to the start of the group so that planned evaluation can be conducted (Craig, 1978; Hadley & Mitchell, 1995; see also Chapter 12, Evaluating Group Counseling and Chapter 15, The Case for Group Research).

A5: Identify *Resources* for Managing the Group Program

Several practical considerations related to resources should be considered prior to implementation. These resources are the nitty gritty necessities that make a plan work.

Fees and Insurance

Fees and group member payment obligations need to be clearly identified. Group charges should be established consistent with agency or organization guidelines and in consideration of the financial status of prospective group members. Many organizations have sliding fee scales to respond to the varying income levels of potential clients.

One of the current challenges in counseling is that of providing services which might be covered in whole or part by insurance. Fees consistent with professional and community standards may vary greatly from reimbursement limits set by insurance plans or health maintenance organizations (HMOs). Further, membership on insurance panels greatly affects reimbursement levels with a late 1990s common effect of reducing fees (Psychotherapy Finances, 1997). A group could thus have some members whose fees are fully paid by insurance, some who have insurance covered by a managed care contract at a discounted fee, members who have no insurance coverage and pay full fee, and members with reduced fees due to income variability.

Funding

Adequate funding must be available to support a group program. Costs typically include budgeted funds for materials, supplies, continuing education, and contingency funds to support professional staff who may need additional group training and/or supervision.

Leaders/Coleaders

A determination of whether it is appropriate for the group to be led by one leader or coleaders should be made. If coleaders are appropriate, the model of leadership they will employ (apprentice model, rotating model, supervision model) should be identified. Leadership styles of coleaders have to be discussed and integrated so that group members are not confused or harmed by different orientations or approaches. In recent research and analysis it is suggested that coleaders need to progress through their own development as a team prior to beginning work with a group (Dugo & Beck, 1997; Wheelan, 1997).

Meeting Space

Identifying available group meeting space in accord with privacy requirements ensures that groups can actually take place in the desired setting. It is not unusual for facilities to lack designated space for groups whether the provider is an agency, business, school or private practice. Flexible negotiating may be necessary to convert space or allocate physical priorities to group work.

Marketing and Recruiting

Any recruitment or marketing must be conducted in light of the setting for the group. Presentations to professional staff about the group program, staff discussion with clients about group benefits, community education presentations, consultation with referral agencies and individuals, community service announcements, media presentations, and internet announcements are among appropriate options.

Other organization settings require alternative strategies. School settings have unique resources, including classroom teachers, administrators who work with at risk students, parents, and students themselves. Business organizations have Employee Assistance Programs, managers and supervisors, inhouse publications, and employees themselves as potential referral sources.

A6: Develop a *Professional Disclosure Statement*

An essential step in the planning process is the preparation of a professional disclosure statement. These printed statements are often required by law and serve to inform potential group members of the group leader's scope of practice, licenses and certifications, specific qualifications in conducting the group or groups being offered, and fees for service (see Fig. 8.1 for an example).

A7: Conduct *Group and Members Preparation*

Screening

Once the counselor has selected the type of group to be conducted, it can be determined whether it is appropriate or not to screen members prior to

Identification:
>   Pat Jones, Adolescent Group Coordinator
>   Community Mental Health Center
>   110 Main Street
>   Central City, Your State
>   Phone: (123) 456-7890

Education:
>   Master's Degree (M.A.) in Community Counseling from State University
>   (CACREP Approved Program) and specialist in advanced counseling
>   from State University

Licensure and Certification:
>   Licensed Professional Clinical Counselor
>   Your State License No. 12345
>   Certified, National Board for Certified Counselors

Professional Associations:
>   American Counseling Association
>   Association for Specialists in Group Work
>   Your State Counseling Association

Scope of Practice:
>   Provision of community counseling services within the mental health
>   setting

Specialization:
>   Group work with adolescent clients in the Mental Health Center who
>   experience behavior, drug, and alcohol issues

Purpose and Goals of Group Counseling:
>   Assist adolescents in resolving conflicts and increasing problem solving
>   skills as they face risk situations

Group Structure:
>   Time limited, closed groups; ongoing open groups; groups are frequently
>   col-ed

Previous Experience Leading Groups:
>   Two years as a junior group coleader and four years as senior group
>   coleader

Fee Schedule:
>   Groups follow the agency fee schedule provided to all clients

Credentialing Agency Address:
>   Counselor Licensing Board
>   123 Central Avenue
>   Capital, Your State

FIGURE 8.1. Sample professional disclosure statement.

admission to the experience. Counseling and psychotherapy groups generally require prescreening to ensure a good match between member and group. When counselors are using psychoeducational or task groups, they may be working with intact groups in which individual member screening is not always possible or necessary.

Informed Consent

A group plan cannot succeed without orientation and education of the actual people who will become its members. Information prepared during preceding planning activities is provided during screening to ensure that prospective members are fully informed, willing, and appropriate to participate in the group. Clearly delivered information about goals of the group, ground rules for participation, possible activities, leader qualifications, and leader and member responsibilities fosters member involvement and ownership of the group experience.

Confidentiality and Its Limits

A delicate balance is required to both educate potential group members to the importance of confidentiality within and outside the group experience and to provide information on the limits of confidentiality (for example, informing members that legal privilege does not extend to group discussions and that the group leader cannot guarantee confidentiality of information shared among group members). Members need to understand that documentation for treatment plans, insurance approval, and claim filing requires that the group leader provide confidential information in writing that may not be protected beyond the sponsoring organization.

A8: Pursue *Professional Development*

Group workers have both opportunity and obligation for continuous learning. In addition to the learning opportunities present in every group session, more formal opportunities for professional enhancement are plentiful. Continuing education through professional meetings, professional development workshops, academic experiences, professional supervision in groups, coleading experiences, professional presentations, and personal development all enhance counselors' abilities to serve group members. Responsible group workers integrate research and practice literature into group design and evaluation.

A9: Be Aware of *Trends and Technological Changes*

Counselors should be aware of and appropriately respond to technological changes and trends as they affect society and the profession.

Managed Care

Mental health delivery systems, including group services, have been significantly affected by legislative health care reform and changes in the insurance industry. Managed care has and will continue to influence many areas of group work including access to services, delivery of group and other treatment modalities, documentation, confidentiality, reimbursement, and outcome evaluation. On the positive side of managed care, there is some indication that group counseling services may become a preferred delivery format in the future for reasons of both economy and effectiveness (Spitz, 1996). Group counselors must be active participants in understanding managed care issues and in developing appropriate responses to them.

Demographics

Counselors, including group counselors, must respond in their training and practice to changing population demographics and client needs. These include, for example, increased sensitivity to multicultural and diversity issues as the population becomes more diverse, responding to AIDS and other serious health trends, and working with an aging population.

Technology

Counselors must keep abreast of technological advances that affect their work. Access to the internet presents both opportunity and challenge in many areas (e.g., in research, information exchange, advertising, and service provision). Counselors must adhere to ethical guidelines related to use of developing technologies (Bloom, 1997; NBCC, 1997a). Preparation and flexibility are essential for future professional success.

☐ Section B: Best Practices in *Performing*: Guidelines

The performance of group counseling involves effectively adapting the group counseling plan to fit situational demands. Seldom will a preconceived plan, no matter how well developed, be implemented without undergoing substantial modification. The counselor must use effective and appropriate competencies and strategies to effect plan revisions, with the goal of meeting group and individual member goals. Although performance is a portion of group leadership (encompassed by planning and processing), it is an essential ingredient. Performance is what most often is thought of as comprising group leadership. It is what the leader actually does during the course of group counseling sessions.

B1: Know Thyself or Cultivate *Self-Knowledge*

As many experts have observed (e.g., Corey & Corey, 1997; Gladding, 1994), it is fundamentally important that group counselors be aware of their strengths and weaknesses and of their stimulus value to others. One of the best ways that future group counselors can become aware of themselves as interpersonal beings is to become a member of one or more therapeutic group experiences and avail themselves of the opportunities to self-disclose and to give and receive feedback in the group setting.

B2 : Effectively Deliver *Group Competencies*

Core Group Competencies

As described in the ASGW Professional Training Standards (ASGW, 1989), all counselors should be able to perform the foundation skills of group work and understand basic knowledge of groups. For example, they should be able to

1. open and close group sessions,
2. encourage the participation of group members, and
3. engage in appropriate self-disclosure in groups. As well, all counselors must possess a working knowledge of groups, including
    1. being able to identify the principles of group dynamics,
    2. describe specific ethical issues that are unique to group work, and
    3. deliver a clear definition of group work.

Counseling Group Competencies

In addition to the core group competencies, counselors specializing in group counseling should be able to effectively implement its skills and should possess knowledge of the group counseling specialty. Among these skills, group counselors should be able to 1) recruit and screen prospective group members, 2) intervene effectively in critical situations that occur during counseling group process, and 3) effectively manage disruptive members. Moreover, knowledge applicable to group counseling must be understood, including the relationship of interpersonal dynamics and interpersonal assessment to group counseling, the advantages and disadvantages of group counseling, and when it is best indicated for use.

B3: Develop, Implement, and Adapt a Group Plan (*Group Plan Adaptation*)

As stated above, group counselors need to learn the conditions under which their plan can be used as is, modified, or reconsidered or abandoned. Group counselors need to develop adequate and reliable professional judgment, such that they can determine when and how to proceed with their groups (Conyne, Wilson, & Ward, 1997; Kottler, 1994a). While this capacity emerges through experience and training, it can be advanced through appropriate supervision and by working in coleadership arrangements where processing of group events and experiences can occur openly and genuinely between sessions.

Choosing Appropriate Interventions

Group counselors need to be able to select interventions from a range of possibilities that fit the presenting situation. Considerations such as intervention level (individual, interpersonal, group), type (conceptual, experiential, structural), and intended intensity (high, medium, low) are important to understand and utilize (Cohen & Smith, 1976; see also Chapters 6 and 13).

B4: Master *Therapeutic Conditions and Dynamics*

Effective group counselors understand what we call the holy trinity of therapeutic conditions and dynamics: 1) group development; 2) process observation; and 3) therapeutic conditions.

Group Development

Many sequential and cyclical models of group development exist (MacKenzie, 1997). The sequential model described in this text is as useful as any particularly because it ties group developmental tasks to each stage. But whichever model is chosen, it can provide the group counselor with a powerful schematic for generally predicting future events and for interpreting occurring ones. Possessing such knowledge allows the group leader to bring perspective to practice and contributes to leader competence and confidence.

Process Observation

Group counselors must be able to assess and diagnose what is occurring in their groups, not only in terms of what is being said (content) but, also, how content is being presented and received (process). Examples of important group process observations include being able to notice levels of participation, influence, styles of decision making, group tone, task and maintenance behaviors, how affect is dealt with, and the operating norms of the group (Hanson, 1972). Noting such processes within sessions and across them helps to determine how the group is working and how members are progressing. (See Appendix E, Gleanings of a Process Observer.)

Therapeutic Conditions

Yalom's (1995) therapeutic conditions or factors are accepted by most experts as axiomatic to effective group counseling and psychotherapy (Crouch,

Block, & Wanless, 1994). The capacity to generate these conditions, such as universality, instillation of hope, and altruism, needs to be well within the repertoire of all group counselors, regardless of theoretical orientation.

B5: Attend to the Here and Now and to *Meaning* Attribution

Group counselors generally can help members find increased therapeutic value in interactions that are focused on present experience and events, followed by aiding members in attributing meaning to (making sense of) their experience (Hill, 1969; Yalom, 1995).

B6: Promote *Collaboration* with Members

Help Members Develop Goals

Groups tend to flounder when members do not understand the general group purpose or if they do not receive help in translating their sometimes vague intentions into more concrete goal statements (Johnson & Johnson, 1997). Working with group members to define feasible and meaningful goals for the group experience is an excellent motivational tool that can accelerate positive outcomes.

Coequal Partners

Leaders and members are coequal partners in group counseling. Leaders are experts in the theory and process of group counseling; members are experts in their own experience and life situation. Working with members and seeking to empower them through activating their own resources represents an important way for group counselors to approach leadership.

B7: Include *Evaluation*

When evaluation occurs in group counseling, it is most likely to be at a group's conclusion and to be formal in nature. However, it is also important for leaders to evaluate each session informally with their group members. Doing so reinforces an ethic of collaborative learning and will help to keep the group on a proper course. This kind of evaluation need not be complex, sophisticated, or lengthy. In fact, we recommend it be simple, friendly, and short, and integrated with discussion. A very usable format is that developed by Hill (1969), called the Post Meeting Reaction Sheet (PMRS), where leaders and members discuss at the end of each session such issues as personal learning, participation levels, and overall satisfaction.

B8: Value *Diversity*

Group counselors need to establish a group value that fully incorporates diversity. An interesting way to think broadly about diversity can be found through considering the term RESPECTFUL, used as an acronym by D'Andrea and Daniels (1997b). The authors argue that counselors should integrate within their work attention to a broad range of client differences, including:

*R*eligious/spiritual identity;
*E*thnic identity;
*S*exual identity;
*P*sychological maturity;
*E*conomic class standing;
*C*hronological challenges;
*T*hreats to one's well being;
*F*amily history;
*U*nique physical characteristics; and
*L*ocation of residence.

B9: Maintain a Constant *Ethical Surveillance*

Group counseling is an intricate, complex intervention that demands great attention, focus, and skill of its practitioners. Ethical challenges can be found in every session. Examples include: How to safeguard and protect the rights of each member while, at the same time, encouraging risk taking; How to develop a common agreement about the sacred trust of confidentiality while explaining to members that it is not possible to guarantee it; How to help members understand the leader's position on a topic while not imposing his or her own values on the member. Group counselors need to develop a solid understanding of the ACA Code of Ethics and Standards of Practice, to employ a process of ethical decision making to help them determine appropriate courses of action in morally or procedurally uncertain instances (Forester-Miller & Davis, 1995), and to be able to consult with competent, trusted colleagues when murkiness or confusion arises.

☐ Section C: Best Practices in *Processing*: Guidelines

Life in general is fast paced. Events and experiences occur as if in a blur. Speed characterizes life in group counseling, as well. So much happens, from so many directions, that group members and group counselors alike often are unable to keep up with, let alone make sense of, what is occurring (Conyne, Wilson, & Ward, 1997). That is why the processing element is so crucial.

C1: Set and Maintain a *Processing Schedule*

Purpose for Processing

Processing is often overlooked in group counseling, taking a back seat to performing and planning. Since it is linked to Planning and Performing, we refer to processing as between session analysis, evaluation, and reflection engaged in by the group counselor in order to guide the group forward productively. Processing by group leaders is necessary in order for them to better understand what occurred, draw meaning from events and experiences, and to make appropriate or necessary adjustments to the plan for next sessions.

Before and After Session Processing

Before and after session processing is similar to processing that may occur within sessions, which is conducted to help members integrate experiential with cognitive learning. However, before and after session processing is distinguishable as a leadership step which is conducted to help the group stay on course and be effective. Never forget, ignore, or avoid making time to process before and after sessions, no matter how difficult it is to schedule or how threatening it may seem to do (Conyne, 1989). Doing so makes a commitment to your learning and to the group and its members.

Before a session, the leader is concerned with 1) adequate preparation and making sure goals and strategies are linked, 2) making sure the session plan matches the developmental progress of the group, and 3) making sure leader roles are clear. After a session, the leader is focused on 1) understanding what occurred, 2) examining member and leader behavior, 3) assessing the relative effectiveness of the session, and 4) seeking to draw deeper meaning from events and experiences.

C2: Engage in *Reflective Practice*

Learn from Experience

Yalom (1995) has identified the *reflective arc* as a critically important insession group leadership activity that is linked to successful outcomes. He contends that here and now experience needs to be considered and understood, resulting in the attribution of meaning (Lieberman, Yalom, & Miles, 1973). This is accomplished by reflecting back (arcing) on concrete group experiences that results in an integration of experiential and cognitive learning. Similarly, Argyris, Putnam, and Smith (1985) discussed the *action scientist* role, Lewin (1951) posited the value of *action research*, and Conyne, Wilson, and Ward (1997) described the group worker as a *reflective practitioner*. These perspectives all accentuate the integrative value of incorporating synthesizing with doing, action with reflection, and theory with practice. Group counselors must actively and systematically allocate time, energy, and focus to learning from their experiences as leaders and to appropriately incorporate learning outcomes into their ongoing groups. For between session processing, assiduously keeping session by session journals, processing before and after sessions with a coleader, peers or supervisor, applying concepts to practice, reviewing session evaluation results, and critiquing video tapes of sessions represent some of the strategies to use in nurturing the reflective practitioner role.

Pragmatic and Deep Processing

Two types of processing between or after sessions are possible: 1) pragmatic processing, and 2) deep processing (Conyne, in press; Conyne, Smith, & Wathen, 1997). In pragmatic processing, the focus is placed on noting and describing the dynamics of members and their interactions, including such matters as who talks to whom and identifying decision making procedures that have been used. In deep processing, leaders probe more intensely the relationship between what has occurred and their values, cognition, and affect. Here, each leader risks confronting himself/herself and each other, intending to move to a deeper level of personal meaning that could have both immediate and lasting impact on their professional practice.

C3: Use *Evaluation* Data *and* Conduct *Follow-Up* Activities

Evaluation is a central part of processing. Utilization-focused evaluation conceptualized by Patton (1997) and applied to group counseling practice requires that evaluation data must be used. That is, unless one is conducting basic experimental research, it is of little value to ask questions about a counseling group that do not have pragmatic importance. Conversely, it is of high value to ask questions and to produce data that are directly relevant to ongoing group issues.

Evaluation Process

Evaluation can be focused on monitoring the ongoing processes and performance of a group. Questions of effort, efficiency, appropriateness, satisfaction, group process, and congruence with the group plan are often important for monitoring (Craig, 1978). In performing guideline B7 we discussed collaborating with group members to include evaluation within each session. In processing, the focus of evaluation is on a) studying evaluation data between sessions, b) designing methods for gathering evaluative data in future sessions, and c) using data produced for making any necessary adjustments in the group plan.

Evaluation Outcomes

Evaluation can also be focused on determining group outcomes. Outcomes address such summative matters as overall satisfaction, involvement, effectiveness, and goal accomplishment. For example, an outcome evaluation can be designed to test if the general purposes of the group and the individual goals of members were met. Quasi- or experimental designs (Campbell & Stanley, 1963) are suited to these kinds of bottom line questions, the answers to which have assumed considerably more significance with the advent of managed care and its emphasis on what works.

C4: Engage in *Consultation and Training with Other Organizations*

As previously noted, group counselors seek out consultation from coleaders, supervisors, and other professionals in the planning, performing, and processing of their groups. They may also be in positions to provide consultation to other individuals or organizations offering group counseling. The provision of consultation stimulates and strengthens group counselors' skills by demonstrating and assisting others in understanding groups and group process. Well trained and experienced group counseling leaders have numerous consultation opportunities including, providing outside group leadership to counselor training groups, conducting workshops, assisting teachers, and serving as members of planning teams in designing and modifying group offerings.

☐ Conclusion

Group counseling is rapidly developing as an essential helping methodology. According to some experts, it and other forms of group work may become the preferred forms of help giving in 21st century America. Given the importance of group counseling, it is necessary that best practices be developed to help guide training, delivery, and research. This chapter represents an effort in presenting these best practices. Its contents emerge from ethical guidelines previously adopted by the Association for Specialists in Group Work, and it is compatible with both the Code of Ethics and Standards of Practice of the American Counseling Association, and ASGW's Best Practices in Group Work Guidelines.

The set of best practices presented in this chapter are organized within three major sections: 1) Planning, 2) Performing, and 3) Processing, as are the learning activities that follow. Implementation of these best practices will assist practitioners in their provision of effective, appropriate, ethical, professional, therapeutic, and useful counseling groups.

☐ Learning Activities

Planning Activities

1. Imagine you are a staff member in a mental health center that has no group services. Generate for your real or imagined setting at least six points you would need to consider in developing a group counseling program. Share and discuss contributions in a small learning group of three to five members. (60 minutes)

2. Using the following elements design a Professional Disclosure Statement for yourself containing appropriate information for a group counselor and present it to a partner or a small group; then reverse or repeat the process. Discuss your similarities and differences. (30–45 minutes)

> Identifying information: Name, business address, phone number
> Education
> License and/or certification
> Professional associations
> Scope of practice
> Specialization
> Purpose and goals of your counseling group
> Group structure
> Previous experience leading groups
> Fee schedule, if appropriate
> Address of credentialing agency (for example, State Licensing Board) if
>   appropriate

Performing Activities

1. Self-assess your strengths and areas for improvement as a group counseling leader. List strengths and improvement areas in two columns. Select one strength and one improvement area and indicate how you might enhance each one. Discuss these with a partner, then reverse roles. (60 minutes)

2. Organize into a group of six people and select a leader. Conduct a 20 minute group discussion addressing the topic, "How I think group counseling can be helpful to people." After 20 minutes, stop the group and engage in an evaluative discussion, asking 1) How did the meeting go? 2) How satisfied were you with your participation? 3) How might we be able to improve our working together, using this information? (40–45 minutes)

Processing Activities

1. Break into pairs to complete the following exercise. Suppose the two of you have just joined as coleaders to offer a counseling group. Individually

identify what characteristics would be important for you to discuss with your coleader to ensure a successful group. Discuss your ideas with your partner. Summarize ideas from your dyad and share with the whole group. (60 minutes)

2. What specific steps would you take to assure adequate processing of your group experience? Prepare your answer, then discuss your steps with others in a small discussion group of three to five participants. (45 minutes).

3. You have assumed a new role in your agency or school as Group Counseling Coordinator. As part of your responsibilities you need to develop procedures to help determine if group counseling services are working. Develop ideas to address this question and discuss your ideas with a partner; reverse roles. (30 minutes)

4. Identify a specific group experience or event you have encountered as a member or leader. Describe its dynamics (pragmatic processing). Go beyond this to identify your thoughts and feelings and, also, what this experience meant to you (deep processing). Share the results of your work with a partner; reverse roles. (60 minutes)

5. Use the check list in Figure 8.2 as a guide for planning a group. Have you done everything you need to do to plan for, perform and process your group experience? For *no* responses, return to this chapter and identify what additional actions you need to take.

Check List Items	Yes	No	NA
Best Practices in Planning Group Counseling			
Have awareness of professional context			
Have reviewed Codes of Ethics			
Have complied with licensure, certification, and accreditation requirements			
Have developed conceptual underpinnings			
Have understanding of the value of group counseling			
Have defined my scope of practice			
Have developed a conceptual framework			
Have completed an ecological assessment			
Have identified and answered key assessment questions			
Have matched group work type to population			
Have implemented program development and evaluation			
Have defined group purpose			
Have defined group goals			
Have complied with fee and insurance policies			
Have secured necessary funding			
Have made leadership\coleadership decision			
Have secured meeting space			
Have completed marketing and recruiting			
Have developed a professional disclosure statement			
Have prepared the group and its members			
Have completed any required screening			
Have provided informed consent			
Have described confidentiality and its limits			
Have identified relevant professional development activities			
Have awareness of relevant trends and technology			
Have understanding of managed care impacts			
Have understanding of client demographics			
Have understanding of technology impacts			

FIGURE 8.2. Best practices in group counseling checklist.

Check List Items	Yes	No	NA
Best Practices in Performing			
Have understanding of personal limits (self-knowledge)			
Have understanding and skill in group competencies			
Have knowledge and skill in core competencies			
Have group counseling competencies			
Have group plan and adaptation contingencies			
Have chosen appropriate interventions			
Have skill in therapeutic conditions and dynamics			
Have understanding of group development			
Have skill in process observation			
Have knowledge of therapeutic conditions			
Have prepared to attend to here and now and meaning attribution			
Have plan to collaborate with group members			
Have plan for member goal development			
Have respect for member contributions			
Have plan to include evaluation			
Have value for diversity			
Have plan to maintain a constant ethical surveillance			
Best Practices in Processing			
Have schedule for processing			
Have purpose for processing			
Have plan for before and after sessions			
Have activities to engage in reflective practice			
Have focus on learning from experience			
Have plan for pragmatic processing			
Have plan for deep processing			
Have plan to integrate evaluation data			
Have made consultation and training contacts			

FIGURE 8.2. Best practices in group counseling checklist (*Continued*).

CHAPTER 9

Rod J. Merta

Multicultural Group Work

☐ Introduction by James P. Trotzer

> Style of leadership and the tools that are prevalent in group work . . . reflect the prevailing politics and values of the time.
>
> W. Lifton (Christensen, 1990, p. 136)

So stated Walt Lifton, group work pioneer, in an interview conducted by the *Journal for Specialists in Group Work* for a series on the History of Group Work. In his observation Lifton captured both a reflective reality and a projective direction which is crucial to group work and particularly relevant to the focus of this chapter, Multicultural Group Work.

As a reflective reality the current sociopolitical climate and emerging cultural pluralism in the United States and the technologically prompted reality of the world as a global community all converge to bring a multiplicity of cultures and diversities into our lives and profession. As a projective direction, the fact that multicultural and diversity factors must be accounted for is no longer a matter for debate. From President Clinton's Initiative on Race to the board room of every international corporation, to the state and federal agencies that must provide health and human services, whether in the public or private sector, the mandate is the same: culture and diversity must be acknowledged, understood, accounted for, and valued.

As the face and fabric of our society and culture change over the next century, counseling as a profession and group work as a particular dimension of that profession must, and will respond to the challenges put forth so eloquently by Dean Mahesh Sharma of Cambridge College (May 8, 1998).

Speaking as an outsider to the profession at a conference on Multicultural and Spiritual Dimensions of Counselor Supervision he put forth four challenges or questions. I paraphrase these challenges as follows:

The Browning of America: How will counseling cope with, account for, and incorporate multicultural factors as the fabric of society changes to a pluralistic configuration of cultural, racial, and ethnic diversity and complexity?

The East versus West: How will counseling acknowledge, account for, cope with, and resolve the philosophy of life differences manifested in an Eastern philosophy that values community and emphasizes ego submersion and a Western philosophy that values individuality and stresses ego emersion?

The Emergence or Reemergence of Spirituality: How will counseling acknowledge, account for, incorporate, and value spirituality with its many faces and facets in the lives of clients?

The Downside of Technology: How will counseling respond to the problems created by the ever increasing impact of technology that a) produces an ever widening gap between the rich and the poor, the "haves and have nots," and b) generates an insidious separation of the humane from the human as technical contact replaces personal touch in the relational realm?

These challenges and issues provide a suitable umbrella for the consideration of multiculturalism in group work.

The challenge of diversity has been taken up with great enthusiasm in the field of group work. The Preamble of the Association for Specialists in Group Work Principles for Diversity Competent Group Workers (ASGW, 1998) avers a commitment to "understanding how issues of diversity affect all aspects of group work" (see Appendix D). Horne and DeLucia-Waack as editors of the *Journal for Specialists in Group Work* have made poignant efforts to spur recognition and utilization of the multicultural perspective in group work. Horne (1994) challenged authors to emphasize multicultural implications in their writings and work and DeLucia-Waack (1996) declared unequivocally that "multiculuralism is inherent in all group work" (p. 218).

I concur with Arredondo (1994) who concluded that all counseling, including group counseling, must be reframed as multicultural counseling. To do so with regard to group work, however, requires that group leaders develop competencies that include cultural awareness and sensitivity relative to their own and other's characteristics of culture and diversity and proficiency in using that competence in forming, leading, and utilizing groups. Failure to do so will produce detrimental effects either out of ignorance or because cultural differences when magnified or denied will undermine therapeutic dynamics (Vacc, 1989). Rather, diversity competent group leaders will have the attitudes and beliefs, knowledge and skills to facilitate a group process where diversity and culture are not only acknowledged, understood, and valued but also mobilized to the therapeutic benefit of the group and its members.

Rod Merta has been and is in the vanguard of multicultural group work. His chapter provides an eminently practical perspective while contributing a cutting edge authenticity that gives the contemporary group worker a reflective reality for the present and a projective direction for the exciting challenges of doing group work in the 21st century.

☐ Overview

While attending a professional conference, I had the opportunity to observe a role play of an interactional group. After a few opening comments from the European-American male group leader, an European-American woman took the lead and disclosed that she was having difficulties with her significant other. Not long into her monologue, an African-American woman suddenly responded with some unsolicited and rather blunt feedback. The African-American woman made it clear that she would not have tolerated such behavior from any man. The group began to go silent and the group leader in an attempt to resuscitate it, initiated a process illumination (see Yalom, 1995) by asking the group what they thought had just happened. The group leader having scanned the group and having noticed that an Asian-American woman appeared uncomfortable with the previous exchange, asked for her to respond to his question. She responded rather nervously that the African-American woman had behaved disrespectfully toward the European-American woman. In a meaningful attempt to norm feedback, the group continued to process the exchange, the reactions to it, and the type of feedback to be used in the future, but no one ever acknowledged that perhaps race, ethnicity, or some other cultural variable had served as a group dynamic impacting the group process.

When observed in daily exchanges, social etiquette or political correctness may compel us to ignore such *group dynamics*, defined as forces operating in a group (Gladding, 1991; Jacobs, Harvill, & Mason, 1994). In contrast, an effective group worker cannot ignore the impact that such forces might have on *group process*, defined as the stages of development of a group and the interactions that characterize each stage (Corey & Corey, 1992). Whereas the content of the group may appear to have been focused on gender, the dynamic that quickly propelled this group from an initial stage interaction to a transition stage interaction appears to have been race/ethnicity. The behaviors of the three women appear to be racially/ethnically stereotypic, with the European-American being all too quick to initiate comment or attempt to dominate, the African-American appearing frank or even aggressive, and the Asian-American appearing uncomfortable with negative feedback and conflict (see Merta, 1995). Recognizing the multicultural (both racial/ethnic and nonracial/ethnic factors) makeup of people, one cannot rule out the possible influence of gender, region of the country, or socioeconomic status (SES) on the observed behaviors of the three women.

A review of the literature in group work reveals that race, ethnicity, and other cultural variables such as ability (mental/physical), age, gender, region of the country, religion, sexual orientation, and socioeconomic status have largely been overlooked as constituting group dynamics that can impact the group process (see Merta, 1995). The focus in multicultural counseling has been on individual counseling rather than on group work (D'Andrea & Daniels, 1997a; Delucia, Coleman, & Jensen-Scott, 1992; Helms, 1990). Only recently has there been a surge of interest in multicultural group work (Conyne, 1998; Corey, 1995; D'Andrea & Daniels, 1997a; Delucia-Waack, 1996; Delucia, Coleman, & Jensen-Scott, 1992; Granrose & Oskamp, 1997; Greeley, Garcia, Kessler, & Gilchrest, 1992; Merta, 1995). A major catalyst for this surge in interest has been the development of the Multicultural Counseling Competencies (Association for Multicultural Counseling and Development, 1996) and the operationalization of these goal like competencies into objective like explanatory statements, strategies, and recommended activities (Sue, Arredondo, & McDavis, 1992). The Association for Specialists in Group Work has adopted the competencies and is adapting them to group work, entitling them the Principles for Diversity Competent Group Workers (ASGW, 1998). See Appendix D.

The multicultural competencies are focused on three *characteristics*: 1) counselor awareness of own assumptions, values, and biases, 2) understanding the world view of the culturally different client, and 3) developing culturally appropriate intervention strategies. Based on these characteristics, a culturally competent counselor is

> one who is actively in the process of becoming aware of her or his own assumptions about human behavior, values, biases, preconceived notions, and personal limitations; who actively seeks to understand the world view of his or her culturally different client without negative judgments; and who is in the process of actively developing and practicing appropriate, relevant, and sensitive intervention strategies and skills in working with his or her culturally different clients (Sue, Arredondo, & McDavis, 1992, p. 482).

In addition, the competencies also focus on three *domains* that interface with each characteristic: 1) attitudes and beliefs, 2) knowledge, and 3) skills. As for the domains, *attitudes and beliefs* refer to a group worker's awareness of his or her stereotypes, biases, and values toward culturally different group members and how these attitudes might affect cross-cultural group work. *Knowledge* pertains to the group worker's understanding of his or her own world view, the world views of his or her group members, and of relevant sociopolitical influences (i.e., immigration, prejudice, discrimination, oppression, and powerlessness). *Skills* refer to the specific interventions and strategies, individual and institutional, to be employed with culturally different group members.

Transferring the multicultural counseling competencies from one modality to another is, in itself, highly beneficial to group workers. In addition, there are facets to group work that are unique to the modality and require a more specialized adaptation of the competencies. The purpose of this chapter is to instill in group workers the importance of having a multicultural perspective and to provide an adaptation of multicultural counseling competencies to group work that is both universal to counselors and unique to group workers that will assist them in leading multicultural groups more effectively. The remainder of the chapter is organized as follows: definitions, multicultural group leadership, and learning activities.

☐ Definitions

In an attempt to reduce ambiguity for the reader, various terms relevant to multicultural group work will be defined, while other terms will be defined as they occur within the text of this chapter. *Culture* has been defined broadly as "any group of people who identify or associate with one another on the basis of some common purpose, need, or similarity of background" (Axelson, 1993, p. 3). The term *value*, "the principles or standards that individuals or groups of people use in determining their behavior"(Axelson, 1993, p. 33), is perceived by the author as constituting the basic element of a culture. *Stereotype* can be defined as "the application to others of personality theories that we all have about people whom we have met or have experienced in some way at some time" (Axelson, 1993, p. 35). African-Americans, American-Indians, Asian-Americans, and Hispanic- and Latino-Americans along with European-Americans will be referred to as *racial/ethnic groups*, while such groups as the elderly, feminists, people from Appalachia, gays and lesbians, people who are deaf, and religious fundamentalists will be referred to as *cultural groups*. In regards to counseling, the term *multicultural* is often used to refer to four racial/ethnic minority groups, while the term *cross-cultural* and *diversity* are used to refer to all cultural groups, racial/ethnic and non-racial/ethnic (Sue, Arredondo, & McDavis, 1992). For the purposes of this chapter, the term *multicultural group work* will be used to refer to all cultural groups. I am well aware of the profound stigma that characterizes race/ethnicity in the U.S. and the negative consequences (i.e., discrimination, segregation, oppression, disenfranchisement, and poverty) that have resulted from that stigmatization. By utilizing the term multicultural group work in reference to all cultural groups, I do not intend to imply that all cultural groups are equally stigmatized nor has stigmatization resulted in equally negative consequences for all groups.

☐ Multicultural Group Leadership

I originally proposed guidelines for effectively leading multicultural groups under the following four categories: 1) multicultural awareness; 2) self awareness; 3) recruitment, screening, selecting, and preparation; and 4) group interventions (Merta, 1995). Continued experience leading multicultural groups and greater familiarity with the multicultural counseling competencies and the growing body of literature in multicultural group work has caused me to both expand and refine my original guidelines into the following competency characteristics for leading multicultural group work: (1) culturally identify oneself vis-à-vis the group members, (2) culturally identify group members, and (3) use culturally appropriate group intervention strategies. Although worded slightly differently, the first and second characteristics mirror the first two multicultural counseling competency characteristics: counselor awareness of own values and biases and counselor awareness of client's world view. The third characteristic focuses on culturally-appropriate intervention strategies relevant to group work and consists of the following:

1. prepare members for multicultural group work;
2. model cultural respect and sensitivity;
3. interact with members in a genuine manner;
4. demonstrate neutral but active leadership;
5. be alert to and work through cultural group conflict; and
6. protect members and the group from cultural group think.

It is important to note that support for these intervention strategies is largely anecdotal rather than empirical. Although largely consistent with the multicultural counseling competencies, basic counseling theory and techniques (Cormier & Cormier, 1991; Young, 1992), and group theory and techniques (Yalom, 1995), they are based primarily on my own experiences leading multicultural groups. To echo D'Andrea and Daniels (1997a), there is great need for systematic research to validate what is being proposed here and elsewhere as being effective in multicultural group work.

Culturally Identify Oneself Vis-À-Vis Group Members

Counselor awareness of own cultural values and biases constitutes the first multicultural counseling competency characteristic (Sue, Arredondo, & McDavis, 1992). Culturally identifying others is not sufficient; but instead, group workers must be willing to identify their own cultural identities vis-à-vis their group members. Group workers must be aware of the relevance of their own cultural variables (e.g., race/ethnicity, SES, gender), values (e.g., traditional versus more androgynous gender roles, extended, nuclear, blended, or single parent families, traditional versus progressive parenting styles), and stereotypes (e.g., Hispanic men as being macho, the elderly as being inflexible, feminists as being male bashers), and how they might function as group dynamics impacting the group process.

   For example, I live in a southwest community that is slightly more Hispanic than Anglo. I lead community substance abuse, anger management, couples, and domestic violence groups in which the adolescent and adult members are predominantly Hispanic—many of whom are of a lower socioeconomic status. I teach counseling and counseling psychology to graduate

students who are predominately female—many of whom identify themselves as feminists. As an Anglo, middle class, middle aged male leading a
variety of weekly guidance/psychoeducational, counseling/interpersonal problem solving, and task/work groups (see ASGW, 1990), my values are constantly impacting on and being impacted by the culturally different people
around me. I am continuously being influenced by various stereotypes that
I harbor for those around me. Unless I can identify my own cultural variables, values, and stereotypes, I will be at a disadvantage in understanding
how much and in what ways my own cultural identity is impacting the
group—limiting my ability to facilitate the group process.

As I begin each anger management or domestic violence group, I am
consciously aware that my race/ethnicity and SES have benefitted me, while
the race/ethnicity and SES have not similarly benefitted most of my Hispanic-American, lower SES group members. Having worked in juvenile and
adult correctional facilities, I am most aware that African-Americans and
Hispanic-Americans and lower SES individuals are over represented in such
facilities and that a similar over representation exists for court mandated
groups. I recognize that various sociopolitical forces (i.e., immigration, prejudice,
discrimination, oppression, poverty, and powerlessness) have significantly
contributed to these differences. I am also aware that higher SES people
engaged in family disputes, who reside in homes with lots of a half acre or
more, are less likely to have their neighbors report them to the police than
lower SES people, who reside in smaller homes, apartments, or mobile
homes. I am aware that my race/ethnicity and SES will prove advantageous
to me should I have to interact with the police and a judge in negotiating a
more positive outcome to a family dispute than has been the case for many
of my group members.

As I begin to employ a treatment model for leading my domestic violence
group, I need to realize that my agency's treatment model reflects a strong
European-American, middle class, feminist perspective that rules out systemic explanations for domestic violence, stereotypes the male as the sole
abuser, and actively imposes values (e.g., shared responsibility for house-
hold chores, parenting, and financial and family decision making) that frequently conflict with the more traditional Hispanic and lower SES values of
my members. As I began to modify this treatment model so as to reduce
what I perceive as being a high degree of value imposition, I begin to question the extent to which my own traditional male values are impacting
these modifications. Another source for value imposition is my general approach to group work. Regardless of group, I prefer a process oriented,
interactional approach (Yalom, 1995) that is dependent on members giving
each other feedback on their attitudes and behaviors—especially those that
impact interpersonal relations. Again, I must ask myself how congruent are
the values inherent within my theoretical approach with the lower SES,
Hispanic male values of my members?

As I engage my group members, I need to be aware of the stereotypes that

I may be harboring for them and how I might counter transfer on to them these untested stereotypes. A few of my members appear to fit the negative macho stereotype of Mexican-American men that I have acquired: attitudes of superiority toward women, domineering and insensitive behaviors toward women, excessive beer drinking and womanizing, and verbal and physical abusiveness (Gutierrez, 1990). Most of the men in my groups vary considerably from these stereotypes. I am often impressed with their interpersonal sensitivity and skills, and despite the aforementioned sociopolitical forces, they convey a strong commitment to monogamy and family.

In addition to culturally defining oneself on the basis of cultural variables, values, and stereotypes, Helms' (1995) six-status White Racial Identity Development (WRID) model, offers the group worker still another means for cultural identification. Helms' (1995) statuses and their corresponding information processing strategies are as follows: *contact* (denial, obliviousness, or avoidance of anxiety evoking racial information), *disintegration* (disorientation, confusion, and suppression of information that would force one to choose between own group loyalty and humanism), *reintegration* (distortion of information in an own group enhancing manner), *pseudo-independence* (reshaping racial/ethnic or cultural stimuli to fit one's own liberal societal framework; *immersion/emersion* (reeducating and searching for internally defined racial and cultural standards), and *autonomy* (flexible analyses and responses to racial material) (see p. 188).

At what status do I find myself when leading groups of lower SES, Hispanic males? It varies. I suspect I started out at the pseudo-independence status by frequently attempting to reshape the men's behaviors, attitudes, and disclosures to fit my own liberal societal framework. I essentially believed that a sensitive and nonjudgmental male could help these men to be less abusive by helping them to adjust to changing gender roles. There are times when the arrogance, sexism, and hostility of a particular member or direct exposure to a severely abused spouse triggers a regressive response within me, and I find myself at the reintegration status by extolling, primarily to myself, the superior traits of the middle SES, Anglo vis-à-vis the lower SES Hispanic. For the most part, greater contact and understanding of my group members' cultural identities, life experiences, and the sociopolitical forces to which they are subjected have resulted in my progression to the immersion/emersion status. I increasingly come to realize that in assessing my group members for the risk of repeated violence, I must recognize and respect value differences as well as testing out stereotypes that I might be harboring. In so doing, I am increasingly capable of developing my own internal standards for evaluating these culturally different men. I have not achieved autonomy status as of yet, but I believe that I am on the right track.

Although originally intended for cultural identification of European-Americans vis-à-vis African-Americans, the WRID was subsequently extended for use with members of the Latino and Hispanic, Asian-American, and Native American groups. I and others (Myers et. al, 1991), have found the WRID useful as a majority identity developmental model—applicable to various nonracial/ethnic cultural groups (i.e., women, gays and lesbians, people with disabilities, lower SES individuals, religious fundamentalists).

Culturally Identify Group Members

Counselor awareness of the client's world view constitutes the second multicultural counseling competency characteristic (Sue, Arredondo, & McDavis, 1992). If cultural differences among group members constitute potential group dynamics that might impact the group process (e.g., cultural group conflict and group think), the group leader needs to be able to assess a group member's world view. As defined by Dana (1993), one's world view takes into account one's group identity (cultural heritage) as well as one's individual identity (self-concept). The group leader needs to have knowledge of a member's cultural heritage and life experiences, and how sociopolitical forces (i.e., immigration, prejudice, discrimination, and oppression) may have impacted him or her. Such cultural awareness requires the group leader to research a given cultural group by means of literature and media, consult with professionals who have had experience with that cultural group, and make direct contact with people of that cultural group. Arredondo et al. (1996) offer specific activities for accessing such resources and obtaining such awareness. Although not a substitute for pregroup research, consultation, and direct contact with the member's culture, contact with a member before and during the group, provides the group leader with an opportunity to culturally identify members. Regardless of group type or cultural composition, the group leader should be alert to and even inquire into—albeit in a respectful and sensitive manner—the cultural identity of group members. Some suggested forms for identifying the cultural identities of group members are as follows: the pregroup screening interview, member disclosure in the form of a round, and ongoing group leader observation and inquiry.

The *pregroup screening interview* is an excellent means for identifying the cultural identities of group members. The inquiry can take the form of dialogue alone or the dialogue can be facilitated by having the prospective member first complete a simple form in which he or she voluntarily identifies himself or herself by relevant cultural variables (e.g., race/ethnicity, religion, region of the country, and sexual orientation), values (e.g., pro–life position on abortion, sexual equality, and youth orientation) and offensive stereotypes (e.g., Hispanic women as being dependent, religious fundamentalists as being rigid in their thinking, lesbians as being masculine in grooming and dress, New Yorkers as being fast paced and rather abrupt). At first glance, some cultural variables appear more readily apparent than others: race/ethnicity or gender in contrast to religion or sexual orientation. In the case of race/ethnicity, I was caught off guard by a member who reacted negatively to being referred to as an Anglo—a popular southwestern designation for European-Americans. The elderly male member disclosed that he was an Irish immigrant, whose family had resisted English domination for too many generations to have such a label forced on him now. As an example of an offensive stereotype I have had several counseling students, who identified themselves as religious fundamentalists, disclose that they are hesitant to share personal values or religious beliefs when participating in departmental groups. When I lightly prodded them, they revealed their frustration with others, who all too often stereotyped them as being pejorative, lacking flexibility, and being opposed to gender equality, gay and lesbian rights, and the needs of unwed teenage mothers. When making such inquiries the group leader needs to avoid being insensitive and unnecessarily intrusive. By introducing the terms cultural variable, values, and stereotypes by means of providing definitions and examples, the group leader can then inquire as to whether any of the variables are personally relevant. Pressure to have members identify themselves on all eight variables (race/ethnicity, ability, age, gender, geographical region, religion, sexual orientation, SES) or any identified values or stereotypes by the leader is neither sensitive nor necessary. In the dialogue or on the aforementioned form, allow the prospective member to select or identify the variables, values, or stereotypes relevant to him or her while ignoring or omitting those that are not.

If the opportunity for prescreening is not available or if you want to have members be aware of the cultural identities of other members, the author recommends facilitating a *round*, a technique in which every member takes a turn responding to a question or topic initiated by the group leader (Gladding, 1991; Jacobs, Harvill, & Mason, 1994). The opening round should ideally be initiated during the first session. The leader should preface the round by stating the importance of being culturally aware of each other and respecting and being sensitive to cultural differences as a norming initiative. As was recommended for the prescreening interview, the leader may wish to introduce the terms cultural variables, values, and stereotypes. Use of the aforementioned form for cultural identification might be used to facilitate the round. Again, members should be encouraged to identify themselves only by those variables, values, and stereotypes that they deem relevant and safe. Since personal disclosures can sometimes take on a self-perpetuating nature, the leader needs to preface the round by cautioning members to disclose only that information they feel comfortable in sharing; and second, the leader needs to be prepared to halt a member's disclosure and check out with the member whether further disclosure is warranted. Such a round may appear rather time consuming, but it certainly could be used in lieu of such traditional ice breakers as having members compare themselves to some animal. If normed and facilitated sensitively, I have found that opening rounds provide validation for group members regardless of cultural identity. With younger or more reticent members, the group leader may wish to first use *dyad* work in preparation for the round. The dyad work could consist of pairing members, having them take turns completing the cultural identification exercise, and then having the dyad partners take turns introducing each other to the group by his or her cultural identity.

With or without cultural identification of group members by means of pregroup screening or completion of a round, the group leader must engage in *ongoing cultural identification* by being alert to member's disclosures and nonverbal behaviors and by being willing to follow-up with inquiries into the nature of a member's cultural identity. In a process oriented, interactional group, Lisa, an Asian-American woman was receiving feedback from other members on her hesitancy to be assertive. Having disclosed her racial/ethnic identity at the start of the group, I was alert to the realization that her cultural identity might be a factor in her hesitancy to be assertive. As the member feedback became more intense, the young woman responded by stating, "I sometimes find it hard to be assertive, because it seems so disrespectful and hurtful." I perceived her words to be culturally relevant and chose that moment to intervene by inquiring as to how such feedback coincided with her own cultural upbringing. She acknowledged that her parents would find such assertiveness disrespectful. Her disclosure had the effect of allowing her more control over the group process.

Being alert to cultural identity involves being observant of a member's nonverbal behaviors as well as his or her verbal disclosures. In another group of graduate students, the topic of men crying led to an exchange on the appropriateness of men crying in various group settings—especially if they were the group leader. One European-American woman discarded any attempt at political correctness on the topic by abruptly interjecting, "I'd have real problems with a male group leader who started crying during a group." As the woman spoke, the author observed another European-American woman grimacing and shaking her head. This woman appeared to be reacting to the values and stereotypes being espoused by the first woman but was hesitating to respond. Due to these nonverbal behaviors, I attempted to draw out this woman by making the following observation and inquiry: "Jean, I can't help but notice that you seem to be reacting to Karen's comments. Would you care to respond to them." Jean's response was as follows: "I just don't think we should limit people to traditional gender roles or behaviors."

When generalizing about or stereotyping other cultural groups, we often fail to take into account between-group differences (e.g., differences between Mexican-Americans and Cuban-Americans) and within-group differences (e.g., differences in acculturation level or socioeconomic status among Mexican-Americans) (Merta, Ponterotto, & Brown, 1992). The cultural identity developmental models constitute a valuable within-group difference for leading multicultural groups (D'Andrea & Daniels, 1997a; Greeley, Garcia, Kessler, & Gilchrest, 1992). These models are cited in both the competencies (Sue, Arredondo, & McDavis, 1992) and in their operationalization

(Arredondo, et al., 1996) as being very instrumental in enhancing a group worker's awareness and knowledge of his or her culturally different group members. Although a variety of these models have been developed for the various racial/ethnic minorities as well as other cultural minorities (see Ponterotto, Casas, Suzuki, & Alexander, 1995), I have become accustomed to and value Atkinson, Morton, and Sue's (1993) Minority Identity Developmental model (MID). As in the case of the majority model (WRID), I have found that use of the MID can be extended to nonracial/ethnic minority groups (e.g., women, gays and lesbians, religious fundamentalists).

The MID model (Atkinson, Morton, & Sue, 1993) consists of the following five stages: conformity, dissonance, resistance and immersion, introspection, and synergistic. Individuals at each stage are characterized by their attitudes toward themselves, members of the same minority, members of different minorities, and toward members of the dominant group. An individual characterized as being in the *conformity stage* is viewed as depreciating himself or herself, his or her own group, and other minority groups, while appreciating and accepting without question the values of the dominant group. In the *dissonance stage*, the individual experiences conflict between depreciating and appreciating attitudes toward self, his or her own group, other minority groups, and the dominant group. At the *resistance and immersion stage*, the individual comes to appreciate self and own group, is torn between empathy for other minority groups and an emerging culturocentrism, and comes to depreciate the dominant group. In the *introspection stage*, the individual experiences conflict between responsibility for and allegiance to one's minority group and one's own personal autonomy, begins to question the unequivocal nature of group appreciation, becomes concerned with his or her ethnocentric basis for judging members of other minority groups, and begins to replace an attitude of complete distrust for the dominant group with a more selective trust and distrust of dominant individuals based on their demonstrated behaviors and attitudes. At the *synergistic stage*, the individual develops a self-appreciating attitude and experiences a sense of self-worth, self-confidence, and autonomy by having established his or her identity as an individual, a member of a minority group, and a member of the dominant culture with an attitude of selective appreciation for the dominant group.

In my graduate classes, which frequently take the form of guidance/psychoeducational groups, I encounter women, who are vigilant of and react to any statements made by me or other students, male or female, that may appear at all gender biased or sexist. In contrast to many other students who would identify themselves as being feminist and strong proponents of gender equality, the aforementioned women appear very angry. As I struggle to establish some semblance of a relationship with these women, their disclosures reveal a history of sexism, discrimination, abusive relationships, and oppression—sociopolitical pressures not unlike those often experienced by racial/ethnic minorities. As to their MID stage identity, I experience many as being at the resistance/immersion stage, in which they relate best to other women, especially women who share their distrust of and disdain for a male dominated society. Women at this stage may often find it difficult to empathize with other minority groups—especially when the latter (e.g., a traditional African-American male or a religious fundamentalist female) are perceived as being in competition or conflict with them. Women at the resistance/immersion stage are apt to be very suspicious of and hostile toward European-American males such as myself. As the group leader, it is not enough for me to culturally define such women in isolation; but instead, I must define them vis-à-vis myself and other group members using the WRID or MID models depending on the cultural variables. By identifying such stage combinations, I will be better prepared to anticipate and facilitate cultural conflicts and identify and delimit cultural group think. For example, a female administrator at the agency where I lead domestic violence groups, was reported to have said that the primary outcome of these male led groups was that of producing more sophisticated male abusers. The comment might have temporarily dislodged me from either a pseudo-independence or immersion/emersion stage and propelled me toward reintegration on the WRID model. While at such a stage, even temporarily, I might be slow to protect a woman at the resistance/immersion stage from cultural conflict or cultural group think or even actively contribute to them.

Use Culturally-Appropriate Group Intervention Strategies

Prepare Group Members for Multicultural Group Work

As noted in the multicultural counseling competencies (Sue, Arredondo, & McDavis, 1992), the culturally skilled counselor must assess the appropriateness of a particular counseling approach for a culturally different client. Group work theories and techniques are not culture free, but like counseling theories and techniques, in general, reflect the values of the dominant or majority culture. The majority culture in the U.S. is usually best epitomized by the middle aged, middle class, European-American male. Nevertheless, for counseling the majority culture might be more accurately identified as middle aged, middle class, European-American, androgynous male or female. Counseling values or human relations norms (i.e., attention to feelings, willingness to show vulnerability, personal and direct expression), as articulated by Kanter (1977), appear to be more representative of females and androgynous males than traditional males. Anecdotal reports of male aversion to counseling and evidence of underutilization of services by men (Feldman, 1990; Pasick, Gordon, & Feldman, 1990) appear to support such a conclusion. The more at variance a prospective group member (e.g., a lower SES, inner city, African-American or Hispanic male adolescent) appears to be from the majority culture, the more important it is for the group leader to culturally identify group members, to facilitate informed consent, and to begin structuring the group experience.

Consistent with ASGW (1989) ethical guidelines for group work, group leaders need to provide prospective members with informed consent. *Informed consent* entails providing a prospective group member information on all aspects of a particular group: the nature or theoretical basis of the group, the various techniques that will be used, and the values or norms, expectations, and characteristics of the group (e.g., nondirective group leadership, nonstructured interactions, self-disclosures of a personal nature with a focus on feelings, and member to member feedback of a candid and possibly negative nature). With such information the prospective member can decide on participating in the group or not. Again, with a more culturally different individual, the group worker needs to emphasize existing cultural differences between the group and the prospective member. Although the group worker can and may need to facilitate informed consent during the first group session, with the culturally different individual, the group worker should attempt to do it during a pregroup screening interview to allow for more individual attention and sensitivity. The member needs to be made aware of the group, initially given the choice of participation, and the opportunity to exit the group at any time (ASGW, 1989). Although involuntary or mandatory group members's choices are reduced, informed consent is even more of a necessity (see Corey, 1995). With court or agency mandated group members, the group worker must not only inform the individual of eliciting cultural differences in regards to the group but often in regards to the agency, legal system, and society as well. With my substance abuse groups, I find myself spending considerable time attempting to explain culturally different and changing mores and laws regarding alcohol and drug use (e.g., stiffer DWI or DUI sentencing, illegalization of marijuana, and differing penalties for cocaine and crack abuse) to my predominately lower SES, Hispanic adolescent group members. To be more effective in facilitating informed consent, the group worker should provide a written description of the group (see Corey, 1995), possibly in the form of a contract and preferably in Spanish or any other language of relevance to prospective members.

Structuring is defined by Cormier and Cormier (1991) as "an interactional process between counselors and clients in which they arrive at similar perceptions of the role of counselor, an understanding of what occurs in the counseling process, and an agreement on which outcome goals will be achieved" (p. 51). Merta (1995) inferred from the literature in multicultural counseling that structuring group work may actually take two forms: 1) informing members prior to and during the group process of what to expect from a particular group, and 2) modifying the group to be more accommodating to culturally different group members. As already noted, this first form of structuring began with the group worker providing the culturally different individual with information on the group to facilitate informed consent. Even after the group has begun, the structuring continues as the group worker must be prepared to interrupt a group session to clarify for a culturally different member any aspect of the group process that appears to be confusing or frustrating. The group worker may wish to use before or after group session contacts with a group member for such efforts at clarification. It may not always be clear to the group worker whether a reticent or apparently contrary group member is sincerely confused as to group expectations or is intentionally resisting them. Negative norming is common in my adolescent substance groups as members either attempt to refocus the attention of the group on the injustices of the agency and/or courts or openly challenge group expectations (e.g., member to member feedback). When a member is consistently resistant or openly defiant, I may initiate a before or after group session contact as follows:

> Arturo, I know you don't believe you should be in this place (residential treatment center). I know you don't believe your drug use is a problem, and I know you don't believe this group is of any use. Nevertheless, I am worried about your drug use, and I believe that you stand to learn more from others in terms of controlling your use of drugs than from me. I need you to be willing to give other members feedback, and you need a good report from me on your participation in the group.

Structuring sometimes requires modeling and practice as well as simple instruction. I find the following five norms to be most helpful when leading these substance abuse groups:

1. confidentiality;
2. one person speaking at a time;
3. no bashing (excessive criticism) other members;
4. no glorifying drugs; and
5. no physical contact.

I carry along a medium size bulletin board on which I have the norms listed as well as the content for that particular group. I have the group start out with a member reviewing the norms. I use a simple grading system for reinforcing group participation that consists of the following:

(−1) failed to attend group, left group without permission, or was asked to leave group;
(0) was disruptive in group but was not asked to leave;
(1) minimal participation but not disruptive;
(2) responds positively when asked;
(3) initiates own positive interaction, and;
(4) consistently assumes positive leadership role.

I post their grades on a bulletin board in their living unit and review the grades with them at the start of each session.

As for the second form of structuring, modifying a group so as to accommodate culturally different members, I purposely structure my substance abuse groups to form a hybrid of guidance/psychoeducational and counseling/interpersonal problem solving groups. In the early sessions, I have the group focus on content and skill building, and as the group progresses, I have them begin to focus on member to member feedback. In regards to giving feedback, I have the members begin with the positive and progress toward the less positive. To allow members a safe means for impacting group content and process I have them complete a brief written evaluation called the Group Response Form. They rate the group on a 5-point Likert scale, identifying anything in the group they liked, and anything in the group that they disliked. In any event, involving culturally different individuals in a group without providing informed consent or without structuring the group experience reflects both insensitivity and ineffectiveness as a group leader.

Model Cultural Respect and Sensitivity

Regardless of the cultures represented in one's group, the group leader must strive to model cultural respect by communicating and demonstrating that all cultures are valued and all members are treated equally. Similarly, the group leader must strive to model cultural sensitivity by being aware of, showing respect for, and protecting the values and personal boundaries of one's members. I have observed that people, including counselors, are often selective as to whom they bestow cultural respect and sensitivity. Whereas a counselor may be theoretically committed to respecting Hispanic-Americans, he or she may be openly contemptuous of traditional Hispanic-American gender roles. Whereas that same counselor may model respect and sensitivity toward a Navajo disclosing traditional religious beliefs, he or she may communicate contempt of an African-American disclosing religious fundamentalist beliefs. Although voicing support for gays and lesbians, a group worker may hasten a gay member relating a romantic encounter to hurry up by unintentionally revealing his or her discomfort. In modeling cultural respect and sensitivity, I do not believe that a group worker can show preferential treatment for one cultural group at the expense of another without alienating culturally different group members. As noted in the first and second competency characteristics, modeling cultural respect and sensitivity is dependent on our cultural awareness of others and ourselves. Cultural disrespect often takes the form of discounting another's values, often out of ignorance of those values, and by proselytizing one's own. Respect comes from increased familiarity with culturally different groups obtained through research, consultation, and especially personal contact. Sensitivity begins with respect and is dependent on one's proficiency at using skills often practiced in individual counseling: core conditions, listening skills, open ended probes, and confrontations (Cormier & Cormier, 1991; Young, 1992). Young (1992) defines confrontation as "an advanced counseling technique that involves facing clients with inconsistencies between affect, cognition, and behaviors (p. 275). I've had success with what I like to call Columbo-style confrontations, in which I assume a slightly confused or self-effacing manner. In the following example, I am employing a Columbo-style confrontation in an attempt to move this entrenched, traditional Hispanic male toward conciliation with his partner while still showing respect for his traditional role in the family:

> Raul, let me see if I have this right. You expect your wife and mother-in-law to apologize for the blow up and respect your role as head of the family, or you're going to continue to live alone in your rented room and see your kids but twice a month. Although I respect your need to be the head of your family, I'm a little confused. I am not sure how living alone and seeing your kids but twice a month is helping you to function as the head of your family.

According to Yalom (1995), *culture building* refers to a collaborative process between leader and members in which the group culture—"an unwritten code of behavioral rules, or norms—must be established that will guide the interaction of the group" (p. 108). Although structuring and culture building are similar concepts, structuring primarily occurs between the leader and an individual member during the prescreening interview and contacts before and after sessions, while culture building involves the leader and all the members and occurs within the session. Yalom contends that the group leader serves as technical expert and a role model in the building of the group culture—for example, modeling norms that emphasize a here and now focus, member to member feedback, and working through conflict. As for a multicultural group, the leader must serve as a technical expert by being knowledgeable of the value differences, stereotypes, majority and minority stage identities, and sociopolitical forces operating within a multicultural group, so as to intervene to work through conflict and avoid cultural group think.

In the aforementioned graduate student group where Jean, the European-American woman, reacted to the other woman for being critical of male group leaders crying during a group. I described how my observation of Jean's nonverbal reactions (i.e., grimacing and shaking her head) had suggested to me that she was reacting to her values being discounted. In my role as technical expert, I believe that I was responsible for being aware of a potential value clash. As both technical expert *and* role model, I was responsible for drawing Jean out and subsequently acting to ensure that both members and cultural perspectives were given equal treatment. It wasn't just Jean's grimacing and head shaking that alerted to me a possible cultural clash on this gender related topic. Jean's hair style, and what I perceived as a masculine style of dress, generated a stereotype for me that led me to believe Jean was very nontraditional in her gender identity, bisexual, or lesbian. There had been no opportunity for a pregroup screening interview and she had chosen not to disclose anything regarding her gender identity or sexual orientation during the opening round or any time since. I was sensitive enough to avoid transcending Jean's personal boundaries by inquiring as to either her gender identity or sexual orientation. I have some knowledge of the sociopolitical forces that people with nontraditional gender identities, bisexuals, or gays and lesbians experience to know that facilitating an identity disclosure, even in a potentially supportive group as this one, would be highly insensitive on my part. Nevertheless, I still felt compelled to draw Jean out on the topic of men crying based on the combination of her nonverbal behaviors as well as the stereotype that I was harboring. I believe that a group leader needs to transcend political correctness by making inquiries into a member's cultural identity, but it is important that the member has at least implicitly approved such inquiries by having taken the initiative in culturally identifying themselves. Although culture building is a group consensual process, the group leader must model cultural respect and sensitivity and must be vigilant and willing to intervene to maintain a culturally respectful and sensitive group culture.

Interact with Group Members in a Genuine Manner

> The multicultural field will continue to incur resistance until training programs can more clearly delineate the field from the concept of political correctness that often precludes the furthering of discussion. Politically correct behaviors may not be highly related to multicultural philosophy, because some of these behaviors are often reactions to political climates or other external factors (Leach & Carlton, 1997, p. 202).

Genuineness (congruence) along with empathy (accurate understanding) and respect (positive regard) were initially identified by Carl Rogers and have long since been deemed basic relationship conditions for or skills in counseling (Cormier & Cormier, 1991). *Genuineness* is defined as "being oneself without being phony or playing a role" (Cormier & Cormier, 1991: p. 25). I applaud the concept of being *politically correct* when it denotes cultural respect and sensitivity, but when it limits the ability of a leader of a multicultural group to be genuine, I perceive it as impeding that group leader in fulfilling the first and second multicultural competency characteristics: culturally identifying self vis-à-vis the group and culturally identifying group members. As a group leader, I may hesitate to openly explore my own cultural identity or the cultural identities of my members because of a fear of being perceived as sexist or racist or because of my own personal discomfort with the risk taking that such exploration often involves. If I do so, I am assuming a politically correct role that is not genuine, and is likely to preclude further group discussion and exploration (Leach & Carlton, 1997).

By being genuine, multicultural group work provides the opportunity for group leader and member alike to take risks in exploring cultural similarities and differences by disclosing one's own values, biases, stereotypes, and personal limitations.

Having stereotypes of other people has become so politically incorrect, that most of us would like to be perceived as not possessing them. Although stereotypes are applied to all groups, can be positive in nature, and may be accurate, stereotypes have been stereotyped, if the reader will pardon my liberal use of the term, as being negative, focused largely on members of racial/ethnic and other cultural minority groups, and as being totally unfounded. Patterson (1996) contends that descriptions of racial/ethnic groups in the multicultural counseling literature (e.g., Asian-Americans will find giving feedback in group uncomfortable and Native Americans will be reluctant to permit outsiders to intervene in their personal problems) constitute a form of professional stereotype that can result in self-fulfilling prophecies for the culturally different. I do not perceive stereotypes as inherently negative, but rather see them as prototypes, defined here as the original or model upon which something is patterned. I believe stereotypes can provide us a useful means for processing information. Stereotypes become negative when our misuse of them causes us to think of, feel about, or act toward another individual of a particular group without then proceeding to test out the stereotype that we harbor toward that group. One of the conclusions identified in the cross-cultural simulation game, BaFa BaFa (Shirts, 1969), is that stereotypes are probably inevitable in the absence of contact with an individual of the group being stereotyped. As stated previously, multicultural group work provides the opportunity for group leader and members alike to take risks by disclosing their own values, biases, stereotypes, and personal limitations, inquiring into the nature of another's world view, and in so doing, explore cultural similarities and differences.

In my anger management groups Ray, a European-American male in his late 60s, triggered for me and other members the stereotype that older people are inflexible—set in their ways and unwilling to consider change (Axelson, 1993; Vacc, DeVaney, & Willmer, 1992). As the group evolved, it became apparent to the group that Ray's abuse of his wife and adult stepdaughter followed a regular pattern. One or both of them would do something to make him angry, he would retreat to his room, drink, and eventually return to be abusive. In exploring his daily routine, it became apparent that Ray had no social outlets other than his immediate family. It was also apparent that Ray was enjoying and apparently benefitting from the group. Whenever a group member would point out Ray's need for other social outlets and begin to brainstorm, Ray would resist. The more Ray resisted, the more the stereotype of inflexibility became apparent. Rather than let the stereotype fester within us, I chose to test it in the following manner:

Ray, whether accurate or not, sometimes elderly people are stereotyped as being inflexible or unwilling to try new things. The group perceives you as being in need of more social outlets and of being resistant to their feedback. Correct me if I am wrong, but it seems there might be a relationship here between the stereotype and your behavior.

Without ever addressing the stereotype directly, Ray did disclose both his loneliness and his age related difficulty in trying to connect with other people. The group responded by validating his feelings and the difficulty, and with his permission, Ray and the group began to brainstorm. Two weeks after the group ended, I received a call from Ray. He wanted me to know of his recent success in avoiding a blow up with his wife and step-daughter. Apparently, he had joined a health club and had opted for the company of others at the club's whirlpool instead of the bottle in his room. Assuming the stereotype was accurate to begin with, Ray's actions have laid it to rest.

Although interacting with group members in a genuine manner, making inquiries into the nature of a member's cultural identity, and testing out our own stereotypes are necessary interventions in a multicultural group, they can be overdone. Use of these interventions do not give a group leader or another group member license to bombard a culturally different person with a whole series of personally, intrusive questions. The group worker must balance genuineness with cultural sensitivity. In the case of Jean, her nonverbal behaviors and my stereotype did not give me license to transcend her personal boundaries by making inquiries as to the nature of her cultural identity. Jean never disclosed that she was bisexual or lesbian nor that she had a nontraditional gender identity. As such, I felt justified only in drawing her out by mentioning that she seemed to be reacting to the comments of the other woman. To be any more intrusive would have been culturally insensitive.

Demonstrate Neutral but Active Leadership

> Democratic leaders set policies through group discussion and decision-making, encourage and help group members to interact, request the cooperation of others, and are considerate of members' feelings and needs (Johnson & Johnson, 1994, p. 178).

Similar to the need for balancing genuineness and sensitivity, the group leader must strive to balance genuineness and respect in the form of equal treatment of group members. Regardless of modality—individual, family, or group—I have found that by occasionally disclosing some of my own values, I increase my cultural similarity with my members but only to the extent that those members share my values. In racially/ethnically and culturally heterogeneous groups, I believe that by disclosing my own values, biases, stereotypes, and personal limitations, my group members perceive my behavior as genuine and often a stimulus for engaging in similar risk taking. Despite the potential gains, I may make such disclosures at the risk of being perceived by some members as being biased. When leading an all male, domestic violence group, I can take much liberty with my disclosures of shared traditional male values. On the other hand, those same disclosures are likely to alienate some of the female members of my couples groups. I recently led a process oriented, interactional group of graduate students in counseling for the purpose of cultural exploration. The group was a racial/ethnic (Hispanic/Anglo) and cultural (female/male) heterogeneous group. As an Anglo male, I believe that I was suspect by some or all of my female and Hispanic male members from the beginning as being Anglo and male biased. Had I attempted to counter that perception by assuming a stance partial to either the female or Hispanic members, I may have been perceived as modeling political correctness by the male and Anglo members of the group and they would have likely followed suit—limiting the degree of risk taking needed for cultural exploration. To avoid perceptions of bias and partiality, I believe the group leader must limit his or his disclosures to reinforcing group norms (i.e., cultural identification, cultural respect and sensitivity, genuineness) and stating universals (i.e., failure to test stereotypes, tendency to be ethnocentric regarding our values, etc.). By intentionally communicating personal values, failing to model cultural respect and sensitivity to all members and cultures represented in a group, permitting stereotypes to be stated but go untested, and extending preferential treatment to any member regardless of cultural identity, the leader is likely to sacrifice the members' perception of him or her as a neutral and objective leader who will facilitate the group impartially.

Such neutrality should not be mistaken for a laissez faire style of group leadership. Lewin identified three styles of group leadership: authoritarian (directive and structured, leader centered), democratic (nondirective but active, group centered), and laissez faire (no structure or direction, group led) (Gladding, 1991). Although the leader should avoid being directive, he or she cannot afford to be laissez faire. By being overly directive, group members are limited in their interaction and hence their cultural exploration. By being too laissez faire, negative norms are as apt to develop as positive ones, conflict will likely be avoided or left to become abusive, and the group is likely to experience cultural group think as the values and stereotypes of the majority will dominate and eventually be imposed on minority members. Helping to build a group culture that is conducive to cultural exploration, managing group conflict, and avoiding cultural group think demands a democratic style of leadership as portrayed by Johnson and Johnson (1994) in the quote at the start of this section.

Be Alert to and Work Through Cultural Group Conflict

Most white people do this patronizing number: They never disagree with you, even when you are talking the worst sort of garbage. It is near impossible to have a decent, human conversation with them. They are so busy trying not to say anything offensive—so busy trying to prove they aren't prejudiced—that they freeze up, get all constricted, formal. They never just talk. (Attributed to the African-American narrator in *Primary Colors: A Novel of Politics*; Anonymous, 1996, pp. 35–36).

Just as political correctness can cause a group leader to interact with culturally different members in a less than genuine manner by failing to explore cultural differences and by opting not to disclose personal biases and limitations or test out stereotypes, it can cause that same group leader to avoid cultural group conflict as illustrated in the quote above. As noted by Yalom (1995), "conflict can be harnessed in the service of the group, if the intensity does not exceed the members's tolerance and the proper group norms have been established" (p. 344). *Conflict resolution* of cultural conflict is properly performed when the group leader does not prematurely rescue members from receiving negative feedback while still insuring that the feedback does not become abusive. But as noted in the group exchange depicted at the start of this chapter, from whose cultural perspective do we define acceptable and abusive conflict? Susan—the European-American woman who initiated the exchange? Doris—the African-American woman who gave her feedback? Lisa—the Asian-American woman who reacted to and was critical of the manner in which the feedback was given? The European-American male group leader who is responsible for conflict resolution? In the aforementioned exchange, the leader chose not to slow the conflict by blocking (raising one's hand much like traffic officer) or cutting off (verbally overriding) either the African-American or Asian-American woman. Had the exchange become abusive as perceived by the group leader, he would need to have acted to halt it. As for norming feedback and modeling conflict resolution, the group leader now has an opportunity with which to do both. Granted, this norming should have begun with the prescreening interview and the first group session with the leader informing members that conflict will not be avoided nor will it be allowed to become abusive. With the group interaction halted, the group leader can facilitate norming as follows:

Leader: What just happened here was one member gave another member feedback. If we value member feedback, we need to feel safe giving each other both positive and negative feedback. Are we uncomfortable with negative feedback or the manner in which it is given? Susan?

Susan: Yes, I felt Doris was a bit abrupt with me, but I do value what she said. In fact, I think she's right in that I should have been more assertive with my boyfriend.

Doris: I didn't mean to ruffle any feathers. I just call them as I see them.

Lisa: Well, maybe I shouldn't be so sensitive. It's just that I come from a family, where raising your voice was said to be disrespectful.

Doris: Okay, but I come from a family, where if you didn't give out a yell, you weren't going to be heard.

Lisa: But you really weren't angry?

Doris: Believe me, if I was angry, you'd know it. Okay, if you work at not being so sensitive, I'll try to be a bit milder.

Leader: I really like what you've done here. You've acknowledged a possible cultural difference and a conflict resulting from it, worked through the conflict, and renormed member feedback.

As noted by Greeley, Garcia, Kessler, and Gilchrest (1992), group workers may hesitate to acknowledge the existence of cultural differences and avoid working through conflict for fear of offending members or making them feel uncomfortable. Such avoidance is unfortunate because acknowledgment of cultural differences and working through cultural conflict can result in greater group cohesiveness as well as greater multicultural awareness.

Protect Group Members from Cultural Group Think

It is essential to differentiate between therapeutic pressure that is part of any group and "undue pressure," which is not therapeutic. The purpose of a group is to help participants find their own answer, not to pressure them into what the group thinks is appropriate (ASGW, 1989, ethical guidelines 6a & b).

Groupthink is the collective striving for unanimity that overrides group members' motivations to realistically appraise alternative courses of actions and, thereby, leads to (a) deterioration of mental efficiency, reality testing, and moral judgment, and (b) ignoring external information inconsistent with the favored alternative course of action (Johnson & Johnson, 1994, p. 255).

The first quote addresses an individual member experiencing value imposition due to undue pressure from the group, the second quote addresses the group as a whole experiencing diminished effectiveness in decision making due to group think. In multicultural groups, I perceive value imposition and ineffective decision making as being the consequences of *cultural group think* (see Merta, 1995). The earlier example of Lisa, the Asian-American woman, who received strong group feedback on the need to be more assertive bordered on undue pressure and could have resulted in value imposition as a consequence of cultural group think. The value of assertiveness for people, in general, and women, in particular, was so strongly held by the group members, that they found it difficult to curtail their zealousness, to consider other values, and to consider other alternatives. My professional preference for assertiveness could have forestalled my attempt to protect Lisa from cultural group think. As noted earlier (Merta, 1995), our effectiveness in leading multicultural groups will be impaired most by the adherence to values that we hold most dear.

The 1957 film, *12 Angry Men*, is an excellent example of diminished effectiveness in decision making due to cultural group think. Twelve European-American male jurists, mostly Anglo-Saxons (i.e., northern Europeans) but a few White ethnics (i.e., eastern and southern Europeans) (see Axelson, 1993), begin deliberating on a first degree murder case. By an 11 to 1 vote for conviction, the dominant group—primarily middle class, Anglo-Saxon, attempts to push through a quick decision by stifling discussion and the consideration of alternative perspectives. Although the initial hold out is of the majority—a middle class, Anglo-Saxon—the various minority group members (i.e., the low SES individual, the elderly person, the immigrant, the blue collar worker, and the person of small physical stature) come forth in sequence to reveal overlooked evidence that gradually reverses support for conviction—culminating in a unanimous vote of not guilty. The film illustrates the deficiencies inherent in homogeneous groups and group think. Homogeneous groups are generally perceived as producing less effective decision making (Johnson & Johnson, 1994), whereas heterogeneous groups are perceived as being more creative and generating more problem solutions for more effective decision making, but only in the absence of group think (Granrose & Oskamp, 1997). This particular group was largely homogeneous, lacking diversity in terms of race/ethnicity as well as gender and other cultural variables. The 1997 version of the film includes African-American and Hispanic-American jurists, but we will have to wait for still another version, perhaps *12 Angry People* or *12 Angry Jurists*, before women are included.

By limiting cultural diversity and by suppressing differing cultural perspectives in the form of cultural group think, groups become more culturally encapsulated (Wrenn, 1985), less creative, and less effective in decision making. Consequently, the group worker must intervene to protect both member and group from cultural group think by ensuring greater cultural diversity within groups and by ensuring that differing cultural perspectives are respected within the group. To ensure more culturally diverse groups, the group worker needs to actively recruit culturally different members (see Merta, 1995), and, whenever possible, form *racial or cultural equality groups*. Equality groups possess equal numbers of the racial/ethnic or cultural groups in a group (e.g., four African-Americans and four European-Americans)—as opposed to having token representation—which reduces the likelihood of value imposition and increases the potential for cultural exploration.

As an example of an individual group member experiencing value imposition due to cultural group think, the case of Lisa is worth reexamining. By being aware that Lisa was Asian American and having knowledge that many Asian-Americans do not always value assertiveness to the extent that many European-Americans do, I was alert to the possibility that cultural differences might constitute a relevant group dynamic. By being aware that despite some diversity within the group (i.e., race/ethnicity and gender), and that the members and leader alike strongly valued assertiveness, I was alert to the possibility of value imposition in the form of cultural group think. In the case of Jean's nontraditional gender identity or sexual orientation, I would have used *process illumination* (Yalom, 1995) by having the group recognize the possibility that their feedback was taking the form of undue pressure and allowing Jean a reprieve while redirecting the group to another concern or topic. I might then have used an out of group contact with Jean to assess her feelings and preferences. Given the less stigmatizing nature of Lisa's cultural identity, there was greater opportunity for immediate cultural exploration for both Lisa and the group. I proceeded as follows:

Leader: Folks, what are we doing here?

Member #1: We're trying to help Lisa.

Leader: Okay, but does anyone else have another perception?

Member #2: Maybe we're putting too much pressure on Lisa?

Leader: Lisa, is member #2's perception correct?

Lisa: Well, I appreciate your help but the feedback was becoming a bit overwhelming.

Leader: Lisa, is there a relationship between you being Asian-American and the group's feedback on assertiveness?

Lisa: Well, sure. I can be assertive and at times, I am. At other times, being assertive makes me feel disrespectful of others.

After initiating Lisa's exploration of assertiveness, I would use some personal disclosure and *consensual validation* (Yalom, 1995) to extend the cultural exploration to the group.

Leader: Like me, it sounds like most of you strongly value assertiveness. I am curious as to how each of you view it and whether there are some of you who question its use at times.

After this initial stage of exploration, I would attempt to expand the group's problem solving efforts.

Leader: Interesting, there is more variation in how we perceive and use assertiveness than I first thought. Recognizing that some form of assertiveness is one option open to Lisa, why don't we make an attempt at identifying some other options that she might care to use.

☐ Learning Activities

In contrast to more traditional didactic approaches (e.g., lecture, class discussion), calls for increased experiential training in multicultural counseling have multiplied resulting in a varied assortment of experiential activities (McRae & Johnson, 1991; Merta, Stringham, & Ponterotto, 1988; Pope-Davis,

Breaux, and Liu; Ridley, Mendoza & Kanitz, 1994; Wehrly, 1991). Experiential training has been defined as "exercises that provide occasions for trainees to personally experience immersion in a culture different from their own" (Ridley, Mendoza, & Kanitz, 1994, p. 263). The purpose of experiential learning is to affect "the learner in three ways: 1) the learner's cognitive structures are altered, 2) the learner's attitudes are modified, and 3) the learner's repertoire of behavior skills is expanded (Johnson & Johnson, 1994, pp. 44–45). I have found three experiential learning activities that I perceive to be effective in training counselors and other helping professionals in both diversity sensitivity and in leading multicultural groups. These learning activities are as follows: Bafa Bafa—a cross-cultural simulation game, the case vignette/role play exercise, and the process oriented, interactional, multicultural group.

BaFa BaFa: A Cross-Cultural Simulation Game

BaFa BaFa (Shirts, 1969) has become one of the most widely used crosscultural simulation games designed to teach cultural awareness. BaFa BaFa is a mythical land with two distinct cultures: Alpha and Beta. Whereas, people from Alpha are warm, friendly, patriarchal, and possess a strong ingroup, outgroup identity, the people from Beta speak a foreign language, and are highly competitive and task oriented. Upon being formerly trained in the rules of one culture, participants must then visit the other culture and must cope on a trial and error basis with no formal instruction. Upon visiting the foreign culture, participants initially become bewildered and eventually become critical of and hostile toward their hosts—labeling them strange or weird. In the postsimulation discussion, participants learn the cultural rules of the foreign culture and with this realization, attitudes reportedly change from hostility to tolerance. Through further discussion, this experience can be generalized to real world cultural groups. As to whether the game alters people's stereotypes and attitudes, the results of research studies appear to be mixed (Peterson, Glover, Romero, & Romero, 1978; Pope-Davis, Breaux, & Lin, 1994). I find BaFa BaFa to be a popular activity for introducing multicultural counseling and group work. Based on participant feedback, participants experience, albeit briefly, the confusion and feelings associated with functioning in a different culture. Subsequent discussions on value differences, attitudes, and stereotypes can be linked to the BaFa BaFa experiences rendering them a little less abstract and a little more real. BaFa BaFa can be ordered from Simulation Training Systems, P. O. Box 910, 218 Twelfth Street, Del Mar, CA 92014-0910, (619) 755-0272.

The Case Vignette/Role Play Approach

The case vignette approach for facilitating multicultural awareness is most frequently attributed to Derald Wing Sue (Sue & Sue, 1990). Although I initially used Sue's case vignettes and his recommended follow-up questions verbatim, I eventually began to develop my own case vignettes and follow-up questions. The idea for the following case vignette was generated by an actual incident reported by a columnist in a local newspaper and I subsequently modified and adopted it by for use in my courses in multicultural counseling and group work:

MIT or the State University?

Ms. Owens is an European-American math teacher at the high school in which you are a counselor. The fact that she is paying you a visit is rather surprising since your past contact with her has been minimal. You know her to be a highly dedicated math teacher, and one who does not hesitate to become involved with her students, especially the more promising female students. Ms. Owens informs you that Rita Hernandez, a Mexican-American senior, who recently received a full scholarship to MIT, has just informed her that due to her parents' wishes, she will be attending the State University. Apparently, Mr. Hernandez, an auto mechanic, does not want his daughter to be moving away from home at such an early age. Ms. Owens finds the situation totally incredulous and requests your help in making Mr. Hernandez realize that he is limiting his daughter's future.

1. Match up individuals in this vignette who are experiencing cultural conflicts and identify them by possible *cultural variables*.

Example:	Rita Hernandez	Mexican-American, Adolescent Traditionalist, Working Class
	Mr. Hernandez	Mexican-American, Middle Aged Traditionalist, Working Class,
	Ms. Owens	European-American, Feminist, Middle Class, Middle Aged

2. Identify the *values* that are possibly in conflict.

Example:	Rita Hernandez	Family, Independence
	Mr. Hernandez	Family, Safety of Daughter
	Ms. Owens	Education, Gender Equality

3. Identify the significant characters in this case vignette in terms of *cultural identity development stage* and potential for transference. Be sure to utilize Helms' (1995) and Atkinson, Morten, & Sue's (1993) cultural identity development models.

Example:	Rita Hernandez	Conformity Stage (MID)
	Mr. Hernandez	Resistance & Immersion (MID)
	Ms. Owens	Pseudo-Independent (WRID)

4. In relation to the significant characters, identify your own cultural identity, values, untested stereotypes, and potential for countertransference. Be sure to use Helms' (1995) cultural identity developmental model.

Example: Author   European-American, Middle Class,
                                Androgynous, Middle Aged,
                                Education, Cultural Sensitivity,
                                & Gender Equality
              Mr. Hernandez   Macho & Out of Touch
              Ms. Owens   Radical & Insensitive Immersion/
                                Emersion (WRID)

After having participants read and complete the follow-up activities, as I
have done above, you can identify volunteers culturally similar to the characters in the case vignette. Have these participants role play their characters
in a brief interaction. Have participants critique the role plays and substitute in new casts of players as needed. Upon observing the role plays and
their reactions to the characters being role played, allow participants the
opportunity to alter their answers. Divide the larger group into small groups
(three to five members) and have them discuss how they culturally identified the characters and themselves. A variation to this approach would be
to have guests (i.e., professionals who have had experience with the cultural groups depicted in the case vignette—a Mexican-American tradition-
alist male and a European-American feminist), participate in the role play,
join in the small group discussions, and later join in the large group discussions. In terms of the multicultural competencies, the initial benefit to be
gained by participating in this learning activity is practice at culturally identifying self and others. Practice with the six culturally appropriate intervention strategies identified in this chapter can easily be facilitated by
having designated participants take turns functioning as group leaders to
role play process oriented, interactional groups (six to eight members) in
which the content of the vignette becomes the content of the group.

A Process Oriented, Interactional, Culturally Heterogeneous Group

Kurt Lewin is credited with having originated experiential learning in the
form of the T (Training) group, the forerunner of today's process oriented,
interactional group and foresaw its potential for diversity sensitivity training (Johnson & Johnson, 1994; Merta, 1995; Yalom, 1995). Yalom's (1995)
theory and techniques, as depicted in his text *Theory and Practice of Group
Psychotherapy*, provide the conceptual framework and necessary interventions for effectively leading a process oriented, interactional group designed
for cultural exploration. The basis of the theory and techniques are described below:

> The focus of the group is to facilitate interpersonal learning by having mem-
> bers disclose and receive feedback from each other in response to here-and-
> now issues and interactions occurring within the group. Because the group is

more interactional, the interpersonal behaviors that a member customarily exhibits outside of group become manifested within the group, which is referred to as a social microcosm. Although the group leader does not assume a directive role, he or she certainly plays a very active one. By a variety of group techniques (i.e., culture building, process illumination, here-and-now activation, consensual validation, and conflict resolution), he or she helps to develop a cohesive group in which members feel safe to disclose and to give and receive feedback, and in which conflict is worked through rather than avoided or left to go unchecked. Members enter the group harboring certain "parataxic distortions"—distorted perceptions or beliefs regarding interpersonal relations that they have not been able to correct during normal social relations. By acknowledging their parataxic distortions at the outset of or any time during the group, members can establish their goals of correcting these distortions and improving their interpersonal relations. For many, if not all, members of a racially heterogeneous, interactional group, the parataxic distortions are likely to take the form of racial biases, stereotypes, ethnocentrism, and ignorance of various multicultural issues and perspectives (Merta, 1995, p. 571).

Although participation in any process oriented, interactional group is apt to result in member to member feedback of a racial/ethnic or cultural nature, cultural exploration, interpersonal change, and practice in multicultural group leadership are more likely to occur if the multicultural group is a planned one. When planning a process oriented, culturally heterogeneous group in which a cultural variable (e.g., race/ethnicity, gender, sexual orientation) will intentionally be explored and discussed, the group leader is advised to recruit, screen, and select members so as to insure the creation of a *racial or cultural equality group*. In so doing, the equally balanced number of members (e.g., four Hispanic and four Anglo) will greatly reduce the risk of cultural group think occurring. Lightly structure the group by having a single theme for each group session, even though issues or topics that spontaneously arise in the group might take precedence. In the group researched by Merta, Romero, and Bennet (1997), the themes consisted of the following: racial/ethnic values and stereotypes, gender roles, cross-cultural dating and marriage, dual career issues, and affirmative action. Finally, have each member identify a personal group goal to work toward (e.g., an Anglo male member might choose to learn if he interacts with women differently than with men; an Hispanic female might choose to learn if she is less independent and assertive than Anglo females). Members should expect alternative or additional goals to spontaneously arise from group feedback. Allow ample time (e.g., 90-minute sessions) and duration (a weekly group for 10 weeks) for group process to occur and for individuals to fulfill their goals. Use of a process observer to provide members feedback on group dynamics and process as well as leadership skills can be a most valuable addition.

10
CHAPTER

Differentiating Groups

Up to this point we have concentrated on the nature of the group process and the integral components that interact to create that process—namely the leader and the members. However, groups have many different facets which come into play in the context of translating group process into practice. The purpose of the next three chapters is to focus on the technical dimensions of group work as a means of providing hands on tools for implementing group programs.

As the field of group work has grown, acquiring merit as a human service modality, it has developed a technology of its own which has both affirmed its validity and enhanced its reliability across client populations and settings. The fact that groups are here to stay is well established. Conyne (1985) observed that "groups are a dominant, omnipresent force in our lives and they most likely will continue to be so well into the future" (p. 61). This is because research and clinical practice have demonstrated that group work is an entity with specific knowledge, procedures, processes, and mechanics that can be beneficially learned, applied, and adapted in most human contexts. The problem is no longer one of proving the potential and relevance of group work in facilitating growth, enhancing productivity, and resolving problems. The problem now is how to most effectively and efficiently utilize group process. This is where the elements of differentiation, organization, and evaluation of groups becomes important. Unless group leaders can effectively do all three, the prospects of establishing effective groups and developing functional group programs are curtailed.

This chapter will focus on the first of these three components of group process. Differentiation will be addressed from the standpoint of process and focus perspectives and via group typology based on the nature of groups and client populations served. In Chapter 11 organization will be discussed in a general to specific manner. Starting with the perspective of outreach and guidelines for planning group programs, we will then delineate group composition factors and technical considerations for forming groups and conclude with an example of a group counseling format. Evaluation will be discussed in Chapter 12 from a practitioner's perspective which differentiates research from evaluation and provides specific tools and suggestions for evaluating process and outcome.

☐ Differentiating Between Groups

The term group usually conjures up the image of a particular type of group or group approach, most likely one the counselor has been exposed to, trained in, or experienced. This often creates a limited purview from which it is difficult to build a flexible and varied group program that will serve a variety of purposes and meet a wide range of client needs. The ability to differentiate between groups based on process characteristics and qualities unique to certain group formats and purposes will provide a solid basis for organizing and implementing appropriate and comprehensive group programs (Trotzer, 1975). Consideration will be given first to process perspectives that attribute contextual diversity to groups and then group typology will be described from both a process and client perspective.

☐ Socio-Process and Psyche-Process Groups

Coffey (1952) initially proposed the idea that groups could be categorized as socio-process groups (task oriented in nature) or psyche-process groups (person oriented in nature). Kemp (1970) expanded on this idea, relating it particularly to group guidance and counseling. A socio-process group is one in which goals are external to the group and involves tasks for which the group is given or assumes responsibility. "The intent of the (socio-process) group and its specific reason for being is not primarily the self-improvement of members" (Dinkmeyer & Muro, 1971, p. 126) but rather it is to accomplish a set task. The socio-process group is thus task oriented and attempts to utilize the resources (members) of the group in the most efficient and effective manner to accomplish its mission. The group is problem oriented only to the point of resolving difficulties that are directly associated with the task or are interfering with the group's progress in working on the task. Members receive gratification and fulfillment as a result of their contribution to the task, their cooperation with other members, and ultimately from the accomplishment of the task itself. The leader is primarily responsible for getting the job done by keeping the group goal oriented, assessing the group's resources, and mobilizing them to achieve its task goal. Examples of socio-process groups are committees, athletic teams, work groups in business and industry—such as quality circles or think tanks—task force groups, and other such groups that interact to attain an end result in the form of a program, policy, product, victory, and so forth.

A psyche-process group is one in which goals come from within the group, particularly from the internal frame of reference of individual group members themselves. The process is person oriented as opposed to task oriented, and individual growth, personal learning, and personal problem solving are the focuses. Group interaction itself is of primary importance. Member satisfaction results from involvement and interaction with group members, increased knowledge about self and others, and from personal problem solving, change, and growth. The leader is responsible to the members, not to a task, and functions to create a therapeutic climate in the group, facilitate interaction, and protect group members if that becomes necessary. Examples of psyche-process groups are counseling and therapy groups, marital enrichment, encounter, sensitivity, and personal growth groups.

Schmuck and Schmuck (1971) noted that both socio- and psyche-process groups can be either individual oriented or group oriented in purpose. That is, the interaction of any group benefits either individuals separately or the group as a unit. For example, classrooms are individual socio-process groups whereas industrial work groups tend to be group socio-process groups. Therapy groups are examples of individual psyche-process groups while T-groups are group psyche-process groups. The individual focus therefore means that results are gauged in terms of what each individual member achieves as a function of group interaction. The group focus by contrast results in increased group efficiency and increased knowledge and awareness of the group process itself.

In most guidance, psychoeducational, counseling, and psychotherapy groups the primary goal is to use the group process for the benefit of individual members. This goal is basic to the nature of therapeutic groups. Therefore, if groups do not promote the best interests of the individuals involved, they are not effectively serving the cause of human growth and development. On the other hand, the group emphasis in certain groups like class meetings, guidance classes, T-groups, consciousness raising groups, and human relations groups may serve an extremely important function in helping members learn cooperation and respect for one another and appreciation of those who have ethnic, racial, or cultural characteristics different from their own.

Although all counseling and psychotherapy groups are basically psyche-process in concept, the socio-process concept is often used, particularly as a basis for leadership strategies. Some leaders prefer to start their groups on a structured task or activity oriented basis. They use tasks to develop a group atmosphere in which members get to know each other, gain trust for one another, and develop cohesiveness through working together on the activities. Gradually then the leader turns the responsibility and focus over to members and facilitates the evolution of the psyche-process so members can get down to the business of working on their own problems and concerns. Conversely, groups such as committees and work teams that are socio-process in concept may utilize psyche-process strategies to get started. Before receiving a specific task to work on, members of the group spend time and effort, often via T-group, encounter group, or human relations methods, getting to know each other and building a group relationship. Emphasis is on acceptance of self and others and interpersonal communication. Once the members have begun to develop a relationship where personal needs are met, they are then assigned a task to accomplish, switching the emphasis of the group from psyche-process to socio-process.

In either of these strategies the leader can move back and forth between the two processes as the group needs dictate. At times the psyche-group may benefit from the structure and responsibility of a task and the socio-group may need to reestablish the person to person quality of their group interaction. So the tenor of the group can change depending on its overall purpose and the needs of the members.

Wilbur and Roberts-Wilbur (1994) further refined the dynamics of socio-process and psych-process into three categories of group processes: Task-process groups, psycho-process groups, and socio-process groups. The task form is characterized by a predetermined task or project to which the group is assigned. The group interacts in a manner that Waldo (1985) typifies as *extrapersonal* where gathering information and completing tasks are predominant activities. The psycho form is designed to change behavior of the group participants, and meets Waldo's (1985) criteria for being *intrapersonal* in nature because the impact of group interaction is realized in the individual lives of the members. In contrast, the socio form is a more cognitive, interactive process where attitudes, values, beliefs, ideas, and opinions are surfaced and examined in a format that qualifies as *interpersonal* (Waldo, 1985) because emphasis is on sharing information, orientation, and discussion (Polcin, 1991). All three forms relate directly to the ASGW group work typologies delineated in Chapter 2.

Finally, a recent development in group work has further exemplified the importance of the process delineations just described. The emergence of the Process Observer as an official entity in groups of all forms has made it possible to directly identify and utilize process components and dynamics to enhance group effectiveness. A process person is incorporated in the group for purposes of tracking process dynamics and bringing observations of such to the attention of the leader and group members. As such process becomes a recognized and considered dimension of the group activity regardless of its purpose and nature (Trotzer, 1997a, 1997b, 1997c, & 1998b). Task groups, class groups, work groups, committees, and leadership teams such as the ASGW Executive Council have all utilized and benefited from inclusion   of
a Process Observer into their deliberations thereby creating a vital link between process and content (Krause & Hulse-Kilacky, 1996).

☐   Different Focuses in Groups

Groups also can be distinguished on the basis of the focus of the interaction in the group. Patterns of communication in a group define its nature and solidify characteristics that can be used to describe it. Several basic focuses tend to occur in groups. Each has advantages and disadvantages. Each can promote the effectiveness of the group or disrupt it. The leader has to be aware of the type of focus that will best serve the interests of members and achieve the group's goals and act to see that that focus is developed and maintained. Each focus is briefly discussed in the following pages.

Here and Now Perspective

This focus is on what is happening to and in the individual and the group at the moment. The concentration is on the action and interaction as it develops in the group. This orientation brings out members' feelings and thoughts that are part of their present awareness and deals with current behavior. It maintains that what individuals are like in the group is representative of their personalities and actions outside the group. The basic assumption is that personality is consistent in human beings and that the group can use what occurs in the group as material for helping members resolve problems outside the group. As Sklare, Keener, and Mas (1990) note: "The group is a microcosm of society, behaviors similar to that which members exhibit outside the group will come to life in the group" (p. 144). The here and now focus is an integral part of growth groups, is highly significant in counseling and psychotherapy groups (Carroll, 1986; Yalom, 1995) and has procedural importance in other groups. The here and now is a firm foundation for beginning communication and relationships because all parties have equal access to the stimuli of interaction. It provides a common starting point and is a necessary component of any effort to increase self-knowledge and improve social adequacy. It is also the perspective that gives feedback its most meaningful impact. However, the here and now also can be a means of avoiding problem issues that involve the outside world. Too much emphasis on the present (in the group) interaction can lead groups away from reality instead of closer to it.

One of the charges leveled against marathon groups and encounter groups is that they become so enmeshed in the here and now interaction of the sessions that little if any transfer of learning occurs. Participants have to wait until another opportunity arises to engage in a similar process to use their newfound insights and skills. This focus also can stymie group members in their development of plans for action that have a future, outside the group application. The group leader therefore must be able to assess when the group needs to get to the here and now but also must sense when that focus is running counter to the process of therapeutic change.

There and Then Perspective

This focus deals with events, behaviors, or feelings that occurred in the past but are still interfering with the adjustment of the individual or the group in the present. This perspective may draw on either conscious or subconscious material in its effort to identify causes and to clarify and resolve problems (Donigian & Malnati, 1997). This perspective should not be misconstrued as displaying dirty laundry or looking for skeletons in someone's closet. The past is a natural element in any person's life and in the group's life and can contribute meaningfully to the helping process if utilized in the proper manner. The individual's past is an extremely important theme in group therapy and has importance, but to a lesser degree, in group counseling. The group's past, typified in comments like "remember last time," is important in growth groups, counseling groups, and therapy groups but has less value except for transition purposes in other groups. The there and then is particularly useful if members have unresolved feelings about past events that are currently stifling growth. Conflicts unsuccessfully dealt with, feelings of guilt, actions that are regretted, and traumatic experiences stemming from rape, physical abuse, incest, or substance abuse are examples of past material that can be brought out and worked through beneficially in the group.

The important thing to remember about this focus is that efforts should always be made to bring the person up to date so that the disclosure does not become just another unsatisfactory means of handling the situation. The past is of value when it can perpetuate adjustment to the present and stimulate growth in the future. Frequently members use the there and then to avoid getting into the here and now problems of their lives. A common ploy in groups is to play the "remember when" nostalgia game as a means of procuring a reprieve from working on problems. The group leader must sense when the there and then is losing its impact in the helping process and help the group move on to a more valuable focus. Similarly the leader must help the group avoid rehashing its past to such an extent that it never catches up to itself. Some groups continually dwell on clarifying past behaviors, perceptions, and intentions. They get to the end of their sessions feeling that they have analyzed their group history without ever having experienced it as a present phenomenon.

Social Value Perspective

This focus basically asks the question "What does society expect and how does that affect me?" It attempts to assess a person's thoughts, feelings, and behaviors in light of their usefulness in daily life. This perspective makes full use of the group as a mini-society reflecting the standards, norms, and expectations of the outside world. The social value focus is the key to reality testing that needs to be done in the group to make the process meaningful for transfer of learning. The basic idea is that if members can provide realistic feedback and evaluations, individuals can make better decisions and develop plans for change that have a higher probability of success. The necessity of this perspective in most groups is obvious, especially when problems are involved. As Glasser (1965) noted, most problems initially reflect a denial or distortion of reality, and if the group does not attempt to reestablish the member's contact with reality, the process has little positive effect. In guidance groups, counseling groups, and therapy groups this perspective is mandatory. In all other groups it is important from the standpoint of credibility. Individual members may resist this perspective because it demands that they face problems in light of others' perceptions and not simply their own. In an effort to protect their members, groups sometimes deny reality and on occasion actually distort it. When this situation occurs, the relevance and usefulness of the group process in solving problems is negated. Whenever leaders become part and parcel of a group's refusal to be a reality check and do not act responsibly to include that focus, they are acting unethically. Sometimes the leader may have to stand alone and confront members with reality in order to force them to deal realistically with each other's problems.

Skills and Tools Perspective

This focus, as the name implies, is concerned with providing group members with the technical means of resolving their problems, living more effective lives, and making growth facilitating decisions. This perspective provides a focus around which entire groups can be built since it concentrates on providing members with certain basic skills that will enhance their personal welfare. A group can be organized to help members learn a variety of skills ranging from decision making to social interaction skills. (Gazda & Brooks, 1985; Johnson & Johnson, 1997). This perspective can perpetuate both preventative and remedial helping group methods. Gazda has promoted this perspective stating "I think we need to employ a model in which, after clients' deficits are identified in the interview format, they are put through a systematic, structured, intensive skills training program" (Ritter, West, & Trotzer, 1987, p. 296). The skills and tools perspective are an essential part of guidance and psychoeducational groups and can be one of the means of implementing action during the work stage of counseling groups. This focus has relevance in therapy groups, incidental impact in growth groups, and selective value in task groups.

The expertise of the leader is especially important to this focus for two reasons. First, he or she must recognize when the lack of certain skills is a major part of a member's or group's problems and be able to act to fill that void in the group. Second, he or she must have the wherewithal to teach the needed skills. The only draw back to this perspective is that it can become a rigid and inflexible means of running groups if the leader begins focusing only on teaching the skills and not on the persons in the group. In other words, the group can develop into a classroom type group with a leader centered structure and academic content but little personal relevance to group members.

Agent of Change Perspective

The philosophical basis for this focus is that each person is responsible for learning about himself or herself, and the group is an arena in which that learning can take place. Reddy (1985) believes this perspective will become increasingly important as group work reaches for its zenith in society's effort to meet personal, social, and business needs. She stated, "with the breakdown of the family unit and a continuing depersonalized society, individuals will be in, if not seek out, small groups of people to fulfill their affiliations, tasks, and personal, interpersonal and organizational needs" (p. 106). The main objective is to change oneself in a desired direction and to help others do the same. Self-acceptance, self-knowledge, and self-responsibility are associated with this perspective. It also contributes to members' understanding and acceptance of others.

The material for group discussion is personal functioning and involves self-disclosure and direct feedback as the principal means of acquiring self-understanding. This focus tends to be the primary emphasis in growth groups because of the basic assumption that participants in these groups are healthy, normal individuals who willingly involve themselves and who are capable of governing their own lives. The advantage of this perspective is that ideally each member chooses the amount of involvement, disclosure, feedback, or change desired. However, in reality, sometimes one has difficulty assessing whether the person, the group, or the leader is the motivating force in the interaction. All helping groups should advocate self-responsibility, but especially in counseling groups members need to *learn* how to be responsible for themselves before they can *practice* it. Therefore the group leader may need to help the group develop this perspective over time rather than use it as the primary means of promoting change throughout the entire group process.

Summary

The perspectives described tend to complement each other in effective groups. Certain focuses may be primary in certain types of groups but the others serve a countering and balancing function in keeping group interaction relevant and therapeutic. Most groups with which the counselor works will utilize all of these focuses to some extent. The typical counseling group may run the full gamut of perspectives during its course. Guidance and psychoedu-cational groups, though mainly concerned with the skills and social value perspectives, will incorporate other focuses as well. Once again the needs of the members and the purposes of the group will determine the validity of the focus that the leader promotes in the group. The leader should not hesitate to redirect the focus when necessary to help groups engage in constructive interaction.

☐ Typology of Group Work

Group workers should have a specific awareness of the many different types of groups relevant to their particular settings. Effective groups in helping settings have in common process characteristics that we've discussed in previous chapters. But they also have unique attributes that differentiate them from each other and broaden the impact of the group process as a means of increasing the counselor's effectiveness. Generally, helping groups can be broken down into six major categories:

1. guidance and life skills groups (psychoeducation),
2. counseling groups,
3. psychotherapy groups,
4. support and self-help groups,
5. consultation groups, and
6. growth groups.

Each category has characteristics relative to focus, leadership, size, and purpose that distinguish it. General traits and characteristics of the broad categories in which each of these groups fit are delineated in Chapter 2. Each of these six major categories and representative types of groups are presented on the following pages.

☐ Guidance and Life Skills Groups

Under the general rubric of psychoeducation, guidance groups are primarily school oriented both conceptually and practically whereas life skills groups have broader applicability to any mental health private practice or agency. Both use a similar format adapting content to the setting and clientele served. The process involved is that of

> providing personally relevant information and skills and encouraging interpersonal interaction, discussion, and sharing in order to help group members understand themselves, their development, and their world, thereby facilitating effective decision-making, appropriate adjustment, and satisfactory personal growth (Trotzer, 1980, p. 342).

The types of guidance groups a counselor should be familiar with are large and small group guidance, classroom meetings, guidance classes, human relations groups, and life skills groups. However, research by Dansby (1996) has found that "types of groups vary greatly by school level with apparently more counseling groups being conducted with younger students and more guidance groups with older students" (p. 238).

Large Group Guidance

Large group guidance is primarily concerned with dispensing information to help in personal planning and decision making. Emphasis is on presenting educational and vocational information of a personally relevant nature in an interesting manner to large numbers of clients who need the same information. Large group guidance is used when information can be presented in a straightforward manner with little risk of misunderstanding. Methods usually involve a presentation in the form of films or lectures followed by an opportunity for discussion and questions. The process is content oriented and cognitive in nature and stresses environmental factors as well as generic personal attributes. The leader generally presents the information and directs and controls discussion.

Large group guidance can be effectively used in orientation and articulation situations to help clients understand a system and how to move through it. Although called large group guidance, it is still advantageous to limit groups to a size where the counselor can keep tabs on how information is being received. A general rule of thumb is to work with groups no larger than the usual class size. Using groups larger than this may get the information to more people at one time but also may inhibit discussion to the extent that the process could become self-defeating. The length of time involved in these groups can vary from 15 minutes to an hour. Longer presentations result in diminishing returns due to the loss of client attention and interest. Large group guidance also helps counselors give out general information in a relatively small amount of time, thus freeing the counselor to concentrate on other aspects of the group program.

Small Group Guidance

Very often small group guidance is an outgrowth of a large group presentation. In a school situation, for instance, scheduling procedures may be explained in a large group, but the actual working out of an individual's schedule can be done in a small group. In fact, it is indeed strange that school counselors who are often saddled with scheduling responsibilities do not opt more frequently for handling this task in small groups rather than on a one on one basis. Time is saved and monotony is lessened for everyone. Small group guidance allows clients to discuss their own situations and allows for asking specific questions. Clients who refuse to ask questions in a large group are much more willing to do so in a small group.

Emphasis in small group guidance is on providing educational, vocational, and personal information. Methods, however, concentrate on the discussion aspect rather than on presentation, and efforts are made to involve all members in the interaction. The process is cognitive stressing both content and skills. Focus is on relating environmental and informational factors to personal goals, values, attitudes, and responsibilities. The leader alternately facilitates group discussion and presents information.

Small group guidance is particularly useful in helping clients develop social skills and decision making skills to help them be more successful in their lives. In addition, vocational and educational planning in small groups for members who have common interests and goals is an efficient use of counselor time. For example, clients desiring to explore common career areas can benefit from small group guidance sessions, sharing their interests, concerns, and knowledge with other clients headed in the same direction. Generally small group guidance is appropriate when clients are beginning to make specific use of information or need to develop some skill to enhance personal effectiveness. Group size should be restricted to 8 to 12 members, because larger groups decrease the probability of interaction by the total group membership. Sessions of 30 to 60 minutes tend to be sufficient, and the frequency of meetings should depend on the topic discussed and the needs of group members.

The content and focus of most guidance groups in schools tend to be categorized in one of the following areas (Thompson & Poppen, 1979):

1. *Self-concept development*. Group sessions address the question of "Who am I?" They are designed to help participants deal with identity crises associated with growing up, develop positive self-concepts, and engage in self-exploration and values clarification.
2. *Student self-discipline*. The focus is on learning to be responsible for self and acting in a responsible manner toward others. Decision making and coping skills are often intrinsically involved.
3. *Effective peer relations*. The emphasis is on understanding and effectively coping with peer pressure and utilizing peer dynamics constructively. Exploration of the impact of peers on individuals is stressed and human relations skills are taught.
4. *Effective interpersonal relationships with nonpeers*. The focus is primarily on developing effective adult-child relationships and communication encompassing teacher-student, parent-child, and other such relationships that involve a transgenerational or hierarchical authority type of interaction.
5. *Academic progress of all learners*. The emphasis is on educational progress in orientation, articulation, and study skills. General educational information and requirements, or teaching specific learning skills, may be involved.

6. *Career development*. Educational-occupational information, career decision making, and vocational development are addressed for the purpose of helping participants make effective career choices.
7. *Effective classroom or work environment*. The focus is on developing a cooperative (cohesive) learning environment and a positive learning atmosphere characterized by effective communication.

Within these broad categories specific group guidance programs are developed and tailored to the specific needs of participants and conditions of the environment (Trotzer, 1980).

Classroom Meetings

Classroom meetings utilize a ready made group situation, although, of course, the situation is limited to schools. School counselors who conduct classroom meetings enhance their own roles in three ways:

1. By direct contact with the counselor, the students become more cognizant of who the counselor is and more familiar with the counselor role.
2. By becoming involved in the classroom milieu, counselors are kept aware of the kinds of experiences and pressures both students and teachers face, which makes them more sensitive to both groups.
3. By developing a working relationship with teachers, school counselors will perpetuate their impact as consultants and referral sources.

The general format and implementation of class meetings is described by Glasser (1969). He discussed three main types of classroom meetings: 1) the social, problem solving meeting where the goal is to change behavior, 2) the open ended meeting where the goal is to change thinking, and 3) the educational-diagnostic meeting where the goal is to determine what students have learned and where weaknesses still exist.

Class meetings can facilitate the development of productive and positive classroom relationships and therefore should involve the entire class. By structuring the meetings into the regular routine students learn that they have a specific time when what they have to say takes precedence over what the teacher or counselor has to say.

Thompson and Poppen (1979) described seven types of classroom meetings based on their focus:

1. *Involvement meetings*: to promote student involvement and sense of belonging.
2. *Rules and responsibilities meetings*: to deal with class operational procedures and expectations.
3. *Thinking meetings*: to increase students' thinking and verbal abilities.
4. *Values clarification meetings*: to clarify personal values and develop tolerance of differences.
5. *Hypothetical dilemmas*: to pose hypothetical problem situations and develop action plans.

6. *Actual problem solving*: to deal with real problems in the classroom.
7. *Class council*: to provide a vehicle for class governance (pp. 157–159).

Whatever the focus, the process is discussion oriented with the goal of maximizing total student participation. Although the process is mainly cognitive, efforts are directed at finding out what the students think. The counselor serves as a facilitator of the discussion and as a model to the teacher who should be present in the class. In this way counselors help teachers develop their own skills so that eventually the counselor can bow out. The meetings should be at least 30 minutes in length but can vary depending on class involvement, topic of discussion, and leader time commitment. Frequency is a key factor, Glasser (1969) maintained that elementary school classes should have a class meeting every day. In secondary schools, one or two meetings a week is a realistic goal for counselors to seek. Thus the counselor's time must be carefully planned. To be effective he or she must develop a programmed sequence of conducting class meetings and training teachers so that as responsibility for one class meeting is turned over to its teacher another class can be added.

Guidance/Psychoeducational Classes

The oldest of any guidance technique was first proposed in the form of vocational guidance classes as part of the school curriculum. Through the years, however, the guidance class gradually became so routine, monotonous, and irrelevant that both counselors and students perceived it as no more than a necessary evil at best. However, with the recent emphasis on career, mental health, and psychological education, the guidance class is once again assuming its meaningful place in school curricula. Guidance classes are courses taught by the counselor whose content and structure are based on guidance and counseling principles. They may be elective or required and usually last for one quarter or semester, during which time students consider personally relevant topics and information in both an experiential and academic manner. They also make use of what Schmuck and Schmuck (1971) called the "splendid myriad of different individual styles and emotional experiences" (p. 4) that make up a classroom group. For best results class size should be limited to approximately 20 people. The format of guidance classes is highly variable, depending on needs of students and the personality of the counselor. However, several forms enjoy fairly consistent emphasis and acceptance among counselors.

Career Guidance Classes

The career guidance class (Hoppock, 1976) helps students make vocational choices based on self-knowledge and knowledge about the world of work.

Students do various career projects, research numerous vocations, and assess their own vocational interests and abilities. Offshoots of this type of group are appearing in greater quantity throughout the educational process. The main purpose of these classes is to prepare students for a vocational choice that is personally satisfying and contributes meaningfully to society.

Feelings Classes

The feelings class as described by Faust (1968) has a guidance class format that concerns itself with the affective domain of students' lives. The purpose of the class is to give attention to the emotional development of the student. Five main ideas are stressed:

1. Many kinds of feelings exist.
2. Nearly everyone experiences all the different feelings.
3. To have these feelings is all right.
4. Having a feeling is different from expressing a feeling.
5. Feelings can be expressed in ways that are not harmful to yourself or others, and in many cases these methods of expression are helpful.

Feelings classes should not be confused with sensitivity training or encounter groups. Rather they are to teach people that knowing how to express a feeling is as important as having the feeling in the first place. The leader must be able to work with clients' feelings in a constructive manner. The critical importance of human emotions which supports such group efforts has been elucidated by Goleman's (1995) national best seller *Emotional Intelligence*.

"Knowing Me" Classes

In these classes students have an opportunity to learn how wonderfully complex and interesting they are as persons. Under the direction of the counselor they engage in a variety of self-assessment and interpersonal learning activities. They discuss results among themselves and hear presentations on various aspects of human development. These classes can be held for any age group, but they are particularly interesting to middle school and junior high students because they are in that no man's land of pre-adolescence where change and the imminence of change are major factors in their experience. The leader must be adept in the psychology of the particular age group with whom he or she is working and have the ability to organize class sessions around the individual differences of class members.

Human Relations Groups

Human awareness and human relations are becoming an increasingly important aspect of the group process. Within the context of education, Birnbaum (1969) stated that human relations training

> holds tremendous potential for improving education by dealing with affective components, reducing unnecessary friction between generations and creating a revolution in instruction by helping teachers to learn how to use the classroom group for learning purposes (p. 82).

Gazda (1971b) added that we have a responsibility to educate children in human relations to prepare them to cope adequately with their ever expanding worlds. Not to do so would be a tragic and inexcusable mistake. In general, human relations groups are a means of contributing to the psychological education of both children and adults. The counselor trained in group process has the resources to be in the forefront of this movement.

Human relations groups can vary in size from six members to six dozen members; the larger groups are broken down into small subgroups all under the direction of one leader. Focus is on development of competencies in communication and relationship formation, and the process entails demonstration, experiential involvement in activities, and group discussion. Under-standing and appreciating individual differences and similarities especially in terms of racial, cultural, and other diversity factors are stressed. The leader structures and guides interaction and facilitates discussion. Sessions are usually organized in a planned sequence and meet for a set number of times. They usually last one to three hours per session or are arranged in a workshop format of longer time periods. Members benefit from involvement in the sessions because the social skills and knowledge of self and others are immediately relevant to their lives.

Life Skills Groups

Life skills groups have many labels but one basic commonality: they use a structured, experiential, group training format to teach participants specific skills that enable them to improve their life adjustment. Gazda has identified four generic life skills areas that delineate the content of these groups. They are:

1. Interpersonal communication or relationships,
2. Fitness and health maintenance,
3. Problem solving and decision making, and
4. Establishing one's personal identity and life's purpose (Ritter, West, & Trotzer, 1987, p. 296).

Training programs in each of these skill areas can be developed that are applicable to four specific settings: community, home, school, and work. Numerous resources have been developed in the life skills area by leaders in the field such as George Gazda (Gazda, 1984b; Gazda & Brooks, 1985) and David Johnson (Johnson, 1972; Johnson & Johnson, 1979; 1997). You also are referred to Drum and Knott's (1977) book *Structured Groups for Facilitating Development* as a prototype work in the life skills area.

The group process model described in Chapters 4 and 5 is a useful resource in organizing and planning groups of a guidance or life skills nature. Figure 10.1 presents the basic content and process components that provide a planning framework for these groups.

Content considerations include selection and development of a general theme based on the needs of the population to be served. Specifications of overall goals emanate from the theme. The nature of the goals brings the sequential order of the program into perspective, with each session addressing relevant topics. Specific objectives for each session are planned and topic related information, activities, and materials are selected for presentation and discussion. Thus as participants move through the sequence of sessions they engage in experiences that culminate in achievement of goals of the program, which, in turn, meet the needs for which the group was organized. However, structuring content is only part of the organizational task; it is the horizontal dimension of the model. The group process also must be accounted for in the planning of topics, selection of activities, and organization of sessions. Group process is the vertical dimension of the model. The sequential interaction between process and content form the basis for an effective group guidance program.

Developmental tasks provide a basis for selecting activities appropriate to the stage of development in which the group is. Accounting for process tasks increases the relevance of activities and facilitates movement to the next stage of the group process. The choice of activities, then, should be based on both process and content considerations. In other words, any activities chosen should facilitate the realization of both process and content objectives. For example, an initial session of a career guidance group might use a get acquainted activity that includes sharing vocational goals along with other "who are you?" tasks. Process and content thus are integrated, providing experiences and an atmosphere conducive to personalized learning relative to the focus of the group guidance program. Individual group sessions can be further organized and planned using phases of a group session described in Chapter 5.

☐ Counseling Groups

The factor that distinguishes counseling groups from guidance groups is that they are problem oriented and remedial in nature. Group counseling

CONTENT									
THEME									
OVERALL GOALS									
SESSIONS	**1**	**2**	**3**	**4**	**5**	**6**	**7**	**8**	**X**
TOPICS									
OBJECTIVES									
ACTIVITIES									
MATERIALS									

SECURITY	Getting Acquainted	⟶
	Setting Boundaries	⟶
	Interpersonal Warm-up	⟶
	Establishing Trust (Basic Rapport)	⟶
ACCEPTANCE	Personal Sharing	⟶
	Giving Feedback	⟶
	Group Cohesiveness	⟶
	Accepting Self	⟶
	Accepting Others	⟶
RESPONSIBILITY	Self Assessment	⟶
	Recognizing Ownership	⟶
	Building Responsibility	⟶
	Giving Respect	⟶
	Doing a Fair Share	⟶
WORK	Problem-Solving	⟶
	Decision-Making	⟶
	Learning and Applying Information and Skills to Personal Life	⟶
	Mobilizing Group Resources	⟶
	Reality Testing	⟶
CLOSING	Unfinished Business	⟶
	Giving Support	⟶
	Confirming and Affirming Growth	⟶
	Saying Goodbye	⟶
		Follow-up

FIGURE 10.1. Group guidance: Program development format.

focuses on helping people explore and confront specific dissatisfactions in their lives with the express purpose of understanding their concerns and discovering and implementing ways of resolving their problems (Trotzer, 1972). The group leader attempts to develop an atmosphere in which members can talk openly about their problems without fear of rejection or reprisal. He or she encourages members to help each other, facilitates communication, protects individuals if that becomes necessary, and functions in many other ways that have already been described. Since members feel safe and have the opportunity to both help and be helped, the process becomes one of conscientious concern for each other. This group also serves as a reality testing ground, where members can try out alternatives and obtain feedback about their probable success prior to attempting to make changes in the real world.

Since group counseling is the primary focus of this book, little additional information about it is necessary at this point. Group size should be limited to 4 to 10 members to preserve the personal focus in the group. Verbal techniques and conscious awareness are emphasized, and groups meet as often and only for as long as is necessary to resolve problems. Session length ranges from 45 to 90 minutes with the ideal length of time being one and one-half to two hours. The focus of the group varies with the nature of the members' problems, and therefore group counseling is a quite flexible tool. The following descriptions of some types of counseling groups attest to this quality of flexibility.

Common Problems Groups

The common problems group (Blocher, 1966) uses the most typical of all group strategies. Most practitioners agree that homogeneous groups have many advantages. Members share concerns and therefore do not feel isolated from the experiences of others. Comments such as "I feel that too," "That's the same problem I have," "We're all in the same boat," and "I'm glad I'm not the only one who has that problem" abound in these groups. Members benefit by observing others working out problems similar to their own. This strategy is highly relevant because it can be adapted to any type of problem that a number of clients have in common. Examples include problems with drugs/alcohol, dating, parents, losses (death or divorce), and so forth. Certain variations can improve the effect of the group, such as using role models or opening the group to new members as individuals resolve their problems and leave.

Case Centered Groups

An alternative to the common problems group is the case centered group (Poppen & Thompson, 1974), which uses a problem solving approach with a heterogeneous group. Whenever the focus is on a problem different from their own, other members are cast in the role of helpers, providing valuable feedback, information, and support based on their own experiences in overcoming that problem or simply offering assistance as interested, concerned, and objective helping persons. Diverse group membership is valuable for motivating interaction and maintaining group interest. Only in extreme circumstances where members' problems are so different that little basis exists for understanding one another is heterogeneity seriously disruptive to the group process. The only disadvantage is that some people may feel the other members cannot help them with their problems because of lack of experience or understanding. Heterogeneous groups are often much more interesting to leaders, making the task of leadership more stimulating

Human Potential Groups

Human potential counseling groups (Otto, 1967) focus on personal strengths and positive resources of the person as a means of overcoming obstacles that are preventing him or her from realizing his or her potential. This type of group is unique due to the process involved. It can be utilized in homogeneous or heterogeneous groups and attempts to resolve problems by concentrating on what individuals can do rather than what they can't do. Members are asked to examine their resources and then apply those resources to their concerns. The key quality of this approach is that it counters effectively the negative connotations and feelings of inferiority usually associated with having problems. Even when group leaders do not adhere completely to this format they incorporate sessions that stress the positives of balance and perspective. By operating from a strength base members grow in self-esteem and self-confidence, improve their self-concepts, and have more positive attitudes toward changing their behaviors, feelings, or cognitions.

Problem Solving Groups

Current dynamics and developments in the mental health field coupled with the economic expediency introduced by managed care have prompted the emergence of counseling groups that are characterized as short term, pragmatic, and solution focused. Problem solving groups are formed of individuals who specify before meeting the problem(s) in concrete terms that each is going to address in the group. The format is then structured and directed by the leader who provides the guidelines, parameters, techniques, and activities for the group to perpetuate the problem solving process. These groups may meet for extended, workshop type time frames (two to three hours) for four sessions over a one month period with a follow-up session, or may be conducted in a day long format with a follow-up session. In any event, the methods utilized reflect the influence of brief family therapy and solution focused therapy along with techniques adapted specifically to problem solving (Trotzer, 1998c; Trotzer, in press).

☐ Psychotherapy Groups

Therapy groups differ from counseling groups more on the basis of who is in them, who leads them, and where they take place than on the basis of process variations or therapeutic dynamics. Clients tend to be more disturbed and often carry a DSM-IV diagnosis. Leaders tend to have had their clinical training in settings that treat mental health disorders, e.g., hospitals, mental health centers, or other outpatient treatment programs. Leaders also tend to have more academic training, clinical experience, and credentials and are usually certified or licensed as psychiatrists, psychologists, clinical social workers, pastoral counselors, or clinical mental health counselors. The majority of therapy groups convene in agency, private practice, or hospital settings (inpatient or outpatient). The factors that delineate counseling from therapy are described in Chapter 2. Yalom (1983) distinguished inpatient from outpatient group therapy by differentiating process based on the level of functionality of the patients. Higher level inpatient groups meet for one hour and fifteen minutes during which time they work through a four phase process of 1) orientation/preparation, 2) agenda formation, 3) agenda filling, and 4) review of the meeting. Lower level inpatient groups meet for only 45 minutes in somewhat smaller groups and work through the same phases but in a much more structured, leader activated manner.

Therapy groups also tend to be open ended and long term. In hospital settings they may meet daily and in outpatient situations they may meet more than once a week as well. For additional information on therapy groups you are referred to Yalom (1983, 1995).

☐ Support and Self-Help Groups

Groups in this category are differentiated by the following traits:

1. Group membership is homogeneous with each member experiencing or having experienced the particular problem that called the group into being,
2. Peer support and assistance takes precedence over expert (professional) resources and assistance, and
3. If a leader is present, he or she is primarily a facilitator and/or also may be in need of the same support as the group members.

Pearson (1986) differentiated between mutual help/self-help groups and support groups on the basis of professional group leadership. He pointed out that any group that "truly functions as a group involves mutual help" (p. 66). Therefore, a distinction must be made between professionally organized and led groups which he calls support groups and groups which are couched in the context of "fellow sufferers giving aid to and receiving assistance from each other" (p. 66) which he calls mutual help or self-help groups.

The rise of self-help and mutual aid groups in contemporary society has been identified by Katz (1981) as an emerging social movement. At the time he estimated that 500,000 self-help groups existed in the U.S. with a membership of 23 million people. That number has since grown extensively. Such observations make group workers take note. What is the appeal of these groups, and in what capacity do professional group workers relate? Silverman's (1985) definition of mutual help groups gives us some clues to answer the first question.

> A mutual help group is an aggregate of people sharing a common problem or predicament who come together for mutual support and constructive action to solve their shared problem. The help offered is based on the participants' experience in coping with their problems and is not the result of any professional training or education group members possess (p. 237).

The appeal, merit, and practicality of these groups are based on members "having been there." Examples of such groups abound starting with Alcoholics Anonymous and all the other anonymouses (narcotics, gamblers, overeaters, etc.). Physical ailments (kidney transplants, cancer, spinal bifida, HIV positive/AIDS), physical disabilities (paraplegics, amputees), and losses of various types (death, divorce) generate many mutual help and support groups. Other self-help and support groups have emerged for those who have lived or do live with and/or care for people with illnesses or difficult circumstances or conditions. Examples include Adult Children of Alcoholics (ACOA), parents of HIV positive/AIDS patients or other ailments and caretakers of aging parents.

While many such groups abound and are appealing, the role of the professional group leader is not all that clear. In fact, Shapiro and Shapiro (1985) warned that the trend toward population specific specialization in group work has produced "an increased reliance on self-help and ingroup chauvinism" which is based on "an underlying notion that only someone who shares an affliction can successfully treat it" (p. 85)—a trend that is counter to the values and power of professional group work. Traditionally competition, skepticism, and distrust has existed between lay experts and professionals who have vied for the same client turf. However, some positive shifts are occurring. Some of the reasons for the shift are the efforts to delineate between professionally led and nonprofessionally led groups, the sharing of expertise both ways, and the concern for valid research to document therapeutic impact.

For more indepth discussion of this group category you are referred to the May, 1986 (Volume 11, Number 2) special issue of the *Journal for Specialists in Group Work* edited by Richard Pearson and to Silverman's (1985) Chapter 12 on mutual help groups in *The Group Worker's Handbook: Varieties of Group Experience* edited by Robert Conyne.

Peer Facilitated Counseling Groups

An emerging development in group counseling that is gaining acceptance and support in a wide range of environments from schools to prisons to community settings is the use of peer counselors as group leaders or coleaders. Kranzow (1973) noted that in peer facilitated groups members frequently are responsive to peer pressures and controls. Peer leaders tend to speak the same language literally and figuratively and members find it easier to identify with and trust the peer leader. Blaker and Samo (1973) pointed out that information gained from peers is usually more impressive than the same information provided by experts. Peer led groups also are applicable to all age levels (Brown, 1965; Gumaer, 1973; Hamburg & Varenhorst, 1972; Vriend, 1969).

Counselors who utilize the peer facilitator approach are themselves extremely important to its success. They must be involved in the selection and training of peer counselors and must be responsible for their supervision once the groups are under way (Tindall, 1989; Tindall & Gray, 1985 & 1989). They serve as a referral source and as a resource in crisis situations. Counselors who pursue this course of action therefore are not only going to make their own jobs easier, but will be able to expand the helping function in their settings.

☐ Consultation Groups

The counselor's consultant role can be immensely expanded through effective use of the group process. As a group specialist the counselor's expertise can be utilized by larger numbers of people across varied settings. In fact, Reddy (1985) emphasized the utility of group expertise in the form of a rhetorical question: "Does 'group specialist' signify a profession or does it represent a set of skills to be used by a broad range of professionals in many different fields?" (p. 105). For our purposes the answer is yes to both questions and the counselor's consultant function is his or her primary means of demonstrating it. In the schools, for example, parents, teachers, administrators, and other professionals can all be conveniently gathered under the umbrella of consultation in the interest of improving their own effectiveness and promoting the welfare of clients. In business and industry consulting groups can be an integral part of Employee Assistance Programs and personnel work (Kirby, 1985).

The leader in these groups performs many of the same functions as in counseling groups, only the purpose and composition of the group varies. Session length and duration are variable depending on the purpose for which the group is organized but usually one to one and one-half hours is a comfortable time period for individual sessions. Group size should be limited to 6 to 10 members for optimum interaction and results. The two basic types of consulting groups are the case centered consulting group and the C-group (Dinkmeyer & Muro, 1971).

Case Centered Consultation Groups

The counselor organizes case centered consultation groups when specific problem situations or cases arise that need the immediate attention of out-side resources to facilitate resolution. Persons involved in these groups in-clude significant others who have some direct relationship to the problem situation or person being discussed. Additional members should be drawn from resource personnel who have expertise that relates to the problem. The exact membership of the group, however, is dependent on the nature of the initiating problem.

The main focus in these groups is on clarifying the problem and the relationship of each member to it and then, through environmental or systemic intervention involving a plan devised by members, acting to deal with that problem. The counselor's role is to facilitate discussion, contrib-ute to it, and serve as a catalyst in getting the group to deal directly with the problem. The leader should first attempt to orient the group toward expressing their perceptions about the problem. Once understanding and consensus has been largely achieved, the leader then can turn the group to consideration of alternative solutions leading to a specific plan of action (Kirby, 1985). If effectively conducted these groups can have a definite impact on improving communication and developing respect between the various participants.

C-Groups

The C-group, developed by Dinkmeyer and Muro (1971), combines didac-tic and experiential procedures to provide group members with practical, relevant training that is generalizable to their professional lives. This ap-proach is labeled C-group because many of the factors that account for its success begin with C. These components are described as follows:

1. The group *collaborates*, works together on mutual concerns.
2. The group *consults*. The interaction within the group helps members de-velop new approaches to issues or problems. . . .
3. The group *clarifies* for each member what it is he or she really believes and how congruent or incongruent his or her behavior is with what he or she believes.
4. The group *confronts*. The group expects each individual to see their own self, purposes, attitudes and to be willing to confront other members of the group.
5. The group is *concerned* and *cares*. It shows that it is involved. . . .

6. The group is *confidential* insofar as personal material discussed in the group is not carried out of the group.
7. The group develops a *commitment to change*.

Participants in the group are concerned with recognizing what they can really only change themselves. They are expected to develop a specific commitment which involves an action they will take before the next C-group meeting to change their approach to a problem. (Dinkmeyer & Muro, 1971, pp. 272–273)

This type of consulting group is useful for all professionals in the helping fields. Participants can develop their helping skills and work out solutions to common problems. Within the school, it's particularly useful for teachers. The emphasis on the teacher-advisor system in schools for example, stresses the need for teachers to develop their helping and group leadership skills.

The C-group can be an effective method of working with families. It can help parents develop the ability to relate to their children and find creative solutions to their problems. The counselor can use these groups to help these people realize they have much in common with other parents and also have the ability to help each other overcome their problems in raising children. The C-group model is also adaptable to business/industry and professional agencies where supervisors, coworkers and colleagues can be assembled for purposes of addressing common problems and issues.

Growth Groups

Growth groups are organized for the purpose of helping psychologically healthy people become more sensitive, aware, fully functioning, and self-actualized through the use of the group process. Members are assumed to be responsible for themselves and capable of handling ambiguous situations and intense personal interaction. They grow by expanding their levels of personal effectiveness.

A great deal of controversy exists over what constitutes a growth group. Certainly titles are no indication of what is involved in the process. The most common types of growth groups, however, are the sensitivity group or T-group and the encounter group. Although commentaries on each of these groups abound, the terminology tends to be so similar that it is often difficult to ferret out distinctions.

One distinction is that the T-group has a distinct point of origin with the National Training laboratory (NTL) in Bethel, Maine. Therefore it has an eminently traceable history, whereas the encounter group has grown out of a broad range of social and psychological endeavors. Significant contributions have certainly been made by Gestalt psychology, by Carl Rogers, and by Institutes such as Esalen in Big Sur, California, but the encounter movement is still a melting pot in which influences are quickly subsumed. Beyond that distinction, however, the encounter group places its primary emphasis on the individual's growth in the group, while sensitivity groups stress individual learning and learning about the group process as well. From this point on, differences become more a matter of degrees than contrasts. Encounter groups use more confrontation, while T-groups emphasize awareness, sensitivity, and learning about self and others. Birnbaum (1969) affirmed that in encounter groups "emphasis is on direct exposure of beliefs and feelings that usually are not put on public display by individuals. The objective is to stimulate an exchange that is inhibited by a minimum of reserve and defensiveness in order to achieve a maximum of openness and honesty" (p. 83). Encounter groups on the whole tend to be more intense and emotional than sensitivity groups. Encounter groups lean toward a problem oriented focus while T-groups tend to be more process oriented. This focus on process is implied in the definition of a T-group by Bradford, Gibb, and Benne (1964):

> A T-group is a relatively unstructured group in which individuals participate as learners. The data for learning are not outside these individuals or remote from their immediate experience with the T-group. The data are transactions among members, their own behavior in the group, as they struggle to create a productive and viable organization, a miniature society (p. 1).

Similarities associated with all growth groups are numerous. They are characterized by open, close, direct psychological contact that stresses spontaneity, freedom of expression, and intense interaction. The focus is on the here and now action of the group and ambiguity is commonly used to generate interaction. Methods utilize verbal and nonverbal techniques aimed at expanding the members' conscious awareness and zeroing in on their feelings and perceptions. One of the major issues in growth groups is the development of trust so that members can be truly themselves in the group. The time span of growth groups is usually brief but intense, ranging from two week workshops and weekends during which members spend many hours together to ongoing sessions over a specific period of time. Spending hours together without interruption often heightens the intensity of interaction. Finally, growth groups are face to face groups with no organizational structure and no imposed tasks and rely heavily on feedback and reinforcement as the tools for self-learning.

Growth groups peaked in popularity during the mid-1960s and early 1970s and in retrospect created two major issues for the field of group work (Dies, 1985). The distinction between growth and remediation was blurred and many of the leaders particularly of the more intensive group experiences had dubious credentials. Thus the issue of quality control always must be raised with growth groups relative to both the nature of the experience and the leadership.

Vriend (1985) noted the critical importance of this issue by delineating between the encounter group model (model B) and the counseling group model (model A). Encounter groups develop their own norms and content, evolve through inevitable stages, function with a facilitator who guides the process but does not determine its nature, and cause (allow) change in members. Counseling groups presuppose a trained group leader who takes responsibility for and determines the structure of the experience, teaches group members therapeutic group behavior, and bases interventions on a rationale emanating from counseling theory (p. 66). Vriend contended that the training of group leaders must be based on the counseling group model for the profession to survive.

Growth Groups in Schools

The encounter group per se has no relevance to the vast majority of counseling programs in schools because of its intense confrontative nature, its assumption of adult maturity, and the time arrangements required to use it. And the impact of encounter groups is hard to determine. Birnbaum (1969) points out this basic weakness, "Because of the failure to follow through with concrete plans for specific action, it (the encounter group) too often remains a memorable experience, but not one that produces change" (p. 96). Some of the encounter methods, however, are useful to the group counselor and can be integrated into group counseling to the mutual benefit of the members and the group process.

Sensitivity groups also have little general relevance to the school. This is mainly because of the misconceptions people have about T-groups as well as for some of the same reasons noted above. However, in specific situations and in certain clearly defined areas a case can be made for using them. Because T-groups stress both self-learning and understanding of the group process they can help well adjusted students become more cognizant of their own self-characteristics and improve their human relations skills. As a social laboratory, it allows group members to gain insight into their own behaviors, develop better understanding of others, and increase their awareness of processes that help and hinder group action. Schmidt (n.d.) described two basic T-group concepts that give the method advantages:

1. People can learn best about themselves by producing behavior, becoming aware of that behavior, analyzing the behavior and its consequences, and then drawing generalizations.

2. People can learn about their own assumptions and values by being placed in a setting where there is considerable ambiguity. The ambiguity permits them to project their own meanings into the situation and to compare their projections with those of their colleagues.

If counselors do decide to use sensitivity type groups, the best procedure is to label them with a less auspicious title and clarify precisely the nature of the process and its objectives before starting the groups.

☐ Conyne's Typology of Group Work Grid

Conyne (1985) has made an admirable effort to categorize the variety in group work by creating the Group Work Grid presented in Figure 10.2. Responding to the observation that "generally missing from our major texts (on group work) is attention to the range of group experiences available today" (p. x), he created this matrix to conceptualize group work as a means of expanding the horizon of group work and consolidating practical understanding about group work. The Group Work Grid is comprised of two major interactive dimensions: 1) the purpose of the group work intervention and 2) the level of the group work intervention. *Purpose* is further delineated into correction and enhancement and *level* is divided into individual, interpersonal, organizational, and community subcategories. Within the purpose dimension is embedded the process factor of whether the group is personal (psyche-process) or task (socio-process) in orientation. The result is a working model of group typology that has both breadth and depth. Each section of the grid represents a type of group that is explicated in the book Conyne edited and entitled, *The Group Worker's Handbook: Varieties of Group Experience* (1985) to which you are referred for further understanding of both the variety of groups and their specific nature.

☐ Client Populations and Group Work

The interaction between specific client populations and settings is another basis for delineating groups. Each client group and setting flavors the group process with unique dynamics and characteristics that leaders must take into account and work with to generate effective therapeutic impact. The parameters of this book do not allow for explication of the almost endless variety of group possibilities based on population and setting, but Seligman (1982) has made an estimable attempt to present a representative sample. You are referred to his book *Group Psychotherapy and Counseling With Specific Populations* as an adjunctive resource in differentiating group work (Trotzer, 1984). In addition, the *Journal for Specialists in Group Work* has made a conscientious effort to publish articles about group work practice that represent the full gamut of settings, group types, and populations.

☐ Learning Activities

The following activities can be used to compare and contrast the basic characteristics of socio- and psyche-process groups. First, divide the class into small groups of four to eight members. Depending on the number of groups you have, give half the groups a socio-process activity such as the NASA space project and the other groups a psyche-process activity like the here

Intervention Level Emphasis

		Correction		Enhancement	
		Personal	Task	Personal	Task
Individual	Type	Personality Change	Rehabilitation	Personal Growth	Skill Development
	Eg.	*Psychotherapy*	*Remedial Social Skills*	*Personal Development*	*Human Relations Skills Training*
Interpersonal	Type	Interpersonal Problem Solving	Resocialization	Interpersonal Growth	Learning
	Eg.	*Counseling*	*Social Control*	*T-Groups*	*Systematic Group Discussion*
Organization	Type	Employee Change	Organizational Change	Management Development	Organization Development
	Eg.	*Employee Assistance*	*Social Climate*	*Team Development*	*Quality Circles*
Community-Population	Type	Secondary/Tertiary Prevention	Community Change	Health Promotion/Primary Prevention	Community Development
	Eg.	*Manual Help*	*Action*	*Life Transition*	*Futuring*

Intervention Level Emphasis

FIGURE 10.2. Conyne's group work grid.

and now face. Next, repeat the process, reversing the activities. Follow-up discussion should focus on distinctions between and similarities of the two processes. In additional discussion, the class can compare the effects of having one process precede the other. In this way elements of leadership strategy in using these processes can be identified.

NASA Space Project

The materials for this socio-process activity are in Figures 10.3, 10.4, and 10.5. First, administer the decision form (Figure 10.3) individually to each group member. After each person has completed an evaluation of the items, give the group another decision form and read the instructions for Decision by Consensus (Figure 10.4). Instruct the group to fill out the group decision

---

Instructions: You are a member of a space crew scheduled to rendezvous with a mother ship on the lighted surface of the moon. Due to mechanical difficulties, however, your ship was forced to land at a spot some 200 miles from the rendezvous point. During reentry and landing, much of the equipment aboard was damaged and, since survival depends on reaching the mother ship, the most critical items available must be chosen for the 200-mile trip. Below are the 15 items left intact and undamaged after landing. Your task is to rank order them in terms of their importance in allowing your crew to reach the rendezvous point. Place the number 1 by the most important item, number 2 by the second most important, and so on through number 15, the least important.

_____ Box of matches
_____ Food concentrate
_____ 50 feet of nylon rope
_____ Parachute silk
_____ Portable heating unit
_____ Two .45 caliber pistols
_____ One case dehydrated milk
_____ Two 100 pound tanks of oxygen
_____ Stellar map (of the moon's constellation)
_____ Life raft
_____ Magnetic compass
_____ 5 gallons of water
_____ Signal flares
_____ First aid kit containing injection needles
_____ Solar powered FM receiver-transmitter

From "Lost on the Moon: A Decision Making Problem," *Today's Education* (1969). Reprinted by permission.

FIGURE 10.3. NASA decision form.

Research in group dynamics has revealed that the manner in which groups utilize their member resources is a critical determinant of how they perform. In this exercise you are asked to use the technique of group consensus. This means that the ranking for each of the 15 survival items must be agreed upon by each member before it becomes a part of the group decision. Consensus is difficult to reach. Therefore, not every ranking will meet with everyone's complete approval. Unanimity, however, is not a goal (although it may be achieved unintentionally), and it is not necessary, for example, that every person be as satisfied as he or she might be if he or she had complete control over what the group decides.

What should be stressed is the individual's ability to accept a given ranking on the basis of logic, whatever his or her level of satisfaction—and his or her willingness to entertain such a judgment as feasible. When the point is reached at which all group members feel this way as a minimal criterion, you may assume that you have reached a consensus as it is defined here and the judgment may be entered as a group decision. This means, in effect, that a single person can block the group, if he or she thinks it necessary; at the same time, it is assumed that this option will be employed in the best sense of reciprocity. Here are some guidelines to use in achieving consensus:

1. Avoid arguing for your own ranking. Present your position as lucidly and logically as possible, but consider seriously the reactions of the group in any subsequent presentations of the same point.
2. Avoid win-lose stalemates in the discussion of rankings. Discard the notion that someone must win and someone must lose in the discussion; when impasses occur, look for the next most acceptable alternative for both parties.
3. Avoid changing your mind only in order to avoid conflict and to reach agreement and harmony. Withstand pressures to yield that have no objective or logically sound foundation. Strive for enlightened flexibility; avoid outright capitulation.
4. Avoid conflict-reducing techniques such as the majority vote, averaging, bargaining, coin flipping, and the like. Treat differences of opinion as indicative of an incomplete sharing of relevant information on someone's part and press for additional sharing—either about task or emotional data—where it seems in order.
5. View differences of opinion as both natural and helpful rather than as a hindrance in decision making. Generally, the more ideas expressed, the greater the likelihood of conflict will be; but the richer the array of resources will be as well.
6. View initial agreement as suspect. Explore the reasons underlying apparent agreements; make sure that people have arrived at similar solutions for either the same basic reasons or for complementary reasons before incorporating such solutions in the group decision.
7. Avoid subtle forms of influence and decision modification; for example, when a dissenting member finally agrees, don't feel that he or she must be rewarded by having his or her own way on some later point.
8. Be willing to entertain the possibility that your group can excel at its decision task; avoid doom saying and negative thinking.

From "Decision by Consensus," Jay Hall (1969). Reprinted by permission.

FIGURE 10.4. Decision by consensus (NASA).

Little or no use on moon	_15_	Box of matches
Supply of daily food required	_4_	Food concentrate
Useful in tying injured together, help in climbing	_6_	50 feet of nylon rope
Shelter against sun's rays	_8_	Parachute silk
Useful only if party landed on dark side	_13_	Portable heating unit
Self-propulsion devices could be made from them	_11_	Two .45 caliber pistols
Food, mixed with water for drinking	_12_	One case dehydrated milk
Fill respiration requirement	_1_	Two 100-pound tanks of oxygen
One of the principal means of finding directions	_3_	Stellar map (of the moon's constellation)
CO_2 bottles for self-propulsion across chasms, etc.	_9_	Life raft
Probably no magnetized poles; thus, useless	_14_	Magnetic compass
Replenishes loss from sweating, etc.	_2_	5 gallons of water
Distress call when line of sight possible	_10_	Signal flares
Oral pills and injection medicine	_7_	First aid kit containing injection needles
Distress signal transmitter; possible communication with mother ship	_5_	Solar-powered FM receiver-transmitter

From "Lost on the Moon: A Decision-Making Problem," *Today's Education* (1969). Reprinted by permission.

FIGURE 10.5. NASA key.

form based on the discussion in the group. Under no circumstances should individuals change their own answers. After the group has completed the task, give them the key (Figure 10.5) and have them calculate their individual scores by totaling the absolute value of the difference between their ranking and the key's ranking on each item. The instructor can calculate the group score to demonstrate the scoring process. The lower the scores the more accurate the ranking of the items in terms of their practical relevance on the moon. Have the group answer questions such as the following:

1. Was the group or the individual more effective in performing the task?
2. Who emerged as the leader in the group?
3. Who seemed to be the expert in the group?
4. Who talked most and least in the group discussion?
5. Who seemed to get the group to accept his or her opinion most often? How did he or she do it?

You may wish to have members discuss these questions prior to determining their scores and then use the scores as a means of assessing the accuracy of the group's perception.

Here and Now Face

The here and now face (Kranzow, 1973) is a psyche-process activity designed to help members disclose and discuss their feelings and emotions. Instruct the members to draw a face that represents the feelings they are experiencing at the present time. Below the face, have them write a verbal description of those feelings and the reasons for them. The discussion should include both what the feelings are and why they exist in the person at the present time. Some leaders use a format statement like "I am feeling (member fills in what) because (member fills in why)." This activity is a means of generating a discussion of the importance of feelings in our lives and brings the group into personal contact with one another.

Cooperation Squares

Cooperation is one of the key components of any task oriented group, and this activity focuses specifically on the factors involved in working together. Make puzzle squares out of cardboard, following the patterns illustrated in Figure 10.6. Six-inch squares are a satisfactory size. Divide the class into groups of five and give each group a package containing five envelopes with equal numbers of pieces but from different puzzles, (five different puzzles to a group). Then read the following instructions and rules:

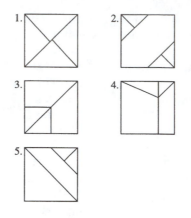

FIGURE 10.6. Puzzle designs.

Directions: In this package are five envelopes, each of which contains pieces of cardboard for forming squares. When the leader gives the signal to begin, it is the task of your group to form five squares of equal size. The task will not be completed until each member has a perfect square of the same size as that held by the other members. The following rules must be followed in working on the problem:

1. No member may speak. The task is to be completed entirely without words.
2. No member may ask another member for a puzzle piece or in any way signal that another person is to give her or him a piece.
3. Members may, however, give pieces to other members.

The instructor's task is to see that the rules are adhered to. Follow-up discussion generated by this activity usually centers around the importance of cooperation and communication in effective group functioning. Conversation may also turn to a consideration of good and bad rules.

Life Picture Map

This psyche-process activity (Kranzow, 1973) is oriented toward helping members develop the time competence perspective so important in self-actualization (Johnson, 1972). Ask group members to draw an illustrated road map that represents their past, present, and future. The map should pictorially depict experiences the members have had, obstacles they have overcome, what their present lives are like, what their goals are for the future, and what barriers stand in the way of accomplishing those goals. Upon completion of the drawings, have the members share their maps with the group, explaining the various illustrations. Follow-up discussion should just be allowed to evolve from a consideration of the pictures.

Paint a Group Picture

This activity essentially combines many of the elements of both psyche-process and socio-process groups. It focuses on the nature of the group itself, its personality and atmosphere, but uses a task approach to do so. Divide the total group into groups of four to eight and supply the subgroups with paper and paints (crayons also will suffice). Ask them to paint a picture as a team that reflects the personality of the subgroup. The picture should be creative and integrate individual efforts. Some leaders require the groups to decide on a group name and sign the picture with it. Materials need not be limited to just paints either. The group can use a variety of media to make a group sculpture or group collage. Discussion should revolve around the experiences of group members in this activity. Feelings of shyness, embarrassment, and artistic inferiority are common. Information about who got the choice spot on the painting, the role of wit, and who emerged as leader also are germane to the discussion. If several groups have participated, each group can present and explain their picture to the rest and describe the interaction that took place.

Eight Topics for Group Discussion

The following eight topics are useful in generating personal discussion in groups and also can be used effectively in determining the locale of problems. The topics can be handled one at a time or in combination. Members can use them in interviewing each other, or they can be incorporated into a general group exercise to stimulate discussion.

1. List three people who have influenced you greatly in your life.
2. Briefly describe three experiences you have had that you feel you will remember the rest of your life.
3. List three things at which you are particularly good.
4. List three things that really interest you.
5. List three things that you would like to accomplish in the future.
6. List three decisions you have made that have changed your life in some way.
7. List three values or beliefs that are important to you and that you live by.
8. List three problems that you have right now that you have not been able to resolve.

The number of things required in each instruction can vary, and directions can be added or substituted depending on the leader's interests and the nature of the group. How each topic is handled is also the prerogative of the leader.

11
CHAPTER

Organizing Group Counseling

Any amount of group knowledge, training, and experience is useless if counselors cannot implement the group process into the framework of their work environments. Even the most conscientious and enthusiastic attempts to use groups will fail if appropriate methods of organizing a group program are not utilized.

☐ Perspective of the Counselor: Outreach

To effectively organize a group, counselors need to develop a dynamic perspective of their role and function. That perspective can be summarized as *outreach*. "Too often, we (counselors) have donned our clinical robes within the safe confines of a remote office and waited for the world to beat a path to our door. The counselor who would work with groups cannot afford the luxury of solitude—it is he/she who must make contact with . . . possible clientele" (Dinkmeyer & Muro, 1971, p. 140).

The counselor must take the responsibility for building a group program based on the knowledge and confidence that the group approach has a great deal to offer. In all probability, most administrators, staff members, and clients will be cognizant of neither the potential of the group process nor the counselor's own expertise in that area.

Another reason for the outreach perspective is to assure the counselor of a solid foundation on which to build a group program. Too often counselors filled with professional zeal have ventured forth on group missions without a clear conception of objectives in mind and have found themselves in the deep water of professional criticism without a lifeboat of accountability to rescue them. To establish groups simply on the merit of the group process itself is not sufficient. As Mahler (1969) pointed out, the fundamental question that must be asked is "for what purpose is this group being organized?" The outreach perspective provides necessary information about the needs of clients in the systems in which they interact so that accurate and clearly defined goals can be established to answer that question. Outreach is the key because it enables the counselor to enter the domain of clients, to penetrate their life spaces, and make contact directly with people and factors relating to their problems. In this manner counselors can not only clarify their own roles and the nature of the group process but also make both of them relevant to their clientele and their environments.

The purpose of this chapter is to provide the counselor with practical methods for setting up a group program. The full gamut of administrative procedures related to group organization and composition are considered. Material for this chapter relies heavily on an experiential basis bolstered by the ever increasing empirical foundation provided by group research. In many cases definitive guidelines for use in organizing group programs remain in a formative state. However, the wealth of clinical knowledge derived from practice provides an invaluable resource in lieu of and in conjunction with research findings (Corey, 1995; Dinkmeyer & Muro, 1979; Gazda, 1984a; Jacobs, Harvill, & Masson, 1988; Mahler, 1969; Ohlsen, Horne, & Lawe, 1988; Yalom, 1995).

Organizational development of group programs is discussed from the perspective of schools or institutional settings and embellished with considerations from agency/practice settings.

☐ Determining the Need

The best way to get a group program off on the right foot is to determine where a need for one exists. Counselors should never organize groups simply because it is part of their professional role or because counselor educators have told them to do so. Groups should only be proposed after the counselor has done some background investigation to determine what the problems are and whether they can be effectively worked with using a group approach. Counselors have many sources of information in this regard, and they should make use of all of them to obtain as comprehensive a picture of needs and problems as possible. In school situations the major sources are students (potential clients), teachers, learning specialists, school psychologists and social workers, administrators, families, cumulative record folders, and databases. In agency/practice settings clients and referral sources such as physicians, pastors, attorneys, and professional colleagues both in and out of your own setting are useful resources. In conducting this needs assessment successfully the counselor must keep two guidelines in mind: 1) the nature of the approach must be outreach, going out to make contact with the various populations and talking with them on their home ground; and 2) the purpose of this contact is to listen and understand not to suggest.

After the counselor has accumulated input and evaluated it carefully, then the time is right for proposals and suggestions.

Potential Clients

Potential clients are the most obvious sources of information and in many respects the most accurate. In schools, of course, the potential clients are students. School counselors can use their normal role contacts with students in guidance and counseling situations to develop a conception of the general concerns and problems of the population they work with. This in itself is not enough, however, since many students will never darken the door of a counselor's office for any reason. The counselor must get out and mingle with students, holding informal conversations with them in the areas where students congregate, such as the student commons, the gym, or hallways. Setting up rap sessions in some classes simply to get student opinions is effective, and even establishing a rap corner or rap room near student gathering places so they can drop by and chat is helpful.

More formal procedures might involve the use of survey instruments. Open ended questionnaires that stimulate reactions (including statements like "the thing I worry most about is . . .") can be used anonymously to tap client opinions of needs. Problem checklists, your own or standardized ones like the Mooney Problem Checklist, can be administered to determine what areas give clients the most concern. In many cases designing the survey instrument yourself is preferable because you can include items that are appropriate to the unique environment in which you work. Another effective method is to use the "agree-disagree" format (see Figure 2.5) and design statements dealing with specific problem areas (like problems with parents) and then let the clients come up with their own conception of the most accurate statements. In these ways the counselor can determine whether the group approach is appropriate or not and for what reasons.

In agency/practice settings one's own caseload is the most viable source of potential group members especially as individual cases emerge that have commonality or needs that are conducive to a group approach.

The importance of understanding the needs of clients before starting groups cannot be overstated. Ponzo (1991) has aptly warned of the dangers of group work that does not address client needs: "Just as nutritious food has no value if it is hostile to the consumer's palate, so too are curative factors or critical factors rendered impotent if they do not match the discriminating wants, needs and desires of our clients" (p. 22).

Faculty/Staff Referral Sources

Another school source of valuable information that often goes untapped is teachers. Yet teachers represent an aggregate of individuals whose cumulative experience in relating to students far surpasses that of any other group. The counselor who cultivates a positive working relationship with them, meets them on their own ground (classroom, faculty lounge, *their* offices, and hallways), and approaches them with a sincere interest in learning from their experience will find the results beneficial. Counselors can use many approaches to obtain vital information from teachers. They can ask permission to attend various department meetings and listen as they discuss students and problems related to their particular areas of interest and expertise. Organizing voluntary rap sessions during coffee breaks and free periods also can be effective. Socializing with them is still the most accepted and best informal way of making contact. Some counselors have developed suggestion boxes so students and teachers can express their concerns and ideas to the counselor. Developing this relationship with teachers helps them feel more a part of the process of organizing the group program rather than feeling it is imposed on them. They begin to be supportive of it rather than threatened by it.

In agency/practice settings directly contacting referral sources to solicit their input as to the types of problems that need attention can be very productive. Once referral sources realize your interest and emphasis is emanating from their input, both your relationship and your client referrals will improve.

Education Specialists

Other resource groups of vital importance in the school are the education and learning specialists. Specialists in learning disabilities and giftedness, school psychologists, social workers and other adjunct educational staff can be polled for input relative to the clientele they serve and problems they address. Attending Individual Education Planning (IEP) meetings, parent conferences, community agency consultations, and other such interactive meetings can provide critical information about special problems and special populations.

Administrators

Sitting down with school administrators for a few minutes of straight talk will usually produce positive results. Administrators inevitably have a pet group of students they are particularly concerned about (usually because they are a pain in the neck, represent the educational system's failure to work, or are a threat to it). If the counselor approaches the administration indicating an interest in helping and a concern for the students, administrators will usually respond, even if they have reservations about counseling or the group process. The counselor must be careful not to make any promises at this point, however, since that might create expectations that are unrealistic. The information received should be contemplated for a time before the counselor returns with positive suggestions and alternatives. Counselors who approach administrators this way often realize greater respect and support from the administration. Administrators soon realize the counselor is making efforts to help students and also to improve the efficiency and effectiveness of the school. Colleagues and administrators in agency/practice environments can provide the same type of input as school officials.

Families

Families represent another source of information for counselors. Counselors in schools find students' parents especially helpful, but more difficult to contact than other sources. The counselor can make use of incidental contacts with parents to garner their opinions and can use the consultation function with parents to do so as well. Questionnaires, preferably brief, can be sent to parents and usually result in an adequate percentage of returns. The counselor's participation in parent programs, parent nights, and parent school organizations (for example, parent teacher associations) is a valid use of counselor time. Counselors can organize sharing/discussion sessions around topics related to student problems, use the "agree-disagree" strategy, and conduct surveys as part of the regular agenda. In any case, families should always be considered as a crucial source of information, since their perspectives are definitely a factor in many of the concerns clients will express in counseling groups.

Cumulative Record Folders and Data Bases

Within schools, counselors can find information in student cumulative folders and data bases that is valuable to needs assessment with respect to groups. The best approach is to do it in an organized manner, using a specific set of criteria for determining problems. If the counselor can organize guidelines for the kind of data being looked for, an aide can do the work of tabulating. Using cumulative folders can often become tedious and yield minimal results, especially if a scatter gun approach is used. The advent of computers and electronic record keeping, however, has greatly enhanced accessibility and efficiency. The best method is to define specific problem behaviors or student characteristics and then accumulate frequencies based on comments and data in the student records. However, with the change in public records laws this source of information may become less informative and less useful.

Examples of data that provide cues to needs that groups may address are demographics on single parent and remarried families where adjustment factors related to death or divorce and blended family living are prominent. Children who are coded as exceptional (learning disabilities or giftedness) often manifest adjustment issues, absences, or other characteristics which may signal problems.

Once the counselor has accumulated information from all these sources and evaluated it, a decision can be made, based on needs, as to how groups can be used and what specific problems will be addressed. At this point the counselor is ready to take the next step of setting goals and recontacting the various groups to inform them of program proposals.

☐ Establishing Goals

Goals are extremely important to group counseling because they provide a direction for both the leader and members and supply an appropriate yardstick for assessing the value of the group experience. They fall into two major categories—general group goals and specific individual goals. *General goals* refer to the overall objectives of the group and are the basic reasons for which it is formed. *Specific goals* are those directly related to individual members and their personal lives. The relationship between the two has been expressed by Dinkmeyer and Muro (1971): "The group counselor and the group must be flexible enough to allow individuals to work on personal concerns, and broad general goals of the group must not be so rigid that the individual is sacrificed to some theoretical construct" (p. 139).

The most important consideration is to determine if group counseling is the most appropriate means of dealing with problems revealed by the needs assessment. Then the counselor must make sure that goals are in accord with and matched to the needs of clients. The counselor's professional judgment must be utilized in this process. Mahler (1969) pinpointed a number of situations that lend themselves to individual counseling, group counseling, or both; they provide useful guidelines in making the decision to use group counseling. These situations are detailed in Figure 11.1. Counselors are not to view group counseling as a cure all; however, they are to make specific professional decisions for or against its use. In this way the possibility of success is enhanced and the usefulness of the group approach assured.

Some of the general goals that have relevance to group counseling are as follows:

1. To develop relationships that will help individual members meet their developmental and psychological needs;
2. To help members in their identity seeking process (Mahler, 1969);
3. To help members change undesirable behaviors (Dustin & George, 1973);
4. To help members develop social skills and resolve problems in social relationships;

Individual counseling tends to be more appropriate:

1. When the client has a crisis problem that is very complicated, both as to causes and possible solutions.
2. When confidentiality is highly essential to protect the client and others.
3. When working through the meaning of test results in terms of one's self-concept.
4. When fear of talking in a group is so extreme that the person does not seem to be able to get started in the group.
5. When an individual is grossly ineffective in relating to his peers and sets off such a strong immediate reaction that the group is more likely to be rejective than acceptant.
6. When a person's awareness and understanding of his or her own feelings, motivations, and patterns of behavior are very limited or so complicated that he or she feels lost and unable to share in a group.
7. When sexual behavior, particularly of a deviate nature, is involved.
8. When one's need for attention and recognition is too extreme to be managed in the group situation.

Group counseling tends to be more valuable in the following areas:

1. Learning to better understand a variety of other people and finding out how others perceive things.
2. Learning a deeper respect for other people, particularly those who are different in many ways from oneself.
3. Gaining greater social skills in talking and relating to others.
4. Learning to share with other people, especially gaining a deeper sense of belonging from participation in a group in which one is a respected and accepted member.
5. Being free to talk about concerns, problems, values, and ideas with others who are facing similar situations.
6. Getting several persons' reactions to one's problems and concerns.
7. Finding support from a group of peers, which is often of greater value to a student than support from an interested adult.
8. Giving each person an opportunity to spend more time with a counselor.
9. Being able to involve oneself rather slowly in the counseling process and to withdraw partially if a discussion becomes too threatening.
10. Giving the counselor a chance to see clients in a broader and more active social setting than individual sessions provide.

FIGURE 11.1. Situational guidelines for use of individual counseling, group counseling, or both.

Both group and individual counseling tend to be equally valuable in the following areas:

1. Being accepted as a worthwhile individual.

2. Being responsible for one's own behavior.

3. Deepening the understanding one has of human behavior.

4. Being able to explore wider variations in one's emotional life and gaining greater confidence in the control of one's emotions.

5. Increasing one's self-confidence and trust in one's own perceptions.

6. Gaining strength to be an individual in one's own right.

7. Examining one's interests and values and moving toward integrating them into a life plan.

From *Group Counseling in the Schools,* C. A. Mahler (1969). Reprinted by permission.

FIGURE 11.1. Situational guidelines for use of individual counseling, group counseling, or both (*Continued*).

5. To help members increase their acceptance and understanding of self and others;
6. To help members deal with an identified and specified problem area they have in common;
7. To help members develop self-confidence and self-responsibility in directing their own lives;
8. To help members deal with concerns and problems related to the educational and vocational decision making process;
9. To help members examine feelings, attitudes, values, and ideas about themselves and their world; and
10. To help members learn new and desirable adaptive behaviors (Dustin & George, 1973).

Certainly many more general goals could be identified, but these are sufficient as examples. Individual goal definition comes later in the process, when group members actually begin to prepare for and interact together in the group. Once these general goals are defined, the counselor must orient all concerned people to the nature of specific and general goals and the group process in order to enlist group members' support and cooperation.

☐ Orienting Significant Others

The principal purposes of orienting significant others are to help them understand the nature and intent of the group process, clarify misconceptions, answer questions, and generally obtain their support and cooperation. Orientation should certainly include all parties who were contacted during the needs assessment period of the organizational plan. They deserve to know what use you have made of the information they shared and in most cases are seriously interested in the suggestions you have developed. Orientation regarding the group process, its nature, and its goals should encompass the vast majority of staff members, referral sources, and, if applicable, the families of those selected for participation.

Counselors have a variety of options available to orient staff members in a school situation. They can organize inservice programs, make presentations at staff meetings, or contact members individually or in small groups (at department meetings). Methods should involve presentation, explanation, and preferably demonstration with a follow-up period allowed for questions. Important topics for orientation might include advantages of the group process (Chapter 2), rationale for group counseling (Chapter 3), the nature of the group process (Chapters 4 and 5), the role of the leader (Chapter 6), ethics and best practices in group work (Chapter 8), and distinctions between types of groups (Chapter 10).

Demonstration is a particularly useful mechanism because staff members have an opportunity to observe the group process firsthand. Organization of a live demonstration group composed of former group members is a useful method for orienting significant others (staff, administrators, parents) to group process and dynamics. This type of procedure may be a bit threatening because the counselor is automatically subjected to evaluation by colleagues. Also, if the group members are from the same school as the staff being oriented, members may feel some anxiety because they are under the scrutiny of past, present, or future teachers. On the other hand former group members are typically the best advocates for group work which tends to counter the anxiety factor. One way around this is to use a videotape that has been properly edited. In any case, the consent of participants must be obtained before proceeding. (If the group members are minors, the written permission of their parents is obligatory.) Another option is to use staff members to role play a typical group counseling session. Staff members thus can experience directly the dynamics involved. A mini-demonstration involving the use of a specific group exercise also may suffice. Finally use of commercial videotapes can also be incorporated into staff orientation (Carroll, 1985; Stockton, 1992).

Whatever approach to orientation is chosen, specific things need to be communicated. Dinkmeyer and Muro (1971) enumerate them:

1. Teachers should be aware of the nature of groups—of how and why students are selected and what their goals are.
2. Faculty members should be aware of the necessity of confidentiality.
3. Teachers should understand that the primary purpose of the group is not to promote a systematic attack on the school, the staff, or society at large.

4. The organizational and mechanical steps of group organization should be explained to the faculty.
5. The counselor should make his or her point of view known to the staff, especially in terms of group composition.
6. The faculty should know that wherever possible the counselor will report back to them on the group's progress. (pp. 141–142)

Generally speaking the same ideas apply to orienting families with the one difference being that they may be more wary and concerned than staff members. Parents can be invited to the school for presentations and demonstrations, met with individually, or talked with over the phone. Sometimes information sent home in the mail is sufficient. But when group members are minors, precautions always should be taken to obtain written, informed consent from parents.

☐ Orienting Potential Clientele

The purposes of orienting potential clients are to help them understand the nature and goals of group counseling, to answer questions, and to elicit and nurture an interest in participation. Zimpfer (1991) in a review of literature pertaining to pretraining and orientation of group members identified three general objectives: 1) clarification of expectations; 2) presentation of guidelines for group participation, and 3) provision of models for effective behavior in groups (p. 264). Bowman and DeLucia (1993) explicated these objectives stipulating the purposes of preparation as: 1) to establish rapport, allay "excessive" anxiety and orient clients to the group; 2) to assess the client's psychological dynamics and interpersonal skills, and 3) to establish therapeutic goals, expectations and a problem focus (p. 68).

Basic forms of orientation are *cognitive*: provision of information; *vicarious*: observation of role models or examples; *experiential*: involvement in a structured experimental activity, and a *combination* of all three (cognitive-vicarious-experiential). These forms can be incorporated into both dyadic and group orientation formats (Bowman & DeLucia, 1993).

Based on the premise that member preparation is an essential task of the group therapist Bowman and DeLucia (1993) conducted a study to determine the impact of preparation relative to enhancing group effectiveness and preventing drop outs. Results of the study 1) supported the positive impact of preparation on client attitudes, beliefs and expectations about group therapy; and 2) confirmed the combination of information, vicarious exposure, and opportunity to practice (cognitive-vicarious-experiential) as the most effective form of preparation. These findings support Korda and Pancrazio's (1989) contention that competent and adequate preparation is one of the key factors that limits negative outcomes in group work.

In a practical sense one of the most effective ways of reaching students in schools is to give presentations in classes that all students must attend. For example, in the high school the counselor can make a presentation in each grade level's English classes. In this way two purposes are served: 1) students are familiarized with the group process and its probable benefit to them; and 2) students increase their general knowledge of the counselor's role and function. This type of systematic approach ensures consistency in presenting group information because counselors can prepare duplicated and audio visual materials to complement a presentation and utilize all the formats described above. Typical topics that could be covered in these presentations are the nature and process of group counseling (Chapters 2, 4, and 5), the role of the group leader (Chapter 6), the role of the group member (Chapter 7) and ethics in group work (Chapter 8). Questions also should be dealt with as they arise. A key part of these sessions should be a mini-demonstration, in which class members participate in a brief but effective small group activity. Many of the activities listed at the end of most chapters of this book lend themselves well to demonstration. In this way students are given not only a cognitive introduction to the group process but an experiential one as well. Another element of a class presentation should be a sign up sheet that members can fill out to indicate their interest in participating in a counseling group. A similar sheet also should be available in the counselor's office for those students who decide to volunteer at a later date. Nelson (1971) warned that volunteers should not be obtained by a show of hands in these presentations because of the possible reactions to popular or unpopular students' actions in responding and the importance of protecting privacy of prospective participants.

The counselor can use regular guidance and counseling contacts to spread the word about group counseling, but, as has already been stressed, this alone is insufficient. Effective orientation of staff, administration, and parents yields positive results because they inform potential clients of the group possibility and may even refer them. Another vehicle is to use the announcement approach, where concise clearly worded blurbs are passed out in classes, posted on bulletin boards, or run in the school newspaper stating that a certain type of group is being organized and that interested students should check with the counselor. Although this smacks a bit of the advertising syndrome, catchy phrases, creative designs, and art forms will attract attention and produce results. One counselor got together with the art department and produced some very effective posters that attracted a substantial number of inquiries and an eventual commitment to group counseling by one-half of those who inquired. Finally, some counselors have mobilized technological resources to set up a Web page where announcements of groups can be posted and a chat room where questions about group counseling can be addressed.

Regardless of the approach used to orient potential clients, some essential items should be included. Muro and Freeman (1968) described them as follows:

1. Students should be told in simple terms about the nature of group counseling. It may be helpful to inform prospective counselees that participants will be given an opportunity to learn more about themselves, their plans, and the ways other students see them.
2. Prospective group members should know that group meetings are confidential and the topics discussed in groups are not for general discussion outside the group meetings.
3. Students should be informed that they are not joining a therapy group. Students frequently associate any type of counseling activity with those who are in some way unhealthy.
4. The counselor should prepare a schedule of the times she or he has available for working with groups. Within this limitation, the number of meetings a week and the duration of counseling should be a topic to be decided after the groups have been formed.
5. Students should know whether or not volunteering to participate would mean they would be selected as group members. It is best to inform teachers and students of the number of students the counselor wishes to have in a group and how the final selection will be made if the number of volunteers is too large.
6. It is beneficial to inform the students that those who wish to participate may be interviewed individually. This will give the counselor an additional opportunity to make decisions about placing the student in a group. In addition, students may wish to ask the counselor personal questions about group participation that may be embarrassing to ask in a class size group (pp. 314–331).

If the counselor has adequately performed the needs assessment and orientation steps, then the time is appropriate to proceed to the actual organization of specific groups. Note that although my primary emphasis is on group counseling, other types of groups described in Chapters 2 and 10 also may be called for at this point. If so the counselor must make the proper administrative arrangements and proceed in the manner prescribed by the nature of the group. For group counseling, however, further organizational steps are usually required before the groups actually convenes.

☐ Selection and Preparation of Group Members

Selection and preparation of group members go hand in hand in the minds of most writers and practitioners (Dinkmeyer & Muro, 1979; Gazda, 1984a; Mahler, 1969; Ohlsen, Horne, & Lawe, 1988) because they are both associated with a pregroup individual interview with prospective group members. Once clients have indicated an interest in participating in group counseling, a good idea is to schedule them for an interview on an individual basis. The important areas of emphasis during this interview should be 1) client expectations, 2) counselor assessment, and 3) client commitment. Corey and Corey (1987) state that the key screening question for the group leader in the pregroup interview is: "Should this particular *person* be included in this particular *group* at this *time* with this *leader*?" (p. 81).

Client Expectations

Purposes of the interview from the client's perspective are to ask questions and develop realistic expectations about the group process. Ohlsen (1970) stated that "clients profit most from a counseling group when they understand what is expected of them before they decide whether to join" (p. 82). They should be informed that responsibility to change and help others change is part of their commitment and that they will be expected to work toward the "mutually aligned goal of personal\social growth" (Dinkmeyer & Muro, 1971, p. 38). Clients should be given an opportunity to describe problems with which they hope the group can help. They should be told that the group will engage in free and honest expressions of feeling and that members will have the opportunity to discuss their own and others' problems constructively. In addition, every effort should be made to dispel any myths the member may have regarding group counseling (Childers & Couch, 1989). If group leaders are interested in eliciting change in group members, clients must be truly ready for constructive group participation.

Counselor Assessment

From the counselor's perspective purposes of the screening interview are to evaluate the client's readiness for group counseling, develop that readiness if it's not present, gather information that will facilitate selection and placement, and generally get to know the client. The counselor's role is not to counsel the client at this point but rather to clarify the nature of the group process and to obtain data that will facilitate decisions in regard to the client's group participation. The counselor's professional judgment is involved here. The impact of each client on other individuals as well as on the total group must be considered. Counselors must keep in mind various factors discussed later in this chapter to facilitate placement of selected members in the most beneficial groups. Generally the counselor must try to determine how each client will best fit into group counseling and organize various groups around that knowledge.

Client Commitment

Nelson (1971) indicated that three steps exist in securing commitment from potential group counseling members. The first is the indication of interest in participating. The second is the individual interview. And the third is arrival at the group session. Of the three he felt that the individual interview may be the most vital. Ohlsen (1970) emphasized the importance of commitment, stating that "those who profit most from group counseling recognize and accept the need for assistance and are committed to talk about their problems, to solve them, and to change their behavior when they are accepted for group counseling" (p. 80). The screening interview should facilitate the securing of this type of commitment.

A pregroup, group meeting is another commonly used screening device. Potential group members are brought together as a group to orient them to the purpose and process, assess their readiness for group counseling, and elicit their commitment. The advantage of this procedure is that the group leader gets a first hand opportunity to assess the interpersonal competence of each member with respect to their ability to function effectively in a group.

Sometimes individual or pregroup group interviews are not convenient or time does not permit them. In that event a wise procedure is to use the initial group session for group screening during which the same objectives and information just discussed are considered. In fact, some group leaders prefer not to have pregroup interviews so as to avoid preconceived attitudes that have a tendency to form as a result of them. These counselors prefer to handle problems of readiness and commitment as they emerge in the group and to use the group as an arena and resource for dealing with them. In most cases however, the counselor will be wise to make some type of pregroup contact, if only to waylay some of the grossly destructive factors and misconceptions that will undoubtedly hamper group progress.

☐ Group Composition Factors

In some respects the group counselor is like a baker who must put together all the right ingredients in the proper proportions in order to come up with a satisfactory product. There are certain factors that must be weighed in the organization of any group. Too much of one thing or too little of another can cause problems. No magic formula exists for putting together all the right ingredients in their proper amounts. Research has not fully delineated specific guidelines either. But practical experience, combined with investigative efforts of researchers has revealed some tendencies the professional counselor as developmental scientist and clinical artist can use to organize groups that are catalytic to therapeutic change (Roark & Roark, 1979).

Homogeneity Versus Heterogeneity

The issue of homogeneous and heterogenous groups was already posed in Chapter 10 in discussing common problems groups and case centered groups.

Both types have advantages and disadvantages, but the counselor who is working with a normal range of clients doesn't have to take a stand at any one particular place on this issue. A more appropriate procedure is to maintain a flexible attitude, making decisions based on the nature of the problems and clients being worked with. Commonality certainly enhances identification and facilitates the cohesive development of the group. But too much similarity can spoil the process and lead to boredom, stagnation, and disinterest. Bach (1954) noted that heterogeneity gives members the experience of learning to relate to different kinds of people. Unger (1989) affirmed this notion stating, "If group therapy is to help one prepare for everyday realities of life, it seems ultimately desirable to emphasize its heterogeneous aspects" (p. 156). However, Mahler (1969) warned that too wide a variation may create problems in communication and relationship formation. Nelson (1971) and Dustin and George (1973) took a more middle of the road perspective and advocated that groups should include some members who have different concerns. All things considered, balance seems to be the key. Groups should have enough diversity to generate interest but also enough commonality to help members feel comfortable and identify with one another. Certain groups that deal with specific concerns like disruptive behavior may tend toward homogeneity, whereas other groups that deal with a broader category of concerns like social competency may be more heterogeneous in nature.

Where clients are in their efforts to deal with an issue also may affect whether homogeneous or heterogeneous groups are more appropriate. For example, McBride and Emerson (1989) noted that for adults molested as children (AMACs), homogeneous groups are more appropriate during the initial phase of treatment because discomfort is eased. However, if clients are further along in their progress, say at the point of dealing with the fact of having been abused (past the denial and denial break through phase) then a more heterogeneous group may be more appropriate.

Counselors must find their own solutions to this issue relying on research, clinical experience, and client input to develop the type of experience that will be most beneficial to the group members and the group's purposes and that will accommodate the counselor's personality and leadership style.

Age and Maturity

For most counseling groups, generally, an advisable procedure is to put members together who are roughly the same age. For noneducational, adult groups this is less important but still a factor. Most practitioners agree that maturity more than age is the key, but leaders hesitate to group on this basis because the specifications of maturity levels have not been clearly delineated. Dinkmeyer and Muro (1971) felt that for organizing groups of children more attention should be given to developmental factors than to chronological ones. Ohlsen (1970) made a far more comprehensive assertion that social maturity is simply more important than age. Until clearer guidelines are established by research, the counselor is generally warranted in using age guidelines in the placement of group members but should temper them by restructuring groups that have obvious inequities in social maturity. Members tend to be more comfortable in their own age groups because of the importance of peer relationships. Any variation of this type of grouping should be done with specific purposes in mind (for example, putting teenagers and parents together to increase communication, connectedness and understanding) or to effect certain special treatment procedures in the group (for instance, using socially competent seniors as models for sophomores who lack certain social skills). On the other hand, some of the most effective, fascinating, and dynamic groups I have led have occurred in working with adults in graduate school and private practice and with children and adolescents in inpatient settings. A broad range of ages were represented, contributing diversity that made these groups complex and resourceful.

Gender

The literature contains general consensus that same gender groups are preferable for preadolescents and mixed gender groups are more appropriate for adolescent and adult groups. Ginott (1968) felt that mixed gender groups were appropriate for preschool children since no compelling reasons exist to separate them. But for school age children he firmly adheres to same gender groups because boys and girls are in the process of developing their masculine and feminine identity. The mixed gender group has merit because it is a more natural environment with immediate relevance to the outside world and is a safe but effective way for males and females to deal with their problems and further their normal social-emotional development (Ohlsen, 1970).

   Mahler (1969) supported the ideas expressed here but did note particular situations that call for one or the other of the gender groupings. Groups organized to work with discipline problem clients are more effective if they include only same gender members, whereas, social problems groups should definitely be mixed. He also pointed out that when counselors are in doubt regarding the gender grouping of clients they should consult the clients. In most cases especially from adolescence on up the inclusion of both sexes stimulates interest even though it may also be a bit threatening to members. The relational developments that result from group interaction between the sexes are valuable regardless of the specific goal for which the group was formed.

Other Factors

Additional factors to consider in the selection and placement of group members are 1) verbal ability, 2) diversity characteristics and personality, and 3) prior acquaintance and friendship. *Verbal ability*, especially its potential, must be assessed so that extreme differences do not interfere with the communication process in the group. If ability is comparable the more expressive members can model verbal behaviors for less expressive members; drawing out a quiet person can be an appropriate goal for a group. But if members who lack verbal abilities and skills are placed with those who verbalize with ease, it can be a very frustrating experience. In fact, if members with low verbal ability are put on the spot by the leader or other members, they can suffer extreme embarrassment which can lead to withdrawal or aggression and cause untold damage to their self-concepts. The best procedure is to work with these members in groups of their own and occasionally admit carefully selected models until they have upgraded their skills and self-confidence.

To consider *diversity characteristics* and *personality* requires a tremendous amount of counselor time and sensitivity but is important as a basic criterion for selection and placement. Understanding the nuances of various cultural, environmental, family, ethnic, racial, and personality factors and their impact on group interaction is a difficult but important task. Diversity is a topic that is addressed in detail in Chapter 9 by Merta. Benefit will result from giving serious attention to these factors prior to the commencement of the group in an effort to address factors that might generate difficulties in the group. Differences, especially those related to culture, ethnicity, and race, should not be a reason for excluding members but should be noted as factors that affect group interaction and have beneficial potential to group members. DeLucia-Waack (1996) stated that "multiculturalism is inherent in all group work and in fact enhances the effectiveness of all group work" (p. 222). Since understanding self and others is an important goal for any group, cultural background, diversity, and personality differences definitely contribute to the broadening of that understanding. In individual cases, however, decisions may have to be made to redirect or omit a person from participation in a specific group based on characteristics that preclude effective adjustment and involvement in that group.

Prior acquaintance and friendship can be touchy subjects in member selection. In some instances including friends in the same group has adverse results because they tend to support one another in a cliquish manner, which deters the group process. Prior friendships also make contact outside the group a more critical and influential factor that can be disruptive and undermining. In addition, including friends in the same group also may have detrimental effects on their friendship. On the other hand, the group can benefit from members whose friendships are the support needed to help them reveal and work on their problems. The group also can improve friendships by helping members learn behaviors that are conducive to deeper understanding and better communication. The best way to decide on this factor is to obtain additional information on the individuals and their friendships and develop clear ground rules relative to outside the group contact and discussions. Rittenhouse (1997) cites the dynamics of feminine psychology which emphasizes relationship as a critical factor in self-esteem and healing as a basis for contact between members outside the group for purposes of support and accountability. To frame such contact therapeutically, however, three parameters must be implemented: 1) contact is voluntary; 2) contact is reported to the group, and 3) contact is not destructive/harmful to the person or disruptive/harmful to the group process.

   In some respect to expect that groups be composed of persons who do not know each other is unrealistic because in many situations groups are composed of persons who relate to each other for some reason and therefore do not qualify as being strangers. The group counselor needs to be concerned with relationships that may interfere with the group process, and in most circumstances even these can be worked with in the group.

   The counselor's main concern regarding these factors is to develop a reasonable balance in the group's composition to facilitate the helping process rather than detract from it. If members are included who function reasonably well in small group situations and if extreme variations are avoided, the resulting effect will most likely be positive.

☐ Technical Considerations

In addition to the various selection and placement factors the group counselor also must be concerned about several technical factors that can enhance the group's effectiveness. Decisions and strategies in these areas affect the nature of the group. These factors also affect the group's initial reaction to the leader, influence effectiveness, and establish the boundaries within which the leader will operate. The major technical factors of group organization are discussed in the following subtopics.

Voluntary Versus Forced Participation

Counselors must make a basic decision about the kind of group member they wish to work with in each group that is organized. The three basic types are volunteers, forced volunteers, and forced participants (nonvolunteers). *Volunteers* decide to participate of their own volition or on the basis of group counseling information they have received from presentations, friends who have participated, or other sources. The volunteer is most likely to benefit from group counseling. Johnson (1963) indicated that clients who are experiencing pain and seek help on their own are easier to work with than those who have been coerced by family or friends. Ohlsen (1970) also affirmed that the volunteer is more apt to profit than the nonvolunteer, and Mahler (1969) maintained that for this reason the decision to partici- pate should be left up to the individual. The counselor who works with volunteers is much more likely to experience success. Volunteering is also an effective means of ensuring commitment since these members take re- sponsibility for thrusting themselves into the interaction of the group. Thus the success of the group process is more assured with volunteers, but the extent of its impact in terms of numbers is limited. Many clients who could benefit from the group process will not freely volunteer, and if counselors restrict themselves to volunteers they will be limiting their effectiveness.

Forced volunteers are like "Mr. or Ms. In Between." They have professed their interest in participating but only because they were cajoled, bugged, or directed to do so. They enter the group under the guise of their volun- teering but experience great ambivalence because of the pressure that was used to help them decide to participate. Forced or prompted volunteers may represent an obstacle in the group because they are hiding behind the facade of willing participation which translates into resistance or because they adopt a passive aggressive posture relative to group pressure. Thus they must resolve their dissonance in regard to being in the group in addi- tion to trying to resolve their problems. With forced volunteers more time must be spent in the initial stages to lay a groundwork of trust and accep- tance. If handled carefully these members can convince themselves that the decision was in their own best interests no matter what its genesis was and then they will commit themselves to the process. But if pushed too fast and too hard they may regret the decision and negate all efforts of the group to help them.

Mahler (1969) advocated required participation for certain clients (for example, acting out boys). He felt that involuntary attendance should be required whenever "group counseling is being used to help people who are causing trouble or having difficulty adjusting to a situation in which they find themselves" (p. 60). The counselor must decide whether the effort of working with *forced participants* will result in positive change or have dimin- ishing returns. Realizing that the returns may be less than hoped for and tend to be in contrast to volunteer groups, the counselor may still be able to work effectively with groups composed of forced participants. Gazda (1968) summarized the whole issue of voluntariness:

> An individual must either have or be capable of developing a desire to change at the time he/she enters a group. Involuntary clients can be assisted, how- ever, if they remain in counseling long enough to experience the beneficial effects of the process (pp. 268–269).

Basically the decision about which kind of group members counselors wil work with is between two main types: 1) members who volunteer and 2 members the counselor feels the group process can help. On the basis o these two criteria counselors can organize all their groups. The only pre-cautions are that selectivity is still important among volunteers and that the counselor must be willing to admit that group counseling cannot help everyone (Childers & Couch, 1989).

Open Versus Closed Groups

Another decision the counselor must make is whether the group will be open or closed. In open groups old members leave and new members rotate in as the group per se continues. In closed groups the same members stay together from the beginning to the end. Both types have advantages, but counseling groups in schools have the tendency to be closed groups. Dinkmeyer and Muro (1971) gave one good reason for this: "A group must develop, it must move through or pass through certain phases for optimal effective-ness. Such movement requires time and a sense of cohesiveness" (p.148).

The introduction of new members can impede this process of develop-ment because it automatically places members at different developmental levels process wise. If the decision is made to open a group to a new mem-ber, the leader should discuss it first with the group and make the integra-tion of the new member the responsibility of the group. The introduction of a new member should be done on a one at a time basis so that the group can more easily absorb the new person without experiencing a great deal of pressure and causing undue regression in the group's development. Cer-tainly adding a new member will cause some growing pains, but if it's done on an individual basis and if a good therapeutic rapport exists among mem-bers, the impact will be slight. In fact, the new member's development will probably be accelerated, and initiating a new member can be a positive experience for the group as well.

In contrast, in agency/practice settings, open ended groups are more typi-cal and practical due to the ebb and flow of case loads and client turnover. More than one member may be added at a time but two or three should be the maximum as three already represents a significant minority with sub-grouping propensities that could undermine the group process. Addition-ally, in inpatient settings where groups meet more frequently or even daily, open ended groups are more common.

In most cases, however, staying with a set group membership is prefer-able because it facilitates the feeling of togetherness, which enhances iden-ification and cohesiveness and helps the group move in a more consistent developmental manner to its culmination point. Within a closed group the possibility is higher that all the business of the group will be finished—new, unfinished, or old—while in an open group new members always introduce new business and their entrance into the group may effect changes that prevent old business from being fully completed. (Frederick S. Perls, Gestalt psychologist and well-known group therapist, used the terms new business, unfinished business, and old business in reference to the material considered in group therapy and encounter group sessions.)

Group Size

No magic number determines the absolute effectiveness of the group counseling process, but reasonable considerations necessitate limiting group size. Roark and Roark (1979) recommend a size range of 5 to 12 members. For practical and therapeutic reasons, however, counseling groups should be limited to 10 or fewer members. Mahler (1969) stated:

> The main dangers of groups with more than ten members are that some members may not get adequate attention or be able to participate fully, that others can avoid involvement, that the counselor may have difficulty giving adequate attention to each member, and that the group may tend to become more of a class than a counseling session (p. 55).

For adolescents and adults, groups of 6 to 10 can be handled effectively by a leader. That size of a group is large enough to maintain interest due to the diversity in the group, gives members an adequate opportunity to participate, and yet is large enough for members to feel safety in numbers. For children, groups of four to six are more appropriate. Mayer and Baker (1967) indicated that the size of groups for children should vary with the age and maturity level of the counselees. Although some group experts stress a specific number, generally the group leader must decide what a workable group size is. This decision should be based on the counselor's own effectiveness and comfort in various sized groups and on knowledge of group members. In most cases the 10-member limit should be adhered to, and therefore the decision applies mainly to establishing what the minimum size will be. My own clinical experience has indicated that the most intense, effective, satisfying and interesting interaction has occurred in groups of five to eight members.

Time and Frequency of Meetings

Roark and Roark (1979) delineated time into calendar time and clock time. *Calendar time* refers to the schedule of group meetings, and *clock time* refers to the length of individual sessions. The optimal frequency of sessions and length of individual meetings have not been definitely established. Both tend to conform to the administrative structure within which the group is formed. In schools individual sessions mirror the length of class periods, and frequency tends to be established on the basis of student and counselor availability. Mahler (1969) stated that groups should meet at least once a week for a minimum of 10 sessions, although urgency may require more frequent meetings. Dinkmeyer and Muro (1971) suggested twice weekly meetings, reducing or increasing frequency with the development of the group. Based on a review of research, Roark and Roark (1979) recommend that closed groups meet twice weekly over a 10 week span. The more often the group meets the greater the tendency to be cohesive; however, members should have time between group sessions to reconsider group interaction, prepare themselves for the next session, and simply relax and unwind. Relative to frequency, weekly sessions are still the most common.

As far as length of each session is concerned the class period approach is practical for schools but isn't necessarily ideal for the group process. Class periods tend to be too short because groups need the first 10 to 15 minutes to warm up and settle down to the work of the group. This time is important and should not be eliminated. Although members can be made aware of it and can work to reduce the amount of time needed for warm up, work time in the group often gets limited to 20 to 30 minutes depending on the length of the class period.

The preferable time period for group counseling is one and one-half to two hours. With more flexible scheduling procedures in some schools the possibility increases to set this amount of time aside for group counseling without raising havoc with the student's schedule. However, the class period is still the primary unit at this point, so the leader should see that groups begin and end promptly. This facilitates maximum use of time and good public relations with other staff members since students don't show up late for their classes. For children, shorter time periods are appropriate, ranging from 20 minutes to an hour depending on the attention span of members and the practical learning and administrative requirements of members' classroom environments.

In agency/practice settings scheduling relative to clock time is not a problem. However, when in the day group sessions are scheduled is crucial. Prime group time is one and one-half to two hours in the late afternoon or evening which is the most convenient time slot for children, adolescents, and adults who must coordinate school, work, and family schedules.

The number of sessions again depends on the goals of the group and the nature of the members. Quarters, semesters, and school years do provide some natural time periods for groups to meet, but they should not be rigidly subscribed to. Interestingly enough, however, even in agency/practice settings clients tend to think and behave on the basis of school year time frames. At least 10 to 12 sessions are necessary for groups to develop a substantial therapeutic group process, and more are preferable. Members need to be informed of the termination date of sessions so they can pace their work accordingly and do not get left in midstream. Even when groups continue on an open ended basis, the advisable procedure is to give members a couple of weeks notice before disbanding, and to have a guideline for departing members to notify the group two to four weeks prior to termination.

Scheduling

In school situations, scheduling is consistently one of the group counselor's biggest headaches, especially if group counseling does not enjoy the support and cooperation of administration and staff. Dansby (1996) simply states that "lack of time and lack of access to the students remain the primary obstacles to conducting groups in schools" (p. 238). For this reason the counselor must do a good job of orienting significant others and networking and developing a positive working relationship with teachers as a preventative and facilitative measure. Whenever possible group meetings should be scheduled during students' free periods or in conjunction with a relevant curriculum offering, such as a "knowing me" class. A second strategy is to rotate meeting times so that students don't miss the same classes all the time. Mahler (1969) suggested an additional strategy for groups organized to help troublemakers. He suggested that groups should meet during the period when the trouble normally occurs. In any event, arranging schedules should take into account both the members' and the counselor's obligations and responsibilities and should show a concern for the perspective of significant others. Clearly relate the schedule to members, stressing the necessity of staying with the schedule but allowing enough flexibility to make justified exceptions.

In agency/practice settings clients' schedules rather than agency or practitioner schedules create the scheduling obstacles. Most of the resistance relative to engaging in and committing to the group is worked through by addressing the scheduling issue. (Scheduling and payment issues are on par with each other for raising and working through resistances.)

Physical Arrangements

To say that the room makes the group, would be an exaggeration but it does help. The physical setting is a significant factor and especially influences the nature of group interaction during the early stages when the development of rapport and establishing member comfort are important. Mahler (1969) stated that the group room should be small but large enough to accommodate everyone without crowding. It should have sufficient privacy so that the group neither distracts others nor is distracted by others. Nothing is more disruptive than to have to compete with noises outside the group and nothing is more embarrassing than having an outsider, especially someone members know, enter the room in the middle of a personal discussion. Muro and Freeman (1968) recommended that the same room should be used for each meeting since roaming seems to hinder group progress. The decision to meet around a table or without one, to use chairs or sit on the floor (with pillows, cushions, or bean bags) is up to the leader and the group. Having a suitable facility is a big help in this regard.

Roark and Roark (1979) extended physical arrangements to include the way in which the room is set up and people are seated advocating a circle format as most conducive to effective group interaction. Donigian and Malnati (1997) also place much emphasis on physical arrangements dynamically in their discussion of proxemics (the physical and emotional distance between members and leader) (pp. 17–19). The decor of the room can contribute to members' comfort, but the leader always must be on the lookout for group members using the setting as a resistance ploy or an excuse not to become involved. No matter how poor the facility is, my experience has been that the group interaction can overcome any physical setting barrier if members develop a supportive milieu and concentrate on each other and the purposes for which they are meeting.

Summary

The basic steps in establishing a group program are as follows:

1. Determine the needs of the clients, utilizing as broad a range of resources as possible.
2. On the basis of the needs assessment determine the relevance of group counseling and establish general goals for which groups are to be organized.
3. Orient significant others in order to help them understand the group process and enlist their support and cooperation in organizing the group program.
4. Orient potential clientele to clarify the nature of the group process and its benefits to them and solicit their interest in participating.
5. Select and prepare group members, preferably on the basis of a screening interview in which questions are answered, assessments are made, expectations are developed, and commitment is obtained.
6. Develop specific groups, taking into account the group composition factors that will result in the most tenable helping relationships. Organize groups in accordance with the specific technical qualities that facilitate positive interaction.
7. Hold the first group meeting.

Learning Activities

De-Mythologizing Group Work Activities

Note: The ideas and contents for the following activities were derived from the Childers and Couch (1989) article entitled "Myths about Group Counseling: Identifying and Challenging Misconceptions."

The scales and activities described below can be used in training group leaders by making use of both scales or in prescreening procedures with prospective group members as a means of generating questions and discussion about prospective group participation. The members' scale has also been useful in initial group sessions to stimulate discussion of member expectations.

Group Member Perception Scale

Provide prospective group members or group members with the scale in Figure 11.2 and have them rate their perception of each item according to the directions.

Individual Members (PreGroup Screening Interview). Review each item with the prospective group member discussing his or her rating and the meaning of it relative to his or her expectations and perceptions of group counseling. Use the statements to explore the member's expectations and as a means of orienting him or her to the nature of the group process.

Group Process Activity. Have group members share their ratings item by item and facilitate a discussion of expectations, perceptions, and concerns that leads to a discussion of group ground rules. A follow-up task is to have the group develop a list of their own reflecting realistic perceptions and characteristics of group counseling.

Group Leader Perception Scale

Provide prospective group leaders or leaders in training with a copy of the scale in Figure 11.3 and ask them to rate the items according to their perception of group counseling and group work. When all participants have completed the rating, have them share their ratings with each other and facilitate a discussion processing the information for the purpose of developing statements which reflect a realistic perspective of groups and group process. The final objective is to have the group compile a list of statements that the group agrees with and which reflects the reality of group dynamics, process, and theory.

Directions: Please read the following statements that represent typical thoughts or feelings people may have about counseling groups. Examine each statement carefully and circle the rating that most accurately represents your thoughts and feelings as you anticipate becoming or being a group member.

My view of this statement is that it is:

Very Inaccurate VI	Somewhat Inaccurate SI	Not Sure NS	Somewhat Accurate SA	Very Accurate VA

Stimulus Statement	**Personal Rating**				
1. Counseling groups are for sick people.	VI	SI	NS	SA	VA
2. Counseling groups force people to lose their identity.	VI	SI	NS	SA	VA
3. In counseling groups you "gotta spill your guts."	VI	SI	NS	SA	VA
4. Group counseling is a second class treatment process.	VI	SI	NS	SA	VA
5. Counseling groups tear down psychological defenses.	VI	SI	NS	SA	VA
6. Counseling groups are confrontative, hostile, and attacking.	VI	SI	NS	SA	VA
7. All counseling groups are "touchy-feely."	VI	SI	NS	SA	VA
8. Counseling groups are artificial and unreal.	VI	SI	NS	SA	VA
9. Counseling groups are environments for brainwashing.	VI	SI	NS	SA	VA

Note: Items adapted from Myths about Group Counseling: Identifying and Challenging Misconceptions, J. H. Childers & R. D. Couch, *Journal for Specialists in Group Work* (1989).

FIGURE 11.2. Group member process perception scale.

Directions: Please rate the following statements about group counseling. Examine each statement carefully and circle the rating that most accurately represents your thoughts and feelings as you anticipate becoming or being a group leader.

My view of this statement is that it is:

Very Inaccurate VI	Somewhat Inaccurate SI	Not Sure NS	Somewhat Accurate SA	Very Accurate VA

Stimulus Statement		**Personal Rating**		
1. Everyone benefits from a group experience.	VI	SI	NS	SA	VA
2. Leaders can compose groups to assure effective outcomes.	VI	SI	NS	SA	VA
3. The group revolves around the "sun" of the leader.	VI	SI	NS	SA	VA
4. Leaders can direct change through the use of structured exercises.	VI	SI	NS	SA	VA
5. The medium of change in groups is an emotional here and now experience.	VI	SI	NS	SA	VA
6. The majority of learning in groups comes from self-disclosure and feedback.	VI	SI	NS	SA	VA
7. One can work effectively with groups without understanding group process and dynamics.	VI	SI	NS	SA	VA
8. Changes in intensive small group experiences are not maintained over time.	VI	SI	NS	SA	VA
9. Discussion of racial-cultural differences will offend group members.	VI	SI	NS	SA	VA
10. Groups can be truly homogeneous.	VI	SI	NS	SA	VA
11. Group member differences do not affect process and outcome of task groups.	VI	SI	NS	SA	VA
12. Group work theory is appropriate for all clients.	VI	SI	NS	SA	VA

Note: Items 1–8 are adapted from Myths about Group Counseling: Identifying and Challenging Misconceptions, J. H. Childers & R. D. Couch, *Journal for Specialists in Group Work* (1989). Items 9–12 are adapted from Multiculturalism is Inherent in all Group Work, J. L. Delucia-Waack, *Journal for Specialists in Group Work* (1996).

FIGURE 11.3. Group leader perception scale.

12
CHAPTER

Evaluating Group Counseling

Evaluating group counseling is pivotal to both the individual group experience and the ongoing group program. Rapin and Conyne (Chapter 8) and ASGW's Best Practices Guidelines (Appendix C) emphasize the critical importance of evaluation by making a specific place for it in planning, performing, and processing group work. Evaluation is particularly important to the group practitioners in the field who wishes to determine whether group counseling is effective or not and who may need such information not only to enhance the quality of the group experience but to justify the viability of groups as a helping modality.

The purpose of this chapter is to examine evaluation from a practical perspective and provide the rationale and resources to assist group workers in effectively evaluating their efforts. Both process and outcome evaluation will be considered and specific techniques and tools will be described. The chapter will culminate with an illustrative group counseling example reflecting in an integrative manner some of the material presented in chapters 10–12. Learning activities will conclude the chapter.

☐ Basic Assumptions

In presenting evaluation as the focus of this chapter the following basic assumptions were made to insure that a practitioner oriented perspective was maintained.

1. Professional counselors are primarily interested in the impact group counseling has in their own settings, and global answers to group questions though relevant are of secondary importance.

2. The typical counselor in most settings does not have the wherewithal in terms of time, interest, skill, and access to financial resources or multi-disciplinary professional expertise needed to conduct significant group counseling research.
3. Group counseling is an effective procedure in helping clients resolve their problems but evaluation is necessary to denote its specific impact.
4. Effective evaluation practices in individual settings will create fertile ground and a solid data base for formalized, extensive, and specific research projects in group counseling.
5. Effective evaluation procedures will—in and of themselves—contribute significantly to the expanding experiential base necessary for conducting successful group counseling.

☐ Methods of Evaluation

The group counselor must develop evaluation procedures that are relevant to counseling via the group process. Just as classroom teachers develop evaluative practices in accordance with subject matter and teaching methods and businesses develop marketing analysis procedures commensurate with their products, so counselors must construct evaluation procedures appropriate to their area of expertise. In doing this the counselor can learn much from the experiences and findings of researchers since many of the factors which undermine research also undermine evaluation. By eliminating or at least decreasing error factors and paying particular attention to specificity, effective evaluation can be implemented. The following discussion describes various procedures to help the counselor assess both the process and the outcomes of group counseling.

Process Evaluation

Process refers to what goes on in the group and has three components: the leader, the members, and the group interaction (Donigian & Malnati, 1997). Efforts to evaluate group process are designed to increase understanding of group dynamics and to help counselors improve effectiveness in utilizing the group as a helping vehicle. Evaluation of process is generally associated with observation, analysis, and feedback. Specific goals include 1) determining leader methods, attitudes, and characteristics to assess the effectiveness of approach; 2) determining member attitudes, reactions, and characteristics to better understand the effect of the group on the individual; and 3) identifying the focus and themes of group interaction to establish their relevance to the goals of the group and its members. Various methods discussed in the following paragraphs lend themselves well to process evaluation.

Expert Evaluation

One method of process evaluation is to ask colleagues or other professionals who have expertise in group counseling to observe your group sessions and give you feedback. This can be done either on a consistent basis as in a supervision relationship or on a selective basis where the expert is asked to observe when the group is at an impasse or not going well. The leader then uses the observer as a resource in finding ways of improving the group interaction. If colleagues are used, follow the procedures detailed in Chapter 6. To prevent distractibility, have the observer watch the group by an indirect means such as a one way mirror or by closed circuit TV. Some counselors have found that observation by a group of experts followed by a roundtable discussion with the leader is professionally growth producing.

Member Process Observer Evaluation

Another method that is gaining wide acceptance is appointing a group member to be the process observer and rotating the responsibility through the group membership as the group progresses. Brief training in process observation is usually necessary but once in motion this approach adds immensely to the group experience. Input from the process observer during the group, at the end of group, and on an impromptu basis stimulates the group and gives each member an additional learning experience as well.

Member Evaluation

Another source of process evaluation is the group participants themselves. Who is really better qualified to evaluate process that those who are affected by it? Some counselors use what might be called 3 × 5 evaluation methods. This format involves giving members 3 × 5 cards at the end of each session and asking them to write down their honest impressions or appraisal of the session. They also may include suggestions for improvement. An alternative is to have cards or sheets printed with a number of descriptive continuums to which members can respond by circling the rating that best represents their reaction to the group (for example, a seven point scale of boring to extremely interesting). The cards (filled out anonymously) are collected by the leader and used to help assess the group's development in an ongoing manner.

Some leaders ask members to keep journals or logs of their reactions to each group meeting, turning them in at the succeeding session (Yalom, 1995). This procedure tends to give a more comprehensive picture of the group process but creates a disadvantage because the counselor is always a week behind. This can be rectified if members are willing to turn in their logs at a time prior to the next meeting. Then leaders can make use of the material and adjust their approaches accordingly. Another option is to simply collect the journals at the end of the entire group process as a learning device for future reference.

Yalom (1995) suggested the use of leader process summaries dictated immediately after each session, typed, and distributed to members between sessions as a means of evaluating group process, facilitating flow from session to session, and extending the depth of group interaction. Group members also can take on this task as a means of presenting their view of the group process.

Evaluation of Audio and Video Replays

The most extensive method of process evaluation uses either recorded or videotaped replays of group sessions. Certainly no better way exists for analyzing one's actions and the interaction of the group than to review and reexperience the action to get a clearer understanding of the process. The major disadvantage of this approach is time. Busy counselors seldom have the opportunity to go over sessions without sacrificing some other aspect of their jobs or personal lives. For this reason tapes tend to be used extensively in training but seldom on the job. One means of circumventing the time problem is to listen to sessions or excerpts that the leader feels left something to be desired, involved a crisis, was particularly therapeutic, contained vital information, or represented significant disclosure. A good idea is to get members used to being recorded so that it doesn't become a disruptive element. Some counselors make the mistake of introducing the tape recorder or videotape at crucial points in the process that they want to look at more closely. They bring the recorder or video camera to the session for the first time and then are surprised when the interaction is completely different. Whether you listen to the sessions or not, get the group accustomed to being taped so you can use the recordings if the need arises. These recorded sessions also can be used to stimulate professional discussion and obtain constructive feedback at staff meetings if permission has been obtained from group members for supervision purposes.

Interaction Evaluation

A more formal method of evaluating the group process is for counselors to familiarize themselves with a group interaction scale such as Bales (1950) Interaction Analysis Scale, the Hill Interaction Matrix (Hill, 1966) or Simon and Agazarians's (1974) Sequential Analysis of Verbal Interaction (SAVI). For extensive discussion of these and other formal instruments of evaluation the reader is referred to DeLucia-Waack (1997b).

Scales can be used by counselors to analyze taped sessions on their own or counselors can train observers to use them. In either case the scales can be used to quantify interaction patterns and evaluate them qualitatively. The conscientious use of these sophisticated methods can yield valuable results for the counselor's own understanding of the group process and as a guide to productive group interaction (Zimpfer, 1986).

Group Themes

The group process can be assessed effectively on the basis of themes or topics the group considers. Bates (1966) and Muro and Denton (1968) first introduced this evaluation procedure with adolescent and college student populations. A theme is a "point of focus in the group's interaction with a clear beginning and stopping point" (Dinkmeyer & Muro, 1971, p. 111). Identification of these themes gives the group leader a solid basis for determining whether the group is engaging in meaningful goal oriented interaction or not. If not, the leader can exert influence to get the members to do so.

Process Evaluation Scales

Two process scales have been developed from material in this text. The Leadership Process Evaluation Scale (Figure 12.1) is constructed from information pertaining to leadership skills found in Chapter 6. The Member Process Evaluation Scale (Figure 12.2) is constructed from descriptions of members' behaviors in Chapter 7.

The Leadership Process Evaluation Scale is helpful in assessing the nature and effectiveness of the counselor as a group leader. Each leader response is observed and identified on the basis of the various skill categories. The impact of that response is then evaluated on a five point scale of Very Effective (5) to Very Ineffective (1). By accumulating frequencies of each skill, leaders can determine the characteristics of their leadership roles, functions, and styles. By calculating means based on the evaluation ratings leaders can determine their effectiveness in using each skill and on an overall basis. Group leaders can use this information to improve their skills and cultivate the use of skills they deem more helpful. They can clearly determine whether they are making appropriate progress in the use of their skills.

The Member Process Evaluation Scale is useful in helping the group leader evaluate the behavior of individual members. It also depicts characteristics of the group interaction at any one point that can be related to the process of group development. Each member should be given an ID number to facilitate the evaluation process. Then members' behaviors are observed and identified according to the categories listed on the scale by placing the member's ID number in the appropriate column. Other than exceptions noted on the scale each member behavior is recorded in the incidence column. Accumulation of behavior frequencies depicts the interaction in the group and tabulation of each member's behaviors results in a profile of that person's participation. Information from this scale helps counselors understand the members and the group process better and gives them definite

Instructions: Observe the group leader, noting each response he or she makes. Identify that response as representative of one of the skill categories listed on the scale. Place an X in the Incidence (*I*) column each time you observe an identifiable skill. Then note the impact of that response by rating the response in the Effectiveness (*E*) column on a 1 to 5 scale:

5 Very Effective: Helpful to the group process and person(s) involved
4 Effective: Helpful to either the group process or person(s) involved
3 Appropriate but neutral in impact
2 Ineffective: Inappropriate or distracts group process or person(s) involved
1 Very Ineffective: Distracts group process and impedes person(s) involved

Be sure to identify each response and evaluate its impact. Frequencies of each skill can be calculated by tabulating the marks in the *I* column. Leader effectiveness means can be determined for each skill as well as on an overall basis by adding the ratings in the *E* column for each skill and across all skills and dividing by the appropriate frequency.

Note: Counselors who use this scale should attach an addendum describing each skill for reference purposes. This information can be obtained from Chapter 6.

Leadership Process Evaluation Scale

I = *Incidence*   5 Very Effective
E = *Evaluation*   4 Effective
3 Neutral
2 Ineffective
1 Very Ineffective

Session No. _____

Skills	I	E	I	E	I	E	I	E	I	E	I	E	I	E	I	E	Freq.	Ave.
Reaction Skills																		
1. Restatement																		
2. Reflection																		
3. Clarification																		
4. Summarization																		
5. Tracking																		
6. Scanning																		
Interaction Skills																		
7. Moderating																		
8. Interpreting																		

(Totals: Freq. / Ave.)

FIGURE 12.1. Leadership process evaluation scale.

	Totals																	
Skills	I	E	I	E	I	E	I	E	I	E	I	E	I	E	I	E	Freq.	Ave.
9. Linking																		
10. Blocking																		
11. Supporting																		
12. Limiting																		
13. Protecting																		
14. Consensus taking																		
Action Skills																		
15. Questioning																		
16. Confronting																		
17. Personal Sharing																		
18. Modeling																		

Leader Effectiveness Mean _____

FIGURE 12.1. Leadership process evaluation scale (*Continued*).

areas that need to be worked on in the group. It also indicates when the group atmosphere is becoming more therapeutic and less resistant and manipulative.

Process evaluation is perhaps the easiest type of evaluation to do. It concerns itself only with what is happening within the confines of the group interaction and does not concern itself with external matters. The process, however, is only important as it relates to the impact witnessed outside the group. As Dies (1985) indicated, one of the bridges that must be built in group research and practice is the bridge between process and outcome. Our attention therefore must turn to the outcomes of group counseling because only in the context of external results is the value of the therapeutic process validated.

Outcome Evaluation

Outcome is what happens in a group member's life as a result of experience in group counseling. Outcome shows how goals, purposes, and objectives for which the group is organized are manifested in terms of change or impact in group members' feelings, thoughts, and behaviors. The degree to which that change occurs determines the relative success or failure of the group process. Evaluation of outcomes is a difficult task because neither the treatment nor the subjects can be adequately controlled, and the evaluation criteria are

Instructions: Provide each group member with an ID number to assist the rating process (e.g., numbers 1–8 or letters A–H for an eight member group). Observe the group interaction, identifying member behaviors according to the categories listed on the scale. Note the incidence of the behavior by placing the member's ID number in the Incidence column each time the behavior occurs. Except for those exceptions noted on the scale, there must be a member ID number recorded for each behavior that can be identified. When the group is completed, total the incidence numbers for each behavior category by counting the number of ID entries in that category. This gives you the frequency of the behavior in the group session. A behavior profile can be developed for each group member by plotting the number of times a member's ID number appeared in each behavior category.

Note: Counselors who use this scale should attach an addendum describing the characteristics of each behavior for reference purposes. This information can be obtained from Chapter 7.

Member Process Evaluation Scale

Session no. _____   Number of Members in Group: _____

Member Behaviors	Incidence	Total
Resisting Behaviors		
1. Monopolizing	_____	_____
2. Excessive Talking	_____	_____
3. Hostility	_____	_____
4. Silence #	_____	_____
5. Withdrawal	_____	_____
6. Absence 0	_____	_____
7. Cross Talking	_____	_____
8. Intellectualizing	_____	_____
9. Old Pro	_____	_____
10. Joker	_____	_____
11. Housekeeper	_____	_____
12. Help Rejecting Complaining	_____	_____
13. Self-Righteous Moralizing	_____	_____
14. Rescuing	_____	_____

FIGURE 12.2. Member process evaluation scale.

Member Behaviors	Incidence	Total
Manipulating Behaviors		
15. Socializing		
16. Scapegoating		
17. Dependency		
18. Submissiveness		
19. Aggression		
20. Criticism		
21. Domination		
22. Mothering		
23. Calculating		
Helping Behaviors		
24. Listening #		
25. Facilitating		
26. Leading		
27. Self-Disclosure		
28. Giving Feedback		
29. Leveling		
30. Keeping Conficence #		
31. Personalizing Communication		
Emotional Behaviors		
32. Venting Negative Feelings		
33. Physical Aggression		
34. Acting Out		
35. Crying		
36. Affection		

\# Behaviors labeled with this sign may be recorded as a group behavior as well as an individual member behavior by simply recording the sign each time the group engages in the behavior.

0 Absence need only be recorded once per session designating those members not present by ID number.

FIGURE 12.2. Member process evaluation scale (*Continued*).

often difficult to define. If change is observed the question of whether it was caused by the group is moot, and if no change occurs, one wonders if the criteria were valid or if the method of evaluating was appropriate.

Despite the difficulty, group counselors can do much to make evaluations of outcomes meaningful and concise in their own settings. It can be done by heeding the various warnings researchers have proffered, by making evaluations an inherent aspect of the group counseling program, and by designing evaluation procedures specifically related to clients, the setting, and the nature of the counseling group. Some of the basic considerations of effective outcome evaluation are discussed in the following subtopics.

Importance of Goals

Although we have discussed goals in regard to organizing group programs, I must emphasize them further here because goals are the roots of effective outcome evaluation. This topic is introduced with an appropriate quotation and warning from Ohlsen (1970):

> A counselor may be tempted to use vague general goals, to select for groups only clients with some common goals, and to ignore individuals' unique goals when appraising clients' growth. . . . Such errors often account for a counselor's failure to obtain significant results when he (or she) tries to assess outcomes of group counseling. Carefully defined, precise goals stated in terms of measurable or observable outcomes are necessary if the counselor is adequately to assess changes in clients (p. 43).

He continued by advising that group counselors should learn from the behavioral counselors:

> They have not attempted to improve the global adjustment of clients. They have merely focused their attentions on one or two precise behaviors, for which they usually have adequate measuring devices to assess predicted changes (p. 255).

Group counselors should address themselves to measuring change in individual members rather than on a total group basis. In this way individual assessment will add up to a composite of group change. Cohn (1967) advocated this approach, considering it the easiest way to demonstrate change as a result of group counseling. Specific goals for individuals in groups must be developed so that evaluation is on an individual basis leading to a cumulative group effect. In other words, *general group goals are important in organizing a group program, but specific individual goals are necessary to determine outcomes.* This perspective is intrinsic to counseling since "counseling's worth rests on the notion of furthering individual development and helping individuals face and learn to deal with painful and distressing problems. Therefore appraisal must focus on individual change" (Ohlsen, 1970, p. 256). Dinkmeyer and Muro (1979) add that each group member should be afforded the opportunity to define and clarify goals that are unique to them within the context of the group.

So the message is clear: to evaluate outcomes of group counseling accurately we must develop individual goals within the group process. With this in mind let's turn our attention to implementation. Some counselors use the screening interview to help clients identify individual goals they wish to work toward in group counseling. Members then come to the first session with certain goals already specified. If this method is used, a natural initiating activity during the first session is to have members share their goals as a means of getting acquainted and establishing a work oriented attitude among members.

Another approach used in brief, solution oriented group counseling is to have members come to group with a detailed description of a problem they wish to solve or issue they wish to resolve. Solutions are then generated in group which upon implementation solve the problem or resolve the issue (based on member reporting data) (Trotzer, 1998c; in press).

Other counselors structure goal setting sessions into the group counseling process, during which each member discusses and selects specific goals on which to work. In this case not only are the counselor and the client aware of the person's goals, but the rest of the group is cognizant of them as well.

Once individual goals are clarified and established, an excellent evaluative device is the behavioral contract (Dustin and George, 1973). Members are asked to specify in writing the actions they will take in an effort to achieve their goals. This contract negotiated in the group is then signed by the client and counselor and witnessed by the group. Each can receive a copy of the others' contracts so that the group can monitor progress and determine if a client successfully fulfilled the contract obligation. It also has built in evaluative criteria and implies or even denotes evaluation procedures. As such its use is recommended as a procedure for outcome evaluation.

Another evaluation method that has great promise and utility for assessing individual change in counseling and therapy groups is called *Goal Attainment Scaling (GAS)* (see Figure 12.3). Developed by Kiresuk and Sherman (1968) and adapted to group counseling by Paritzky and Magoon (1982), GAS is a standard score device which translates any group member's goal into a measurable form using a 5 point scale from minus 2 (much worse than expected) to plus 2 (much better than expected). This procedure requires each group member to identify specific, concrete, measurable, problem solving goals they want to attain. The individual's goal is then represented as 0 (expected outcome) and serves as the target for which the member is to strive. A reasonable unit of variation from the target is determined to complete the scale in increments of 1 unit per integer above and below the target. Progress is then periodically assessed by the members and leader. The overall objective is to demonstrate progress and ultimately to be on target. This procedure allows for individualized group member goals and

Name: _____

Goal Statement: (expected outcome) _____

_____

_____

Scale Value	Scale Level Descriptor	Specific Problem Solving Behavior
+2	Much better than expected outcome	
+1	Better than expected outcome	
0	Expected outcome	
−1	Worse than expected outcome	
−2	Much worse than expected outcome	

FIGURE 12.3. Goal attainment scaling (GAS).

provides a means of clearly identifying progress. Combining GAS scores across all group members demonstrates the overall effectiveness of the group counseling process.

Self and Other Reports

Two important sources of outcome data are the clients themselves and those important others who have extensive contacts with them. If change occurs, it must be recognized by the party who changes and by those with whom that party interacts and relates. Cohn (1967) identified the distinguishing quality between self-reports and other reports of client changes when he wrote, "In both cases subjectivity operates, but in one case it is subjectivity of the (clients) involved, and in the other the subjectivity of a not-so-interested observer" (p. 31). In other words, self- and other reports tend to have inherent bias due to their subjective nature, but this in no way precludes their importance to the evaluation of outcomes. In fact, these reports are really front line evaluation procedures because of their kinship to the group process itself. Since group counseling is a people oriented process, its effects have people oriented meanings. Thus the counselor should be immensely interested in whether clients themselves think they have changed and whether others around them concur. Ample evidence is available to indicate that what one thinks and perceives affects what one does. These thoughts need to be gotten out in the open as a means of gaging the influence of the group process on members and to assess the reception of significant others to member changes. Once reports have been obtained their validity or invalidity can always be tested.

The self-report can take many forms ranging from feedback given directly to the counselor or group to the use of instruments like Q-sorts, rating scales, semantic differentials, or personality inventories. The general purpose is to provide a self-based evaluation of the client's experience or change. In many cases researchers have found that no changes were noted on formal criteria (such as standardized instruments) but that group members reported positive reactions to their experience (Trotzer, 1971; Trotzer & Sease, 1971). Thus the self-report can serve an especially important function if discrepancies are found or if no changes are evident on selected formal criteria. If discrepancies occur, the counselor must investigate the possible causes which often leads to productive changes in the group process, individual members, or both. If no changes are noted on other criteria counselors are compelled to reassess their criteria in light of positive self-reports of group members.

As far as other reports are concerned, Ohlsen (1970) pointed out that "when counseling is effective, important others should notice some of the changes in behavior and attitudes" (p. 258). If those around the client perceive changes, most likely the change has been extensive enough to overcome the normal expectations that tend to resist acknowledgement of change. If others notice it, most likely it exists. But this prompts an additional motive for using self- and other reports. Sometimes changes clients make have an adverse effect on their relationships with important others. Cohn (1967) stated that counselors must find out whether "changes in growth in a given member act as a freeing device for other persons to whom he (or she) significantly related or whether individual growth will cause a disruptive pattern in his (or her) group relationship outside of counseling" (p. 19). In the latter case the group member may need assistance in coping with problems generated as a result of efforts to change. Such input addresses the systemic nature of the change process reflecting the resistance to change or the acknowledgement of change in the client's world outside the group, both of which are critical to an individual member's success in implementing changes in their life.

Those persons involved in these evaluative reports are generally the clients themselves, parents, and other family members, teachers, coworkers, colleagues, supervisors, and selected peers both in and out of group. The counselor can use formal or informal methods in obtaining their reports. An informal method might entail devising a brief rating sheet that concentrates on the specific problem area the client is addressing and administering it periodically to the client and selected significant others. A comparison of the raters' perceptions of changes can then be made. This procedure is advantageous because it alerts those around the client to the client's efforts and generates more positive expectations. The balancing effect of both the client's and others' perspectives counters bias. *Note*: When using significant others or any outside referent, be sure to build in appropriate release of information mechanisms.

Other useful methods of acquiring significant other reports are Q-sorts, semantic differentials, rating scales, open ended questionnaires, and structured face to face interviews. These procedures enable respondents to express their personal perspectives relative to the change process and provide a basis for determining whether change has occurred in the interpersonal realm of the member's experience. In most cases it is preferable to use methods involving both self- and other perceptions in order to obtain a more comprehensive, balanced and accurate evaluation of change.

Outcome Criteria

The selection of criteria for the evaluation of outcomes must be done in accordance with the points already considered. The criteria must be adaptable to the individual goals of the client, not the client to the criteria. Criteria must be specific and observable or measurable so that it can be validated. For groups conducted in schools, Cohn (1967) added another guideline that criteria "should probably be limited to variables that can be demonstrated to have some rather direct bearing on the child's school performance" (p. 32). A more general application of this idea is that criteria chosen should have a direct impact on the client's performance in the setting in which the group is organized and in the client's living environment. However, tangential criteria should not be excluded if they pertain to the individual goals of the client.

Cohn (1967) delineated two kinds of criteria, behavioral and affective (including attitudes, feelings, and values), both of which have relevance to group counseling. In schools the most readily available criteria are the educational variables of grades (in specific classes), grade point average (GPA), and a host of standardized tests (especially achievement and aptitude). Numerous other tests and inventories also can be called on to measure a variety of other variables. Examples include acceptance of self and others (Berger, 1952), self-concept (Tennessee Self Concept Scale-Counseling Form, Fitts, 1965), dogmatism (Rokeach, 1960), and many other personality type measures. (See also DeLucia-Waack, 1997b).

Before counselors choose to use any of these or other criteria they must ask the following questions:

1. Is this criteria merely convenient or does it actually measure a relevant variable?
2. Can this criteria be related to the individual goals of the clients?
3. Is change in a positive direction on these criteria indicative of change that results in problem resolution?
4. Can results be described simply and clearly to the client and significant others?
5. Will results reflect the influence of the group counseling process?

If criteria are selected in this manner, the counselor will have a creditable basis on which to support claims regarding the efficacy of the group counseling process.

Follow-up Procedures

Probably the most serious concern in the helping professions is whether positive change that is realized at the end of treatment is maintained over time. A related question is whether a latent effect occurs that generates positive change sometime after the treatment is completed. These same questions plague the group counselor. Mahler, (1969) felt that "if we use immediate criteria measures the outcomes of a short group counseling program might be somewhat superficial" (p. 210). He stressed therefore that follow-up is more important than immediate results. Cohn's (1967) guidelines also emphasize that delayed evaluation is preferable.

The follow-up idea is extremely important in evaluation of group counseling outcomes. Counselors should make every effort to maintain contact with their former group members over an extended period of time to keep tabs on whether changes (actual or professed at the close of group counseling) have been integrated into the client's life style. This need not take an inordinate amount of time. But contact either personally or by questionnaire should be made, and data should be tabulated for reference purposes. Some counselors follow a general routine of contacting ex-group members after three months and again after six months. Others operate on a more casual basis with no specific schedule. They simply keep in touch with group clients over a period of time. Another method is to reconvene the entire group periodically for follow-up sessions to find out how members have progressed. These sessions often turn into extremely interesting and revealing interactions. In any event, the extent to which changes are retained is a good indicator of the potency of the group process in helping individuals resolve their problems.

☐ Summary

The key to effective evaluation of group counseling is to relate process and outcome. An overemphasis of one or the other therefore will be detrimental to both (Krause & Hulse-Killacky, 1996). A philosophy of multiple assessment will greatly increase the reliability and importance of evaluation procedures. Obtaining data and feedback from a variety of relevant sources serves to clarify the nature of the group process and delineate its effect on the group members. The three principal concepts to keep in mind are 1) make evaluation an inherent and established part of a group program; 2) develop relevant general goals based on assessed needs for organizing groups, but concentrate on specific individual goals to assess outcomes; and 3) utilize evaluation results to improve the group process, increase the expertise of the group leader, and establish group counseling as an accountable procedure in helping people solve their problems.

☐   Illustrative Group Counseling Example

An Interpersonal Problem Solving Group in a Mental Health Center

The counseling group described below took place in a mental health center (Trotzer, 1985). The group consisted of eight adult members, five female and three male, and was facilitated by a male-female coleadership team. All group members were referred to group counseling by their individual therapists at the center. Group members had become involved in individual therapy for a variety of reasons but were referred to the group to work specifically on the interpersonal dimensions of their lives. The group met for a total of 30 hours including an intake/orientation interview, an exit interview and 14 two-hour group sessions over a four month period.

Overview of the Group Process

Orientation/Intake Interview

The coleaders conducted an intake interview with each of the prospective group members for purposes of screening, orientation, and goal setting. The individual's therapist also was contacted with the client's permission to obtain relevant information. During this one hour interview each client was helped to identify interpersonal problem areas in his or her life and asked to specify particular problems or issues he or she wanted to work on in the group. Group ground rules were explained and questions were answered. The client was introduced to the Goal Attainment Scaling process (Figure 12.3) described earlier in the chapter, and a commitment to group participation was obtained.

Based on the content of the intake interviews the leaders determined to utilize a semi-structured approach to the group introducing specific activities related to relevant topics as well as providing for open ended, problem focused interaction. The nature of the clients' interpersonal problems indicated that attention to four specific interpersonal skill areas would be a helpful adjunct to the group counseling process. These areas were communication skills, social skills, assertiveness skills, and conflict resolution skills. Consequently, two sessions were devoted to each of these areas. (Refer to Chapter 11 for a specific format for organizing a group counseling program.)

Sessions 1 and 2

These sessions were primarily devoted to the forming and security aspects of the group. Members became acquainted with one another through structured activities and began engaging in self-disclosure and giving feedback. Group rules were reiterated and clarified and time was devoted to making contact on a person to person basis. Each person also shared why they were in the group, what issues they wanted to work on, and something about their current status.

Sessions 3 and 4

The focus of these sessions was on communication in a context of building cohesiveness and acceptance in the group. Members engaged in lab activities related to active listening and practiced various forms of interpersonal communication (Miller, Nunnally & Wackman, 1975). Time also was spent identifying the specific interpersonal problem areas in clients' lives that served as content for the process of learning effective communication skills.

Sessions 5 and 6

Social skills were emphasized in these sessions combining the use of role playing and behavior rehearsal with out of group tasks and assignments to facilitate the learning of social skills. The principle of ingroup and out of group connectedness thus was established prior to any intensive consideration of interpersonal problems. In addition, the perspective of responsibility for self and individuation/differentiation in the context of the group was explored.

Sessions 7 and 8

Assertiveness principles and techniques were integrated into these sessions thereby extending the responsibility dynamics introduced previously. Members practiced assertiveness skills in the group and targeted situations where they could use them outside the group.

Sessions 9 and 10

Lab activities teaching the various strategies of conflict resolution and helping group members identify their own tendencies in conflict situations were used. Conflict situations in each client's life were identified and analyzed from the viewpoint of effective conflict resolution thus introducing the dynamics of the work stage of the group process. Conflict resolution contracts were drawn up for each member with respect to a relationship outside the group.

Note: The approximate ratio of structured activity to spontaneous interaction for these first 10 sessions was 1 to 1½ hours structure to ½ to 1 hour open ended. The last four sessions, however, were heavily oriented toward the open ended form of interaction following the lead of members as they zeroed in on the specific problems in their lives.

Sessions 11–14

The focus of these sessions was directed by the content of problems on which group members were working. A check in system was used where each group member updated the group as to his or her progress and indicated whether or not specific attention (time) was needed during the session. A goal board was constructed so that members could be quickly apprised of each other's goals and progress. Sessions were primarily work oriented and devoted to making plans, testing them in the social laboratory of the group, and reporting on their efforts outside the group. The final session involved reviewing individual and group progress, making commitments to continue working individually, and saying goodbye.

Exit Interview

An exit interview was conducted by the coleaders with each group member and centered around the Goal Attainment Scale procedure that had been introduced in the orientation session and developed during the group meetings. Emphasis was on helping the individual assess and take credit for his or her own efforts and change and determining the overall effectiveness of the group counseling process.

Follow-up

A three month follow-up questionnaire and survey consisting of two parts was sent to group members by the leaders. Part 1 consisted of questions related to the client's individual goals/progress and current status. Part 2 consisted of questions designed to solicit feedback relative to the group process experience and merits of group counseling for interpersonal problem solving.

☐ Learning Activities

The learning activities described in this section are primarily designed to prepare the group counselor for the orientation aspects of organizing a group program. A secondary gain, however, is the development of leadership skills and expansion of the counselor's repertoire of group activities and experiences. Use these activities in conjunction with the material covered in Chapters 10–12.

Class Presentation

Using material from the various chapters of this book, prepare and deliver a 15–20 minute talk on group counseling designed to clarify potential clients' understanding of the group process and inspire their interest in participating. After the talk conduct a question and answer discussion in which class members, posing as potential clients, ask questions that typically might emerge in such meetings. Upon completion of this discussion ask the class to critique the presentation noting strengths, weaknesses, and possible omissions and revisions.

Staff Orientation

Have class members pose as teachers, referral sources, administrators, or parents and present a brief description (15–20 minutes) of the distinctions between different types of groups. Follow up the presentation with a demonstration that involves all or some of the members so that they will be able to experience the nature of one of the types of groups firsthand. Conduct a follow-up discussion to answer questions. Class members should try to anticipate typical questions teachers, administrators, referral sources, or parents might ask. Finally, critique the presentation.

Demonstration Videotape

Using class members or other persons develop a videotape that can be used to demonstrate the group counseling process. Making it could be a class project with one member designated as the leader and other members playing various member roles. This tape can serve as a means of stimulating class discussion about the group process and the leadership role. It can be shown to counselors in the field, referral sources, teachers, administrators, and families to get their reactions and feedback. The tape may be a useful resource to the student going into his/her internship or the counselor going into the field. It could also be duplicated for use on the job.

Demonstration Activities Project

Instruct each class member to compile a list of three to five group activities that could be used in a classroom situation, with prospective clients, or in a staff orientation session to experientially present the group process. These activities must be obtained from sources other than this book and must be written up in detail covering goals, materials needed, procedures, instructions, and the population for whom each activity is best suited.

Each class member then can be asked to demonstrate one of the activities in class. Duplicating these papers so that each class member can have a copy is a good way of supplying valuable material for future reference. These activities will also serve as a resource in leading groups since counselors will be able to adapt them readily to group sessions.

13
CHAPTER

Communication Activities in Groups

Structured activities in groups have emerged as a viable and integral component of group work and as a vital element in facilitating the group process (Bates, Johnson & Blaker, 1982; Corey, Corey, Callahan, & Russell, 1982; Gladding, 1994; Jacobs, Harvill, & Masson, 1988; Johnson & Johnson, 1997; Ohlsen, Horne, & Lawe, 1988). Labeled variously as group procedures or techniques, structured exercises, catalytic activities, or human relations activities, they all can be subsumed under the general rubric of communication activities, the term we will use to identify them in this chapter. Although the genesis of communication activities is difficult to determine, the activities themselves have emanated from a wide range of psychological, sociological, communicational, and educational endeavors. Because of the growing reliance on and use of communication activities and the increased awareness of their existence and utility in both professional circles and the public sector, a special need is for the group leader to have an understanding of their nature and use. Perhaps Bates, Johnson, and Blaker (1982), who call communication activities catalytic activities, have stated the perspective toward communication activities best: "Catalysts are not the most important part of a leader's arsenal but they do provide added potential for leading creatively" (p. 162).

The proliferation of information regarding communication activities in the literature is almost at a saturation point. With the general emphasis on human relations training, diversity and multicultural awareness, the expansion and adaptation of the growth group on college campuses and in society at large, the appeal of encounter groups as a form of white collar hippie movement and the use of sensitivity training, T-Groups and quality circles in business and industry, the amount of professional material is almost overwhelming. However, the low key hysteria (both for and against) communication activities fanned in the sixties and seventies by the popular media (Howard, 1968; Human Potential, 1970) has evolved into a more professional perspective that emphasizes pragmatism, ethics, and conceptual validity. The initial confusion in the public sector—and to some extent in professional circles—as to the use of communication activities in groups has largely been clarified. The mention of communication activities is less likely to conjure up comments about touchy feely experiences, brain washing, seduction, or unethical practice, but such issues are still cause for concern because they represent a potential threat to group counseling and can curtail the effective use of communication activities in the helping process. This threat has long been recognized by many professionals in counseling and psychotherapy who strongly voiced the need to develop ethical standards and guidelines to regulate the use of these activities and to ensure leader competence (Lakin, 1969, 1970; The Personnel and Guidance Journal, Vol. 50, No. 4, 1972; Verplanck, 1970; Whiteley, 1970). Their concerns have produced the ethical and training standards that now epitomize both the training and the practice of professional group leaders with respect to communication activities (Association for Specialists in Group Work, 1991). (See also Chapter 8 and Appendices A, B, and C.)

The purpose of this chapter is to address the nature and use of communication activities as a means of assisting group leaders in resolving the normal dilemmas that arise when consideration is given to using them in groups. The chapter will 1) present a model for categorizing communication activities, 2) discuss a rationale for their use, 3) identify guidelines for selection, 4) describe psychodrama as a particular form of communication activity, and 5) conclude with sample communication activities that reflect the chapter's contents.

☐ Categorizing Communication Activities

Despite the plethora of terms and the variation in definitions, certain characteristics generally distinguish communication activities from other group procedures and methods used by group leaders. First, communication activities call for specific directions and parameters that give group members a format and/or a focus for their interaction. Whenever the leader makes "an explicit and directive request of a member for the purposes of focusing on material, augmenting or exaggerating affect, practicing behavior or solidifying insight" he or she is using a form of communication activity (Corey, Corey, & Callahan, 1982, p. 1). Second, communication activities often entail the use of materials or props for carrying out the activity (for example, pencils, paper, paint, material objects, and so forth). Finally, communication activities can be standardized to a large degree, enabling leaders to use them in adapted form with a minimum of alteration in a variety of group settings and with diverse clientele.

Leader Attitude Toward Communication Activities

The group leader's attitude toward communication activities should reflect a professional commitment to ethical standards and his or her personal responsibility to group members. Communication activities are only tools that must be used judiciously to enhance the group process for the benefit of group members. These activities are not mechanisms that should be exploited, used to generate emotional highs, or entertain group participants. Any experimentation should be done for specific purposes, such as determining the impact of a technique to ensure its most effective use in a group counseling setting or familiarizing group leaders with an activity so that they have more confidence in using it. Communication activities should not become ends in themselves and should always relate directly to the group process and the needs of group members. They must be consistent with the rationale and philosophy of the group leader and have a specified purpose from a pragmatic (group related) and conceptual (theory related) perspective.

Identifying Traits of Communication Activities

Figure 13.1 presents a model comprised of two dimensions that is helpful in differentiating the nature of communication activities. The first relates to the *focus* of the activity and is divided into two parts, intrapersonal and interpersonal. *Intrapersonal activities* are designed to help people engage in the introspective process that leads to greater self-knowledge. They emphasize a greater understanding of one's inner self as the basis for making constructive decisions, living a more effective life, changing one's feelings, thoughts, or behaviors, and actualizing one's potential. They stress personal learning about the subject of self. *Interpersonal activities* are designed to help people explore, understand, and improve their relationships with others. Their focuses are on the social self and human relationships. Activities revolve around interpersonal interaction, and emphasis is on relational qualities and characteristics that enhance effective communication, promote meaningful human encounters, and facilitate meeting social-psychological needs.

The second dimension of the model involves the *process of communication* used in the activity and is divided into verbal and nonverbal categories. *Verbal activities* concentrate on the use of words as the primary means of communication. The form of verbal exchange may make use of either the speaking or writing capacities of the participants. *Nonverbal activities* encompass a broad range of media from art forms to body language to internal communication processes. The nonverbal dimension of communication activities is identified by the fact that the primary action takes place without the use of or dependence on words.

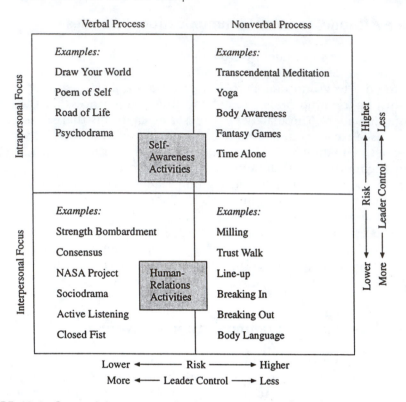

FIGURE 13.1. Categorizing communication activities. (Adapted from a model presented by Roy Evans, clinical psychologist, Minnesota State Prison, during a group counseling workshop at the University of Wisconsin-River Falls, Summer, 1972. Reprinted by permission.)

The combination of these two dimensions provides us with a perspective for assessing the nature of communication activities. *Verbal intrapersonal activities* help individuals examine themselves and then verbally share their perceptions in the form of self-disclosure. Examples include such activities as Draw Your World, Poem of Self, Road of Life, and Life Story. Psychodrama is a very sophisticated form of this type of activity. *Nonverbal intrapersonal activities* provide a format for introspection but the experience takes place totally within the confines of the individual and is not accessible to others except through that person's verbal interpretation of what was experienced. Examples of ingroup activities include meditation, yoga, body awareness exercises, Fantasy Games (Schutz, 1967), and Time Alone (Katz, 1973). Out of group activities may involve a variety of creative writing activities or tasks. (See Wenz & McWhirter (1990) and Gladding (1992a; 1992b) for specific writing activities that can be incorporated into group work.) Most of these activities include some type of sharing, but their main thrust is or providing each person with an internal experience for personal enrichment, problem solving and learning.

One prominent example of an intrapersonal activity that has a long history of effectiveness in group counseling is journaling (Riordan, 1996; Riordan & Matheny, 1972). Referred to variously as diary writing, journaling, or keeping a log, Riordan (1996) has dubbed the use of writing as an adjunctive dimension of counseling as *scriptotherapy*. In groups members are asked to or recommended to keep a journal of their thoughts, feelings and experiences over the course of the group. This serves the purpose of intrapersonal processing and effectively develops a conceptual bridge for members between group sessions. As a communication exercise specific instructions can be given as follows:

> When you have finished the session, take 15 minutes to record your observations and feelings (Riordan & White, 1996, p. 97).

These entries can be collected and reviewed by the group leader or simply left to be a personal summary and a possible stimulus for members to voluntarily relate or share in the course of group interaction.

Verbal interpersonal activities are designed to engage people in interaction with others and are characterized by dependence on verbal feedback and sharing. Examples include Strength Bombardment, Consensus, Active Listening, and The Closed Fist. Sociodrama is a form of this type of exercise but in an expanded sense. Sociodrama focuses on common problems in social relationships that all group members can benefit from working on and uses mainly verbal role playing techniques to do so. *Nonverbal interpersonal activities* are designed to provide members with experiences in interpersonal relationships without using the normal communication channel of words. Although these activities usually entail a verbal follow-up, the main action takes place during the activity. Any clarification, interpretation, sharing, or feedback takes place after the experience which is then subject to modification when translated into the verbal domain. Activities such as Trust Walk, Milling, Lineup, Breaking In, and body language activities are examples.

Generally speaking we can classify all verbal and nonverbal intrapersonal activities as *self-awareness activities*. Similarly, verbal and nonverbal interpersonal activities can be labeled *human-relations activities*. No absolute rigidity exists in this model because many activities include both verbal and nonverbal components and some also may incorporate all four quadrants of the diagram. Also, many exercises can be altered to fit the various categories with just a little creativity on the part of the group leader. In effect then, this model is a reference for determining the characteristics of communication activities. As such it is a useful resource in training group leaders to select and use communication exercises in groups.

Some specific considerations of this model have direct relevance to group counseling. The group counseling process is primarily a verbal process whose

effectiveness depends on communication among group members. Therefore the leader must always incorporate a verbal sharing component into
any activity that is used.

Activities should always end up in the verbal interpersonal realm. In point
of fact, the processing phase when using communication exercises is the
most important dimension (DeLucia-Waack, 1997a). Kees and Jacobs (1990)
emphasize that

> without adequate processing the leader cannot be sure of what learning has
> taken place. If done correctly, processing can provide members with addi-
> tional learning about themselves and other members of the group. Through
> processing, members may also develop a plan of action for transferring this
> learning to their lives outside the group (p. 23).

Processing in the verbal interpersonal domain facilitates greater group cohesiveness and communication and alleviates problems of member disso-
ciation that sometimes occur, especially with nonverbal and intrapersonal
activities. It also enables members to benefit from each other's experiences
and encourages modeling and identification. DeLucia-Waack (1997a) notes
that processing by both individuals and the group is critical. "The effectiveness of group work interventions and strategies is greatly increased when
the intervention (*communication activity*) is processed (*verbally*) at the individual (*intrapersonal*) and group (*interpersonal*) level" (p. 3).

Two underlying continuums also are part of this model and warrant careful attention by the group leader. The first is the element of risk involved in
using these activities. At the beginning of the Chapter I mentioned some
general concerns with communication activities, but here I will be more
specific. Verbal activities are less risky than nonverbal in the perception
of both group members and significant others outside the group. This is
especially true in school situations and with adolescent groups. Nonverbal activities should be carefully selected and used judiciously. Extensive physical contact and physically dangerous activities should be avoided.
Risk also is somewhat higher in intrapersonal activities than in interpersonal ones. The risk here is psychological in nature because of the focus
on self-disclosure. Usually a person can give feedback more easily than be
self-disclosing and can talk more easily about what is happening between
people than engage in introspection. In other words, low level self-assessment activities and interpersonal activities should take precedence over
exercises requiring in depth self-disclosure until the group is ready for them.
In this way an atmosphere of trust and acceptance can be established that
reduces the risk of sharing more private thoughts about one's self and one's
problems.

Bates, Johnson, and Blaker (1982) in adapting this model noted that a
within quadrant intensity factor mirrors the overall risk dimension. Within
each section activities can be refined more definitively on the basis of being

low, medium, or high in intensity. Group leaders can thus select activities that are appropriate to the level of group interaction and commensurate with the nature of group dynamics.

The second continuum is leader control. The amount of control the leader has in guiding, facilitating, and limiting the interaction in using communication activities is directly related to their nature. Verbal activities lend themselves to much greater control than do nonverbal. At least when members are talking the leader can tune in to consistencies and discrepancies between members' words and their experiences. In nonverbal activities much of this awareness can be lost or hidden. And nonverbal communication by its very nature is much more difficult to follow anyway. Because the experience takes place without the usual verbal cues of the expressive domain, the leader has less contact with it. Similarly interpersonal activities are more conducive than intrapersonal to leader direction, especially in the nonverbal intrapersonal area. To maintain a common level of involvement in these activities is difficult because some members may go very deep and others may do nothing. The result thus can be detrimental to group cohesiveness and progress.

These considerations should not deter group leaders from using communication activities in their groups, but they should be aware of these issues and take them into account in choosing and implementing activities. Risk will always be involved because change and growth don't occur without it. Control problems always will exist because of individual uniqueness, the diversity of member commitment and involvement, and the nature of the group process. Leaders must act to reduce these problems by carefully utilizing techniques that are consistent with their philosophies and rationales of group counseling and that are best suited to the needs of the group members.

☐ Rationale and Use of Communication Activities

By viewing the group as an on going developmental process and each group session as a mini-reflection or prototype of that process, we can build a rationale for using communication activities. This rationale provides a framework that encompasses individual differences in group leadership styles and can help alleviate problems of explanation and justification for the group leader. To relate communication activities to the group counseling process, I will discuss their purposes and how they are introduced into the group. The three basic ways of using communication activities are to: initiate, facilitate, and terminate (conclude or close). Each will be described separately (Trotzer, 1973).

Initiation

Communication activities can be used in group counseling to initiate the group process. This includes beginning the overall group process, starting individual sessions within that process, and interjecting a new or different focus during the group session. For example, at the first session of a 10 session counseling group of graduate students, the leader asked members to describe themselves in the third person as if they were their own best friend. The members described themselves using their first names and "he" or "she" rather than "I" or "me." In this way the leader initiated an activity that set the tone for both that particular session and the overall group process. Members began the process of getting to know one another and sharing themselves with others. The self-consciousness created by the newness of the group and having to talk about themselves was lessened because members could step outside themselves and speak more objectively. This example points out one of the purposes in initiating activities: giving members a structured format in which they can have a common experience. Some of the discomfort of beginning the group was lessened, and the common focus established a basis on which the group process could build.

Hetzel, Barton and Davenport (1994) reported that the use of structured activities was particularly useful in beginning their men's groups. They observed that "a few exercises were helpful during the initial sessions of the group in developing a sense of trust among members, but no more than one activity should be included during each session" (p. 59). Their use of communication activities in an initiating manner thus helped the individual members and the group process get off to a constructive start.

Stockton, Rohde, and Haughey (1994) found that structured group exercises at the beginning of each session resulted in participants being significantly more satisfied with their group experiences. In addition, they discovered that groups where structured activities were used did significantly less recycling to earlier developmental group tasks and stages.

A second purpose for using communication activities to initiate is to orient the group toward a topic that will be useful to effective group functioning and the helping process. The intent is not to precipitate anything in the group but rather to aid the group members in learning to function as a group. For example, a group of male high school juniors was formed because of their disruptive classroom behaviors. They exhibited a great deal of discomfort, resistance, and distrust during their first two sessions. The counselor suggested the trust walk as an initiating activity for the third session. The trust walk made the issue of trust concrete since each individual experienced being dependent on another person and being responsible for another person. When the activity was over, the leader helped group members express their feelings about the experience and make the transition from being trusting and trustworthy in the activity to being so in the group and in their own lives.

Using communication activities to start group interaction lessens the discomfort created by the ambiguity of an unstructured situation. Members are able to loosen up and lower interpersonal barriers, thus opening channels of communication that can subsequently be used to confront and resolve problems in the group. Also, the simulation experience and modeling effect of the activities help group members learn important aspects of effective interpersonal communication and group dynamics.

Counselors who use communication activities to initiate group interaction gain the benefit of group control. They become the experts who direct the group interaction, lifting this responsibility from the members' shoulders. The counselor becomes the guide, and members become the guided. Structuring group interaction by using an activity gives the counselor a better sense of what is going on and what to expect. This provides the leader with a kind of security that is not as readily accessible to the leader who does not initiate. Leaders who are more comfortable and effective in structured settings or who want to make things happen (Poppen & Thompson, 1974) tend to use more initiating activities. In fact, some leaders resemble orchestra conductors or movie directors, putting together activity after activity and molding and directing the group process from start to finish.

One drawback to using communication activities for initiating purposes is that the counselor may create a dependency situation in which members expect the counselor to provide the direction all the time. To circumvent this possibility, the leader must be able to integrate the initiating activity into the group process and facilitate the shift of responsibility back to the members. The communication activity should not be an isolated experience but an integral part of the life cycle of the counseling group.

Another difficulty is in choosing appropriate initiating activities. The counselor's choice of an activity should be based on his or her knowledge of both the group process and the unique qualities of group members. For best results, leaders should choose activities with which they are familiar. Even then, at times an activity will not be effective. This situation may be avoided if the leader maintains a tentative attitude when suggesting activities and remains sensitive to the group's reaction as the activities are being described. Leader willingness to alter or change the activity based on members' reactions usually enhances success. Having more than one activity in mind also gives the leader flexibility in dealing with situations created by member resistance or by the failure of a particular activity to work.

Finally, when leaders use initiating activities they provide members with targets toward which to direct their resistance. Members can grasp the opportunity to be uncooperative in a very specific way. However, resistance is normal and if the leader is prepared for it the activity also can serve as a means of dealing with it in a constructive manner. Since members know clearly what is expected of them, they can direct their resistance at a nonpersonal target but also are likely to experience group pressure to participate. The end result is that through the activity members often find that their reasons for resistance are unwarranted and can comfortably make the transition from resistance to cooperation and involvement.

Facilitation

The primary purpose of using communication activities to facilitate is to help the group use its resources to the fullest extent (Poppen & Thompson, 1974). For example, a group of sixth grade girls who were central figures in cliques found it difficult to talk to one another without getting into heated arguments. The group leader used active listening as an activity to help them learn listening skills and thereby improve their communications with one another. The girls not only began to relate to each other in the group but used their listening skills with noticeable effect in the classroom.

The main point to keep in mind when using communication activities to facilitate the group counseling process is that the activities should be derived from or suggested in response to a situation or dynamic that has emerged in the group. A typical facilitating activity is role playing. Role playing is a procedure in which a problem is dealt with by having the principals involved act it out in the safety of the group with other members participating as actors or observers. For example, a ninth grade girl was discussing her problem of communication with her parents about dating and curfews. The counselor asked the girl to role play a typical conversation with her parents on this topic, using other members as auxiliaries. The counselor directed the role playing by keeping the actors in character and guiding them through the use of role reversals, alter egos, and role substitutions. When the role playing was over the leader facilitated a follow-up discussion to consolidate what had transpired regarding the problem. In this particular case, role playing also was used to help the girl try out some alternative approaches to the problem.

Facilitating activities help to clarify problem situations, present alternatives, alleviate anxiety producing circumstances, and break through impasses that occur in groups. They can be used to perk up the group interaction when normal communication channels break down. They can help a group consider an issue that they feel is relevant but don't know how to approach. Facilitation procedures should be catalytic, stimulating, and enhancing to group interaction without creating a noticeable structure that will distract members from their stated purposes.

Facilitating activities usually enjoy ready acceptance by group members. Because they are based directly on the interaction of the group, their probability of success is increased. Since facilitating activities are designed to provide avenues for reaching goals set by the group and do not suggest content, the group experiences an autonomy and responsibility with respect to the nature and focus of the material discussed. Facilitating techniques thus help members learn their responsibility in the group and at the same time help the leader establish guidelines and boundaries within which the group interaction occurs.

The facilitative use of communication activities is difficult to master. Its relevance and effectiveness is dependent on the leader's creativity, spontaneity, and sensitivity in here and now situations. The leader must exhibit a willingness to follow and respond rather than lead and direct. A facilitative leader must have a capacity to tolerate ambiguity, allowing the group to take responsibility for its own direction. Responding effectively requires a knowledge and awareness of numerous activities that are usable in groups. This knowledge should include details of procedure, applicability, and probable effects of each activity. The ability to respond with the right activity at the right time has to be developed through experience in the leadership role.

Termination

Communication activities are useful at the end of individual group sessions, when individual members terminate, and when the total group is being disbanded. In all cases their major purposes are to consolidate and integrate what has been learned in the group and generate closure. More specifically, they help members clarify and review what has transpired, provide reinforcement for changes that have been made, and encourage members to implement these changes in their daily lives.

Terminating activities that bring closure to a group provide a jumping off place for members. For example, a go-round at the end of a session asking members for their reactions to the session or to the problems or topic under consideration creates a format in which members can express their feelings before the group disperses. An activity such as this aids both the leader and members in understanding where the group is and provides a natural ending point.

The impact of termination activities removes some of the awkwardness associated with closure. It helps individual members say goodbye and gives the group an opportunity to send them off on a positive note. For example, a member of a therapy group for prison inmates obtained a parole. At the member's last session, the leader suggested an adaptation of the Hope Chest activity in which group members presented the departing member with symbolic gifts they felt would enhance his success in readjusting to society. The gifts served to pinpoint the gains he had made and warned of vulnerabilities that still needed attention. In addition, the positive feelings generated had a remarkable effect on the group itself that was evident in their efforts to work on their own problems during the following weeks.

When a group is being disbanded members usually recognize that termination is called for but experience some ambivalence about it, especially if a sense of belongingness and cohesiveness have developed in the group. This desire to "end but not yet" triggers the enthusiastic involvement typifying the ending phase of a group and may even result in members suggesting their own closing activities. For example, during the final session of a group of college freshmen who initially were having a difficult time adjusting to a large university, one member suggested that each member show how he or she felt about every other member. Members individually went around the group expressing their feelings toward each other, first nonverbally and then verbally. This activity clarified the relationships between individual members and also focused on their learning in the area of developing relationships.

Ambivalent feelings about terminating also may affect group leaders. They may feel reluctant to disband a group because of the effort expended in getting it to function effectively. Or they may feel that something the group— or an individual in the group—needs for a more complete or well rounded experience has been overlooked or neglected. In either case a closing activity may be useful. For example, during the course of a human relations group composed of high school seniors, the group members had looked critically at themselves and each other offering constructive criticism to each other but focusing primarily on their weaknesses in relating to others. The leader felt a balance was needed, and he also felt a great deal of personal involvement in the group. Therefore, he suggested a segment of the technique called Strength Bombardment in which every member including the leader gave every other member only positive feedback. This activity helped to remove some doubts that members had about relating to others and served to strike a balance between critical and positive feedback. It brought the group together and helped them realize how much they had learned about themselves and each other. It also showed emphatically that, regardless of difficulties a person may have to resolve, strengths and other good qualities can aid and sustain them in that process.

Termination activities involve very little risk. The group is generally cohesive and cooperative at this point, ensuring the effectiveness of most activities suggested. And since members recognize that the group is ending, the chances of opening new problems or going overboard emotionally are small. One drawback is that the high degree of closeness and satisfaction the group may experience may not be present in the daily lives of individual members. This could create distortion in their perceptions of the group counseling process and temporarily block out the effort that was involved in getting to the ending point. It may even give rise to wishes to prolong the group, which the leader must handle warmly but firmly. This reaction is a normal phenomenon associated with the completion of difficult but successful projects and is soon replaced with a more realistic perspective.

Flexibility of Communication Activities

Many communication activities can be used in all of the ways previously described. They can be revised and adapted to fit into the group process as initiating, facilitating, or terminating activities. Most also can be redesigned to conform to a leader's particular style or to meet the unique needs of a particular group. The main point is that all communication activities are intended to provide a means by which group members can interact with each other (Blaker & Samo, 1973). They can and do add flexibility and breadth to the group counseling process. But it must be remembered that the focus of the group is on persons and purposes—in that order—and that communication activities are only important and useful to the extent they contribute to the therapeutic growth of individuals in the group and resolution of problems for which the group was formed.

☐ Guidelines for Selecting Communication Activities

The group counseling process can be greatly enhanced by the proper selection and judicious use of communication activities. For example, McMillon (1994) found that intentionally structured groups had a positive impact on problem solving and interpersonal communication among a population of underprepared, first year minority college students. However, naive and careless use of structured activities casts a bad reflection on the counselor and the group counseling process and may endanger group members in a psychological, moral, or physical sense.

Blaker and Samo (1973) warned that communication games can become ends in themselves in the hands of incompetent leaders who discover their potential for reducing inhibitions. However, communication activities do aid the group process if selected for a specific purpose and introduced in the right way (Trotzer, 1973). The following guidelines are designed to help the group leader make wise choices in selecting communication activities for use in the group counseling process (Trotzer & Kassera, 1973).

1. *Select activities on the basis of their purpose, relevance, and desired outcome.* This is the most important rule and supersedes all other considerations. Communication activities should not be implemented because they produce emotional highs. All too frequently popularity and familiarity are the only bases for selecting an exercise rather than the why and wherefore of its use. The impact of an activity should be considered above all else, and if that impact is not in accord with the needs of the members and the purposes of the group, the activity should not be used.

Jacobs, Harvill and Masson (1988) suggest seven generic reasons or purposes for using communication exercises:

1. To generate discussion and participation.
2. To get the group focused on a common topic or issue.
3. To shift or deepen the focus.
4. To provide an opportunity for experiential learning.
5. To increase the comfort level.
6. To provide the leader with useful information.
7. To provide fun and relaxation.

These process parameters provide a general framework within which specific activities can be selected.

2. *Select activities that have a solid conceptual framework and rationale relative to human growth and development.* Activities should not be selected on the basis of pragmatism alone. Each activity also should have a psychological, conceptual basis that validates its use from a theoretical perspective. This guideline serves as a check and balance to the often intuitive use of structured activities that can initiate interactions that are not consistent with principles of human growth and development, the group leader's philosophy, and/or the psychological rationale of the group.

3. *Select activities that are familiar and comfortable for you to use.* The enthusiasm and confidence of the leader in presenting an activity are often the cues that mark its reception by the members. The leader's discomfort with a technique will be picked up by the group and could cause resistance to and even the failure of the activity. Activities that have been experienced should take precedence over those that have been observed or read about. Don't use techniques you have heard about just to see what will happen. To increase your repertoire of activities, first attempt new techniques under controlled conditions so that the process can be carefully observed and the impact or outcome evaluated.

4. *Select activities that are primarily verbal rather than physical.* Physical contact is often the first issue raised against the use of communication activities in group counseling and should be included only after careful consideration. Members' cultural, religious, and personal values and beliefs may mitigate against activities that involve physical contact. Consequently activities need to be selected and adapted to facilitate inclusion and participation rather than resistance, intrusion, or exclusion. From a leader's perspective, Birnbaum (1969) noted that nonverbal techniques require a minimum of experience and knowledge to stimulate an initial response but demand a maximum of expert knowledge and sophistication to extract a positive educational outcome. Most desired outcomes in group counseling can be attained either by verbal or nonverbal activities that involve a minimum of physical contact. For example, hand or arm holding in a trust walk is acceptable, but the extended physical contact of an activity such as body sculpturing (Schutz, 1967) is better avoided. Remember that any nonverbal activity should always involve a verbal sharing component. This enables the leader to assess more accurately the effect of the activity and to make the necessary adjustments to handle problems.

In addition, modifications that accommodate individual belief systems and religious or cultural mores can be made to generate inclusion rather than to delimit the group from access to a particular experiential learning activity that involves touch. For example, in a mixed gender training group that included a male whose religious practice forbade physical contact with females, the leader enlisted his assistance as a verbal consultant to the group as they addressed the task of getting the group physically into a two foot square area. He participated verbally by contributing suggestions as to strategy and was thus included in the activity and could participate directly in the processing portion of the activity. In this particular case it also enabled the group to expand its diversity awareness and sensitivity and enabled the individual to share his beliefs without threat of rejection or judgment.

5. *Select activities that do not require labels or can be labeled with terms that do not carry connotations of negativity or overtones that stigmatize.* Many times people react to the connotations of names without knowing the real nature of the process to which the name is given. In selecting and discussing activities, group leaders should take that tendency into account. Often the same activity can have many different labels. "Let's see if you can show us how you reacted in that situation" could be termed psychodrama, sociodrama, or role playing. However, there is a considerable difference in connotation between labeling it psychodrama as opposed to role playing. Activities selected should be explained in everyday language or in neutral terms.

6. *Select activities commensurate with the maturity level of group members.* The members' abilities to immerse themselves in an activity without undue difficulty, tension, or embarrassment is extremely important to the effective use of any technique. Similarly, the activity should have characteristics that appeal to members' interests. If members feel they are being manipulated, talked down to, or treated without respect, they will resist and shun involvement. If the activity itself is unattractive or unstimulating, they will lose interest or be easily distracted. For example, the use of puppets to aid third graders in exploring their feelings may be more effective than role playing. Eighth graders, however, would probably prefer role playing, and adults may benefit from a full blown psychodrama integrated into the session. If a leader feels a particular activity has merit and accomplishes a desired purpose, it can most likely be modified to fit the age level and maturity of the group. In fact, this type of leader action is constructive because it indicates the leader is person oriented rather than technique oriented and is willing to alter activities to meet the needs of the group.

7. *Select activities that are adaptable to the physical setting in which the group is meeting.* If the physical setting does not allow for an activity to be fully experienced or interferes with its being carried out, the activity should be avoided. For a large group that meets in a small room, using dyads for a verbal activity requiring high concentration may create confusion and interfere with accomplishing the purpose intended. Similarly, techniques that require members to leave the room should be carefully screened and

explained and are best avoided if any indications are present that clients may not be able to handle the activity responsibly. The loss of leader control in these activities could result in misunderstanding from outside observers who witness the actions of group members as well as from the members themselves.

8. *Select activities that allow for maximum member participation.* Some activities require physical skills or emotional endurance that may be frightening, distasteful, or overtaxing to some group members. Physical activities always should be prefaced with a caution to members and an option to observe rather than participate. Strenuous activities are best avoided. Activities that require members to move in a way that might cause embarrassment should be used only when members have been advised in advance of this factor. For example, for some activities members might prefer to wear jeans rather than dresses or skirts. Selection should take into account the psychological, intellectual, and experiential levels of group members. Techniques requiring extensive self-disclosure and feedback may not allow for maximum participation if members are at different levels with respect to trust and acceptance or if they have varied skill capacities or experiential contact with communication activities. In addition, consideration of cultural and diversity factors is necessary to facilitate maximum relevance and participation.

9. *Select activities that allow group members to control their own involvement.* Guideline 8 is directed at external factors that must be considered to promote maximum member participation in an activity. Guideline 9 focuses on internal factors that allow for maximum involvement by each individual member. Communication activities should promote personal freedom and empowerment not simply reduce inhibitions. Techniques that force members to do something they are not ready for or find too threatening should be avoided. Birnbaum (1969) pointed out that confrontation techniques, for example, are easy to implement but very difficult to handle constructively because of the psychological pressure placed on individuals being confronted. Members should be allowed to decide how they will involve themselves and to what depth they will go. Activities that interfere with an individual's right to personal privacy or undermine his or her free agency should not be used in group counseling. A general guideline that states *participation is expected but the depth of involvement and sharing is up to each individual* included in the instructions or groundrules often alleviates the undue pressure dimension of communication exercises.

10. *Select activities that will result in outcomes you are sure the group and you as a leader can handle.* Activities that precipitate the expression of strong feelings are always risky and should be used with extreme caution. If the possibility of loss of control is apparent in the use of any technique, it is best avoided. Leaders must always consider their own capabilities and the composition of the group in selecting activities. As member involvement increases and leader experience expands, the range and depth of activities

that can be effectively utilized increases. However, experience is not a license to experiment freely; it is rather a safeguard against the inappropriate handling of member reactions. A conscientious concern for the hidden psychological triggers embedded in activities is a necessary component for effective leadership when using communication activities.

11. *Select activities that can be culminated in the time available in the group meeting.* Leaders should have a good idea about how much time is necessary to fully implement an activity. Nothing is more frustrating to a leader or to group members than to run out of time in the middle of an activity in which everyone is involved and interested. Select activities that can be presented, experienced, and processed during the time limits of the group. Don't begin an activity that can't be worked through before the session ends. And hurrying to get through an activity usually defeats its whole purpose by forcing members to concentrate on the activity rather than on themselves or each other. If an activity has not been satisfactorily concluded at the end of the time period, sometimes the better procedure is to hold the group over rather than to have members leave with unexpressed or unresolved feelings that could produce misunderstandings or disgruntlement detrimental to the group.

12. *Select activities that are easily processable and integrate effectively into the flow of group interaction.* In order to counter the myopic tendencies produced by structured activities, select communication activities on the basis of their processability. Key processability features are 1) the interaction generated is reflective of the group process, and 2) the content is relevant to group member problems or purposes for which the group was formed. Activities that produce experiences that the leader and members can effectively integrate into the flow of the group interaction are preferable to those that are self-contained or require extensive translation to make them fit. A distinctive trait of a processable activity is that the group moves directly back into their interactive pattern without spending excessive time and energy finishing or closing the activity.

☐ Psychodrama: A Special Form of Communication Activity

Psychodrama is both a group process in and of itself and a tool to be used in the context of group counseling and therapy. As such, it is a sophisticated and elegant form of communication activity and therefore merits separate consideration in the context of this chapter.

Psychodrama was conceived and nurtured into being by Viennese psychiatrist, J. L. Moreno (1964) who brought it with him to New York in 1925. Using the tools of the stage and the conceptual framework of psychology he and his students developed psychodrama into an entity in and of itself with wide ranging application to therapy across many populations and settings. Psychodrama is now an approach to therapy with training programs and skilled practitioners who practice it exclusively. However, it is also a viable tool for group leaders to learn and use in the context of other group process applications.

The calling card or seminal identifying trait of psychodrama is *action*. It is a form of therapy or training in which participants enact or reenact situations in their lives that are of emotional significance to them. The process is active, not passive and relies on behavioral expression rather than verbal description. The environment (where the action takes place) provides free space that can be used expressively whether it occurs in an office, in a classroom, or on a stage. The main actor essentially performs therapy on him or herself.

The key conceptual dynamic of psychodrama is known as *surplus reality*. This term refers to the perspective that whatever is occurring in the action whether it is drawn from the past, present, or future, and whether it represents reality or fantasy, it is all happening in the here and now. As such, the present is expanded experientially to encompass the whole of life experience.

Psychodrama has a distinct quality that enables greater honesty to occur with less effort. It requires more energy and purposeful honesty to disclose what cannot be seen by others (that which occurs outside the group or is hidden inside the person) than to acknowledge what is occurring before the group in the here and now. Thus, psychodrama is useful in helping people deal with issues in their lives that are often harder to talk about than to act out.

Techniques

Psychodrama can be credited with the development and adaptation of numerous techniques that have utility to the group practitioner whether the form of psychodrama is applied or not. Several examples are briefly described in the following subtopics.

The Soliloquy

Taken from drama where an actor steps out of the context of the play to express a supplementary perspective to the audience, this technique is essentially designed to help a client think out loud.

The Double

Another person assumes the place of the main actor to assist him or her in expressing his or her experiences. The double plays a key role in helping that which cannot be expressed to emerge and bringing out distortions in that which is expressed. The double can take many forms such as the following:

1. Colorless double: relies primarily on restatement
2. Satirical double: uses humor and paradox in responding
3. Passionate double: expresses the emotions of the main character
4. Oppositional double: takes an opposing side in order to create a dialogue between sides
5. Physical double: mirrors gestures, behavior, and body language
6. Multiple double: represents different aspects of the person such as their past, present, and future or his or her thoughts, feelings, and actions.

The double is also referred to as the alter ego to emphasize the role as an extension of the person who is the central focus.

Magic Shop

This technique casts the therapist or other group member in the role of a shopkeeper who barters with clients for qualities, values, and experiences they want based on the principle that they must give something valuable (pay a price) to get something valuable. (Additional techniques are described in the learning activities section of this chapter).

   The psychodrama process is composed of five elements and three phases which combine to create the therapeutic context.

Five Elements

The Stage

The stage is the arena of action. Everything that happens on it occurs in the here and now. It is a space limited only by the imagination and creativity of participants and the director. It is the area where the drama occurs and is differentiated from the area which contains the observers or audience.

The Protagonist

The protagonist is the main actor, the star of the psychodrama. He or she is the one who is working through a problem or issue in action. He or she is performing therapy on him or herself, but is also the one who defines the limits of the drama (is in charge of how far the action will go). The protagonist acts out his or her problem from a subjective point of view.

The Auxiliaries

The auxiliaries are the extensions of the world of the protagonist. They are the supporting cast who assist the protagonist in carrying out the drama.

Operating from an objective point of view the auxiliaries perform three important supplementary functions besides assisting the protagonist. They provide support for the protagonist, they give input to the director, and they are therapeutic agents to the main actor helping him or her clarify, understand, and modify his or her life experience. More skill is required of auxiliaries than of protagonists which is one reason that trained auxiliaries are often included in groups that utilize psychodrama.

The Director

The director is the one in charge of producing the drama. He or she has the technical skills and tools necessary to help the protagonist act out his or her story and mobilize auxiliaries to that end. The director is in charge of the entire process of the psychodrama not just the action. He or she plays three key roles in the process. Besides being producer, he or she is also analyst and therapist merging, combining, and separating these roles in the best interests of the main actor. The director must not only be skilled in psychodrama, but also must be able to trust it as the final arbiter and guide in the therapeutic process (Moreno, n.d.).

The Audience

The audience represents the world and is the source for both protagonists and auxiliaries. Audience members are all participants even if their role is that of spectator. They are particularly essential with respect to the sharing phase of psychodrama where the audience gives back to the protagonist in exchange for that which was given them.

Three Phases

The Warm-up

Purposes of the warm-up phase are to assist participants in connecting with each other, develop an atmosphere of rapport and safety, and generate content out of which can emerge the selection of a protagonist. As such, the security stage tasks of getting acquainted, interpersonal warm-up, and trust building are addressed along with the acceptance stage tasks of personal sharing and building cohesiveness and closeness.

The warm-up is the precursor to the action and sets the atmosphere in which the drama can unfold. It usually involves a structured activity that will generate personal content in the form of issues or problems that will lend themselves to being acted out in a psychodrama. Many of the activities at the end of chapters in this book are effective tools for the warm-up phase of psychodrama. The purpose of the warm-up is to generate interaction between participants that enables them to open up and share experiences thereby assisting the director in identifying a potential protagonist.

The Drama

The drama phase is the action or core of the psychodrama. Once the protagonist has been elicited he or she works with the director to act out the story. The arena is divided into stage and audience and the play is carried out to a suitable end point using auxiliaries as appropriate.

The Sharing

Once the protagonist has reached the climax and ends his or her story, the final phase of the psychodrama is invoked by the director. This is the follow-up to the drama where the audience shares with the protagonist what his or her story has meant to them. This is not a time for analysis, advice giving, or therapy. It is a time when members of the audience give a piece of themselves to the main actor. This is crucial for closure for both the protagonist and the audience and is the phase in which the impact of the drama is generalized beyond the designated client-protagonist.

Phases of psychodrama are recycled each time a drama is enacted much like groups recycle stages as they evolve to deeper or different levels of interaction. Each of these phases and each of these elements are central to the psychodrama's effective use. Training in psychodrama is eminently available and a recommended adjunct to group leadership training. Much of the psychodrama literature (especially that of J. L. Moreno and Zerka Moreno) is published by and available from Beacon House, Inc., P.O. Box 311, Beacon, NY 12508. Additional resources are Greenberg (1974) and Leveton (1977).

☐ Concluding Comments

Resources for finding communication activities to utilize in group work abound. Some of them are Johnson (1981); Johnson and Johnson (1997); Pfeiffer and Jones (1969–85); Bates, Johnson, and Blaker (1982); Jacobs, Harvill, and Masson (1988); Stevens (1972); Simon, Howe, and Kirchenbaum (1972); Thompson and Poppen (1979) and Rosenthal (1998). However, selection and implementation are the bailiwick of the professional leader.

Communication activities are valuable tools in facilitating the group process and improving individual self-understanding. They contribute to the helping process and give both leaders and members a means of coping with problems that are a part of therapeutic group interaction. There are, however, precautions that must be considered. These activities should not be viewed as an end in themselves but rather as means to an end. They should be used with considerable discretion and only in the context of ethical practice.

☐ Learning Activities

Communication activities described in the following pages are organized around their primary use in initiating, facilitating, or terminating the group process. Remember, however, that these activities are flexible and can be used in ways other than described here.

Initiation

Describe Yourself as Your Own Best Friend

The purpose of this activity is to help members get to know one another through the process of self-disclosure. The anxiety of talking about oneself is reduced by the objective third person approach, which helps members cope with the discomfort of the group environment and feelings of self-consciousness.

   Have group members individually describe themselves as their own best friend using their name ("This is my friend John . . .") and the appropriate third person pronoun referent (he or she). Each member can be his or her own best friend or describe their self as a best friend would. After each person has completed his or her description, other members can ask questions to obtain or clarify information. These questions are also in the form of the third person. (e.g., "What does John like about himself?") The person responds to the questions in the third person. The leader's role is to help members maintain the third person approach and to ask leading questions as a guide or model for other members. Also an effective approach is to have the leader be the first person to do the activity. In this way he or she can set the tone for the group, model self-disclosure, and demonstrate how the activity should be done.

Name Tags, "able" and "ing"

This is a good beginning activity, especially in groups where members are not familiar with each other (Kranzow, 1973). Have members make name tags that state their name and include three words ending in "ing," and three words ending in "able" that describe what they are like. The six words should describe their personality traits (e.g., interesting, loving, irritable, likable). Encourage members to be creative and invent words that best fit their personality (e.g., funning, angerable). After name tags are completed have members introduce themselves to one another. ("My name is Toni, and I am fascinating . . ." or "I see your name is John, and you are memorable. . ."). After the participants have had the opportunity to meet each other, convene the total group and have the members explain why they chose the words they did. Other group members also can respond by adding "ing" or "able" words they think are appropriate to individual members.

Building Blocks Go-Round

This is another good initiating activity that breaks the ice of a new group and helps members get to know each other—at least by name—very quickly. Sit in a circle and have one member start by stating his or her name. The person next to him or her must repeat the first member's name and then give her or his own. This continues with each person repeating the names of every preceding person until each member can flawlessly state every other person's name in the group. Then add a piece of information, such as how each is feeling at the moment, and repeat the entire process using names and feelings. You can continue to build in this way, adding categories such as major interest, goal in life, main concern, marital status, job, and so forth. Choose items of information that will be most conducive to group growth and sharing. You may want to intersperse position changes in the group during this activity to help members remember persons rather than positions and sequences. This activity, especially the name part, can be repeated at the beginning of the first few sessions until people are completely sure of one another's names. This takes very little time and removes some of the natural embarrassment and frustration members experience when they know they should remember a person's name but don't and are afraid to ask.

Draw Your World

This activity initiates the process of self-disclosure in the group and incorporates a visual dimension into the process of sharing. Provide group members with a sheet of paper with a large circle on it and ask them to create a picture that represents their world. They may use symbols, pictures, words, or phrases or a combination. The purpose is to portray their personal world as they see it and as they fit into it. When the picture is completed have members embellish their pictures with the following information: At each of the four corners of your world (N, S, E, W) write two words or brief phrases that describe: 1) How your family sees you; 2) How your friends see you; 3) How your colleagues or coworkers see you; and 4) How you see yourself. Have each member show their picture to the group and describe his or her world and answer questions about it. When all have shown their pictures, have them share the descriptions. Additional perceptions that may be solicited are those of employer, teachers, students, neighbors, etc.

Appleton and Dykeman (1996) have suggested a modification of this activity that has worked effectively with Native American groups. They call it Make a Picture of Your World. They distribute magazines to the group and ask members to do a rapid perusal of them and tear or cut out pictures that reflect who they are and their world. Members then form these pictures into a collage depicting their life which is then shared with the group. Processing is integrated into the sharing to generate group interaction.

Lifeline Activity

Miller (1993) describes this activity as "a near surefire, bona fide strategy in fostering self-disclosure, group cohesion and group feedback" (p. 51). Use the following instructions to introduce the activity:

> Draw a horizontal line across your card (usually a 5 × 7 index card). Put a dot at each end of the line. Over the left dot, place a zero. This dot represents your birthday. Write your birthdate under this dot. The dot on the right represents your death. This next part is optional. Over the right dot, put a number which indicates your best guess as to how many years you will live. Now place a dot which indicates where you are right now on the line between birth and death. Above the line, experiences that were positive, happy, or rewarding should be plotted chronologically. Below are plotted experiences that were negative, unhappy, or painful. The distance above or below the line indicates the degree of positive or negative impact or feeling. Try to write at least two or three positive and negative events or experiences in such a way that you will be able to identify them. Take your time and when you are finished put down your pencil so I will know you've finished. (p. 52)

Processing will require consideration of time limitations and be adapted to the nature and purposes of the group. Modifications for children, adolescents, and adults will also be necessary as developmental dynamics impact both the product developed and the resulting process.

Facilitation

Role Playing

Role playing is one of the most flexible facilitation techniques in group counseling and every counselor should develop expertise in its use. Role playing in its simplest form means reenacting or acting out a situation in the group as if it were occurring in actuality. Role playing makes use of simulation and modeling to help group members look more intensely at problem areas, both for deeper understanding of their concerns and for alternative solutions. It provides members with a highly realistic basis for transfer of learning to the real environment making the prospect of change less threatening and the implementation of change less difficult.

Role playing can be appropriate any time a member gets into a descriptive discourse of a problem situation that involves other people. It is especially helpful when a person is having difficulty expressing a situation clearly or if a story seems to have discrepancies. Ask whether the member is willing to role play the situation and, if so, ask for a brief description of the people and setting. Select other group members to play the roles of the people involved, and have the member give the participants a brief run down on the personalities of the people they are playing. Then begin the role play, making sure that participants stay in their roles until the role play is concluded or is concluded by the leader or member. Some leaders prefer to run through the whole situation whereas others approach it in small vignettes, stopping along the way to assess what is happening, to ask for feedback, or to point out something relevant to the problem. Make sure sufficient time is available when a role play is completed for discussion in which participants and observers can reflect on what happened.

Many role playing techniques can be used by a counselor. A few examples are briefly described below:

Open Chair Technique. In this particular technique only one role player is involved. It is useful when the problem under consideration involves only the member and one other person. Two chairs are placed facing each other and the member sits in one and the counselor in the other. A conversation is started, and as soon as it gets going the counselor leaves the chair. The client continues the conversation playing both roles, moving to the appropriate chair to speak for each party.

The open chair technique is also effective when an individual is struggling with inner conflicts that can be polarized into a dialogue depicting the two sides of the struggle.

Role Reversal. This technique is similar to the Open Chair except that two persons (or more) are involved throughout the role play. The member and the other person begin a conversation and at an appropriate point the leader intervenes to make them switch chairs and roles. The leader helps the conversation continue smoothly through the switch by repeating the last line that was stated before the reversal. In this way the continuity of the role play is maintained, and participants get to look at things from each other's point of view.

Role Substitution. In many role playing situations a useful technique is to have the main participant stand back and watch him or herself in action. Once a role playing situation is in full swing the counselor can ask another member to play the part of the main actor. The role play continues with the main person watching his or her double in operation, trying to glean a greater awareness of the situation.

Alter Ego. To facilitate clearer and deeper understanding in a role play, the leader may ask a group member to become an alter ego to one or several of the participants. This person is a helper to the person in the role, representing some aspect of that person. The alter ego can operate independently or can be given specific instructions such as "interject now, and express the feelings of the person in the role." This technique is very useful but requires some training and practice before a member can function effectively in the role of alter ego.

By combining any number of these techniques and extending the time and scope of the role play, the group leader can create a full scale sociodrama or psychodrama if that is beneficial to the member or the group. In school settings sociodramas are quite appropriate whereas psychodrama is relevant in treatment programs for chemically dependent clients and in a wide variety of out patient therapy groups.

The Line Up

Many times groups get into discussions that involve being more than or less than something. Some members may see themselves as more quiet or more shy than other people in social situations. Or some members may feel they are more trusting or committed in the group. The lineup is a useful facilitating technique in such situations. Clearly define the issue in terms of a continuum (most talkative to least talkative in social situations), and establish two points in the room to represent the two ends of the continuum. Then have members place themselves on the continuum where they feel most comfortable or that most accurately describes them. The first time through each member chooses a spot on the line but no ties are permitted (two or more people at the same point). When the line has been established repeat the activity, but this time each person's position is determined by the other members. Follow-up discussion can focus on the discrepancies and consistencies between the two lineups and the natural tendency for clustering in the middle on most issues. An additional procedure is to do a follow-up line up where each person places themselves where they would like to be. This helps members set goals to work toward in the group.

Katz (1973) has suggested another version of the line up. Place the group members in a straight line in the middle of the room (order is not important). Then designate the wall in front of the members as one endpoint of the continuum and the wall behind them as the other endpoint. Ask members to close their eyes and on a signal move to the spot where they feel they belong on the continuum. In this way the intragroup comparative nature of the exercise is minimized and each member reacts more independently and personally to the continuum issue itself.

Relationship Analysis

Many group members have relationship problems. Poppen and Thompson (1974) suggested a format to help members assess what is happening in their relationships and with the group's help identify whether they are balanced (mutually respectful). This procedure involves five basic steps:

1. Describe the relationship.
2. Specify the limits (specific boundaries) in the relationship.
3. State the responsibilities each person has in the relationship.
4. Note the degree of freedom within the relationship.
5. Designate the amount of personal recreation (time alone) for each person in the relationship.

Discuss each step in the group and determine if the relationship is unbalanced and what can be done to achieve mutual respect in the relationship. The basic ideas behind this facilitative technique are that: 1) all relationships have some limits and some specific areas of freedom; 2) every person should have designated responsibilities (even a child); and 3) personal recreation time (time alone) is important. If members can learn these principles, they can act constructively in resolving many of their relationship problems.

Three Things I'd To Like to Change

This activity can be used to facilitate a work oriented focus on specific problems of group members. Many times group members have difficulty resolving their problems because they do not know exactly what they want to change. This activity helps them identify clearly the areas that need changing. Have members write down three things about themselves that they would like to change. Have each member share their list with the group, giving brief explanations of each item. Then have each member select one area from the list and describe it in more detail following these four basic behavioral steps:

1. Describe what you do not like about the way you are (*problem*).
2. Describe how you would like to change (*goal*).
3. Discuss with the group how you might be able to change and form a strategy for doing so (*plan*).
4. Try out the plan, and report back to the group on your progress (*follow-up*).

For the last two steps some counselors like to use the contract system (Dustin & George, 1973), where the group member writes up a plan as if it were a contract and signs it in the group's presence. This increases the specificity of the plan, promotes the individual's commitment to it, and gives the group a solid basis for holding the member accountable and reinforcing, encouraging, and evaluating the member's progress. This same procedure can be used for each of the desired changes noted on the initial lists.

Button and Flower Technique

Thomas, Nelson, and Sumners (1994) recommend an activity the helps members "recognize the connection between current situations that automatically elicit strong negative feelings" and abusive experiences from their past (p. 108). Paper, pen, and a box of buttons are needed for this activity. Each member is asked to draw a flower composed of petals, each of which describes a repetitive situation where he or she experiences strong negative reactions. When completed a button is placed on a flower petal of one member (representing a situation that pushes his or her button), and the situation is processed in the group to assist the person in identifying, understanding, and dealing with the situation and the real origin of his or her feelings. This technique is used facilitatively over time and is particularly helpful in groups where members are dealing with and working through repercussions of traumatizing experiences.

Write Your Play

Thomas, Nelson, and Sumners (1994) use this activity to help members "realize the complex nature of breaking the abuse cycle and the tendency to continually replay the victim, caretaker or abuser role with their partners, families and peers" (p. 108). Each group member is helped to describe in detail recurring situations in their lives where interactions are characterized by the same negative, destructive, and self-defeating dynamics and behaviors. Relative to that scenario, each member is then asked to: 1) Name the play; 2) Identify the roles played by the member and others involved; 3) Describe the plot (pattern); and 4) Recognize the familiar ending. Once the play has been fully developed the member is asked to rewrite the play giving it: 1) A new name; 2) New roles; 3) A new plot with different behaviors leading to 4) A new ending. Processing has deep impact on the life of the member whose play it is and on the members who enact similar scenarios in their lives leading to empowerment and breaking the abuse cycle.

Termination

Crystal Ball

This terminating activity requires the use of some object that resembles a crystal ball. Members are asked to think about the future and consider what and where they would like to be five years hence. (The timeframe is arbitrary and can be varied according to the age level and particular setting of the group). The crystal ball is then passed from person to person and members describe as imaginatively and creatively as possible what they see for themselves in the future. Another way of proceeding is to have members project what they see in the future for their fellow members. This activity tends to give members a future orientation but is based in large measure on the learning and experiences that has taken place in the group.

3 × 5 Evaluation

Some leaders like to get feedback regarding the group process at the end of each session. A kind of ongoing evaluation takes place that serves the leader's purposes for planning and revision and also helps members assess their experiences during that particular session. One means of doing this is to distribute 3 × 5 cards on which members anonymously express their reactions, opinions, or suggestions about the group session. This evaluation can be done during the last five minutes of each session and cards can be deposited in a box as members leave. This activity also provides a cue to members that time is up and yet allows an opportunity for the expression of any feelings that members were not able to state during the meeting. Over time these cards can supply counselors with valuable feedback about their effectiveness and the progress of the group.

Hope Chest

This activity is helpful for closing a group on a positive note, accentuating the qualities of interpersonal support that have developed. Ask the group members to silently consider their hopes and wishes for every other member in the group. Pass out blank sheets of paper to members and have them write at the top "Hope Chest for (their own names)." Then have the members pass their sheet to the person on their right. When the exchange is made ask each member to draw a symbol or picture, designate a gift, or write a statement that reflects specific hopes for the person whose name appears at the top. Continue this process until each person in the group has made an entry on each sheet. When the sheets return to their owners, each member reviews the information and in turn holds up his or her Hope Chest for the group to see. The members then explain their contributions as feedback and acknowledgement. A variation of this technique is to have members exchange symbolic gifts that represent wishes for one another.

Harman and Withers (1992) use a modification of the Hope Chest as follows: A blank sheet of paper is taped to each member's back. Members are given magic markers and 30 minutes to write comments reflecting their hopes for each other. Colors are alternated to camouflage the source of feedback. Upon completion of the time period, sheets are removed and each member reads and reflects on the comments. The feedback and experience are processed in the group as a closing activity.

CHAPTER

Family Theory as a Group Resource

The impetus for including a chapter relating family theory and systems thinking to group process emanated from a variety of sources not the least of which was my own evolutionary development as a professional. Trained initially in an individually oriented, primarily Rogerian model that emphasized necessary and sufficient therapeutic conditions in the counselor-client relationship and the mobilization of the inner resources of the client to resolve his or her problems, I quickly realized that a major discrepancy existed between what happened in the counselor's office and what happened in the client's life. The helping process that relied on the therapeutic relationship to mobilize intrapsychic forces for the purpose of implementing change often was insufficient to overcome the insurmountable obstacles presented by the client's social system.

☐ Introduction: The Case for Integration

In an effort to improve the transferability of the therapeutic process to the ongoing life experiences of clients, I became interested in the group process, which because of its nature as a social milieu, offered advantages (as noted in Chapter 2) that greatly enhanced the probability of constructive change. However, even the group process was limited in that it could only represent reality. As a social laboratory group members could approximate the real world, but a gap still existed between their experiences in the group and their experiences outside the group.

The desire to work directly with a piece of client reality instead of a second hand account or an approximation, coupled with the observation that in both individual and group counseling problems typically had a family connection, resulted in my becoming involved in family counseling. However, my evolution was far from complete. The old expression *what goes around comes around* typifies what happened next. I moved from a position at a university where I was training counselors in all three modalities to a position as a practicing clinician where I was immersed in using all three modalities. This shift produced a basic dilemma because unilateral decisions as to appropriate modality and approach were not always easy to make. Consequently, questions of whether these three modalities were mutually exclusive, sequential, or tangential with areas of commonality as well as uniqueness were raised. Whether I wanted to or not, I had to grapple with the challenge of integration. This chapter is part of my response to that issue—particularly from the perspective of relating group process and family theory.

Integrating Group and Family Counseling

Efforts to develop a conceptual and pragmatic interface between group counseling and family counseling as differentiated but related therapeutic modalities have been emerging in the literature, in training, and in clinical practice for at least three decades. From the group perspective, Ohlsen (1979) noted the high incidence of counselors doing marital work and compiled a set of articles that applied group methodology to couples. West and Kirby (1981) followed suit demonstrating the relevance of group methods in dealing with family issues and problems. Becvar (1982) reviewed literature comparing the family and other small groups and concluded that small group theory is a valid and useful resource in understanding and working with families. In 1982, the Association for Specialists in Group Work created a Commission on Family Counseling specifically to address the relationship between family counseling and group counseling. That commission presented an initial program at the 1984 American Association for Counseling and Development Convention in Houston, Texas comparing and contrasting group and family counseling (Ritter, West, & Trotzer, 1987). The Commission also presented a subsequent program in New York in 1985 on integrating and differentiating group and family counseling in theory, training, and practice (Trotzer, West, Ritter & Malnati, 1985), and a program in Chicago, Illinois entitled, Group and Family Perspectives on a Simulated Family Session (Trotzer, West, Ritter, Malnati & Hovestadt, 1987).

The fact that family counseling has emerged as a therapeutic modality in its own right is reflected in the growth of marriage and family training programs and the incorporation of such training into counselor education programs (Hovestadt, Fennell, & Piercy, 1983). The growth of professional organizations promoting marriage and family counseling such as the American Association for Marriage and Family Therapy (AAMFT), the American Family Therapy Association (AFTA), the International Association for Marriage and Family Counseling (IAMFC), and Division 43 (Family Psychology) of the American Psychological Association (APA) also attest to the emergence and relevance of family theory and family therapy. While the popularity of marriage and family counseling has prompted some counseling practitioners to make exclusionary commitments to family therapy as the modality of choice across the board, a strong case exists for family theory and family therapy to be a resource to the other counseling modalities as well as being a preferred interventive entity in its own right. In fact, Horne (Campbell, 1992) has framed family counseling as one of the developmental phases the counseling profession has gone through in its maturing process. He noted that the sequence of individual counseling, group counseling, marriage and family counseling, and currently multicultural counseling are substantiated as critical stages of development in the counseling profession with a cumulative effect on training and practice.

Current research and clinical practice supports the idea that a group and family specialization is not only viable, but recommended as a future oriented training necessity (Shapiro & Shapiro, 1985). Ruevini (1985) in addressing the critical issues facing group work in the future observed the following:

> Group workers . . . should realize that they need to involve themselves not only with the important issues of group methodology, research and the effectiveness of various available theoretical frameworks, but also with issues of the viability, importance and central position of the family group as a critical factor in people's lives (p. 88).

He goes on to promote training in family therapy as an essential component of group leadership training. Matthews (1992) proceeds a step further by examining and explicating the link between general systems theory (GST) and group process.

The purpose of this chapter is to present the utility of family theory as a resource in group counseling. The basic premise is that just as group theory and techniques can be useful in understanding and helping families (Becvar, 1982) so family theory and techniques can be useful in understanding and helping individuals in groups. (See Trotzer responses in Donigian & Hulse-Killacky, 1999). This chapter will first differentiate between group and family dynamics and then discuss family theory as a group resource. Family theory in relationship to group process and content and as a basis for developing group techniques will also be presented. Guidelines and precautions for using family based group techniques will be discussed, and the chapter will conclude with group learning activities derived from a family theory base.

☐ Differentiating the Family Group from the Counseling Group

A family is a group with a history, structure, and organizational hierarchy which the counselor must join while a counseling group consists of individuals brought together by a counselor to create its own history and structure. The family group will continue regardless of interventive efforts while a counseling group will dissolve (Trotzer, 1988). Consequently, the family is a unit of relational reality that has continuity over time while the counseling group is artificially created to approximate relational reality which is time limited.

Tavantzis and Tavantzis (1985) noted additional differences between the family group and the counseling group. In counseling groups the purpose is to enable members to interact as equals in a safe environment where mutual help is a derived norm. The thrust is to create the possibility for members to share their vulnerabilities and experiment with new attitudes and behaviors. The leader often takes a responsible role in creating a safe atmosphere, but greatly relinquishes that role to the group as the group evolves. As Pistole (1997) notes: "In a family, the parents remain the authority and source of security and protection. In groups, the counselor's goal is to relinquish this position and manage the multiple relationships more as a partner" (p. 12).

In family groups, hierarchies take precedence over equality relative to membership, and the security of the group is more than an artifact of the group process. Vulnerability and freedom are greatly curtailed by the family members "shared history and interlocking roles and patterned behavior" (Tavantzis & Tavantzis, 1985, p. 4). The therapist must be continuously cognizant of the safety factor in the family as it extends beyond the therapy room. Hansen (Ritter, West, & Trotzer, 1986) observed that if people get nicked up in individual counseling or chewed up in group they can still turn to others for support and sustenance. But, if they get nicked up in family counseling, the most meaningful people in their lives are doing the attacking (p. 297). Thus, family members both bring their stressful environments with them and take them home while group members can get respite from their stressors in either environment (the group or their life) by moving from one to the other. However, one advantage of group work is that generic similarities between the counseling group and the family group can bring family issues to life in the group while providing a space where those issues can be examined without the contingent threat of family retaliation (Pistole, 1997).

In counseling groups (with some exceptions) membership is primarily voluntary whereas in family counseling members often attend involuntarily (parents bring children; wives coerce husbands). The advantage of working with a family is that you get to work with a piece of reality without having to rely on second hand accounts (individual counseling) or approximations of reality (group counseling). However, the disadvantage is that the resistance factors are accentuated. As Yalom (Forester-Miller, 1989) observes in groups and families "some of the basic processes are the same in that you are using interpersonal analysis" (p. 198). The difference is that "there are ongoing relationships in the family that you want to alter, where the group is much more a kind of dress rehearsal for life" (p. 198).

While family theory and group theory both address the process involved in their respective units, the focus of change differs. In family counseling the unit of change is either the family with subsequent impact on the individual or change in the individuals with subsequent impact on the family system. In groups, however, the unit of change is the individual.

Hovestadt (Ritter, West, & Trotzer, 1987) stated that the purpose of change in family counseling is to generate a higher level of functioning and satisfaction in the family system which is in contrast to group counseling where the goal is to improve the functioning of the individual (p. 296). In addition, the epistemology of the change process differs. Most individual and group approaches tend to be based on linear thought process models of causation whereas family counseling is based on systemic thinking which posits circularity with patterns and sequences as the causal framework (Couch & Childers, 1989). Change then only occurs when the pattern or sequence of interaction—rather than the individual per se—is modified. However, both modalities are interventive in nature attempting to utilize and/or create interpersonal dynamics that will result in therapeutic change. This particular factor paves the way for integration between the two modalities as will be explicated in the remainder of this chapter.

☐ Family Theory as a Resource

The significance and centrality of family data and experience are not new ideas in a therapeutic sense. Freud relied on family data particularly from a person's infancy to explain psychodynamically the characteristics of personality development. Adler emphasized the impact of a person's childhood family recollections in regard to the development of social interest and the emergence of his or her private logic and basic mistakes. However, family dynamics remained only a factor in the conceptualization of human problems. The family was treated vicariously within the individual and the subsequent resolution of family dynamics was left unaddressed until the family theorists and their systemic orientation emerged in the 50s and 60s (Zuk, 1971). Since then, the field of family theory and therapy has blossomed into a fully developed conceptual and clinical entity as a bonafide approach to resolving human problems (Mikesell, Lusterman & McDaniel, 1995).

Family theory provides conceptual models that relate directly to group counseling in terms of process, content, and techniques. For group leaders who wish to utilize family theory as a resource, understanding the following conceptual components is recommended as a minimum basis for incorporating family concepts into group counseling:

1. Overview of the growth and development of family theory and family therapy (Barnard & Corrales, 1979; Goldenberg & Goldenberg, 1996; Nichols, 1984);

2. The family as a system, i.e., systemic thinking from both a structural and strategic perspective (Madanes, 1981; Minuchin, 1974);
3. Intergenerational family dynamics (Boszormenyi-Nagy & Krasner, 1986; Boszormenyi-Nagy & Spark, 1973; Bowen, 1966);
4. The developmental life cycle of the family (Carter & McGoldrick, 1988; Walsh, 1982);
5. The impact of divorce and the dynamics of single parent and remarried (blended) families (Cantor & Drake, 1983; Sager, Brown, Crohn, Engel, Rodstein, & Walker, 1983; Visher & Visher, 1979, 1988);
6. The importance, impact, and relevance of ethnicity, diversity, and culture in family systems (McGoldrick, Giordano, & Pearce, 1996).

An introductory course in marriage and family counseling will address most of the above noted material and a follow-up course in marriage and family theories and techniques will provide the conceptual depth necessary to use family theory as a resource in leading groups.

Family Theory and Group Process

The family is a social unit that teaches its members about social interaction and supplies them with skills, perceptions, and rules relative to how one is affected by and acts in social (interpersonal) situations. In group counseling each individual member reflects his or her family heritage—a factor which significantly affects the process of group development. For example, "attachment theory describes individual and dyadic aspects of significant relationships that develop within the family and so it can be an aid in exploring and interpreting behavior in adult relationships" (Pistole, 1997, p. 10). Such family theory constructs that explain the dynamics of family influence can be useful in helping group leaders address the tasks involved in starting a group and building a cohesive group structure while accounting for individual differences. For example, a person raised in an enmeshed family (Minuchin, 1974) may experience great difficulty connecting in the group during its initial stages due to loyalty or guilt issues, while a person raised in a disengaged family (Minuchin, 1974) may rapidly identify with the group but have difficulty or actually resist forming a committed attachment. Such reactions emanate from family based social expectations and rules that influence members behaviors and experiences in the group. As such, family theory provides a useful perspective as group members negotiate ground rules and establish group norms.

Family theory also provides process tools for the group leader. For example, Zuk (1981) has identified three key roles that the therapist plays in negotiating the therapeutic process. These roles are that of celebrant, go-between, and side taker.

The _celebrant_ is the role of official who presides over significant events such as a minister presides over a marriage or a judge over a trial. This role is crucial in establishing that an interaction or a problem is real and definitive so that it can be treated as a fact of life. By this means problems are acknowledged and established as the focus of attention.

The *go-between* is the mediator role. This role is facilitative in nature enabling people with different perspectives to connect with and understand each other. The go-between sees that communication occurs, makes sure everyone is heard, and serves as the channel for translating differences into understandings.

The *side taker* is the influence dimension of the counselor role where he or she judiciously chooses to take sides in the best interests of generating constructive change and problem resolution.

Based on the premise that a family therapist cannot help but be drawn into emotional intensity among clients, these roles enable him or her to act constructively in spite of becoming emotionally inducted into the family system. The same dynamics affect the group leader when group members become engaged in intense interpersonal interactions. As such, being cognizant of and able to utilize these roles are valuable process assets to group leadership.

Another systemic construct that relates directly to the group process is the separateness-belongingness dimension of human experience. "The oscillation between individualizing and grouping or differentiation and integration according to GST (general systems theory) is the basic dialectic of all human systems" (Matthews, 1992, p. 162). In groups this dynamic is manifested in the members' "conflict between responsibility to self and responsibility to the group" (Matthews, 1992, p. 163) and in the vacillating balance between the individual influencing the group and the group influencing the individual. "Therapy conducted in groups has the advantage of treating the members in the context of this fundamental dance of life" (Matthews, 1992, p. 163).

Applying this construct to process, Matthews (1992) summarizes the essence of leadership as delineating "whether differentiation or integration is needed" (p. 163) and deciding "whether to pull members together as a group or let them differentiate as individuals" (p. 163). The "orchestration of such decisions is the way (leaders) guide a group through its developmental stages" (p. 163).

The process applications of family theory to group counseling are innumerable. As groups develop cohesiveness, they take on more characteristics and traits that make them just like a family in many respects. As Saygal (1996) observed, "healthy functioning families, as any well functioning groups, respect diverse perspectives and individual differences, embrace an overall mood of warmth and caring and operate via clear yet flexible structures" (p. 81). The reverse of these characteristics can also be true generating dysfunction in both a family and a group. However, as noted by Gazda (Ritter, West, & Trotzer, 1987), groups can generate feelings that are similar to families but certain dimensions are always missing. Therefore, family theory is useful in understanding and guiding the group process, but should not be used as a means of recreating group experiences that are meant to be family experiences. Rather groups are arenas for recapitulating family dynamics for the purpose of reconstructing emotional experiences for corrective therapeutic reasons (Yalom, 1995).

☐ Family Theory and Group Content

In terms of content, a significant portion of problems and issues raised in group counseling are directly or indirectly related to family. Trotzer's (1985) Interpersonal Problem Matrix designates marital and family problems as a major subgroup of the category conflicts in relationships (p. 101). Yalom (1985) stated that "without exception patients enter group therapy with a history of a highly unsatisfactory experience in their first and most important group—their primary family" (p. 15). Although somewhat overstated for counseling groups, family experience does provide developmental and residual problems that are often addressed in groups. Satir (1972) stated simply that "troubled families make troubled people" (p. 18), and their troubles (or problems) tend to emerge in counseling groups.

Ruevini (1985) acknowledged the family as the source of pain in a past, present, and future sense, but also credits it as a major source of productive and positive support—especially in periods of crisis. Family theory, therefore, is a vital resource relative to the content of problems addressed in groups both from the standpoint of clearly delineating their nature and developing practical and realistic interventive strategies the individual member can use in dealing with them. For example, adolescent counseling groups typically address problems related to the existence and nature of boundaries established by significant adults in their lives, the resulting dynamics of differentiation, and the emerging generation gap. Subsequently, constructs drawn from the adolescent stage of the family life cycle are particularly applicable (Carter & McGoldrick, 1988; Walsh, 1982). In groups for young adults, understanding and utilizing individuation and differentiation concepts and helping group members establish and communicate *positions* where they are separate from but connected to parents, siblings, and family are helpful group resources (Bowen, 1966).

Content applications of family theory are even more germane to group counseling than the process dimensions. Increased familiarity with the dynamics and perspectives of family life in relationship to individual development will enhance understanding of group member problems and improve the probability of constructive resolution strategies and potential change. Therefore, family theory has a direct relationship to the therapeutic impact of group counseling and therapy.

☐ Family Theory and Group Techniques

One primary vehicle for integrating family theory constructs into group counseling is the structured group technique. As noted in Chapter 13 structured activities have utility as initiating, facilitating, and terminating tools in groups (Bates, Johnson, & Blaker, 1982; Trotzer, 1973). Coupled with family theory as an idea generation base (Trotzer, 1985), the group counselor can develop a myriad of activities that enhance group process and surface relevant material for group interaction.

Family based group techniques are advantageous for both intrapersonal and interpersonal reasons. Intrapersonally, such techniques are engaging because they tap a common experience, i.e., everyone has a family background. In addition, one's own family background is an arena where each person is more expert than anyone else. Thus, a common focus is generated where everyone has something meaningful to contribute. Interpersonally, a family focus stimulates generic curiosity. Since everyone is a member of a family, each person tends to reflect on how his or her family is different from or similar to other families. Family based group techniques provide a natural bridge between members facilitating cohesiveness and creating a context where similarities and differences can be acknowledged. Thus commonality and connectedness is enhanced *and* diversity and uniqueness is promoted. Effectively used, family based group techniques will facilitate the group process and generate foci in accordance with the problem solving purpose of the group's existence. Several examples of such techniques follow.

☐ Family Based Group Techniques

Family Rules and Group Rules

One of the fundamental constructs of family theory is based on the premise that the family is a system. A system is a number of parts related in such a way that a change in one part affects all other parts (Barnard & Corrales, 1979). Systems operate on the basis of rules which are communicated to its members in either spoken form (verbalized edicts that specify expectations and consequences) or unspoken form (nonverbalized operational rules that only family members know). These rules create the basis of group members' social expectations referred to previously. An activity entitled Rules Grew Up With that surfaces these expectations is particularly useful as an initiating activity in the early stages of group counseling. The activity is as follows:

Rules I Grew Up With (Instructions)

1. Explain the difference between spoken and unspoken rules (Barnard & Corrales, 1979).

2. On a blank sheet of paper create two columns, one labeled Spoken and the other Unspoken.
3. Have group members list examples of rules they grew up with in the appropriate columns.
4. Have group members share their lists and explain their entries.
5. Process the activity in relation to member expectations about the group and relate the material to ground rules for group interaction.

The Rules I Grew Up With activity facilitates the expression of group members' expectations and begins the process of forming group norms. Group ground rules whether established by leader directive or group consensus are reflective of spoken rules and norms which evolve in groups are reflective of the unspoken variety. Just as families need effective boundaries, so do groups. In group counseling therapeutic ground rules and norms can be forged out of the composite of group members' experiences with family rules. This activity also lays the ground work for helping members adjust to environments with differing boundaries (e.g., school or work setting) and modifying expectations that have been molded in family environments that are contributing to adjustment problems. Therefore, the material generated by this activity has both process and content relevance.

Sibling Position and Group Relationships

The family theory contention that significant aspects of a person's personality are forged in the family is useful in facilitating the development of relationships in the group. Constructs such as Toman's (1976) family constellation and ordinal position in the sibling hierarchy lend themselves well to an activity that effectively assists group members in connecting relationally. The following activity helps group members get acquainted and form relational bonds.

Sibling Position Personality Activity (Instructions)

1. Have group members identify themselves according to their birth order (oldest, second, middle, youngest, only, or an appropriate modification of such e.g., oldest of the second set of three) and include details such as gender of siblings and spacing chronologically. Instruct the person to refrain from giving details as to their experience in that position.
2. Ask the group to discuss what they know about each person based on their birth order identification only: e.g., "What do you know about John who is the oldest of three with two younger sisters?" The focus person only listens during this discussion.
3. After each person's traits are proscribed by the group, ask that person to respond with their perspective of themselves (verification, clarification, refinement, modification, or disconfirmation).
4. After each member has been processed individually, discuss how differ-

ent combinations of sibling position personalities might be expected to relate: e.g., "How would a youngest and an oldest relate?" or "What might be happening between an oldest and a second child?"

Process the activity in light of possible group dynamics and interaction patterns in the group. Discussion usually brings the group's attention to itself and the relationships forming as a result of group interaction. This activity is particularly useful in the cohesiveness stage of the group and helps members get to know each other quickly and effectively without excessive emphasis on self-disclosure.

Family Legacy as a Group Resource

Intergenerational family constructs are particularly useful in the work or problem solving stage of the group. Decision making in personal, interpersonal, vocational, and spiritual spheres of life are often influenced by the legacies a person inherits from his or her family of origin. An activity entitled Houses in Your Life is useful in exploring the psychodynamic forces operating in group members' lives.

Houses in Your Life (Instructions)

1. Have group members draw caricatures or bring photographs of the following family homes:
   a. Maternal grandparents
   b. Paternal grandparents
   c. Parents (step-parents if applicable)
   d. Current home (if different from parents)
   Note: Extended generational homes such as great grandparents' homesteads or immigrant families' original homeland domiciles can also be included.
2. Have members identify and share the following information relative to each home:
   a. A significant memory
   b. Traits, attitudes, or values associated with that home or generation.
3. Process the shared information in light of each member's current life style, decisions and problems.

Family of origin dynamics tend to be intricately involved in most problems group members discuss. This activity facilitates emergence of legacy material that tends to remain beneath the surface when considering here and now problems and future oriented decisions. Consequently, a broader base of information becomes available to the individual and the group that can be mobilized as part of the problem solving process. These examples illustrate how family theory can be integrated into the group process through the vehicle of a structured group technique. (Additional activities are described at the end of the chapter.) However, the material from family theory also can be integrated without reliance on structured techniques. Using the leadership tools described in Chapter 6, group leaders can introduce family dynamics in the context of using their reactive, active, and interactive skills to carry out their leadership functions.

☐ Guidelines and Precautions

Although family based group techniques are relatively easy to develop and utilize, there are several important guidelines and precautions that must be observed.

1. *Remember the loyalty factor.* Whenever individuals are invited or induced to discuss their family, an automatic loyalty conflict is created—particularly if negative information is involved. Consequently, group leaders must learn the skill of multi-directed partiality (Boszormenyi-Nagy & Krasner, 1986). This skill enables the counselor to be partial to both the discloser's side and the family's side without taking sides, thus enabling a constructive dialogue to ensue between the sides in the safety of the group context. Raising the family's side of a group member's perspective enables the group member to disclose without feeling like a traitor because the group leader demonstrates fairness and caring not only for the member but for his or her family as well.

2. *Seek resources not skeletons.* The purpose of family based group techniques is to generate material that will provide understanding of the individual member and assistance in helping that member deal with his or her problems or concerns. While family material can be extremely enticing from an interest perspective, leaders must avoid getting distracted by family story telling. If the material emerging cannot be directly related to the group process or the concerns of the individuals, measures should be taken to redirect the discussion.

3. *Avoid meddling in families.* A basic premise of group counseling is that the group can only directly affect persons who are in the group. This fact must be recognized and continually reaffirmed when using family based group techniques. Leaders must avoid doing long distance family therapy or turning group members into therapists for their own families. The tendency to meddle in families must be watched for and curtailed. Keeping the focus on the person rather than the family during sharing and discussion will circumvent the tendency to dabble in family dynamics without a clear purpose with respect to the individual member.

4. *Build family based group techniques from concepts rather than content.* Most people are private where information related to their families is concerned. This is particularly true in certain cultures and ethnic groups. Group techniques should be created out of a sound conceptual framework and not merely for the purpose of eliciting particular information. The structure of the technique should be such that members do not feel threatened by the content of the desired disclosure. Apprise group members of the construct

undergirding the activity which relates to all group members so that they will feel comfortable in supplying the subsequent information.

5. *Avoid family based techniques which elicit emotionalized or traumatic disclosures.* Family encounters often produce the most painful emotional reactions. Psychological wounds garnered in the context of family relationships tend to produce emotional responses whether they represent recent or old wounds. Leaders must be sensitive to the traumatizing potential in family based activities, discard high risk activities, and modify instructions to temper the level of emotional impact.

Note: In therapy groups with members who have experienced intrusive acts in a family context (e.g., incest or sexual, physical, emotional abuse) this guideline does not constitute avoidance, but rather a monitoring of disclosures to maintain a pace and focus that facilitates therapeutic working through of such experiences (Courtois & Leehan, 1982).

☐ Concluding Comment

Family theory provides a vast resource base for the group counselor. Whether used from a dynamic perspective as a means of understanding and assisting group members, as a catalyst relative to group process and content, or translated into group techniques, it is a valuable entity for extending the group practitioner's expertise. When used ethically and wisely, the impact and utility of group work as a therapeutic modality will be enhanced.

☐ Learning Activities

The learning activities that follow are divided into five loosely defined categories based on the nature of their conceptual origins, the content produced, or the general focus of the activity. The categories are

1. impact of the family,
2. exploring family dynamics,
3. individual development in a family context,
4. exploring legacy dynamics, and
5. couple's group activities.

Impact of the Family

Introduction Dyads: The Family Perspective

This activity is an excellent initiating activity for groups. Using a format of revolving dyads, have group members introduce themselves from the following perspectives:

1. *Grandparent (legacy) Perspective*: Introduce yourself as if your grandparents were introducing you: "This is my grandson/daughter (name). He/she. . . ."
2. *Family of Origin Perspective*: Introduce yourself as your parents would introduce you: "This is my son/daughter (name). He/she. . . ."
3. *Sibling Perspective*: Introduce yourself as your siblings (brother/sister) would introduce you: "This is my brother/sister (name). He/she. . . ."
4. *Intimate Partner Perspective*: Introduce yourself as your intimate partner (spouse, lover, finance', etc.) would introduce you: "This is my (husband/wife, etc.) (name). He/she. . . ."
5. *Family of Creation Perspective*: Introduce yourself as your children would introduce you: "This is my mother/father (name). He/she. . . ."
6. *Self Perspective*: Introduce yourself as you would introduce you: "My name is ____. I am. . . ."

Step family perspectives can be added or substituted depending on the group. For any perspective that does not currently exist or apply (e.g., member does not have children or was an only child), the member should make up an introduction as they would like it to be if it did exist. Each member can also be given a 3 × 5 card to record significant traits that emerge from each introduction. These data can be self-recorded or the result of feedback from the partner who picks out one or two traits that stood out in the introduction.

Additional note: A God, Higher Power, or Supreme Being perspective reflecting the spiritual dimension of human experience can also be incorporated into the dyadic rounds (e.g., "Introduce yourself as God or a Higher Power would introduce you.)

When all perspectives have been shared convene the total group and process the activity from the perspective of how it helped group members get to know one another and how family relationships affect personality development and identity.

Exploring Family Dynamics

Family Tree

One of the places where love and belonging is crucial to the growth and development of a person is in the family. This activity is designed to help each person consider how family background has contributed to who he or she is today. Furnish each person with paper and crayons for drawing. On the paper have group members draw a symbolic tree. The type of tree should represent each person's family; its color should symbolize feelings about childhood, the ground should represent the nature of growth and development, and the background should indicate dominant childhood memories.

After members complete the drawings (10 minutes), pair members off and have them explain their drawings to each other. Have them discuss how they fit into their respective families at the present time (15 minutes).

Form groups of four (two pairs) and have each person discuss their partner's tree and family relationship, pointing out things that seem interesting and significant (25 minutes).

Family Sculpture

Another activity that demonstrates the love and belonging aspect of family relationships is the family sculpture. Select a volunteer to create a family sculpture using other group members. Have him or her design a sculpture of his or her family that represents the relationships as he or she sees them. The sculptor should include him- or herself in the sculpture. When completed have the sculptor assume the position of him- or herself in the finished product. Then have the sculptor describe why he or she placed each person in the position he or she did and what his or her own relationship to the family is. After that discussion have the same volunteer form another family sculpture using different members of the group (the first sculpture should remain intact except for the sculptor). The second sculpture should be a desired picture of the family (how the person would like it to be). If the same people are used remind each person to remember their original position so the first sculpture can be reformed for comparison and contrast. Follow-up discussion should deal with similarities and differences between the two sculptures. You can repeat this several times but usually once or twice is sufficient to generate meaningful discussion. This technique is very useful as a tool in helping clients who are experiencing problems in their families.

Draw Your Childhood Table

Instructions:

1. On a large sheet of paper draw the shape of the table your family ate at when you were growing up (as a child between ages 7 and 12 if you want to raise school age family dynamics or as a teenager between ages 13 and 17 if you want to raise adolescent family dynamics).
2. Place members of your family around the table in their usual places using rectangles around names of males and circles around females. Identify parents and include yourself. An example is provided in Figure 14.1.
3. On the surface of the table write descriptors (words and phrases) which describe the family atmosphere and what it was like for you to live in this family.
4. Near each member at the table write at least two phrases or comments that describe his or her personality.
5. Have each member share their family table with the group.

If used as a homework task, have members write a one page description of their family of origin.

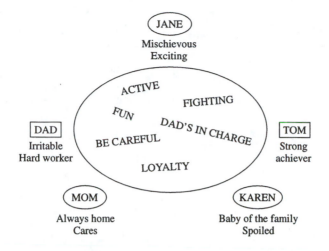

FIGURE 14.1. Example of table with family members seated in regular positions for meals plus words to describe personalities and feelings.

This activity can be modified to the present family table and used to explore current family dynamics. Another version is to have members do both their childhood and current family tables. Processing then involves comparing and contrasting one's experience in family of origin and family of creation.

Another effective method of processing the material from this activity is to use the *family-o-gram technique*. Each person at the table is assigned a typical statement or comment that typifies their personality and role in the family. These statements are assigned to group members who represent the family members. The focus group member then stands in the center of a circle organized in the seating arrangement depicted in the family table. Starting with a parent figure the member rotates around the table receiving the phrases consecutively in a rapid fire manner. Each family member attempts to capture both the content and affect of the message. Have the focus member rotate around the table at least three times without interruption or discussion. The family-o-gram is concluded by having each family member repeat their phrase or statement at the same time attempting to solicit the focus member's attention while he or she stands still with his or her eyes closed. The activity is then processed in light of the messages and perceptions the group member carries with him or her from his or her family experiences. (See Trotzer, 1998a for additional features of this activity.)

Belongingness-Separateness Activity

All families provide their members with two basic experiences growing up: experiences of belongingness and experiences of separateness. These

Belongingness		Separateness	
Free Choice	Forced	Encouraged	Discouraged

FIGURE 14.2. Sample sheet of belongingness-separateness activity.

experiences combine to create a dynamic force in identity development (Trotzer & Trotzer, 1986). Belongingness experiences are of two types: those that are engaged in freely and with enthusiasm and those that are forced upon children and participated in with some resistance. Separateness similarly is divided into activities that were encouraged and discouraged (Figure 14.2).

Pass out a sheet with columns as identified in Figure 14.2 and have group members identify belongingness and separateness experiences they had in their families growing up.

Have group members share their experiences either column by column or overall. Process the information in terms of the impact of these experiences on the respective identity, personality, and values of each person in the group. This activity is effective in helping members get to know each other on a deeper level and begins to surface the unmet needs and strengths in group member's lives.

Individual Development in a Family Context

Individuals In the Family Life Cycle

Pass out the diagram found in Figure 14.3. Have group members plot the following information about themselves and their family.

1. Place a dot and the initials of each family member (parents, spouse, siblings, children, grandparents, self) on the birth to death individual development (ID) line.
2. If married, draw a line from the age at which marriage occurred (ID line) to the marriage dot on the family life cycle (FLC) line. (If divorce and/or remarriage has occurred, add that information by identifying age at divorce on the ID line and draw a line from age at remarriage to the marriage dot on the FLC line.)

FAMILY LIFE CYCLE (FLC) LINE

Establishment	New Parent	Pre-school	School Age	Adolescent	Young Adult	Launching	Parental Middle Years	Aging Family (72) (78)

Spouse's Death

INDIVIDUAL DEVELOPMENT (ID) LINE

Marriage

Birth	2	6	12	18	(22-24)	30	40	50	60	70	Death

Developmental Tasks

Trust   Autonomy   Initiative   Identity (Who am I?)   Differentiation —Seeker Self —Merger Self   Generativity   Integrity

FIGURE 14.3. Individual and family development.

3. Life expectancy date: Have males draw a line from their current age on the ID line to the dot representing 72 (male life expectancy) on the FLC line. Have females draw a line from their current age to the dot representing 78 (female life expectancy) on the FLC line.
4. Family life cycle data: Draw a line straight up from the age of your oldest child on the ID line to the FLC line. (This approximates the family life cycle stage the family is in.) If a step-family is involved, draw a line straight up from the age of the oldest child in each biological family unit.

The information charted can be processed as a means of getting acquainted and understanding the context in which each member is living. Data such as individual development via decade of life, stage of the family life cycle, years left to live and/or years of married life left, and complexity of living in single or remarried families all tend to emerge in the sharing and provide valuable material for developing closeness, acceptance, and understanding in the group and pinpointing problem areas.

Family Life Cycle Analysis

This activity is designed to help members look specifically at their experiences in their family from a developmental perspective.

Instructions: Answer the following questions or respond to the directives relative to your family's current position in the family life cycle. Briefly review the typical stages of family life (Trotzer & Trotzer, 1986, pp. 225–234).

1. In what stage of development is your family at this time? Explain why you made that assessment. (Remember some families may be in more than one stage at any one time.)
2. Write one sentence describing how each person in your family is currently experiencing the family (include yourself), e.g., if you have five people in your family write five sentences.
3. What issues or problems is your family currently dealing with that are typical of the family's stage of development.
4. What is your family doing to deal with the issues or problems listed above?
5. Describe the nature or condition of the marital relationship in your family. Indicate how it contributes and/or hinders the family's ability to deal with the tasks and problems of its developmental stage.

Have each group member share their analysis with the group for the purpose of pinpointing common issues and problems emanating from the stages of family development represented.

This activity is useful in agenda setting as group members identify issues they are struggling with that can be worked on in the group.

Five Roles Activity

Everyone plays many different roles as a normal part of daily life. Some of these roles are more important than others, and some roles cause conflicts with others. This activity is designed to help members clarify their values with regard to several of the most important roles they play. Have each group member write five commonly played roles on five different 3 × 5 cards. Seat the group in a circle with their roles on their laps. Citing a crisis mandate (e.g., "Something happens in your life and because of that circumstance you must give up one role.") ask them to decide individually which role they would be most willing to give up. Have them crumple up that card and throw it into the middle of the circle. Continue the same process without discussion until each member has one role left. Then have the members discuss why they kept that particular role, how they decided to eliminate the other roles, and what their feelings were as they proceeded to discard roles.

An alternative procedure is to have a discussion after each decision and an extensive discussion relative to priorities and values at the end.

Another modification is to make certain roles mandatory as part of the five, such as job, parent, spouse. This creates a set of dynamics (sometimes referred to as systems clash) that typifies the stressors in each person's life when demands of job, personal interests, and family compete for time and energy. Process the activity in terms of daily decisions made to allocate time, energy, and resources to these roles and relative to priorities and values that often conflict with behavior and create stress and tension in daily living.

Expectations and How We Live

Describe the chart in Figure 14.4. (*Note*: Categories on this chart are generic and can be modified, deleted, or expanded to be more relevant to the members of your group.) The instructions are as follows:

1. Fold the sheet so that only the Importance column is showing and rank the categories 1 through 9 based on their importance to you where 1 represents the most important. (This is the *cognitive* dimension and typifies ideal or value based priorities.)
2. Fold the sheet so that only the Time column is showing and rank the categories 1 through 9 on the basis of actual time spent in doing the activities of that category where 1 represents the most time spent. (This is the *behavioral* dimension and represents how time is allocated.)
3. Fold the sheet so that only the Satisfaction column is showing and rank the categories 1 through 9 on the basis of personal satisfaction experienced in each category where 1 represents the most satisfaction. (This represents the *affective* dimension and reflects the nature of inner emotions related to experience.)

Categories	Importance	Time	Satisfaction
1. **Work:** This category includes all jobs or tasks you perform for which you are paid. (Include full time and part time) (School, full time or part time fits here)			
2. **Family:** This category includes activities and time spent with all or some (at least one) members of your nuclear family, meaning parent(s) and children.			
3. **Extended Family:** (Family of origin) This category includes time and activities with members of your extended family (parents, siblings, grandparents, aunts, uncles, etc.)			
4. **Marriage:** This category includes time spent specifically with your spouse exclusive of other family members. (Includes social activities together)			
5. **Personal:** This category includes individual activities and interests you pursue apart from your family/ marriage/work. (Hobbies, recreation, time alone, etc.)			
6. **Organizations:** This category includes time and activities in groups you belong to such as civic or professional groups, community organizations, clubs, etc.			

7. **Domestic:** This category includes activities or tasks you are responsible for to run and maintain your household e.g., chores, cleaning, cooking, house maintenance, etc.			
8. **Church:** This category includes church related and other activities that have a spiritual dimension and require time and commitment to pursue.			
9. **Step Family:** This category includes all activities with step-children if you differentiate them from the family category above.			
10. Write your own: _____			

FIGURE 14.4. Expectations and how we live.

4. Unfold the sheet so all rankings can be compared. Have each member analyze their rankings for congruence (importance, time, and satisfaction are directly related) or incongruence (discrepancies exist between the importance, time, and satisfaction columns).
5. Have group members share their rankings and analysis in the group.

This activity is particularly useful in groups where stress and stress management are topics of importance.

Exploring Legacy Dynamics

Family Genogram Activity

Genograms are useful tools in helping group members explore their personhood and legacy. The instructions that follow are for a limited or working genogram that can be constructed quickly. For more extensive information about genograms refer to McGoldrick and Gerson (1985).

1. Construct a genogram of your family consisting of at least three generations of persons that you have known personally or know about through other family members.
2. Be sure to include both sides of your parents' families and in cases of step-families include significant generational relationships such as step-grandparents.
3. Most genograms will include:
   a. your generation (spouse and/or siblings)
   b. your children (if applicable)
   c. your children's children (if applicable)
   d. your parents
   e. your grandparents
   f. your great-grandparents
4. Indicate birth order via gender, sequence, and age. (See Figure 14.5 for example.)
5. Use circles to designate females and squares to designate males.

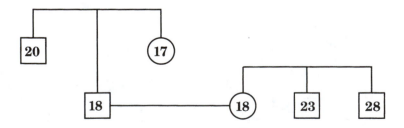

FIGURE 14.5. Example of sibling level.

6. Indicate deaths by placing an X over the person indicating their age at time of death, date of death, and cause.
7. Indicate divorces with slashes through the line connecting the two persons and separations with dashes.
8. Use dash lines to indicate adoption.
9. Place a star by those family members you resemble the most.
10. Place a check mark by those family members you resemble the least.
11. Optional: Identify facts, traits or tendencies in your family such as alcohol/substance abuse, diseases (cancer, heart attacks, etc.) by appropriate designations (e.g., circle alcohol/substance abuser in red).

Creating a genogram is a good homework assignment and can be used for both getting to know one another and exploring a person's background in greater depth in relation to a particular problem such as substance abuse. Have group members present their completed genograms to the group and then brainstorm possible dynamics that may be operating in the person's life. Some groups continue to develop genograms over the course of the group process so the technique has both short term and long range utility.

Marriage and Family: The Impact of Legacy

The following activity may be used in total or in part to help group members explore the impact of their family of origin and family legacy on their lives particularly in the context of current family relationships. The activity can be administered as a homework task or used as a guide to structuring discussion around each of the topics built into the activity.

The Revolving Slate. Growing up in our family of origin often produces resolutions about marriage and family that we find are tested once we become married and have a family. We are often surprised, shocked, or even disappointed that patterns or traits are repeated even when we had determined they would not be.

1. Make a list of statements you recall making as you grew up in your family that reflect how you wanted your marriage and family life to be. Most of these statements will take the form of resolutions or vows starting with stems such as:
   • When I'm married. . . .
   • The person I marry will (will not). . . .
   • I will never. . . .
   • My children will (will not). . . .
2. Indicate which of the preceding statements are the most important to you and why.
3. Have you altered any of the preceding statements or found any to be inaccurate. If so, how does that make you feel and how did the change occur?

Adopting-Adapting. Growing up in our family of origin produces certain experiences and values that we wish to emulate in our own marriage and family. Complete the following tasks to help you discover how the positives in your family legacy have influenced you.

1. Make a list of experiences in your family of origin that have resulted in treasured memories.
2. Complete the following statement: The traits and values I admire most about my family are. . . .
3. Identify one of your treasured memories that you would like to *adopt* or have *adopted* in your marriage or family of creation in the same way you experienced it. Explain why and indicate problems you have or may have in doing so.
4. Identify one of your treasured memories you would like to *adapt* or have *adapted* in your marriage or family of creation. Explain how you would like to modify (or have modified) it and why.

Opposing-Rejecting. Growing up in our family of origin produces certain experiences and impressions we want to negate or avoid reconstructing in our own marriage and family. Complete the following tasks to help you discover how the negatives in your family legacy have influenced you.

1. Make a list of experiences in your family of origin that have resulted in negative memories.
2. Complete the following statement: The traits I consider undesirable and the values I disagree with in my family of origin are. . . .
3. Identify one thing you will do or have done in your family of creation that makes sure the negative experience you had will not be repeated. Explain how that change will affect your children's experience.
4. Identify how one of the above listed experiences could be (or has been) handled differently in your marriage or family of creation. Indicate how you discovered the means of changing it.

Decisions Across the Generations

Every generation is faced with choices and decisions which must be made in the course of forming its identity in and impact on the flow of life. These decisions may be repetitive emerging in every generation or may be unique to the historical time frame or context in which the person and family is. This activity is designed to explore the generational relatedness or non-relatedness of personal decisions. It is best conducted as an out of group process where group members actually discuss with grandparents and parents what they consider their most important decisions were and are. In the absence of the opportunity to obtain the data first hand, the group member can project the data from memory or conjecture. Have group members identify the most important decisions (specific choices) that their 1) grand-parents made, are making, and must make; 2) parents made, are making, and must make; and 3) they have made, are making, and must make. Upon completion, have group members share the data comparing and contrasting their contemporary generational decisions (problems and issues) with those of the previous two generations. Process the activity in light of common and different problems and in terms of assets and resources that are available from past generations that can be mobilized in resolving current problems.

Couples Groups

The activities that follow are particularly appropriate to couples groups where intimate partners can benefit from sharing with each other as well as in the group. The resource for these and other couples activities is *Marriage and Family: Better Ready Than Not* by Trotzer and Trotzer (1986).

Expecting To Be Loved

One of the most significant aspects of an intimate relationship is the love dimension. However, the definition of love and more particularly how it is expressed is the root of many relational issues. The following activity is useful in helping couples assess and express their similarities and differences relative to the behavior of demonstrating love. Have each group member rank the five categories described in Figure 14.6 on the basis of their own preference for giving and receiving love. Then have them rank their perception of their intimate partner's preferences for giving and receiving love. Use 1 to represent the top preference.

When the individual rankings are completed have each couple share their rankings with each other using them as a basis for discussion. When the couple dyads are finished, reconvene the group and process the activity in light of gender preferences and characteristics and personality traits of the couples and individuals in the group.

Attraction Dimension in Couples

The following activity is a good get acquainted activity because it focuses couples on a typically positive time in their lives and provides a comfortable channel for couples to share themselves with each other. The instructions are as follows:

1. Complete the following statements with respect to your partner. Share your responses with your partner.
   a. When I first met you I was attracted to you because. . . .

Five Categories Relative to Expressing Love	Me	Spouse
1. **WORDS**: One way to express love is simply by saying "I love you," or "You look nice in that dress," or "I like the way you did that." Verbal statements affirming love bring a great deal of emotional security to some of us.	____	____
2. **GIFTS**: A second love language is gifts. They need not be expensive to be valuable. A gift says, "He or she was thinking of me when we were apart." You cannot select a gift without thinking about the person to whom you will give it. It is a deliberate act of love.	____	____
3. **ACTION**: Doing things for your spouse can be a powerful communication of love. Cooking a meal, washing dishes, dusting, vacuuming the floor, taking out the garbage, putting gas in the car, etc., are all ways of expressing love.	____	____
4. **TIME**: Spending quality time with your spouse is also a means of expressing love. Quality time is giving your spouse your undivided attention. Whether you are sitting on the couch, taking a walk, or sharing a meal at a quiet restaurant, when you focus on listening and sharing with your spouse, you are communicating love.	____	____
5. **TOUCH**: Physical touch is recognized as an important way to express love. Kissing, embracing, holding hands, sexual intercourse, or other affectionate physical contacts are a means of communicating love.	____	____

FIGURE 14.6. Expecting to be loved.

  b. When I got to know you I was attracted to you because. . . .
  c. Now I am attracted to you because. . . .
2. Tell the story of your courtship and marriage. (Use this task as a means for couples to introduce themselves to the group.)
  a. *His turn*: Share with the group how you met and became involved with each other
  b. *Her turn*: Describe how you decided to get married
3. In the columns in Figure 14.7 indicate specific examples of things that attract you to your partner. Fit them into the category you believe is most appropriate.

Similarities (How we are alike)	Differences (How we are different)	Exchanges (How we contribute to each other)

FIGURE 14.7. Sample sheet for categorizing specific things that attracted one to his or her partner.

a. Share the column information in same gender subgroups. Each partner shares his or her perception of the attraction dimension in his or her intimate relationship.
b. Reconvene the group and discuss the importance of attraction as a relationship characteristic in intimate relating.

Basic Arenas of Marital Conflict

Distribute and briefly explain the diagram located in Figure 14.8 (Trotzer & Trotzer, 1986, pp. 185–187). Have each couple identify a list of specific issues from their own relationship that relate to the four arenas of marital conflict. Have them identify three issues they would be willing to discuss in the group. Convene the group and have each couple share the issues they would like to discuss and give a brief description of them to the group. When all couples have shared their issues, form an agenda for group work either by selecting a problem/issue of common concern to the couples in the group or by having each couple identify a priority issue. Organize the work of the group around the agenda making sure each couple's issue or version of the issue is addressed.

Relationship Analysis Inventory

Give a brief introduction to the activity by describing the four component parts of an intimate relationship (Trotzer & Trotzer, 1986, pp. 162–170). Have partners complete the Relationship Analysis Inventory (Figure 14.9) individually and then share their results with each other. Have them identify the area(s) they want to work on in the group. Have each couple share what they learned about their relationship with the group and use the information to solidify the group and create a work focus.

The Relationship Analysis Inventory also can be used as a homework

FIGURE 14.8. Basic arenas of marital conflict.

task for the couple to work on together. Each couple then presents their analysis to the group. The results are processed as a means of identifying work areas and setting agendas for the group and the individual couples.

Marital Vows Activity

Marriage vows raise the issue of commitment and their content elicits the definitions and values that undergird that commitment. The following activity is appropriate for both premarital and postmarital couples groups and can be utilized as either a group activity or a combined couple and group activity. If a combined approach is used, the sequence can be either couple-group or group-couple. Results will vary based on sequence, but the end result will be a deeper understanding, appreciation, and meaning for couples relative to their own commitment to each other and for the group relative to the importance of commitment in marriage. The instructions are as follows:

Group-Couple Sequence: Read the example of typical marriage vows below and then as a group create a generic version emphasizing the elements the group feels are most important. You may wish to use either traditional or contemporary language.

INSTRUCTIONS: Select an intimate relationship you are currently involved in (boy/girl friend, fiance', spouse, intimate partner) and fill in the columns below as follows:

1. Togetherness: Indicate those activities the two of you participate in together.
2. Apartness: Indicate those activities you engage in separate from your partner.
3. Pushing-Resisting: a) Identify the things about you your partner does not like or wishes you would change. b) Identify the things about your partner that you do not like and wish he/she would change.
4. Leading-Supporting: a) Identify the things you take the initiative in while your partner gives you his/her support and encouragement. b) Identify the things your partner takes the initiative in where you give him/her your support and encouragement.

1. Togetherness	2. Apartness	3. Pushing-Resisting	4. Leading-Supporting
		a)	a)
		b)	b)

FIGURE 14.9. Relationship analysis inventory

445

Marriage Vows

(name) , will you have _(name)_ as your(husband/wife)? Will you live with (him/her) according to God's will? Will you love and comfort (him/her), honor and support (him/her), in times of joy and trial, as long as you both shall live?

I, _(name_ , take you, _(name)_ , to be my (wife/husband) from this day forward, as long as I live; to be with you in times of joy and suffering and wealth and poverty; to love and honor you, according to God's will; I therefore pledge you my faithfulness.

Each couple then uses the generic form as a stimulus to develop their own personalized version which is then shared with the group. (For the _Couple-group Sequence_ simply modify the steps as follows: Typical marriage vows, personalized marriage vows (couple), and generic marriage vows (group).

As a group, discuss and respond to the marriage vows shared and then have couples review and, if desired, refine or revise their vows based on input from the discussion. Using the group leader as presider, each couple may wish to recite their vows to each other in the presence of the group as a recommitment experience.

Marriage: The Sexual Dimension

Sex in marriage serves four basic functions. Sex is the means of expressing and experiencing intimacy. Sex is the means of meeting each persons need for sexual gratification and release. Sex is the means by which partners reproduce themselves (biological reproduction). Sex is the means by which physical pleasure and enjoyment is experienced. All are important facets of the sexual dimension of the marriage relationship. The instructions for this activity are as follows:

1. Personally rank _intimacy, need, pleasure,_ and _reproduction_ in order of priority for you as a person (Trotzer & Trotzer, 1986, pp. 181–185).

   ____ Intimacy   ____ Need
   ____ Pleasure   ____ Reproduction

2. Share your ranking and your explanation with your partner.
3. Suggested Personal Sharing Tasks (Between Partners)
   a. Share a special memory of your sexual life together.
   b. Share the most enjoyable aspect of sex for you.
   c. Share one thing you would like to change or add to your sex life.
   d. Identify differences between you and your partner with respect to sexual relating.
   e. Discuss how you think you obtained your perspective and values relative to sex (what influences you to see sex as you do?)
   f. Share your perception of the current state of your sexual relating.

g. What sexual experience(s) do you anticipate with each other? (Share your sexual fantasies).
4. Have a group discussion of the four dimensions of sexuality reviewed in the opening paragraphs of this activity. Discuss similarities and differences relative to:
   a. Values and religious perspectives,
   b. Influence of legacy and family of origin,
   c. Gender perspectives, and
   d. Developmental dynamics (age, family status, etc.).

Rex Stockton
Paul L. Toth

The Case for Group Research

☐ Introduction by James P. Trotzer

I have always construed the relationship between *teaching, practice,* and *research* in group work to be a series of overlapping, interlocking circles of equal size held together by a central core circle of *training.* The role of teaching is to supply theory and techniques in a manner that incorporates, integrates, and connects the arenas of research and practice. Training as the core connecting construct generates the overall relevance of all three areas whether in the form of graduate training for the group counselor or continuing education training for the group practitioner. The actual manifestation of this model, however, is difficult to find in reality.

Several dynamics account for this apparent conundrum. First, it appears that research and practice each have an inherent nature which acts to drive them in different directions both away from each other and out of the overlapping, interlocking relationship with teaching. The hearts of the group practitioner and the group researcher seem to strive for a different destiny. Second, the very nature of research and clinical practice seem to mitigate against alliance. Research prompted by a commitment to objectivity and guided by scientific rigor seems to generate a different essence than practice prompted by human compassion and guided by intuitive creativity. Finally, the settings in which research and practice tend to occur (universities, institutes, and colleges versus schools, community mental health agencies, and private practice) place different demands on the progenitors and have vastly different resources to mobilize and limitations with which to contend.

In my previous editions of this text I opted to emphasize a practitioner oriented evaluation perspective as the pragmatic response to the research-practice dilemma. However, that resulted in a perspective that only perpetuated the above noted splitting dynamics. I have attempted to remedy that problem in this edition by adding this chapter entitled The Case for Group Research: A Practitioner Friendly Proposition by Rex Stockton and Paul Toth. The evolution of this addition and relevance of the chapter to the overall perspective of the book is elaborated as follows.

Research or Evaluation: The Practitioner's Dilemma

Conscientious group counselors are usually confronted with a conflict between a professional obligation to do all they can to expand and clarify the knowledge and understanding of group counseling and a role responsibility to extend and apply group counseling to the greatest number of clientele as is meaningfully possible. The former attempts to involve counselors as responsible contributors to the broad professional community of group counselors, and the latter relates specifically to the service function of counselors in the particular settings in which they work. The research perspective is emphasized by many of the counselor's trainers, because of the research orientation of higher education, and by the professional literature and professional associations. The role perspective is nurtured by the work setting, where the interest is in the counselor's impact rather than on his or her knowledge of the field or reputation in professional circles. Fulfilling the expectations of both the profession and the job requires at least a superhuman effort and in most cases is realistically impossible. This situation causes pressures and frustration that can curtail the effectiveness and personal satisfaction of the group counselor.

Common reactions to this dilemma reflect extremes in commitment as well as compromise. At one extreme, are those counselors who look at the complexity and demands of group counseling, the need for accountable action, and the requirements of a research orientation and decide (actively or by default) to do nothing. Therefore they neither initiate a group program nor do they become embroiled in a situation they feel would only add difficulty and pressure to their already strenuous roles. At the other extreme are those counselors who completely buy into the research orientation and expend all their energies designing and implementing projects to further the cause of science with respect to group counseling. Because of the consuming nature of a research perspective, these counselors often end up neglecting or failing to do justice to their other important role responsibilities. Their clientele therefore do not receive adequate overall professional attention and are sacrificed for the sake of research. Finally, compromisers try to appease both the research requirements and the demands of the setting by doing research of convenience and expedience. In most cases their efforts yield minimal results, because the methodology is poor.

The obvious conclusion is that none of these approaches provides a viable answer for the group counselor. Clients suffer or much effort is exerted in meaningless endeavors which tend to harm the group process more than help it. Counselors who wish to use groups must therefore develop a more practical and realistic perspective if they are to effectively resolve the research-practice dilemma. They can do this by carefully appraising the demands of 1) their environment, 2) a group counseling program, 3) meaningful research, and 4) the counselor role and by making constructive decisions based on the reality of those demands.

A Realistic Perspective

An assessment of the four areas just mentioned points out the following: 1) Within every counselor's work environment are clientele whose needs can be most adequately met through the development of a group program. Group work should therefore be incorporated into the guidance/psychoeducation, counseling, therapy, and consulting functions of the counselor in an effort to facilitate individual adjustment, improve the learning environment, and generally enhance the mental health of clients they serve. 2) A successful group program requires careful planning and preparation and entails a substantial time commitment to make it beneficial. Therefore counselors must place group work high on their priority lists if they are to give groups the amount of attention they need and deserve. 3) Potentially significant research requires more money and other resources than is typically available in practice settings (Mahler, 1969), close involvement with specialists from professionally allied fields, such as psychometrists and statisticians (Cohn, 1967), and a great deal of time and effort. In most cases substantial, well designed, sophisticated, and carefully conducted studies are necessary to answer the key questions that group counseling poses. The typical group counselor does not have the time, resources, opportunity, expertise and/or interest to initiate this kind of effort. 4) The counselor's role, for all the attention it has received, still remains somewhat nebulous and tenuous and at best is less than ideal in practice (Trotzer & Kassera, 1971). The inclusion of a concentrated group research orientation, therefore, may serve to confuse the issue further. It might also alienate potential clients. As a result group counselors can best carry out their responsibilities by cultivating certain perspectives that ameliorate the research-practice conundrum while accelerating and implementing their professional role.

Leave the Major Burden of Research to Researchers and Become a Collaborator with Group Researchers

Since most studies are generated by graduate students and other professionals whose requirements and job descriptions primarily entail research, the practitioner need not assume further responsibilities in this area. Ohlsen

(1970) stated, "Considering (their) commitment to service, the time required to obtain adequate financial support for research, the difficulties involved in appraising outcomes of counseling and (their) own feelings about (their) research skills, one would not expect the practitioner to do much research" (pp. 284–285). A suitable role for the practitioner is to become a collaborator with group researchers (Dies, 1985; McCoy, 1997; Riva & Kalodner, 1997), participate in well designed and carefully conceived research projects, and offer his or her groups to researchers for studies and data collection.

Become a Consumer of Research

The procedures and findings of research projects reported in various professional journals and at professional meetings and conventions are an invaluable source of help to the group counselor. As a consumer, the group counselor can integrate this information into practice to make the group process even more effective. Dinkmeyer and Muro (1971) confirmed this point of view stating that the "practicing counselor is more a research consumer than he(she) is a producer" (p. 303).

Being a consumer is made convenient by professional journals such as those listed in Figure 15.1. In addition, efforts such as David Zimpfer's critical reviews of group research on selected topics frequently published in the *Journal for Specialists in Group Work* are reflective of efforts made by journals to produce user friendly research data. (See "Review of Group Literature" section of *JSGW* Volumes 14–17, 1989–1992). A resource such as Zimpfer's (1984) *Bibliography* is also a helpful resource to consumers. A fine example of a recent comprehensive review of group research is Horne and Rosenthal (1997).

Concentrate on Developing Experience and Expertise as a Group Leader

One of the major weaknesses of many group counseling research projects is that they do not utilize leaders who have extensive group counseling

1. *Group Dynamics: Theory, Research and Practice*
2. *International Journal of Group Psychotherapy*
3. *Journal for Specialists in Group Work*
4. *Journal of Child and Adolescent Group Therapy*
5. *Journal of Group Psychotherapy, Psychodrama, and Sociometry*
6. *Small Group Behavior*
7. *Small Group Research*
8. *Social Work With Groups*
9. *Group Psychology and Psychotherapy*

FIGURE 15.1. Professional journals for group research

experience and competence (Cohn, 1967; Mahler, 1969). Thus when the research fails to attain significance it may be a result of low level leader expertise rather than lack of power in the group counseling process. By building one's expertise in practice, the counselor will contribute to a more extensive population of competent group leaders who can be called upon for help in research projects (Dies, 1983).

Become an Evaluator of Group Counseling in Your Own Setting

Even though counselors may not be in the position to do research, that does not negate their responsibility for evaluation of the effectiveness of group counseling in their own environments. Cohn (1967) emphasized that the practitioner needs "to be persuaded that evaluation is necessary to determine actual outcomes rather than depending solely upon his (her) own individual perception of outcomes" (p. 28). Counselors must be interested in assessing the results of their group programs. They need to be accountable to their clients, themselves, and their profession, and an evaluation emphasis can meet that need. In addition, evaluation results are grist for the research mill and often provide the seeds from which research projects grow.

Research Versus Evaluation

The basic difference between evaluation and research is that *evaluation* is concerned with what is happening or what has happened in order to determine the value and worth of the assessed occurrence in that situation, while *research* is designed to assess the nature and impact of a particular treatment for purposes of predicting and generalizing to other situations. Research also entails a formal design for comparison and replication purposes and incorporates the use of descriptive and inferential statistical methods. Research makes use of accumulated knowledge and procedures that compose a professional discipline in their own right. Evaluation is less formal and is not restricted by rigorous statistical and procedural limits. Its procedures are associated with the specific area being evaluated rather than with an outside body of professional knowledge. An analogy might be that evaluation is to the group counselor as teacher-made tests are to the classroom instructor. In both cases the practitioner utilizes information from formal testing or research methods but adapts it to fit particular subjects, methods, clientele, and environments. Evaluation uses discovered results as a means of developing, revising, or consolidating a very specific treatment (in this case group counseling). Research is more oriented toward defining overall group counseling characteristics in order to standardize the process as a formal and specified procedure of the counseling profession.

With the above noted delineations in mind, I am happy to bring this introduction to a close by presenting the chapter, The Case for Group Research: A Practitioner Friendly Proposition. Rex Stockton and Paul Toth do a superb job of presenting the case for research that is relevant to the group counselor in training and or in practice. Rex Stockton is a premier group researcher, a recognized leader and a published contributor in the group research field. He and his protege and now colleague at Indiana University—Paul Toth, have collaborated extensively in group research and writing for publication. On two recent occasions (1997) their work has been acknowledged for excellence and given the Outstanding Research Award and the Outstanding Article of the Year Award by the Association for Specialists in Group Work. Therefore, it is with a great deal of admiration and respect that I introduce you to their chapter on group research.

Group Research: A Practitioner Friendly Proposition

Note: The authors acknowledge the invaluable assistance of Amy Gibson Nitza in researching the material used in this chapter.

Practitioners often feel removed from the work of research. We are aware that most of our readers will not be researchers and many group workers do not feel comfortable in a research environment. This is also seen in the broader field of counseling and psychotherapy where there has been a historic division between practice and research. Hill and Corbett (1993) make the point that research does not seem able to keep up with practice. This is because research attempts to test interventions developed in clinical settings instead of addressing the needs of clinical practice by developing interventions in the counseling laboratory. It is very important that practice be informed by systematic research that will enable the practitioner to have access to the most appropriate interventions available.

The fact that many practitioners shy away from clinical research is no surprise. From their first statistics and research courses people begin to avoid that which they have difficulty with or are not introduced to in a way that makes practical sense. Group workers may feel they have not been adequately trained in research methodology. Or, they may feel that those who do research carry out their studies in a world removed from day to day practice. So, we hope that this chapter will give the reader an appreciation as to what research can do in terms of influencing practice. Both authors are researchers *and* practitioners who value research and enjoy pursuits of acquiring new knowledge. Whether research is analyzing basic information that might influence group practice in general or evaluating factors that have an impact on a particular group program, applying scientific reasoning to group work enhances practice, teaching, and continued studies. Let us begin by talking about basic scientific inquiry and some of the effects of research in the field of counseling.

In the life time of many readers, polio infantile paralysis was a scourge. During the summer months, when it frequently raged, many localities had to close swimming pools, theaters, and other places where children liked to congregate. A multitude of resources went into developing iron lungs and other methods to treat the consequences of the disease. One of the authors vividly recalls stories in his local newspaper of improved treatments of those who were affected by the disease. However, it wasn't until the development of vaccines that prevented polio that the epidemic was stopped. Prior to this, energy and resources that were poured into developing ways to treat the illness were well spent. However, in this case, the best payoff went into the fundamental research that developed the vaccine. Having effective treatment procedures and instruments is important, not having to use these procedures and instruments is even better. In many cases basic scientific research provides us with the methodology to investigate better treatment and prevention. Practice can be enhanced by the application of knowledge which was uncovered through scientific research.

To put scientific research in the mental health field into perspective let us consider the case of depression. Depression is a mood disorder that affects an estimated two to three percent of men and four to nine percent of women at any given time. Moreover, 10% of men and 20% of women in the population are at risk for developing depression at some time in their lives (Kahn, 1993). Counselors who have practiced any length of time inevitably have worked with depressed clients. Seasoned counselors will be old enough to remember when mood disorders, especially major depressive disorder, were treated much less effectively than they are today. Two areas of inquiry have helped us understand and treat depression more effectively: 1) the advent of medication that affects certain synaptic responses in the brain, and 2) the development of treatment that affects a person's self-perceptions. Basic scientific research has provided the field with a better understanding of the brain's biochemical functions and the importance of cognitive and behavioral interventions on the treatment of depression.

Biological research into chemical processes that occur in the brain resulted in the development of drugs that regulate those processes and help control depression. Initially, it was unclear to researchers which neurotransmitters were involved with depression, so the earlier drugs were developed to target a wide area of the brain. Further research helped pin-point a specific neurotransmitter, serotonin, as being involved in depression. This enabled a new group of drugs, selective serotonin reuptake inhibitors (SSRIs), to be developed, and they have been quite successful in the treatment of depression (Goldenberg, 1990). Thus, an organized program of research has helped a large number of people suffering from depression.

A similar programmatic research approach focused on the cognitive aspects of depression. In 1967 Seligman and Maier began a cognitive revo lution in psychotherapy treatment not by initially working with human clients, but by painstakingly investigating responses of animals to inescapable situations. The laboratory work of Seligman and Maier (1967), Overmeier and Seligman (1967), Maier and Seligman (1976) and Maier, Seligman, and Solomon (1969) found that if animals were presented with a mild electric shock when they had no opportunity to escape, they would continue to take shocks even when escape was made available (Rosenhan & Seligman, 1989). If escape was hopeless, the animals became helpless and passive and did not engage in behavior (escape) that would ultimately benefit them. This exploration with animals led Seligman and others to investigate this phenomenon further. They discovered that learned helplessness also occurs in humans. With this information in mind, they hypothesized that persons with depression could be helped by changing their cognitions from thinking they are ineffective in controlling life events to believing they can have an impact on their future.(Rosenhan & Seligman, 1989). Helpful therapeutic treatment for depression has come from researching learned helplessness in people.

The research of Seligman and others is an illustration of how inquiry works in the sciences. In order for a problem to be understood and appropriate solutions to the problem developed, it is important to understand its basic components. Breaking down a problem and researching its component parts offers glimpses of insight into the workings of the entire piece.

Experimental Method

In the classic experimental method, a researcher attempts to test a hypothesis by experimentally manipulating one variable (the independent variable) to measure its effects on another variable (the dependent variable). In order to show that there is a causal relationship between these two variables, the researcher must carefully rule out other possible, or extraneous, hypotheses (Ingersoll, in press). One way this is done is to control, to the extent possible, outside factors that are irrelevant to the purpose of the study, but that nevertheless may have an effect on the outcome. These factors are known as extraneous variables. Many steps are typically taken by investigators in order to control or eliminate the impact of extraneous variables. The most powerful method of doing so is randomization. If participants are randomly assigned to treatment or control conditions, it can be assumed that extraneous variables are relatively equal across groups; such variables are thus not likely to significantly impact results (Ingersoll, in press). When randomization is not possible, other methods of controlling for extraneous variables can be used. One such method is to carefully match (matching) the participants in experimental groups on these variables. For example, if researchers were concerned about gender as an extraneous variable, they could ensure that there were equal numbers of males and females in each group. Another method is to hold the extraneous variable constant for all participants (for example, selecting only female subjects for the study).

The problem of extraneous variables becomes even more challenging in group research. This is because of the complexity of the group experience. Interactions among group members and leaders create many extraneous variables not present in other types of research. The work of Stockton and Morran (1981) is an example of using an experimental design to control for extraneous variables. In this study group members were instructed to give feedback to each other and then to rate the credibility, desirability, impact, and helpfulness of the feedback they received. Group researchers know that extraneous variables such as social influence and other effects resulting from interpersonal communication may influence the type of feedback members give to each other. So, in order to control for these effects in this study, members were instructed to write down their feedback before being asked to orally communicate it. Additionally, members rated feedback from others anonymously. Using these methods allowed the researchers to state with more confidence that experimental results were due to the effects of the feedback and not other interactional factors.

In addition to the problem of extraneous variables, Fuhriman and Burlingame (1994) mention several types of methodological problems in the group research to date. They conclude that the most serious threats to the soundness of the research base involve construct validity issues. Specifically, although many studies report positive client outcomes as a result of group therapy, few studies actually describe in detail the characteristics of the therapy or the therapist. Thus, it is very difficult to determine what it was that actually occurred to produce the positive outcomes. Another construct validity problem is the way in which outcomes are measured. "The sheer volume of measures being used in the group literature makes it virtually impossible to delineate the nature of reliable effects to be expected" (Fuhriman & Burlingame, 1994, p. 70). Thus, it is often difficult to discern specifically what occurs in group therapy that makes it effective and what types of results can be expected. Such methodological problems may make it difficult for the group practitioner to translate research results into useful information that can be applied to their own work.

Expanding the Use of the Scientific Method

The scientific method, the standard approach to scientific inquiry, is able to provide answers to many significant questions. However, this type of tightly controlled research can not answer all the complex questions within the human domain. Research into problems of human interaction are too complex to be answered with absolute clarity. Depending on the methods employed, certain facets of the truth are revealed. Since it is tremendously difficult to control for extraneous variables in the life of the group, it be comes all the harder to make group research fit into a nicely designed package that is free from error and clean of confounding elements. Therefore, it is typical for a study to answer only a part of the question being explored by the investigation. A study that investigated the effects of structured group exercises on group counseling is a good illustration of both limitations and usefulness of this type of research. Stockton, Rohde, and Haughey (1994) had participants in an experimental condition begin their group sessions with a 20 minute structured exercise. The researchers assumed that this structure would affect the following developmental variables: cohesion, engagement, avoidance, and conflict. The researchers also thought that satisfaction with the experience would be higher for those involved in the exercises than those who were not. The results of this study suggest support for the effectiveness (with some important cautions) of structured group exercises early in group development. Though this was a relatively sophisticated study, there were limitations. In this case, groups focused on personal growth instead of pathology, and participants were quite similar as to socioeconomic and academic variables. Even with these qualifications, the study provided some support for the use of low risk structured exercises. It remains to be seen whether or not these findings would also apply to different types of groups with different types of participants. This was one study that answered only a portion of the overall question being posed by the investigators, but still added to the overall knowledge of group work and offered suggestions for future studies. This is how research works—the researcher discovers a bit of new information as he or she moves along *and* poses new or additional questions to examine via continued research.

Given the complexity of interpersonal interactions that are magnified in group therapy, it is especially important for group researchers to expand our use of the scientific method. Polkinghorne (1988) wrote: "knowledge is understood to be the best understanding that we have been able to produce thus far, not a statement of what is ultimately real" (p. 2). Polkinghorne went on to say that science should not be an endeavor that, like cooking, follows certain procedures so as to produce certain results. Instead, science should become "the creative search to understand better, and it uses whatever approaches are responsive to the particular questions and subject matters addressed" (p. 3). Likewise, Wampold (1986) wrote that research should consider "using any methodology, provided the methodology is appropriate to answer the research question and provided the methodology is applied correctly" (p. 38). Additionally, using one type of research method often provides insights that can be explored using another approach. For example, by using qualitative research methods and procedures (interviews) McDonnell (1996) has recently elaborated in rich detail the experiences of beginning group leaders as they start and work their way through their first group leadership experiences. Using this information it is possible to devise experimental studies that will address the same issues. An area young in its theoretical development, group work has much to gain from such a cooperative and interactional system. The vital importance of practitioners in the early and continued development of other applied fields such as medicine and engineering attests to the possibilities for group counselors to make the same kind of contributions to group work.

Group Research that Works

Stockton and Hulse (1983), in writing about group research, have noted "if the profession does not assume responsibility for intellectual inquiry, which might provide answers to basic questions concerning effective practice, the field cannot advance" (p. 303). The use of therapeutic groups is firmly established in the practice of human service disciplines. For example, in the fields of counseling, psychology, psychiatry, and nursing the overall effectiveness of therapeutic group work has been well established (Bednar & Kaul, 1994; Fuhriman & Burlingame, 1994). In group work especially, practice and research have been uninterested partners (Bednar & Kaul, 1994; Fuhriman & Burlingame, 1994).

We do have significant information about applied practice. A variety of studies and synthesizing reviews have impacted current practice. Research has helped mold ideas of what is best practice. For example, conventional wisdom in the 1960s and 1970s had assumed that powerful negative feedback was appropriate in early therapeutic group development. This view held sway until the research of Jacobs and Spradlin (1974), in a series of analogue studies, demonstrated that in a laboratory setting much better results were produced by beginning with positive feedback. This was followed by research on actual counseling groups done at Indiana University which have supported the notion that feedback can have a positive impact on group members and be seen as helpful if the feedback meets some of the following qualifications: 1) corrective feedback is given after the group moves along in the developmental process (Morran, Stockton, & Harris, 1991; Morran, Stockton & Robison, 1985; Stockton & Morran, 1981); 2) positive feedback is given prior to corrective feedback (Davies & Jacobs, 1985; Morran, Stockton, & Harris, 1991; Stockton & Morran, 1981); and 3) corrective feedback focuses on specific behaviors (Morran, Stockton, & Harris, 1991).

Another illustration of the impact of research on group practice is a seminal study by Liberman, Yalom, and Miles (1972) that explored the role of leadership in encounter groups and helped to shape the practice of therapeutic group leadership. Their study set out to examine the relationship between outcome, leader techniques, and group process variables. Though this study has limitations, it continues to have important impact on the field of group research. In this study, 210 undergraduate students participated in 1 of 18 groups, that met for 12 weeks for a total of 30 hours. Group leaders were chosen from a variety of ideological schools to allow for an investigation of the impact of leader technique on outcome. Outcome was measured using a psychological test battery given before the group began, at the completion of the group, and at a six month follow-up. There were several important findings from this study. Outcome results indicated that approximately 33% of the participants underwent moderate or considerable positive change, while approximately 15% of the participants experienced negative change. "The encounter group, thus, clearly influenced change, but for both better and worse" (Yalom, 1985, p. 499). Another important finding was that certain leader behaviors had a large impact on the effectiveness of a group. Important leader behaviors were broken down into four basic leadership functions:

1. *emotional stimulation* included such activities as challenging, confronting, and modeling risk taking and self disclosure;
2. *caring* included such things as support, acceptance, and genuineness;
3. *meaning attribution* involved explaining, interpreting, and providing a cognitive framework for change; and,
4. *executive functions* included activities that provide structure in the group, such as setting norms and limits, managing time, and suggesting procedures in the group.

Leader behaviors were strongly related to outcome but were not related to the ideological school of the leader. This study showed that it was what the leader did, not whose theory he or she followed, that had the greatest influence on outcome. This study has obviously influenced Yalom (1995), who has cited it in his well known book *The Theory and Practice of Group Psychotherapy*. Thus, this study then influences anyone who has used his book or been taught from his ideas.

Another study that has had significant impact on group therapy focused on the role of the leader in providing optimum group structure. Until the work of Bednar, Melnick, and Kaul, (1974), the conventional wisdom in group work called for a very low level of structure within the group. However, Bednar, Melnick, and Kaul's (1974) review of small group research led them to believe that a lack of structure in the early stages of a group may actually impede the development of group process. Groups with low structure often suffered from high dropout rates, high levels of distress, and avoidance of interpersonal communication.

Bednar, Melnick, and Kaul (1974) argued that the implementation of a certain degree of structure in early group sessions would facilitate and enhance the development of group process. More specifically, he argued for the use of pretherapy training to help clarify role expectations for clients, including modeling, practicing of good group behaviors, and helping clients develop an understanding of group development.

Like a good scientist practitioner, Bednar implemented a research program to investigate his theoretical formulations. Through a series of studies he and his colleagues (Evensen & Bednar, 1978; Lee & Bednar, 1977) examined different aspects of the theory. These studies were designed to examine the effects of group structure, in the form of pretherapy training, on people with varying levels of risk taking dispositions (i.e., high risk takers versus low risk takers). Consistent with Bednar's theory, results of the studies indicated that high risk takers exposed to a high level of structure in pretherapy training were more involved than others in self-disclosure and exchanging interpersonal feedback. These subjects also reported higher levels of group cohesion and depth of communication. High levels of structure were also shown to be particularly influential in increasing the amount of self-disclosure and interpersonal feedback in those with low risk taking dispositions (Evensen & Bednar, 1978; Lee & Bednar, 1977).

Through these research studies, Bednar was able to gain empirical support for his ideas. The work of Bednar and his colleagues has had a major impact on the way the majority of group workers think about and plan for the initial stages of group counseling. Although there is still much to be learned about this topic, it does demonstrate that a well developed and implemented program of research, that looks at a topic in a variety of ways, can have a beneficial effect on or provide insights into good practice.

Understanding and Engaging in the Research Process

This section will discuss ways to sharpen research and evaluation skills for those either in graduate school or those who have completed graduate work and wish to increase their knowledge and ability in this area. It is our hope that training programs will provide more focus on group research since graduate schools are one of the major ways people develop research skills. Gelso (1993) tells us that graduate school training has a great impact on the student's attitude toward research and his or her commitment toward continued research after graduation. The result of a positive research training experience may be the development of practitioners who are excited about inquiry and able to become good consumers, perhaps even taking part in research themselves. Medicine and other fields are filled with examples of practitioners who have applied their research skills, curiosity and creativity to solving major medical and social problems. The same may also be true of group counseling, but practitioners need to first apply research skills to the work they do.

Wampold (1986) has suggested that research training employ a model familiar to clinical instruction. This is a sound idea not only for graduate instruction but also for developing research and evaluation in the practice setting. Just as students in counseling begin their clinical training by developing beginning skills, beginning researchers (practitioners or students) should start by developing basic research skills. For example, in order to insure that the first counseling experience is a positive one, the student's first client is often a classmate from whom the student can receive encouragement and nonthreatening direction (after all, the peer playing the client will have to be the counselor as well). Likewise, in order to make a counselor's first evaluation or research project a positive experience it should be nonthreatening, fairly simple in design and analysis, and of interest to the counselor.

Taking Wampold's (1986) suggestion to train counselors to do research by using a model similar to clinical training has implications for the practice setting as well. Just as students who graduate with a masters or doctoral degree in counseling continue to benefit from on going supervision, consultation, mentoring, and peer discussion, so also persons in the field benefit from these on going experiences in their clinical work (Stockton & Toth, 1997). Likewise, one will become a more astute researcher from supervised practice, inter- and intra-agency consultation, and peer group discussions focused on research. A supportive research environment in which to proceed with research efforts is essential to successful outcomes. As Gelso (1993) and Gelso, Mallinckrodt, and Judge, (1996) have stressed, a research environment can be created in any setting whenever there is a critical mass of individuals and resources available. Since early efforts so heavily influence later paths, it is essential to gain support from peers and a working alliance with supervisors in order to maximize chances for early success. Moreover, research training at the postgraduate level is available. The American Educational Research Association (AERA) offers professional workshops in research methods at their annual conventions. Divisions of the American Counseling Association (ACA) like the Association for Specialists in Group Work (ASGW) sponsor informal discussions at their annual conventions, also. The ASGW gatherings provide opportunities for persons less experienced in group research to ask questions and engage in dialogue with those who are more experienced. It is an opportunity to discuss research ideas and problems with peers experienced in a variety of group research methods. It can be a golden opportunity for those beginning research projects to employ the collective wisdom of seasoned professionals before they get their programs off the ground. Moreover, ASGW sponsors group research papers at their annual conferences and the annual convention of the ACA. These are additional opportunities to hear what types of research are being done in the field.

An example of following a developmental model of research training comes from an advanced group counseling course taught by Toth at the University of Iowa. In this course group research was introduced in a nonthreatening way. Students began a project by reviewing journal articles. Next, they conducted a literature review that was informed by their perusal of journal articles. This research project required students to design a study that could be conducted at the local community counseling center where they had participated in field observations throughout the semester. So, the students' inquiries were informed both by literature in the field and by what they observed in the practice setting. The instructor focused on positively reinforcing students' research activities and maximizing success through early introduction to a minimally intimidating research involvement (Gelso, 1993).

Another example of the importance of graduate student research in group counseling is found in the work of the group research team developed by Stockton at Indiana University. The research team has been engaged in a long term program of inquiry. The team has been composed of faculty members and students in training (who, in some cases, continue working with the team following their graduation). Beginning with an earlier focus on such factors as cohesion, goal setting, self-disclosure, and feedback, in the past few years the team has also been concerned with group leader instruction. Two primary questions have guided the work: What is it that group leaders need to know? And, what teaching methods are best suited to the instruction of group leaders? Thus, the goal of the team is to be able to richly describe a group experience from the perspective of members as they are trying to make changes in their lives and also from the perspective of leaders as they attempt to apply skills they have learned. Students are involved in this apprenticeship type program at the level they are prepared and feel comfortable. Typically they begin with necessary activities that do not require high technical sophistication, e.g., library literature reviews, assisting in preparing information, administering and collecting forms for research projects, and coding data. At the same time these activities are taking place, team members are involved in weekly seminars. At these meetings current projects are discussed or future projects contemplated. These projects range from dissertations to pilot studies to long term continuing projects. The discussions range from practical support for data gathering to brainstorming about beginning projects to research design or statistical analysis.

Program Evaluation

The purpose of this section is to discuss the importance of evaluation research in the field of social sciences. More specifically, information regarding how to carry on program evaluation, and questions one might ask in this endeavor are given.

Counselors are increasingly being called upon to be accountable for the work that they do. As funding becomes less available, it is being left up to human service professionals to document the effectiveness of their programs. This is particularly true in the world of managed care, but is also increasingly true in all other areas of counseling. Private practitioners, counseling centers, and other provider programs that do not begin to inform consumers' representatives of their worth are likely to be undercut by other competition, or simply cut out of the mental health provider system. Correspondingly, school counselors are also increasingly called upon to provide evidence of the efficacy of their services. Evaluating group counseling and psychoeducational programs in the school setting is advised in order to justify to the principal, superintendent, or board of education the necessity of spending valuable resources on such programs. Thus, more and more often counselors are expected, even required, to be involved in program evaluation. Often they may be put in charge of putting together and implementing such an evaluation. Therefore, it is increasingly important that counselors be knowledgeable about and skilled in program evaluation. Evaluating your group counseling programs for school settings provides data to support the work that you are doing as well as gives you information about the quality of the work you are doing. By evaluating your group counseling programs you can begin to create a reciprocal relationship between program quality and evidence of efficacy.

We know that many counselors practice, at least part time, in an independent setting. It is just as incumbent upon counselors in private practice to evaluate the efficacy of their work. All counselors have an ethical obligation to evaluate their work as well as to utilize practices that have a research base to illuminate practice. At an earlier time it was fine for counselors to rely on clinical accounts and client customer satisfaction to claim success. The only people who needed to be convinced that therapy had something to offer were the clients themselves. The clients kept returning, the counselor continued to be paid, and everyone was happy. However, times have changed, and counselors are asked to provide evidence of the efficacy of their work. Horne (1995) wrote that "our livelihood is beginning to depend on our ability to justify our services" (p. 2). Now it is not only middle persons like managed care corporations that are looking for evidence of therapeutic results but the whole fabric of the counseling endeavor including consumers, advocates, overseers, providers and sources of funding.

Evaluation Procedures

Before proceeding with any evaluation of a program, it is important to determine specifically what information is being sought. In other words, why is the evaluation being done. For example, sometimes program evaluation is necessary to provide accountability for government sponsored programs or for other funding agencies, such as managed care providers or foundations. Program evaluations are also used for purposes of policy making. Often, decisions such as whether or not to continue a program or how much financial and political support it will receive are based on outcome data (Hosie, 1994). Other times, program evaluations are conducted by conscientious counselors who simply want to get an idea of the effectiveness of their programs and make improvements where needed. It is important to keep the purpose of your evaluation in mind while planning. Some issues to consider when planning the evaluation include what services will be evaluated, how the data will be collected, who will be involved in and/or affected by the evaluation, and how the information will be used. It is important to make explicit the information you are looking for by developing a specific list of questions to be answered in the evaluation.

Some types of evaluation will involve the use of written evaluation instruments. Published instruments may be acquired from several sources. There are many self-report type instruments published in journal articles that may be reproduced and used at no cost. Other standardized instruments may be purchased from publishing companies. Other resources include compendiums of reviews and test descriptions; the best known of these is the *Mental Measurements Yearbook* series published by the Buros Institute of Mental Measurement (Impara & Plake, 1998). Often journal articles will describe instruments. An excellent example of such an article is by DeLucia-Waack (1997b), which describes a number of instruments designed specifically to measure the efficacy of groups. Readers interested in group assessment will find this resource particularly helpful.

You may want to develop your own instrument: It may be helpful or even necessary to develop a questionnaire to answer dilemmas that are unique to your agency. Developing your own instruments will help to ensure that data collected corresponds specifically to the information you are seeking (Fairchild & Seeley, 1996). If you are going to develop your own instrument you should consider consulting with a specialist since the application of psychometric procedures takes particular training. Below we discuss some self-developed evaluation instruments. It should be noted that many of the following examples of programmatic evaluation are rather simple in their executions. Nevertheless, they are still important in that they answer specific questions raised by specific counseling situations in the field. They help to discern the program's strengths and weaknesses and offer bits and pieces of important information to the broader field of group counseling.

A review of the group counseling literature by Auger (1997) discussed nine different approaches to group program evaluation that have been or can be used in school settings:

> group member postgroup evaluations;
> postgroup evaluation by student members' parents;
> group members' formative evaluations;
> ratings by teachers or parents of group members;
> self-report questionnaires;
> single subjects designs;
> independent observation of group process;
> using both pre and postgroup ratings of group members; and
> formal evaluation instruments that examine group process.

Postgroup evaluations can be accomplished in a number of ways. Group members can be asked open ended questions at the conclusion of the group that will serve to elicit evaluative responses. For example, members can be asked: "Were you able to discuss your problems in the group?" A Likert type scale, where students are asked to respond to a series of questions on a 5 point continuum, could be used at the group's conclusion to determine group effectiveness.

An example of a postgroup evaluation was provided by Bruckner and Thompson (1987). They set out to evaluate their developmental group guidance program for students in grades 4 through 6. In this program, group sessions were held with each classroom for 30 minutes each week. Sessions included instructional lessons as well as group discussions about topics of concern to students. To evaluate this program, a simple sentence completion form was given to each student in grades 4–6. The form was adapted from previously developed sentence completion tests that were found in journals. The form was brief, containing only nine items. Examples of the items include the following:

1. I think coming to the guidance room is _____.
2. The counselor could do better if _____.
3. If I had my choice I (would) (would not) come to the guidance room with my class.

Students' responses were given ratings from 1 (clearly positive) to 5 (clearly negative), and scores were averaged in order to give average response ratings for each grade level. In addition to the number ratings, students' actual written comments were used to give the counselors suggestions and ideas for improving the program. Besides being used for the counselors own purposes, the information was used for several other purposes: 1) results were presented to the principal as part of the counselor's annual evaluation; 2) they were shared with a team appointed by the governor to assess the impact of elementary school guidance, and 3) they were used as a needs assessment for developing the group guidance program for the following year. Thus, a simple and quick evaluation proved very beneficial in a variety of ways.

Another good example of an evaluation of a group counseling program was done by the bereavement directors of two hospice programs (Houseley, 1996). The directors wanted to investigate the effectiveness of the children's grief groups they conducted. This evaluation involved administering pre and posttest measures to the participant children and their parents, as well as to a control group of children and families that the directors recruited from local public schools. The evaluators of the hospice groups designed their study to answer specific questions:

1. Do the children feel differently about themselves after participating in the grief support group?
2. What are the children's perceptions of the effectiveness of grief support groups following their participation?
3. What are strengths and weaknesses of the group experience as perceived by the children?

4. What were the undesirable outcomes of participation in the group?
5. What was the effectiveness of the group as reported by the parents?

To answer these questions, the children in both groups were given the Death Concept Scale and the Piers Harris Self-Concept Scale. The parents in both groups were administered the Child Behavior Checklist and an Information Questionnaire. In addition, semi-structured interviews were designed and administered to the children and parents in the treatment group. In general, the investigators found that participation in the groups was effective and beneficial. This study is a good example of an evaluation designed to meet the needs of the program itself. By planning out the questions to be answered, the investigators were able to design an effective combination of quantitative and qualitative measures to assess the effectiveness of their program. While the evaluation was effective and helpful, it was also simple enough to be performed by practitioners without an extensive research background.

Another example of the effectiveness of field evaluation for therapy groups can be seen in a study by Toth (1997) and a colleague at a large university counseling center. In order to determine the effectiveness of their grief therapy group for college students who had suffered the death of a significant other, Toth and his colleague conducted an evaluation of their grief group. Five students who had experienced loss by death within the last two years participated in a short term grief therapy group. They agreed to fill out measures to determine the severity of their bereavement and their experiences in the group at four times during the eight treatment sessions.

In this study, the group leaders used the Brief Grief Experience Inventory (Lee, Munro, & McCorkle, 1993) to measure the extent of each clients' bereavement and progress in symptom reduction, and had members write a journal entry four times during the course of the therapy expressing their perceptions of significant events that took place in the group. For their journal entries members were asked to comment on the following questions:

1. Describe a personally significant experience from today's group session. Please be as specific as you can about the event. What made this particular experience meaningful? Was the event helpful? If so, how was it helpful?
   a. List two thoughts about the experience.
   b. List two feelings regarding the experience.
   c. List two physical reactions to the experience.

2. Are there any other thoughts or feelings you wish to discuss about today's group session? Do you have any other comments you would like to share?

This study is an example of how evaluation procedures can be utilized and helpful information can be gathered even with a small number of participants and lack of experimental control. Even though statistically significant results would not be expected from a sample size as small as this, significant policy information regarding the members' group experiences was gathered. When examining the group members' responses to questions posed to them it was clear that the members experienced a good deal of therapeutic gain. Nearly all the members appreciated the feeling of universality they shared with others. Sharing their grief with others interrupted the members' feelings of isolation and despair. They began to talk about feeling normal in spite of these unusual feelings they were having. The members were also grateful to have a forum to deal with these feelings. The group provided a safe place to explore thoughts and feelings they were not able to share with peers.

Even a study with a small number of participants, though not experimentally significant, can provide useful information. The next time a group like this was done, the leaders were more informed about how to meet members' needs. Recommendations that were made after reviewing the data included: 1) taking more group time to involve members in interpersonal interaction as well as honoring the time members need to tell their grief stories; 2) a longer period for treatment could prove helpful since eight one and one-half hour sessions did not seem to be enough time to members or leaders; and, 3) consider group as a mode for treating distress due to losses other than death (Toth, 1997).

Curriculum evaluation in classroom settings can help improve the quality of teaching and may result in more highly trained counselors. For example, Toth taught the here and now intervention to masters level group counseling students (Toth & Stockton, 1996), and wanted to add another intervention to this skill based curriculum. With help from an advanced doctoral student at the University of Iowa, he developed a training program to teach group leaders to give and facilitate feedback in interpersonal therapy groups (Toth & Erwin, in press). In order to help determine the efficacy of this technique, they utilized many of the above mentioned evaluation techniques with his introduction to group counseling course. Toth and Erwin wanted to know whether or not students' self-confidence about giving and facilitating feedback improved through the training interval. They wanted to know the students' experiences in the training program, i.e., did students find this training helpful, enjoyable, and/or stimulating? In order to discover this information they constructed evaluation measures specifically for these purposes. Students responded to a survey measuring their confidence in making feedback interventions prior to and after being trained in the intervention. Students also responded to a series of questions and were asked to comment on various aspects of the training program so that the researchers could determine the most interesting, helpful, and useful portions of the training. The evaluation helped clarify the researchers' perceptions of the program and supplied valuable data regarding the students' perceptions of the program and development of self-confidence. This evaluation enabled the researchers to make decisions about how to best meet students' training needs in the face of classroom and curricular limitations.

How to Access Information

When doing research the first step that one has to take is to get informed. The researcher has to find information in the field that already exists about the topic. Alternatively, before you find out about a topic you may have a question that you are interested in pursuing. This question may be what inspires you to pursue further understanding. However, it is the review of literature that gives a grounding for your further pursuits of the problem in question. A good review allows the investigator to establish what is already known about a topic. There should be a logical progression of knowledge, or at least some understanding of gaps in the knowledge base. When completed, the review should be able to demonstrate the need for the next logical study in the area being examined.

Current group text books play an important role in dissemination of research knowledge as it applies to group practice. However, there is always a lag time between the knowledge base available and the publication of any text. Another source of research information is reviews done by writers who compile, analyze, and make sense of what we know about an area in a research review. There are a number of good reviews regarding group research: e.g., the well known chapter in *The Handbook of Psychotherapy and Behaviors Change* by Bednar and Kaul (1994), *The Handbook of Group Psychotherapy* by Fuhriman and Burlingame (1994), and reviews of literature in the counseling journals such as Kivlinghan's (1985) review of feedback. A recent set of reviews in group research are contained in the November 1997 special issue on research of the *Journal for Specialists in Group Work* (Vol. 22, No. 4). Reading these reviews can help one gain perspective on what groups are, and why they work the way they do, and how to be most effective as a group leader.

A good first step in undertaking any research or evaluation project is to find out what work has already been done in that area, as well as what other professionals are currently doing. Methods for investigation have changed quite dramatically in recent years with advances that have been made in technology. In the not so distant past reviewing the literature on a topic involved proceeding manually through card catalogs with note cards in hand to take notes. Collecting information today is a much different process. With use of a computer it is possible to gain access to a vast amount of information electronically. This information comes in a variety of forms, including electronic data bases and Internet sites. It is also possible to communicate with other professionals through list servs and mailing lists. While the use of such resources may initially seem intimidating, becoming familiar with them can make the task of collecting information a much easier and faster process.

Databases of research formerly available only as print indexes, such as Educational Research and Information Clearinghouse (ERIC) and PsychLit, are now published on CD-ROM and are available at many libraries. These databases allow the user to quickly generate lists of publications on topics of interest. They also offer the advantages of "being able to experiment with various keywords, follow interesting leads (e.g., the works of a particular author), and limit the final output to only those references that are right on target . . ." (Sexton, Whiston, Bleuer, & Walz, 1997, p. 132).

Even newer and more easily accessible resources are available over the Internet. Today, it is possible to access an incredible amount of information from professional organizations, online journals, and even from live communication with other professionals. A big advantage to using the Internet is that most sites are frequently updated, so that the user often has access to the most current information available. Such a vast amount of information is now available that it can be difficult to know where to begin. Efficiently searching the Internet for information has become a skill in and of itself. However, there are several key sites which can provide good starting points for the professional interested in gathering information about group counseling. A list of actual site addresses can be found in Figure 15.2.

The Educational Research and Informational Clearinghouse (ERIC) which produces the CD-ROM database discussed above, also has a web site with an excellent selection of helpful resources. In addition to searching their database online, the user can browse through digests, which are two page research syntheses on various topics. These digests include a summary of the current research on the topic as well as a list of references. If the user is unable to find the information they are seeking, the AskERIC function allows the user to send an e-mail message with a specific question. A personal response will be returned within two business days.

Professional organizations such as the American Counseling Association (ACA), the American Educational Research Association (AERA) and the American Psychological Association (APA) also have web sites that are full of helpful information. For example, at the ACA website counselors can chat with colleagues on the World Counseling Network, which holds regularly scheduled discussions on specified topics. The AERA website contains online journals and publications; this site allows you to search abstracts of AERA journals from 1966–1996. It also provides access to list servs such as the Education Research List, which is a forum for general discussion of education research. Similar resources are available at the APA website; you

1. American Counseling Association: http://www.counseling.org/
2. American Educational Research Association: http://aera.net
3. American Psychological Association: http://www.apa.org/
4. Association for Specialists in Group Work: http://psyctcl.sghms.ac.uk/ mirrors/asgw/index.html
5. Educational Research and Information Clearinghouse: http://ericr.syr.edu

FIGURE 15.2. Internet sites of interest to group counselors.

can browse APA journals by topic, for example, as well as get access to PsychInfo database online.

Of particular interest to group counselors may be the Association for Specialists in Group Work (ASGW) website. At this site a counselor can gain access to information on all aspects of group work by selecting the Resources for Group Workers icon, which provides links to many excellent resources on all aspects of group work. The research area of this site may be particularly useful to counselors embarking on a research or evaluation project. The electronic listserv Groupstuff, operated by Stockton, can also be accessed from the resources icon of the ASGW site. Through this listserv, counselors can exchange information, questions, ideas, and feedback related to group topics. For example, the authors' research team recently sent out a survey regarding group therapists' uses of the therapeutic factors in their group work. The survey responses will be used in an upcoming research project.

There are numerous other sites with a seemingly endless amount of information available over the Internet. Perhaps the best way to learn about what is available is to just explore; the possibilities are almost endless. The sites mentioned here and listed in Figure 15.2 are good starting points.

Summary

As we have pointed out, research plays a very important role in the way we think about and conduct group practice. In this chapter we have identified some of the problems and challenges inherent in doing research in general and in group work specifically. We have tried to present to the reader the trade offs that are inevitably necessary in conducting this type of research. In doing this, we have used actual studies to illustrate how the knowledge base in group work has developed through a combination of research and evaluation approaches. We have noted that research knowledge develops incrementally and stressed the importance of programmatic efforts to this end. Finally, we have emphasized the value of becoming familiar with the literature and have encouraged our readers to develop and carry out their own studies.

REFERENCES

Alberti, R. E. (Ed.). (1977). *Assertiveness: Innovations, applications, issues.* San Luis Obispo, CA: Impact Publishers.

Alberti, R. E., & Emmons, M. L. (1995a). *Your perfect right: A guide to assertive behavior* (6th ed.). San Luis Obispo, CA: Impact Publishers.

Alberti, R. E., & Emmons, M. (1995b). *Your perfect right: A manual for assertiveness trainers.* San Luis Obispo, CA: Impact Publishers.

Allport, G. W. (1960). *Becoming.* New Haven, CT: Yale University Press.

American Counseling Association. (1995). *Code of ethics and standards of practice.* Alexandria, VA: Author.

American Group Psychotherapy Association. (1991). *Guidelines for ethics.* New York: Author.

American Psychological Association. (1992). Ethical principles of psychologists and code of conduct. *American Psychologist, 47,* 1597–1611.

Anderson, A. R. (1969). Group counseling. *Review of educational research, 39,* 209–226.

Anderson, J. (1984). *Counseling through group process.* New York: Springer.

Anonymous. (1996). *Primary colors: A novel of politics.* New York: Warner Books.

Appleton, V. E., & Dykeman, C. (1996). Using art in group counseling with Native American youth. *Journal for Specialists in Group Work, 21*(4), 224–242.

Argras, W. S. (Ed.). (1978). *Behavior modification: Principles and clinical applications* (2nd ed.). Boston: Little Brown.

Argyris, C., Putnam, R., & Smith, D. M. (1985). *Action Science.* San Francisco, CA: Jossey-Bass.

Arredondo, P. (1994). Multicultural training: A response. *The Counseling Psychologist, 22,* 308–314.

Arredondo, P., Toporek, R., Brown, S. P., Jones, J., Locke, D. C., Sanchez, J., & Stadler, H. (1996). Operationalization of the multicultural counseling competencies. *Journal of Multicultural Counseling and Development, 24,* 42–78.

Association for Multicultural Counseling and Development. (1996). *Multicultural competencies.* Alexandria, VA: Author.

Association for Specialists in Group Work. (1982). Group work and organizational development. *Journal for Specialists in Group Work, 7*(1).

Association for Specialists in Group Work. (1982). Special issue: Ethical issues in group work. *Journal for Specialists in Group Work, 7*(3), 138–214.

Association for Specialists in Group Work. (1989). *Ethical guidelines for group counselors.* Alexandria, VA: Author.

Association for Specialists in Group Work. (1990). *Professional standards for the training of group workers.* Alexandria, VA: Author.

Association for Specialists in Group Work. (1990). Special issue: Ethical and legal issues in group work. *Journal for Specialists in Group Work, 15*(2), 66–127.

Association for Specialists in Group Work. (1991). *Professional training standards for the training of group workers.* Alexandria, VA: Author.

Association for Specialists in Group Work. (1992). ASGW: Professional training standards for group workers. *Journal for specialists in group work, 17*(1), 12–19.

Association for Specialists in Group Work. (1997). Special issue: Group research—encouraging a collaboration between practitioners and researchers. *Journal for Specialists in Group Work, 22*(4), 226–297.

Association for Specialists in Group Work. (1998). *Principles for diversity competent group workers*. Alexandria, VA: Author.

Atkinson, D. R., Morton, G., & Sue, D. W. (1993). *Counseling American minorities* (4th ed.). Dubuque, IA: Brown & Benchmark.

Aubrey, R. F. (1973). Organizational victimization of school counselors. *The School Counselor, 20*, 346–353.

Auger, R. W. (1997). Evaluating the effectiveness of counseling groups in schools. Unpublished manuscript.

Axelson, J. A. (1993). *Counseling and development in a multicultural society*. (Rev. ed.). Monterey, CA: Brooks/Cole.

Bach, G. R. (1954). *Intensive group psychotherapy*. New York: Ronald Press.

Bach, R. (1970). *Jonathan Livingston Seagull: A story*. New York: Macmillan.

Bales, R. F. (1950). *Interaction process analysis*. Cambridge, MA: Addison-Wesley.

Bandura, A. (1969). *Principles of behavior modification*. New York: Holt, Rinehart, and Winston.

Barnard, C. P., & Corrales, R. G. (1979). *The theory and technique of family therapy*. Springfield. IL: Charles C. Thomas.

Bates, M. (1966). Themes in group counseling with adolescents. *Personnel and Guidance Journal, 44*, 568–575.

Bates, M., Johnson, C. D., & Blaker, K. E. (1982). *Group leadership: A manual for group counseling leaders* (2nd ed.). Denver: Love.

Beck, A. T., & Weishaar, M. E. (1995). Cognitive therapy in R. J. Corsini & D. Wedding (Eds.), *Current psychotherapies* (4th ed., pp. 285–320). Itasca, IL: F.E. Peacock.

Becvar, D. (1982). The family is not a group—or is it? *Journal for Specialists in Group Work, 7*(2), 88–95.

Bednar, R., & Kaul, T. (1994). Experiential group research: Can the canon fire? In A. E. Bergin & S. I. Garfield (Eds.), *Handbook of psychotherapy and behavior change* (4th ed., pp. 631–663). New York: Wiley.

Bednar, R. L., & Langenbahn, D. M. (1979). Structure and ambiguity: Conceptual and applied misconceptions. *Journal for Specialists in Group Work, 4*, 170–175.

Bednar, R., Melnick, J., & Kaul, T. (1974). Risk, responsibility and structure. *Journal of Counseling Psychology, 21*(1), 31–37.

Bemak, F., & Epp, L. R. (1996). The 12th curative factor: Love as an agent of healing in group psychotherapy. *Journal for Specialists in Group Work, 21*(2), 118–127.

Benjamin, A. B. (1987). *The helping interview with case illustrations*. Boston: Houghton Mifflin.

Berger, E. M. (1952). The relationship between expressed acceptance of self and expressed acceptance of others. *Journal of Abnormal and Social Psychology, 47*, 778–782.

Bieschke, K. J., Matthews, C., & Wade, J. (1996). Training group counselors: The Process observer method. *Journal for Specialists in Group Work, 21*(3), 181–186.

Birnbaum, M. (1969). Sense about sensitivity training. *Saturday review*, November 15, 82–89.

Blaker, K. E., & Samo, J. (1973). Communications games: A group counseling technique. *The School Counselor, 21*, 46–51.

Blocher, D. (1966). *Developmental counseling*. New York: Ronald Press.

Bloom, J. W. (1997). Guidelines for the new world of webcounseling. *NBCC NewsNotes, 14*(2), 1–2.

Bonney, W. C. (1969). Group counseling and development processes. In G. M.Gazda (Ed.), *Theories and methods of group counseling in the schools*. Springfield, IL: Charles C. Thomas.

Boszormenyi-Nagy, I., & Krasner, B. R. (1986). *Between give and take: A clinical guide to contextual therapy*. New York, NY: Brunner/Mazel.

Boszormenyi-Nagy, I., & Spark, G. M. (1973). *Invisible loyalties: Reciprocity in family therapy.* Hagerstown, MD: Harper & Row.

Bowen, M. (1966). The use of family theory in clinical practice. *Comprehensive Psychiatry, 7,* 345–374.

Bowman, V. E., & DeLucia, J. L. (1993). Preparation for group therapy: The effects of preparer and modality on group process and individual functioning. *Journal for Specialists in Group Work, 18*(2), 67–79.

Bradford, L. P., Gibb, J., & Benne, K. (1964). *T-group theory and laboratory methods.* New York: Wiley.

Brammer, L. M., & Shostrum, E. L. (1976). *Therapeutic psychology: Fundamentals of counseling and psychotherapy* (3rd ed.). Englewood Cliffs, NJ: Prentice-Hall.

Breier, C. A. (1997). Group counseling is like. . . . *Together, 25*(2), 12.

Brown, S. L. (1991). *Counseling victims of violence.* Alexandria, VA: American Counseling Association

Brown, W. F. (1965). Student to student counseling for academic adjustment. *Personnel and Guidance Journal, 43,* 811–816.

Bruckner, S. T., & Thompson, C. L. (1987). Guidance program evaluation: An example. *Elementary School Guidance and Counseling, 21*(3), 193–196.

Burke, M. T., & Miranti, J. G. (Eds.). (1992). *Ethical and spiritual values in counseling.* Alexandria, VA: American Counseling Association.

Campbell, D., & Stanley, J. (1963). *Experimental and quasi-experimental designs for research.* Chicago: Rand McNally.

Campbell, L. (1992). An interview with Arthur M. Horne. *Journal for Specialists in Group Work, 17*(3), 131–143.

Campbell, L. (1996). Samuel T. Gladding: A sense of self in group. *Journal for Specialists in Group Work, 21*(2), 69–80.

Cantor, D. W., & Drake, E. A. (1983). *Divorced parents and their children.* New York: Springer.

Caple, M. C., & Cox, P. L. (1989). Relationships among group structure, member expectations, attraction to group and satisfaction with the group experience. *Journal for Specialists in Group Work, 14*(1), 16–24.

Carroll, H. A. (1969). *Mental hygiene: The dynamics of adjustment* (5th ed.). Englewood Cliffs, NJ: Prentice-Hall.

Carroll, M. R. (1973). The regeneration of guidance. *The School Counselor, 20,* 355–360.

Carroll, M. R. (1985). Critical issues in group work in education: Now and 2001. *Journal for Specialists in Group Work, 10*(2), 98–102.

Carroll, M. R. (1986). *Group work: Leading in the here and now.* Alexandria, VA: American Counseling Association.

Carroll, M. R., & Wiggins, J. D. (1997). *Elements of group counseling: Back to the basics* (2nd ed.). Denver, CO: Love.

Carter, E. A., & McGoldrick, M. (Eds.). (1988). *The family life cycle: A framework for family therapy* (2nd ed.). New York: Gardner Press.

Cartwright, D. (1951). Achieving change in people: Some applications of group dynamic theory. *Human Relations, 4,* 381–392.

Childers, Jr., J. H., & Couch, R. D. (1989). Myths about group counseling: Identifying and challenging misconceptions. *Journal for Specialists in Group Work, 14*(2), 105–111.

Christensen, E. W. (1990). Walter Lifton's Pioneering contributions to group work. *Journal for Specialists in Group Work, 15*(3), 132–140.

Clark, A. J. (1989). Questions in group counseling. *Journal for Specialists in Group Work, 14*(2), 121–124.

Clark, A. J. (1992). Defense mechanisms in group counseling. *Journal for Specialists in Group Work, 17*(3), 151–160.

Clark, A. J. (1993). Interpretation in group counseling: Theoretical and operational issues. *Journal for Specialists in Group Work, 18*(4), 174–181.

Clark, A. J. (1997). Projective identification as a defense mechanism in group counseling. *Journal for Specialists in Group Work, 22*(2), 85–96.

Coffey, R. S. (1952). Socio and psyche group process: Integrated concepts. *Journal of Social Issues, 8,* 65–74.

Cohen, A. M., & Smith, R. D. (1976). *The critical incident in growth groups: Theory and technique.* La Jolla, CA: University Associates, Inc.

Cohn, B. (1964). Group counseling with adolescents. In B. Cohn (Ed.), *Collected articles: The adolescent and group counseling* (unpublished). Board of Cooperative Educational Services. Yorktown Heights, NY, 10598.

Cohn, B. (Ed.). (1967). *Guidelines for future research on group counseling in the public school setting.* Washington, DC: American Personnel and Guidance Association.

Cohn, B. (1973). Group counseling presentation. Spring Group Guidance Conference, University of Wisconsin-Oshkosh.

Combs, A. W., & Snygg, D. (1959). *Individual behavior* (Rev. ed.). New York: Harper & Row.

Conyne, R. K. (Ed.). (1985). *The group worker's handbook: Varieties of group experience.* Springfield, IL: Charles C. Thomas.

Conyne, R. K. (1989). *How personal growth and task groups work.* Newbury Park, CA: Sage.

Conyne, R. K. (1996). The Association for Specialists in Group Work training standards: Some considerations and suggestions for training. *Journal for Specialists in Group Work, 21*(3), 155–162.

Conyne, R. K. (1998). What to look for in groups: Helping trainees become more sensitive to multicultural issues. *Journal for Specialists in Group Work, 23*(1), 22–32.

Conyne, R. K. (In Press). *Failures in group work: How we can learn from our failures.* Thousand Oaks, CA: Sage

Conyne, R. K., Dye, A., Gill, S. J., Leddick, G. R., Morran, D. K., & Ward, D. E. (1985). A retrospective of "critical issues." *Journal for Specialists in Group Work, 10*(2), 112–115.

Conyne, R. K., Dye, H. A., Kline, W. B., Morran, D. K., Ward, D. E., & Wilson, F. R. (1992). Context for revising the Association for Specialists in Group Work training standards. *Journal for Specialists in Group Work, 17*(1), 12–19.

Conyne, R. K., Harvill, R. L., Morganette, R. S., Morran, D. K., & Hulse-Killacky, D. (1990). Effective group leadership: Continuing the search for greater clarity and understanding. *Journal for Specialists in Group Work, 15*(1), 30–36.

Conyne, R. K., Smith, J., & Wathen, S. (1997, October). *Co-leader and supervisor processing of group phenomena.* Paper presented at the annual meeting of the North Central Association for Counselor Education & Supervision, St. Louis, MO.

Conyne, R. K., Wilson, F. R., & Ward, D. (1997). *Comprehensive group work: What it means & how to teach it.* Alexandria, VA: American Counseling Association.

Conyne, R., Wilson, F. R., Kline, W., Morran, D. K., & Ward, D. (1993). Training Group Workers: Implications of the new ASGW training standards for training and practice. *Journal for Specialists in Group Work, 18*(1), 11–23.

Corey, G. (1995). *Theory and practice of group counseling* (4th ed.). Monterey, CA: Brooks/Cole.

Corey, G., & Corey, M. S. (1977). *Groups: Process and practice.* Monterey, CA: Brooks/Cole.

Corey, G., & Corey, M. S. (1987). *Groups: Process and practice* (3rd ed.). Monterey, CA: Brooks/Cole.

Corey, G., & Corey, M. S. (1997). *Groups: Process and practice* (5th ed.). Monterey, CA: Brooks/Cole.

Corey, G., Corey, M. S., & Callahan, P. (1990). Role of group leader's values in group counseling. *Journal for Specialists in Group Work, 15*(2), 68–74.

Corey, G., Corey, M. S., Callahan, P., & Russell, J.M. (1982). *Group techniques.* Monterey, CA: Brooks/Cole.

Corey, G., Corey, M. S., & Callahan, P. (1993). *Issues and ethics in the helping professions* (4th ed.). Pacific Grove, CA: Brooks/Cole.

Corey, G., Corey, M. S., Callahan, P., & Russell, J. M. (1992). *Group techniques* (2nd ed.). Pacific Grove, CA: Brooks/Cole.

Corey, M. S., & Corey, G. (1992). *Groups: Process and practice* (4th ed.). Pacific Grove, CA: Brooks/Cole.

Cormier, W. H., & Cormier, L. S. (1991). *Interviewing strategies for helpers: Fundamental skills and cognitive behavioral interventions* (3rd ed.). Pacific Grove, CA: Brooks/Cole.

Corsini, R. (1968). Immediate therapy in groups. In G. M. Gazda (Ed.), *Innovations in group psychotherapy* (pp. 15–41). Springfield, IL: Charles C. Thomas.

Cottingham, H. F. (1973). Psychological education, the guidance function and the school counselor. *The School Counselor, 20,* 340–345.

Couch, R. D., & Childers, Jr., J. H. (1989). A discussion of differences between group therapy and family therapy: Implications for counselor training and practice. *Journal for Specialists in Group Work, 14*(4), 226–231.

Council for Accreditation of Counseling and Related Educational Programs (CACREP). (1993). *CACREP accreditation standards and procedures manual.* Alexandria, VA: Author.

Courtois, C. A. (1988). *Healing the incest wound: Adult survivors in therapy.* New York: Norton.

Courtois, C. A., & Leehan, J. (1982). Group treatment for grown-up abused children. *Personnel and Guidance Journal, 60*(9), 564–566.

Craig, D. P. (1978). *Hip pocket guide to planning and evaluation.* Austin, TX: Learning Concepts.

Crouch, E., Block, S., & Wanless, J. (1994). Therapeutic factors: Interpersonal and intrapersonal mechanisms. In A. Fuhriman & G. Burlingame (Eds.), *Handbook of group psychotherapy: An empirical and clinical synthesis* (pp. 269–315). New York: Wiley.

Crowley, P. M. (1989). Ask the expert: A group teaching tool. *Journal for Specialists in Group Work, 14*(3), 173–175.

D'Andrea, M., & Daniels, J. (1997a). Multicultural group counseling. In S. Gladding (Ed.), *New developments in group counseling* (pp. 105–110). Greensboro, NC: ERIC Clearinghouse on Counseling & Student Services.

D'Andrea, M., & Daniels, J. (1997b). RESPECTFUL counseling: A new way of thinking about diversity counseling. *Counseling Today, 40,* 30–31, 34.

Dana, R. H. (1993). *Multicultural assessment perspectives for professional psychology.* Boston: Allyn & Bacon.

Dansby, V. S. (1996). Group work within the school system: Survey of implementation of leadership role issues. *Journal for Specialists in Group Work, 21*(4), 232–242.

Davies, D., & Jacobs, A. (1985). "Sandwiching" complex interpersonal feedback. *Small Group Behavior, 16*(3), 387–396.

Davis, L. E. (1979). Racial composition of groups. *Social Work, 24,* 203–218.

Davis, L. E. (1984). *Ethnicity in social group practice.* New York: Haworth.

DeLucia, J. L., Coleman, V. L., & Jensen-Scott, R. L. (Eds.). (1992). Counseling with multicultural populations (Special Issue). *Journal for Specialists in Group Work, 17*(4), 235–242.

DeLucia, J. L. (1991). An interview with H. Allen Dye: Perspectives on the field of group work. *Journal for Specialists in Group Work, 16*(2), 67–73.

DeLucia-Waack, J. L. (1996). Multiculturalism is inherent in all group work. *Journal for Specialists in Group Work, 21*(4), 218–223.

DeLucia-Waack, J. L. (1997a). The importance of processing activities, exercises and events to group work practitioners. *Journal for Specialists in Group Work, 22*(2), 82–84.

DeLucia-Waack, J. L. (1997b). Measuring the effectiveness of group work: A review and analysis of process and outcome measures. *Journal for Specialists in Group Work, 22*(4), 277–293.

DePree, M. (1989). *Leadership is an art.* New York: Dell Publishing.

Dies, R. R. (1983). Bridging the gap between research and practice in group psychotherapy. In R. R. Dies & K. R. MacKensie (Eds.), *Advances in group psychotherapy: Integrating research and practice* (pp. 1–26). New York: International Universities Press.

Dies, R. R. (1985). Research foundation for the future of group work. *Journal for Specialists in Group Work, 10*(2), 68–73.

Dinkmeyer, D. D., & Muro, J. (1971). *Group counseling: Theory and practice.* Itasca, IL: F.E. Peacock.

Dinkmeyer, D. D., & Muro, J. J. (1979). *Group counseling: Theory and practice* (2nd ed.). Itasca, IL: F.E. Peacock.

Donigian, J. (1993). Duality: The issue that won't go away. *Journal for Specialists in Group Work, 18*(3), 137–140.

Donigian, J., & Hulse-Killacky, D. (1999). *Critical incidents in group work* (2nd ed.). Pacific Grove, CA: Brooks/Cole.

Donigian, J., & Malnati, R. (1997). *Systemic group therapy: A triadic model.* Pacific Grove, CA: Brooks/Cole.

Donnelly, T. A. (Producer), & Friedkin, W. (Director). (1997). *12 Angry Men* (Film). (Available from MGM Worldwide Television Productions, Inc. Orion Home Video)

Drum, D. J., & Knott, J. E. (1977). *Structured groups for facilitating development: Acquiring life skills, resolving life themes and making life transitions.* New York: Human Sciences Press.

Dugo, J. M., & Beck, A. P. (1997). Significance and complexity of early phases in the development of the co-therapy relationship. *Group Dynamics: Theory, Research, and Practice 1,* 294–305.

Dustin, R., & George, R. A. (1973). *Action counseling for behavior change.* New York: Intext Educational Publishers.

Dye, A. (1981). Challenges to ethical behavior in group work. *Counseling and Values, 25,* 227–235.

Dyer, H. S. (1967). *The discovery and development of educational goals.* Princeton: Educational Testing Service.

Egan, G. (1986). *The skilled helper* (3rd ed.). Pacific Grove, CA: Brooks/Cole.

Ellis, A. (1971). *Growth through reason: Verbatim cases in rational-emotive psychotherapy.* Palo Alto, CA: Science and Behavior Books.

Evan, R. (1972). *Group counseling workshop.* River Falls, WI: University of Wisconsin–River Falls.

Evensen, E. P., & Bednar, R. I. (1978). Effects of specific cognitive and behavioral structure on early group behavior and atmosphere. *Journal of Counseling Psychology, 25,* 66–75.

Fairchild, T. N., & Seeley, T. J. (1996). Evaluation of school psychological services: A case illustration. *Psychology in the Schools, 33,* 46–55.

Faust, V. (1968). *The counselor-consultant in the elementary school.* Boston: Houghton Mifflin.

Feldman, L. B. (1990). Fathers and fathering. In R. L. Meth & R. S. Pasick (Eds.), *Men in therapy* (pp. 88–107). New York: Guilford Press.

Fitts, W. H. (1965). *Manual: Tennessee (Department of mental health) self concept scale.* Counselor Recordings and Tests, Box 6184, Nashville, TN. 37212.

Fitz-Gibbon, C. T., & Morris, L. L. (1987). *How to design a program evaluation.* Newbury Park, CA: Sage.

Fonda, F. (Producer), & Lumet, S. (Director). (1957). *12 Angry Men* (Film). (Available from MGM Worldwide Television Productions, Inc. United Artists)

Forrester-Miller, H. (1989). Dr. Irving Yalom discusses group psychotherapy. *Journal for Specialists in Group Work, 14*(4), 196–201.

Forrester-Miller, H., & Davis, T. E. (1995). *A practitioner's guide to ethical decision making.* Alexandria, VA: American Counseling Association.

Forrester-Miller, H., & Duncan, J. A. (1990). The effects of dual relationships in the training of group counselors. *Journal for Specialists in Group Work, 15*(2), 88–93.

Forrester-Miller, H., & Rubenstein, R. L. (1992). Group counseling: Ethics and professional issues. In D. Capuzzi & D. R. Gross (Eds.), *Introduction to group counseling* (pp. 307–323). Denver, CO: Love.

Forsyth, D. R. (1990). *Group dynamics.* (2nd ed.). Monterey, CA: Brooks/Cole.

Fuhriman, A., & Burlingame, G. M. (Eds.). (1994). *Handbook of group psychotherapy: An empirical and clinical synthesis.* New York: Wiley.

Fukuyama, M. A., & Coleman, N. C. (1992). A model for bicultural assertion training with Asian-Pacific American college students: A pilot study. *Journal for Specialists in Group Work, 17*(4), 210–217.

Fullmer, D. W. (1971). *Counseling: Group theory and system*. New York: Intext Educational Publishers.

Gawrys, J., Jr., & Brown, B. O. (1963). Group counseling: More than a catalyst. *The School Counselor, 12,* 206–213.

Gadza, G. M. (1968). Preface. *Journal of Research and Development in Education, 2,* 1–2.

Gazda, G. M. (1971a). *Group Counseling: A developmental approach*. Boston: Allyn & Bacon.

Gazda, G. M. (1971b). *Human relations development: A manual for educators*. Boston: Allyn & Bacon.

Gazda, G. M. (1984a). *Group counseling: A developmental approach* (3rd ed.). Boston: Allyn & Bacon.

Gazda, G. M. (1984b). Multiple impact training. In D. Larson (Ed.), *Teaching psychology skills: Models for giving psychology away.* (pp. 87–101). Monterey, CA: Brooks/Cole.

Gazda, G. M., & Brooks, D. K., Jr. (Eds.),(1985). The development of the social/life skills training (theme issue). *Journal of Group Psychotherapy, Psychodrama and Sociometry, 38,* 1–68.

Gadza, G. M., Duncan, J. A., & Meadows, M. E. (1967). Group counseling and group procedures: Report of a survey. *Counselor Education and Supervision, 6,* 306–310.

Gazda, G. M., & Larson, M. J. (1968). A comprehensive appraisal of group and multiple counseling research. *Journal of Research and Development in Education, 1*(2), 57–132.

Gelso, C. J. (1993). On the making of a scientist-practitioner: A theory of research training in professional psychology. *Professional Psychology: Research and Practice, 24,* 468–476.

Gelso, C. J., Mallinckrodt, B., & Judge, A. B. (1996). Research training environment attitudes toward research, and research self-efficacy: The revised research training environment scale. *The Counseling Psychologist, 24,* 304–322.

Gendlin, E. T., & Beebe. J. (1968). An experimental approach to group therapy. *Journal of Research and Development in Education, 2*(2), 19–29.

Gilmer, B. V. H. (1970). *Psychology*. New York: Harper & Row.

Ginott, G. M. (1968). A functional approach to group counseling. In G. M. Gazda (Ed.), *Basic approaches to group psychotherapy and group counseling*. Springfield, IL: Charles C. Thomas.

Gladding, S. T. (1984). The metaphor as a counseling tool in group work. *Journal for Specialists in Group Work, 9*(3), 151–156.

Gladding, S. T. (1990). Coming full circle: Reentry after the group. *Journal for Specialists in Group Work, 15*(2), 130–131.

Gladding, S. T. (1991). *Group work*. New York: Merrill.

Gladding, S. T. (1992a). *Counseling as an art: The creative arts in counseling*. Alexandria, VA: American Counseling Association.

Gladding, S. T. (1992b). *Uses of metaphors and poetry in counseling*. (videotape). Available from American Counseling Association. 5999 Stevenson Ave., Alexandria, VA 22304.

Gladding, S. T. (1994). *Group work: A counseling specialty*. Englewood Cliffs, NJ: Prentice-Hall.

Glass, S. (1978, March). Group work in the 80s: What's next after encounter groups? Luncheon address at the meeting of the Association of Specialists in Group Work, Washington, DC.

Glasser, W. (1965). *Reality therapy*. New York: Harper & Row.

Glasser, W. (1969). *Schools without failure*. New York: Harper & Row.

Glasser, W., & Wubbolding, R. (1995) Reality therapy. In R. Corsini and D. Wedding (Eds.), *Current psychotherapies* (5th ed., pp. 293–321). Itasca, IL: F.E. Peacock.

Goldenberg, I., & Goldenberg, H. (1996). *Family therapy: An overview* (4th ed.). Monterey, CA: Brooks/Cole.

Goldenberg, M. M. (1990). *Pharmacology for the psychotherapist*. Muncie, IN: Accelerated Development.

Goldman, L. (1962). Group guidance: Content and process. *Personnel and Guidance Journal, 39,* 518–522.

Goleman, D. (1995). *Emotional intelligence*. New York: Bantam Books.

Granrose, C. S., & Oskamp, S. (Eds.). (1997). *Cross-cultural work groups*. Thousand Oaks, CA: Sage.

Greeley, A. T., Garcia, V. L., Kessler, B. L., & Gilchrest, G. (1992). Training effective multicultural group counselors: Issues for a group training course. *Journal for Specialists in Group Work, 17*(4), 197–209.

Greenberg, J. A. (1974). *Psychodrama: Theory and therapy.* New York: Behavioral Publications.

Gumaer, J. (1973). Peer-facilitated groups. *Elementary School Guidance and Counseling, 8,* 4–11.

Gumaer, J. (1982). Ethics and the experts: Insight into critical incidents. *Journal for Specialists in Group Work, 7*(3), 154–161.

Gutierrez, F. J. (1990). Exploring the macho mystique: Counseling Latino men. In D. Moore & F. Leafgren (Eds.), *Problem solving strategies and interventions for men in conflict.* Alexandria, VA: American Counseling Association.

Hadley, R. G., & Mitchell, L. K. (1995). *Counseling research and program evaluation.* Pacific Grove, CA: Brooks/Cole.

Hall, J. (1969). *Decision by consensus.* Teleometrics International.

Hamachek, D. E. (1971). *Encounters with the self.* New York: Holt, Rinehart, and Winston.

Hamachek, D. E. (1978). *Encounters with the self* (2nd ed.). New York: Holt, Rinehart, and Winston.

Hamburg, B. A., & Varenhorst, B. B. (1972). Peer counseling in secondary school: A community mental health project for youth. *American Journal of Orthopsychiatry, 42,* 566–581.

Hansen, J. C., Warner, R. W. ,& Smith, E. J. (1980). *Group counseling: Theory and process.* Chicago: Rand McNally College Publishing.

Hanson, P. G. (1972). What to look for in groups. In J. W. Pfeiffer & J. E. Jones (Eds.), *1972 Annual handbook for group facilitators* (pp. 21–24). La Jolla, CA: University Associates.

Harman, M. J., & Withers, L. (1992). University students from homes with alcoholic parents: Considerations for therapy groups. *Journal for Specialists in Group Work, 17*(1), 37–41.

Harmin, M., Kirschenbaum, H., & Simon, S. B. (1973). *Clarifying values through subject matter,* Minneapolis: Winston Press.

Havighurst, R. J., & Neugarten, B. L (1968). *Society and education* (3rd ed.). Boston: Allyn and Bacon.

Hayes, R. I. (1987). A message from the president-elect. *ASGW Newsletter, 15*(3), 1–6.

Helms, J. E. (1990). Generalizing racial identity interaction theory to groups. In J. E. Helms (Ed.), *Black and white racial identity: Theory, research, and practice* (pp. 187–204). Westport, CT: Greenwood Press.

Helms, J. E. (1995). An update of Helm's white and people of color racial identity models. In J. G. Ponterotto, J. M. Casas, L. A. Suzuki, & C. M. Alexander (Eds.), *Handbook of multicultural counseling* (pp. 181–198). Thousand Oaks, CA: Sage.

Herlihy, B., & Corey, G. (1996). *ACA ethical standards casebook* (5th ed.). Alexandria, VA: American Counseling Association.

Hesse, H. (1971). *Siddartha.* New York: Bantam Books.

Hetzel, R. D., Barton, D. A., & Davenport, D. S. (1994). Helping men change: A group counseling model for male clients. *Journal for Specialists in Group Work, 19*(2), 52–64.

Hetzel, R., Stockton, R., & McDonnell, K. (1994) Trends in training group counselors. Paper presented at the American Counseling Association Annual Convention, Minneapolis, MN.

Higgs, J. A. (1992). Dealing with resistance: Strategies for effective groups. *Journal for Specialists in Group Work, 17*(2), 67–73.

Hill, C. E., & Corbett, M. M. (1993). A perspective on the history of process and outcome research in counseling psychology. *Journal of Counseling Psychology, 40,* 3–24.

Hill, S. F. (1969). *Learning thru discussion.* Beverly Hills, CA: Sage.

Hill, W. F. (1966). *Hill interaction matrix (HIM) monograph.* Los Angeles: University of Southern California, Youth Studies Center.

Hinckley, R. G., & Herman, L. (1951). *Group treatment in psychotherapy.* Minneapolis: University of Minnesota Press.

Ho, M. K. (1984). Social group work with Asian/Pacific-Americans. *Social work with groups, 7,* 49–61.

Hogan, R., Curphy, G. J., & Hogan J. (1994). What we know about leadership: Effectiveness and personality. *American psychologist*, 49(6), 493–504.

Homans, G. C. (1950). *The human group*. New York: Harcourt, Brace, Jovanorich.

Hoppock, R. (1976). *Occupational information* (4th ed.). New York: McGraw-Hill.

Horne, A. M. (1994). Developing group work for diverse groups. *Journal for Specialists in Group Work*, 19(3), 138–139.

Horne, A. M. (1995). Editorial. *Journal for Specialists in Group Work, 20*(1), 1–2.

Horne, A. M., & Rosenthal, R. (1997). Research in group work: How did we get where we are? *Journal for Specialists in Group Work, 22*(4), 228–240.

Hosie, T. W. (1994). Program evaluation: A potential area of expertise for counselors. *Counselor education and supervision, 33,* 349–355.

Housley, P. C. (1996). *The use of qualitative and quantitative measures in program evaluation: A practical example.* Paper presented at the annual meeting of the National Association of School Psychologists, Atlanta, GA.

Hovestadt, A. J., Fennell, D., & Piercy, F. P. (1983). Integrating marriage and family therapy within counselor education: A three level training model. In B. F. Okun & S. T. Gladding (Eds.), *Issues in training marriage and family therapists* (pp. 31–41). Ann Arbor, MI: ERIC/CAPS.

Howard, J. (1968). Inhibitions thrown to the gentle winds. *Life,* July 12, 48–65.

Huhn, R. P., Zimpfer, D. G., Waltman, D. E., & Williamson, S. K. (1985). A survey of programs of professional preparation for group counseling. *Journal for Specialists in Group Work, 10*(3), 124–133.

Hulse, D. (1985). Overcoming the social-ecological barriers to group effectiveness: Present and future. *Journal for Specialists in Group Work, 10*(2), 92–97.

Hulse, W. C. (1950). The therapeutic management of group tension. *American Journal of Orthopsychiatry, 20,* 834–838.

Hulse-Killacky, D. (1986). The classroom as a group: How to survive and thrive as leaders and teachers. *Educational Dimensions, 2*(1), 1–2, 8.

Hulse-Killacky, D. (1996). Using the classroom as a group to integrate knowledge, skills and supervised practice. *Journal for Specialists in Group Work, 21*(3), 151–213.

Human potential: The revolution of feeling. (1970). *Time,* November 9, 54–58.

Impara, J. C., & Plake, B. S. (Eds.). (1998). *The thirteenth mental measurements yearbook.* Lincoln, NE: University of Nebraska Press.

Ingersoll, G. (In press). Applying experimental methods in diabetes education research and evaluation. *The Diabetes Educator.*

Ipaye, T. (1982). Introducing group counseling into Nigerian secondary schools: Report of a three-year experience. *International Journal for the Advancement of Counseling, 5,* 35–47.

Ivey, A. E., & Alschuler, A. S. (1973). An introduction to the field. *Personnel and Guidance Journal, 51,* 591–597.

Jacobs, A., & Spradlin, W. W. (1974). *Group as agent of change.* New York: Behavioral Publications.

Jacobs, E. E., Harvill, R. L., & Masson, R. L. (1988). *Group counseling: Strategies and skills.* Monterey. CA: Brooks/Cole.

Jacobs, E. E., Harvill, R. L., & Masson, R. L. (1994). *Group counseling: Strategies and skills* (2nd ed.). Monterey, CA: Brooks/Cole.

James, W. (1890). *The principles of psychology.* Vol. 1. New York: Holt.

Janis, I. L. (1971). Groupthink. *Psychology Today, 6,* 43–46, 74–76.

Janis, I. L. (1972). *Victims of groupthink: A psychological study of foreign policy decisions and fiascos.* Boston: Houghton-Mifflin.

Johnson, D. W. (1972). *Reaching out: Interpersonal effectiveness and self-actualization.* Englewood Cliffs, NJ: Prentice-Hall.

Johnson, D. W. (1981). *Reaching out: Interpersonal effectiveness and self actualization* (2nd ed.). Engelwood Cliffs, NJ: Prentice-Hall, Inc.

Johnson, D. W., & Johnson, F. P. (1979). The use of counseling groups to improve interpersonal skills. *Journal for Specialists inGroup Work, 4*(4), 211–215.

Johnson, D. W., & Johnson, F. P. (1982). *Joining together: Group theory and group skills* (2nd ed.). Englewood Cliffs, NJ: Prentice-Hall.

Johnson, D. W., & Johnson, F. P. (1994). *Joining together: Group therapy and group skills* (5th ed.). Boston: Allyn & Bacon.

Johnson, D. W., & Johnson, F. P. (1997). *Joining together: Group theory and group skills* (6th ed.). Englewood Cliffs, NJ: Prentice-Hall.

Johnson, J. A. (1963). *Group therapy: A practical approach.* New York: McGraw-Hill.

Jourard, S. (1968). *Disclosing man to himself.* Princeton: Van Nostrand.

Journal for Specialists in Group Work. (1979). Special issue: Group counseling and the dynamic of structure. *4*(4), Author.

Journal for Specialists in Group Work. (1985). Special issue: Critical issues in group work: Now and 2001. *10*(2), Author.

Juntunen, C. L., Cohen, B. B., & Wolszon, L. R. (1997). Women and anger: A structured group. *Journal for Specialists in Group Work, 22*(2), 97–110.

Kahn, A. P. (1993). *Encyclopedia of mental health.* New York: Facts on File.

Kane, C. (1995). Fishbowl training in group process. *Journal for Specialists in Group Work, 20*(3), 183–188.

Kaneshige, E. (1973). Cultural factors in group counseling and interaction. *Personnel and Guidance Journal, 51*, 407–412.

Kanfer, F. H., & Goldstein, A. P. (Eds.). (1975). *Helping people change.* New York: Pergamon Press.

Kanter, R. M. (1977). Women in organizations: Sex roles, group dynamics, and change strategies. In A. G. Sargent (Ed.), *Beyond sex roles.* St. Paul, MN: West Publishing Co.

Kaplan, H. I., & Saddock, B. J. (1993). *Comprehensive group psychotherapy* (3rd ed.). Baltimore: Williams and Wilkens.

Kassera, W., & Kassera, M. (1979). Energizers as group openers. *Journal for Specialists in Group Work, 4*(4), 201–205.

Katz, A. H. (1981). Self-help and mutual aid: An emerging social movement. *Annual Review of Sociology, 7*, 129–155.

Katz, R. (1973). *Preludes to growth: An experimental approach.* New York: Free Press.

Keel, L. P., & Rapin, L. S. (1997, April). *Bridging with group workers on best practice standards.* Roundtable seminar presented at the annual meeting of the American Counseling Association, Orlando, FL.

Kees, N. L., & Jacobs, E. (1990). Conducting more effective groups: How to select and process group exercises. *Journal for Specialists in Group Work, 15*(1), 21–29.

Kemp, C. G. (1970). *Group counseling: A foundation for counseling with groups.* Boston: Houghton Mifflin.

Kirby, J. (1985). *Consultation: Practice and practitioner.* Muncie, IN: Accelerated Development.

Kiresuk, T. J., & Sherman, R. E. (1968). Goal attainment scaling: A general method for evaluating community mental health programs. *Community Mental Health Journal, 4*, 443–453.

Kirschenbaum, H. (1977). *Advanced value clarification.* LaJolla, CA: University Associates.

Kitchener, K. S. (1984). Intuition, critical evaluation and ethical principles: The foundation for ethical decisions in counseling psychology. *The Counseling Psychologist, 12*, 43–55.

Kivlinghan, D. M. (1985). Feedback in group psychotherapy: Review and implications. *Small Group Behavior, 16*, 373–385.

Klein, E. B. (1985). Group work: 1985 and 2001. *Journal for Specialists in Group Work, 10*(2), 108–111.

Kline, W. B. (1990). Responding to "problem" members. *Journal for Specialists in Group Work, 15*(4), 195–200.

Korda, L. J., & Pancrazio, J. J. (1989). Limiting negative outcome in group practice. *Journal for Specialists in Group Work, 14*(2), 112–120.

Koss, M., Goodman, L., Fitzgerald, L., Russo, N. F., Keita, G. P., & Browne, A. (1994). *No safe* place: *Male violence against women at home, at work and in the community.* Hyattsville, MD: American Psychological Association.

Kottler, J. A. (1992). *Compassionate therapy: Working with difficult clients.* San Francisco, CA: Jossey-Bass.

Kottler, J. A. (1994a). *Advanced group leadership.* Pacific Grove, CA: Brooks/Cole.

Kottler, J. A. (1994b). Working with difficult group members. *Journal for Specialists in Group Work, 19*(1), 3–10.

Kranzow, G. W. (1973). *Peer counseling handbook. ESEA Title III.* Peer Counseling Project. Special Education District of Lake County, 4440 W. Grand Ave., Gurnee, IL: 60031.

Krause, K., & Hulse-Killacky, D. (1996). Balancing process and content in groups: A metaphor. *Journal for Specialists in Group Work, 21*(2), 90–93.

Krumboltz, J. D., & Thoreson, L. E. (Eds.). (1976). *Counseling methods.* New York: Holt.

Kubie, L. (1958). *Neurotic distortion of the creative process.* Lawrence, KS: University of Kansas Press.

Laird, D. A., & Laird, E. (1967). *Psychology: Human relations and motivation.* New York: McGraw-Hill.

Lakin, M. (n.d.) On the distinctions between group psychotherapy and dyadic psychotherapy. (audio tape). Available from Counselor Recordings and Tests. Box 6184 Acklen Station, Nashville, TN 37212.

Lakin, M. (1969). Some ethical issues in sensitivity training. *American Psychologist, 24,* 923–928.

Lakin, M. (1970). Group sensitivity training and encounter: Uses and abuses of a method. *Counseling Psychologist, 2*(2), 66–70.

Lakin, M. (1979). What's happened to small group research? Epilogue. *Journal of Applied Behavioral Science, 15,* 424–427.

Landreth, G. L (1973). Group counseling: To structure or not to structure. *The School Counselor, 20,* 371–374.

Lange, A. J., & Jakubowski, P. (1976). *Responsible assertive behavior: Cognitive/behavioral procedures for trainers.* Champaign, IL: Research Press.

Leach, M. M., & Carlton, M. A. (1997). Toward defining a multicultural training philosophy. In D. B. Pope-Davis & H. L. K. Coleman (Eds.), *Multicultural counseling competencies: Assessment, education and training, and supervision* (pp. 184–208). Thousand Oaks: CA: Sage.

Leary, T. (1957). *Interpersonal diagnosis of personality: A functional theory and methodology for personality evaluation.* New York: The Ronald Press.

Lee, E., Munro, B. H., & McCorkle, R. (1993). A shortened version of an instrument measuring bereavement. *International Journal of Nursing Studies, 30,* 213–226.

Lee, F., & Bednar, R. I. (1977). Effects of group structure and risk-taking disposition on group behavior, attitudes and atmosphere. *Journal of Counseling Psychology, 24,* 191–199.

Leveton, E. (1977). *Psychodrama for the timid clinician.* New York: Springer.

Lewin, K. (1951). *Field theory in social science.* New York: Harper.

Lieberman, M., Yalom, I., & Miles, M. (1973). *Encounter groups: First facts.* New York: Basic Books.

Lifton, W. (1966). *Working with groups* (2nd ed.). New York: Wiley.

Lindt, H. (1958). The nature of therapeutic interaction of patients in groups. *International Journal of Group Psychotherapy, 8,* 55–69.

Lloyd, A. (1990). Dual relationships in group activities: A counselor education/accreditation dilemma. *Journal for Specialists in Group Work, 15*(2), 83–87.

Luft, J. (1963). *Group processes: An introduction to group dynamics.* Palo Alto, CA: National Press Books.

Luft, J. (1970). *Group process: An introduction to group dynamics* (2nd ed.). Palo Alto, CA: National Press Books.

Luft, J. (1984). *Group process: An introduction to group dynamics* (3rd ed.). Palo Alto, CA: Mayfield Publishing.

MacDevitt, J. W. (1987). Conceptualizing components of group counseling. *Journal for Specialists in Group Work, 12*(2), 76–84.

MacKenzie, K. R. (1997). Clinical application of group development ideas. *Group dynamics: Theory, research & practice, 1,* 275–287.

Madanes, C. (1981). *Strategic family therapy.* San Francisco: Jossey-Bass Publishers.

Mahler, C. A. (1969). *Group counseling in the schools.* Boston: Houghton Mifflin.

Maier, S. F., & Seligman, M. E. P. (1976). Learned helplessness: Theory and evidence. *Journal of Experimental Psychology, 105*(1), 3–46.

Maier, S. F., Seligman, M. E. P., & Solomon, R. L. (1969). Pavlovian fear conditioning and learned helplessness: Effects on escape and avoidance behavior of (a) the CS-US contingency and (b) the independence of the US and voluntary responding. In Campbell & Church (Eds.), *Punishment and adverse behavior.* New York: Appleton.

Makuch, L., Robison, F. F., & Stockton, R. (1998, January). Leadership characteristics inventory: Development and tryout. Presentation at the 6th National Group Work Conference. Tucson, AZ.

Maples, M. F. (1992). STEAMWORK: An effective approach to team building. *Journal for Specialists in Group Work, 17*(3), 144–150.

Maslow, A. H. (1943). A theory of human motivation. *Psychological Review, 50,* 370–396.

Maslow, A. H. (1954). *Motivation and personality.* New York: Harper.

Maslow, A. H. (1962). *Toward a psychology of being.* Princeton: Van Nostrand.

Maslow, A. H. (1967). Self actualization and beyond. In J. F. T. Bugenthal (Ed.), *Challenges of humanistic psychology* (pp. 279–286). New York: McGraw-Hill.

Maslow, A. H. (1970). A theory of human motivation. In *Motivation and personality* (2nd ed.). New York: Harper and Row.

Matthews, C. O. (1992). An application of general systems theory (GST) to group therapy. *Journal for Specialists in Group Work, 17*(3), 161–169.

May, R. (1953). *Man's search for himself.* New York: Norton.

Mayer, G. R., & Baker, P. (1967). Group counseling with elementary school children: A look at group size. *Elementary School Guidance and Counseling, 1,* 140–145.

McBride, M. C., & Emerson, S. (1989). Group work with women who were molested as children. *Journal for Specialists in Group Work, 14*(1), 25–33.

McClure, B. A. (1989). What's a meta-phor? *Journal for Specialists in Group Work, 14*(4), 239–242.

McClure, B. A. (1990). The group mind: Generative and regressive groups. *Journal for Specialists in Group Work, 15*(3), 159–170.

McCoy P. C. (1997). Group research: A practitioner's perspective. *Journal for Specialists in Group Work, 22*(4), 294–296.

McCue-Herlihy, B. (1996). A student's perspective on learning to do group work. *Journal for Specialists in Group Work, 21*(3), 169–171.

McDonnell, K. A. (1996). *A qualitative study of beginning therapy group leaders.* Unpublished manuscript, Indiana University at Bloomington.

McGoldrick, M., & Gerson, R. (1985). *Genograms in family assessment.* New York: W.W. Norton.

McGoldrick, M., Giordano, J., & Pearce, J. K. (1996). *Ethnicity and family therapy* (2nd ed.). New York: The Guilford Press.

McKay, M., & Paleg, K. (Eds.). (1992). *Focal group psychotherapy.* Oakland, CA: New Harbinger.

McManus, P. W., Redford, J. L., & Hughes, R. B. (1997). Connecting self to others: A structured group for women. *Journal for Specialists in Group Work, 21*(1), 22–30.

McMillon, H. G. (1994). Developing problem solving and interpersonal communication skills through intentionally structured groups. *Journal for Specialists in Group Work, 19*(1), 43–47.

McRae, M. B., & Johnson, S. D. (1991). Toward training for competence in multicultural counselor education. *Journal of Counseling and Development, 70,* 131–135.

McRoy, C. R., & Brown, B. M. (1996). Effect of conceptual level of group conflict interaction. *Journal for Specialists in Group Work, 21*(1), 11–17.

Meichenbaum, D. (1977). *Cognitive behavior modification: An integrative approach.* New York: Plenum.

Meichenbaum, D. (1985). *Stress innoculation training.* New York: Pergamon Press.

Merta, R. J. (1995). Group work: Multicultural perspectives. In J. G. Ponterotto, J. M. Casas, L. A. Suzuki & C. M. Alexander (Ed.). *Handbook of multicultural counseling* (pp. 567–585). Thousand Oaks, CA: Sage.

Merta, R. J., Ponterotto, J. G., & Brown, R. D. (1992). Comparing the effectiveness of two directive styles in academic counseling of foreign students. *Journal of Counseling Psychology, 39,* 214–218.

Merta, R. J., Romero, J., & Bennett, M. (1997, August). *Therapeutic factors in process-oriented multicultural group work.* Poster session presented at the annual conference of the American Psychological Association, Chicago, IL.

Merta, R. J., & Sisson, J. A. (1991). The experiential group: An ethical and professional dilemma. *Journal for Specialists in Group Work, 16*(4), 236–245.

Merta, R. J., Stringham, E. M., & Ponterotto, J. G. (1988). Simulating culture shock in counselor trainees: An experiential exercise for cross-cultural training. *Journal of Counseling and Development, 66,* 242–245.

Merta, R. J., Wolfgang, L., & McNeil, K. (1993). Five models for using the experiential group in the preparation of group counselors. *Journal for Specialists in Group Work, 18*(4), 200–207.

Mikesell, R. H., Lusterman, D-D., & McDaniel, S. H. (1995). *Integrating family therapy: Handbook of psychology and systems theory.* Washington DC: American Psychological Association.

Miller, M. J. (1993). The lifeline: A qualitative method to promote group dynamics. *Journal for Specialists in Group Work, 18*(2), 51–54.

Miller, S., Nunnally, E. W., & Wackman, D. B. (1975). *Alive and aware: Improving communication in relationships.* Minneapolis, MN: Interpersonal Communication Programs.

Minuchin, S. (1974). *Families and family therapy.* Cambridge, MA: Harvard University Press.

Moreno, J. L. (1964). *Psychodrama* (Vols. I–III). New York: Beacon House.

Moreno, Z. (n.d.) *Psychodramatic rules, techniques and adjunctive methods.* (monograph). New York: Beacon House.

Morran, D. K. (1992). An interview with Rex Stockton. *Journal for Specialists in Group Work, 17*(1), 4–9.

Morran, D. K., & Stockton, R. (1985). Perspectives on the development of group psychotherapy research programs. *Journal for Specialists in Group Work, 10,* 186–191.

Morran, D. K., Stockton, R., & Harris, M. (1991). Analysis of group leader and member feedback messages. *Journal of Group Psychotherapy, Psychodrama, and Sociometry, 44*(3), 126–135.

Morran, D. K., Stockton, R., & Robison, F. F. (1985) Feedback exchange in counseling groups: An analysis of message content and receiver acceptance as a function of leader versus member delivery, session and valence. *Journal of Counseling Psychology, 32*(1), 57–67.

Moustakas, C. (1972). *Teaching as learning.* New York: Ballantine Books.

Muro, J. J., & Freeman, S. L. (1968). *Readings in group counseling.* Scranton, PA: International Textbook.

Muro, J. J., & Denton, G. (1968). Expressed concerns of teacher-education students in counseling groups. *Journal of Teacher Education, 19,* 465–470.

Myers, L. J., Speight, S. L., Highlen, P. S., Chikako, I. C., Reynolds, A. L., Adams, E. M., & Hanley, C. P. (1991). Identity development and world view: Toward an optimal conceptualization. *Journal of Counseling and Development, 70,* 54–63.

Napier, R. W., & Gershenfeld, M. K. (1993). *Groups: Theory and experience.* (5th ed.). Boston: Houghton Mifflin.

National Association of Social Workers. (1993). *Code of ethics of the National Association of Social Workers.* Washington, DC: Author.

National Board for Certified Counselors. (1989). *Code of ethics.* Greensboro, NC: Author.

National Board for Certified Counselors. (1997a, Fall). Standards for the ethical practice of webcounseling. *NBCC Newsnotes, 14*(2), 3–4.

National Board for Certified Counselors. (1997b, Fall). State counselor licensure/certification: September 15, 1997. *NBCC NewsNotes, 14*(2), 6b–6e.

National Education Association. (1969). Lost on the moon: A decision making problem. *Today's Education, 58*(2), 55–56.

Nelson, R. C. (1971). Organizing for group counseling. *Personnel and Guidance Journal, 50*, 25–28.

Nichols, M. (1984). *Family therapy: Concepts and methods.* New York: Gardner Press.

Ohlsen, M. M. (1970). *Group counseling.* New York: Holt, Rinehart & Winston.

Ohlsen, M. M. (1974). *Guidance services in the modern school* (2nd ed.). New York: Harcourt Brace Jovanovich.

Ohlsen, M. (1977). *Group counseling* (2nd ed.). New York: Holt, Rinehart and Winston.

Ohlsen, M. M. (Ed.) (1979). *Journal for Specialists in Group Work, 4*(2).

Ohlsen, M. M., Horne, A. M., & Lawe, C. F. (1988). *Group counseling* (3rd ed.). New York: Holt, Rinehart and Winston.

Osborne, N. L. (1990). Ben Cohn: Group counseling and the acting-out underachieving adolescent. *Journal for Specialists in Group Work, 15*(1), 2–9.

Otto, H. (1967). *Guide to developing your potential.* New York: Scribners.

Overmeier, J. B., & Seligman, M. E. P. (1967). Effects of unescapable shock upon subsequent escape and avoidance learning. *Journal of Comparative and Physiological Psychology, 63*, 23–33.

Paritzky, R. S., & Magoon, T. M. (1982). Goal attainment scaling models for assessing group counseling. *Personnel and Guidance Journal, 60*, 381–384.

Pasik, R. S., Gordon, S., & Feldman, L. B. (1990). Fathers and fathering. In R. L. Meth & R. S. Pasick (Eds.), *Men in therapy* (pp. 152–180). New York: Guilford Press.

Patterson, C. H. (1996). Multicultural counseling: From diversity to universality. *Journal of Counseling and Development, 74*, 227–231.

Patton, M. Q. (1997). *Utilization-focused evaluation.* (3rd ed.). Thousand Oaks, CA: Sage.

Pearson, R. E. (1981). Basic skills for leadership of counseling groups. *Counselor Education and Supervision, 21*(1), 30–37.

Pearson, R. E. (1986). Guest editorial. *Journal for Specialists in Group Work, 11*(2), 66.

Pedersen, P. B. (1998). The cultural context of the American counseling association code of ethics. *Journal of Counseling and Development, 76*, 23–28.

Personnel and guidance journal. (1972). *50*(4).

Petersen, C., Glover, J. A., Romero, D., & Romero, P. (1978). The effects of a cross-cultural simulation game on participants' personal characteristics. *Social Behavior and Personality, 6*(1), 21–26.

Peterson, J. V., & Nisenholz, B. (1995). *Orientation to counseling* (3rd ed.). Boston: Allyn & Bacon.

Pfeiffer, D. C., & Jones, J. E. (1969–1985). *A handbook of structured experiences for human relations training* (Vols. I–X). San Diego, CA: University Associates.

Pierce, K. A., & Baldwin, C. (1990). Participation versus privacy in the training of group counselors. *Journal for Specialists in Group Work, 15*(3), 149–158.

Pistole, M. C. (1997). Attachment theory: Contributions to group work. *Journal for Specialists in Group Work, 22*(1), 7–21.

Platt, J., & Spivak, G. (1976). *Workbook for training in interpersonal problem-solving thinking* Philadelphia: Department of Mental Health Sciences, Hahnemann Community Mental Retardation Center.

Polcin, D. (1991). Prescriptive group leadership. *Journal for Specialists in Group Work, 16*(1) 8–15.

Polkinghorne, D. E. (1988). *Narrative knowing and the human sciences.* Albany, NY: SUNY Press

Ponterotto, J. G., Casas, J. M., Suzuki, L. A., & Alexander, C. M. (Eds.). (1995). *Handbook of multicultural counseling.* Thousand Oaks, CA: Sage.

nzo, Z. (1991). Critical factors in group work: Clients perceptions. *Journal for Specialists in Group Work, 16*(1), 16–23.

pe-Davis, D. B., Breaux, C., & Liu, W. M. (1994). A multicultural immersion experience: Filling a void in multicultural training. In D. B. Pope-Davis, H. L. K. Coleman (Eds.), *Multicultural counseling competencies: Assessment, education and training, and supervision* (pp. 227–241). Thousand Oaks, CA: Sage.

ppen, W. A., & Thompson, C. L. (1974). *School counseling: Theories and concepts.* Lincoln, NE: Professional Educators Publications.

wdermaker, F. B., & Frank, J. D. (1953). *Group psychotherapy.* Cambridge, MA: Harvard University Press.

well, J. (1969). *Why am I afraid to tell you who I am?* Niles, IL: Argus Communications.

ychotherapy Finances. (1997, May). 1997 fee, practice and managed care survey. *Psychotherapy Finances, 23*(5), 1–12.

pin, L. S., & Keel, L. P. (1996a, January). *Best practice guidelines for group workers: Enhancing ACA's 1995 Code of Ethics.* Seminar presented at the Association for Specialists in Group Work 4th National Group Work Conference, Athens, GA.

pin, L. S., & Keel, L. P. (1996b, April). *Best practice guidelines for group workers: Applying ACA 1995 Code of Ethics.* Seminar presented at the annual meeting of the American Counseling Association, Pittsburgh, PA.

pin, L. S., & Keel, L. P. (1997, February). *ASGW members' roundtable on group best practice guidelines: Input to Ethics Committee.* Seminar presented at the Association for Specialists in Group Work 5th National Group Work Conference, Athens, GA.

pin, L. S., & Keel, L. P. (1998). ASGW best practices in group work. (Adopted by ASGW Executive Board March 29, 1998).

ths, L. E., Harmin, M., & Simon, S. B. (1966). *Values and teaching.* Columbus, OH: Charles E. Merrill Publishing.

ddy, W. B. (1985). The role of change agent in the future of group work. *Journal for Specialists in Group Work, 10*(2), 103–107.

ncken, R. H. (1989). *Intervention strategies for sexual abuse.* Alexandria, VA: American Counseling Association.

dley, C. R., Mendoza, D. W., & Kanitz, B. E. (1994). Multicultural training: Reexamination, operationalization, and integration. *The Counseling Psychologist, 22*, 227–289.

ordan, R. J. (1996). Scriptotherapy: Therapeutic writing as a counseling adjunct. *Journal for Counseling and Development, 74*, 263–269.

ordan, R. J., & Matheny, K. B. (1972). Dear diary: Logs in group counseling. *The Personnel and Guidance Journal, 50*, 379–382.

ordan, R. J., & White, J. (1996). Logs as therapeutic adjuncts in group. *Journal for Specialists in Group Work, 21*(2), 94–100.

ttenhouse, J. (1997). Feminist principles in survivors groups: Out-of-group contact. *Journal for Specialists in Group Work, 22*(2), 111–119.

tter, K. Y., West, J. D., & Trotzer, J. P. (1986). Comparing family counseling and group counseling: An interview with George Gazda, James Hansen, and Alan Hovestadt. *Journal of Counseling and Development, 65*(6), 295–300.

va, M. T., & Kalodner, C. R. (1997). Group research: Encouraging a collaboration between practitioners and researchers. *Journal for Specialists in Group Work, 22*(4), 226–227.

ark, A. E., & Roark, A. B. (1979). Group structure: Components and effects. *Journal for Specialists in Group Work, 4*(4), 186–192.

binson, III, E. H. (Ed.). (1980). Life coping skills through the group medium. *Journal for Specialists in Group Work, 5*(3).

gers, C. R. (1951). *Client-centered therapy.* Boston: Houghton Mifflin.

gers, C. R. (1952). Barriers and gateways to communication. *Harvard Business Review, 30*(4), 46–52.

gers, C. R. (1961). *On becoming a person.* Boston: Houghton Mifflin.

Rogers, C. R. (1962). The interpersonal relationship: The core of guidance. *Harvard Educational Review, 32,* 416–429.

Rogers, C. R. (1967). The process of the basic encounter group. In J. F. T. Bugental (Ed.). *Challenges of humanistic psychology.* New York: McGraw-Hill.

Rogers, C. R. (1970). *Carl Rogers on encounter groups.* New York: Harper & Row.

Rokeach, M. (1960). *The open and closed mind.* New York: Basic Books.

Rosenhan, D. L., & Seligman, M. E. P. (1989). *Abnormal psychology* (2nd ed.). New York. W.W. Norton and Co.

Rosenthal, H. G. (Ed.) (1998). *Favorite counseling and therapy techniques: 51 therapists share their most creative strategies.* Bristol, PA: Accelerated Development.

Rossel, R. D. (1981). Word play metaphor and humor in the small group. *Small Group Behavior, 12*(1), 116–136.

Ruevini, U. (1985). The family as a social support group now and 2001. *Journal for Specialists in Group Work, 10*(2), 88–93.

Rugel, R. P. (1991). Closed and open systems: The tavistock group from a general system perspective. *Journal for Specialists in Group Work, 16*(2), 74–84.

Rybak, C. J., & Brown, B. M. (1997). Group conflict: Communication patterns and group development. *Journal for Specialists in Group Work, 22*(1), 31–51.

Sager, C. J., Brown, H. S., Crohn, H., Engel, T., Rothstein, E., & Walker, L. (1983). *Treating the remarried family.* New York: Brunner/Mazel.

Satir, V. (1972). *Peoplemaking.* Palo Alto, CA: Science and Behavior Books.

Sayger, T. V. (1996). Creating resilient children and empowering families using a multi family group process. *Journal for Specialists in Group Work, 21*(2), 8–89.

Schmidt, E. H. (n.d.). Sensitivity training: A report and critique. University of California, Los Angeles. Graduate School of Business.

Schmuck, R. A., & Schmuck, P. A. (1971). *Group processes in the classroom.* Dubuque, IA William C. Brown.

Schmuck, R. A., & Schmuck, P. A. (1985). *Group processes in the classroom.* Dubuque, IA William C. Brown.

Schutz, W. (1967). *Joy.* New York: Grove Press.

Seigelman, E. (1983). *Personal risk: Mastering change in love and work.* New York: Harper and Row.

Seligman, M. (Ed.). (1982). *Group psychotherapy and counseling with special populations.* Baltimore, MD: University Park Press.

Seligman, M. P. (1995). The effectiveness of psychotherapy: The Consumer Report study. *American Psychologist, 50,* 965–974.

Seligman, M. E. P., & Maier, S. F. (1967). Failure to escape traumatic shock. *Journal Experimental Psychology, 74,* 1–9.

Sexton, T. L., Whiston, S. C., Bleuer, J. C., & Walz, G. R. (1997). *Integrating outcome research into counseling practice and training.* Alexandria, VA: American Counseling Association.

Shapiro, J. L., & Shapiro, S. B. (1985). Group work to 2001: HAL or haven (from isolation *Journal for Specialists in Group Work, 10*(2), 83–87.

Sharma, M. (1998, May). Welcoming Remarks. Multicultural and Spiritual Dimensions of Counselor Supervision Workshop. Cambridge College, Boston, MA.

Shaw, M. E. (1981). *Group dynamics: The psychology of small group behavior.* New York: McGraw Hill.

Shirts, R. G. (1969). *Bafa Bafa: A cross culture simulation.* Del Mar: CA: Simulation Training Systems.

Shostrom, E. L. (1967). *Man the manipulator: The inner journey from manipulation to actualization.* New York: Abingdon Press.

Silverman, P. R. (1985). Tertiary/secondary prevention: Preventive intervention—The case for mutual help groups. In R. Conyne (Ed.), *The group worker's handbook: Varieties of group experience* (pp. 237–258). Springfield, IL: Charles C. Thomas.

Simon, A., & Agazarian, Y. (1974). Sequential analysis of verbal interaction (SAVI). In A. Simon & E. G. Boyer (Eds.), *Mirrors for behavior III: An anthology of observation instruments* (pp. 543–564). Wyncote, PA: Communication Materials Center (Rice's Mill Road).

Simon, S. B., Howe, L. M., & Kirschenbaum, H. (1972). *Values clarification: A handbook of practical strategies for teachers and students*. New York: Hart Publishing.

Sklare, G., Keener, R., & Mas, C. (1990). Preparing members for "here and now" group counseling. *Journal for Specialists in Group Work, 15*(3), 141–148.

Sklare, G., Thomas, D. V., Williams, E. C., & Powers, K. A. (1996). Ethics and an experiential "here and now" group: A blend that works. *Journal for Specialists in Group Work, 21*(4), 263–273.

Slavson, S. R. (1952). The dynamics of group work. In D. F. Sullivan (Ed.), *Readings in group work*. New York: Associated Press.

Sleek, S. (1995). Group therapy: Tapping the power of team work. *APA Monitor, 26*(7), 1, 38–39.

Spitz, H. I. (1996). *Group psychotherapy and managed mental health care: A clinical guide for providers*. New York: Brunner/Mazel.

Stevens, J. O. (1971). *Awareness: Exploring, experimenting, experiencing*. Moab, UT: Real People Press.

Stockton, R. (Presenter)(1992). Developmental aspects of counseling: Process, leadership and supervision, I, II, III (videotapes). Alexandria, VA: American Counseling Association.

Stockton, R., & Hulse, D. (1983). The use of research teams to enhance competence in counseling research. *Counselor Education and Supervision, 22,* 303–310.

Stockton, R., & Morran, D. K. (1981). Feedback exchange in personal growth groups: Receiver acceptance as a function of valence, session and order of delivery. *Journal of Counseling Psychology, 28,* 490–497.

Stockton, R., & Morran, D. K. (1982). Review and perspective of critical dimensions in therapeutic small group research. In G. Gazda (Ed.) *Basic approaches to group psychotherapy and group counseling* (pp. 37–83). Springfield, IL: Charles C. Thomas.

Stockton, R., Morran, D. K., & Velkoff, P. (1987). Leadership of therapeutic small groups. *Journal of Group Psychotherapy, Psychodrama, and Sociometry, 38,* 157–165.

Stockton, R., Rohde, R. I., & Haughey, J. (1994). The effects of structured group exercises on cohesion, engagement, avoidance and conflict. *Small Group Research, 23,* 155–168.

Stockton, R. & Toth, P. L. (1996). Teaching group counselors: Recommendations for maximizing preservice instruction. *Journal for Specialists in Group Work, 21*(4), 274–282.

Stockton, R., & Toth, P. L. (1997). Applying a general research training model to group work. *Journal for Specialists in Group Work, 22*(4), 241–252.

Sue, D. W., Arredondo, P., & McDavis, R. J. (1992). Multicultural counseling competencies and standards: A call to the profession. *Journal of Counseling and Development, 70,* 477–486.

Sue, D. W., & Sue, D. (1990). *Counseling the culturally different: Theory and practice*. New York: John Wiley.

Sullivan, H. S. (1953a). *Conception of modern psychiatry* (2nd ed). New York: W.W. Norton.

Sullivan, H. S. (1953b). *The interpersonal theory of psychiatry*. New York: W.W. Norton.

Tavantzis, T. N., & Tavantzis, M. T. (1985). Boundaries between family and group therapy. Paper presented at American Association for Counseling and Development National Convention. New York, NY.

Thomas, M. C., Nelson, C. S., & Sumners, C. M. (1994). From victims to victors: Group process as the path to recovery for males molested as children. *Journal for Specialists in Group Work, 19*(2), 102–111.

Thompson, C. L., & Poppen, W. A. (1979). *Guidance activities for counselors and teachers*. Monterey, CA: Brooks/Cole.

Tiedeman, D. V., & Tiedeman, A. L. M. (1973). Guidance in learning: An examination of roles in self-centering during thinking. *The School Counselor, 20,* 334–339.

Tindall, J. A. (1989). *Peer power: Book 2, applying peer helper skills* (2nd ed.). Muncie, IN: Accelerated Development.

Tindall, J. A., & Gray, H. D. (1985). *Peer power: Becoming an effective helper. Book I-Introductory program* (2nd ed.). Muncie, IN: Accelerated Development.

Tindall, J. A., & Gray, H. D. (1989). *Peer counseling: In-depth look at training peer helpers* (3rd ed.). Muncie, IN: Accelerated Development.

Toffler, A. (1970). *Future shock*. New York: Random House.

Toman, W. (1976). *Family constellations* (3rd ed.). New York: Springer.

Toth, P. L. (1997). A short-term grief and loss therapy group: Group members' experience. *Journal of Personal and Interpersonal Loss, 2*, 83–103.

Toth, P. L., & Erwin, W. J. (in press). Applying skill-based curriculum to teach feedback in groups: An evaluation study. *Journal of Counseling and Development*.

Toth, P. L., & Stockton, R. (1996). A skill based approach to teaching group counseling interventions. *Journal for Specialists in Group Work, 21*(2), 101–109.

Trotzer, J. P. (1971). Process comparison of encounter groups and discussion groups using video taped excerpts. *Journal of Counseling Psychology, 18*, 358–361.

Trotzer, J. P. (1972). Group counseling: Process and perspective. *Guidelines for Pupil Services, 10*, 105–110.

Trotzer, J. P. (1973). Using communication exercises in groups. *Personnel and Guidance Journal, 51*, 373–377.

Trotzer, J. P. (1975). The counselor and the group: Differentiating to facilitate practice. *Guidelines for Pupil Services, 14*, 11–16.

Trotzer, J. P. (1977). *The counselor and the group: Integrating theory, training and practice*. Monterey, CA: Brooks/Cole Publishing Company.

Trotzer, J. P. (1979). Developmental tasks in group counseling: The basis for structure. *Journal for Specialists in Group Work, 4*(4), 177–185.

Trotzer, J. P. (1980). Develop your own guidance group: A structural model for planning and practice. *The School Counselor, 27*(5), 341–349.

Trotzer, J. P. (1984). Brief reviews. *Journal of Psychology and Theology, 12*(3), 248.

Trotzer, J. P. (1985). Interpersonal problem solving: The group counseling approach. In R. K. Conyne (Ed.). *The group worker's handbook: Varieties in group experience* (pp. 91–112). Springfield, IL: Charles C. Thomas.

Trotzer, J. P. (1988). Group and family interface. *Together, 16*(2), 6, 8.

Trotzer, J. P. (1997a). Gleanings of a process observer. *Together, 25*(2), 7.

Trotzer, J. P. (1997b). Gleanings of a process observer. *Together, 25*(3), 6.

Trotzer, J. P. (1997c). Gleanings of a process observer. *Together, 26*(1), 6.

Trotzer, J. P.(1997d). Problem-solving (Solution focused and brief) Group counseling: A working model. Workshop presented at the Association for Specialists in Group Work 5th National Conference. Athens, GA.

Trotzer, J. P. (1997e) Treating violence and conflict in families. ACA Profesional Development Workshop. American Counseling Association, 5999 Stevensen Avenue, Alexandria, VA.

Trotzer, J. P. (1998a). Draw your family table/family-o-gram. In H.G. Rosenthal (Ed.), *Favorite counseling and therapy techniques: 51 therapists share their most creative strategies* (pp. 179–181). Bristol, PA: Accelerated Development.

Trotzer, J. P. (1998b). Gleanings of a process observer. *Together, 26*(2), 6.

Trotzer, J. P. (1998c). Problem solving (Solution-focused and brief) group counseling: A working model. Association for Specialists in Group Work 6th National Group Workers Conference. Tucson, AZ.

Trotzer, J. P. (In press). Problem solving group therapy. In R. Corsini (Ed.). *Handbook of innovative therapy* (2nd ed.). New York: John Wiley & Sons.

Trotzer, J. P., & Kassera, W. J. (1971). Do counselors do what they're taught? *The school counselor, 18*(5), 335–341.

Trotzer, J. P., & Kassera, W. J. (1972). *Effect of human relations experience on prospective teachers' attitudes and self concept.* River Falls: University of Wisconsin-River Falls.

Trotzer, J. P., & Kassera, W. J. (1973). Guidelines for selecting communication techniques in group counseling. *The School Counselor, 20*(4), 299–301.

Trotzer, J. P., & Sease, W. A. (1971). The effect of group-centered and topic-centered methods on volunteer college students' self concepts. *Journal of College Student Personnel, 12,* 292–296.

Trotzer, J. P., & Trotzer, T. B. (1986). *Marriage and family: Better ready than not.* Muncie, IN: Accelerated Development.

Trotzer, J. P., West, J., Ritter, K., & Malnati, R. (1985). Integrating and differentiating group and family counseling in theory, training and practice. Presentation at the American Association for Counseling and Development National Convention. New York, NY.

Trotzer, J. P., West, J., Ritter, K., Malnati, R., & Hovestadt, A. (1987). Group and family perspectives on a simulated family session. Presentation at the American Association for Counseling and Development National Convention. Chicago, IL.

Truax, C. B., & Carkhuff, R. R. (1967). *Toward effective counseling and psychotherapy: Training and practice.* Chicago: Aldine.

Tubbs, S. L., & Moss, S. (1978). *Interpersonal communication.* New York: Random House.

Tuckman, B. W. (1965). Developmental sequences in small groups. *Psychological Bulletin, 63*(6), 384–399.

Tuckman, B. W., & Jensen, M. C. (1977). Stages of group development revisited. *Group & Organizational Studies, 2*(4), 419–427.

Unger, R. (1989). Selection and composition criteria in group psychotherapy. *Journal for Specialists in Group Work, 14*(3), 151–157.

Vacc, N. A. (1989). Group counseling: C.H. Patterson—A personalized view. *Journal for Specialists in Group Work, 14*(1), 4–15.

Vacc, N. A., DeVaney, S. B., & Willmer, J. (1992). *Experiencing and counseling multicultural and diverse populations* (3rd ed.). Bristol, PA: Accelerated Development.

Verplanck, W. S. (1970). Trainers, trainees and ethics. *Counseling Psychologist, 2*(2), 71–75.

Visher E. B., & Visher, J. S. (1979). *Stepfamilies.* New York: Brunner/Mazel.

Visher, E. B., & Visher, J. S. (1988). *Old loyalties, new ties: Therapeutic strategies with stepfamilies.* New York: Brunner/Mazel.

Vorrath, H. H. (n.d.). *Positive peer culture: Content, structure and process.* Red Wing, MN: Red Wing State Training School.

Vorrath, H., & Brendtro, L. (1974). *Positive peer culture.* Chicago: Aldine.

Vorrath, H., & Brendtro, L. (1985). *Positive peer culture* (2nd ed.). Chicago: Aldine.

Vriend, T. J. (1969). High-performing inner city adolescents assist low-performing peers in counseling groups. *Personnel and Guidance Journal, 47,* 897–904.

Vriend, T. J. (1985). We've come a long way group. *Journal for Specialists in Group Work, 10*(2), 63–67.

Waitley, D. E. (1978). The psychology of winning. Nightengale-Conant Corporation, 7300 North Lehigh Avenue, Chicago, IL 60648.

Waldo, M. (1985). A curative factor framework for conceptualizing group counseling. *Journal of Counseling and Development, 64,* 52–58.

Walsh, F. (Ed.). (1982). *Normal family processes.* New York: The Guilford Press.

Wampold, B. E. (1986). Toward quality research in counseling psychology: Curricular recommendation for design and analysis. *The Counseling Psychologist, 14,* 37–48.

Ward, D. (1993). An interview with Bob Conyne. *Journal for Specialists in Group Work, 18*(3), 99–108.

Wehrly, B. (1991). Preparing multicultural counselors. *Counseling and Human Development, 24,* 1–24.

Welfel, E. R., & Kitchener, K. S. (1992). Introduction to the special section: Ethics education—An agenda for the 90s. *Professional psychology: Research and practice, 23*(3), 179–181.

Wenz, K., & McWhirter, J. J. (1990). Enhancing group experience: Creative writing exercises. *Journal for Specialists in Group Work, 15*(1) 37–42.

West, J. D., & Kirby, J. (Eds). (1981). Troubled family interactions and group intervention. *Journal for Specialists in Group Work, 6*(1).

Wheelan, S. A. (1997). Co-therapists and the creation of a functional psychotherapy group: A group dynamics perspective. *Group Dynamics: Theory, Research, and Practice, 1*, 306–310.

White, R. W. (1966). *Lives in progress.* New York: Holt, Rinehart, & Winston.

Whiteley, J. M. (1970). Special section: Some ethical questions. *Counseling Psychologist, 2*(2).

Whitman, J. S., Morgan, L. B., & Alfred, A. R. (1996). Graduate students as co-leaders of groups: A trainees experience. *Journal for Specialists in Group Work, 21*(3), 187–193.

Williams, G. T. (1990). Ethical dilemmas in teaching a group leadership course. *Journal for Specialists in Group Work, 15*(2), 104–113.

Wilbur, M. P., & Roberts-Wilbur, S. (1994). Group work with men's beliefs. *Journal for Specialists in Group Work, 19*(2), 65–82.

Wolpe, J. (1990). *The practice of behavior therapy.* Elmsford, NY: Pergamon Press.

Wrenn, C. G. (1962). *The counselor in a changing world.* Washington DC: American Personnel and Guidance Association.

Wrenn, C. G. (1971). The attitude of caring. *Education News,* January.

Wrenn, C. G. (1985). Afterward: The culturally encapsulated counselor revisited. In P. Pedersen (Ed.), *Handbook of cross-cultural counseling and therapy* (pp. 323–330). Westport, CT: Greenwood.

Wright, E. W. (1963). Group procedures. *Review of Educational Research, 33, 205–213.*

Wubbolding, R. (1991). *Understanding reality therapy.* New York: Harper & Row (Perennial Library).

Yalom, I. D. (1970). *The theory and practice of group psychotherapy.* New York: Basic Books.

Yalom, I. D. (1975). *The theory and practice of group psychotherapy* (2nd ed.). New York: Basic Books.

Yalom, I. D. (1983). *Inpatient group psychotherapy.* New York: Basic Books.

Yalom, I. D. (1985). *The theory and practice of group psychotherapy* (3rd ed.). New York: Basic Books.

Yalom, I. D. (1995). *The theory and practice of group psychotherapy* (4th ed.). New York: Basic Books.

Young, M. E. (1992). *Counseling methods and techniques: An eclectic approach.* New York: Merrill.

Zimpfer, D. G. (1984). *Group work in the helping professions: A bibliography* (2nd ed.). Muncie, IN: Accelerated Development.

Zimpfer, D. G. (1986). Planning for groups based on their developmental phases. *Journal for Specialists in Group Work, 11*(3), 180–187.

Zimpfer, D. G. (1991). Pretraining for group work: A review. *Journal for Specialists in Group Work, 16*(4), 264–269.

Zimpfer, D. G. (1989–1992). Review of group literature section. *Journal for Specialists in Group Work.*

Zuk G. H. (1971). Family therapy during 1964–1970. *Psychotherapy: Theory, Research and Practice, 8,* 90–97.

Zuk G. H. (1981). *Family therapy: A triadic based approach* (Rev. ed.). New York: Human Sciences Press.

APPENDIX A: Association for Specialists in Group Work: Professional Standards for the Training of Group Workers
(Adopted April 20, 1991)

☐ Preamble

All counselors should possess a set of core competencies in general group work. These basic knowledge and skills provide a foundation which specialty training can extend. Mastery of the core competencies does not qualify one to independently practice any group work specialty. Specialists in group work must possess advanced competencies relevant to a particular group work type.

The Association for Specialists in Group Work (ASGW) advocates for the incorporation of core group competencies as part of the Masters level training required in all counselor education programs. The Association also supports preparation of group work specialists at the Masters level. ASGW further supports the continued preparation of group work specialists at the post-Masters level (Ed.S. or Certificate, Doctoral, Continuing Education, etc.), recognizing that recommended levels of group work specialty training in many programs will need to be accomplished following completion of the Masters Degree.

This revision of the *Professional Standards for Training of Group Workers* contains two levels of competencies and related training that have been identified by the ASGW Standards Committee: (a) *Core Group Competencies*: The minimum core of group worker competencies and related training necessary for all counselors, including knowledge, skills, and practice (Minimum: 10 clock hours; Recommended: 20 clock hours); and (b) For Group Work *Specialists*: Advanced competencies that build on the generalist core in the four identified group work specialties of:

- *Task/Work groups,* including knowledge, skills, and supervised practice beyond core group training (Additional minimum: 30 clock hours; Recommended: 45 clock hours);

- *Guidance/Psychoeducation groups,* including knowledge, skills, and supervised practice beyond core group training (Additional minimum: 30 clock hours; Recommended: 45 clock hours);
- *Counseling/Interpersonal Problem-Solving groups,* including knowledge, skills, and supervised practice beyond core group training (Additional minimum: 45 clock hours; Recommended: 60 clock hours);
- *Psychotherapy/Personality Reconstruction groups,* including knowledge, skills, and supervised practice beyond core group training (Additional minimum: 45 clock hours; Recommended: 60 clock hours).

☐ Definitions

Group Work

Group work is a broad professional practice that refers to the giving of help or the accomplishment of tasks in a group setting. It involves the application of group theory and process by a capable professional practitioner to assist an interdependent collection of people to reach their mutual goals, which may be personal, interpersonal, or task-related in nature.

Core Training in Group Work for All Counselors

All professional counselors should possess basic, fundamental knowledge and skills in group work. Moreover, this set of competencies provides a basic foundation upon which specialization training in group work is built.

Core training group work competencies does not prepare a counseling professional to independently assume responsibility for conducting any of the specialty groups to be defined in these Standards. Additional focused training is required for independent practice in a specialty, as detailed below.

Group Work Specializations

The trainee may proceed beyond core training in group work to specialize in one or more advanced areas of practice. It is to be expected that all Counseling programs would provide core training in group work to all students and most would offer additional training in at least one of the other specializations. Definitions of each specialization follow.

Task/Work Groups

Much work in contemporary Western society is accomplished through group endeavor. The task/work group specialist is able to assist groups such as task forces, committees, planning groups, community organizations, discussion groups, study circles, learning groups, and other similar groups to correct or develop their functioning. The focus is on the application of group dynamics principles and processes to improve practice and the accomplishment of identified work goals.

Guidance/Psychoeducation Groups

Education and prevention are critically important goals for the contemporary counselor. The guidance/psychoeducation group specialist seeks to use the group medium to educate group participants who are presently unaffected about a potential threat (such as AIDS), a developmental life event (such as a transition point), or how to cope with an immediate life crisis (such as suicide of a loved one), with the goal of preventing an array of educational and psychological disturbance from occurring.

Counseling/Interpersonal Problem-Solving Groups

The group worker who specializes in counseling/interpersonal problem-solv-ing seeks to help group participants to resolve the usual, yet often difficult, problems of living through interpersonal support and problem-solving. An additional goal is to help participants to develop their existing interpersonal problem-solving competencies that they may be better able to handle future problems of a similar nature. Nonsevere career, educational, personal, social, and developmental concerns are frequently addressed.

Psychotherapy/Personality Reconstruction Groups

The group worker who specializes in psychotherapy/personality reconstruction seeks to help individual group members to remediate their in-depth psychological problems. Because the depth and extent of the psychological disturbance is significant, the goal is to aid each individual to reconstruct major personality dimensions.

☐ Training Standards

A. Core Group Work for All Counselors: Knowledge Competencies

All counselors can effectively:

1. State for the four major group work specializations identified in this document (task groups, guidance groups, counseling groups, psychotherapy groups) the distinguishing characteristics of each, the common-

alities shared by all, and the appropriate instances in which each is to be used.

2. Identify the basic principles of group dynamics.
3. Discuss the basic therapeutic ingredients of groups.
4. Identify the personal characteristics of group workers that have an impact on members; knowledge of personal strengths, weaknesses, biases, values, and their effect on others.
5. Describe the specific ethical issues that are unique to group work.
6. Discuss the body of research on group work and how it relates to one's academic preparation in either school counseling, student personnel education, community counseling, mental health counseling, or other specialized studies.
7. Define the process components involved in typical stages of a group's development (i.e., characteristics of group interaction and counselor roles).
8. Describe the major facilitative and debilitative roles that group members may take.
9. State the advantages and disadvantages of group work and the circumstances for which it is indicated or contraindicated.
10 Detail therapeutic factors of group work.
11. Identify principles and strategies for recruiting and screening prospective group members.
12. Detail the importance of group and member evaluation.
13. Deliver a clear, concise, and complete definition of group work.
14. Deliver a clear, concise, and complete definition of each of the four group work specialities.
15. Explain and clarify the purpose of a particular form of group work.

Core Group Work Training for All Counselors: Skill Competencies

All counselors are able to effectively:

1. Encourage participation of group members
2. Observe and identify group process events.
3. Attend to and acknowledge group member behavior.
4. Clarify and summarize group member statements.
5. Open and close group sessions.
6. Impart information in the group when necessary.
7. Model effective group leader behavior.
8. Engage in appropriate self-disclosure in the group.
9. Give and receive feedback in the group.
10. Ask open-ended questions in the group.
11. Empathize with group members.

12. Confront group members' behavior.
13. Help group members attribute meaning to their experience.
14. Help group members to integrate and apply learnings.
15. Demonstrate ASCW ethical and professional standards in group practice.
16. Keep the group on task in accomplishing its goals.

Core Group Work Training

Knowledge

Core training in group work should include a minimum of one course. Contained in this course should be attention to competencies in the Knowledge and in the Skills domains.

Skills Through Supervised Practice

The Practice domain should include observation and participation in a group experience, which could occur in a classroom group.
 —**Minimum** amount of supervised practice: *10 clock hours.*
 —**Recommended** amount of supervised practice: *20 clock hours.*

B. Group Work Specializations: Knowledge, Skill, and Supervised Practice Domains

The counselor trainee, having mastered the core knowledge and skill domains displayed above, can specialize in one or more advanced areas of group work practice. These advanced specially areas are Task/Work groups, Guidance/Psychoeducation groups, Counseling/Interpersonal Problem-Solving groups, and Psychotherapy/Personality Reconstruction groups. The advanced knowledge and skill competencies associated with each of these specialties are presented below.

Task/Work Groups

Knowledge Competencies

In addition to Core knowledge, the qualified Task/Work group specialist can effectively:

1. Identify organizational dynamics pertinent to task/work groups.
2. Describe community dynamics pertinent to task/work groups.
3. Identify political dynamics pertinent to task/work groups.
4. Describe standard discussion methodologies appropriate for task/work groups.

5. Identify specific ethical considerations in working with task/work groups.
6. Identify program development and evaluation models appropriate for task/work groups.
7. List consultation principles and approaches appropriate for task/work groups.

Skills Competencies

In addition to Core skills, the qualified Task/Work group specialist is able to effectively:

1. Focus and maintain attention on task and work issues.
2. Obtain goal clarity in a task/work group.
3. Conduct a personally selected task/work group model appropriate to the age and clientele of the group leader's specialty area(s) (e.g., school counseling).
4. Mobilize energies toward a common goal in task/work groups.
5. Implement group decision-making methods in task/work groups.
6. Manage conflict in task/work groups.
7. Blend the predominant task focus with appropriate attention to human relations factors in task/work groups.
8. Sense and use larger organizational and political dynamics in task/work groups.

Specialist Training: Task/Work Groups

Knowledge

Course work should be taken in the broad area of organization development, management, and/or sociology such that the student understands organizational life and how task groups function within it. Course work also should be taken in consultation.

Skills Through Supervised Practice

In addition to Core training acquired through observation and participation in a group (10 clock hours minimum; 20 clock hours recommended), practice should include:

    —**Minimum** amount of *30 clock hours* should be obtained in co-leading or leading a task/work group in a field-practice setting supervised by qualified faculty or staff personnel.

    —**Recommended** amount of *45 clock hours* should be obtained in co-leading or leading a task/work group in a field-practice setting supervised by qualified faculty or staff personnel.

Guidance/Psychoeducation Groups

Knowledge Competencies

In addition to Core knowledge, the qualified Guidance/Psychoeducation group specialist can effectively:

1. Identify the concepts of primary prevention and secondary prevention in guidance/psychoeducation groups.
2. Articulate the concept of "at risk" in guidance/psychoeducation groups.
3. Enumerate principles of instruction relevant to guidance/psychoeducation groups.
4. Develop a knowledge base relevant to the focus of a guidance/psychoeducation group intervention.
5. List principles involved in obtaining healthy and/or at risk members for guidance/psychoeducation groups.
6. Describe human development theory pertinent to guidance/psychoeducation groups.
7. Discuss environmental assessment as related to guidance/psychoeducation groups.
8. Discuss principles of structure as related to guidance/psychoeducation groups.
9. Discuss the concept of empowerment in guidance/psychoeducation groups.
10. Identify specific ethical considerations unique to guidance/psychoeducation groups.
11. List advantages of guidance/psychoeducation groups and where indicated and contraindicated.

Skills Competencies

In addition to Core skills, the qualified Guidance/Psychoeducation group specialist can effectively:

1. Plan a guidance/psychoeducation group in collaboration with "target" population members or representatives.
2. Match a relevant guidance/psychoeducation topic with relevant (and currently "unaffected") target group.
3. Conduct a personally selected guidance/psychoeducation group model appropriate to the age and clientele of the group leader's specialty area (e.g., student personnel education).
4. Design a guidance/psychoeducation group plan that is developmentally and practically sound.
5. Present information in a guidance/psychoeducation group.
6. Use environmental dynamics to the benefit of the guidance/psychoeducation group.
7. Conduct skill training in guidance/psychoeducation groups.

Specialist Training: Guidance/Psychoeducation Groups

Knowledge

Course work should be taken in the broad area of community psychology, health promotion, marketing, consultation, and curriculum design.

Skills Through Supervised Practice

In addition to Core training acquired through observation and participation in a group (10 clock hours minimum; 20 clock hours recommended), practice should include:

—**Minimum** amount of *30 clock hours* should be obtained in co-leading or leading a guidance/psychoeducation group in a field-practice setting supervised by qualified faculty or staff personnel.

—**Recommended** amount of *45 clock hours* should be obtained in co-leading or leading a guidance/psychoeducation group in a practice setting supervised by qualified faculty or staff personnel.

Counseling/Interpersonal Problem-Solving Groups

Knowledge Competencies

In addition to Core knowledge, the qualified Counseling/Interpersonal Problem-Solving group specialist can effectively:

1. State for at least three major theoretical approaches to group counseling the distinguishing characteristics of each and the commonalities shared by all.
2. Identify specific ethical problems and considerations unique to group counseling.
3. List advantages and disadvantages of group counseling and the circumstances for which it is indicated or contraindicated.
4. Describe interpersonal dynamics in group counseling.
5. Describe group problem-solving approaches in relation to group counseling.
6. Discuss interpersonal assessment in group counseling.
7. Identify referral sources and procedures in group counseling.
8. Describe group formation principles in group counseling.

Skills Competencies

In addition to Core skills, the qualified Counseling/Interpersonal Problem-Solving group specialist can effectively:

1. Recruit and screen prospective counseling group members.
2. Recognize self-defeating behaviors of counseling group members.
3. Conduct a personally selected group counseling model appropriate to the age and clientele of the group leader's specialty area(s) (e.g., community counseling).
4. Develop reasonable hypotheses about nonverbal behavior among counseling group members.
5. Exhibit appropriate pacing skills involved in stages of a counseling group's development.
6. Intervene effectively at critical incidents in the counseling group process.
7. Work appropriately with disruptive counseling group members.
8. Make use of the major strategies, techniques, and procedures of group counseling.
9. Use procedures to assist transfer and support of changes by group counseling members in the natural environment.
10. Use adjunct group counseling structures such as homework (e.g., goal setting).
11. Work cooperatively and effectively with a counseling group co-leader.
12. Use assessment procedures in evaluating effects and contributions of group counseling.

Specialist Training: Counseling/Interpersonal Problem-Solving Groups

Knowledge

As much course work in group counseling as possible is desirable, but at least one course beyond the generalist is necessary. Other courses in the Counseling program should provide good support for the group counseling specialty.

Skills through Supervised Practice

In addition to Core training acquired through observation and participation in a group (10 clock hours minimum; 20 clock hours recommended), practice should include:

—**Minimum** amount of *45 clock hours* should be obtained in co-leading or leading a counseling/interpersonal problem-solving group in a field practice setting supervised by qualified faculty or staff personnel.

—**Recommended** amount of *60 clock hours* should be obtained in co-leading or leading a counseling/interpersonal problem-solving group in a field-practice setting supervised by qualified faculty or staff personnel.

Psychotherapy/Personality Reconstruction Groups

Knowledge Competencies

In addition to Core knowledge, the Psychotherapy/Personality Reconstruction group specialist can effectively:

1. State for at least three major theoretical approaches to group psychotherapy the distinguishing characteristics of each and the commonalities shared by all.
2. Identify specific ethical problems and considerations unique to group psychotherapy.
3. List advantages and disadvantages of group psychotherapy and the circumstances for which it is indicated or contraindicated.
4. Specify intrapersonal and interpersonal dynamics in group psychotherapy.
5. Describe group problem-solving approaches in relation to group psychotherapy.
6. Discuss interpersonal assessment and intervention in group psychotherapy.
7. Identify referral sources and procedures in group psychotherapy.
8. Describe group formation principles in group psychotherapy.
9. Identify and describe abnormal behavior in relation to group psychotherapy.
10. Identify psychopathology as related to group psychotherapy.
11. Describe personality theory as related to group psychotherapy.
12. Detail crisis intervention approaches suitable for group psychotherapy.
13. Specify diagnostic and assessment methods appropriate for group psychotherapy.

Skill Competencies

In addition to Core skills, the qualified Psychotherapy/Personality Reconstruction group specialist can effectively:

1. Recruit and screen prospective psychotherapy group members.
2. Recognize self-defeating behaviors of psychotherapy group members.
3. Describe and conduct a personally selected group psychotherapy model appropriate to the age and clientele of the group leader's specialty area (e.g., mental health counseling).
4. Identify and develop reasonable hypotheses about nonverbal behavior among psychotherapy group members.
5. Exhibit appropriate pacing skills involved in stages of a psychotherapy group's development.
6. Identify and intervene effectively at critical incidents in the psychotherapy group process.
7. Work appropriately with disruptive psychotherapy group members.

8. Make use of the major strategies, techniques, and procedures of group psychotherapy.
9. Provide and use procedures to assist transfer and support of changes by group psychotherapy members in the natural environment.
10. Use adjunct group psychotherapy structures such as psychological homework (e.g., self-monitoring, contracting).
11. Work cooperatively and effectively with a psychotherapy group co-leader.
12. Use assessment procedures in evaluating effects and contributions of group psychotherapy.
13. Assist individual change along the full range of development, from "normal" to "abnormal" in the psychotherapy group.
14. Handle psychological emergencies in the psychotherapy group.
15. Institute hospitalization procedures when appropriate and necessary in the psychotherapy group.
16. Assess and diagnose mental and emotional disorders of psychotherapy group members.

Specialist Training: Psychotherapy/Personality Reconstruction Groups

Knowledge

Course work should be taken in the areas of group psychotherapy, abnormal psychology, psychopathology, and diagnostic assessment to assure capabilities in working with more disturbed populations.

Skills Through Supervised Practice

In addition to Core training acquired through observation and participation in a group (10 clock hours minimum; 20 clock hours recommended), practice should include:

—**Minimum** amount of *45 clock hours* should be obtained in co-leading or leading a psychotherapy/personality reconstruction group in a field-practice setting supervised by qualified faculty or staff personnel.

—**Recommended** amount of *60 clock hours* should be obtained in co-leading or leading a psychotherapy/personality reconstruction group in a field-practice setting supervised by qualified faculty or staff personnel.

APPENDIX B: Code of Ethics and Standards of Practice

As Approved by Governing Council
April 1995
Effective July 1, 1995

☐ Preamble

The American Counseling Association is an educational, scientific and professional organization whose members are dedicated to the enhancement of human development throughout the life span. Association members recognize diversity in our society and embrace a cross-cultural approach in support of the worth, dignity, potential, and uniqueness of each individual.

The specification of a code of ethics enables the association to clarify to current and future members, and to those served by members, the nature of the ethical responsibilities held in common by its members. As the code of ethics of the association, this document establishes principles that define the ethical behavior of association members. All members of the American Counseling Association are required to adhere to the Code of Ethics and the Standards of Practice. The Code of Ethics will serve as the basis for processing ethical complaints initiated against members of the association.

Section A: The Counseling Relationship

A.1. Client Welfare

a. *Primary Responsibility.*
   The primary responsibility of counselors is to respect the dignity and to promote the welfare of clients.
b. *Positive Growth and Development.*
   Counselors encourage client growth and development in ways that foster the clients' interest and welfare; counselors avoid fostering dependent counseling relationships.

c. *Counseling Plans.*

Counselors and their clients work jointly in devising integrated, individual counseling plans that offer reasonable promise of success and are consistent with abilities and circumstances of clients. Counselors and clients regularly review counseling plans to ensure their continued viability and effectiveness, respecting clients' freedom of choice. (See A.3.b.)

d. *Family Involvement.*

Counselors recognize that families are usually important in clients' lives and strive to enlist family understanding and involvement as a positive resource, when appropriate.

e. *Career and Employment Needs.*

Counselors work with their clients in considering employment in jobs and circumstances that are consistent with the clients' overall abilities, vocational limitations, physical restrictions, general temperament, interest and aptitude patterns, social skills, education, general qualifications, and other relevant characteristics and needs. Counselors neither place nor participate in placing clients in positions that will result in damaging the interest and the welfare of clients, employers, or the public.

A.2. Respecting Diversity

a. *Nondiscrimination.*

Counselors do not condone or engage in discrimination based on age, color, culture, disability, ethnic group, gender, race, religion, sexual orientation, marital status, or socioeconomic status. (See C.5.a., C.5.b., and D.l.i.)

b. *Respecting Differences.*

Counselors will actively attempt to understand the diverse cultural backgrounds of the clients with whom they work. This includes, but is not limited to, learning how the counselor's own cultural/ethnic/racial identity impacts her or his values and beliefs about the counseling process. (See E.8. and F.2.i.)

A.3. Client Rights

a. *Disclosure to Clients.*

When counseling is initiated, and throughout the counseling process as necessary, counselors inform clients of the purposes, goals, techniques, procedures, limitations, potential risks and benefits of services to be performed, and other pertinent information. Counselors take steps to ensure that clients understand the implications of diagnosis, the intended use of tests and reports, fees, and billing arrangements. Clients have the right to expect confidentiality and to be provided with an explanation of its limitations, including supervision and/or treatment team professionals; to obtain clear information about their case records; to participate in the ongoing counseling plans; and to refuse any recommended services and be advised of the consequences of such refusal. (See E.5.a. and G.2.)

b. *Freedom of Choice.*

Counselors offer clients the freedom to choose whether to enter into a counseling relationship and to determine which professional(s) will provide counseling. Restrictions that limit choices of clients are fully explained. (See A.1.c.)

c. *Inability to Give Consent.*

When counseling minors or persons unable to give voluntary informed consent, counselors act in these clients' best interests. (See B.3.)

A.4. Clients Served by Others

If a client is receiving services from another mental health professional, counselors, with client consent, inform the professional persons already involved and develop clear agreements to avoid confusion and conflict for the client. (See C.6.c.)

A.5. Personal Needs and Values

a. *Personal Needs.*

In the counseling relationship, counselors are aware of the intimacy and responsibilities inherent in the counseling relationship, maintain respect for clients, and avoid actions that seek to meet their personal needs at the expense of clients.

b. *Personal Values.*

Counselors are aware of their own values, attitudes, beliefs, and behaviors and how these apply in a diverse society, and avoid imposing their values on clients. (See C.5.a)

A.6. Dual Relationships

a. *Avoid When Possible.*

Counselors are aware of their influential positions with respect to clients, and they avoid exploiting the trust and dependency of clients. Counselors make ever effort to avoid dual relationships with clients that could impair professional judgment or increase the risk of harm to clients. (Examples of such relationships include, but are not limited to, familial, social, financial, business, or close personal relationships with clients.) When a dual relationship cannot be avoided, counselors take appropriate professional precautions such as informed consent, consultation, supervision, and documentation to ensure that judgment is not impaired and no exploitation occurs. (See F.1.b.)

b. *Superior/Subordinate Relationships.*

Counselors do not accept as clients superiors or subordinates with whom they have administrative, supervisory, or evaluative relationships.

A.7. Sexual Intimacies With Clients

a. *Current Clients.*
Counselors do not have any type of sexual intimacies with clients and do not counsel persons with whom they have had a sexual relationship.
b. *Former Clients.*
Counselors do not engage in sexual intimacies with former clients within a minimum of two years after terminating the counseling relationship. Counselors who engage in such relationship after two years following termination have the responsibility to thoroughly examine and document that such relations did not have an exploitative nature, based on factors such as duration of counseling, amount of time since counseling, termination circumstances, client's personal history and mental status, adverse impact on the client, and actions by the counselor suggesting a plan to initiate a sexual relationship with the client after termination.

A.8. Multiple Clients.

When counselors agree to provide counseling services to two or more persons who have a relationship (such as husband and wife or parents and children), counselors clarify at the outset which person or persons are clients and the nature of the relationships they will have with each involved person. If it becomes apparent that counselors may be called upon to perform potentially conflicting roles, they clarify, adjust, or withdraw from roles appropriately. (See B.2. and B.4.d.)

A.9. Group Work

a. *Screening.*
Counselors screen prospective group counseling/therapy participants. To the extent possible. counselors select members whose needs and goals are compatible with goals of the group, who will not impede the group process, and whose well-being will not be jeopardized by the group experience.
b. *Protecting Clients.*
In a group setting, counselors take reasonable precautions to protect clients from physical or psychological trauma.

A.10. Fees and Bartering
(See D.3.a. and D.3.b.)

a. *Advance Understanding.*
Counselors clearly explain to clients, prior to entering the counseling relationship, all financial arrangements related to professional services including the use of collection agencies or legal measures for nonpayment. (A.11.c.)

b. *Establishing Fees.*

In establishing fees for professional counseling services, counselors consider the financial status of clients and locality. In the event that the established fee structure is inappropriate for a client, assistance is provided in attempting to find comparable services of acceptable cost. (See, A.10.d., D.3.a., and D.3.b.)

c. *Bartering Discouraged.*

Counselors ordinarily refrain from accepting goods or services from clients in return for counseling services because such arrangements create inherent potential for conflicts, exploitation, and distortion of the professional relationship. Counselors may participate in bartering only if the relationship is not exploitive, if the client requests it, if a clear written contract is established, and if such arrangements are an accepted practice among professionals in the community. (See A.6.a.)

d. *Pro Bono Service.*

Counselors contribute to society by devoting a portion of their professional activity to services for which there is little or no financial return (pro bono).

A.11. Termination and Referral

a. *Abandonment Prohibited.*

Counselors do not abandon or neglect clients in counseling. Counselors assist in making appropriate arrangements for the continuation of treatment, when necessary, during interruptions such as vacations, and following termination.

b. *Inability to Assist Clients.*

If counselors determine an inability to be of professional assistance to clients, they avoid entering or immediately terminate a counseling relationship. Counselors are knowledgeable about referral resources and suggest appropriate alternatives. If clients decline the suggested referral, counselors should discontinue the relationship.

c. *Appropriate Termination.*

Counselors terminate a counseling relationship, securing client agreement when possible, when it is reasonably clear that the client is no longer benefiting, when services are no longer required, when counseling no longer serves the client's needs or interests, when clients do not pay fees charged, or when agency or institution limits do not allow provision of further counseling services. (See A.10.b. and C.2.g.)

A.12. Computer Technology

a. *Use of Computers.*

When computer applications are used in counseling services, counselors ensure that: 1) the client is intellectually, emotionally, and physically capable of using the computer application; 2) the computer application is appropriate for the needs of the client; 3) the client understands the purpose and operation of the computer applications; and 4) a follow-up of client use of a computer application is provided to correct possible misconceptions, discover inappropriate use, and assess subsequent needs.

b. *Explanation of Limitations.*

Counselors ensure that clients are provided information as a part of the counseling relationship that adequately explains the limitations of computer technology.

c. *Access to Computer Applications.*

Counselors provide for equal access to computer applications in counseling services. (See A.2.a.)

Section B: Confidentiality

B.1. Right of Privacy

a. *Respect for Privacy.*

Counselors respect their clients' right to privacy and avoid illegal and unwarranted disclosures of confidential information. (See A.3.a. and B.6.a.)

b. *Client Waiver.*

The right to privacy may be waived by the client or their legally recognized representative.

c. *Exceptions.*

The general requirement that counselors keep information confidential does not apply when disclosure is required to prevent clear and imminent danger to the client or others or when legal requirements demand that confidential information be revealed. Counselors consult with other professionals when in doubt as to the validity of an exception.

d. *Contagious Fatal Diseases.*

A counselor who receives information confirming that a client has a disease commonly known to be both communicable and fatal is justified in disclosing information to an identifiable third party, who by his or her relationship with the client is at a high risk of contracting the disease. Prior to making a disclosure the counselor should ascertain that the client has not already informed the third party about his or her disease and that the client is not intending to inform the third party in the immediate future. (See B.1.c and B.1.f)

e. *Court Ordered Disclosure.*

When court ordered to release confidential information without a client's permission, counselors request to the court that the disclosure not be required due to potential harm to the client or counseling relationship. (See B.1 .c.)

f. *Minimal Disclosure.*
When circumstances require the disclosure of confidential information, only essential information is revealed. To the extent possible, clients are informed before confidential information is disclosed.

g. *Explanation of Limitations.*
When counseling is initiated and throughout the counseling process as necessary, counselors inform clients of the limitations of confidentiality and identify foreseeable situations in which confidentiality must be breached. (See G.2.a.)

h. *Subordinates.*
Counselors make every effort to ensure that privacy and confidentiality of clients are maintained by subordinates including employees, supervisees, clerical assistants, and volunteers. (See B.1.a.)

I. *Treatment Teams.*
If client treatment will involve a continued review by a treatment team, the client will be informed of the team's existence and composition.

B.2. Groups and Families

a. *Group Work.*
In group work, counselors clearly define confidentiality and the parameters for the specific group being entered, explain its importance, and discuss the difficulties related to confidentiality involved in group work. The fact that confidentiality cannot be guaranteed is clearly communicated to group members.

b. *Family Counseling.*
In family counseling, information about one family member cannot be disclosed to another member without permission. Counselors protect the privacy rights of each family member. (See A.8., B.3., and B.4.d.)

B.3. Minor or Incompetent Clients

When counseling clients who are minors or individuals who are unable to give voluntary, informed consent, parents or guardians may be included in the counseling process as appropriate. Counselors act in the best interests of clients and take measures to safeguard confidentiality. (See A.3.c.)

B.4. Records

a. *Requirement of Records.*
Counselors maintain records necessary for rendering professional services to their clients and as required by laws, regulations, or agency or institution procedures.

b. *Confidentiality of Records.*
Counselors are responsible for securing the safety and confidentiality of any counseling records they create, maintain, transfer, or destroy whether the records are written, taped, computerized, or stored in any other medium. (See B.1.a.)

c. *Permission to Record or Observe.*
Counselors obtain permission from clients prior to electronically recording or observing sessions. (See A.3.a.)

d. *Client Access.*
Counselors recognize that counseling records are kept for the benefit of clients, and therefore provide access to records and copies of records when requested by competent clients, unless the records contain information that may be misleading and detrimental to the client. In situations involving multiple clients, access to records is limited to those parts of records that do not include confidential information related to another client. (See A.8., B.1.a., and B.2.b.)

e. *Disclosure or Transfer.*
Counselors obtain written permission from clients to disclose or transfer records to legitimate third parties unless exceptions to confidentiality exist as listed in Section B.1. Steps are taken to ensure that receivers of counseling records are sensitive to their confidential nature.

B.5. Research and Training

a. *Data Disguise Required.*
Use of data derived from counseling relationships for purposes of training, research, or publication is confined to content that is disguised to ensure the anonymity of the individuals involved. (See B.1.g. and G.3.d.)

b. *Agreement for Identification.*
Identification of a client in a presentation or publication is permissible only when the client has reviewed the material and has agreed to its presentation or publication. (See G.3.d.)

B.6. Consultation

a. *Respect for Privacy.*
Information obtained in a consulting relationship is discussed for professional purposes only with persons clearly concerned with the case. Written and oral reports present data germane to the purposes of the consultation, and every effort is made to protect client identity and avoid undue invasion of privacy.

b. *Cooperating Agencies.*
Before sharing information, counselors make efforts to ensure that there are defined policies in other agencies serving the counselor's clients that effectively protect the confidentiality of information.

Section C: Professional Responsibility

C.1. Standards Knowledge

Counselors have a responsibility to read, understand, and follow the Code of Ethics and the Standards of Practice.

C.2. Professional Competence

a. *Boundaries of Competence.*
Counselors practice only within the boundaries of their competence, based on their education, training, supervised experience, state and national professional credentials, and appropriate professional experience. Counselors will demonstrate a commitment to gain knowledge, personal awareness, sensitivity, and skills pertinent to working with a diverse client population.

b. *New Specialty Areas of Practice.*
Counselors practice in specialty areas new to them only after appropriate education, training, and supervised experience. While developing skills in new specialty areas, counselors take steps to ensure the competence of their work and to protect others from possible harm.

c. *Qualified for Employment.*
Counselors accept employment only for positions for which they are qualified by education, training, supervised experience, state and national professional credentials, and appropriate professional experience. Counselors hire for professional counseling positions only individuals who are qualified and competent

d. *Monitor Effectiveness.*
Counselors continually monitor their effectiveness as professionals and take steps to improve when necessary. Counselors in private practice take reasonable steps to seek out peer supervision to evaluate their efficacy as counselors.

e. *Ethical Issues Consultation.*
Counselors take reasonable steps to consult with other counselors or related professionals when they have questions regarding their ethical obligations or professional practice. (See H.1)

f. *Continuing Education.*
Counselors recognize the need for continuing education to maintain a reasonable level of awareness of current scientific and professional information in their fields of activity. They take steps to maintain competence in the skills they use, are open to new procedures, and keep current with the diverse and/or special populations with whom they work.

g. *Impairment.*
Counselors refrain from offering or accepting professional services when their physical, mental or emotional problems are likely to harm a client or others. They are alert to the signs of impairment, seek assistance for

problems, and, if necessary, limit, suspend, or terminate their professional responsibilities. (See A.11.c.)

C.3. Advertising and Soliciting Clients

a. *Accurate Advertising.*
There are no restrictions on advertising by counselors except those that can be specifically justified to protect the public from deceptive practices. Counselors advertise or represent their services to the public by identifying their credentials in an accurate manner that is not false, misleading, deceptive, or fraudulent. Counselors may only advertise the highest degree earned which is in counseling or a closely related field from a college or university that was accredited when the degree was awarded by one of the regional accrediting bodies recognized by the Council on Postsecondary Accreditation.

b. *Testimonials.*
Counselors who use testimonials do not solicit them from clients or other persons who, because of their particular circumstances, may be vulnerable to undue influence.

c. *Statements by Others.*
Counselors make reasonable efforts to ensure that statements made by others about them or the profession of counseling are accurate.

d. *Recruiting Through Employment.*
Counselors do not use their places of employment or institutional affiliation to recruit or gain clients, supervisees, or consultees for their private practices. (See C.5.e.)

e. *Products and Training Advertisements.*
Counselors who develop products related to their profession or conduct workshops or training events ensure that the advertisements concerning these products or events are accurate and disclose adequate information for consumers to make informed choices.

f. *Promoting to Those Served.*
Counselors do not use counseling, teaching, training, or supervisory relationships to promote their products or training events in a manner that is deceptive or would exert undue influence on individuals who may be vulnerable. Counselors may adopt textbooks they have authored for instruction purposes.

g. *Professional Association Involvement.*
Counselors actively participate in local, state, and national associations that foster the development and improvement of counseling.

C.4. Credentials

a. *Credentials Claimed.*
Counselors claim or imply only professional credentials possessed and

are responsible for correcting any known misrepresentations of their credentials by others. Professional credentials include graduate degrees in counseling or closely related mental health fields, accreditation of graduate programs, national voluntary certifications, government-issued certifications or licenses. ACA professional membership, or any other credential that might indicate to the public specialized knowledge or expertise in counseling.

b. *ACA Professional Membership.*
ACA professional members may announce to the public their membership status. Regular members may not announce their ACA membership in a manner that might imply they are credentialed counselors.

c. *Credential Guidelines.*
Counselors follow the guidelines for use of credentials that have been established by the entities that issue the credentials.

d. *Misrepresentation of Credentials.*
Counselors do not attribute more to their credentials than the credentials represent, and do not imply that other counselors are not qualified because they do not possess certain credentials.

e. *Doctoral Degrees From Other Fields.*
Counselors who hold a master's degree in counseling or a closely related mental health field, but hold a doctoral degree from other than counseling or a closely related field do not use the title, "Dr." in their practices and do not announce to the public in relation to their practice or status as a counselor that they hold a doctorate.

C.5. Public Responsibility

a. *Nondiscrimination.*
Counselors do not discriminate against clients, students, or supervisees in a manner that has a negative impact based on their age, color, culture, disability, ethnic group, gender, race, religion, sexual orientation, or socioeconomic status, or for any other reason. (See A.2.a.)

b. *Sexual Harassment.*
Counselors do not engage in sexual harassment. Sexual harassment is defined as sexual solicitation, physical advances, or verbal or nonverbal conduct that is sexual in nature, that occurs in connection with professional activities or roles, and that either: 1) is unwelcome, is offensive, or creates a hostile workplace environment, and counselors know or are told this; or 2) is sufficiently severe or intense to be perceived as harassment to a reasonable person in the context. Sexual harassment can consist of a single, intense or severe act or multiple persistent or pervasive acts.

c. *Reports to Third Parties.*
Counselors are accurate, honest, and unbiased in reporting their professional activities and judgments to appropriate third parties including

courts, health insurance companies, those who are the recipients of evaluation reports, and others. (See B.1.g.)

d. *Media Presentations.*

When counselors provide advice or comment by means of public lectures, demonstrations, radio or television programs, prerecorded tapes, printed articles, mailed material, or other media, they take reasonable precautions to ensure that 1) the statements are based on appropriate professional counseling literature and practice; 2) the statements are otherwise consistent with the Code of Ethics and the Standards of Practice; and 3) the recipients of the information are not encouraged to infer that a professional counseling relationship has been established. (See C.6.b.)

e. *Unjustified Gains.*

Counselors do not use their professional positions to seek or receive unjustified personal gains, sexual favors, unfair advantage, or unearned goods or services. (See C.3.d.)

C.6. Responsibility to Other Professionals

a. *Different Approaches.*

Counselors are respectful of approaches to professional counseling that differ from their own. Counselors know and take into account the traditions and practices of other professional groups with which they work.

b. *Personal Public Statements.*

When making personal statements in a public context, counselors clarify that they are speaking from their personal perspectives and that they are not speaking on behalf of all counselors or the profession. (See C.5.d.)

c. *Clients Served by Others.*

When counselors learn that their clients are in a professional relationship with another mental health professional, they request release from clients to inform the other professionals and strive to establish positive and collaborative professional relationships. (See A.4.)

Section D: Relationships With Other Professionals

D.1. Relationships With Employers and Employees

a. *Role Definition.*

Counselors define and describe for their employers and employees the parameters and levels of their professional roles.

b. *Agreements.*

Counselors establish working agreements with supervisors, colleagues, and subordinates regarding counseling or clinical relationships, confidentiality, adherence to professional standards, distinction between public and private material, maintenance and dissemination of recorded information, workload, and accountability. Working agreements in each instance are specified and made known to those concerned.

c. *Negative Conditions.*
Counselors alert their employers to conditions that may be potentially disruptive or damaging to the counselor's professional responsibilities or that may limit their effectiveness.

d. *Evaluation.*
Counselors submit regularly to professional review and evaluation by their supervisor or the appropriate representative of the employer.

e. *In-Service.*
Counselors are responsible for in-service development of self and staff.

f. *Goals.*
Counselors inform their staff of goals and programs.

g. *Practices.*
Counselors provide personnel and agency practices that respect and enhance the rights and welfare of each employee and recipient of agency services. Counselors strive to maintain the highest levels of professional services.

h. *Personnel Selection and Assignment.*
Counselors select competent staff and assign responsibilities compatible with their skills and experiences.

I. *Discrimination.*
Counselors, as either employers or employees, do not engage in or condone practices that are inhumane, illegal, or unjustifiable (such as considerations based on age, color, culture, disability, ethnic group, gender, race, religion, sexual orientation, or socioeconomic status) in hiring, promotion, or training. (See A.2.a. and C.5.b.)

j. *Professional Conduct.*
Counselors have a responsibility both to clients and to the agency or institution within which services are performed to maintain high standards of professional conduct.

k. *Exploiting Relationships.*
Counselors do not engage in exploitive relationships with individuals over whom they have supervisory, evaluative, or instructional control or authority.

l. *Employer Policies.*
The acceptance of employment in an agency or institution implies that counselors are in agreement with its general policies and principles. Counselors strive to reach agreement with employers as to acceptable standards of conduct that allow for changes in institutional policy conducive to the growth and development of clients.

D.2. Consultation (See B.6)

a. *Consultation as an Option.*
Counselors may choose to consult with any other professionally competent persons about their clients. In choosing consultants, counselors

avoid placing the consultant in a conflict of interest situation that would preclude the consultant being a proper party to the counselor's efforts to help the client. Should counselors be engaged in a work setting that compromises this consultation standard, they consult with other professionals whenever possible to consider justifiable alternatives.

b. *Consultant Competency.*

Counselors are reasonably certain that they have or the organization represented has the necessary competencies and resources for giving the kind of consulting services needed and that appropriate referral resources are available

c. *Understanding with Clients.*

When providing consultation, counselors attempt to develop with their clients a clear understanding of problem definition, goals for change, and predicted consequences of interventions selected.

d. *Consultant Goals.*

The consulting relationship is one in which client adaptability and growth toward self-direction are consistently encouraged and cultivated. (See A.1.b.)

D.3. Fees for Referral

a. *Accepting Fees from Agency Clients.*

Counselors refuse a private fee or other remuneration for rendering services to persons who are entitled to such services through the counselor's employing agency or institution. The policies of a particular agency may make explicit provisions for agency clients to receive counseling services from members of its staff in private practice. In such instances, the clients must be informed of other options open to them should they seek private counseling services. (See A.10.a., A.11.b., and C.3.d.)

b. *Referral Fees.*

Counselors do not accept a referral fee from other professionals.

D.4. Subcontractor Arrangements.

When counselors work as subcontractors for counseling services for a third party, they have a duty to inform clients of the limitations of confidentiality that the organization may place on counselors in providing counseling services to clients. The limits of such confidentiality ordinarily are discussed as part of the intake session. (See B.1.e. and B.1.f.)

Section E: Evaluation, Assessment, and Interpretation

E.1. General

a. *Appraisal Techniques.*

The primary purpose of educational and psychological assessment is to

provide measures that are objective and interpretable in either comparative or absolute terms. Counselors recognize the need to interpret the
statements in this section as applying to the whole range of appraisal
techniques, including test and nontest data.

b. *Client Welfare.*

Counselors promote the welfare and best interests of the client in the
development, publication, and utilization of educational and psychological assessment techniques. They do not misuse assessment results and
interpretations and take reasonable steps to prevent others from mis-
using the information these techniques provide. They respect the client's
right to know the results, the interpretations made, and the bases for
their conclusions and recommendations.

E.2. Competence to Use and Interpret Tests

a. *Limits of Competence.*

Counselors recognize the limits of their competence and perform only
those testing and assessment services for which they have been trained.
They are familiar with reliability, validity, related standardization, error
of measurement, and proper application of any technique utilized. Counselors using computer-based test interpretations are trained in the construct being measured and the specific instrument being used prior to
using this type of computer application. Counselors take reasonable measures to ensure the proper use of psychological assessment techniques by
persons under their supervision.

b. *Appropriate Use.*

Counselors are responsible for the appropriate application, scoring, interpretation, and use of assessment instruments, whether they score and
interpret such tests themselves or use computerized or other services.

c. *Decisions Based on Results.*

Counselors responsible for decisions involving individuals or policies that
are based on assessment results have a thorough understanding of educational and psychological measurement, including validation criteria,
test research, and guidelines for test development and use.

d. *Accurate Information.*

Counselors provide accurate information and avoid false claims or misconceptions when making statements about assessment instruments or
techniques. Special efforts are made to avoid unwarranted connotations
of such terms as IQ and grade equivalent scores. (See C.5.c.)

E.3. Informed Consent

a. *Explanation to Clients.*

Prior to assessment, counselors explain the nature and purposes of assessment and the specific use of results in language the client (or other

legally authorized person on behalf of the client) can understand, unless an explicit exception to this right has been agreed upon in advance. Regardless of whether scoring and interpretation are completed by counselors, by assistants, or by computer or other outside services, counselors take reasonable steps to ensure that appropriate explanations are given to the client.

b. *Recipients of Results.*

The examinee's welfare, explicit understanding, and prior agreement determine the recipients of test results. Counselors include accurate and appropriate interpretations with any release of individual or group test results. (See B.1.a. and C.5.c.)

E.4. Release of Information to Competent Professionals

a. *Misuse of Results.*

Counselors do not misuse assessment results, including test results, and interpretations, and take reasonable steps to prevent the misuse of such by others. (See C.5.c.)

b. *Release of Raw Data.*

Counselors ordinarily release data (e.g. protocols, counseling or interview notes, or questionnaires) in which the client is identified only with the consent of the client or the client's legal representative. Such data are usually released only to persons recognized by counselors as competent to interpret the data. (See B.1.a.)

E.5. Proper Diagnosis of Mental Disorders

a. *Proper Diagnosis.*

Counselors take special care to provide proper diagnosis of mental disorders. Assessment techniques (including personal interview) used to determine client care (e.g., locus of treatment, type of treatment, or recommended follow-up) are carefully selected and appropriately used. (See A.3.a. and C.5.c.)

b. *Cultural Sensitivity.*

Counselors recognize that culture affects the manner in which clients' problems are defined. Clients' socioeconomic and cultural experience is considered when diagnosing mental disorders.

E.6. Test Selection

a. *Appropriateness of Instruments.*

Counselors carefully consider the validity, reliability, psychometric limitations, and appropriateness of instruments when selecting tests for use in a given situation or with a particular client.

b. *Culturally Diverse Populations.*
   Counselors are cautious when selecting tests for culturally diverse populations to avoid inappropriateness of testing that may be outside of socialized behavioral or cognitive patterns.

E.7. Conditions of Test Administration

a. *Administration Conditions.*
   Counselors administer tests under the same conditions that were established in their standardization. When tests are not administered under standard conditions or when unusual behavior or irregularities occur during the testing session, those conditions are noted in interpretation, and the results may be designated as invalid or of questionable validity.
b. *Computer Administration.*
   Counselors are responsible for ensuring that administration programs function properly to provide clients with accurate results when a computer or other electronic methods are used for test administration. (See A.12.b.)
c. *Unsupervised Test-Taking.*
   Counselors do not permit unsupervised or inadequately supervised use of tests or assessments unless the tests or assessments are designed, intended, and validated for self-administration and/or scoring.
d. *Disclosure of Favorable Conditions.*
   Prior to test administration, conditions that produce most favorable test results are made known to the examinee.

E.8. Diversity in Testing

Counselors are cautious in using assessment techniques, making evaluations, and interpreting the performance of populations not represented in the norm group on which an instrument was standardized. They recognize the effects of age, color, culture, disability ethnic group, gender, race, religion, sexual orientation, and socioeconomic status on test administration and interpretation and place test results in proper perspective with other relevant factors. (See A.2.a.)

E.9. Test Scoring and Interpretation

a. *Reporting Reservations.*
   In reporting assessment results, counselors indicate any reservations that exist regarding validity or reliability because of the circumstances of the assessment or the inappropriateness of the norms for the person tested.
b. *Research Instruments.*
   Counselors exercise caution when interpreting the results of research instruments possessing insufficient technical data to support respondent results. The specific purposes for the use of such instruments are stated explicitly to the examinee.

c. *Testing Services.*
Counselors who provide test scoring and test interpretation services to support the assessment process confirm the validity of such interpretations. They accurately describe the purpose, norms, validity, reliability, and applications of the procedures and any special qualifications applicable to their use. The public offering of an automated test interpretations service is considered a professional-to-professional consultation. The formal responsibility of the consultant is to the consultee, but the ultimate and overriding responsibility is to the client.

E.10. Test Security

Counselors maintain the integrity and security of tests and other assessment techniques consistent with legal and contractual obligations. Counselors do not appropriate, reproduce, or modify published tests or parts thereof without acknowledgment and permission from the publisher.

E.11. Obsolete Tests and Outdated Test Results

Counselors do not use data or test results that are obsolete or outdated for the current purpose. Counselors make every effort to prevent the misuse of obsolete measures and test data by others.

E.12. Test Construction

Counselors use established scientific procedures, relevant standards, and current professional knowledge for test design in the development, publication, and utilization of educational and psychological assessment techniques.

Section F: Teaching, Training, and Supervision

F.1. Counselor Educators and Trainers

a. *Educators as Teachers and Practitioners.*
Counselors who are responsible for developing, implementing, and supervising educational programs are skilled as teachers and practitioners. They are knowledgeable regarding the ethical, legal, and regulatory aspects of the profession, are skilled in applying that knowledge, and make students and supervisees aware of their responsibilities. Counselors conduct counselor education and training programs in an ethical manner and serve as role models for professional behavior. Counselor educators should make an effort to infuse material related to human diversity into all courses and/or workshops that are designed to promote the development of professional counselors.

b. *Relationship Boundaries with Students and Supervisees.*
Counselors clearly define and maintain ethical, professional, and social relationship boundaries with their students and supervisees. They are aware of the differential in power that exists and the student's or supervisee's possible incomprehension of that power differential. Counselors explain to students and supervisees the potential for the relationship to become exploitive.

c. *Sexual Relationships.*
Counselors do not engage in sexual relationships with students or supervisees and do not subject them to sexual harassment. (See A.6. and C.5.a.)

d. *Contributions to Research.*
Counselors give credit to students or supervisees for their contributions to research and scholarly projects. Credit is given through coauthorship, acknowledgment, footnote statement, or other appropriate means, in accordance with such contributions. (See G.4.b. and G.4.c.)

e. *Close Relatives.*
Counselors do not accept close relatives as students or supervisees.

f. *Supervision Preparation.*
Counselors who offer clinical supervision services are adequately prepared in supervision methods and techniques. Counselors who are doctoral students serving as practicum or internship supervisors to master's level students are adequately prepared and supervised by the training program.

g. *Responsibility for Services to Clients.*
Counselors who supervise the counseling services of others take reasonable measures to ensure that counseling services provided to clients are professional.

h. *Endorsement.*
Counselors do not endorse students or supervisees for certification, licensure, employment, or completion of an academic or training program if they believe students or supervisees are not qualified for the endorsement. Counselors take reasonable steps to assist students or supervisees who are not qualified for endorsement to become qualified.

F.2. Counselor Education and Training Programs

a. *Orientation.*
Prior to admission, counselors orient prospective students to the counselor education or training program's expectations, including but not limited to the following: 1) the type and level of skill acquisition required for successful completion of the training, 2) subject matter to be covered, 3) basis for evaluation. 4) training components that encourage self-growth or self-disclosure as part of the training process, 5) the type of supervision settings and requirements of the sites for required clinical

field experiences, 6) student and supervisee evaluation and dismissal policies and procedures, and 7) up-to-date employment prospects for graduates.

b. *Integration of Study and Practice.*
Counselors establish counselor education and training programs that integrate academic study and supervised practice.

c. *Evaluation.*
Counselors clearly state to students and supervisees, in advance of training, the levels of competency expected, appraisal methods, and timing of evaluations for both didactic and experiential components. Counselors provide students and supervisees with periodic performance appraisal and evaluation feedback throughout the training program.

d. *Teaching Ethics.*
Counselors make students and supervisees aware of the ethical responsibilities and standards of the profession and the students' and supervisees' ethical responsibilities to the profession. (See C.1. and F.3.e.)

e. *Peer Relationships.*
When students or supervisees are assigned to lead counseling groups or provide clinical supervision for their peers, counselors take steps to ensure that students and supervisees placed in these roles do not have personal or adverse relationships with peers and that they understand they have the same ethical obligations as counselor educators, trainers, and supervisors. Counselors make every effort to ensure that the rights of peers are not compromised when students or supervisees are assigned to lead counseling groups or provide clinical supervision.

f. *Varied Theoretical Positions.*
Counselors present varied theoretical positions so that students and supervisees may make comparisons and have opportunities to develop their own positions. Counselors provide information concerning the scientific bases of professional practice. (See C.6.a.)

g. *Field Placements.*
Counselors develop clear policies within their training program regarding field placement and other clinical experiences. Counselors provide clearly stated roles and responsibilities for the student or supervisee, the site supervisor, and the program supervisor. They confirm that site supervisors are qualified to provide supervision and are informed of their professional and ethical responsibilities in this role.

h. *Dual Relationships as Supervisors.*
Counselors avoid dual relationships such as performing the role of site supervisor and training program supervisor in the student's or supervisee's training program. Counselors do not accept any form of professional services, fees, commissions, reimbursement, or remuneration from a site for student or supervisee placement.

i. *Diversity in Programs.*
Counselors are responsive to their institution's and program's recruit-

ment and retention needs for training program administrators, faculty, and students with diverse backgrounds and special needs. (See A.2.a.)

F.3. Students and Supervisees

a. *Limitations.*

Counselors, through ongoing evaluation and appraisal, are aware of the academic and personal limitations of students and supervisees that might impede performance. Counselors assist students and supervisees in securing remedial assistance when needed, and dismiss from the training program supervisees who are unable to provide competent service due to academic or personal limitations. Counselors seek professional consultation and document their decision to dismiss or refer students or supervisees for assistance. Counselors assure that students and supervisees have recourse to address decisions made, to require them to seek assistance, or to dismiss them.

b. *Self-Growth Experiences.*

Counselors use professional judgment when designing training experiences conducted by the counselors themselves that require student and supervisee self-growth or self-disclosure. Safeguards are provided so that students and supervisees are aware of the ramifications their self-disclosure may have, on counselors whose primary role as teacher, trainer, or supervisor requires acting on ethical obligations to the profession. Evaluative components of experiential training experiences explicitly delineate predetermined academic standards that are separate and not dependent on the student's level of self-disclosure. (See A.6.)

c. *Counseling for Students and Supervisees.*

If students or supervisees request counseling, supervisors or counselor educators provide them with acceptable referrals. Supervisors or counselor educators do not serve as counselor to students or supervisees over whom they hold administrative, teaching, or evaluative roles unless this is a brief role associated with a training experience. (See A.6.b.)

d. *Clients of Students and Supervisees.*

Counselors make every effort to ensure that the clients at field placements are aware of the services rendered and the qualifications of the students and supervisees rendering those services. Clients receive professional disclosure information and are informed of the limits of confidentiality. Client permission is obtained in order for the students and supervisees to use any information concerning the counseling relationship in the training process. (See B.1.e.)

e. *Standards for Students and Supervisees*

Students and supervisees preparing to become counselors adhere to the Code of Ethics and the Standards of Practice. Students and supervisees have the same obligations to clients as those required of counselors. (See H.1.)

Section G: Research and Publication

G.1. Research Responsibilities.

a. *Use of Human Subjects.*
Counselors plan, design, conduct, and report research in a manner consistent with pertinent ethical principles, federal and state laws, host institutional regulations, and scientific standards governing research with human subjects. Counselors design and conduct research that reflects cultural sensitivity appropriateness.

b. *Deviation from Standard Practices.*
Counselors seek consultation and observe stringent safeguards to protect the rights of research participants when a research problem suggests a deviation from standard acceptable practices. (See B.6.)

c. *Precautions to Void Injury.*
Counselors who conduct research with human subjects are responsible for the subjects' welfare throughout the experiment and take reasonable precautions to avoid causing injurious psychological, physical, or social effects to their subjects.

d. *Principal Researcher Responsibility.*
The ultimate responsibility for ethical research practice lies with the principal researcher. All others involved in the research activities share ethical obligations and full responsibility for their own actions.

e. *Minimal Interference.*
Counselors take reasonable precautions to avoid causing disruptions in subjects' lives due to participation in research.

f. *Diversity.*
Counselors are sensitive to diversity and research issues with special populations. They seek consultation when appropriate. (See A.2.a. and B.6.)

G.2. Informed Consent

a. *Topics Disclosed.*
In obtaining informed consent for research, counselors use language that is understandable to research participants and that: 1) accurately explains the purpose and procedures to be followed; 2) identifies any procedures that are experimental or relatively untried; 3) describes the attendant discomforts and risks; 4) describes the benefits or changes in individuals or organizations that might be reasonably expected; 5) discloses appropriate alternative procedures that would be advantageous for subjects; 6) offers to answer any inquiries concerning the procedures; 7) describes any limitations on confidentiality; and 8) instructs that subjects are free to withdraw their consent and to discontinue participation in the project at any thee. (See B.1.f.)

. *Deception.*
Counselors do not conduct research involving deception unless alterna-

tive procedures are not feasible and the prospective value of the research justifies the deception. When the methodological requirements of a study necessitate concealment or deception, the investigator is required to explain clearly the reasons for this action as soon as possible.

c. *Voluntary Participation.*

Participation in research is typically voluntary and without any penalty for refusal to participate. Involuntary participation is appropriate only when it can be demonstrated that participation will have no harmful effects on subjects and is essential to the investigation.

d. *Confidentiality of Information.*

Information obtained about research participants during the course of an investigation is confidential. When the possibility exists that others may obtain access to such information, ethical research practice requires that the possibility, together with the plans for protecting confidentiality, be explained to participants as a part of the procedure for obtaining informed consent. (See B.1.e.)

e. *Persons Incapable of Giving Informed Consent.*

When a person is incapable of giving informed consent, counselors provide an appropriate explanation, obtain agreement for participation and obtain appropriate consent from a legally authorized person.

f. *Commitments to Participants.*

Counselors take reasonable measures to honor all commitments to research participants.

g. *Explanations After Data Collection.*

After data are collected, counselors provide participants with full clarification of the nature of the study to remove any misconceptions. Where scientific or human values justify delaying or withholding information, counselors take reasonable measures to avoid causing harm.

h. *Agreements to Cooperate.*

Counselors who agree to cooperate with another individual in research or publication incur an obligation to cooperate as promised in terms of punctuality of performance and with regard to the completeness and accuracy of the information required.

I. *Informed Consent for Sponsors.*

In the pursuit of research, counselors give sponsors, institutions, and publication channels the same respect and opportunity for giving informed consent that they accord to individual research participants. Counselors are aware of their obligation to future research workers and ensure that host institutions are given feedback information and proper acknowledgment.

G.3. Reporting Results

a. *Information Affecting Outcome.*

When reporting research results, counselors explicitly mention all variables and conditions known to the investigator that may have affected the outcome of a study or the interpretation of data.

b. *Accurate Results.*

Counselors plan, conduct, and report research accurately and in a manner that minimizes the possibility that results will be misleading. They provide thorough discussions of the limitations of their data and alternative hypotheses. Counselors do not engage in fraudulent research, distort data, misrepresent data, or deliberately bias their results.

c. *Obligation to Report Unfavorable Results.*

Counselors communicate to other counselors the results of any research judged to be of professional value. Results that reflect unfavorably on institutions, programs, services, prevailing opinions, or vested interests are not withheld.

d. *Identity of Subjects.*

Counselors who supply data, aid in the research of another person, report research results, or make original data available take due care to disguise the identity of respective subjects in the absence of specific authorization from the subjects to do otherwise. (See B.1.g. and B.5.a.)

e. *Replication Studies.*

Counselors are obligated to make available sufficient original research data to qualified professionals who may wish to replicate the study.

G.4. Publication

a. *Recognition of Others.*

When conducting and reporting research, counselors are familiar with and give recognition to previous work on the topic, observe copyright laws, and give full credit to those to whom credit is due. (See F.1.d. and G.4.c.)

b. *Contributors.*

Counselors give credit through joint authorship, acknowledgment, footnote statements, or other appropriate means to those who have contributed significantly to research or concept development in accordance with such contributions. The principal contributor is listed first and minor technical or professional contributions are acknowledged in notes or introductory statements.

c. *Student Research.*

For an article that is substantially based on a student's dissertation or thesis, the student is listed as the principal author. (See F.1.d. and G.4.a.)

d. *Duplicate Submission.*

Counselors submit manuscripts for consideration to only one journal at a time. Manuscripts that are published in whole or in substantial part in another journal or published work are not submitted for publication without acknowledgment and permission from the previous publication.

e. *Professional Review.*

Counselors who review material submitted for publication, research, or other scholarly purposes respect the confidentiality and proprietary rights of those who submitted it.

Section H: Resolving Ethical Issues

H.1. Knowledge of Standards

Counselors are familiar with the Code of Ethics and the Standards of Practice and other applicable ethics codes from other professional organizations of which they are member, or from certification and licensure bodies. Lack of knowledge or misunderstanding of an ethical responsibility is not a defense against a charge of unethical conduct. (See F.3.e.)

H.2. Suspected Violations

a. *Ethical Behavior Expected.*
   Counselors expect professional associates to adhere to Code of Ethics. When counselors possess reasonable cause that raises doubts as to whether a counselor is acting in an ethical manner, they take appropriate action. (See H.2.d. and H.2.e.)
b. *Consultation.*
   When uncertain as to whether a particular situation or course of action may be in violation of Code of Ethics, counselors consult with other counselors who are knowledgeable about ethics, with colleagues, or with appropriate authorities.
c. *Organization Conflicts.*
   If the demands of an organization with which counselors are affiliated pose a conflict with Code of Ethics, counselors specify the nature of such conflicts and express to their supervisors or other responsible officials their commitment to Code of Ethics. When possible, counselors work toward change within the organization to allow full adherence to Code of Ethics.
d. *Informal Resolution.*
   When counselors have reasonable cause to believe that another counselor is violating an ethical standard, they attempt to first resolve the issue informally with the other counselor if feasible, providing that such action does not violate confidentiality rights that may be involved.
c. *Reporting Suspected Violations.*
   When an informal resolution is not appropriate or feasible, counselors, upon reasonable cause, take action such as reporting the suspected ethical violation to state or national ethics committees, unless this action conflicts with confidentiality rights that cannot be resolved.
f. *Unwarranted Complaints.*
   Counselors do not initiate, participate in, or encourage the filing of ethics complaints that are unwarranted or intend to harm a counselor rather than to protect clients or the public.

H.3. Cooperation With Ethics Committees.

Counselors assist in the process of enforcing Code of Ethics. Counselors cooperate with investigations, proceedings, and requirements of the ACA

Ethics Committee or ethics committees of other duly constituted associations or boards having jurisdiction over those charged with a violation. Counselors are familiar with the ACA Policies and Procedures and use it as a reference in assisting the enforcement of the Code of Ethics.

☐ Standards of Practice

All members of the American Counseling Association (ACA) are required to adhere to the Standards of Practice and the Code of Ethics. The Standards of Practice represent minimal behavioral statements of the Code of Ethics. Members should refer to the applicable section of the Code of Ethics for further interpretation and amplification of the applicable Standard of Practice.

Section A: The Counseling Relationship

Standard of Practice One (SP-1)
Nondiscrimination

Counselors respect diversity and must not discriminate against clients because of age, color, culture, disability, ethnic group, gender, race, religion, sexual orientation, marital status, or socioeconomic status. (See A.2.a)

Standard of Practice Two (SP-2)
Disclosure to Clients

Counselors must adequately inform clients, preferably in writing, regarding the counseling process and counseling relationship at or before the time it begins and throughout the relationship. (See A.3.a.)

Standard of Practice Three (SP-3)
Dual Relationships

Counselors must make every effort to avoid, dual relationships with clients that could impair their professional judgment or increase the risk of harm to clients. When a dual relationship cannot be avoided, counselors must take appropriate steps to ensure that judgment is not impaired and that no exploitation occurs. (See A.6.a. and A.6.b.)

Standard of Practice Four (SP-4)
Sexual Intimacies with Clients

Counselors must not engage in any type of sexual intimacies with current clients and must not engage in sexual intimacies with former clients within a minimum of two years after terminating the counseling relationship. Counselors who engage in such relationship after two years following termination have the responsibility to thoroughly examine and document that such relations did not have an exploitative nature.

Standard of Practice Five (SP-5)
Protecting Clients During Group Work

Counselors must take steps to protect clients from physical or psychological trauma resulting from interactions during group work. (See A.9.b.)

Standard of Practice Six (SP-6)
Advance Understanding of Fees

Counselors must explain to clients, prior to their entering the counseling relationship, financial arrangements related to professional services. (See A.10.a-d. and A.11.c.)

Standard of Practice Seven (SP-7) Termination

Counselors must assist in making appropriate arrangements for the continuation of treatment of clients, when necessary, following termination of counseling relationships. (See A.11.a.)

Standard of Practice Eight (SP-8)
Inability to Assist Clients

Counselors must avoid entering or immediately terminate a counseling relationship if it is determined that they are unable to be of professional assistance to a client. The counselor may assist in making an appropriate referral for the client. (See A.11.b.)

Section B: Confidentiality

Standard of Practice Nine (SP-9)
Confidentiality Requirements

Counselors must keep information related to counseling services confidential unless disclosure is in the best interest of clients, is required for the welfare of others, or is required by law. When disclosure is required, only information that is essential is revealed and the client is informed of such disclosure. (See B.1.a.-f.)

Standard of Practice Ten (SP-10)
Confidentiality Requirements for Subordinates

Counselors must take measures to ensure that privacy and confidentiality of clients are maintained by subordinates. (See B.1.h.)

Standard of Practice Eleven (SP-11)
Confidentiality in Group Work

Counselors must clearly communicate to group members that confidentiality cannot be guaranteed in group work. (See B.2.a.)

Standard of Practice Twelve (SP-12)
Confidentiality in Family Counseling

Counselors must not disclose information about one family member in counseling to another family member without prior consent. (See B.2.b.)

Standard of Practice Thirteen (SP-13)
Confidentiality of Records

Counselors must maintain appropriate confidentiality in creating, storing, accessing, transferring, and disposing of counseling records. (See B.4.b.)

Standard of Practice Fourteen (SP-14)
Permission to Record or Observe

Counselors must obtain prior consent from clients in order to electronically record or observe sessions. (See B.4.c.)

Standard of Practice Fifteen (SP-15)
Disclosure or Transfer of Records

Counselors must obtain client consent to disclose or transfer records to third parties, unless exceptions listed in SP-9 exist. (See B.4.e.)

Standard of Practice Sixteen (SP-16)
Data Disguise Required

Counselors must disguise the identity of the client when using data for training, research, or publication. (See B.5.a.)

Section C: Professional Responsibility

Standard of Practice Seventeen (SP-17)
Boundaries of Competence

Counselors must practice only within the boundaries of their competence. (See C.2.a)

Standard of Practice Eighteen (SP-18)
Continuing Education

Counselors must engage in continuing education to maintain their professional competence. (See C.2.f.)

Standard of Practice Nineteen (SP-19)
Impairment of Professionals

Counselors must refrain from offering professional services when their personal problems or conflicts may cause harm to a client or others. (See C.2.g.)

Standard of Practice Twenty (SP-20)
Accurate Advertising

Counselors must accurately represent their credentials and services when advertising. (See C.3.a.)

Standard of Practice Twenty-One (SP-21)
Recruiting Through Employment

Counselors must not use their place of employment or institutional affiliation to recruit clients for their private practice. (See C.3.d.)

Standard of Practice Twenty-Two (SP-22)
Credentials Claimed

Counselors must claim or imply only professional credentials possessed and must correct any known misrepresentations of their credentials by others. (See C.4.a.)

Standard of Practice Twenty-three (SP-23)
Sexual Harassment

Counselors must not engage in sexual harassment. (See C.5.b.)

Standard of Practice Twenty-four (SP-24)
Unjustified Gains

Counselors must not use their professional positions to seek or receive unjustified personal gains, sexual favors, unfair advantage, or unearned goods or services. (See C.5.e.)

Standard of Practice Twenty-five (SP-25)
Clients Served by Others

With the consent of the client, counselors must inform other mental health professionals serving the same client that a counseling relationship between the counselor and client exists. (See C.6.c.)

Standard of Practice Twenty-six (SP-26)
Negative Employment Conditions

Counselors must alert their employers to institutional policy or conditions that may be potentially disruptive or damaging to the counselor's professional responsibilities, or that may limit their effectiveness or deny clients' rights. (See D.1.C.)

Standard of Practice Twenty-seven (SP-27)
Personnel Selection and Assignment

Counselors must select competent staff and must assign responsibilities compatible with staff skills and experiences. (See D.1.h.)

Standard of Practice Twenty-Eight (SP-28)
Exploitive Relationships with Subordinates

Counselors must not engage in exploitive relationships with individuals over whom they have supervisory, evaluative, or instructional control or authority. (See D.1.k.)

Section D: Relationship With Other Professionals

Standard of Practice Twenty-Nine (SP-29)
Accepting Fees from Agency Clients

Counselors must not accept fees or other remuneration for consultation with persons entitled to such services through the counselor's employing agency or institution. (See D.3.a.)

Standard of Practice Thirty (SP-30)
Referral Fees

Counselors must not accept referral fees. (See D.3 b.)

Section E: Evaluation, Assessment, and Interpretation

Standard of Practice Thirty-one (SP-31)
Limits of Competence

Counselors must perform only testing and assessment services for which they are competent. Counselors must not allow the use of psychological assessment techniques by unqualified persons under their supervision. (See E.2.a.)

Standard of Practice Thirty-Two (SP-32)
Appropriate Use of Assessment Instruments

Counselors must use assessment instruments in the manner for which they were intended. (See E.2.b.)

Standard of Practice Thirty-three (SP-33)
Assessment Explanations to Clients

Counselors must provide explanations to clients prior to assessment about the nature and purposes of assessment and the specific uses of results. (See E.3.a.)

Standard of Practice Thirty-four (SP-34)
Recipients of Test Results

Counselors must ensure that accurate and appropriate interpretations accompany any release of testing and assessment information. (See E.3.b.)

Standard of Practice Thirty-five (SP-35)
Obsolete Tests and Outdated Test Results

Counselors must not base their assessment or intervention decisions or recommendations on data or test results that are obsolete or outdated for the current purpose. (See E.11.)

Section F: Teaching, Training, and Supervision

Standard of Practice Thirty-six (SP-36)
Sexual Relationships with Students or Supervisees

Counselors must not engage in sexual relationships with their students and supervisees. (See F.1.c.)

Standard of Practice Thirty-seven (SP-37)
Credit for Contributions to Research

Counselors must give credit to students or supervisees for their contributions to research and scholarly projects. (See F.1.d.)

Standard of Practice Thirty-eight (SP-38)
Supervision Preparation

Counselors who offer clinical supervision services must be trained and prepared in supervision methods and techniques. (See F.1.f.)

Standard of Practice Thirty-nine (SP-39)
Evaluation Information

Counselors must clearly state to students and supervisees in advance of training, the levels of competency expected, appraisal methods, and timing of evaluations. Counselors must provide students and supervisees with periodic performance appraisal and evaluation feedback throughout the training program. (See F.2.c.)

Standard of Practice Forty (SP-40)
Peer Relationships in Training

Counselors must make every effort to ensure that the rights of peers are not violated when students and supervisees are assigned to lead counseling groups or provide clinical supervision. (See E.2.e.)

Standard of Practice Forty-one (SP-41)
Limitations of Students and Supervisees

Counselors must assist students and supervisees in securing remedial assistance, when needed, and must dismiss from the training program students and supervisees who are unable to provide competent service due to academic or personal limitations. (See F.3.a.)

Standard of Practice Forty-two (SP-42)
Self-Growth Experiences

Counselors who conduct experiences for students or supervisees that include self-growth or self disclosure must inform participants of counselors' ethical obligations to the profession and must not grade participants based on their nonacademic performance. (See F.3.b.)

Standard of Practice Forty-three (SP-43)
Standards for Students and Supervisees

Students and supervisees preparing to become counselors must adhere to the Code of Ethics and the Standards of Practice of counselors. (See F.3.e.)

Section G: Research and Publication

Standard of Practice Forty-four (SP-44)
Precautions to Avoid Injury in Research

Counselors must avoid causing physical, social, or psychological harm or injury to subjects in research. (See G.1.c.)

Standard of Practice Forty-five (SP-45)
Confidentiality of Research Information

Counselors must keep confidential information obtained about research participants. (See G.2.d.)

Standard of Practice Forty-six (SP-46)
Information Affecting Research Outcome

Counselors must report all variables and conditions known to the investigator that may have affected research data or outcomes. (See G.3.a.)

Standard of Practice Forty-seven (SP-47)
Accurate Research Results

Counselors must not distort or misrepresent research data, nor fabricate or intentionally bias research results. (See G.3.b.)

Standard of Practice Forty-eight (SP-48)
Publication Contributors

Counselors must give appropriate credit to those who have contributed to research (See G.4.a. and G.4.h.)

Section H: Resolving Ethical Issues

Standard of Practice Forty-nine (SP-49)
Ethical Behavior Expected

Counselors must take appropriate action when they possess reasonable cause that raises doubts as to whether counselors or other mental health professionals are acting in an ethical manner. (See H.2.a.)

Standard of Practice Fifty (SP-50)
Unwarranted Complaints

Counselors must not initiate, participate in, or encourage the filing of ethics complaints that are unwarranted or intended to harm a mental health professional rather than to protect clients or the public. (See H.2.f.)

Standard of Practice Fifty-one (SP-51)
Cooperation with Ethics Committees

Counselors must cooperate with investigations, proceedings, and requirements of the ACA Ethics Committee or ethics committees of other duly constituted associations or boards having jurisdiction over those charged with a violation. (See H.3.)

References

The following documents are available to counselors as resources to guide them in their practices. These resources are not a part of the Code of Ethics and the Standards of Practice.

American Association for Counseling and Development/Association for Measurement and Evaluation in Counseling and Development. (1989). The responsibilities of users of standardized tests (revised). Washington, DC: Author.

American Counseling Association. (1988). American Counseling Association Ethical Standards Alexandria, VA: Author.

American Psychological Association. (1985). Standards for educational and psychological testing (revised). Washington, DC: Author.

American Rehabilitation Counseling Association, Commission on Rehabilitation Counselor Certification, and National Rehabilitation Counseling Association. (1995). Code of professional ethics for rehabilitation counselors. Chicago, IL: Author.

American School Counselor Association. (1992). Ethical standards for school counselors. Alexandria, VA: Author.

Joint Committee on Testing Practices. (1988). Code of fair testing practices in education. Washington, DC: Author.

National Board for Certified Counselors. (1989). National Board for Certified Counselors Code of Ethics. Alexandria, VA: Author.

Prediger, D. J. (Ed.). (1993, March). Multicultural assessment standards. Alexandria, VA: Association for Assessment in Counseling.

APPENDIX C: Association for Specialists in Group Work Best Practice Guidelines

Approved by the Executive Board March 29, 1998
Prepared by Lynn Rapin and Linda Keel,
ASGW Ethics Committee Co-Chairs

The Association for Specialists in Group Work (ASGW) is a division of the American Counseling Association whose members are interested in and specialize in group work. We value the creation of community; service to our members, clients, and the profession; and value leadership as a process to facilitate the growth and development of individuals and groups.

The Association for Specialists in Group Work recognizes the commitment of its members to the Code of Ethics and Standards of Practice (as revised in 1995) of its parent organization, the American Counseling Association, and nothing in this document shall be construed to supplant that code. These Best Practice Guidelines are intended to clarify the application of the ACA Code of Ethics and Standards of Practice to the field of group work by defining Group Workers' responsibility and scope of practice involving those activities, strategies and interventions that are consistent and current with effective and appropriate professional ethical and community standards. ASGW views ethical process as being integral to group work and views Group Workers as ethical agents. Group Workers, by their very nature in being responsible and responsive to their group members, necessarily embrace certain potential for ethical vulnerability. It is incumbent upon Group Workers to give considerable attention to the intent and context of their actions because the attempts of Group Workers to influence human behavior through group work always have ethical implications. These Best Practice Guideline address Group Workers' responsibilities in planning, performing and processing groups.

☐ Section A: Best Practice in Planning

A.1. Professional Context and Regulatory Requirements

Group Workers actively know, understand and apply the ACA Code of Ethics and Standards of Best Practice, the ASGW Professional Standards for the Training of Group Workers, these ASGW Best Practice Guidelines, the ASGW diversity competencies, the ACA Multicultural Guidelines, relevant state laws, accreditation requirements, relevant National Board for Certified Counselors Codes and Standards, their organization's standards, and insurance requirements impacting the practice of group work.

A.2. Scope of Practice and Conceptual Framework

Group Workers define the scope of practice related to the core and specialization competencies defined in the ASGW Training Standards. Group Workers are aware of personal strengths and weaknesses in leading groups. Group Workers develop and are able to articulate a general conceptual framework to guide practice and a rationale for use of techniques that are to be used. Group Workers limit their practice to those areas for which they meet the training criteria established by the ASGW Training Standards.

A.3. Assessment

a. *Assessment of self.* Group Workers actively assess their knowledge and skills related to the specific group(s) offered. Group Workers assess their values, beliefs and theoretical orientation and how these impact upon the group, particularly when working with a diverse and multicultural population.
b. *Ecological assessment.* Group Workers assess community needs, agency or organization resources, sponsoring organization mission, staff competency, attitudes regarding group work, professional training levels of potential group leaders regarding group work; client attitudes regarding group work, and multicultural and diversity considerations. Group Workers use this information as the basis for making decisions related to their group practice, or to the implementation of groups for which they have supervisory, evaluation, or oversight responsibilities.

A.4. Program Development and Evaluation

a. *Group Workers identify the type(s) of group(s) to be offered and how they relate to community needs.*

b. *Group Workers concisely state in writing the purpose and goals of the group.* Group Workers also identify the role of the group members in influencing or determining the group goals.

c. *Group Workers set fees consistent with the organization's fee schedule, taking into consideration the financial status and locality of prospective group members.*

d. *Group Workers choose techniques and a leadership style appropriate to the type(s) of group(s) being offered.*

e. *Group Workers have an evaluation plan consistent with regulatory, organization and insurance requirements where appropriate.*

f. *Group Workers take into consideration current professional guidelines when using technology, including but not limited to Internet communication.*

A.5. Resources

Group Workers coordinate resources related to the kind of group(s) and group activities to be provided, such as: adequate funding; the appropriateness and availability of a trained co-leader; space and privacy requirements for the type(s) of group(s) being offered; marketing and recruiting; and appropriate collaboration with other community agencies and organizations.

A.6. Professional Disclosure Statement

Group Workers have a professional disclosure statement which includes information on confidentiality and exceptions to confidentiality, theoretical orientation, information on the nature, purpose(s) and goals of the group, the group services that can be provided, the role and responsibility of group members and leaders, Group Workers' qualifications to conduct the specific group(s), specific licenses, certifications and professional affiliations, and address of licensing/credentialing body.

A.7. Group and Member Preparation

a. *Group Workers screen prospective group members if appropriate to the type of group being offered.* When selection of group members is appropriate, Group Workers identify group members whose needs and goals are compatible with the goals of the group.

b. *Group Workers facilitate informed consent.* Group Workers provide in oral and written form to prospective members (when appropriate to group type): the professional disclosure statement; group purpose and goals; group participation expectations including voluntary and involuntary membership; role expectations of members and leader(s); policies related to entering and exiting the group; policies governing substance use; policies and procedures governing mandated groups (where relevant); documentation requirements; disclosure of information to others; implications of out-of-group contact or involvement among members; procedures for consultation between group leader(s) and group member(s); fees and time parameters; and potential impacts of group participation.

c. *Group Workers obtain the appropriate consent forms for work with minors and other dependent group members.*

d. *Group Workers define confidentiality and its limits (for example, legal and ethical exceptions and expectations; waivers implicit with treatment plans, documentation and insurance usage).* Group Workers have the responsibility to inform all group participants of the need for confidentiality, potential consequences of breaching confidentiality and that legal privilege does not apply to group discussions (unless provided by state statute).

A.8. Professional Development

Group Workers recognize that professional growth is a continuous, ongoing, developmental process throughout their career.

a. *Group Workers remain current and increase knowledge and skill competencies through activities such as continuing education, professional supervision, and participation in personal and professional development activities.*

b. *Group Workers seek consultation and/or supervision regarding ethics concerns that interfere with effective functioning as a group leader.* Supervisors have the responsibility to keep abreast of consultation, group theory, process, and adhere to related ethics guidelines.

c. *Group Workers seek appropriate professional assistance for their own personal problems or conflicts that are likely to impair their professional judgement or work performance.*

d. *Group Workers seek consultation and supervision to ensure appropriate practice whenever working with a group for which all knowledge and skill competencies have not been achieved.*

e. *Group Workers keep abreast of group research and development.*

A.9. Trends and Technological Change

Group Workers are aware of and responsive to technological changes as they affect society and the profession. These include but are not limited to changes in mental health delivery systems; legislative and insurance industry reforms; shifting population demographics and client needs; and technological advances in Internet and other communication and delivery systems. Group Workers adhere to ethical guidelines related to the use of developing technologies.

☐ **Section B: Best Practice in Performing**

B.1. Self Knowledge

Group Workers are aware of and monitor their strengths and weaknesses and the effects these have on group members.

B.2. Group Competencies

Group Workers have a basic knowledge of groups and the principles of group dynamics, and are able to perform the core group competencies, as described in the ASGW Professional Standards for the Training of Group Workers. Additionally, Group Workers have adequate understanding and skill in any group specialty area chosen for practice (psychotherapy, counseling, task, psychoeducation, as described in the ASGW Training Standards).

B.3. Group Plan Adaptation

a. *Group Workers apply and modify knowledge, skills and techniques appropriate to group type and stage, and to the unique needs of various cultural and ethnic groups.*
b. *Group Workers monitor the group's progress toward the group goals and plan.*
c. *Group Workers clearly define and maintain ethical, professional, and social relationship boundaries with group members as appropriate to their role in the organization and the type of group being offered.*

B.4. Therapeutic Conditions and Dynamics

Group Workers understand and are able to implement appropriate models of group development, process observation and therapeutic conditions.

B.5. Meaning

Group Workers assist members in generating meaning from the group experience.

B.6. Collaboration

Group Workers assist members in developing individual goals and respect group members as co-equal partners in the group experience.

B.7. Evaluation

Group Workers include evaluation (both formal and informal) between sessions and at the conclusion of the group.

B.8. Diversity

Group Workers practice with broad sensitivity to client differences including but not limited to ethnic, gender, religious, sexual, psychological maturity, economic class, family history, physical characteristics or limitations and geographic location. Group Workers continuously seek information regarding the cultural issues of the diverse population with whom they are working both by interaction with participants and from using outside resources.

B.9. Ethical Surveillance

Group Workers employ an appropriate ethical decision making model in responding to ethical challenges and issues and in determining courses of action and behavior for self and group members. In addition, Group Workers employ applicable standards as promulgated by ACA, ASGW, or other appropriate professional organizations.

☐ Section C: Best Practice in Group Processing

C.1. Processing Schedule

Group Workers process the workings of the group with themselves, group members, supervisors or other colleagues, as appropriate. This may include assessing progress on group and member goals, leader behaviors and techniques, group dynamics and interventions; developing understanding and acceptance of meaning. Processing may occur both within sessions and before and after each session, at time of termination, and later follow up, as appropriate.

C.2. Reflective Practice

Group Workers attend to opportunities to synthesize theory and practice and to incorporate learning outcomes into ongoing groups. Group Workers attend to session dynamics of members and their interactions and also attend to the relationship between session dynamics and leader values, cognition and affect.

C.3. Evaluation and Follow-Up

a. *Group Workers evaluate process and outcomes.* Results are used for ongoing program planning, improvement and revisions of current group and/or to contribute to professional research literature. Group Workers follow all applicable policies and standards in using group material for research and reports.
b. *Group Workers conduct follow-up contact with group members, as appropriate, to assess outcomes or when requested by a group member(s).*

C.4. Consultation and Training with Other Organizations

Group Workers provide consultation and training to organizations in and out of their setting, when appropriate. Group Workers seek out consultation as needed with competent professional persons knowledgeable about group work.

Please direct comments to Lynn Rapin at rapinls@email.uc.edu and/or Linda Keel at LP-Keel@neiu.edu

APPENDIX D: Association for Specialists in Group Work Principles for Diversity-Competent Group Workers

Approved by the Executive Board August 1, 1998
Prepared by Dr. Lynn Haley-Bañez, Dr. Sherlon Brown, and Dr. Bogusia Molina
Consultants: Dr. Michael D'Andrea, Dr. Patricia Arrendondo, Dr. Niloufer Merchant, and Sandra Wathen

☐ Preamble

The Association for Specialists in Group Work (ASGW) is committed to understanding how issues of diversity affect all aspects of group work. This includes but is not limited to: training diversity-competent group workers; conducting research that will add to the literature on group work with diverse populations; understanding how diversity affects group process and dynamics; and assisting group facilitators in various settings to increase their awareness, knowledge, and skills as they relate to facilitating groups with diverse memberships.

As an organization, ASGW has endorsed this document with the recognition that issues of diversity affect group process and dynamics, group facilitation, training, and research. As an organization, we recognize that racism, classism, sexism, heterosexism, ableism, and so forth, affect everyone. As individual members of this organization, it is our personal responsibility to address these issues through awareness, knowledge, and skills. As members of ASGW, we need to increase our awareness of our own biases, values, and beliefs and how they impact the groups we run. We need to increase our awareness of our group members' biases, values, and beliefs and how they also impact and influence group process and dynamics. Finally, we need to increase our knowledge in facilitating, with confidence, competence, and integrity, groups that are diverse on many dimensions.

☐ Definitions

For the purposes of this document, it is important that the language used is understood. Terms such as "dominant," "nondominant," and "target" persons and/or populations are used to define a person or groups of persons who historically, in the United States, do not have equal access to power, money, certain privileges (such as access to mental health services because of financial constraints, or the legal right to marry, in the case of a gay or lesbian couple), and/or the ability to influence or initiate social policy because of unequal representation in government and politics. These terms are not used to denote a lack of numbers in terms of representation in the overall U.S. population. Nor are these terms used to continue to perpetuate the very biases and forms of oppression, both overt and covert, that this document attempts to address.

For the purposes of this document, the term "disabilities" refers to differences in physical, mental, emotional, and learning abilities and styles among people. It is not meant as a term to define a person, such as a learning disabled person, but rather in the context of a person with a learning disability.

Given the history and current cultural, social, and political context in which this document is written, the authors of this document are limited to the language of this era. With this in mind, we have attempted to construct a "living document" that can and will change as the sociopolitical and cultural context changes.

☐ The Principles

I. Awareness of Self

A. Attitudes and Beliefs

1. Diversity-competent group workers demonstrate movement from being unaware to being increasingly aware and sensitive to their own race, ethnic and cultural heritage, gender, socioeconomic status (SES), sexual orientation, abilities, and religion and spiritual beliefs, and to valuing and respecting differences.
2. Diversity-competent group workers demonstrate increased awareness of how their own race, ethnicity, culture, gender, SES, sexual orientation, abilities, and religion and spiritual beliefs are impacted by their own experiences and histories, which in turn influence group process and dynamics.
3. Diversity-competent group workers can recognize the limits of their competencies and expertise with regard to working with group members who are different from them in terms of race, ethnicity, culture (including language), SES, gender, sexual orientation, abilities, religion, and

spirituality and their beliefs, values, and biases. (For further clarification on limitations, expertise, and type of group work, refer to the training standards and best practice guidelines, Association for Specialists in Group Work, 1998; and the ethical guidelines, American Counseling Association, 1995.)

4. Diversity-competent group workers demonstrate comfort, tolerance, and sensitivity with differences that exist between themselves and group members in terms of race, ethnicity, culture, SES, gender, sexual orientation, abilities, religion, and spirituality and their beliefs, values, and biases.

B. Knowledge

1. Diversity-competent group workers can identify specific knowledge about their own race, ethnicity, SES, gender, sexual orientation, abilities, religion, and spirituality, and how they personally and professionally affect their definitions of "normality" and the group process.

2. Diversity-skilled group workers demonstrate knowledge and understanding regarding how oppression in any form—such as, racism, classism, sexism, heterosexism, ableism, discrimination, and stereotyping—affects them personally and professionally.

3. Diversity-skilled group workers demonstrate knowledge about their social impact on others. They are knowledgeable about communication style differences, how their style may inhibit or foster the group process with members who are different from themselves along the different dimensions of diversity, and how to anticipate the impact they may have on others.

C. Skills

1. Diversity-competent group workers seek out educational, consultative, and training experiences to improve their understanding and effectiveness in working with group members who self-identify as Indigenous Peoples, African Americans, Asian Americans, Hispanics, Latinos/Latinas, gays, lesbians, bisexuals, or transgendered persons and persons with physical, mental/emotional, and/or learning disabilities, particularly with regard to race and ethnicity. Within this context, group workers are able to recognize the limits of their competencies and: a) seek consultation, b) seek further training or education, c) refer members to more qualified group workers, or d) engage in a combination of these.

2. Group workers who exhibit diversity competence are constantly seeking to understand themselves within their multiple identities (apparent and unapparent differences), for example, gay, Latina, Christian, working-class, and female, and are constantly and actively striving to unlearn the various behaviors and processes they covertly and overtly communicate that perpetuate oppression, particularly racism.

II. Group Worker's Awareness of Group Member's Worldview

A. Attitudes and Beliefs

1. Diversity-skilled group workers exhibit awareness of any possible negative emotional reactions toward Indigenous Peoples, African Americans, Asian Americans, Hispanics, Latinos/Latinas, gays, lesbians, bisexuals, or transgendered persons and persons with physical, mental/emotional, and/or learning disabilities that they may hold. They are willing to contrast in a nonjudgmental manner their own beliefs and attitudes with those of Indigenous Peoples, African Americans, Asian Americans, Hispanics, Latinos/Latinas, gays, lesbians, bisexuals, or transgendered persons and persons with physical, mental/emotional, and/or learning disabilities who are group members.

2. Diversity-competent group workers demonstrate awareness of their stereotypes and preconceived notions that they may hold toward Indigenous Peoples, African Americans, Asian Americans, Hispanics, Latinos/Latinas, gays, lesbians, bisexuals, or transgendered persons and persons with physical, mental/emotional, and/or learning disabilities.

B. Knowledge

1. Diversity-skilled group workers possess specific knowledge and information about Indigenous Peoples, African Americans, Asian Americans, Hispanics, Latinos/Latinas, gays, lesbians, bisexuals, and transgendered people and group members who have mental/emotional, physical, and/or learning disabilities with whom they are working. They are aware of the life experiences, cultural heritage, and sociopolitical background of Indigenous Peoples, African Americans, Asian Americans, Hispanics, Latinos/Latinas, gays, lesbians, bisexuals, or transgendered persons and group members with physical, mental/emotional, and/or learning disabilities. This particular knowledge-based competency is strongly linked to the various racial/minority and sexual identity development models available in the literature (Atkinson, Morten, & Sue, 1993; Cass, 1979; Cross, 1995; D'Augelli & Patterson, 1995; Helms, 1992).

2. Diversity-competent group workers exhibit an understanding of how race, ethnicity, culture, gender, sexual identity, different abilities, SES, and other immutable personal characteristics may affect personality formation, vocational choices, manifestation of psychological disorders, physical "dis-ease" or somatic symptoms, help-seeking behavior(s), and the appropriateness or inappropriateness of the various types of and theoretical approaches to group work.

3. Group workers who demonstrate competency in diversity in groups understand and have the knowledge about sociopolitical influences that

impinge upon the lives of Indigenous Peoples, African Americans, Asian Americans, Hispanics, Latinos/Latinas, gays, lesbians, bisexuals, or transgendered persons and persons with physical, mental/emotional, and/or learning disabilities. Immigration issues, poverty, racism, oppression, stereotyping, and/or powerlessness adversely impacts many of these individuals and therefore impacts group process or dynamics.

C. Skills

1. Diversity-skilled group workers familiarize themselves with relevant research and the latest findings regarding mental health issues of Indigenous Peoples, African Americans, Asian Americans, Hispanics, Latinos/Latinas, gays, lesbians, bisexuals, or transgendered persons and persons with physical, mental/emotional, and/or learning disabilities. They actively seek out educational experiences that foster their knowledge and understanding of skills for facilitating groups across differences.
2. Diversity-competent group workers become actively involved with Indigenous Peoples, African Americans, Asian Americans, Hispanics, Latinos/Latinas, gays, lesbians, bisexuals, or transgendered persons and persons with physical, mental/emotional, and/or learning disabilities outside of their group work/counseling setting (community events, social and political functions, celebrations, friendships, neighborhood groups, etc.) so that their perspective of minorities is more than academic or experienced through a third partner.

II. Diversity-Appropriate Intervention Strategies

A. Attitudes and Beliefs

1. Diversity-competent group workers respect clients' religious and/or spiritual beliefs and values, because they affect worldview, psychosocial functioning, and expressions of distress.
2. Diversity-competent group workers respect indigenous helping practices and respect Indigenous Peoples, African Americans, Asian Americans, Hispanics, Latinos/Latinas, gays, lesbians, bisexuals, or transgendered persons and persons with physical, mental/emotional, and/or learning disabilities and can identify and utilize community intrinsic help-giving networks.
3. Diversity-competent group workers value bilingualism and sign language and do not view another language as an impediment to group work.

B. Knowledge

1. Diversity-competent group workers demonstrate a clear and explicit knowledge and understanding of generic characteristics of group work and theory

and how they may clash with the beliefs, values, and traditions of Indigenous Peoples, African Americans, Asian Americans, Hispanics Latinos/Latinas, gays, lesbians, bisexuals, or transgendered persons and persons with physical, mental/emotional, and/or learning disabilities.

2. Diversity-competent group workers exhibit an awareness of institutional barriers that prevent Indigenous Peoples, African Americans, Asian Americans, Hispanics, Latinos/Latinas, gays, lesbians, bisexuals, or transgendered members and members with physical, mental/emotional, and/or learning disabilities from actively participating in or using various types of groups, that is, task groups, psychoeducational groups, counseling groups, and psychotherapy groups or the settings in which the services are offered.

3. Diversity-competent group workers demonstrate knowledge of the potential bias in assessment instruments and use procedures and interpret findings, or actively participate in various types of evaluations of group outcome or success, keeping in mind the linguistic, cultural, and other self-identified characteristics of the group member.

4. Diversity-competent group workers exhibit knowledge of the family structures, hierarchies, values, and beliefs of Indigenous Peoples, African Americans, Asian Americans, Hispanics, Latinos/Latinas, gays, lesbians, bisexuals, or transgendered persons and persons with physical, mental/emotional, and/or learning disabilities. They are knowledgeable about the community characteristics and the resources in the community as well as about the family.

5. Diversity-competent group workers demonstrate an awareness of relevant discriminatory practices at the social and community level that may be affecting the psychological welfare of persons and access to services of the population being served.

C. Skills

1. Diversity-competent group workers are able to engage in a variety of verbal and nonverbal group-facilitating functions, dependent upon the type of group (task, counseling, psychoeducational, psychotherapy), and the multiple, self-identified status of various group members (such as Indigenous Peoples, African Americans, Asian Americans, Hispanics, Latinos/Latinas, gays, lesbians, bisexuals, or transgendered persons and persons with physical, mental/emotional, and/or learning disabilities). They demonstrate the ability to send and receive both verbal and nonverbal messages accurately, appropriately, and across/between the differences represented in the group. They are not tied down to one method or approach to group facilitation and recognize that helping styles and approaches may be culture-bound. When they sense that their group facilitation style is limited and potentially inappropriate, they can anticipate and ameliorate its negative impact by drawing upon other culturally relevant skill sets.

2. Diversity-competent group workers have the ability to exercise institutional intervention skills on behalf of their group members. They can help a member determine whether a "problem" with the institution stems from the oppression of Indigenous Peoples, African Americans, Asian Americans, Hispanics, Latinos/Latinas, gays, lesbians, bisexuals, or transgendered persons and persons with physical, mental/emotional, and/or learning disabilities, such as in the case of developing or having a "healthy" paranoia, so that group members do not inappropriately personalize problems.

3. Diversity-competent group workers do not exhibit a reluctance to seek consultation with traditional healers and religious and spiritual healers and practitioners in the treatment of members who are self-identified Indigenous Peoples, African Americans, Asian Americans, Hispanics, Latinos/Latinas, gays, lesbians, bisexuals, and transgendered persons and/or group members with mental/emotional, physical, and/or learning disabilities when appropriate.

4. Diversity-competent group workers take responsibility for interacting in the language requested by the group member(s) and, if not feasible, make an appropriate referral. A serious problem arises when the linguistic skills of a group worker and a group member or members, including sign language, do not match. The same problem occurs when the linguistic skills of one member or several members do not match. This being the case the group worker, should a) seek a translator with cultural knowledge and appropriate professional background, and b) refer to a knowledgeable, competent bilingual group worker or a group worker competent or certified in sign language. In some cases, it may be necessary to have a group for group members of similar languages or to refer the group member for individual counseling.

5. Diversity-competent group workers are trained and have expertise in the use of traditional assessment and testing instruments related to group work, such as in screening potential members, and they also are aware of the cultural bias/limitations of these tools and processes. This allows them to use the tools for the welfare of diverse group members following culturally appropriate procedures.

6. Diversity-competent group workers attend to as well as work to eliminate biases, prejudices, oppression, and discriminatory practices. They are cognizant of how sociopolitical contexts may affect evaluation and provision of group work and should develop sensitivity to issues of oppression, racism, sexism, heterosexism, classism, and so forth.

7. Diversity-competent group workers take responsibility in educating their group members to the processes of group work, such as goals, expectations, legal rights, sound ethical practice, and the group worker's theoretical orientation with regard to facilitating groups with diverse membership.

☐ Conclusion

This document is the "starting point" for group workers as we become increasingly aware, knowledgeable, and skillful in facilitating groups whose memberships represent the diversity of our society. It is not intended to be a "how to" document. It is written as a call to action and/or a guideline and represents ASGW's commitment to moving forward with an agenda for addressing and understanding the needs of the populations we serve. As a "living document," the Association for Specialists in Group Work acknowledges the changing world in which we live and work and therefore recognizes that this is the first step in working with diverse group members with competence, compassion, respect, and integrity. As our awareness, knowledge, and skills develop, so too will this document evolve. As our knowledge as a profession grows in this area and as the sociopolitical context in which this document was written changes, new editions of these Principles for Diversity-Competent Group Workers will arise. The operationalization of this document (article in process) will begin to define appropriate group leadership skills and interventions as well as make recommendations for research in understanding how diversity in group membership affects group process and dynamics.

☐ References

American Counseling Association. (1995). *Code of ethics and standards.* Alexandria, VA: Author.

Association for Multicultural Counseling and Development. (1996). *Multicultural competencies.* Alexandria, VA: American Counseling Association.

Association for Specialists in Group Work (1991). *Professional standards for training of group workers. Together, 20,* 9–14.

Association for Specialists in Group Work (1998). Guidelines for best practice. *Journal for Specialists in Group Work, 23,* 237–244.

Atkinson, D. R., Morten, G., & Sue, D. W. (Eds.). (1993). *Counseling American minorities* (4th ed.). Madison, WI: Brown & Benchmark.

Cass, V. C. (1979). Homosexual identity formation: A theoretical model. *Journal of Homosexuality, 4,* 219–236.

Cross, W. E. (1995). The psychology of Nigrescence: Revising the cross model. In J. G. Ponterotto, J. M. Casas, L. A.Suzuki, & C. M. Alexander (Eds.), *Handbook of multicultural counseling* (pp. 93–122). Thousand Oaks, CA: Sage.

D'Augelli, A. R., & Patterson, C. J. (Eds.). (1995). *Lesbian, gay and bisexual identities over the lifespan.* New York: Oxford University Press.

Helms, J. E. (1992). *A race is a nice thing to have.* Topeka, KS: Context Communications.

APPENDIX E: Gleanings of a Process Observer

James P. Trotzer

In ancient times when grain was harvested by hand, it was common for the villagers to follow the reapers and collect for themselves the remnants of the crop. In this way, members of the community benefited from the work of the farmer and represented a form of sharing and caring. This was called gleaning. The objective of this column is to share with the ASGW community the gleaning of my work as the Process Observer at ASGW Executive Council meetings.

I. The Process Observer: Gleanings as to Role and Function

The Process Observer is a catalytic agent who functions in a task group for the specific purpose of enhancing process dynamics for the benefit of product results. Consequently, the guiding principle of process observation must be related to the purpose of the job rather than how it is carried out. I suggest the general objective of process observation is: To make the Implicit Explicit so that task group members have greater Choice-Ability.

This principle relates to at least three domains of the group enterprise: 1) The Intrapersonal Domain: dynamics of personality within individual members of the group, 2) The Interpersonal Domain: dynamics of members relating to each other in the group process, and 3) The Interactional Domain: dynamics involving interaction of content, group process and individual personalities. Attending to these arenas is intensely engaging, optimally energizing and critically helpful to the Process Observer in sticking with the task of process observation, especially when content focus and interaction invites professional or personal participation in the group.

In this way, the Process Observer is partly like the mold that forms jello, leaving its imprint and giving shape to jello salad, and partly like the gelatin that stimulates the ingredients to gel together. Thus the personality of the Process Observer and his/her perspective of process is critical. Just as

551

no one group leader is exactly like another, no one Process Observer will have the same catalytic effect as another.

The Process Observer can function in many ways, both intentionally by initiative and responsively by invitation. For example, the Process Observer may reflect, monitor, facilitate, interrupt, analyze or confront the group. When these activities stimulate rather than deter progress, clarify rather than distort perception, improve rather than impede communication and help focus rather than distract the group, the Process Observer is an asset. As such, a neutral or detrimental Process Observer is a liability to the group.

It is becoming clear to me, then, that the Process Observer must be a formal position in the group rather than a part of a member's role or an informal adjunct to the group. By having a defined position with the ASGW Executive Board, I am both recognizable and accountable, features which give me a sense of identity and value in the group. This realization attests to the farsighted wisdom of the leaders of ASGW, who saw the value of adding the position of Process Observer to its leadership team.

II. Next Issue: Gleanings as to Effective Process

In my last column, I proposed that the general objective of process observation in a task group is: "To make the implicit explicit so that task group members have greater choice-ability." The implications of this objective manifest themselves in the functionality, productivity and perspective of the group; either enhancing or detracting from its effectiveness. This column's purpose is to identify several ways in which process affects the group's interaction and results.

Process is Prophetic

The foundation for effective problem-solving and conflict resolution is effective group process. Groups have easier and more successful experiences dealing with emerging issues and problems when we put forth an early effort to attend to process. Impasse and polarization arise with conflict when group process is defective or ignored. This stalls the group, undermines morale and impedes productivity. On the other hand, good process facilitates problem resolution and stimulates cooperation while valuing differences and respecting individuality.

A potent indicator of poor process is the escalation of tension and anxiety over time rather than an ebb and flow in relationship to topics and issues pertinent to the group's content or task. Unattended, that anxiety and tension becomes part of the fabric and context of the group rather than a companion to issues, topics and problems experienced in the normal course of addressing the group's agenda.

Process is Prototype

The nature of the process in the leadership group of an organization (in this case the ASGW Executive Council) provides the prototype for the subgroups of the organization as a whole. Process-wise: AS GOES THE LEADERSHIP TEAM SO GOES THE ORGANIZATION. If the group process reflects collaboration, cooperation and communication, the organizational derivatives follow suit. If process reflects individual vs. group initiatives or adversarial or competitive dynamics, the organization will reflect that style of process in doing its work. Thus process permeates the structure of a task group thereby influencing its over-all productivity.

Process is Perspective

The manner in which a task group incorporates differences, diversity and multicultural characteristics of its members provides the perspective the organization will hold and the attitude it will convey not only to its members but to people outside the organization. This perspective becomes the norm of the group as a whole and the model by which it functions. For example, a task group valuing differences, diversity and multicultural complexity in its deliberations might ask the following catalytic question at a process level: "IS DIVERSITY CORE AND COMMONALITY CONTEXT?"or "IS COMMONALITY CORE AND DIVERSITY CONTEXT?" Following either route for effective process can lead to productivity. However, ignoring this may result in a form of "GROUPTHINK" that produces results devoid of diversity and multicultural dynamics, reflecting overt or covert insensitivity or bias.

Process has Power

Since the endemic nature of process as manifested in a task group is prophetic of the group's functionality, prototypical of the group's productivity, and provocative of the group's perspective, the power of process is eminently evident. Therefore as a process observer, it is essential that I work to make process awareness an integral part of leader and member consciousness as they relate to each other and the task of the group.

III. Methods of Process Observation

The functional role of the process observer in a task group is "to make process awareness an integral part of leader and member consciousness as they relate to each other and the task of the group." The purpose of this column is to identify methods by which the process observer can carry out that function. Integrating these methods into the fabric of group inter-action formulates the process observer's particular role characteristics and generates the specific impact of process observation.

Feedback by Invitation

The leader or members of the task group can solicit input from the process observer periodically during the course of meeting, at critical junctures or stuck points during interaction, or as part of closure and review of the group's work. In any case, the tenor of solicited feedback should balance credit and acknowledgment with constructive criticism or corrective in-quiry. Presenting input in an observational manner tempered by tentative-ness rather than absoluteness facilitates positive group functioning.

Taking Initiative to Intervene

The process observer's autonomy as a defined group position provides a springboard from which s/he can make initiatives in the best interests of group productivity. Initiatives relative to group process are apropos when the group ignores process, engages in distracting or destructive process, or overlooks process resources in addressing their task. The process observer's style of intervention may vary from "process bulldog," holding the group accountable for good process to "cuddly kitten," encouraging, supporting and smoothing to facilitate good process.

Getting the Group to Process Process

Soliciting process input and discussion from the group is a very effective way to generate effective process. This not only raises their awareness but their expertise and serves to soften the process observer's role boundaries, helping him/her avoid the trap of being perceived as a process "expert" adjunct to the group rather than as an integral part of the group. Leading questions or requests such as, "I'm wondering what each of you is experi-encing at this time given the intense interaction that just occurred," or "Maybe, we could take a few minutes to process what is going on inside and between us," can be useful in helping the group attend to its own process.

Physical Location and Process Perspective

The physical positioning of the process observer affects both the group's interaction and the process observer's perspective. Location, in and of itself, has meaning, e.g., sitting in the circle vs. outside the circle, or sitting next to the leader vs. across from the leader. Changing location, periodically and strategically, varies the process observer's perspective. Modifying location (e.g., moving in and out of the group) is also useful to accentuate process dynamics. Generally, maintaining a mobile physical position in the group is advantageous to effective process observation.

Tuning Process Observation to Group Development

The content of process input needs to reflect the developmental dynamics and stage of the specific task group. The ASGW Executive Board met three times in the course of the year for (marathon-type) meetings. While all three meetings attended to ASGW business, forming dynamics and informality characterized the first meeting as members got acquainted with each other, defined their respective roles and formulated their group style of addressing business. The second meeting had an intense work orientation in preparation for the ACA World Conference. Formality characterized the third meeting as the leadership attended to presiding over the conference, culminating official business, and preparing for passing on the mantle of leadership. As such, process input was attuned to the developmental level of the group. Fine tuning feedback to reflect, inform and facilitate group development enhances group functionality and secures the process observer role as an asset to the group.

IV. Reflections on What I Have Learned

In the past three issues of Together I presented my perspectives on 1) the role and function of the Process Observer (Vol. 25, No. 2, p. 7), 2) the impact of process observation in task groups including the nature of effective and defective process (Vol. 25, No. 3, p. 6), and 3) methods of process observation (Vol. 26, No. 1, p. 6). In this column I present a reprise of my learning and offer a prospective to further enhance the emerging merit and utility of process observation generally as a group work specialization and specifically as an emphasis in ASGW.

The Emergence of Leadership: A Process Within a Process

While group process is an integral dimension of every task group, a parallel process is also evident to the Process Observer. That process involves the emergence of leadership and is formally and informally embedded in the overall group process.

In ASGW, the formal means of emergent leadership is assured by having past, present and future presidents serve as voting members of the Executive Board. This ensures evolution of leadership, but the means by which the transition takes place is still vital to the group process. How presidential representatives interact, communicate, solidify and transfer their respective leadership roles directly bears upon and impacts the group process of the Board and the organization as a whole.

The informal dynamics of emergent leadership have to do with individual personalities in the group (e.g. specific participants in ASGW Executive Board meetings including non-voting attendees) and the effect of significant others not physically present but prominent in the minds of the participants. Past leaders (fondly referred to as "ghosts of leadership past and present") and active members, whose efforts and work affect the organization, have impact upon task group dynamics and decisions. Effective Process Observers pay heed to these formal and informal dynamics in order to deliver sophisticated and compelling process assistance.

The Complexity of Group Process in a Technological World

The advent of using e-mail and fax machines has become a techno-process endemic to the work of the ASGW Executive Board and the organization as a whole. This techno-process, spurring the efficient and rapid exchange of information, enhances the content orientation of the group's purpose (providing participants are in the loop and keep up with increasing communications). Although techno-process is definitely aligned with the content orientation of the group's purpose it may impede the person orientation of the group's process by eliminating significant amounts of face-to-face communication.

Still unresolved, this startling realization became the most challenging dilemma of my Process Observer experience with ASGW: face-to-face vs. techno-process communication. From my perspective, the personal nature of face-to-face communication is more complicated and requires more relational work than the techno-process that only enhances content. Therefore, in order to provide effective observation, a Process Observer will either have to keep tabs on every member's e-mail messages (a Herculean task) or hold group members accountable to talk to one-another with full access to all the personal and interpersonal cues that attend face-to-face interaction. I opt for the latter approach

Effective Task Group Process Criteria: Balancing Being and Belonging in the Course of Producing

With being involving the expression of one's individuality, uniqueness and diversity in the face of solidarity; and belonging involving cooperating, complementing, connecting and communicating in the course of group interaction; a critical question emerged during the course of my process observation: "Can individual members be and belong in the course of doing the group's task?" In response to this question, I took balanced and appropriate (well-timed) actions to promote, facilitate and enhance being and belonging. I found that the more I took such actions, the more effective the group addressed its tasks.

In Closing: An Outcome and an Invitation

As a result of my Process Observer experience, this past semester I incorporated a Process Observer into my masters level group counseling class for the first time. I appointed a Process Observer for each session and provided them with training material consisting of the first three columns in this series. The results were vitally beneficial to both the overall class experience and the students' learning. I recommend it highly.

Finally, the ASGW Executive Board has incorporated a Process Observer for the past 5 or 6 years. A significant number of ASGW members have advanced the cause of process observation via demonstration, participation, incorporation and publication. I believe there are sufficient resources to form a Process Observer Interest Group within ASGW. If you are interested in forming and participating in such a group, please contact me at the address below. The potential for process application of group work and process observers in group work is unlimited. Let's realize that potential.

Comments may be directed to: James P. Trotzer, Ph.D., 39 Mill Road, Hampton, NH 03842.

INDEX

ABOUT THE AUTHOR

James P. Trotzer is currently a consultant, group leader, and trainer for ETC Professional Services. He received his M.A and Ph.D. degrees from the University of Colorado and completed a year of post-doctoral family therapy training in the Family Psychiatry Department of the Eastern Pennsylvania Psychiatric Institute. He is a Fellow and active member of the Association for Specialists in Group Work (ASGW) and is a member of the American Counseling Association (ACA), the International Association of Marriage and Family Therapy (IAMFT), and the Association of Multicultural Counseling and Development (AMCD).

Dr. Trotzer's professional writing includes twenty-one journal articles, two monographs, several books and book chapters, and a meditation series entitled "Renewing Your Mind: Meditations for Mental Health." His published books include *Marriage and Family: Better Ready than Not*, which he co-authored with his wife, Toni, and *The Counselor and The Group: Integrating Theory, Training, and Practice*, now in its third edition. He also serves on the editorial board of the *Journal for Psychology and Theology*.

Dr. Trotzer's clinical experience encompasses over twenty-five years as a counselor, psychologist, group therapist, marriage and family therapist, consultant, and clinical supervisor. For ten years, he served as executive director of the Renew Counseling Center in Rye, New Hampshire, a non-profit mental health agency. Additionally, he has over twenty years of experience in private practice. He has served as a visiting professor in Germany, Taiwan, and Japan and as an adjunct professor of counselor education at the Johns Hopkins University, Temple University, and the Rosemead School of Psychology at Biola University. He has been recognized professionally by ASGW, which awarded him its President's Award for Extraordinary Service in 1989 and its Professional Practice Award in 1996.

A noted workshop leader, public speaker, and presenter, Dr. Trotzer has recently presented programs both nationally and internationally on topics such as "Treating Violence and Conflict in Families," "Counseling the Post-Divorce Family," "Family Therapy as a Group Resource," and "Problem-Solving (Solution-Focused and Brief) Group Counseling." Dr. Trotzer brings a wealth of knowledge, wisdom, and experience to his audiences, and his presentations are noted for their practicality, experiential involvement, and humor.